Legal Research and Writing

Michael D. Murray

and

Christy Hallam DeSanctis

Foundation Press
2005

© 2005 By FOUNDATION PRESS

      395 Hudson Street
      New York, NY 10014
      Phone Toll Free 1–877–888–1330
      Fax (212) 367–6799
      fdpress.com
Printed in the United States of America

ISBN 1–58778–897–7

TEXT IS PRINTED ON 10% POST CONSUMER RECYCLED PAPER

Acknowledgments

Many people have supported our efforts in writing this book over the last four years. The authors particularly want to thank Steve Errick at Foundation Press, for all of his efforts and for never giving up.

Several other people also are owed our gratitude for their unwavering support of our professional endeavors and participation in the process resulting in this book. Professor Murray would like to single out his research and teaching assistants: Lindsay Beyer, Brian George, Aaron Goldberg, and Maurice Holman at the University of Illinois College of Law, and Renee Auderer, Jeannie Bell, Jonathan Blitz, John Challis, and Katalin Raby at Saint Louis University School of Law; and the Saint Louis University School of Law students who allowed us to use their work as writing examples: Jeannie Bell, Kevin Etzkorn, Josh Knight, Kirsten Moder, Allison Price, Gaylin Rich, Jerrod Sharp, Katherine Weathers, and Cherie Wyatt. Special thanks also are due to Professor Murray's assistant at the University of Illinois, Deanna Shumard, whose support above and beyond the call of duty is remarkable and much appreciated.

Professor DeSanctis would like to recognize Kristen E. Murray, the Associate Director of the Legal Research and Writing program at George Washington University for her outstanding assistance running the program, friendship, unabashed humor, and superb insight on how to teach students to write well (what would I do without you?); Professor Lorri Unumb, the Director of Legal Writing at Charleston School of Law, and my predecessor at GW, for teaching me not only how to teach legal writing but also how to run a great program (and for being an inspiration); the 2004–2005 GW Law Dean's Fellows for their energy and unceasing desire to make teaching legal research and citation interesting, rewarding and fun; and the 2004–05 Writing Fellows at GW for their amazing talent as writing tutors and, in particular, their assistance with the Appendix on grammar rules.

The authors thank their legal research and writing colleagues who reviewed and commented on the text: Kenneth Chestek (University of Indiana–Indianapolis School of Law), Jane Ginsburg (Columbia Law School); Terri LeClercq (University of Texas School of Law); Pamela Lysaght (University of Detroit Mercy School of Law); Joanna Mossop (Columbia Law School); Kristen Murray (George Washington University Law School); Suzanne Rowe (University of Oregon School of Law); Ann Davis Shields (Washington University School of Law); Judith Smith (Columbia Law School); Mark Wojcik (John Marshall Law School); and Cliff Zimmerman (Northwestern University School of Law). This book is the better for their kind and generous review and input.

Professor Murray also thanks his friends and former colleagues at Saint Louis University School of Law who encouraged and supported him, especially Donald King, Alan Weinberger, Ann Cronin, Carol Needham, and Pete Salsich, and his friends and colleagues at the University of Illinois College of Law, especially Shannon Moritz, Amy Gajda, Tom Ginsburg, Heidi Hurd, Richard Kaplan, Jay Kesan, Andy Leipold, George

Mader, David Meyer, Jim Pfander, Aylon Schulte, Charles Tabb, and Michael Vogel. And Professor Murray would like to give special recognition to Professor Louis Henkin and Professor and United States District Judge Jack Weinstein, who taught him what it means to care about the law.

Professor DeSanctis also thanks the following people: Linda A. Shashoua for her unwavering support in this endeavor and all of my others, as well as her guidance, friendship, and expertise in putting thoughts into both writing <u>and</u> music; Michael S. Levine, my "chief of staff," for his friendship and for sharing with me his thoughts and insights from almost ten years of teaching legal writing; Dr. George D. Gopen, for teaching me everything I know about reader and listener expectations; the Honorable John W. Bissell, for the opportunity to work with a true wordsmith and master of the English language; Scott A. Sinder, for teaching me how to write anything in one hour (and a Supreme Court brief in a weekend), for demonstrating why good writing matters, and for the experience working with a fabulously creative, yet very methodical, legal mind; Pam Chamberlain for her institutional know-how and priceless advice on how the GW program operates; and to all of the past, present and future GW LRW adjunct professors, from whom I have learned and continue to learn an enormous amount about a practice-oriented approach to teaching legal writing.

Dedication

To Denise, Olivia, and Dennis, who make it fun;
To my sisters, Margaret, Mary, Jeannette, Anne, and Laura,
who proved to me that the benefits of a
teaching career outweigh all the costs.

M.D.M.
St. Louis, MO
May 2005

To Michael B. DeSanctis,
a truly phenomenal lawyer ... and so much more.

C.H.D.
Washington, DC
May 2005

About the Authors

Professor Michael D. Murray teaches Art Law, Civil Procedure, First Amendment and Censorship, Introduction to Advocacy, and Legal Research and Writing at the University of Illinois College of Law. He graduated summa cum laude from Loyola College in Maryland and was a Harlan Fiske Stone Scholar at Columbia Law School. Professor Murray was a member of a national champion Jessup International Law Moot Court team at Columbia, and notes editor of the Columbia Journal of Transnational Law. After law school, he clerked for United States District Judge John F. Nangle, Eastern District of Missouri and Chair of the Judicial Panel on Multidistrict Litigation, and practiced commercial, intellectual property, and products liability litigation for seven years at Bryan Cave law firm in St. Louis. After leaving private practice, Professor Murray taught at Saint Louis University School of Law from 1998-2002. He has published several books and will publish several more in 2005, including: Adversarial Legal Writing and Oral Argument (Foundation Press, forthcoming 2005); Appellate Advocacy and Moot Court (Foundation Press, forthcoming 2005); Art Law: Cases and Materials (William S. Hein 2004); Civil Rules Practice 3d (Thomson West, forthcoming 2005); The Deskbook of Art Law (Oceana 2004, 2005); First Amendment and Censorship (Oceana 2005); Jurisdiction, Venue, and Limitations 3d (Thomson West, forthcoming 2005); Legal Research Methods (Foundation Press, forthcoming 2005); Legal Research, Writing, and Analysis (Foundation Press, forthcoming 2005); Missouri Products Liability 2d (Thomson West 2002); Objective Legal Writing and Analysis (Foundation Press, forthcoming 2005).

Professor Christy Hallam DeSanctis teaches Introduction to Advocacy and Legal Research and Writing at the George Washington University Law School, where she is the Director of the Legal Research and Writing Program and Law School Writing Center. She graduated from Duke University and New York University School of Law. Prior to joining the George Washington University Law School faculty, Professor DeSanctis practiced at the Washington, D.C., law firm of Collier Shannon Scott, PLLC, where she remains of counsel. At Collier, she focused on trial and appellate litigation at both the state and federal level, including in the U.S. Supreme Court, and worked on a variety of regulatory and legislative matters before a number of federal agencies and Congress. In addition, she published articles relating to major legislative efforts with which she was directly involved, including terrorism insurance legislation and federal health and financial privacy regulations. Professor DeSanctis began teaching as an adjunct faculty member in George Washington University Law School's legal research and writing program in 2002. She was appointed Director of the writing program in 2004. In the 2005–2006 academic year, she also will implement and direct a new series of courses focused on academic legal writing. Professor DeSanctis has also taught undergraduate English courses at the University of Maryland, including a course in argumentation developed from principles of Classical Rhetoric. She will complete a Masters in English, with a minor in Rhetoric and Composition, at Maryland in early 2006.

Preface

The target audience

If you are a first year law student beginning your study of legal analysis, research, and writing, then you have come to the right book. The authors wrote this book primarily for use in a first year legal research and writing or legal method course. We crafted the topics and examples for first year readers, and we do not presume that you will bring extensive knowledge of the law, legal system, or legal reasoning and analysis to your study of this book. What is necessary is that you have an open mind and the ability to critically analyze language, arguments, concepts, and complicated writing.

This book teaches legal method, which consists of the skills necessary to determine legal issues (legal questions that need to be answered) from a given situation or set of facts, to research the law that speaks to these issues, and to analyze the law as you find it. Law school is designed to equip you with the skills to find and apply the law to new situations. You will learn a great deal of legal principles in law school and many ways to approach and think about legal problems, but in essence, the goal of legal education is to enable you to teach yourself the law governing any given situation, as it exists now and as it will exist in the future. Your legal method or legal research and writing course usually is the first course to teach you these skills directly and to evaluate your progress in learning them. This course partners with other basic doctrinal courses, such as torts, contracts, property, and civil procedure, so that you will learn basic principles of law along with the skills necessary to analyze them.

Many of you have come to law school with a background in English, political science, government, philosophy, or history. These disciplines are useful for the study of law, because the law requires careful, correct reading, critical thinking, and the study of historical situations that inform our legal system to this day. But the study and practice of law is not exactly similar to these disciplines, which should come as welcome relief to those of you who did not pursue one of these typical "pre-law" type degrees. In many ways, the law is like a science, relying on known proofs and applying them in a logical way to new situations. However, the law will not always seem like a science to the actual scientists or mathematicians reading this book, because the law does not always point to one correct answer, but frequently to multiple logical and probable outcomes, all of which can be correct if they are justified by proper legal methods. The law is a lot like theology or the study of religion, because it relies on authority — the holy books and scriptures of the law — which must be painstakingly analyzed in order to figure out how to apply them to new situations in a just and equitable manner. In short, there is no one set of skills that you need to bring to law school to succeed, and it is very safe to say that many people with a skill set just like yours have gone before you and excelled.

This book also teaches communication through legal writing and oral advocacy. Once again, it is not necessary that you start off your study of legal research and writing with great writing skills in order to make use of this book, although we will assume that you have a good command of written English and the basic elements of style. We will not cover such elements in any detail in this book, except in those instances where we have perceived that students or lawyers in general have significant difficulty. Entering a legal writing course with strong general writing skills and lots of writing experience will be an advantage in terms of your ability to organize your thoughts and express your ideas on paper, but, as we hope will be evident after reading this work, it is not a towering advantage. Legal writing is not like creative writing or literary composition or poetry. It can be mastered as quickly by students with little writing experience as those with vast experience. The objectives and skills taught in this book allow everyone to have a fair chance to express legal information clearly, concisely, and correctly, no matter what their prior background and experience is.

Why would anyone want to write like a lawyer?!

By now, you may be asking yourself, "Why should I want to write like a lawyer? Lawyers are terrible writers!" It certainly is true that lawyers are held up to popular ridicule for writing that is prolix, overly complex, obfuscatory, and disingenuous. Whether it be for the fine print on the back of a standard form contract, or the complex and convoluted letter sent to a client to explain what the lawyer has done, or a brief loaded with purple prose and Latin and French terms that befuddles and angers a judge, the work product of lawyers constantly is used as an example of what is wrong with modern communication, not what is right.

This situation is unfortunate, because a lawyer's ability to research and analyze the law and communicate these findings and the advice that goes with them is the lawyer's stock and trade. While lawyers easily understand the importance of proper research and analysis, they often neglect communication. As a result, people admire lawyers for their keen skills in reasoning and problem solving but laugh behind these same lawyers' backs (sometimes to their faces) because of their writing. Be assured that this book attempts to correct these problems, not contribute to them. The root causes of the basic complaints of prolixity, excessive complexity, and dishonesty or obfuscation are many and varied, but the problems can be targeted and eliminated.

Communication in writing

Even at the dawn of a new century, much of a lawyer's communication needs to be in writing. Clients, supervisors, other lawyers, and the judges and law clerks of the court system are not going to sit still while you orally attempt to explain the intricacies of the legal problem at hand, the details of the facts, the complex facets of the cases and legal rules that govern the situation, and the proper outcome you are explaining and advocating. Instead, you will have to write down this information in a letter, memorandum, or court brief. That is where some lawyers apparently switch off their highly tuned skills and crank out work product that suffers from the problems popular society scornfully refers to as "legalese" or "legal gobbledygook."

Why are lawyers notoriously wordy? A knee-jerk appraisal may be that lawyers generally love the sound of their own voice, even the inner voice used when drafting a legal document, and therefore cannot cut themselves off. Others probably subscribe to the philosophy that more is better: if I write more, people will think I've done more research, given it more thought, been more thorough, and have more to show to justify my fee. Others lack confidence in determining what to put in and what to leave out, so they err on the side of inclusion.

As an entering law student, you may be in a different place with difference influences driving you toward excessive verbosity. For several undergraduate years, you may have been told to meet minimum page expectations of fifteen, twenty, thirty or more pages. In order to meet such requirements, you may have developed a talent for padding. You might have explained things four times if you wanted to, inserted many huge quotes from your sources, and watched the pages fly off the printer. After you graduate from law school to legal practice, if you continue in this manner, it will be a hindrance in legal contexts. Your audience members — clients, supervisors, colleagues, judges, and law clerks — will have no desire to wade through unnecessary words and paragraphs and pages. Long-winded attorneys in person and in writing incur resentment and disdain, and do a disservice to their clients.

Complexity is a different animal. No one will tell you the law is uncomplicated. Indeed, you will soon find out how complicated it can be. But your written and oral communication should never mirror the same complexity as the legal issues you are writing about. A truly great lawyer takes the complex and explains it in a simple, straightforward, and easily understandable manner. Part of this skill is knowing what and how much to write about in a given document, and part of it is being able to master a legal topic so well that you can explain it to anyone. As discussed throughout this book, you always must try to write with your audience in mind. Make it clear, and make it appropriately simple for the audience at hand, and they will appreciate it and value your writing more because of it.

The impulse to obfuscate can be traced to the same source as the impulse to mislead and defraud. The latter sins quite clearly are unethical and impermissible, not to mention terrible for your client's case and your reputation and future effectiveness as a attorney. But obfuscation is a slower, more indirect form of cheating the reader. The lawyer who attempts to cloud or distort the meaning of the law or who piles on complexity with the sole purpose of defeating the reader's ability to grasp and deal with the true issues of the case, is achieving the same end as an outright lie. In its most frequent incarnation, obfuscation is a tool of lawyers who do not want to be pinned down to a potentially troublesome set of facts or legal positions, allowing a certain amount of wriggle room to escape if the positions they took earlier in the case turn out to be incorrect or unwieldy.

Our goal is to prevent you from developing these bad habits or to break you of them if they already exist. We constantly will remind you to write **clearly, concisely,** and **correctly**. To address verbosity, we advocate page limits of three, five, seven, and ten pages on legal writing assignments that increase in complexity and in the number of issues involved. We have yet to hear complaints about being able to fill up that many pages. Instead, the challenge is to be able to edit your work so as to fit it in that number of pages. Clarity in terms of language and an appropriate level of complexity is the goal we advocate for writing that is composed for a specific audience. We implore you as a law student and future lawyer to avoid the dark path of obfuscation and always to attempt to state the facts and the law honestly and correctly.

Audience-specific writing

The writing you will be asked to do in a legal research and writing or legal method course will be audience-specific writing. Legal writing always is targeted to a specific audience, and the content, tone, and especially the level of objectivity concerning your findings and conclusions about the law will vary according to the persons to whom you are writing. This book is divided according to the main division in legal writing forms: **objective writing** and **advocacy or adversarial legal writing**. The initial chapters will focus on objective, informative writing, the prime example of which is an office memorandum, and the later chapters will focus on writing as a partisan and advocate, using the examples of trial court briefs for a pretrial motion to dismiss and a motion for summary judgment and appellate briefs. Oral advocacy in trial and appellate courts is dealt with in a separate chapter at the end of the book.

Contents

Chapter 1. Introduction to the Process of Law 1
  I.   Legal method 1
  II. The law 1
  III. Sources of the law—primary and secondary 2
  IV. The role of a lawyer 3

Chapter 2. Rules of Law and Legal Reasoning 5
  I.   A rule of law 5
  II. Finding, breaking down, and outlining a rule of law 5
       A. Sources of the law 5
       B. Breaking down a rule of law into its parts 6
       C. Outlining the parts of a rule 6
       D. Use of the outline of parts for structure 8
  III. Legal reasoning 8

Chapter 3. The Life of a Case, State and Federal Court Systems, and Jurisdiction 17
  I.   The life of a case in civil litigation 17
  II. State and federal court systems 23
       A. Federal system 24
       B. California 26
       C. New York 27
       D. Texas 28
  III. Hierarchy of judicial authority 28
  IV. Jurisdiction 32
       A. Jurisdiction as a place 32
       B. Personal jurisdiction 33
       C. Subject matter jurisdiction 35

Chapter 4. Determining the Rule from a Single Case or Other Authority 39
  I.   Determining the rule from constitutions, statutes, or administrative
       regulations 39
  II. Finding the rule in a case 41
       A. The legal method of judges 41
       B. The Borrowed Rule 43
       C. The Applied Rule or Precedent 43
       D. How do you phrase the applied rule? 46
       E. The holding of the case and dicta 49

**Chapter 5. Determining the Applicable Rule Through Statutory Interpretation and
Analysis of Multiple Authorities** 51
  I.   Statutory and rule interpretation 52

II. Analysis of multiple authorities: potentially controlling v. persuasive authority 65
    A. You must know what jurisdiction's law applies 65
    B. Constitutions, statutes, and administrative rules and regulations from the
       applicable jurisdiction always are controlling authority 66
       1. Timing determines the weight of these authorities 66
       2. Cases can and will interpret and modify constitutions, statutes, and
          regulations 66
    C. Cases that are potentially controlling authority 66
       1. Federal law issues in federal court 67
       2. State law issues in state court 68
       3. Federal law issues in state court 69
       4. State law issues in federal court 71
    D. Determining if "potentially controlling" authorities are actually controlling 72
       1. Facts and issues of the case 72
       2. Is the case still good law? 73
       3. Has the case been superseded by more recent, equally authoritative cases,
          statutes, or rules? 74
    E. Relative weight of controlling authorities 75
    F. Primary persuasive authority 77
       1. Relative weight of primary persuasive authorities 78
          a. Dicta from controlling cases 78
          b. Non-controlling cases from the jurisdiction whose law applies 78
          c. Out-of-jurisdiction cases – holding and dicta 79
          d. Out-of-jurisdiction statutes and regulations 80
          e. Dicta from out-of-jurisdiction cases 80
       2. Factors that affect the weight of primary persuasive authorities 80
III. Secondary authority 82
IV. Drafting the rule in a rule section: reconciling, synthesizing, harmonizing
    the various authorities 84
       1. Do start with constitutions, statutes, or regulations 87
       2. Otherwise, start with a watershed opinion 87
       3. Do not change the order or basic contents of the elements of a much
          borrowed rule 87
       4. Do try to reconcile your authorities; do not formulate a rule with
          inherent contradictions 87
       5. List interpretive rules and exceptions after the main rule 88
       6. List sub-rules on elements of the rule in the TREATment of the
          individual element 89
       7. Do accept the possibility that two competing rules might exist 90
V. Rule synthesis 90

Chapter 6. Organization of Legal Writing 95
I. Thesis heading 95
II. Rule section 97
    A. Statement of legal principles and requirements that govern the issue 97
    B. Interpretative rules 98
III. Explanation section and explanatory synthesis 99

      A. Purpose of the explanation section 99
      B. Explanatory synthesis 101
      C. Comparing unsynthesized and synthesized explanation sections 104
      D. Use of secondary authorities 108
      E. Explanation of rules not found in cases 109
  IV. Application section 110
  V. Thesis restated as a conclusion 112
  VI. Other structural formats 113
  VII. Identifying multiple issues 114
      A. What are the separate legal questions you have to answer? 114
      B. Which elements or factors of the rules and sub-rules of the rules are at issue? ... 115
  VIII. Structuring the discussion of multiple issues 116

Chapter 7. The Office Memorandum and the Client Letter 119
  I. Focusing on the reader of the office memo 119
  II. Attention levels of the law-trained reader 120
  III. Structure of the office memorandum 121
  IV. Drafting the Caption 123
  V. Drafting the Issues or Questions Presented 124
  VI. Drafting the Brief Answers or Conclusions 126
  VII. Drafting the Statement of Facts 129
  VIII. Drafting the Discussion Section 132
  IX. Drafting the Conclusion 136
  X. Client letters 137
  XII. Sample office memoranda 138
  XIII. Sample client letters 157

Chapter 8. Editing and Fine-Tuning Your Writing 161
  I. Style issues for the office memorandum 161
    A. Plain English 161
      1. Avoid legalese 161
      2. Be concise 161
      3. Limit your use of the passive tense 162
    B. Quotations 162
      1. Never plagiarize 163
      2. Do not quote so much that the quotes attempt to replace your own analysis of the issues 163
      3. Proper quotation technique 164
      4. When to use quotation marks 164
      5. The mechanics of quotation 165
      6. Quote accurately 166
    C. Parentheticals 166
    D. Discuss dicta correctly so as not to trick the reader into thinking it is holding from a case 167
      1. Obvious and not so obvious ways to discuss a court's holding ... 167
      2. How do you avoid saying "holding"? 168
      3. Avoid using the word "dicta" in your writing 169

E.	Formality of language	169
	1. Do not use slang and colloquialisms	170
	2. Avoid slash constructions unless that is the actual word, phrase, or address that you are quoting or referring to	170
	3. Avoid contractions but do use shorthand words and phrases	171
	4. Do not use symbols except where required	171
	5. Avoid first-person and second-person references	172
	6. Do not use rhetorical questions	173
	7. Write out dates	173
F.	Internal consistency and parallelism	173
G.	Sexist language	174
H.	References to cases and courts	175
I.	Citation to authority	175
	1. The Golden Rule	175
	2. Jump cites must be provided	176
	3. Cite all the sources you need, but do not string cite	176
J.	Tone: humor and excessive emotion is out; vivid and engaging work is in	177
II.	Fine tuning with alternative modifications of the TREAT format	178
III.	Editing tips	181
A.	Write early, rewrite often	181
B.	Employ more than one editing and proofreading technique	182
C.	Stay objective	182
D.	Track the language of the authorities when applying the rule to your facts	182
E.	Be as definite as you can be	183
F.	Statement of facts: how much is too much?	183
G.	Editing the discussion section	183
	1. Side issues, interesting questions	183
	2. Redundancy is bad	184
	3. Too many authorities?	184
Chapter 9. Legal Citation		185
Part I. The ALWD Citation Manual		185
I.	Citation sentences and citation clauses	186
A.	Citation sentence	187
B.	Citation clauses	187
II.	Introductory phrases (ALWD R. 44)	189
III.	Shorthand devices for repeat citations (ALWD 10, 11)	192
I.	Style of the case (ALWD R. 12)	193
A.	Certain words are omitted	193
B.	Use ALWD standard abbreviations	194
II.	Required information for cases	196
A.	Page spans and jump cites (pinpoint cites or pin cites)	196
B.	Court information	197
III.	Subsequent history	198
IV.	Parentheticals (ALWD R. 12.11)	198
V.	Short forms for cases	199
VI.	Citation forms for other authorities	200

Part II. The Bluebook (a uniform system of citation) 203
    I.   Citation sentences and citation clauses 203
        A. Citation sentence 204
        B. Citation clauses 204
    II.   Introductory phrases (BB 4.1) 206
    III. Shorthand devices for repeat citations (BB 10.9 and B5.2) 209
    I.   Style of the case (BB 10) 212
        A. Certain words are omitted 213
        B. Use Bluebook standard abbreviations 213
    II.   Required information for cases (BB 10.1) 215
    III. Subsequent history 219
    IV. Parentheticals (BB 10.6) 219
    V.   Short forms for cases (BB 10.9 and B5.2) 220
    VI. Citation forms for other authorities 221

Chapter 10. Introduction to Legal Research and Printed Sources of the Law 225
    I.   Initial assessment of the problem 225
        A. Determining what is at issue 225
        B. Background research into the area of law 226
        C. Background research into the facts 228
        D. Background information of the "how to do it" kind 228
            1. Your colleagues, and other lawyers you know 229
            2. Practice guides and practice-oriented continuing legal
               education (CLE) materials 229
            3. The agency or court 229
            4. Pleading and practice form books 229
    II.   Planning your research 230
    III. Performing the research using printed sources of the law 231
        A. Determining the scope of the research 231
        B. Legal research sources 231
    IV. Reaching your goal and knowing when you are finished 235

Chapter 11. Federal and State Reporters of Cases 237
    I.   Case reporters and elements of reported opinions 237
        A. Case reports and reporters 237
        B. "Unpublished" cases 237
        C. State trial level court opinions 238
        D. Appellate level court opinions 238
        E. Reporting in two or more different reporters 238
        F. Elements of reported opinions 239
            1. The title (also called the caption or style) of the case 239
            2. The citation 239
            3. The court 240
            4. Docket number 240
            5. Date of the decision and opinion 240
            6. Synopsis (a/k/a prefatory statement, heading, summary) 240
            7. Headnotes and syllabi 241

8. Names of counsel 241

9. Facts 241

10. Opinions of the court and separate opinions of judges 241

11. Decision—the judgment, order, or decree 242

    G. Official and unofficial reporters 243

II.   Federal court reports 243

    A. United States Supreme Court cases 243

    B. Federal court of appeals cases 244

    C. Federal district court cases 245

    D. Other volumes for federal cases 246

III.   State court reports, West's National Reporter System, and regional reporters 246

    A. State court cases 246

        1. Official reporters 246

        2. Regional reporters—official and unofficial 247

        3. West's state-specific publications 247

        4. West's reprint editions of one state's cases 248

        5. Topical, subject matter reporters 248

    B. The National Reporter System 248

Chapter 12. Case Finders and Verification Sources: Digests, Annotated Law Reports, and Shepard's Citations 251

I.   Digests 251

    A. Finding cases on point using digests 251

        1. Catch words, concepts from legal issues 251

        2. Look up these words, concepts and phrases in your digest's indices 252

        3. If you run short, search more broadly, think of synonyms 252

    B. West's digests—key number system 252

    C. How do you find what topics and key numbers to look up 253

    D. West's digest series 255

        1. West's United States Supreme Court Digest 255

        2. Federal Practice Digest 255

        3. Regional digests 255

        4. State digests 255

        5. American Digest System 256

            a. Century Edition Digest 1658-1896 256

            b. Decennial Digests 1897-2001 256

            c. General Digests 2001-Present (in progress) 256

        6. Specialized digests 256

    E. Other digests 256

II.   Annotated law reports 257

    A. What are annotations and annotated law reports 257

    B. What are annotations used for 257

    C. Who writes them 257

    D. American Law Reports—the granddaddy of them all 258

        1. Function of A.L.R.s 258

        2. Limitations of A.L.R.s 258

        3. How to find relevant A.L.R.s 259

4. A.L.R. series 259
5. Updating older A.L.R.s 259
6. Verifying the accuracy of A.L.R.s 260
III. The wonderful world of Shepard's citations 260
A. Frank to the rescue! 260
B. What can you accomplish with Shepard's citations 260
1. Finding the parallel citations to cases 260
2. Trying to find out if the case is still "good law" 261
1. Shepard's can be used to find the direct history of the case 261
2. Shepard's can also be used to find most (hopefully all) of the
indirect history of the case 261
3. What are these codes used in Shepard's 261
4. Can Shepard's miss negative subsequent history? 262
5. How do you compensate for this? 262
6. Should the codes alone be enough to cause you to doubt a case? 262
C. Trying to find other cases using "one good case" with Shepard's 263
D. Shepard's for non-cases 263
E. Which Shepard's do you use 263
F. Updating Shepard's 264
G. Shepard's and KeyCite on-line 264

**Chapter 13. Secondary Sources of the Law: Encyclopedias, Treatises,
Law Reviews, and Periodicals** 267
I. Encyclopedias 267
A. A few words about anything and everything; in depth information
on nothing 267
B. When to use encyclopedias 267
C. Main examples 268
1. Corpus Juris Secundum (C.J.S) 268
a. How do you find information on your topic? 268
b. Can you cite to C.J.S.? 268
2. American Jurisprudence Second (Am. Jur. 2d) 268
3. Am. Jur. Proof of Facts; Am. Jur. Trials; Am. Jur. Legal Forms and
Pleading and Practice Forms 269
4. State encyclopedias 269
II. Treatises and hornbooks vs. practice guides and CLE publications 269
A. Citation to treatises—gold mine or fool's gold? 270
B. How do you use treatises 271
C. Updating 271
III. Restatements—not your ordinary treatise 271
IV. Uniform laws 272
V. Law reviews, law journals 272
A. This can be complicated 272
B. More than you can shake a stick at 273
C. The table of contents is easy to find 273
D. Are you supposed to be impressed? 273

  F. Compared to other secondary authorities, where do law review
    articles rank? 274
  G. Finding law review articles 274
 VI. Other periodicals 274

Chapter 14. Court Rules, Local Rules, and Loose-leaf Services 277
 I. Court rules 277
  A. Federal rules of "general" application 277
  B. Sources regarding the federal rules of general application 278
  C. Other federal rules 281
  D. Secondary sources for commentary, interpretation of rules 281
 II. Federal and state court local rules 282
 III. State general rules of procedure 285
 IV. Drafting reports ("legislative history") of the federal rules 285
 V. Citator services 286
 I. Why are loose-leaf services created? 286
  A. To keep things current 286
  B. Information overload! 286
 II. Types of loose-leaf service 287
 III. Publishers 287

Chapter 15. Constitutions and Federal, State, and Municipal Legislation 289
 I. The Constitution of the United States of America 289
 II. Primary sources for researching and interpreting the Constitution 289
  A. Annotated constitutional law materials 290
   1. United States Code Annotated, Constitution of the United States
    Annotated 290
   2. United States Code Service, Constitution 290
   3. The Constitution of the United States of America (Library of
    Congress Edition) 290
   4. Digests 290
   5. ALR annotations 291
   6. Shepard's 291
  B. On-line access 291
 III. Secondary sources for interpretation 291
  A. Collections of commentary and bibliographies 291
  B. Leading treatises on constitutional law 291
  C. Framers' intent and founding fathers' information 292
  D. The Constitutional Convention 292
 V. State constitutions 292
 I. How federal laws are made 292
  A. Forms of congressional action 293
   1. Bills 293
   2. Joint resolutions 293
   3. Concurrent resolutions 293
   4. Simple resolutions 293
  B. Introduction and referral to committee 294

C. Consideration by committee—public hearings and markup sessions 294
D. Committee action 294
E. House floor consideration 295
F. Resolving differences 295
G. Final steps 295
II. Publication of federal laws 296
A. Slip Laws—Statutes-at-Large—United States Code 296
B. Slip laws 296
C. Statutes at Large 297
D. United States Code 298
E. The 50 Titles of the United States Code 298
III. Researching federal statutory law 300
A. United States Statutes at Large 300
    1. Public laws 300
    2. Private laws 300
    3. Treaties 300
B. Early publication of new laws and amendments to existing laws 301
    1. U.S.C.C.A.N. 301
    2. U.S.C.S. Advance Service 301
    3. Slip Laws, U.S. Law Week, Westlaw, and Lexis 301
C. Codifications and subject organization 302
    1. United States Code 302
    2. West's United States Code Annotated 302
    3. United States Code Service 303
I. Session laws 304
II. Codifications of state laws 304
III. Annotated statutes 304
IV. On-line services 305
IV. Multiple states sources 305
V. Municipal law 305

Chapter 16. Legislative History 307
I. What is legislative history? 307
II. For what purposes is legislative history used? 307
III. Legislative history as legal authority 308
IV. What documents and materials make up legislative history? 309
V. How to compile a legislative history 311
A. Compiled legislative histories 311
B. To do a legislative history of a bill passed in 1970 to the present 312
C. To do a legislative history of any bill introduced before 1970 313
    1. To find committee reports and documents 313
    2. To find committee hearings 314
    3. To find committee prints 314
    4. To find floor debates 314

Chapter 17. Federal Regulatory and Administrative Law.. 315
    I.   Why regulatory and administrative functions are delegated by Congress
          and the executive branch 315
    II.   Types of Administrative Law 315
    III.   The federal register 316
    IV.   Code of Federal Regulations 317
          A. C.F.R.'s organization 318
          B. Locating relevant and current C.F.R. provisions on-line 319
              1. Westlaw and Lexis 319
              2. Internet 319
          C. Locating relevant and current C.F.R. provisions by the book 319
          D. Updating C.F.R. provisions 320

Chapter 18. Computer Assisted Legal Research 321
    Part I. Computer assisted legal research using Westlaw and Lexis 321
    I.   On-line services 321
    II.   Do they replace law libraries? 321
    III.   Before you log on: planning your research 322
          A. Initial assessment of the problem 323
          B. Write down a plan for each issue you have to research 323
    IV.   Databases 323
    V.   Boolean searching: formulating your search requests 325
          A. Key words, catch phrases, and concepts from legal issues 325
          B. Think synonyms 326
          C. Terms and connectors: what logical connections between the terms
             do you want 326
              1. Connectors 327
              2. Expanders and alternative forms 328
              3. Plurals and possessive forms 329
              4. Acronyms, abbreviations, and compound words 330
              5. Phrases 330
           D. Putting it all together—use expanders and connectors to make a
             better search 331
          E. Revise and re-search again and again 331
          F. Advanced searching: fields, date restrictions, locate and focus 331
              1. Field and segment searching 331
              2. Date restrictions 332
              3. Searching for particular headnotes (keynotes) 333
              4. Locate (or focus) 334
    VI.   Natural language searching... 334
          A. It is not logical enough 334
          B. It does not find synonyms 334
          C. You cannot be certain you have exhausted the field 335
    VII. KeyCite™ and Shepard's™ Citations 335
    Part II. Computer assisted legal research using the internet and world wide web 336
    I.   Comparison of the on-line fee based services and free internet services 336
    II.   Why would you use the internet for legal research 339

III.   Appropriate uses of the internet as a tool for legal research 340
IV.   Resources for legal research on the internet 341
    A. Directory sites and legal search engines 342
        1. Findlaw 342
        2. Cornell Legal Information Institute 342
        3. LexisONE 342
    B. Web sites that contain good links to legal resources 343
        1. ABA Legal Technology Resource Center 343
        2. American Law Sources Online 343
        3. CataLaw 343
        4. Heiros Gamos 343
        5. Internet Legal Resource Guide 343
        6. Law.com Dictionary 344
        7. LLRX 344
        8. Megalaw 344
        9. Virtual Chase 344
    C. Sites for federal court opinions, statutes and regulations 344
        1. Cornell Law School's Legal Information Institute 344
        2. U.S. Supreme Court 344
        3. Individual federal court sites 345
        4. Government Printing Office 345
        5. FirstGov 345
    D. Sites for state court cases and regulations 345
    E. Federal legislative history 346
    F. Administrative agency opinions 346
    G. More mainstream search engines 346
        1. Google 347
        2. Alta Vista 347
        3. Fast 347

Chapter 19. Strategies for Research and Determining When You are Finished 349
  I.   Initial assessment of the problem 349
    A. What is at issue? 349
    B. Background research into the area of law 349
    C. Background research into the facts 350
    D. Background information of the "how to do it" kind 350
  II.   Planning your research 350
  III.   Performing the research 351
    A. What determines the scope of the research 351
    B. Sample research plans 351
  IV.   How do you know when you are finished? 354
    A. Several recent controlling authorities that agree 355
        1. Finding paydirt! 355
        2. Not finding anything? 355
        3. How do you "keep looking?" 355
        4. Old cases are not by definition bad cases 355
        5. Why controlling authorities are of paramount importance 356

      6.   Statutes and rules are controlling 356

      7.   A whole new regime? 356

      8.   What are "statutory" research issues? 357

  B. Several good, recent, persuasive authorities 358

      1.   Reality check 358

      2.   Comfort level 358

      3.   Good authority for big picture, policy issues 358

      4.   More analogous facts 358

  C. Reconciling/distinguishing authority 359

  D. Nagging questions? 359

Chapter 20. Adversarial Legal Writing 361

  I.   Differences between objective and adversarial legal writing 361

  II.   The nature of the adversarial system 362

  III.   Strategies and goals for zealous representation in the adversarial context 362

    A. Follow the fifteen minute rule and write clearly and concisely 362

    B. Know your audience and write with your audience in mind 364

    C. Concede facts and give up arguments when it will benefit your client to
        do so; do not concede when it will not 364

    D. Know the facts and the law, and know your options 365

Chapter 21. Pretrial Motions 367

  I.   Structure of pretrial motions and memoranda in support 367

    A. The structure of the memorandum in support 368

    B. The structure of the memorandum in opposition 368

    C. The structure of the reply 369

  II.   The Caption, Title, and Pre-introduction 369

  III.   The Introduction 371

    A. The objective of the introduction 371

    B. The importance of the introduction 371

    C. The drafting of the introduction 371

      1.   Movant's introduction 371

      2.   Opponent's introduction 374

    D. Themes in the introduction 375

    E. Length of the introduction 376

    F. Sample introductions 376

  IV.   The Statement of Facts 379

    A. Drafting the statement of facts 379

      1.   Advocacy through narrative reasoning and story telling 379

      2.   Legal conclusions vs. factual conclusions 381

    B. Limits on drafting the facts – style and good taste 382

    C. Do you cite authority in the statement of facts? 385

    D. In what order do you have to present the facts? 386

    E. Sample statement of facts 386

  V.   Argument 389

    A. Goal for the argument 390

      1.   Client oriented 390

	2.	Persuasive	390
	3.	Correct legal standards—no cheating!	391
	4.	Movant's advice	391
	5.	Opponent's advice	391
		a. Be open and discuss the law as it is, but argue for a change	391
		b. Change the issues, and argue a legal position that you can defend	392
	B.	Structure – TREAT format	392
		1. Argumentative thesis headings	392
		2. Forming a favorable rule for the rule section	393
		3. Use interpretive rules that support the client's case	396
		4. Use of explanatory synthesis in the explanation section	397
		5. Movant's anticipation and handling of negative authority	400
		6. Opponent's handling of negative authority	401
	C.	How much of a TREAT to give – procedural vs. substantive issues and counter-arguments	402
		1. Procedural versus substantive	402
		2. Anticipating counter-arguments	403
	D.	How many issues do you TREAT in a given motion?	404
VI.		The Conclusion Section	407
VII.		Formatting a trial level brief	408
VIII.		Style issues of motions	409
	A.	Tone and formality	409
	B.	Footnotes	410
		1. It looks bad	410
		2. Some people never read footnotes	411
		3. Footnotes are a nuisance	411
		1. Side issues that deserve brief attention	411
		2. Additional facts of some interest to the analysis	411
		3. Tertiary legal support for the argument	411
	C.	Parentheticals	412
IX.		Finishing the memorandum in support	412
	A.	Cite-checking	412
	B.	Proof-reading	412
	C.	Editing	413

Chapter 22. Motions to Dismiss 415
I.	Initial pretrial motion for defendant	415
II.	Motion to dismiss for lack of jurisdiction over the subject matter - Fed. R. Civ. P. 12(b)(1)	415
III.	Motion to dismiss for lack of jurisdiction over the person - Fed. R. Civ. P. 12(b)(2)	416
IV.	Motion to dismiss for improper venue - Fed. R. Civ. P. 12(b)(3)	418
V.	Motion to dismiss for insufficiency of process or service of process - Fed. R. Civ. P. 12(b)(4),(5)	418
VI.	Motion to dismiss for failure to state a claim upon which relief may be granted - Fed. R. Civ. P. 12(b)(6)	419

VII.   Format of motions to dismiss and the opposition to the same 420
VIII. Sample motions 421

Chapter 23. Motions for Summary Judgment 435
   I.   Federal rule of civil procedure 56(c) 435
         A. Material facts 435
         B. Genuine dispute 436
         C. The burden shifts 437
         D. Judgment must be appropriate as a matter of law 437
   II.   Cross-motions for summary judgment 437
   III. Structure and format of a summary judgment motion and opposition 438
   IV.   Sample motions 439

Chapter 24. Appellate Advocacy: Appeals, Writs, Standards of Review 459
   I.   Introduction to the appellate process 459
         A. It is hard to win on appeal 459
         B. Quality is much better than quantity 459
   II.   Types of appeals and appellate writs 460
         A. Appeal after a final judgment 460
         B. Interlocutory appeals 460
         C. Extraordinary writs – writs of mandamus, writs of prohibition 461
   III. Standards of review 463
         A. Determinations of law – "de novo" standard of review 464
         B. Determinations of fact by the jury standard of review 464
         C. Determinations of fact by the trial court in a bench trial –
             "clearly erroneous" standard of review 465
         D. Mixed questions of law and fact standards of review 465
         E. Review of trial court's rulings on proceedings before and during the trial –
             "abuse of discretion" standard of review 466
         F. Trial court's evidentiary determinations – "abuse of discretion" standard
             but the discretion is more limited 467
   IV.   The record on appeal 467
         A. What is the "real record" on appeal – district court record or
             transmitted record? 468
         B. Supplementing the transmitted record 468
         C. What the transmitted record contains 468
         D. Appellant's and appellee's duties regarding the record 469

Chapter 25. Appellate Briefs 471
   I.   The importance of advocacy in writing in the appellate context 471
   II.   What briefs are allowed? 471
   III. Structure of appellate briefs and appellate writs 472
         A. Structure of writs of mandamus and prohibition 472
         B. Structure of interlocutory appellate briefs 473
         C. Structure of appellate briefs in the U.S. Supreme Court 473
             1. Caption (on the Cover) 473

    2. Questions Presented for Review (or Issues Presented, Points of Error, Points Relied On, Points for Review) 475
        a. Questions presented in an intermediate level appellate court 475
        b. Questions presented in a court of last resort 476
    3. Parties to the Proceeding 477
    4. Table of Contents 477
    5. Table of Authorities 478
    6. Opinions and Orders Entered in the Case (or Opinions Below) 481
    7. Statement of Jurisdiction 481
    8. Constitutional, Treaty, Statutory, and Administrative Law Provisions 481
    9. Statement of the Case (Including Statement of Facts and Proceedings Below) 482
    10. Statement of Facts 482
        a. Persuasive facts vs. argument 483
        b. Accuracy 483
        c. Highlighting good facts and downplaying bad facts 485
        d. Level of detail 486
        e. Divide facts with subheadings 487
        f. Citations to the record 487
        g. Party names 487
        h. Abbreviations and acronyms 488
        i. Tell your client's story 488
    11. Standard of Review 488
    12. Summary of Argument 489
    13. Argument 489
    14. Conclusion 489
    15. Appendices 490
  IV. Drafting the argument 490
    A. Use argumentative thesis headings 490
    B. Policy counts more on appeal, and precedent becomes a two-way street 491
    C. The continuing benefits of explanatory synthesis 492
    D. Be assertive rather than critical about the court below and your opponent's arguments, and remember the standard of review 492
    E. Minimize alternative arguments 493
    F. As in other litigation documents, limit the use of footnotes, overuse of emphasis, and lengthy quotes 493
  V. Drafting an answering brief 493
  VI. Drafting the reply brief 495
  VII. Sample brief grading sheets 496
  VIII. Sample briefs 500

Chapter 26. Oral Advocacy at Pretrial, Trial and Appellate Stages 611
  I. Background principles of the practice of oral argument 611
    A. It is an efficient use of the court's time and resources 612
    B. It allows a judge to question the two sides about the motion or appeal 612
    C. It can assist a judge in making up her mind 612
  II. Oral argument in trial level courts prior to trial 613

	A.	"No oral argument" jurisdictions	613
	B.	"Motion Day" or "Law Day" Jurisdictions	613
	C.	"Open Court" Jurisdictions	614
	D.	Informal matters and "show up" jurisdictions	614
	E.	The necessity to "notice up" motions	614
	F.	Style of oral argument in trial courts in the pretrial period	614
III.		Oral argument during a trial	615
IV.		Appellate oral argument	615
V.		How to prepare for oral argument	616
	A.	Know every case and legal authority inside and out	616
	B.	Write an outline, not a script	617
	C.	Prepare an introduction	617
	D.	Themes are not just for briefs	621
	E.	Try to anticipate likely questions, and work out good answers to them	621
	F.	Organize your materials for easy access	621
	G.	Go and do some field research – see how this is done	622
	H.	How do you get to the Supreme Court? – practice, practice, practice	622
VI.		Moot court judges	623
VII.		Decorum, appearance, and delivery	624
VIII.		Constructing the argument	626
IX.		Questions from the panel	626
X.		Other considerations	632
	A.	Winning points	632
	B.	Candor toward the court	633
	C.	Finishing your argument	633
	D.	Pay attention to the stop sign	633
	E.	Wait and listen to the whole question	634
	F.	Give a direct "yes-no" answer to a "yes-no" question; then explain	634
	G.	Unexpected events	634
	H.	Poker face	634

Chapter 27. Strategies for Moot Court and Beyond ... 637
I.		Moot court competitions	637
	A.	A taste of practice	637
	B.	Devil's advocacy skills	638
II.		Ideal traits for a moot court partner	639
	A.	Dedicated and hardworking	639
	B.	Available	639
	C.	Balanced	640
	D.	Good match for your strengths and weaknesses	641
III.		Interpreting moot court rules	641
	A.	Read the rules	642
	B.	United States Supreme Court rules	642
		1. Rules on typesetting and printing	642
		2. Brief covers	642
		3. Brief length	643
	C.	Page limits and typeface rules	643

	D.	Binding	644
	E.	Outside assistance	644
IV.		Analyzing a moot court problem	646
	A.	Careful reading	646
	B.	Handling the facts	646
		1. Put the facts in chronological order	646
		2. Separate good facts from bad facts	647
		3. Make reasonable and logical inferences from the facts	647
		4. Group the facts by topic and subject matter and look for themes	648
		5. Return to the facts again and again	649
	C.	Issue spotting	650
		1. Harmless error, appealable error, preservation, and clear error	650
		2. Jurisdictional errors in the trial court	652
		3. Appellate court jurisdictional issues	652
		4. Constitutional defects of justiciability	654
	D.	Appellant's determination of which issues to raise	655
	E.	Appellee's determination of which issues to rebut	656
V.		The collaborative writing process	657
	A.	Write a complete first draft of the brief as early as you can	657
	B.	Write multiple drafts	658
	C.	Meet frequently with your teammates and let them comment on each draft	658
	D.	Talk about each section the first week, each paragraph the second and third weeks, and each sentence and word the last week	658
	E.	Thoroughly discuss each authority	659
	F.	Use another team or persons briefing the opposite position if the rules allow it	659
	G.	Use all the outside help the rules allow	659

Appendix A. Preparing a Case Brief or Case Analysis for Class 661
Appendix B. Common Errors in Grammar and Punctuation 665
Appendix C. Preparing For and Taking Exams 677

Chapter 1

Introduction to the Process of Law

I. LEGAL METHOD

"Legal method" is an expression to describe the fact that the practice of law at all levels and in all places of employment requires a methodology whereby each participant in the process must properly research and find the law, interpret the law, explain the law to others, and, if that is your role in the legal process, to advocate a certain interpretation of the law that may require the law to be modified, revoked, or extended. This process fits within the three general terms of legal method: **research**, **analysis**, and **communication**. These are the skills that a first year legal research and writing or legal method course is attempting to teach you.

The first things a law student should attempt to grasp is what is the law, where does the law come from, and what is the lawyer's role in the legal process. These three ideas necessarily feed into each other as discussed below.

II. THE LAW

A nutshell definition of the law is easy to state, but you will spend the better part of your law school career trying to get your arms around this concept. The law is authority—that which we hold to be authoritative in governing, regulating, and adjudicating human interaction in a civilized society. The law is the body of statutes, ordinances, administrative rules and regulations, treaties, executive orders, judicial opinions, legal principles, and interpretations of all of these sources, that govern human actions and relations. Generally speaking, the law is "that which is laid down, ordained, or established" and "which must be obeyed and followed by citizens subject to sanctions or legal consequences" within a given geographical or other defined area. See Black's Law Dictionary 795 (5th ed. 1979).

A brief civics lesson may aid this introduction to the definition of the law. Recall that as a citizen of a country, the United States for example, you are a citizen of a community—a village or township or city or other municipal area—and a citizen of a county or parish, and a citizen of a state, and a citizen of a country, and a citizen of the world. All of these levels of relationship—let's call them government for lack of a better word—can regulate your activities by passing statutes, rules, ordinances, acts, laws, regulations, executive orders, treaties, or international conventions. All of them have legislative entities (town councils, county councils, boards of alderman, state legislatures, national or federal legislatures, and international legislatures, such as the United Nations), executive entities (mayors, county executives, governors, presidents, secretaries general), regulatory bodies (zoning boards, licensing bureaus, housing commissions, state and federal regulatory and administrative agencies), and judicial entities (justices of the peace, municipal courts, state and federal trial courts and appellate courts, administrative law judges, arbitral tribunals, and the International Court of Justice). All of these can contribute to the law by creating it, modifying it, interpreting it in official or advisory capacities, and by applying it to particular persons and situations.

It may sound impossible to find the law on any single topic given the breadth of these definitions. But in actuality, necessity dictates that the law must be organized and recorded in a certain number of sources (albeit a growing number of sources), and the process of finding the law directs your attention to the most likely sources for the law on the topic at hand so that you can find the applicable law with the greatest ease and convenience.

III. SOURCES OF THE LAW—*PRIMARY* AND *SECONDARY*

The three main sources of the law are **legislation** (including statutes, ordinances, laws, codes, charters, treaties and other international agreements, and constitutions), **administrative rules and regulations** (including rules, regulations, decrees, orders, and licenses promulgated by administrative agencies, non-legislative governmental entities, and other regulatory boards and commissions), and **judicial opinions** from cases that have come before the courts. These will be referred to as **primary sources** of the law or **primary authorities**. You also must refer to commentary and interpretations of the law written by legal scholars, judges, legislators, and legal practitioners in treatises, restatements of the law, hornbooks, law review articles, annotations, encyclopedias, legislative history documents, and other compilations. These will be referred to as **secondary sources** of the law or **secondary authority**.

Example: Primary and Secondary Authority

In a certain town, dogs were allowed to run loose and several people were bitten by dogs running wild in public places. The local legislature passed an ordinance (**legislation - primary authority**) making dog owners responsible for all injuries caused by their dogs who were not kept on a leash. An administrative agency, the Bureau of Parks and Recreation passed a **regulation (primary authority)** further interpreting the ordinance to require leather or metal chain leashes and collars on dogs. A lawsuit arose and was resolved in a **judicial opinion (primary authority)** wherein a dog owner was held not to be responsible when their dog unexpectedly broke free from his strong leather collar and leash and bit someone.

Later, a law professor studied this area of law, and wrote a law review article (**secondary authority**) explaining that the judicial opinion above has interpreted the ordinance and regulation to require that dog owners be at fault before they will be responsible for unleashed dog injuries. She explained that the legislature could have

---

> imposed a strict liability standard, but the courts have interpreted the statute to require negligence or fault on the part of the dog owner. The law professor's article explains the effect of the primary authorities, but it does not change the law.

It is very important to get a good grip on these definitions because they are used throughout this book. The difference between primary and secondary authority is crucial. As the name indicates, primary authorities carry much more weight in determining what the law is on any topic. Primary authorities will determine the law for every situation where the primary authorities speak to the legal issue, and secondary authorities are only used to explain or supplement primary authorities. Secondary authorities can be of great assistance to lawyers in interpreting the law in areas where the law is unclear or ambiguous, and this kind of commentary can be very persuasive to lawyers, legislators, and judges, but secondary authorities cannot create law. At most, they can provide guidelines for courts or legislatures to act in areas that are not yet defined by a primary authority or where a change in the law is needed.

IV. THE ROLE OF A LAWYER

The nature of lawyering is to determine what the law is and how it is likely to affect a "client" in a given situation. That is what lawyers get paid to do. The client can be a person or business entity that hires the lawyer, or a private or public entity that employs the lawyer, or a court or judicial body in which the lawyer is employed. A good lawyer in each of these sectors can tell you what the current law is, predict how the law will work in various real or hypothetical situations, and advise the "client" on what to do or what to avoid doing in those situations.

When a person goes to a medical doctor's office, they often chat for a while about their problems, called "symptoms" in that context, and the doctor may or may not do some fact gathering on his or her own, through a physical examination or by questioning the person. At the end of the visit, the doctor tells the patient (his client, if you will) what he or she thinks the problem is and prescribes a solution. Medical doctors do not often create the impression that they have to scurry off to their library or jump on the computer very often to look up the problems that their patients are having and the probable solutions to these problems.

As a lawyer, you will not enjoy that luxury. Rarely will you know what the law is ahead of time. You will know a great deal of legal principles in many areas of the law, and a number of actual legal rules of general and specific application, but these will not be enough to answer even the average question that reaches your desk. What usually happens is that a client or a supervisor will come into your office with a problem that has legal implications, and you will listen to the problem, ask questions to gain additional information relating to the problem, and then go to your sources in the library or on-line and attempt to figure out what to do or what will happen based on the law that applies to the problem. Occasionally, you will have had this exact issue come up recently, and you will already know what happens and what to do about it. When this happens, you should gloat and enjoy a momentary feeling of great wisdom and power, and then go and double-check yourself by looking it up and making sure you still are the master of this legal information.

The process of finding the law—looking it up, finding the proper sources, compiling the information, following up on leads, and using what you have found to find other sources—is the first essential skill of a lawyer, which is referred to as **research**. The process of determining what legal issues are implicated by the facts of the problem and what sources should be consulted, reviewing and analyzing what these sources say, and reaching a conclusion about what the law is regarding the problem, is the second essential skill, referred to as **analysis**. The third part of the process is being able to communicate your findings to a variety of persons—your colleagues where you are working, senior lawyers in your firm, your clients, the courts, your opponents, and various governmental or regulatory bodies. A lawyer practicing by himself or herself with no client, no opponent, no court, or no other audience is not doing much practicing. This skill will be referred to as **communication**, and much of the focus of this book will be on communication in writing.

Chapter 2

Rules of Law and Legal Reasoning

I. A RULE OF LAW

The process of law involves the research, analysis, and communication of a **rule of law**, which may be defined as:

RULE OF LAW

A statement of the legal principles and requirements that govern the analysis of the legal issue at hand.

Earlier, we mentioned the concept of a **legal issue**:

LEGAL ISSUE

An individual legal question implicated by a problem (a set of facts) that needs to be answered in order to render advice concerning the problem.

Each legal issue has a rule of law that governs the analysis of the issue. You must find the correct rule and apply it to the facts of the problem to answer the legal issue you are analyzing.

II. FINDING, BREAKING DOWN, AND OUTLINING A RULE OF LAW

A. Sources of the law

You find rules of law in the sources of the law we discussed above, both primary and secondary sources. As an example, if a client has a question about dog bite liability—his dog bit a Girl Scout after she rang his door bell and shouted at the dog—you would look for the rule of law that governs liability of dog owners for their dog's bites. The legal issue is: Will my client be liable for this dog bite injury? To research this issue, you would probably look for a statute or other form of legislation, an administrative rule or regulation, or one or more **cases**—reports of judicial opinions in prior lawsuits and other legal actions—in your state that discuss dog bites and dog owner liability to see what the rule is.

Let's suppose you are in the State of Apex,[1] and you did not find any legislation or regulations, but you came across two cases, <u>Smithy v. Jonesy</u>, 123 W.2d 345, 347 (Apex 1965), and <u>Johnson v. Anderson</u>, 789 W.2d 234, 237 (Apex Ct. App. 1st Dist. 1989),[2] that both say the following about dog bite liability: "In Apex, a dog owner is liable for all injuries caused by his dog unless the dog is provoked by the victim." Assuming you did not find any other authorities on Apex law that add to, change, or state a different wording of the rule or a different rule altogether, you have the rule of law that governs this issue.

B. Breaking down a rule of law into its parts

The first thing to do when you find a rule of law is to break it down into its parts. The **elements of a rule** are those facts that must be present in the case or the separate factors or conditions that must be considered and satisfied in order for the rule to be triggered. If the rule requires three facts to be present, it has three elements. If you are an advocate in a lawsuit seeking to apply the rule in your client's favor, the elements are the facts that you have to prove in order for your client to prevail. The opponent in the same lawsuit must try to disprove (or prove the absence of) one or more elements so that it will prevail.

In the example above, the rule as stated in the cases was: "In Apex, a dog owner is liable for all injuries caused by his dog unless the dog is provoked by the victim." This rule can be broken down into three elements: (1) a dog that is owned by the person from whom the victim seeks recovery, (2) an injury caused by the dog, and (3) a lack of provocation by the victim.

Some rules are not phrased in a form with one or more required elements. Rules can be stated so as to require the consideration of a number of **factors** or **considerations**, all of which do not have to be present for the rule to be triggered as long as some of the factors are satisfied. Other rules are phrased as a **balancing test** wherein a certain number of factors are balanced against other factors to determine the outcome. You must read the authorities carefully to determine what form the rule is taking, but no matter what the form of the rule is, it is still possible to break it down into the separate parts that must be considered (or balanced) in the application of the rule.

C. Outlining the parts of a rule

The parts of a rule often are listed in outline form. One of the purposes of this is to create a ready made organizational structure for discussion of the rule in writing. The three required elements you found for dog bite liability in Apex may be outlined as follows:

---

[1] Fictitious jurisdictions are popular in law school. Apex is our fictitious jurisdiction. You should assume that it is a state of the United States, located in between New York and California.

[2] Naturally, these two cases do not exist. From time to time we will invent cases to illustrate certain principles of legal analysis and communication. The citations do follow proper Bluebook citation form (<u>see</u> Chapter 9, <u>infra</u>), but the actual volume abbreviation ("W." for Western Reporter), page numbers, and dates given in the citations are imaginary. West Group does not publish a "Western" regional reporter as you will learn in Chapter 11.

1. Ownership;
2. Injury;
3. No provocation.

Sometimes the authorities that gave you the rule do the breaking down work for you. <u>Smithy v. Jonesy</u> might have laid out the rule on dog bite liability as follows:

"In order to recover, a dog-bite victim must prove the following:

1. Defendant owned the dog;
2. Plaintiff suffered actual physical injury to his or her person;
3. Plaintiff did not provoke the dog into attacking."

Your personal outline of the elements of the rule still can be stated as:

1. Ownership;
2. Injury;
3. No provocation.

If there were a different rule in Apex that incorporated a balancing test, for example, balancing the amount of provocation, if any, against the viciousness of the dog's attack, you might outline the rule as follows:

1. Ownership;
2. Injury;
3. The severity of the attack was disproportionate to the provocation.

The outline of the rule still can be stated in three parts even though this rule would work differently than the first rule because of the balancing test in the third part of the rule. You would consider whether the dog was provoked into attacking, but even if provoked, the victim might still recover if the attack was disproportionately severe compared to the provocation. For instance, a person might shake a fist at a dog and shout "Down boy!" and receive a nip from the dog (a proportionate attack) and not recover, but if the person were mauled by the dog, he might recover because the attack was disproportionately severe. If you decide that the analysis of severity and provocation is complicated enough to warrant a further breakdown of the rule into subparts, you might outline the rule as follows:

1. Ownership;
2. Injury;
3. Balancing of
    a. the severity of the attack and
    b. the provocation of the dog.

As will be seen below, the outline you come up with merely should be an aid to help you with your analysis and explanation of the rule. There is no need to over-complicate the situation. However, if the authorities provide a ready made outline for a rule, it is a good idea to try to use the outline from the authorities for the convenience of the people to whom you will communicate your analysis.

D. Use of the outline of parts for structure

Chapter 6 discusses the creation of an overall outline for your writing based on the outline of the elements or parts of the legal rules involved. As a preview of this, you could outline a memorandum about dog-bite liability in the following way:

Thesis: The Homeowner will be liable for the injuries to the Girl Scout caused by his dog.

1. <u>Ownership</u>
   Sub-Thesis: It is undisputed that the Homeowner owned the dog.
2. <u>Injury</u>
   Sub-Thesis: It is undisputed that the Girl Scout was injured by the dog.
3. <u>No provocation</u>
   Sub-Thesis: The Girl Scout did not do anything to provoke the dog within the meaning of this element under the law.

III. LEGAL REASONING

Legal writing requires a logical and orderly construction. An explanation of legal principles, whether it be in an informative memorandum to a client or an advocate's brief to the court, generally requires the use of the following types of reasoning:

> ### RULE-BASED REASONING:
>
> The answer is X because the authorities establish the rule that governs this situation, and the rule requires certain facts to be present, and these facts are present, so the application of the rule to the facts produces X result.

This type of reasoning reflects a simple logical syllogism:

The answer is X if there are certain facts present

All of the required facts are present

∴ The answer is X.

The converse also is true:

> The answer is X if there are certain facts present
>
> Not all of the required facts are present
> _____
>
> ∴ The answer is not X.

Using our dog-bite example, the syllogism would be:

> The owner will be liable for his dog's bite if he owned the dog, the dog caused the injury to the plaintiff, and the plaintiff did not provoke the dog.
>
> The facts indicate that the owner owned the dog, the dog caused the injury to the plaintiff, and the plaintiff did not provoke the dog.
> _____
>
> ∴ The owner will be liable for his dog's bite.

Rule-based reasoning is the most common form of logical reasoning in legal writing because legal analysis basically is the analysis of the applicable legal rules and how they apply to the situation at hand. The organizational framework for legal writing taught in this book—**TREAT**—is derived from this type of legal reasoning. **TREAT** stands for <u>T</u>hesis, <u>R</u>ule, <u>E</u>xplanation of how the rule works in various situations, <u>A</u>pplication of the rule to the facts of the present situation, <u>T</u>hesis restated as conclusion. This will be discussed at greater length in Chapter 6.

ANALOGICAL REASONING
(Reasoning by Analogy):

The answer is X because this situation is like the situation in prior cases and in those cases X was the answer.

Very often, you will use analogical reasoning in your writing to try to link your case to other similar cases in which the outcome was favorable. If the court agrees that the cases are similar and that there are no legally significant differences, the court should handle the present case in the same way to produce the same result as in the prior cases. The converse of this type of reasoning is used to argue that a certain case should not determine the outcome of the case at hand because there are legally significant differences. For example:

CONVERSE ANALOGICAL REASONING
(Distinguishing Negative Authority):

Although the result in two prior cases was X, X should not be the result in this case because of certain legally significant differences.

You may combine the two, so as to analogize to the good prior authorities and distinguish yourself from the bad:

Although the result in GHI v. JKL and MNO v. QRS was X, X should not be the result in this case because of . . . [legally significant differences]. Instead, the court should follow STU v. WXY because of . . . [important similarities]. In STU the result was Y, so Y should be the result in the case at hand.

Reasoning by analogy is used frequently in legal writing because the American legal system follows the common law tradition wherein courts follow **precedent**, the record of determinations of similar cases handed down from year to year and age to age. Precedent can be binding or merely persuasive, but it is a cornerstone of the legal reasoning process. This topic is discussed in greater detail in Chapters 5 and 6 and Appendix A.

Often the legal rules used in the rule-based reasoning syllogism require explanation and illumination to demonstrate for the reader why your prediction of the outcome is legally sound and likely to occur. Analogical reasoning is used within the rule-based reasoning syllogism to further the overall discussion by showing how the rule itself or the elements of the rule are supposed to work by discussing and analogizing to or from certain actual circumstances (cases) where the rule was applied to produce a certain outcome. This use of analogical reasoning in the context of an explanation section also is discussed in Chapter 6.

POLICY-BASED REASONING:

The answer should be X because X furthers the public policies of this area of the law.

Policy-based reasoning most often is used to buttress an argument that already is supported by primary authorities. You are arguing that the answer is X not only because the authorities had X result, but also because X result satisfies public policies that are important to this area of the law. Occasionally, when primary sources (cases, statutes, administrative rules) of the law fail you or are absent, and there is no binding authority, the only argument you can make is a policy-based argument.

The following is an example[3] of policy-based reasoning used in legal writing:

---

[3] These authorities are fictitious.

For centuries, the law has recognized the immorality of executing severely mentally deficient persons or persons with severe learning disabilities. Robert R. Writter, <u>The History of Capital Punishment in England and the United States</u> 234-36 (1978). As early as 1782, in the case <u>The King v. Smith</u>, 99 Eng. Rep. 339, 342 (K.B. 1782), the King's Bench court stated that "the marginal satisfaction of blood lust and vengeance secured through the execution of a recognizable moron is far outweighed by the need for mercy and higher justice." Seventeen states have banned the execution of persons whose multi-phasic intelligence quotient ("IQ") is less than 70, making them borderline to profoundly mentally retarded. R. Randall Peters, <u>Capital Punishment Mistakes</u>, 99 Colum. L. Rev. 23, 45 n.76 (1999) (citing state statutes). Although defendant Jones repeatedly has scored a 69 on the multi-phasic IQ test and thus is susceptible to capital punishment at present under the laws of Texas, the court should recognize that Jones's severely limited mental capacity mitigates against the imposition of the ultimate penalty in this case.

A brief example of three forms of argument—rule-based, analogical, and policy-based—together in a discussion that follows the TREAT format of Chapter 6 is the following:

Thesis	Mr. Charles Client, the homeowner ("Homeowner"), is liable for the injuries inflicted on the Girl Scout ("Scout") by his dog.
Rule	In Apex, a dog owner is liable for all injuries caused by his dog unless the dog is provoked by the victim. <u>Smithy v. Jonesy</u>, 123 W.2d 345, 347 (Apex 1965); <u>Johnson v. Anderson</u>, 789 W.2d 234, 237 (Apex Ct. App. 1st Dist. 1989). The elements of a cause of action for dog-bite liability are therefore: (1) defendant's ownership of the dog, (2) injuries caused by the dog, and (3) lack of provocation of the dog by the plaintiff. <u>See</u> <u>Smithy</u>, 123 W.2d at 347.
Explanation of the Rule	Provocation requires an active, physical threat to the dog. <u>See id.</u> at 348 (provocation occurred when small boy hit a dog over the head with a stick several times before the dog bit the boy); <u>Johnson</u>, 789 W.2d at 239 (no provocation when dog attacked a postal worker who had walked up the front walk and opened the front storm door of the house to place a package inside). A non-threatening act such as walking up to a door and opening the door in the normal course of a postman's duties was not provocative within the meaning of the rule.

	<u>Johnson</u>, 789 W.2d at 239. The underlying public policy behind the Apex rule is that persons "attacked by a domesticated animal when the person is acting peaceably and not directly threatening the animal" shall recover from the owner of the animals. <u>See</u> Chester A. Scootch, <u>Apex Animal Laws</u> 234 (1953). Although Professor Scootch was referring to the Roaming Livestock Damage Act, Apex Rev. Stat. § 222.1234 (1944), there is no practical difference between livestock who are roaming loose on the property and domestic animals, such as dogs, who are encountered on the property. <u>See</u> Scootch, <u>supra</u>, at 235. The law provides a remedy for injuries suffered when "the victim is acting peaceably and the dog is not." Mary M. Quitecontrary, <u>When a Best Friend Bites: Dog Bite Liability in Apex</u>, 345 U. Apex L. Rev. 122-23 (1979).
Application of the Rule	In the instant case, there is no dispute that the Homeowner's dog attacked and caused injury to the Scout, an eight-year old girl, when she climbed the front stoop of Homeowner's home and rang the doorbell with the intention to sell Girl Scout cookies. Thus, the first two elements of this cause of action are established. In reference to the third element, lack of provocation, the Scout did nothing to threaten the dog, let alone strike the dog, in contrast to the plaintiff in <u>Smithy</u>. Like the plaintiff in <u>Johnson</u>, plaintiff was using a public walkway that led to the front door of the house to engage in her business. Ringing a doorbell is not a provocative action, and it is certainly no more provocative than opening the front door of the home where the dog is found. Although the postman in <u>Johnson</u> was acting in the ordinary course of his daily duties and the Scout here was doing something outside of her ordinary activities, this should not be viewed as a legally significant difference precluding the Scout from recovery. Recovery by the Scout furthers the policy of allowing recovery where the victim was acting peaceably and the dog was not.
Thesis Restated as Conclusion	Therefore, the Homeowner must compensate the Scout for her injuries in this case.

The first paragraph sets out the overall rule-based reasoning for this discussion. The thesis is the first sentence of the discussion, followed by the rule itself. The second paragraph explains how the rule works and starts the process of analogical reasoning, while the third paragraph engages in policy-based reasoning. Secondary sources written by legal scholars were used because the lawyer writing the above discussion did not think the issues were sufficiently resolved by the two cases that were on point. The fourth paragraph completes the analogical reasoning by showing how the present situation with the Girl Scout is closely analogous to the <u>Johnson</u> case, in which the plaintiff prevailed, but not at all analogous to the <u>Smithy</u> case, where the child with the stick did not prevail. The fifth paragraph finishes the policy-based reasoning, to back up the analysis of the primary authorities in the first four paragraphs. The last sentence of the example is a conclusion—the same thesis that started the discussion, but here restated as a conclusion—which completes the rule-based reasoning syllogism.

NARRATIVE REASONING:

The answer should be X. The fact that A is present supports X; the fact that B is here supports X; the fact that C is present supports X; the fact that D is here supports X . . . [and so on].

The fourth type of reasoning used in legal writing is the form most commonly used by non-lawyers in making a point. A narrative argument is made by stating your thesis and listing the supporting facts or factors. For example, a newspaper editorial will not necessarily lay out a governing rule and show how each requirement of the rule is met [rule-based reasoning], or analogize the present situation to earlier authoritative examples [analogical reasoning], rather it will state a position and float out the details and examples the back up the position. Consider the following example:

In the New York metropolitan area, the vast majority of folks seem content to spend large chunks of their waking hours inhaling fumes in bumper-to-bumper traffic . . . Some people even see clogged streets as an indicator of prosperity—great for the economy and the area's future.

[THESIS:] This mindset does not augur well for th[e] future. [FACT 1:] Travel times in the region are 40 percent longer than they would be if traffic flowed freely, according to the Texas Transportation Institute, which reviewed 1996 data from 70 metropolitan regions. [FACT 2:] Fuel wasted annually in traffic jams amounts to 51 gallons per capita and 63 gallons per driver. [FACT 3:] Congestion's cost—adding the price of delay and wasted gas—makes the New York region second in the nation in dollars squandered, wasting $9.8 billion in 1996, just behind Los Angeles.

This is not, of course, a new problem. [FACT 4:] A mid-1980's congestion study clocked the average commute to Manhattan from eight communities, all of them a mere 15 miles away. Under free-flow conditions, reaching Manhattan took anywhere from 20 minutes (Sheepshead Bay, Brooklyn) or 21 minutes (Yonkers) to no more than 34 minutes (Little Neck, Queens). Rush-hour trips from these points took anywhere from a maximum of 47 minutes (Yonkers) to 49 minutes (Sheepshead Bay) or 1 hour 10 minutes (Little Neck). Things have only gotten worse since then. . . .

Editorial Observer: The Traffic Congestion Strangling New York, N.Y. Times (Aug. 12, 1999), at http://www.nytimes.com (last visited Aug. 13, 1999).

The author led up to the thesis with a brief introduction, then supported it by listing four facts. It is a straight-forward practice, and can be quite effective in legal contexts. Most legal writing requires a statement of the facts that are important to the matter at hand, and narrative skills will enable you to make this a strong part of your writing. A statement of facts is not supposed to be directly argumentative, so a thesis sentence is not customarily inserted in the statement, but with good story-telling skills, the message of the fact statement will be clear. Compare the following statements of the facts in the Girl Scout dog bite case:

#1   On April 7, 1999, the Girl Scout walked up to the Homeowner's house. She rang the doorbell. Homeowner's dog approached her and bit her on the arm three times. She was injured.

#2   Sally Peterson is an eight year old girl, weighing only fifty-five pounds and standing four feet six inches tall. She is a member of the Girl Scouts of America. For the last two years, Sally has sold Girl Scout cookies in Homeowner's neighborhood. On April 7, 1999, at 11:30 a.m., Sally was walking with her mother, Janice Peterson, on Homeowner's street, going from door to door selling cookies. She was wearing her regulation Girl Scout uniform. As she reached each house on the street, Sally would let go of her mother's hand and walk from the public sidewalk up the front walkway and front stoop to ring the doorbell and call out, "Girl Scout cookies!" She followed this same practice at Homeowner's door. Homeowner's Doberman pinscher dog was not in sight when Sally rang the doorbell, but the dog immediately came tearing around the corner of the house, and leaped on top of Sally, sinking its teeth into her arm. Her mother responded to Sally's screams as quickly as she could, but she could not pry the dog off of Sally. A neighbor, Ralph Jones, happened to be driving by and saw the attack and heard Sally's and her mother's screams. He stopped his car and ran up to the stoop where he was able to rescue Sally from the dog's jaws. Sally had deep cuts in three places on her right arm and received 150 stitches at the Dayton County Hospital emergency room. She was bruised and scarred all along her right arm and shoulder and had to wear her right arm in a sling for three weeks. Her injuries prevented her from attending the annual Girl Scout camp-out and kept her off the soccer team for the last four weeks of the season and the play-offs.

The second statement of facts is not simply more detailed than the first, it communicates a message to the reader—a thesis—without overtly stating it. The message is that Sally was a non-threatening person, acting peacefully, using public walkways, and the dog reacted viciously, without there being any threat or provocation to the dog or the house or its owner, and Sally was severely injured by the dog's attack. Other details, such as her small size, the Girl Scout uniform, the breed of dog, the fact that she screamed, the fact that she was taken to the emergency room, and the gruesome and long-lasting nature of her injuries, all go toward painting a sympathetic picture of Sally for the reader. Example #2 uses narrative reasoning to drive home these points. It is clear that the writer of #2 is someone who is on Sally's side, and the intended audience might be someone who has to decide whether Sally should recover for her injuries.

In other contexts and with other audiences, it would not be necessary or proper to include the same details. Certainly, if we represented the dog owner, we would draft this statement differently, such as the following:

> On the morning of April 7, 1999, Sally Peterson was moving about the neighborhood of Jones' house, selling cookies. She was ringing doorbells and shouting "Girl Scout cookies!" at every house on the street. Her raucous approach to her task attracted the attention of Jones' family dog, Benji, and when Sally approached Jones' door, Benji approached her. Sally yelled "Girl Scout cookies!" right at the dog, and apparently swung her basket of cookie boxes in the direction of Benji's head. Benji responded according to his training, and acted to restrain Sally in the only way available to a dog, by fixing its mouth around Sally's arm. Benji was then tackled by Sally's mother and a passerby, and a considerable melee developed in which Benji and Sally were wrestled back and forth. In the skirmish, Sally turned up with several cuts on her arm, and Benji with cuts above his left eye and around the corners of its mouth. Both Sally and Benji required stitches for their injuries.

The focus of this statement is directed away from Sally, and it tries to cast a sympathetic light on the dog, and by association, the dog's owner. It sounds as if Sally did quite a bit of shouting and performed other threatening actions in this example. We intentionally used the phrase "On the morning of . . ." It may have been 11:30 a.m., but if the reader gets the idea that Sally was disturbing an otherwise peaceful morning, that might help. We used the dog's name, "Benji," to make the dog sound a little more like a friendly family pet, rather than a snarling, drooling, killing machine. This tactic would not work if the dog's actual name was "Killer" or "Fang" or "Psycho" or "Cujo." The dog is given a lot of credit for acting responsibly and predictably—our example inserts the helpful facts that the dog had training in protecting the house from unwelcome visitors and acted according to that training. In actuality, your clients may not have these facts going for them. Lastly, we gave fairly significant mention of the dog's injuries. This is a gamble, because you don't want the reader to be angered by a perceived attempt to trivialize injuries to a human being and over-aggrandize injuries to an animal. But it is a calculated risk. We inserted these facts to show that the "melee" was rough and tumble, and to suggest that there were a lot of ways Sally's arm could have gotten cut up in the fray, not just the obvious "the dog bit her too hard." Getting the reader at least to consider alternative causes of Sally's injuries will help the dog owner.

Chapter 3

The Life of a Case, State and Federal Court Systems, and Jurisdiction

A great deal of the research and analysis you will perform in the first semester of the first year of law school will involve **cases**. Cases are the reported opinions of courts at various stages of a lawsuit or other legal action. An understanding of the life of a case, the differences between the state and federal fora where cases are filed in the United States, and the three uses of the term "jurisdiction," is essential to the understanding of the system of precedent and the concepts of controlling and persuasive authority. These concepts will be of paramount importance in all of your first year classes.

This chapter may overlap with some of the material that you will cover in your first year civil procedure course, but it will not replace this material. Our aim is to give a broad foundation and teach key concepts that are necessary for your analysis of cases and the precedential effect of judicial opinions at different stages of a lawsuit and from different courts and different court systems. If your civil procedure professor uses different words or places different emphasis on matters discussed in this chapter, remember to follow the civil procedure professor's instruction for purposes of that course and final exam.

I. THE LIFE OF A CASE IN CIVIL LITIGATION[1]

The **plaintiff** is the person who brings the case. A case may have more than one plaintiff, and the plaintiff need not be a human being. Corporations, for example, also can be plaintiffs.

Plaintiff initiates a case by filing a **petition** or **complaint** in a court. The petition or complaint lays out the plaintiff's allegations against the party who is sued, who is called the **defendant**. The level of court where lawsuits are initiated is known as the **trial court**. Trial court personnel (**trial judges** and their staffs of law clerks and court clerks) administer the lawsuit. When formal requests (which are called **motions**) are made by the parties to the court (the verb is **to move** the court), or disputes and other matters arise in the course of the lawsuit, a trial judge handles them.

---

[1] Our examples throughout this chapter will refer to civil litigation, not criminal litigation.

Plaintiff's complaint or petition will assert one or more **claims** (also known as **causes of action**) against the defendant. A claim or cause of action is a legal term for the facts and circumstances that give a person a right to demand legal relief of some kind from another person or entity. Plaintiff alleges a set of facts and circumstances in one or more **counts** in its petition, each count representing a separate claim, and then makes a **demand for relief** (also known as a **prayer for relief**). The relief or remedy sought from the other person can take the form, among other things, of monetary damages, or the doing or refraining from doing of some act, or a demand to turn something over or give something back. The claims asserted in the complaint or petition may be related or unrelated to each other.

Defendant has several options in how to respond to the complaint or petition. Defendant either: (1) **answers** (verb) by filing an **answer** (noun); or (2) files an answer and a **counterclaim** against the plaintiff; or (3) files a **motion to dismiss** the petition or complaint. A **counterclaim** lays out allegations and asserts one or more claims of the defendant against the plaintiff, and if the defendant prevails on the counterclaim, it will offset the plaintiff's recovery, if any, by the amount recovered on the counterclaim. A **motion to dismiss** asserts that the complaint is improper in some manner (for example, the court has no jurisdiction over the case or the parties, or service of process was improper, or the complaint does not state a claim, or there is some other defect in the pleadings), and asks the court to throw the case out of court then and there.

Plaintiff either: (1) files an answer to defendant's counterclaim if one was filed; (2) files a **reply** to defendant's answer; or (3) files an **opposition** or **response** to the motion to dismiss. If there is more than one defendant, the matter can get complicated very quickly. One defendant may answer, while another will move to dismiss, and a third may answer and file a counterclaim. Plaintiff will respond separately to what each defendant did.

If a motion to dismiss was filed by a defendant, and an opposition or response was filed by the plaintiff, the defendant files a **reply** to the opposition or response. The court will rule on the motion, and if the motion is denied, defendant then goes ahead and files an answer with or without a counterclaim, as discussed above. After this, the parties can bring additional motions or start the process of **discovery** of facts from the other parties.

As mentioned above, a **motion** is a formal request by a party for the court to do something. For example, a party may ask the court, among other things, to dismiss the plaintiff's complaint, to grant the party additional time to do something, to allow the party to file something that normally is not filed, to submit a document in a form that requires permission, or to grant the party judgment prior to trial.

The following is the pattern of a typical motion brought in a trial court:

MOVANT'S ACTION   OPPONENT'S REACTION

(a) Movant files **Motion**

(b) Opponent files **Opposition**

(c) Movant files **Reply**

(d) Additional responses?

(e), (f) **Disposition** by the court

a. The party bringing the motion is called the **movant**. The motion sets out the grounds (legal and factual) that support the court's granting of the relief sought.

b. The party against whom the motion is brought is called the **opponent** or the **non-moving party**. The opponent files an **opposition** or **response** to the motion. The opposition lays out the reasons why the motion should not be granted.

c. The movant can file a **reply** to the opposition or response, which attempts to address and rebut the grounds asserted in the opposition for not granting the motion.

d. The opponent might try to file additional responses—for example, a **surreply** to the reply. This usually is not attempted, and in many courts the trial judge will have to grant you **leave** to file the surreply. If leave is granted and the surreply is filed, the surreply may only address the new issues, arguments, or authorities raised in the reply. In the event that the opponent filed a surreply, the movant might try to file a **rebuttal** (sometimes called a **sursurreply**) to the surreply. This almost certainly will require leave from the trial judge to file, and the judge will not be pleased with the movant for requesting this. The rebuttal may only address the new issues, arguments, or authorities raised in the surreply. The process might continue. The opponent, desperate to have the last word, might try to file a **surrebuttal** to the rebuttal (or **sursursurreply** to the sursurreply). Rather than grant leave to file this document, the court will prefer to kill the parties and their lawyers for filling up the file with paper.

e. When the briefing is completed, it is time for **disposition** of the motion by the court. In many courts, motions are ruled on through **oral argument**. In some jurisdictions, the court sets motions for argument, but in other places a party (usually the **movant**) "**notices up**" a hearing, which means the party picks a date and time for the hearing often by signing up with the court on its calendar, and sends the court and all the other parties a **notice of hearing**, which describes the motion and sets out the date and time for the hearing. However the date and time are set, the parties **appear** before the court on the designated date and time and **argue** the motion, and the trial judge who heard the argument sometimes **rules** on the motion right then and there. The court will either **grant** the motion (sometimes called **sustaining** the motion), or **deny** it (sometimes called **overruling** the motion), or it may **grant it in part, and deny it in part**, which means the movant gets some, but not all of the relief it sought.

f. In other courts, the court will not have oral argument on motions. The court rules on motions based on the papers (the motion, memoranda in support, oppositions, replies, etc.) filed with the court. The parties do not appear before the trial judge on the motion and do not know when they will get a ruling. Even in these courts, a party can request that oral argument be had on a particular motion, but this kind of request routinely is denied.

You can only learn so much about the facts of your case from your client and private investigators and third parties. You also need to get your opponent's version of the events. Fortunately, there is an orderly process by which the parties in civil litigation learn information about the case from each other, called **discovery**. This is how it works:

a. The parties ask each other questions in writing that require a sworn answer (in other words, the party answering is supposed to state, "I swear that the above responses are true and correct"). These are called **interrogatories**.

b. The parties ask each other for documents and data, files, objects, and any other item they think has something to do with the case. These are called **requests for production of documents and things** or simply **document requests**.

c. The parties ask each other to admit certain information. These are called **requests for admissions**. If a party admits something, the other parties can rely on that admission as an established fact in the case without doing anything more to prove that fact (barring some extraordinary occurrence whereby the court allows the party to withdraw the admission).

d. The parties can take **depositions** of the other party, or the party's representatives if it is a corporation or business entity, and any **witnesses** (people who know something about the facts of the case or the transactions and occurrences from which the case arises). The verb is "**to depose**" a witness. The parties take the witness to a conference room and ask the witness anything and everything they want to have answered that has any connection or relevance whatsoever to the case. The witness is placed under oath (solemnly swears to tell the truth, the whole truth, and nothing but the truth) and a **court reporter** sits and takes down all the questions and the answers and anything else that anyone sitting in the conference room says, creating a **record** of the deposition. If you do not want something to be taken down, you must go **off the record**. The record is transcribed by the court reporter into a **transcript** of the deposition which you can flip through like a book.

e. If you think someone is holding back information from you, or not cooperating, or not playing on the up and up in discovery, you can bring a **motion to compel** and request the court to assist you in getting the information you think is being withheld. The court will either **compel the production** of the information or deny the request.

After discovery is completed or nearly completed, the defendant and the plaintiff typically will evaluate whether to move the court for **summary judgment**. A summary judgment motion argues that the **material facts** in the case (those facts necessary to the court's determination of the claims on which movant is seeking summary judgment) are not in dispute, and based on these material undisputed facts, the movant is entitled to judgment as a matter of law. The rules allow a summary judgment motion to be brought at any time in the case, but it often makes the most sense to bring it after discovery is completed because at that point you should know all of your opponent's facts. The movant must prove that the material facts are not in dispute by showing that her opponent has admitted the facts, or stipulated to the facts, or none of the parties have ever asserted and produced evidence that suggests that the facts are other than as stated in the summary judgment motion. A summary judgment motion asserts that no **trial** is needed in the case, because the whole point of a trial is to establish the facts necessary to make a determination of who wins. If no material facts are in dispute, then there is no need for a trial.

If no one wins on summary judgment, the case proceeds to **trial**. A trial involves the following:

a. If a **jury** of your peers and equals hears the evidence and determines what the facts are (in other words, the jury is the **finder of fact**), and applies the law to those facts to determine the winner, then this is called a **jury trial**. The jury is instructed in the law by the trial court in its **jury instructions**.

b. If the court itself (the trial judge) hears the evidence and determines what the facts are (in other words, the trial judge is the finder of fact), and then applies the law to the facts to determine the winner, this is called a **bench-tried case**, or a **bench trial**, or a **non-jury trial**.

c. **Evidence** is taken during the trial. Evidence is something that is offered as a fact or something that makes the existence of a fact more or less likely; in other words, something that **proves** or **disproves** a fact at issue in the case. Evidence consists of the **testimony** of live witnesses, **deposition testimony** (taken from a transcript of the deposition), documents, exhibits and things, admissions of the parties, charts, photographs, maps, drawings, diagrams, movies, tapes (audio and video), and any other means devised by the attorneys for proving or disproving a fact. The **rules of evidence** provide the criteria for the trial court to determine what comes in (and is considered by the finder of fact) and what stays out.

d. In a jury trial, the jury enters a **verdict** in favor of one side and against the other, and the trial judge will enter a **judgment** that follows the direction of the verdict, unless the party against whom the jury rendered its verdict files a **post-trial motion**. A **post-trial motion** will argue that the jury made an erroneous application of the law or made improper determinations of the facts or both, or asserts other errors in the trial, and asks the court to throw the verdict out or grant a new trial—a "do-over." If the verdict is thrown out, the trial judge either orders a **new trial** or goes ahead and enters **judgment notwithstanding the verdict** in favor of the moving party. In Latin, this phrase appears as *judgment non obstante veredicto*, giving us the initials **judgment NOV** or **JNOV** to refer to the procedure (although in federal courts, it is now referred to as **judgment as a matter of law or JAMOL**). After sorting out all of these **post-trial motions for new trial** or for **judgment NOV** or **judgment as a matter of law**, the trial court enters a **judgment** in the case. When a judgment is entered that resolves all the claims of all the parties in the case, it is referred to as a **final judgment**.

The loser at trial in a civil case can take an **appeal** to the **intermediate level appellate court** (if there is one in that jurisdiction). The party who brings the appeal usually is called the **appellant** or **petitioner**, and she assigns "**errors**" to the trial court in its rulings on the law, on the admission or exclusion of evidence, on procedures during the trial or before trial, and anything else unfair or prejudicial that allegedly occurred in the course of the litigation. The appellant files an **appellant's brief** or **opening brief**. The opponent usually is called the **appellee** or **respondent**. The appellee files an **appellee's brief** (or **answering brief** or **opposition brief**). Then the appellant might file a **reply brief**. At present, **oral argument** is available in most appeals, but some appellate courts are moving away from this practice and require the parties to make a special demand for oral argument before it will be scheduled in an appeal.

If unsuccessful, the appellant can try to take an appeal to the highest level appellate court, called the **court of last resort** in the state or federal system. These courts usually have the right to pick and choose what cases they take, so this second appeal is not guaranteed. In other words, in the United States, you generally only get one appeal as of right, and if you want more, you must seek and obtain permission to file subsequent appeals. If you make it to the highest court in the jurisdiction, the titles of the parties may change; for example, an appellant may now go by the name of **petitioner** and an appellee may be called a **respondent**.

If an appeal is unsuccessful, the appellate court **affirms** the decision of the lower court. If an appeal is successful, the appellate court **reverses** the decision of the lower court, and either issues an opinion that corrects the lower court's determination of what the law is or how the law works in the situation before the court (a legal determination), or points out one or more procedural errors of the lower court (an error concerning the procedures employed or enforced by the lower court before or during the trial, the admission or exclusion of evidence, or how motions were handled), and indicates that a party's rights were prejudiced by the error. If the appeal makes a legal determination, the appellate court can simply enter judgment in favor of the appellant, but if the court finds a procedural error, the court usually **remands** the case back to the trial court for further proceedings.

II. STATE AND FEDERAL COURT SYSTEMS

Citizens of the United States are subject to two sovereigns—state (or local) authorities and national (federal or United States) authorities. Each person is governed by the laws both of the state where they live and by the country where they live. Thus, the laws of the United States, which are referred to as federal law, govern everyone living in the United States, while the laws of Michigan only govern people who are living or conducting business in Michigan.

Laws of your country, the United States of America (Federal Law)	⇨ YOU ⇦	Laws of your state (State or Local Law)

Each sovereign has its own court system. Each sovereign has trial level courts and an appellate court of last resort. The federal system and most states have an intermediate level appellate court. The court system of each state enforces the laws of the state. The federal court system operates in every state of the United States, and so there are federal courts that are physically located in each state to enforce the federal laws of the United States that are applicable in every state of the United States.

Depending on who you are (for example, a citizen or non-citizen of the state or of the United States, or a foreign ambassador), or the subject matter of your action (what you did, or what was done to you—discussed below under the topic of **subject matter jurisdiction**), you may become involved in a state action or a federal action or subject to suit in both fora. For example, on occasion, the same conduct may provide grounds for a legal action in both a state court in your state and the federal court that sits in your state. If you are in Montana and you take a gun and rob a bank, and in your escape you shoot two people who were blocking your way as you ran to your getaway car, you might be prosecuted in a Montana state court for murder or felony murder and also prosecuted in the United States District Court for the District of Montana (a trial level court in the federal court system, located in Montana) for bank robbery and use of a firearm in connection with a bank robbery, both of which are federal crimes. If you are a citizen and resident of Texas and you have been swindled out of $100,000 by a Wisconsin citizen and resident, you might sue that person for fraud in state court in Wisconsin or in the United States District Court for the Eastern District of Wisconsin (a federal trial level court located in Wisconsin).

Different states have different names for their courts, while the federal system uses the same terminology wherever the courts are located. For example, compare the terms used in the federal system and in the states of California, New York, and Texas:

A. Federal system

Court of Last Resort	United States Supreme Court
Intermediate Level Appellate Court	United States Court of Appeals
Trial Court - General Jurisdiction	United States District Court
Trial Court - Limited Jurisdiction	United States Bankruptcy Court | United States Tax Court

As discussed above, the federal government maintains a court system that operates in each state of the union. The organization of the courts in the federal system is uniform throughout the United States. The federal trial level courts are called the **United States District Courts**. Each of the fifty states has one or more **districts**, which correspond to a geographic region; for example, North, South, East, West, Middle, or Central. Federal trial courts in states with one district are called the United States District Court for the District of [State]; for example, the United States District Court for the District of Maryland; the United States District Court for the District of Kansas. The District of Columbia is one district, and the court there is called the United States District Court for the District of Columbia. Federal trial courts in states with multiple districts are identified as the United States District Court for the [geographic region] District of [State]; for example, the United States District Court for the Eastern District of Missouri, the United States District Court for the Southern District of New York, the United States District Court for the Central District of Illinois, the United States District Court for the Middle District of Georgia. Each federal district court is subdivided into **courts**, which are identified by a number or a letter or by the judge's name. The courts are presided over by a **United States District Judge** or a **United States Magistrate Judge**. On a tier below the district courts are the federal trial level courts with more limited jurisdiction—the **United States Bankruptcy Court** and the **United States Tax Court.**

The intermediate level appellate courts in the federal system are known as the **United States Courts of Appeals**. The United States Courts of Appeals are located in thirteen circuits, eleven of which encompass the fifty states. The remaining two are the United States Court of Appeals for the District of Columbia Circuit, which hears appeals from the United States District Court for the District of Columbia; and the United States Court of Appeals for the Federal Circuit, which hears appeals from the United States Court of International Trade and certain federal administrative boards. The Federal Circuit also hears all appeals in patent cases even though patent cases are filed and tried in every United States District Court across the country.

The circuits are broken down as follows:

Federal Circuit Courts

1st Circuit Court of Appeals	Maine, Massachusetts, New Hampshire, Puerto Rico, and Rhode Island

2nd Circuit Court of Appeals	New York, Vermont, and Connecticut

3rd Circuit Court of Appeals	Pennsylvania, New Jersey, Delaware, and the Virgin Islands

4th Circuit Court of Appeals	Maryland, North Carolina, South Carolina, Virginia, and West Virginia

5th Circuit Court of Appeals	Louisiana, Texas, and Mississippi

6th Circuit Court of Appeals	Michigan, Ohio, Kentucky, and Tennessee

7th Circuit Court of Appeals	Illinois, Indiana, and Wisconsin

8th Circuit Court of Appeals	North and South Dakota, Minnesota, Nebraska, Iowa, Missouri, and Arkansas

9th Circuit Court of Appeals	California, Oregon, Washington, Arizona, Montana, Idaho, Nevada, Alaska, Hawaii, Guam, and the Northern Mariana Islands

10th Circuit Court of Appeals	Colorado, Kansas, New Mexico, Oklahoma, Utah, and Wyoming, plus those portions of the Yellowstone National Park extending into Montana and Idaho

11th Circuit Court of Appeals	Alabama, Georgia, and Florida

District of Columbia Circuit Court of Appeals	The United States District Court for the District of Columbia, the United States Tax Court, and appeals from many administrative agencies of the federal government

Federal Circuit Court of Appeals	The U.S. Court of International Trade, U.S. Claims Court and the Court of Veterans' Appeals and patent appeals

The court of last resort in the federal system is the **United States Supreme Court** with its nine **justices**, all of whom sit to hear each appeal.

B. California

Court of Last Resort	Supreme Court of California
Intermediate Level Appellate Court	Court of Appeal of California
Trial Court - General Jurisdiction	Superior Court of California

California has a fairly typical structure to its court system. The trial level court of general jurisdiction where cases start out is called the **Superior Court of California.** There is a superior court for each county (for example, the Superior Court, San Mateo County). The courts are divided into **departments** where the superior court judges are assigned; for example, Judge Ronald E. Cappai, Superior Court, Los Angeles County, Department 23.

There is an intermediate level appellate court in California called the **Court of Appeal of California.** Note that the word "appeal" is singular—that is unusual to see because most jurisdictions call it a court of appeals. The court of appeal is divided into six appellate districts, numbered First Appellate District through Sixth Appellate District, and two of the larger districts (the First District in the area of San Francisco and the Second District in the area of Los Angeles) are subdivided into multiple divisions. Therefore, you might find your case in the Court of Appeal, First Appellate District, Division 3. The court of appeal hears appeals from superior courts in panels of three **justices**.

Superior court judges have some appellate duties. Appeals in "limited civil cases" (in California, where $25,000 or less is at issue) and misdemeanors are heard by the **appellate division of the superior court**, where superior court judges are assigned to three judge panels to hear the appeals. When a small claims case is appealed, a superior court judge decides the appeal. Another exception to the rule that all appeals from the superior court go to the court of appeal is death penalty cases, which are appealed directly from the superior court to the Supreme Court of California.

The court of last resort in California is called the **Supreme Court of California.** There are seven **justices** on the Supreme Court of California who all sit together to hear each appeal, which is called sitting **en banc.**

C. New York

Court of Last Resort	New York Court of Appeals
Intermediate Level Appellate Court	New York Supreme Court, Appellate Division
State Trial Court - General Jurisdiction	New York Supreme Court
County Trial Court - Limited Jurisdiction	County Court, Family Court, Surrogate's Court
Local Trial Court - Limited Jurisdiction	City Court, District Court (Long Island), Town Court, Village Court / Civil Court (NYC), Criminal Court (NYC)

New York is quite different from other court systems. The state trial level court of general jurisdiction in New York is called the **New York Supreme Court.** That is not a misprint. Each trial judge is a **justice**! There is a supreme court for each county. The supreme courts are divided into **parts** where the justices sit. At the county level, there also are lower courts with more specific subject matter jurisdiction, called the **County Court,** the **Family Court,** and the **Surrogate's Court.** Outside New York City, there is a third tier of limited jurisdiction courts called the **City Courts, District Courts** (found on Long Island), **Town Courts** and **Village Courts.** In New York City, the second tier of trial level courts below the supreme court are called the **Civil Courts** and **Criminal Courts.**

The intermediate level appellate court in New York is called the **New York Supreme Court Appellate Division.** It is divided into four numbered **departments.** Appellate division **justices** sit in panels of three and hear civil and criminal appeals from the supreme courts. Appeals from second tier trial level courts in the First and Second Departments go to the **Supreme Court Appellate Term.**

The court of last resort is called the **New York Court of Appeals,** and there are seven **judges** who sit **en banc** on this court. Thus a judge (of the Court of Appeals) may overturn the opinion of a justice (of the Supreme Court) in New York.

D. Texas

Courts of Last Resort	Supreme Court of Texas	Court of Criminal Appeals of Texas

Intermediate Level Appellate Court	Court of Appeals of Texas

State Trial Court - General Jurisdiction	District Court of Texas

County Trial Court - Limited Jurisdiction	County Court, County Court at Law, Probate Court

Local Trial Court - Limited Jurisdiction	Municipal Courts, Justice of Peace Courts

Texas also has a fairly complicated court system. The state trial level courts are called **District Courts of Texas**, and although they correspond to a county, they are numbered. For example, the 238th District Court of Midland County, Texas. Many counties have more than one numbered district. For example, Collin County, Texas has the 219th, 296th, and 366th District Courts. There is one **judge** in each district.

Below the district courts are courts of more limited jurisdiction, also associated with a county, called the **County Courts**, **County Courts at Law**, and the **Probate Courts**. Some counties are large enough to have more than one of the limited jurisdiction courts; for example, Probate Court No. 2, Dallas County, Texas. Even lower are courts at the local level, cities and townships, called the **Municipal Courts** and **Justice of Peace Courts.**

The intermediate level appellate court in Texas is called the **Court of Appeals of Texas**. There are fourteen courts of appeals that are numbered and identified by the city where they sit; for example, Third Court of Appeals, Austin. Houston has two—the First and the Fourteenth Courts of Appeals. The court of appeals hears civil and criminal appeals from the district courts and county courts in panels of three **justices**.

The are two courts of last resort in Texas—one for civil appeals, called the **Supreme Court of Texas**, and one for criminal appeals, called the **Court of Criminal Appeals of Texas**. The Supreme Court of Texas has nine **justices** and the Court of Criminal Appeals of Texas has nine **judges**. Both courts hear cases **en banc.**

III. HIERARCHY OF JUDICIAL AUTHORITY

One of the key concepts to master in legal analysis is the weight to be given to different judicial opinions based on the level of the court that issued the opinion. The structure of the court systems described above—trial level court to intermediate level appellate court to court of last resort within each system—is known as a **hierarchy of judicial authority.**

It refers to the power of courts higher up in the same hierarchy to **reverse** or **affirm** the decisions of the courts below it in the same hierarchy. It also refers to the principle that the **decisions of the courts higher up in the hierarchy are controlling authority for any courts directly below the court within the same hierarchy.**

If you think of an appeal as climbing the hierarchy of judicial authority, then the hierarchy of controlling authority uses the same path but in reverse. Appeals climb the hierarchy, while controlling authority descends the hierarchy. For example, the following are three separate hierarchies of judicial authority:

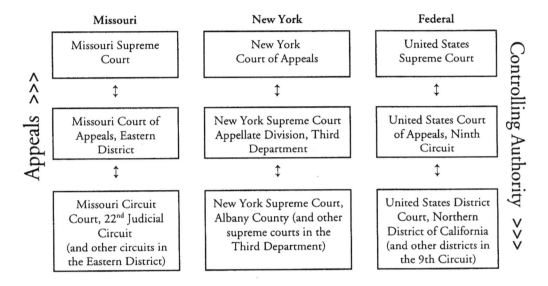

◆ **Courts on the same tier** — do not bind each other.

If a court is on the same tier with another court, it will not control the decisions of that court. Thus, a trial level court of general jurisdiction in a state will not control the decisions of another trial level court of general jurisdiction in the same state. Of course, it will not bind any court of another state on the same tier or a higher tier. In the above chart, the decisions of judges of the Missouri Circuit Court, 22nd Judicial Circuit, St. Louis City, are not binding on the judges of the Missouri Circuit Court, 21st Judicial Circuit, St. Louis County. That said, many courts on the same level will look to other decisions from courts on that same level as **persuasive** authority, but not binding authority.

◆ **Judges on the same court** — do not bind each other.

Even the decisions of judges sitting on the same court are not binding on other judges of the court because the judges are all working for a court that is on the same tier of the hierarchy. For example, the decisions of one judge of the New York Supreme Court,

Albany County, are not binding on the other judges of the New York Supreme Court, Albany County, because these courts are on the same tier. A court does not bind itself.

Individual trial courts and appellate courts may decide to deviate from this rule. A trial court may initiate a "bench rule" that requires all judges on the court to follow the decisions of all other judges on the court until and unless those decisions are overturned or otherwise become bad law. It is up to the judges of the court to decide how strenuously they will follow this rule. Similarly, an appellate court may adopt a "panel rule" that any decision of a three judge panel of the appellate court is to be followed by all subsequently assembled panels of the court unless the opinion is called into question by an intervening en banc opinion of the court or by an opinion of the court of last resort.

◆ **En banc opinions of an intermediate level appellate court** — bind all judges on that court

An exception to the general rule that a court does not bind itself is the situation of an intermediate level appellate court that sits **en banc** (all available judges on the court sit together to hear the case) to reconsider a case. These opinions are binding on each judge and subsequently assembled panel of judges of the intermediate level appellate court. The same is not true of courts of last resort, who often sit en banc to hear every case, and do not bind themselves to follow each decision that the court renders under the general principle that a court does not bind itself. Thus, an en banc decision of the United States Court of Appeals for the Ninth Circuit binds each subsequently assembled three-judge panel of the Ninth Circuit, but an en banc decision of the United States Supreme Court, which always sits en banc to hear each case, does not bind future decisions of the United States Supreme Court.

◆ **Courts that are not in the direct line of appeal** — do not bind lower courts.

A court must be in the direct line of appeal in the hierarchy to bind a court on a lower tier, even if the two courts belong to the same state or federal court system. If, for example, there are multiple districts or divisions or circuits of an intermediate level appellate court in the same jurisdiction, as was the case in all of the court systems discussed above, only the district or division that hears appeals from the state trial level court will bind that court with controlling authority. For example:

> ➢ The Missouri Court of Appeals, Eastern District hears the appeals from the Missouri Circuit Court, 22nd Judicial Circuit, St. Louis City, so it binds the judges of that court and all of the other Missouri Circuit Courts located in territory of the Eastern District. However, the Missouri Court of Appeals, Western District and the Missouri Court of Appeals, Southern District do not bind the Missouri Circuit Court,

22nd Judicial Circuit, St. Louis City or any other circuit court found within the territory of the Eastern District.

➤ The United States Court of Appeals for the Ninth Circuit will control the decisions of all of the United States District Courts located in the territory of the Ninth Circuit, such as the United States District Court for the District of Oregon or the United States District Court for the Central District of California, but it does not bind any district court located outside of the Ninth Circuit, such as the United States District Court for the Western District of Tennessee or the United States District Court for the District of Maryland.

Once again, states may decide to deviate from this rule and adopt a rule that all opinions of the intermediate level appellate courts are binding on all trial level courts wherever they are located within the state. Illinois is one such state that has adopted this rule.[2]

◆ **Courts of last resort** — control all courts in the same hierarchy.

The highest court in any jurisdiction controls all courts in the same hierarchy of judicial authority. The Illinois Supreme Court controls the decisions of each district of the Illinois Appellate Court and all of the Illinois Circuit Courts, because all of these courts are below it in the same hierarchy. The United States Supreme Court controls the decisions of the United States Courts of Appeals for all the circuits and all the United States District Courts, because all of these courts are below it in the same hierarchy.

◆ **Courts of one hierarchy** — do not bind courts of another hierarchy, but the court of last resort of one hierarchy can bind courts of a second hierarchy if the first hierarchy's law is being applied by the courts of the second hierarchy.

The decisions of a court higher up in one jurisdiction's hierarchy are not necessarily controlling in courts outside the hierarchy, even if the courts outside are on a lower tier in their own hierarchy.

➤ In general, courts in the Minnesota state court system do not bind the courts in the Wisconsin court system, nor those in the federal court system, not even the federal courts that sit within the territory of Minnesota.

---

[2] See State Farm Fire and Cas. Co. v. Yapejian, 605 N.E.2d 539 (Ill. 1992) (decisions of one appellate district are not binding on other appellate districts but are binding on all circuit courts across the state).

The exception is if a court of one state is applying another state's law, or a federal court is applying state law, or a state court is applying federal law. In other words, a court of one hierarchy is applying the law of another hierarchy in a case.[3] In these instances, the highest court of the hierarchy whose law is being applied will control the decisions of a court in another hierarchy. Decisions of lower tiered courts of the hierarchy whose law is being applied do not have this power. For example,

> ➤ The Wisconsin Supreme Court does not control the decisions of any Georgia court or federal court unless the non-Wisconsin court is applying Wisconsin law in the case it is adjudicating. The decisions of the Wisconsin Court of Appeals (an intermediate level appellate court) will not bind the decisions of a non-Wisconsin court even if the court is applying Wisconsin law.

It is important to note that the United States Supreme Court does not automatically control the decisions of state courts, because they are outside of the federal court hierarchy, unless the issue that concerns the state court is a matter of federal law, such as a decision interpreting the United States Constitution. Although the United States Supreme court is popularly referred to as the "highest court in the land," the United States Supreme Court only is the highest court of the federal court hierarchy, not the highest court of every hierarchy in the United States. This concept is discussed further in Chapter 5.

IV. JURISDICTION

The term "jurisdiction" is used three different ways in legal parlance. The root of the word means "to speak the law," and all of the uses of the word deal in some way with an entity's (for example, a court's) ability to exercise power over something or someone. Jurisdiction is the power to apply and enforce the law in a given place (Jurisdiction as a place), or with regard to certain persons and entities (Personal Jurisdiction), or with regard to certain kinds of claims and legal actions (Subject Matter Jurisdiction).

A. Jurisdiction as a place

The first usage of the term jurisdiction is a geographic description of a place where an identifiable set of laws and rules applies, and an identifiable entity has the power to enforce those laws and rules within that geographical area. The term refers to the limits and

---

[3] The reasons why courts are called upon to apply the law of another jurisdiction in various instances are the subject matter of complicated areas of the law known as conflicts of law and choice of law, which are taught in second semester or advanced civil procedure courses. Suffice to say that courts are, on occasion, required to apply the law of another jurisdiction, be it another state, or federal law, or the law of another nation.

boundaries of the area where that identifiable entity has this power. The State of New Jersey is a jurisdiction where New Jersey laws and rules apply, and the government and courts of the state can enforce those laws and rules. The United States is a jurisdiction where federal law can be applied and enforced. A police department has a jurisdiction. That concept means that the entity has power within the area referred to as its jurisdiction, and does not have that power outside its jurisdiction. This is the use of the term referred to when you say, "He was escorted out of the jurisdiction," or "Another jurisdiction's law applies to this case."

Venue is a companion term that refers to an individual court's power to adjudicate cases in a certain geographic area. Jurisdiction most often is defined and limited by the constitution of the state or nation, whereas venue most often is defined and limited by statute. A state may ordain in its constitution that all trial level courts of the state have the power (jurisdiction) to hear all cases arising in the state, but the legislature may carve up the state into smaller venues where an individual court will have the right (the venue power) to hear cases that arise in its particular county or other defined location. For example, the Missouri Circuit Court for the 22nd Judicial Circuit has the power (jurisdiction) to adjudicate cases that arise anywhere in the State of Missouri, but the venue of the court is limited to cases that arise in St. Louis City, not St. Louis County, or any other county in the state. The Missouri Constitution gives each Missouri Circuit Court the power to hear cases arising in the State of Missouri, but further legislation defines the proper venue of the Missouri Circuit Court for the 22nd Judicial Circuit to be cases that arise in St. Louis City. The fact that the Missouri Circuit Court for the 22nd Judicial Circuit has the power to adjudicate cases that arise anywhere in the State of Missouri means that if a case is transferred to that court from another Missouri Circuit Court, for reasons of prejudice or improper venue,[4] the court has the power (jurisdiction) to adjudicate the transferred case even though initially it would not have been the proper venue for the case.

B. Personal jurisdiction

The second usage of the term jurisdiction is the concept of **personal jurisdiction**, and refers to a court's power over the parties to the action. A court must have personal jurisdiction over a party to the case in order for the court to render an enforceable judgment against that party. Generally, a party must have some notice that the court is exercising power over it, which is effectuated by **service of process** on the party. Service of process merely perfects the potential power that the court already had with regard to the party—

---

[4] This often is seen in criminal cases which obtain a great deal of publicity in the location where the crime occurred before the trial of the case. The criminal defendant may feel he has been tried in the local press before getting his day in court, and may seek to have a change of venue to a different court in a different part of the state where his case did not receive as much or any attention in the local media.

if the court has no power over someone, service of process will be of no avail. The three main sources of a court's power to issue process that can be served against a party, so that the court can perfect its power to render judgment against that party, are:

1. **Presence**—If the party, whether it be an individual, a corporation, or another type of entity, is present within the jurisdiction and venue of the court, the court can exert power over it. The party is said to be "found" within the jurisdiction. States have inherent power (sovereignty) over the territory of the state, so if a person is present there, the state has power over that person to adjudicate claims concerning that person. In simple terms, a citizen and resident of a jurisdiction, whether it be a human being who has decided to settle there indefinitely, or a corporation or business entity that has its headquarters or its principal place of business within the jurisdiction or who constantly does business there, will be subject to the power of the courts of that jurisdiction. Beyond that, the boundaries of "presence" within the state or other jurisdiction is a complicated legal concept, and it will be addressed in great detail in your civil procedure course.

2. **"Gotcha" service within the jurisdiction**—As of the publication date of this book, service of process on a person who is temporarily found within the state or other jurisdiction is still considered adequate means for a court to obtain power over that person. Some authorities have questioned the viability of this doctrine under the modern requirements of the Due Process Clause (discussed in the section below), but the doctrine still is alive. Thus, if you are served with process while passing through a state, even if you only are there for a few seconds, you still will be subject to the power of the courts of that state.

3. **Long Arm jurisdiction**—In modern times (post-1900), the above sources of power over individuals and corporations began to be perceived as too limited, and the concept of Long Arm jurisdiction was born. The name is derived from the phrase, "the long arm of the law," and refers to a court's power to issue process against an entity that is outside the physical boundaries of the jurisdiction (for example, the state) if that entity performed certain acts that had an effect in the state and if that entity has some minimal connection (called a **nexus**) with the state. If the requirements for the issuance of process are met, and service of process is accomplished according to the laws of the place where the entity is found, then the entity can be haled (or hauled) into the court. There are two requirements that must be met to make the issuance of process and the exercise of power proper:

    a. <u>Statutory Requirement</u>—The action must arise from an activity in the state or having an effect in the state. Many states define the kinds of activities that trigger the exercise of extraterritorial jurisdiction in a **Long Arm Statute**. Typically, the activities include: (1) doing business in the state; (2) making a contract in the state; (3) committing a tort that causes injury in the state; (4) owning or possessing property in the state; or (5) conceiving a child in the state. As mentioned, the lawsuit must arise from the entity's contact with the state while engaging in a defined activity. In states that use a defined list of activities, it is not enough for a person to have done something in the state at one time if the lawsuit has nothing to do with that contact with the state. For example, a defendant may at one time have conceived a child in the state, but if the lawsuit is a property dispute that has nothing to do with that child or with the child's mother, Long Arm jurisdiction will not exist. Another example where Long Arm jurisdiction will not lie is a lawsuit that involves the enforcement of a promise to a real estate broker who is a citizen of the state, but the promise was made outside the state by a non-citizen and non-resident of the state, and the contract was to have been performed outside the state.

Other states have a Long Arm Statute or have developed a body of state law that allows the exercise of extraterritorial jurisdiction in the state to the full extent of the Due Process Clause (discussed in the section below). Even in these states, the lawsuit must arise from one of the party's contacts with the state in order for the exercise of extraterritorial jurisdiction to be appropriate.

b. **Due Process Requirement**—The exercise of Long Arm jurisdiction also must satisfy the requirements of the Due Process Clause of the 14th Amendment of the United States Constitution. The Due Process Clause requires:

(1) That the entity have certain "minimum contacts" with the state. These contacts must not be "random and fortuitous," but instead must show a "purposeful availment" of the benefits and protections of the laws of the state; and

(2) That the exercise of Long Arm jurisdiction be "reasonable" and not offend "traditional notions of fair play and substantial justice." Courts look to see if the defendant's actions in the state were such that she reasonably should have anticipated being subject to suit in that state.

Substantial constitutional case law that you will study in your civil procedure course defines just what these Due Process requirements mean.

C. Subject matter jurisdiction

The final use of the term jurisdiction refers to **subject matter jurisdiction**. Courts can be limited in the subject matter of the cases that they can adjudicate. Subject matter jurisdiction is a creature of statutory and constitutional law—the limitations on the power of a court to hear certain subject matter come from the federal or state constitutions, statutes, or the rules of the court or court system itself.

State trial level courts often have **unlimited** or **universal** or **general jurisdiction** over matters that arise in the state. This means that any action that is properly brought in that state and is not within the exclusive subject matter jurisdiction of another court (for example, a federal court), is fair game to be filed in that court.

Federal courts all have **limited jurisdiction**, meaning that the subject matter of cases that federal courts can hear is limited by the United States Constitution and federal statutes. If your case does not meet one of the limited criteria for federal jurisdiction, it cannot be brought in federal court, and if it is brought there, it can be dismissed or remanded to a proper court.

Exclusive jurisdiction may be granted to a certain court by statute; for example, a federal statute may state that all cases arising under the statute must be brought in the United States District Courts. The opposite of this is **concurrent jurisdiction**, whereby the same type of action can be brought either in federal or state court.

Appellate courts, particularly the courts of last resort, most often have very limited jurisdiction whereby parties seeking to have a case heard in these courts must **request a transfer** to the court or **petition** the court for the issuance of a **writ of certiorari**, or **writ of mandamus**, or other writ, to allow the case to be heard by the court.

Federal subject matter jurisdiction is limited to **federal question jurisdiction** and **diversity jurisdiction**. **Federal question jurisdiction** requires that a claim in the case must arise under a federal statute or a federal administrative rule or regulation. There is a "**well pleaded complaint**" **rule**, meaning that the federal nature of the action must appear from the plaintiff's pleadings; it is not enough that the defendant can answer the complaint and assert a **defense** that arises under a federal statute. If the federal nature of the claim is not apparent from the complaint, the case cannot be removed to federal court.

Diversity jurisdiction over an action requires diverse parties and an amount in controversy of at least $75,000. **Diverse parties** means that all plaintiffs must be "citizens" of different states from all defendants. All plaintiffs need not be from the same state, nor do all defendants need to be from the same state, as long as there is no plaintiff who is from the same state as any of the defendants. An **amount in controversy of $75,000** means that the damages that the plaintiff lawfully seeks, or the value of the property at stake, or the amount owed under the contract, or any other lawful calculation of the amount one party might gain and the other might lose, must add up to at least $75,000. If the criteria of diverse parties and $75,000 in controversy both are met, the case properly can be adjudicated by a federal court even though the case involves a state law claim that could very well have been brought in a state court.

Preemption of subject matter is a term referring to the concept whereby a federal law or federal legal regime is drafted so as to supplant all state law on that topic. The power to preempt is found in the Supremacy Clause of the United States Constitution. U.S. Const. art. 6, cl. 2. If an area is preempted, no state can maintain and enforce its own law in that area, and if a state court hears such a claim, it must apply and follow the federal law on the topic. If the preemptive law is also drafted with exclusive jurisdiction in federal court over claims arising within the area, then an action that is filed in state court may be removed to federal court. Examples of areas of the law that have been preempted by federal law are copyright, patents, employee retirement income and security plans, and the labeling of insecticides, fungicides and rodenticides.

In certain instances, an action brought in state court that could have been brought in federal court, because there is diversity or federal question jurisdiction over the action, may be **removed** by a defendant from the state court and refiled in the United States District Court of the state and district where the state court is located. This is known as **removal jurisdiction**. In diversity cases, only an out-of-state defendant (a defendant who is not a citizen or resident of the state in which the state court action is filed) may remove the case to federal court. There were historical reasons for this practice, largely based on the perception that out-of-state defendants got a raw deal in state courts, and were better treated by the distinguished federal judges in the courthouse across the street from the state court. At present, the perception of prejudice is fading away, but removal jurisdiction lingers on, perhaps driven by the defense bar who sees that jury verdicts generally are larger in state courts (especially in state courts in large cities) than in the federal courts sitting in the same locale.

The right to remove a case on diversity grounds is further limited by time—if the case lingers in state court for one year, the right to remove vanishes. And if the removal was technically improper at the time of removal (in other words, there were no proper grounds for federal jurisdiction), then the federal court can remand the case back to state court.

Chapter 4

Determining the Rule from a Single Case or Other Authority

The starting point of legal analysis is to identify the rule of law that governs the analysis of the legal question at hand. This is the material that will go in the rule section of your discussion. With constitutions, statutes, and regulations, determining the rule is not the hard part—constitutions, statutes, and regulations are rules, and if a constitutional, statutory, or regulatory provision is on point, the terms of the provision state the rule, or at least they are the starting point of the rule section. Figuring out the meaning of the terms of the constitution, statute, or regulation through the process of statutory interpretation is the tricky part, and that will be discussed in the next chapter.

Figuring out the rule or rules that were applied by a court in its decision is not always simple. This chapter discusses how to read and analyze a court order or opinion in order to determine the rule of the law that was applied by the court to produce the outcome in the case. This rule, which is part of the holding of the case, represents the precedent for which the case stands, and in conjunction with the rule(s) from the other sources you are relying on, makes up the rule in your jurisdiction that answers the legal question you are researching.

I. DETERMINING THE RULE FROM CONSTITUTIONS, STATUTES, OR ADMINISTRATIVE REGULATIONS

There is no trick to finding the rule of law in a constitution, statute, or administrative regulation; the constitution, statute, or regulation itself <u>is</u> the rule on the legal issues described in the title and text of the provision. The challenging part is finding the correct laws and statutory sections and interpreting the language of the provisions. You must research and analyze the constitutional, statutory, and administrative law of your jurisdiction to determine which parts of which laws and regulations actually speak to the issue at hand, which we will discuss in the chapters on research. Once you find the correct sections, you have the rule, and will proceed through the process of statutory interpretation to figure out what the terms of the statute mean.

When presenting the rule in writing—for instance, in the rule section of your discussion—you must quote the exact terms of the constitution, statute, or regulation that pertain to your legal issue, which are referred to as the **operative** or **pertinent** or **applicable terms** of the statute or regulation. It is not proper to paraphrase the terms of a constitution, statute, or regulation. There is no guesswork involved in figuring out the terms of the rule from a constitutional, statutory, or regulatory source, because you simply look to the terms on the page in front of you, but you should only quote the operative or pertinent or applicable terms when you draft the rule section so as not to bore or distract your reader with irrelevant information. For example:

Your client has waited four years after a car accident to decide she wants to sue the other driver. She asks you if it is too late to sue. You understand her cause of action to be for negligence, and you correctly deduce that the answer to the time issue will be covered by a statute, which in this case is called a "statute of limitations." You find the following statute in Apex:

Apex Rev. Stat. § 300.2-102. Limitations on Tort and Contract actions.

All actions of libel, slander, intentional torts, negligence, fraud, negligent misrepresentation, and for breach of contract (except contracts for the provision or payment of money, which are covered by section 300.2-101), shall be brought within five years of the date the cause of action accrued.

You have the rule, no question, but you would write it up as follows:

> "All actions of . . . negligence . . . shall be brought within five years of the date the cause of action accrued." Apex Rev. Stat. § 300.2-102 (1997).

Quoting only these terms is most helpful for the reader, because the rest of the statute is irrelevant to the legal issue you are researching. Remember to use ellipses (". . .") to show where you took information out of the statute.[1]

There are issues raised by this rule: What does "accrued" mean, and when did this action accrue? There will be cases interpreting this and other language in the rule, and applying the rule in various situations, all of which can be discussed in separate TREAT sections in your paper. But the starting point in the rule section is the language of the statute quoted above.

A constitution, statute, or regulation represents the official language of a rule of law created by those persons and entities who have been charged with the making of laws and regulations—our legislators and administrative and regulatory agencies. That is the reason why lawyers do not paraphrase the terms of statutes. Contrast this with the courts, who are not charged with making laws, but instead create law in the form of legal precedent as a byproduct of their primary, adjudicatory function. Because constitutions, statutes, and regu-

---

[1] Ellipses are used to show the place of text that has been removed. Three ellipsis dots are used if the removal was in the middle of a sentence ("John fell . . . and broke his leg."). Four ellipsis dots are used of the material was taken at the end of a sentence ("John fell into a hole . . . . Marsha came to rescue him."). Additional rules on ellipses are presented in Appendix B, Section II(C).

lations are the official versions of rules created by the persons charged with rule-making, you must give them priority in your discussion of the sources for a rule of law on your issue. If a constitution, statute, or regulation is found to be on point, it must be quoted first in a rule section. Other authorities (cases, law review articles, treatises, scholarly commentary and critique) may interpret the provision, and these can affect the meaning and effect of the provision, but the official language that you would present first in your rule section remains that which is printed in the constitution, statute, or regulation.

II. FINDING THE RULE IN A CASE

As mentioned above, judges are not charged with the official task of making law. Their primary task is to find and apply the law so as to adjudicate disputes that come before them, not to make new law. People criticize judges and courts for "judicial legislating" and "judicial activism"—terms referring to some courts' tendency to go out of their way to set down a certain rule in a case, thereby taking on a positive or normative role traditionally assigned to lawmakers. But these judicial activists are the exception, not the rule, among jurists.

Nevertheless, we have told you that judicial opinions are a primary source of the law, and it is true that judges can create or modify or abandon rules of law. In most circumstances, rules are made or modified as a by-product of the judge's adjudicatory functions. The description of this process leads neatly into a discussion of what you must look for in order to find the rule of law that the case stands for, which is a major part of the holding of the case, and represents the precedent that is set by the case.

A. The legal method of judges

A judge is in a similar position as a lawyer in private or public practice when it comes to the methodology for solving the problems that reach the judge's desk. Judges (and the lawyers who work for them, who typically are called law clerks or staff attorneys) receive a set of "problems" in the form of a lawsuit, and when they have to make a decision concerning one of these problems, they turn to the same sources of the law as the attorneys who appear before them. Yes, the court has the benefit of the briefs and legal memoranda that this book is training you to write and which are supplied to the court by the counsel for both sides in the case, but woe to the judge or law clerk who simply takes a lawyer's word on what the law is without checking it out for herself. Judges and their legal staff must find the sources and analyze what they say to determine what the law is on each issue that arises in the case before them.

The difference is that judges then get to implement the rule. They get to apply the rule to real persons in actual, concrete situations, and when they do this they have created a precedent for how the rule works in a specific situation.

Judges report their decisions at the trial level in the form of a written **order** (also called at various times a **memorandum and order, order and memorandum,** or **order and judgment**), and at the appellate level, in a written **opinion**. It is in these orders and opinions that new law is made, most often in small, incremental steps, as the judge explains what the law is, what it means, and how it is going to work in the situation at hand. This brings us to the topics of the "**Borrowed Rule**" and the "**Applied Rule**" or "**Precedent**" established by the case.[2]

METHODOLOGY OF COURT OPINIONS:

Problem = Motion or Lawsuit that presents an issue to resolve

Borrowed Rule(s)
Legal principles that govern the issue taken from earlier statutes, administrative rules and regulations, cases, or other authorities

▼   ▼

| If the court applies a borrowed rule to the case without interpreting, modifying, or changing the legal effect of the borrowed rule in any way . . . | If the court interprets, modifies, or changes the legal effect of a borrowed rule . . . |

▼   ▼

| The borrowed rule is applied by the the court to resolve the case. The borrowed rule is part of the holding, and the legal opinion written by the court becomes one more precedent on the borrowed rule. | **"Applied" Rule**
The court has processed the borrowed rule. It may have created a new rule—the "applied rule"— or added new interpretive rules. The applied rule is applied by the court to resolve the case. The applied rule is part of the holding, and the legal opinion written by the court becomes a **precedent** on the applied rule. |

---

[2] The terms used in this chapter — **Borrowed Rule and Applied Rule** — were adopted by the authors to describe concepts that are familiar to all lawyers and legal academics, but the actual terms we are using will not be familiar to them. Various legal writing academics have chosen different terms for these same concepts over the years, and there is little uniformity in the choices, so you should presume that anyone who has not read this book will not understand what you mean by the terms **Borrowed Rule** and **Applied Rule** until you explain the concepts for which they stand. We are using the terms "**precedent**" and "**holding**" in the manner that they commonly are understood in the legal community.

B. The Borrowed Rule

Because judges follow the same methodology as practitioners in looking up and determining what the law is on a given issue, they often include in their writing a statement of the applicable rule of law on the issue that was found in earlier authorities. Thus, the court borrows or adopts this statement of the rule for its own opinion, and we may refer to this statement as the **borrowed rule**.

The borrowed rule may be the rule of law that was applied by the court to make its decision, thus becoming part of the holding, and the case becomes one more precedent on the meaning and application of the borrowed rule. However, it does not have to be. It is important to remember that the borrowed rule *is not necessarily the rule of law that is applied by the court* and it is not necessarily part of the holding and the precedent set by the case. In fact, the borrowed rule is considered part of the holding (and a precedent on the borrowed rule) *only* when the court did nothing in its discussion of the rule to alter, interpret, add to, or abandon all or part of the borrowed rule. If the court does not discuss or explain what the borrowed rule means, and simply applies it to the facts before her, then the borrowed rule *is* the rule from the case that is part of the holding and the case is one more precedent on the borrowed rule.

It is noteworthy if the case uses a particular borrowed rule when there is more than one rule or more than one wording of the rule being used in the jurisdiction. Occasionally, two versions of a rule on a given legal issue will compete at the same time in the same jurisdiction, and one version will have more or different requirements than the other. In these situations, you may uncover a line of cases following each competing rule, and so it is noteworthy which version of the rule the case you are looking at has adopted.

C. The Applied Rule or Precedent

Typically, a court will explain the borrowed rule and how it works in various situations. When a judge does this, attorneys reading the order or opinion of the court can rely on the analysis and interpretation written by the judge about the borrowed rule of law. This discussion of the rule can modify the rule, and an attorney can use the judge's opinion as a source not only for the wording of the rule borrowed from an earlier source, but also for the meaning and interpretation of the words in the rule. This may cast a new light on one or more terms of the borrowed rule, or alter the way we should think about these terms.

The court, in analyzing the case and applying the borrowed rule(s) to the case, may:

◆ **Interpret** a borrowed rule—The court may write a new interpretive rule on the borrowed rule. The court may apply the rule or an element of the rule in such a way that legal effect of the rule or an element of the rule is changed in a legally significant way.

◆ <u>**Modify**</u> a borrowed rule—The court may add an element or factor to the rule or take away an element or factor from the rule. The court may redefine or even reword a rule or an element of a rule, changing its legal effect.

◆ <u>**Abrogate**</u> (or <u>**Overturn**</u> or <u>**Strike Down**</u>) the entire borrowed rule or part of the rule—This is much more common with courts of last resort that have the last word on the law of a given jurisdiction. In regard to statutory law, a court usually will only strike a statute down because of a state or federal constitutional defect in the law or because the law clashes with federal or international law under the Supremacy Clause of the United States Constitution.

The following are examples of what can happen to a borrowed rule. The first situation is a court that inherits a rule and does nothing to interpret, modify, or change the rule in a legally significant way:

Example 1

The Borrowed Rule in the Apex case you are reading, <u>Billy v. Tilly</u>, 887 W.2d 234, 236 (Apex 1996), states:

To prevail on a claim for injuries caused by a dog, a plaintiff must plead and prove: (1) ownership of the dog by the defendant; (2) causation of the injury by the dog; and (3) lack of provocation of the dog. <u>Lori v. Benji</u>, 667 W.2d 234, 236 (Apex 1993).

The judge applies the rule—"The defendant owned the dog, the defendant's dog bit the plaintiff, and the plaintiff had done nothing to provoke the dog. The plaintiff wins."

This case applies the borrowed rule to the case as it found it. <u>Billy</u> becomes one more precedent on the borrowed rule laid down in <u>Lori</u>.

The second example is a case that writes new rules—in this case, interpretive rules—on certain elements of the main rule:

Example 2

The borrowed rule in the Apex case you are reading, <u>Willy v. Gilly</u>, 987 W.2d 134, 136 (Apex 1998), states:

To prevail on a claim for injuries caused by a dog, a plaintiff must plead and prove: (1) ownership of the dog by the defendant; (2) causation of the injury by the dog; and (3) lack of provocation of the dog. <u>Blue v. Bingo</u>, 667 W.2d 234, 236 (Apex 1993).

> The judge goes on to state: "The concept of 'ownership' of the dog is not limited to a person having actual possession of title to the animal, but includes a person who harbors or has control over a dog." Later, the judge states: "Provocation requires an actual physical attack on the dog; verbal attacks do not count."

We now know two things about the rule on dog bite liability in Apex that we did not know from a reading of the borrowed rule: ownership is not limited to title, and includes harboring and controlling a dog, and provocation requires a physical attack, while verbal attacks are excluded. The borrowed rule has been modified by this judge. In the one instance, "ownership" has been expanded; in the other instance, "provocation" has been limited.

Occasionally, a judge will reject or abandon certain terms of the rule, as in the following example:

Example 3

The borrowed rule in the case <u>Garfield v. John</u>, 777 W.2d 333, 335 (Apex 1989), is presented as follows:

The rule in Apex on liability for damages caused by a domestic cat has traditionally been phrased to require proof that: (1) the defendant owned and controlled the cat; (2) the injury was caused by the cat; (3) the plaintiff did not provoke the cat; and (4) the cat weighed more than eight pounds at the time of the attack. <u>Tigre v. Gato</u>, 456 W.2d 654, 658 (Apex 1956).

The court then states: "The last requirement concerning the weight of the cat has never been applied by any court in Apex as a basis for granting or denying relief to any plaintiff. The requirement is dead letter, and the Court will give it no consideration in this matter."

We now know that the court in question will only apply the first three elements of the cat bite rule, and this opinion will be authority for the argument that the rule now only has three elements in Apex.

The court may add to the requirements of the rule, as follows:

Example 4

The borrowed rule in the case <u>Ivan v. Igor</u>, 676 W.2d 545, 548 (Apex Ct. App. 1st Dist. 1985), is stated as follows:

The rule from <u>In re Debbie</u>, 345 W.2d 987 (Apex. Ct. App. 1st Dist. 1965), was that "a party wishing to exercise the option of waiving the right to a trial

> by jury must give notice of this decision to the other party in the matter."
> <u>Id.</u> at 988.
>
> The court goes on to say: "In addition, the party must not only give notice
> of the exercise of the option to her opponent, but must do so promptly, at the
> earliest opportunity in the case."

The rule has been altered by adding an additional requirement or at least a modification of an existing requirement. Attorneys should look at the requirements of the rule differently because of this opinion.

When the court is finished, it will apply the rule as modified to the facts of the case to determine the outcome. It is the modified version of the rule actually used to determine the outcome of the case that is most important to the analysis of the case. We will call this the "**applied rule**" or the "**precedent**" set by the case. By this definition, the precedent is equivalent to the holding of the case, and the holding of the case determines the precedential value of the case. The definition of holding is:

> **Holding:**
>
> A sentence or a short discussion (no more than a paragraph), which explains in legal terms the rule(s) of law that were used to resolve the legal issues in the case, and how they were applied, so as to explain why the prevailing party won.

In legal analysis, lawyers refer to a precedent as a set of facts and circumstances that show how a borrowed rule or applied rule works. "This case is precedent for the proposition that . . ." The applied rule is the rule you will use in the drafting of the rule section of your discussion.

D. How do you phrase the Applied Rule?

You have two choices in how to phrase the applied rule from a case: you can write the borrowed rule followed by the modifications that this case has rendered to the borrowed rule, thus revealing the applied rule in a paragraph, or you can try to synthesize what the case has done to the borrowed rule into a single, revised version of the rule—thus, revealing the applied rule in a single sentence. Which option you should take depends on the historical status of the borrowed rule and your ability to write a coherent applied rule in a single sentence. There are some guidelines to follow:

◆ Never change the wording of rules from constitutions, statutes, and administrative regulations.

If a case modifies a rule taken from a constitution, statute, or administrative regulation, write up the modification separately, after you have you laid out the pertinent terms of the constitution, statute, or regulation. This follows the rule discussed above that states that you never should paraphrase or rephrase the terms of a statute or regulation.

◆ Do not change the wording of a much cited historical rule. Write the modification second.

A borrowed rule sometimes achieves the status of a judicially made statute; all the cases in your jurisdiction cite the same rule as *the* rule on the issue, and the rule is always phrased using the exact same language—same terms, same number of elements—even if the "original" case that is cited for that language changes from case to case. In these instances, you should respect the authorities in your jurisdiction, and start off your rule section with the traditional, historical version of the borrowed rule, followed by a separate discussion of the ways in which the borrowed rule has been modified. In this way, the whole rule section reveals the applied rule.

◆ Synthesize the applied rule if it makes a clear, succinct, and coherent statement of the applied rule. Do not synthesize if it forces you to write a long, overly complicated, run-on sentence for the rule.

In some instances, it is appropriate to modify the actual wording of the borrowed rule when you present it as the applied rule in your rule discussion. The court in Example 4 above added a new requirement that affected one of the existing elements of the rule. The rule and the modification are short enough and simple enough that when we present the applied rule, we would go ahead and add the change:

Synthesized Statement of the Applied Rule

A party wishing to exercise the option of waiving the right to a trial by jury must give notice of this decision to the other party in the matter promptly, at the earliest opportunity in the case. <u>Ivan v. Igor</u>, 676 W.2d 545, 548 (Apex Ct. App. 1st Dist. 1985); <u>In re Debbie</u>, 345 W.2d 987, 988 (Apex Ct. App. 1st Dist. 1965).

<u>In re Debbie</u> was the source of the Borrowed Rule, and <u>Ivan</u> added to the rule, so both cases should be mentioned. There are no quotation marks around the rule because the exact wording we have presented does not appear in either of the sources we have cited, although the meaning of the rule would be apparent to anyone reading the two cited sources.

Example 2 above is different. The terms of the borrowed rule have not been altered directly, but we now know a lot more about what two of those terms mean. If we were presenting the applied rule in a rule section, we would not try to cobble together the two sources and make a single statement of the rule. Do not produce something like the following:

DO NOT WRITE A RULE SECTION LIKE THIS:

To prevail on a claim for injuries caused by a dog, a plaintiff must plead and prove: (1) ownership of the dog by the defendant, which is not limited to a person having actual possession of title to the animal, but includes a person who harbors or has control over a dog; (2) causation of the injury by the dog; and (3) lack of provocation of the dog, meaning lack of an actual physical attack on the dog, because verbal attacks do not count. Billy v. Tilly, 887 W.2d 234, 236 (Apex 1996); Lori v. Benji, 667 W.2d 234, 236 (Apex 1993).

This looks too strange. Simply cobbling the two together makes a long, complicated and cumbersome rule that is too wordy to be useful in the application of the law to the facts. Judges and other audiences will not trust your synthesis of the two authorities if the end product looks like a Frankenstein monster.

Instead of the above, put these interpretative sub-rules where they belong—in the subsections of the discussion that handle these particular elements of the rule (which will be referred to in Chapter 6 as sub-TREAT sections):

Rule on Main Issue:

To prevail on a claim for injuries caused by a dog, a plaintiff must plead and prove: (1) ownership of the dog by the defendant; (2) causation of the injury by the dog; and (3) lack of provocation of the dog. Billy v. Tilly, 887 W.2d 234, 236 (Apex 1996); Lori v. Benji, 667 W.2d 234, 236 (Apex 1993).

Sub-Rule on Ownership (from the sub-TREAT on Ownership):

The concept of "ownership" of the dog is not limited to a person having actual possession of title to the animal, but includes a person who harbors or has control over a dog." Billy, 887 W.2d at 236.

Sub-Rule on Provocation (from the Sub-TREAT on Provocation):

Provocation requires an actual physical attack on the dog; verbal attacks do not count. Id.

Example 3 dropped the fourth element of the borrowed rule. In expressing this change, we would not simply rewrite the rule with the last element lopped off. Instead, we would give notice to our reader that there was a fourth element, but it is no longer applicable:

> The rule in Apex on liability for damages caused by a domestic cat has traditionally been phrased to require proof that: (1) the defendant owned and controlled the cat; (2) the injury was caused by the cat; (3) the plaintiff did not provoke the cat; and (4) the cat weighed more than eight pounds at the time of the attack. Tigre v. Gato, 456 W.2d 654, 658 (Apex 1956). The fourth element, the weight of the cat, has fallen out of favor with courts in Apex, and no longer is applied. See Garfield v. John, 777 W.2d 333, 335 (Apex 1989).

You certainly should not lop off the last element if this were a much cited historical rule or a rule from a statute or administrative rule or regulation. By presenting the borrowed rule first followed by the modification, the reader is given the correct rule, but she will not be surprised if she goes and reads cases that still list four elements to the rule.

E. The holding of the case and dicta

The definition of holding is:

> #### Holding:
>
> A sentence or a short discussion (no more than a paragraph), which explains in legal terms the applied rule(s) of law that were used to resolve the legal issues in the case, and how they were applied, so as to explain why the prevailing party won.

The holding is a combination of the applied rules and a discussion of how the rules were applied to the pertinent facts in the case to produce the result. A proper description of the holding would discuss all three of these things—the applied rules, pertinent or relevant facts, and how the rules were applied to the facts to bring about the result in the case.

There is a holding on each separate ultimate issue raised by the parties in support of their demands for relief. An appellate opinion will typically take up and resolve a number of independent issues, each of which is offered by the appellant as a ground for reversal of the judgment below, and each of which produces a separate holding.

Dicta is a legal discussion in the case that is not part of the holding. Sometimes it is more troublesome to figure out what is dicta than what is the holding. Consider the following definition:

Dicta:

Anything in a case (any statement about the law, any legal analysis, any discussion of an element or factor or consideration) that is irrelevant to and unnecessary for the outcome of the case. If the discussion of the law you are looking at has no impact on the outcome of the case (the decision of the court as to who won and who lost and why), then it is dicta.

When you are confused as to whether it is holding or dicta, think about the following:

◆ Did the court make its decision halfway through the case, and announced it, but went on to discuss several elements, items, or factors anyway? If so, the items that are discussed after the court made up its mind are probably dicta.

◆ Did the court say that it was not reaching certain issues? This is a dead giveaway that any discussion of these issues is dicta.

◆ Did the court predict an outcome for a future case if the facts or circumstances were different? That kind of prediction is dicta.

◆ If you simply dropped the issue or the discussion of the issue from the case—removed every mention of it—would it still be possible to:
  a. Figure out why the prevailing party prevailed?
  b. State the factors, policies and considerations that brought about the decision?
  c. Explain the rule(s) or element(s) that were analyzed and applied to determine the outcome?
  d. State the facts that the court found to be important to the decision?

If you answer YES to a, b, c, and d, you have dicta.

Dicta can be important. As you will see in the chapters that follow, lawyers and judges often will be very curious to find out what other courts have said in previous cases, especially cases from a higher court in the appropriate hierarchy of judicial authority, no matter if the statements are holding or dicta. Dicta can be a useful predictor of what the court that uttered the dicta will do in a future case where the issue discussed in the dicta is finally reached and resolved by the court. The important distinction is that a lower court is not bound by dicta, while it may be bound by the holding, so the distinction does matter for that purpose.

Chapter 5

Determining the Applicable Rule Through Statutory Interpretation and Analysis of Multiple Authorities

You now are ready to try your hand at real life legal analysis. This chapter discusses how to read and analyze multiple authorities, including statutes, rules and regulations, court orders and opinions, in order to determine the rule of the law that applies to your issue in your jurisdiction. In order to do this, you must build on what you already have learned:

◆ You must know which of your sources are primary authorities and which are secondary (Chapter 1).

◆ You must understand the holding of the cases you have found and their applied rules in order to determine their place in the body of controlling or potentially controlling law you are constructing on the issue (Chapter 4).

◆ You must understand what was dicta in these cases, so that you can start building up a store of persuasive authority on the issue (Chapter 4).

◆ You must understand the hierarchy of judicial authority in your jurisdiction so that you can properly rank the cases you have found (Chapter 3).

◆ You must understand the priority of statutes and regulations and how to deal with subsequent interpretations of these sources by cases and legal commentators (Chapters 4 and 5).

A collection of sources must be ordered in terms of priority between primary authorities and secondary authorities and potentially controlling authorities and non-controlling or persuasive authorities. Then you can determine which authorities, if any, are actually controlling, and which are relegated to the persuasive pile. Finally, you must analyze the precedents from each of the authorities and attempt to reconcile them so that you can make one coherent presentation of the rule.

You will recall from Chapter 1 that **primary authorities** are **legislation** (including statutes, ordinances, laws, codes, treaties, charters, and constitutions), **administrative rules and regulations** (including court rules and the regulations, decrees, orders, licenses, and interpretations promulgated by administrative agencies, non-legislative governmental entities, and other regulatory boards and commissions), and **judicial orders and opinions**. **Secondary authorities** are everything else—namely, commentary and interpretations of the law written by legal scholars, judges, legislators, and legal practitioners in treatises, restatements of the law, hornbooks, law review articles, annotations, encyclopedias, legislative history documents, and other publications.

The next concept to grasp is **controlling authority** (also known as **binding** or **mandatory authority**) and **persuasive authority**. Controlling authority must be followed by courts and legal practitioners. It controls the rule that determines the issue you are researching.

Persuasive authority is everything else that is not controlling authority. It does not have to be particularly persuasive to keep its name. Persuasive authority merely is a generic term to refer to all authority that is not controlling authority. Persuasive authority need not be followed. A court might follow persuasive authority if the court finds it to be useful for the resolution of the issue at hand, but the court does not have to follow it. In that persuasive authority will be followed from time to time as long as it does not contradict controlling authority, attorneys must analyze persuasive authority along with any controlling authority on the issue.

Only primary authorities have the potential to be controlling authority, but not every primary authority is even potentially controlling.

> **Only primary authorities from the jurisdiction whose law applies to your case have the potential to be controlling.**

Whether or not they actually are controlling depends on factors we will discuss in a moment. If they are not controlling, they will be relegated to the "persuasive authority" pile.

> **Secondary authorities may be used as persuasive authorities, but they never are controlling.**

Within the stack of persuasive authority, we will study how to rank your persuasive authorities by order of their "persuasiveness."

I. STATUTORY AND RULE INTERPRETATION

Before you go further, you must come to grips with the process of interpreting a statute or administrative rule or regulation. Although a statute or regulation is a rule, and the text of a statute or regulation is the starting point of any rule section in which there is an applicable statute or regulation, a lawyer simply cannot rely on the bare terms of the statute to prove to the reader what the rule means. Instead, she must engage in the process of statutory and rule interpretation.

The process potentially takes you through the consideration of many sources beyond the actual text of the statute, and it is complicated enough to warrant an entire course of study in law school. The following discussion is not intended to replace this course of study; rather, we will lay out in outline form the steps of the process, from textual analysis, to contextual analysis, to secondary sources of interpretation.

The chart on the next page depicts the process of statutory interpretation. The initial section indicates that the interpretation starts with the text, and thus is referred to as the "textual" part of the analysis. The second step is a "contextual" analysis—looking to the context of the relevant statutory section, meaning other provisions of the statute or the code, to find support for an interpretation of the section. A textual or contextual analysis may be assisted by the application of one or more principles of interpretation, often referred to as "canons of construction." These canons allow lawyers and judges to make more uniform and predictable interpretations of statutory language in certain specific contexts described in the canons. Cases may then interpret the terms directly or provide new or modified meanings to the terms by the way the cases apply the terms to certain facts and situations.

Legislative history (discussed in Chapter 16) also may be used as a record of contemporaneous construction of the terms of the statute by the legislators as they prepared to pass these terms into law. Although not part of the statute, and thus not primary authority, legislative history is more authoritative than secondary authority that merely comments on and construes the statute after it has been passed into law. Thus, as discussed below, when the text and context and the general principles of interpretation fail to identify one conclusive meaning of the terms of the statute, legislative history is the next best step in proving that your own interpretation is the correct one.

Secondary authority, in the form of treatises, law review and journal articles, and other forms of commentary, can be used to support an interpretation of the statutory terms. Rarely would such commentary swing the vote of your audience by itself, but it can be very useful in buttressing a textual, contextual, or legislative history driven interpretation.

The process of interpretation described here refers to the determination of the meaning of the terms of the statute on the day that it was passed into law in the jurisdiction. The next step in the analysis, beyond interpretation of the terms, is to consider how the statute has been changed by later primary authorities, namely statutory amendments and case law. This is discussed later in this chapter.

THE PROCESS OF STATUTORY INTERPRETATION[1]

Interpretive Aid	Nature of the Authority	Uniform Statute and Rule Construction Act
Text	Primary	Sections 1, 2, 19
Text of the statutory provision		
Definitions in the statute		
Context	Primary	Section 2
Definitions in other parts of the code		
Usage of similar terms in other parts of the code		
Common or technical meaning of terms		
Meaning derived from provisions in the same title of the code		
Meaning derived from the purpose of the act or regime that created the provision		
Principles of Construction	Neither.	
Baseline definitions in USRCA §§ 3-7 (if adopted in your jurisdiction)	These are rules for how to read text and context.	Sections 3-7
Federal Dictionary Act, 1 U.S.C. §§ 1-7		
Prospective operation of statutes (vs. retrospective operation)		Section 8
Severability of invalid provisions		Section 9
Irreconcilable statutes or provisions Later statutes prevail Comprehensive revision eliminates prior inconsistent laws		Section 10
Enrolled bill text controls over errors in codified version and later publications		Section 11
Incorporation by reference rules		Section 12

---

[1] This section of this chapter is largely derived from the Uniform Statute and Rule Construction Act (ULA 1995) ("USRCA"), which is itself a revision of the Model Statutory Construction Act (ULA 1965, rev'd 1975), and the order of presentation follows the order suggested in Peter B. Maggs, Statutory Interpretation - Copyright (2001), text available at http://home.law.uiuc.edu/ ~pmaggs/ constat.htm.

Headings and titles are not used unless they were drafted by the legislature and included in the enrolled bill passed by the legislature		Section 13
Rules concerning repeal of statutes and repeal of repealing statutes		Sections 14-16
General rules (maxims) of construction		Sections 18, 20
Judicial Construction of the Statute (in cases applying the statute)	Primary	Section 20
Courts have the power to interpret and apply the law, and may change the meaning and effect of the statute as a by-product of this power		
Legislative History	Although not primary, these aids are more authoritative and persuasive than the secondary sources discussed below	
Contemporaneous constructions in House, Senate, and Conference committee reports		Section 20(b), (c)
Amendments and changes in the bill, in committee or on the floor of the chamber		Section 20(c), (d)
Answers to specific questions in floor debate and committee reports		Section 20(c), (d)
Commentary	Secondary	
Official commentary in the statute		
General commentary in treatises, law reviews and other secondary authorities		
Similar Statutes	Primary, but not controlling, and used in a way that simulates secondary authority	Section 20(b)
Uniform Laws		
Construction of similar statutes in other jurisdictions, using text, context, judicial decisions, legislative history, and commentary		

GENERAL PRINCIPLES OF STATUTORY INTERPRETATION

Reading the text of a statute is, of course, the first step in the process, but, as will be painfully clear to you after a few weeks of law school, words do not always mean what a layperson might think they mean when the words appear in a legal document. This is especially true of statutory terms. The following are some general principles of interpretation of statutory language—the canons of construction—that are applied in the United States:

PRINCIPLE I. THE TEXT OF A STATUTE IS THE PRIMARY, ESSENTIAL SOURCE OF ITS MEANING

The Uniform Statute and Rule Construction Act § 19 (ULA 1995) ("USRCA") confirms the general principle that the first step of any statutory interpretation is the text of the statute. The following guidelines on how to approach the reading of the text apply:

A. If the statute contains a definition of a word, its meaning is determined by the definition.

If the statute discusses the term "beverage," and the statute contains a definition of the term "beverage" as meaning "alcoholic drinks and carbonated sodas," it would be proper to construe the term "beverage" as including beer, wine, liquor, cola, root beer, orange soda, and tasteless malt beverages, but it would not be proper to include water and natural fruit juices.

B. If the statute does not contain a definition of a word, its meaning is determined by:

1. Common usage of the terms, including:

a. A meaning that is so obvious to the judge that no authority is cited

You do not have to prove to the court the obvious meaning of terms. Judges should know that "feline" refers to cats and "canine" refers to dogs. More exotic terms (ursine, equine, or porcine) may require a little support. When in doubt, provide support for the obvious, but do it clearly and succinctly.

b. Dictionary definitions

Legislators are presumed to know the common dictionary meanings of the words that they use in legislation, so if they intend a different meaning or only one of several possible dictionary meanings, they should spell it out clearly in the statute.

c. Usage of the same word elsewhere in the same statute

This is part of the contextual analysis. The applicable statutory provision may not contain definitions of several of its terms, but the provision usually will have been passed as part of a larger act, which may contain definitions of terms that were accepted by the legislature when they passed the entire act. In the absence of contrary evidence, the meaning given to the same terms at the same time by the same legislators is powerful evidence that the terms all carry the same meaning.

d. Usage in other statutes, legislative materials, and other public documents

A more tenuous position is to point to definitions found in the same code (the codification of all of the jurisdiction's statutory law), even definitions that were passed into law years before or years after the statutory provision at hand. Under this theory, the legislature is supposed to be aware of the meaning of all terms used in the code of the jurisdiction, so if they use the same terms later, they are presumed to carry the same meaning as when the legislature used them earlier. Of course, the legislators may want to preclude this by defining the terms to mean what they want them to mean, as discussed above.

e. Common law meaning of a term

Again, in the absence of contrary evidence, if a term has a defined legal meaning in the common law developed by a chain of cases, then the legislators are presumed to be aware of this common law legal meaning and are further presumed to have intended the term to have this meaning when they intentionally used the term in the statute. As discussed above, legislators are free to depart from a common law legal meaning of a term by defining the term in the statute.

2. Technical or particular meaning of words that have acquired a technical or particular meaning in a given context

Much like the term of art or trade usage concept from contract law, certain words have well known legal meanings when used in a specific context. The word "freight" has a particular meaning in the context of sales of goods (it means the fee paid for shipping goods with a carrier of goods, such as a trucking company or railroad), which is different from the layperson's understanding of "freight," meaning the goods that are being shipped. The legislators are presumed to know these technical meanings, so if they draft sales of goods legislation and use the word "freight," it will be construed to have the same meaning it usually has in sales contexts. If the legislators do not intend the term to carry the particular meaning it would carry in the subject matter context of the statute, they would have to define the term to remove the presumption.

3. Legal meaning as defined in the Dictionary Act, 1 U.S.C. §§ 1-7

In 1 U.S.C. §§ 1-7, Congress has taken the time to define some terms that often appear in federal legislation. For example, 1 U.S.C. § 1 provides, "words importing the singular include and apply to several persons, parties, or things; words importing the plural include the singular; words importing the masculine gender include the feminine as well; . . . the words 'person' and 'whoever' include corporations, companies, associations, firms, partnerships, societies, and joint stock companies, as well as individuals."

4. Legal meaning as defined by state statute or common law

The USRCA recognizes that certain terms have an established meaning under the common law and state statutory law. For example, "shall" and "must" express a duty, obligation, requirement, or condition precedent. "May" confers a power, authority, privilege, or right. Use of a word of one gender includes corresponding words of the other gender. Use of a verb in the present tense includes the future tense.

5. The context in which the terms appear

Meaning can be derived from context, as discussed above.

6. The rules of English grammar

Most of us would like to believe that English is a precise enough language for the law, but consider the following:

Dog owners shall not bring dogs into the park unless they are leashed.

Is it the dogs that must be leased, or the owners?
And how are we to interpret these phrases:[2]

The ladies of the church have cast off clothing of every kind, and they may be seen in the church basement Friday.

This afternoon there will be a meeting in the south and north ends of the church. Children will be baptized at both ends.

Eight new choir robes are currently needed, due to the addition of several new members and to the deterioration of some older ones.

---

[2] See Hawes Publications Funny Items from the Internet, "Actual "Gems" from Church Bulletins" http://www.execpc.com/hawes/humor.htm#item4 (visited Jan. 3, 2001).

Although the principle stands, be careful about the English language letting you down in the end.

PRINCIPLE II. PROSPECTIVE AND RETROSPECTIVE OPERATION

A statute only operates prospectively unless the statute expressly provides otherwise or its context requires that it operate retrospectively. This principle is an issue of fairness and due process. Cases operate retrospectively because they deal with the legal interpretation and effect of past events that gave rise to claims, but statutes and regulations operate prospectively to define future rights and liabilities. If a statute is passed to prohibit certain behavior, a person is permitted to behave in the proscribed way up to the effective date of the statute. Then, if she quits her bad behavior at the moment before the statute goes into effect, she will not be punished under the statute. For example, if a client was growing marijuana in his basement, and discovers that Congress has just passed a law making the growing of marijuana in basements illegal as of July 1, 2002, the client can throw out his pots of pot on June 30, 2002, and not suffer prosecution under this particular law (but no opinion is offered as to his culpability under other laws already in effect on and before June 30, 2002).

However, some statutes must operate retrospectively, as in the situation where the statute regulates activities, events, rights, or duties that happened in the past. For example, a statute providing for the distribution of reparations for victims of the September 11, 2001 terrorist attack necessarily operates retrospectively to define and regulate rights that arose in the past. Most procedural and jurisdictional statutes operate without regard to when the events on the merits of the suit occurred, so the terms retroactive and prospective do not have an impact on their operation.

PRINCIPLE III. SEVERABILITY OF INVALID PROVISIONS

If a provision of a statute or its application to any person or circumstance is held invalid, the invalidity does not affect other provisions or applications of the statute that can be given effect without the invalid provision or application, and to this end the provisions of the statute are severable. One bad section or provision does not destroy the operation of the rest of the statutory terms and provisions as long as one can make sense of the requirements of the remaining provisions without reference to or use of the stricken terms.

PRINCIPLE IV. STATUTES WHOSE TERMS CONFLICT

If statutes enacted into law in the same jurisdiction appear to conflict, they must be construed, if possible, to give effect to each. If the conflict is irreconcilable, the later enacted statute governs. Legislators are presumed to have known of the conflict and are understood to have passed a law that changed the rules of the earlier statute even if they did not specifically take the steps to show that the earlier legislation was being repealed. However, an earlier enacted specific, special, or local statute prevails over a later enacted general statute unless the context of the later enacted statute indicates otherwise. Statutes with particular subject matter (for example, licensing of bicycles), as opposed to general legislation (for example, regulating all vehicles) may be interpreted as surviving the passage of the later, generally worded statute unless it is clear that the legislators intended to change the rules for all moving vehicles including bicycles. If the general statute has provisions that address bicycles, then the intent of the legislators to regulate bicycles is made clear.

PRINCIPLE V. COMPREHENSIVE REVISIONS OF THE LAW

If a statute is a comprehensive revision of the law on a subject, it prevails over previous statutes on the subject whether or not the revision and the previous statutes conflict irreconcilably. From time to time, legislators pass into law a new statutory regime that is intended to regulate all aspects of a certain legal subject matter.

In 1973, Congress passed into law the Employee Retirement Income Security Act (ERISA), which was intended to establish a new legal regime governing all aspects of employee benefit plans and retirement plans. The sweeping nature of the legislation was clear from the language of the act. Therefore, any federal laws governing aspects of employee benefits and retirement income plans that were on the books prior to 1973 will be deemed to have been supplanted by ERISA unless Congress indicated otherwise in the legislative history or text of the ERISA statute.

PRINCIPLE VI. STATUTES INCORPORATING ANOTHER STATUTE OF THE SAME JURISDICTION

A statute that incorporates by reference another statute of the same jurisdiction is deemed to incorporate a later enactment or amendment of the other statute. If a state's sales of artwork statute incorporates by reference a definition or regulation of the payment of freight from the Uniform Commercial Code enacted in the same state, and the definition or regulation of freight is later updated, the newer, updated version of the freight provision is deemed to be incorporated into the sales of artwork statute unless the legislators indicate something to the contrary.

PRINCIPLE VII. USE OF HEADINGS AND TITLES

Headings and titles may <u>not</u> be used in construing a statute unless they are contained in the enrolled version of a federal statute or in the final version of the statute as passed into law by a state or local legislature. This provision points out the possibility that the legislature did not draft the heading or title of the statute that appears in the code. Other government agencies, such as the Congressional Office of Law Revision Counsel, take the laws that are passed and assign them to subject matter classifications within the codified body of the jurisdiction's laws, and these entities may have been responsible for creating a heading or title of the provision when they inserted it into the code. If Congress or the state or local legislature is not responsible for the heading or title, which would be revealed by looking at the final version of the statute that was voted on and passed into law by the legislature, then the heading or title should have no impact on the interpretation of the law. If the heading or title was drafted by the legislature, it simply is part of the terms of the statute, and can be used for interpretation.

PRINCIPLE VIII. REVISIONS TO STATUTES

A statute that is revised, whether by amendment or by repeal and reenactment, is a continuation of the previous statute and not a new enactment to the extent that it contains substantially the same language as the previous statute. The coverage of the law does not skip a beat while the new amendment has passed, but has not gone into effect.

PRINCIPLE IX. REPEAL OF A REPEALING STATUTE

The repeal of a repealing statute does not revive the statute originally repealed or impair the effect of a savings clause in the original repealing statute. If the legislature intends this effect, it must expressly state it in the new legislation.

PRINCIPLE X. EFFECT OF AMENDMENT OR REPEAL OF CIVIL STATUTES ON CIVIL CLAIMS

Except as to procedural provisions, an amendment or repeal of a civil statute does not affect a pending action or proceeding or a right accrued before the amendment or repeal takes effect. A pending civil action or proceeding may be completed, and a right that has accrued (meaning that you already acquired the right before the enactment of the new law) may be enforced through new litigation as if the statute had not been amended or repealed.

For example, if you had the right to sue a health care provider for strict liability for implanting a defective heart valve at the time the valve was found to be defective (which is the time your right to sue accrued), you still can bring suit or continue to pursue a legal action for strict liability against the health care provider even if the legislature passes a law that forbids strict liability claims against health care providers. You had the right, and the new law does not take it away. This follows the general principle that statutes only operate prospectively. However, if your valve was installed and found to be defective after the legislation was passed, your right to sue for strict liability is extinguished, or more accurately stated, it never accrued.

Procedural provisions, meaning rules and regulations that regulate the conduct of litigation rather than the substantive rights of the parties, are not subject to this principle. Therefore, if the procedural rules on the requirements for the filing of summary judgment motions change while your law suit is pending, you must follow the new rules.

This general principle applies to civil (non-criminal) statutes. A different rule applies to certain criminal statutes, as discussed in the next section.

PRINCIPLE XI. EFFECT OF AMENDMENT OF CRIMINAL SENTENCING PROVISIONS ON PENDING CRIMINAL ACTIONS

If a penalty for a violation of a statute is reduced by an amendment, the penalty, if not already imposed, must be imposed under the statute as amended. This principle is based on concepts of due process and freedom from cruel and unusual punishment. If the public opinion as to the proper sentence for a crime is lessened, the criminal should get the benefit of the lesser sentence.

PRINCIPLE XII. GENERAL AVOIDANCE OF INTERPRETATIONS THAT DOOM A STATUTE TO FAIL

The law has come to recognize these general rules of thumb of what to avoid when you are attempting to find the proper interpretation of a statute. Each of these principles indicates that an interpretation should not wind up declaring a meaning of the statute that would cause the statute or its objectives to fail and the statute to be declared unenforceable. Legislators are presumed not to have intended to pass futile and ineffective laws that are doomed to fail. Therefore, **a statute is construed so as to:**

A. avoid an unconstitutional result;
B. avoid a result that violates international law or an international treaty;
C. avoid extraterritorial effect;
D. avoid an absurd result;
E. avoid an unachievable result;
F. to have uniform nationwide or statewide application;
G. to give effect, if possible, to its entire text;
H. to give effect, if possible, to its objective and purpose;
I. to give effect to any carefully crafted compromises embodied in the statute.

PRINCIPLE XIII. "EJUSDEM GENERIS" MAXIM

Statutory maxims that are phrased in Latin used to be bantered about quite a bit in legal parlance. "Ejusdem generis" is one that still is used in legal circles today. The principle takes two forms in the construction of a statute:

A. the meaning of a word is limited by the series of words or phrases of which it is a part;
B. the meaning of a general word or phrase following two or more specific words or phrases is limited to the category or class established by the specific words or phrases.

For example, if a park regulation allows " household pets" to run free from noon to 4:00 p.m., and the regulation constantly refers to "dogs and cats" in the context of the term "household pets," it may be argued that the regulation was intended to be limited to common domestic pets, and not to exotic pets, such as wolves, tigers, pythons, and tarantulas, even though some people like to keep these pets in their household.

If a bankruptcy law provision allows a debtor to keep "televisions, refrigerators, washers, dryers, dishwashers, microwaves, ranges, ovens, and *other common household goods*" free from execution as part of the homestead exception in the bankruptcy code, it may be argued that this exception was not mean to cover extremely valuable artwork or an elaborate collection of beer brewing equipment. Even though these items may be found in the same home, they are not of the same class or category as the goods specifically mentioned in the section.

PRINCIPLE XIV. STATUTES ON THE SAME SUBJECT

Statutes on the same subject are construed together even if they were enacted or adopted at different times. This general rule is useful and practical, especially when entities such as the Congressional Office of Law Revision Counsel take statutes that were passed at different times and group them into the same section of the code because of their subject matter. This principle allows a lawyer to construe the provisions together to make sense of the code as a whole.

PRINCIPLE XV. LANGUAGE EXCLUDED FROM SUPPLANTING LEGISLATION

If language of an earlier statute on the same subject is excluded from a later statute that replaces it, the excluded language should not be read back into the later statute. If the legislature intended the old language to go back into effect, they should not have left it out of the supplanting legislation.

PRINCIPLE XVI. INTERPRETATION OF DEFINITIONS OF CRIMES

Definitions of crimes are interpreted narrowly to give the benefit of the doubt to the accused. Our system of justice and due process affords many protections to the accused, and this principle is one of them.

PRINCIPLE XVII. STATUTES IN DEROGATION OF THE COMMON LAW

The rule of common law that a civil statute in derogation of the common law is construed strictly does not apply to statutes enacted in the twentieth century. This reflects the fact that our society is well along the way to being a society whose laws primarily are defined by statutes and administrative rules and regulations, so there is no need to apply an old maxim of interpretation that had meaning when the law was largely defined by the common law created by judges.

PRINCIPLE XVIII. ADDITIONAL AIDS TO CONSTRUCTION

If, after considering the text and context of a statute in light of the above rules, the meaning of the text or its application still is uncertain, the following aids to construction may be considered:

A. a settled judicial construction in another jurisdiction as of the time of the borrowing of a statute borrowed from the other jurisdiction;

B. a previous statute, or the common law, on the same subject;

C. related statutes;

D. a judicial construction of the same or similar statute;

E. an administrative construction of the same or similar statute;

F. the circumstances that prompted the enactment or adoption of the statute, the "mischief" that the statute was meant to correct;

G. the purpose of a statute as determined from the legislative or administrative history of the statute;

H. the historical development of other legislation on the same subject;

I. whether the legislature reenacted a statute or an administrative agency readopted a rule without changing the pertinent language after a court or agency construed the statute; and

J. treatises and articles by leading experts on the subject.

PRINCIPLE XIX: LEGISLATIVE HISTORY

Although listed last, legislative history certainly is not the least used tool of statutory interpretation. Lawyers and judges alike give considerable weight to the contemporaneous interpretations of the terms of statutes that are reported by the very legislators who later voted the statute into law. The most authoritative sources of these constructions are house, senate, and conference reports (discussed in Chapter 16). Therefore, house, senate, and conference committee reports frequently are used to confirm the interpretation given by application of principles I to XVIII above, and they may be used to resolve an ambiguity left after applying principles I to XVIII above.

Federal legislative history usually is more thoroughly documented and almost always more accessible than the legislative history of state or local legislative bodies. To the extent that the information is available, the courts will make use of other legislative materials, including:

A. proposed or adopted amendments, preambles, statements of intent or purpose, findings of fact, notes indicating source, contemporaneous documents prepared as a part of the legislative or rule-making process, fiscal notes, and committee reports; and

B. the record of legislative or administrative agency debates and hearings.

When ascribing weight to evidence of meaning of this kind, not found in committee reports, the greatest weight is given to materials that:

    A. are shown by the record to have been considered by the legislature before passage or adoption, rather than materials not shown by the record to have been so considered;

    B. were available to the legislature before passage or adoption, instead of materials not so available;

    C. formed the basis for the language in the statute, rather than materials that did not form the basis for the language; and

    D. were not revised after they were considered by Congress, rather than materials that were so revised.

Thus, the interpretation of any given statute can be a wonderful journey through a vast collection of sources of meaning, and we only are discussing the interpretation of the statute's meaning on the day it went into law. The statute is just the starting point of legal analysis to determine the actual rules that govern a legal issue. After passage of a statute, cases and other authorities can interpret the terms of the statute and change their legal effect, as will be discussed in the remainder of this chapter.

II. ANALYSIS OF MULTIPLE AUTHORITIES: POTENTIALLY CONTROLLING V. PERSUASIVE AUTHORITY

A. You must know what jurisdiction's law applies

You cannot tell a thing about an authority, whether it be a case or a statute or a rule or a regulation, if you do not know what jurisdiction's law applies to your issue. Every issue is governed by a certain set of laws—one state's law or federal law or another country's law. You will not have an issue that is governed by both state and federal law, and a single issue cannot be governed by two different states' laws or by one state's law and by federal law. For example, your issue cannot be governed by both Indiana and Michigan law, nor by Indiana and federal law.

Please note that we are using the word "*issue*," not case or lawsuit. Within a given case, lawsuit, or client situation, different issues may be governed by different laws, state or federal or foreign, but each individual issue is governed by one jurisdiction's laws. This paragraph (and this chapter) is too short to try to explain the legal rules and principles that answer the question of which jurisdiction's law applies, which are known as **conflicts of law** and **choice of law** rules, because these rules and principles make up an entire course of study in law school. Nevertheless, you must have an answer to this question before you properly can evaluate the authorities you have found. For now, the people assigning you problems to work on will tell you to assume that a certain state's law applies ("assume that the law of Oregon applies to this question"), and you will research and analyze the law with that assumption in mind.

B. Constitutions, statutes, and administrative rules and regulations from the applicable jurisdiction always are controlling authority

If a constitution, statute, or administrative rule or regulation from your jurisdiction is on point—namely, it deals with the subject matter of your issue—then it is controlling. There is no guesswork involved. In addition, because constitutions, laws, and administrative rules and regulations are created by the persons charged with law-making and rule-making in our country, you also must give these sources priority in your construction and eventual presentation of the rule on the issue.

If you have a statute and one or more regulations on point, present and discuss the statute first, followed by the regulations. For example, if your issue involved securities law, and arose under the Securities Exchange Act of 1934 (the statute) and Rule 10b-5 (an administrative regulation promulgated under the statute), you would present the pertinent terms of the statute first, followed by the pertinent terms of the regulation. After that, you can get into the cases that interpret the statute and regulation.

1. Timing determines the weight of these authorities

Timing is the big issue with constitutions, statutes, and regulations. You must find the most recent version of the constitution, statute, or regulation, and the most recent amendments. If you are looking at an earlier version of a statutory section, and that version has been amended, superseded, or struck from the books, you have nothing. An out of date constitution, statute, or regulation is no authority at all.

2. Cases can and will interpret and modify constitutions, statutes, and regulations

Although constitutions, statutes, and regulations are given priority in the discussion of a rule, cases subsequent to the constitution, statute, or regulation will interpret and often change the effect of the rule. The courts cannot repeal a statute, but they can take the guts out of it by construing it in such a way that it no longer has any practical application. In addition, courts can nullify (strike down, or abrogate) a statute on state or federal constitutional grounds. If the legislature does not like what the courts are doing when the courts interpret and apply a statute, they can amend the statute to make it clear how they want it to work.

C. Cases that are potentially controlling authority

Cases are **potentially controlling authority** if they are:

◆ issued by a higher court
◆ in the direct hierarchy of judicial authority in the applicable jurisdiction

Potentially controlling cases are actually **controlling** if:

◆ the holding of the case discusses and resolves the issue at hand (in other words, the case is "**on point**")
◆ the case still is good law
◆ the case has not been replaced or superseded by more recent controlling authority

We looked at the concept of the hierarchy of judicial authority in Chapter 3. The hierarchy of judicial authority for the jurisdiction whose law applies determines what cases are potentially controlling no matter what the actual forum of the case is. Thus, as you will soon see, if a case is governed by a state's law, even if the case is filed in a federal court, the federal court should follow the hierarchy of judicial authority of the state whose law applies, not the federal hierarchy. It is the applicable law and not the forum that determines what cases are potentially controlling.

1. Federal law issues in federal court

Example: Federal issue filed in the United States District Court for the District of Alaska

U.S. Supreme Court	When the issue is governed by federal law, U.S. Supreme Court cases are potentially controlling in all federal courts.	Alaska Supreme Court	When the issue is federal, the Alaska Supreme Court cannot issue controlling authority.

U.S. Court of Appeals, Ninth Circuit	Ninth Circuit cases construing federal law are potentially controlling in all district courts in the Ninth Circuit, including the District of Alaska.	Alaska Court of Appeals	Alaska Court of Appeals cannot issue controlling authority when the issue is federal.

U.S. District Court, District of Alaska	**Opinions of the District of Alaska cannot control other courts on the same or a higher tier, but would be highly persuasive.**	Alaska Superior Court	A trial level court binds no other court on the same or higher tier, but this court also is in the Alaska hierarchy, not the federal hierarchy.

In the federal system in a federal question case, the U.S. Supreme Court controls all of the U.S. Courts of Appeals and U.S. District Courts. Each circuit of the U.S. Court of Appeals controls the district courts within that circuit, but it cannot bind the other circuits, and it cannot bind the district courts in the other circuits. A decision from one three-judge panel of a Court of Appeals does not bind the other panels within the same circuit, but an **en banc** opinion of all the judges on the court controls each subsequently assembled three-judge panel in that circuit. A U.S. District Court's opinions bind no other districts, and do not even bind the other judges within the same district, although these opinions should be regarded as highly persuasive.

2. State law issues in state court

Example: Alaska law issue filed in the Alaska Superior Court

U.S. Supreme Court	U.S. Supreme Court cases do not control, not even if they are construing Alaska law.	**Alaska Supreme Court**	**When the issue is governed by Alaska law, Alaska Supreme Court cases are potentially controlling in all Alaska courts.**

U.S. Court of Appeals, Ninth Circuit	Ninth Circuit cases do not control, not even if they are construing Alaska law.	**Alaska Court of Appeals**	**Alaska Court of Appeals is not divided into districts, so its cases construing Alaska law are potentially controlling in all superior courts in the state.**

U.S. District Court, District of Alaska	District of Alaska opinions do not control, not even if they are construing Alaska law.	Alaska Superior Court, 3rd Judicial District, Anchorage	A trial level court binds no other court on the same or higher tier, but its opinions should be regarded as highly persuasive.

As to state law issues, the highest court within the state whose law is being applied is the highest authority on that state's law. The U.S. Supreme Court's opinions on that state's law (if there are any) are not binding. The opinions of any federal court or other states' courts are not binding on the courts of the state whose law is being applied.

In Alaska, the Alaska Supreme Court can control all of the courts in Alaska. The Alaska Court of Appeals (which is not divided into districts) can control all of the trial level courts in Alaska. The Alaska Superior Courts and other trial level courts in Alaska do not control any other courts, but their opinions should be regarded as highly persuasive.

3. Federal law issues in state court

Example: Federal issue filed in Alaska Superior Court

U.S. Supreme Court	When the issue is governed by federal law, the Alaska court will look to the U.S. Supreme Court for evidence of what federal law requires, so U.S. Supreme Court opinions are potentially controlling.	Alaska Supreme Court	When the issue is federal, the Alaska Supreme Court cannot issue controlling authority, and its opinions, if any, on federal law will not be regarded as very persuasive.

U.S. Court of Appeals, Ninth Circuit	Ninth Circuit cases construing federal law are highly persuasive, but not controlling.	Alaska Court of Appeals	Alaska Court of Appeals cannot issue controlling authority when the issue is federal, and its opinions on federal law are not very persuasive.
U.S. District Court, District of Alaska	A trial level court binds no other court on the same or higher tier, but its opinions are persuasive.	Alaska Superior Court	A trial level court binds no other court on the same or higher tier, and its opinions on federal law are not persuasive.

A state court applying another jurisdiction's law is supposed to figure out how the other jurisdiction's courts would interpret and apply the jurisdiction's law in the situation before it. The court will look to the legislature and the court of last resort in the applicable jurisdiction for compelling evidence of what that jurisdiction's law is on the issue at hand. Intermediate level appellate courts' opinions will be regarded as highly persuasive evidence of the jurisdiction's law, but not controlling authority. As always, trial level opinions will be regarded merely as persuasive at best. Thus, with regard to an Alaska Superior Court applying federal law, including the United States Code and the United States Constitution, the court will follow U.S. Supreme Court's opinions as controlling authority. The court will not be controlled by the opinions of the U.S. Court of Appeals for the Ninth Circuit or any other circuit of the federal court of appeals. These opinions will not be ignored; they will be considered as highly persuasive authority of what federal law requires, but not as controlling authority. There is no way to predict that an Alaska state court judge will give any higher regard to the Ninth Circuit's opinions as opposed to other circuits of the United States Courts of Appeals even if her federal colleagues across the street in the U.S. District Court for the District of Alaska would be compelled to follow them.

In the same way, state appellate court decisions on federal law (if any), whether they be from the same state or another state, are not binding on a state court applying federal law, and trial court opinions from the federal or state system still do not control. These opinions will be regarded as persuasive at best, although a well written federal trial level opinion probably will be considered more persuasive than a state court's opinion, but less persuasive than an equally well written federal court of appeals' opinion on federal law because the one federal court is on a higher tier than the other.

4. State law issues in federal court

Example: Alaska state law issue filed in the U.S. District Court for the District of Alaska

U.S. Supreme Court	U.S. Supreme Court cases do not control, not even if they are construing Alaska law. They are low in persuasive value at best.	Alaska Supreme Court	When the issue is governed by Alaska law, a federal court sitting in diversity will follow Alaska Supreme Court cases as potentially controlling authority.

U.S. Court of Appeals, Ninth Circuit	Ninth Circuit cases do not control, not even if they are construing Alaska law. They are low in persuasive value at best.	Alaska Court of Appeals	Alaska Court of Appeals cases construing Alaska law are not potentially controlling, but will be regarded as highly persuasive.

U.S. District Court, District of Alaska	District of Alaska opinions do not control, and are low in persuasive value at best.	Alaska Superior Court, 3rd Judicial District, Anchorage	A trial level court's opinions are not binding, but the opinions of an Alaska trial court will be regarded as persuasive.

A federal court sitting in diversity and applying state law to the matter before it will look to the applicable state's legislature and the state's court of last resort as controlling authority on the state's law. Thus, the United States District Court for the District of Alaska applying Alaska law to the case before it should consider itself bound by decisions of the Alaska Supreme Court. Decisions of the Alaska Court of Appeals will be regarded as highly persuasive, but not controlling. The court is not bound by decisions of the U.S. Court of Appeals for the Ninth Circuit or the U.S. Supreme Court even if they are applying Alaska law, although as a practical matter, if there are any decisions of these courts on

Alaska law, they may be considered persuasive by the court. Trial level opinions will be considered as persuasive authority at best.

D. Determining if "potentially controlling" authorities are actually controlling

Throughout this chapter, we have been discussing **potentially controlling authority** and non-controlling authority (otherwise known as **persuasive authority**). The applicable law and its associated hierarchy of judicial authority determines what cases are potentially controlling, but not all of them necessarily are controlling. In order to determine if a given potentially controlling case is actually controlling, you must consider the following:

1. Facts and issues of the case

The facts and issues of the potentially controlling case you are examining can determine whether it ultimately will control your client's case. If the facts of the earlier case are similar to your own case, then the application of the rule to those facts is likely to work the same way as in your case, and the earlier case can control the outcome of your case. But if the facts in the case you are examining are significantly different (or at least there are legally significant differences), then the application of the rule to the facts of the earlier case does not necessarily predict how the rule should work in your case. In this situation, the case is referred to as inapposite, and it will not control your case. It may be regarded as persuasive, but not controlling.

Similarly, if the issue in the case that you are examining is different than the issue in your client's case, then the applied rule used in the earlier case to resolve that issue probably will be different from the rule that applies to the issue in your client's case, and the holding of the case on that issue will be different, so the case will not control your client's case. One example of this is if there was a different claim or cause of action involved in the earlier case. If the earlier case involved the construction and alleged breach of a lease in a bankruptcy proceeding, the issues in the earlier case are not necessarily the same as in a normal breach of contract case, and the decision in the earlier case will not control the later breach of contract case. It does not matter if the case you are examining has some issues different and some the same, the only issues that should be the same or very similar are the ones governed by the applied rule that you have determined to apply in your client's case.

The facts and issues both may be different. For example, if a potentially controlling dog-bite case involved a dog with rabies who bit a person and gave him rabies, and your client's case has no rabid dog in it, the earlier case probably will not be controlling. There are bound to be legally significant differences between issues concerning provocation and the reasonableness of the response of a rabid dog on the one hand and provocation and response of a healthy dog on the other. You do have to make sure whether it is controlling by doing additional research to check if other courts have or have not equated rabid dogs with regular dogs or whether court have distinguished one from the other. Assuming no other authority has made the connection one way or the other, you can assert that there is a legally significant difference so as to distinguish the rabid dog case.

We previously described a similar process of distinguishing "bad" cases—those that do not support your thesis—from "good" cases that do support your thesis when you are reporting the results of your research and analysis. Here, we are determining what the rule is in the jurisdiction, and we are trying to decide which cases to include in the formulation of the rule. The cases with facts and issues that are the same or similar to the client's case will be used in formulating the rule whether or not the outcome of the cases goes the way of your client. Thus, the designation of "good" and "bad"—namely, supportive of your thesis and unsupportive—does not apply at this stage. You have not determined the applicable rule for the issue; therefore, you will not have a thesis on the issue.

Later, when you have determined the rule and you are explaining the rule in your writing, you will deal with the "bad," potentially controlling cases by trying to find a legally significant difference in either the facts or the issues or both so as to distinguish the case. And even if you like the case, you should perform the same analysis of the facts and the issues so that you will be aware if your opponent can easily distinguish a case upon which you are relying.

2. Is the case still good law?

A case can go bad. Not simply from long shelf-life, but because things can happen to cases. An easy concept to grasp is if the case whose opinion you are reading goes up on appeal and gets reversed or vacated; the opinion is gone. Nothing remains that you would want to rely on. Reversal means the case you were thinking of relying on now has no precedential value, unless another court finds the dead case and resurrects it by adopting its holding and reasoning in a new case. Absent this kind of resurrection, the case is dead letter, and you should give it no further attention.

In similarly dramatic fashion, a case may be discussed by a later authority of the proper jurisdiction and in the course of that discussion the later authority decides to cancel the precedential value of the case at which you were looking (for example, "The Court will no longer follow the rule in <u>Smithy v. Jonesy</u>"). The verbs used for this are overruling or overturning or abrogating the earlier case. The opinion you were thinking of using now has no precedential effect and should be disregarded.

A more indirect attack, but no less effective, is if a later case simply issues an opinion on the same question of law and same legal issue that is the opposite of the opinion in the earlier case, with or without mentioning the earlier case. The more recent opinion supersedes and replaces the earlier opinion. It is not accurate to call this reversing or vacating the case, because those terms refer to an appellate court's action on direct appeal from a case, but the earlier case is effectively canceled. More recent cases may recognize that this implicit overruling has taken place, so you should be on the lookout for these clues in your research.

It matters dearly what court and what level of court is launching the attack on your authority. The court that is overruling the earlier opinion should be a court on the same level or a higher level of the same hierarchy of judicial authority in order for the action to have real effect. In other words, if a trial level court issues an opinion stating, "This court will no longer follow the Supreme Court's opinion in <u>Smithy v. Jonesy</u>," you should view this as the trial court taking off into strange unchartered waters and not as a true overruling of the <u>Smithy</u> case. If you are researching Virginia law, and you find a Maryland case that states that it will no longer follow the Virginia case that you were evaluating, this is of minor interest to you in your calculation of Virginia law on the issue. Maryland courts, no matter how highly placed in their own hierarchy, cannot overturn or otherwise cancel the effect of any Virginia court opinion.

A later court, on the same or a higher level of the applicable hierarchy of judicial authority, may severely criticize the opinion upon which you were thinking of relying. If the criticism is about the very part of the opinion you were looking at, and the criticism indicates that the more recent case thinks that part of the earlier case is wrong, then the earlier case probably is bad law on this issue. Continue your research, because another recent opinion may disagree with the court that criticized the first opinion, and in fact it may criticize the second opinion in turn. You must gather all these cases and sort them out to see where the chips fall.

It matters what the criticism is. If the criticism is not so much about how the earlier case was incorrect as to the law, but instead is commenting that the rule is harsh, overly complicated, or unusual compared to law of other states, then it is not time to throw out the rule from the earlier case. Judges may grumble about the applicable law of their jurisdiction but still faithfully apply it in case after case.

We have been talking about the action of abrogation or criticism from a case higher up or on the same level of the hierarchy of judicial authority. If the criticism comes from outside the hierarchy, for example, from a court in other state, then there is little need to get exercised. The out-of-jurisdiction opinion is merely one more piece of persuasive authority that goes the other way from the earlier case; it cannot overrule or abrogate an opinion from another jurisdiction.

3. Has the case been superseded by more recent, equally authoritative cases, statutes, or rules?

Even if later cases from the same hierarchy of judicial authority do not overrule or severely criticize the earlier opinion you are examining, it may be that the case simply is out of date, and there are newer, fresher cases on the same point of law that should be used in formulating the rule. Later cases can replace the authority you are looking at by restating the same rule or advancing it further through modification and adaptation, not necessarily by stating a new rule on the same legal topic which would overrule the earlier authority. In those circumstances, the more recent cases are better authority, and you should rely on them and use them to formulate the rule in the jurisdiction.

> Q: What happens if an intermediate level appellate court that is controlling changes the law stated in the last opinion of the court of last resort?
>
> A: The newer controlling authority controls. It will be subject to correction by the court of last resort, but until that happens, it controls.

A similar but more significant thing happens when a statute or administrative rule or regulation supersedes an existing line of cases and sets down the rule in that area of the law. We have discussed how statutes and regulations are given priority, and in these circumstances, the statute or regulation replaces the cases to the extent that the rule stated in the statute or regulation overlaps the rule from the cases; if one or more parts of the area of law defined in the cases is untouched by the statute or regulation, then that part of the law from the earlier cases can survive. This process of a statute superseding an earlier case often is commented on or "recognized" by later cases in the same or other jurisdictions or by legal commentators in secondary authorities, so keep a weather eye open for these clues in the course of your research.

After a statute is passed or a regulation is promulgated, cases interpret and apply the statute or regulation, and these more recent authorities color how the statute or regulation works and how it should be applied. Thus, the legislature can "overrule" a line of cases by passing a new statute on the same topic, but the courts can have the last word by interpreting what the statute means and how it works. Lawyers watch from the sidelines, waiting to see where the dust settles, and then they rush in and analyze the dust.

E. Relative weight of controlling authorities

Once you have performed the above analysis, you will know which of your authorities, if any, are actually controlling. You still need to evaluate the weight of each controlling authority, because all controlling authorities are not created equal.

Relative Weight of Controlling Authorities
Most Recent
Watershed Cases
Close Facts
Bad Subsequent History
Unpublished

All else being equal, **recent controlling authorities** are better than older controlling authorities. At least in theory, the more recent authorities have had the chance to survey the older authorities and comment on, change, add to them, so they are more valuable to the researcher. Simply stated, you should look for the most recent and complete statements of the law on the topic. That said, there is nothing inherently wrong with an old case, as long as there are no newer cases on the same issue of law from the same or a higher court.

We say, "**all else being equal**," to indicate the possibility that all else may not be equal. For example, an earlier case may be on all fours with the facts of your case, more so than any more recent opinion. The factual similarity may make the older case more valuable to you than any more recent opinion. The older case may have been written by a famous judge or justice, and you will decide to cite this giant of the law before going into the more recent cases written by lesser luminaries. The earlier case may be a "**watershed case**" that is constantly recited and followed by later opinions, giving it a special status in the formulation of the rule on the issue.

Facts are a very important way to rank your controlling authorities. As suggested above, cases that are closer to your facts and situation will be more important than cases with significantly different facts. If the differences are legally significant, the case is inapposite and distinguishable, and you should treat it as a persuasive authority.

Subsequent history can affect a case. In addition to the things that can happen to make the case "bad" law—being reversed, overruled, abrogated, superseded, or significantly criticized by a later authority—the case may have been interpreted by subsequent cases and limited to a specific set of facts or circumstances. You will then be limited in how you can use the case, unless your client's case fits within the narrowly defined set of facts or circumstances.

Unpublished opinions present a special headache. From time to time, a court in the applicable hierarchy of judicial authority will have issued one or more unpublished opinions in the area of the law governing your issue. "Unpublished" means the case was not published in an official reporter of the court's cases (see Chapter 11), but you found it through computer assisted legal research or other means. Courts have various reasons for this practice. The judges whom we have had the opportunity to hear speak about this swear that it is not because their court has done a "quick and dirty" opinion in a case, and want the opinion to slip by relatively unnoticed if possible. These judges say they make the determination not to publish a case if the case lacks precedential value because it is redundant of other established cases and adds nothing to the jurisprudence of the jurisdiction on this area of the law. Nevertheless, in the course of our practice, we found on several occasions that unpublished opinions were the *only* opinions available on a given issue.

The local rules of the courts where you will be practicing often will limit when you can cite to and use an unpublished opinion; these rules typically limit the usage by prohibiting it. If the use of unpublished authority is prohibited, you might as well set these opinions aside for the time being. They should not be used in the rule section to formulate the governing rule on your issue, but they may be used later in the explanation section of your work if your work is not going to be filed with a court. Even if you are practicing in a jurisdiction whose local rules allow citation to unpublished opinions, unpublished opinions still should fall to the bottom of your controlling authority pile. Their facts may raise them back up a notch, but the spectre of "unpublished" is hard to exorcize. Note well: unpublished opinions do not fall into the persuasive authority pile just because they are unpublished. The local rules of the court may make them non-authority if they cannot be cited or relied upon, but aside from that, the fact that they are unpublished does not turn them from potentially controlling authority to persuasive authority.

F. Primary persuasive authority

You now have ranked your controlling authorities (if any), and you may have tossed some potentially controlling authorities on to the persuasive authority pile. In many instances, you will have enough to formulate the rule of law that governs the issue at hand based on your controlling authorities. But assuming there are gaps and incomplete coverage of the issue, you may have to resort to using some persuasive authority to flesh out the rule.

There is a great divide between controlling and persuasive authority. Do not lose sight of the importance of controlling authority. No matter how wonderfully written and close to your client's facts a persuasive authority may be, it cannot replace or supersede even the lowest of your controlling authorities. The outcome of your client's situation will be determined by whatever controlling authority exists on your issue. Persuasive authority fills in the gaps when the controlling authority is absent and is used to help explain how the controlling authority should be interpreted and applied. Persuasive authority thus can play a critical role in your legal analysis of the issue, but it is always secondary to the role of controlling authority.

The persuasive authority pile has primary authorities in it and secondary authorities. We will first address cases as primary persuasive authorities, because the use of statutes and rules from other jurisdictions is more limited. Remember, if a statute or administrative regulation is from the applicable jurisdiction and it is on point, it is always controlling, so in this section, we are only talking about statutes or regulations from other jurisdictions. As with controlling authority, some persuasive authorities are better than others.

1. Relative weight of primary persuasive authorities

Relative Weight of Persuasive Authorities
Dicta from controlling authorities
Same jurisdiction but parallel hierarchy
Most recent
Close facts
Same or similar law - uniform laws, model codes
Bad subsequent history
Unpublished

a. Dicta from controlling cases

The best persuasive authority is dicta from a controlling authority. As previously explained, only the holding of a case is binding on courts lower down in the same hierarchy of judicial authority. Dicta is not binding. But a trial court is loath to pretend that a court higher up in the chain has not gone on record that the law should be a certain way or that the outcome of the case they are writing about would be different if different facts and circumstances were present. Today's dicta is tomorrow's binding law, and courts are alerted to that by carefully considering the dicta written by their superiors. If the courts are paying attention, you should, too.

b. Non-controlling cases from the jurisdiction whose law applies

The next best kind of primary persuasive authority is a non-controlling case from the jurisdiction whose law applies (for example, a Georgia state court where Georgia law applies), but which is from a parallel hierarchy of judicial authority, not the same hierarchy that your case is in based on the court in which it is filed. In many jurisdictions, the intermediate level appellate court is divided into districts or circuits, only one of which will hear appeals from the court where the client's matter will be filed. Therefore, in most of these court systems, only one district or circuit—the district or circuit that hears the appeal—can issue controlling authority for your client's case. However, cases from the other districts or circuits of the same intermediate level appellate court also are valuable, because these courts have day to day experience applying the law of the applicable jurisdiction and are presumed to have tremendous expertise in this law. If, for example, your case is controlled by opinions of the United States Court of Appeals for the First Circuit, you should consider the opinions of the other circuits of the federal court of appeals and cases from the United States District Courts to be highly persuasive. If your case is controlled by the Florida First District Court of Appeal, you should consider the opinions of the Second, Third, Fourth, and Fifth Districts of the Court of Appeal and the trial level courts in Florida to be highly persuasive.

Regardless of whether the case actually is controlling, a trial court is very interested in following the opinions and recommendations of courts in the same court system. Therefore, the opinions of these courts interpreting the applicable law should be given great weight as persuasive authority—certainly more weight than any of the categories of cases described below.

c. Out-of-jurisdiction cases – holding and dicta

Once you have exhausted cases from your jurisdiction and its hierarchy of judicial authority (subsection (a) above) and cases from the same jurisdiction but a parallel hierarchy of judicial authority (subsection (b) above), you may look to other jurisdictions to see what their courts have said about the law in the area you are examining. These cases are far less persuasive than those discussed in subsections (a) and (b), because the law these courts are applying is not the applicable law and the courts are not presumed to have any experience or expertise in the applicable law. Even if the law in the other jurisdictions is manifestly similar to the applicable law, the courts in the applicable hierarchy are completely free to disregard the out-of-jurisdiction authority for any reason or no reason at all. The out-of-jurisdiction courts have no power at all over the courts of the applicable jurisdiction.

The most advantageous way to use this kind of persuasive authority in legal writing is to buttress an argument that you have already proven with cases and authorities from your own jurisdiction. You will argue, "Not only does our state, New York, hold this as the rule, but Vermont and Connecticut and Rhode Island do, too [citing Vermont authority, Connecticut authority, and Rhode Island authority]." But before you get to the writing stage, when you are constructing the rule that governs your issue, reference to other jurisdictions' law simply is a good check to make sure your analysis has not gone off the deep end. These cases are not controlling and are not as persuasive as the other authorities we have looked at above, but they can be a good reality check.

The second use of out-of-state authority is to find cases that are closer to your client's facts than any cases from the applicable jurisdiction, and to show that under the law of the other jurisdiction, the outcome of these cases supports your formulation of the rule that governs the issue and your thesis on the most likely result from the application of the rule to the facts of your case. An out-of-jurisdiction case that is on all fours with your client's case still cannot trump a case from the jurisdiction whose law governs the action at hand, but it can give support for your formulation of the law, and eventually, when you report your findings, for your thesis. These cases will almost always be discussed in the explanation section of your work, but if there is little or no controlling authority on point, they may be used in the rule section.

The opinions of neighboring states (in a state court case) and sister districts within the same circuit (in a federal case) are **not** all the more persuasive as a result of geography. There are some attorneys who have bought into the myth that if your case is governed by federal law and it is filed in the Eastern District of Wisconsin, the opinions of the Western District of Wisconsin and the other district courts found within the coverage of the Seventh Circuit (the district courts of Indiana and Illinois) are all the more persuasive because of geography. They might believe that if your case is governed by North Carolina law, then cases from Virginia, West Virginia, Tennessee, Alabama, Georgia, and South Carolina take on special weight because of geographic proximity. This is a popular myth, but there is no legal foundation to support the myth. You should look to other criteria, such as the facts of the case, the quality of the research and analysis evidenced in the opinion, and the similarity of the law of the jurisdiction to the applicable jurisdiction's law.

d. Out-of-jurisdiction statutes and regulations

At the rule formulation stage, out-of-jurisdiction statutes and regulations are somewhat useful as a check on your formulation of the applicable jurisdiction's law, but other than that, they do not carry a great deal of persuasive authority. When you get to the writing stage, you may attempt to show that the statutory law of another jurisdiction is virtually the same as your jurisdiction's law (perhaps a "uniform law" has been adopted by both jurisdictions), and thereby attempt to give more persuasive weight to the cases and other authorities that discuss the other jurisdiction's statutory regime. For example, the version of the Uniform Commercial Code (UCC) enacted in any given jurisdiction is likely to be very similar if not identical to the version enacted in many other jurisdictions, and cases interpreting the identical language of another jurisdiction's UCC statute will be of greater persuasive value than cases interpreting language from other statutes that differ from the applicable jurisdiction's laws.

e. Dicta from out-of-jurisdiction cases

Dicta from an out-of-jurisdiction persuasive authority is weaker than the case's holding. Since we already are talking about precedent that has a fairly low level of persuasiveness, when we step down to the level of dicta, the persuasive value is very weak, indeed. We would not recommend taking this kind of authority into account in formulating the applicable rule in your jurisdiction unless you absolutely have to.

2. Factors that affect the weight of primary persuasive authorities

Persuasive authority is affected by the same factors as controlling authority. Recent cases are generally better than older cases. The subsequent history of a case can affect its value through reversal, overruling, severe criticism, or a limitation on the scope of the case. More recent statutes, regulations, or cases can supersede the authority of earlier cases. Unpublished opinions are somewhat suspect, and we would avoid using an unpublished out-of-jurisdiction persuasive authority unless there truly was nothing else out there on the issue at hand. This might be the case with an extremely new, cutting edge legal topic, or an area of law so strange and undeveloped that there is a drastic lack of authority of any kind on point in the United States.

Facts are always important, as strongly analogous cases are far better than tangentially analogous cases. You probably should never even think about citing a persuasive authority unless its facts are analogous to your own—the law in the nation would be pretty bare if you cannot find even one analogous case.

Additional factors affect the value of primary persuasive authority. The relative prestige of the issuing court can make a case more or less persuasive. Most lawyers would agree that a case from the U.S. Supreme Court is more valuable than a case from the Idaho Supreme Court (unless, perhaps, your issue involved potato farming). It is possible that the courts of the applicable jurisdiction might regard the courts or certain judges of another jurisdiction with some suspicion or disdain. Some jurisdictions are considered by other jurisdictions to be a little on the flaky side. This is an unusual circumstance, to be sure, but one of which you should be aware. Sometimes the distance or lack of familiarity between two jurisdictions breeds contempt. Largely urban jurisdictions may suspect the authority from largely rural jurisdictions, and vice-versa; one region may question the propriety of the authority from other regions. Some federal circuit courts are considered to be highly politicized, and their opinions are scrutinized with more care than opinions from other circuits. This situation is far from ideal, and while no attorney should advocate for the perpetuation of this kind of prejudice in this day and age, a smart attorney will weigh the popular folklore into her calculation of which cases are more persuasive than others. Pay attention to these factors as you get into practice; the biases and prejudices of one law firm or judge that you are working for may be different from the average prejudices of your jurisdiction.

We hinted above that the subject matter of the opinion may affect whether the opinion should be valued more highly or not. Some courts have day-to-day experience and have developed expertise with certain kinds of cases, while other courts rarely if ever have a case with that subject matter. An opinion from a New York court or Second Circuit panel on securities law is most likely stronger than a Montana securities law case. It's not that the judges in Montana are slow or cannot understand securities law, but this may be the first securities law opinion they have rendered in several years, whereas the New York and Second Circuit courts handle dozens of such cases every year. The United States District Court for the Southern District of New York and the United States Court of Appeals for the Second Circuit used to be famous for their opinions on copyright law because the major music, theater, art, and publishing industries of the United States were located in that district and circuit and the vast majority of copyright cases were resolved there. Today, these industries are more decentralized, but it is likely that this reputation for excellence lives on in some litigants' and judges' minds.

The relative prestige of the judge who wrote an opinion can affect the value of the opinion. The opinions of certain "giants" of the law—people like Learned Hand, Benjamin Cardozo, Oliver Wendell Holmes, and several others—can go a long way no matter how old their opinions are. You will learn of these giants in your law school classes. This factor usually only works in one direction—an opinion from a relatively unknown judge still will be given its proper weight as persuasive authority, but if the judge is a well known scholar, the opinion will be given even more weight.

The contents of the opinion itself should not be neglected. If you compare what the court says and what it actually does and find a mismatch, that is a bad situation for the case. Well-reasoned, thorough opinions are better than poorly reasoned and cursory opinions.

With appellate cases, the number of judges who signed off on the opinion can affect its value. En banc opinions without dissenters are the best; a full panel opinion (all the judges voted the same way) is better than a split panel. A clear majority opinion (5 yes to 4 no, 4 yes to 3 no) is much better than a plurality opinion where there is no numeric majority (for example, a plurality of 4 vote yes for one reason, 2 concur in that result but for a completely different reason, 2 vote no for a third reason, 1 votes no for yet another reason).

Concurring opinions are suspect, and we would only cite one from a judge on the highest court in the jurisdiction. Concurring opinions at the intermediate level appellate court level do not carry a lot of weight. Dissenting opinions have no value, unless they are so well written and well reasoned that they have to become the law some day. Even so, try your best not to use them.

Certain trends in the law can affect the weight of opinions that follow the trend and those that buck the trend. An example of this kind of occurrence from two decades or so ago was the shift from the concepts of contributory negligence and assumption of risk in negligence law to comparative negligence and comparative fault. Cases that picked up on the comparative fault trend began to gain more and more credibility as the trend spread and the jurisdictions who adopted the trend grew in number. On the other hand, if a case is catching a wave that is brand new—on the cutting edge—it will probably be a good idea to avoid that case until the trend turns from a "fad" to a "widespread development in the law."

None of the biases or trends discussed above can turn an inapposite, out-of-jurisdiction sow's ear of a case into a silk purse authority from the proper jurisdiction. The key elements to a primary persuasive authority are (1) jurisdiction—is it from the applicable jurisdiction or not; (2) facts—are they analogous or not; and (3) is the authority good law or not. Every other factor discussed above is minor and secondary compared to these three.

III. SECONDARY AUTHORITY

Secondary authority should rarely be used in the actual formulation of the rule on an issue. If there absolutely is **no** controlling authority, and the persuasive authority from the applicable jurisdiction is sparse or weak, then you might turn to secondary authorities for rule formulation. Secondary authorities are wonderful sources of legal principles and instructions in how to interpret legal rules, but it is an alarming situation when you see a lawyer cite a secondary authority in the rule section as the source for the rule on a given issue. In a situation where the only authority on point is out-of-jurisdiction authority, secondary authorities can share the stage at the same time with the primary authorities, but when primary authorities from the applicable jurisdiction exist, secondary authorities must take a back seat.

Occasionally, a court **adopts** a secondary authority as the applicable rule for the jurisdiction. If it is a primary controlling authority that adopts a secondary authority, then the controlling authority bootstraps the secondary authority into prominence. The secondary authority may be elevated to become the centerpiece of your discussion, but only because a primary controlling authority did the elevating. For example, if the <u>Smithy</u> case, a controlling authority from your jurisdiction, adopted section 43 of the Restatement (Second) of Contracts, you would present the rule as coming from <u>Smithy</u>, and then go on to explain that <u>Smithy</u> got it from the Restatement. In writing, you would cite and discuss <u>Smithy</u> as the source of the rule in addition to citing section 43 of the Restatement as a resource <u>Smithy</u> used in formulating the rule.

When evaluating the weight of secondary authorities, the name of the game is prestige—the prestige of the author(s) or the prestige of the work (the treatise, the hornbook, the law review article, the Restatement) itself. Certain works are as good as gold, and courts find these sources to be extremely persuasive, and value what they say just below precedent from the applicable jurisdiction. In our experience, Wright and Miller's <u>Federal Practice and Procedure</u> and <u>Moore's Federal Practice</u> are this kind of source, as are the Restatement of Contracts and the Restatement of Torts. Devitt and Blackmar's <u>Federal Jury Practice and Instructions</u> is regarded as the bible on jury instructions in federal court.

Before we get too far with this, let us make the following observation: some students come away from their first year classes with the impression that the Restatement of Contracts, the Restatement of Torts, the U.C.C., and the Model Penal Code are the best authorities on the law of their respective areas that you can find. This is inaccurate. Secondary authorities control no court's decision; their power is only the power of persuasion. As a general rule, never discuss secondary authority before primary controlling authority or primary persuasive authority from the applicable jurisdiction. It can be discussed before primary persuasive authorities from other jurisdictions if the secondary authority is strong enough. Secondary authority can add a great deal of credence to your rule formulation and rule explanation if an important treatise or other weighty authority comes to the same conclusions that you reach. But there is no substitute for primary controlling authority.

Pay attention to the author of the secondary authority you are evaluating. Certain authors are legendary in their field, and will command a great deal of respect; thus, they are highly persuasive. Example of these persons, and the subjects they are known for, are Professor Prosser on Torts, Judge Weinstein on Evidence, Professor Nimmer on Copyright, Professor Newberg on Class Actions, Professors Farnsworth, Williston, and Corbin on Contracts (individually, not as a team), Professor Miller and Judge Wright on Federal Practice and Procedure, and Professor McCormick on Evidence and Federal Procedure.

This list is far from exhaustive, but we will leave it to your own law school professors to tell you who their dream dates are.

Certain authors are local heroes, and will be highly persuasive in the jurisdiction where they are famous. For example, Judge Weinstein and Professors Korn and Smit are local experts on the New York Civil Practice Laws and Regulations. Judge Traynor's writings and opinions on California law are given special weight. Some judges reach the status of national heroes: Holmes, Cardozo, John Marshall, Brandeis, and Learned Hand certainly qualify in this category. Listen for the rapt awe and tearful delivery in your other professors' voices when they speak a judge's name, and you will find other names to add to this list.

When evaluating a law review or law journal article, there is little to distinguish one article from another on the same topic other than the status and prestige of the individual authors of the articles and whether the articles appear to be well researched, well organized, well reasoned, and well written. Articles written by law professors, practitioners, government officials, and judges generally are more valuable and persuasive than articles written by law students. Beyond that, look for well known names as the author—heroes and legends in their field—to the extent that you recognize any of the names.

Similar to primary authorities, up-to-date, timely secondary sources are better than old ones, all else being the same. If you are working with a crusty old treatise or a law review article that is decades old on a topic of the law that enjoys frequent development and upheaval (securities law, intellectual property law, and employment law being good examples, as compared to contracts or torts), then you should try to find some up to the minute secondary authorities. If the area of law you are researching has at some point undergone a major revolution through the passage of groundbreaking legislation, any article or treatise chapter written on that topic prior to the revolution practically will be useless. For example, any article or treatise written on employee benefits and retirement plans prior to the passage of ERISA will be highly suspect, and any article on bankruptcy law written before the passage of the current Bankruptcy Code will not be of much use to you. The chapters on research methods found later in this book will reaffirm this concept.

IV. DRAFTING THE RULE IN A RULE SECTION: RECONCILING, SYNTHESIZING, HARMONIZING THE VARIOUS AUTHORITIES

When you have compiled your authorities, you must analyze them together in order to determine the applicable rule in your jurisdiction. The process has several steps depicted in the following chart, each of which will be explained more completely below:

❶ Start with the highest and most recent controlling authority:
   ◆ If you have a constitution, statute, or regulation, start with these authorities in the order listed - constitution first, statute next, regulation third;
   ◆ If instead you have a watershed case that is controlling, start with that;
   ◆ If instead your best authority is a case from the court of last resort, take the most recent opinion from that court, and start with that;

◆ If these first three criteria do not apply, start with the most recent actual controlling authority that is on point;

◆ Only if none of the above applies would you consider turning to non-controlling authority—primary or secondary.

◆ Don't expect to use all of your authorities.

❷ Reconcile differing statements or phrasings of the rule from controlling authorities, and attempt to synthesize the rule into one coherent statement of the legal principles that govern the issue.

◆ DON'T change the wording of or paraphrase rules from constitutions, statutes, administrative regulations, and watershed cases.

◆ Unless an applied rule can be written smoothly and effectively in one sentence or phrase, write the rule first with modifications second.

❸ Write the rule first, interpretative rules second, and exceptions to the rule third.

◆ Write interpretive sub-rules on elements of the rule in the section or sub-TREAT discussion that discusses that element of the rule. Write exceptions to the sub-rules after you lay out the sub-rules themselves.

❹ Do not write a rule with inherent contradictions.

❺ Do accept the <u>remote</u> possibility that two competing rules on the same issue might exist in the same jurisdiction.

ILLUSTRATION:

You are choosing authorities that define the rule governing an issue in a suit pending in Missouri Circuit Court, 22nd Judicial Circuit, where Missouri law is the applicable law. In this chart the better authorities to choose to define the rule appear higher and to the left in the chart. Lesser authorities appear lower and to the right. In choosing authorities, move from the top left to the lower right.

Controlling Authorities	Non-Controlling (Persuasive) Authorities			
Missouri Authorities		Non-Missouri Authorities		
Missouri Constitution Missouri Statutes Missouri Regulations Missouri Supreme Court Cases, esp. Watershed Cases Missouri Court of Appeals, Eastern District Cases	Remember, non-controlling authorities cannot contradict or supersede controlling authorities	Federal authorities do not control	Other states' authorities do not control	Secondary authorities never control
	Missouri Court of Appeals, Southern and Western District Cases			
	Missouri Trial Court Cases			
▲ Only the above authorities can control this issue	▲ The above authorities are highly persuasive	U.S. Supreme Court Cases	Other states' courts of last resort	Restatements of the Law; commentary and annotations on uniform laws, model codes
		U.S. Court of Appeals Cases	Other states' intermediate level appellate court	
		U.S. District Court Cases	Other states' trial courts	
		Similar federal statutes and regulations	Similar state statutes and regulations	Secondary Authority

When you have your authorities that you want to use in formulating the rule, you must piece together what you learn from each authority and figure out how to discuss it so as to make one coherent expression of the rule.

1. Do start with constitutions, statutes, or regulations

With constitutions, statutes, or regulations, do start with the pertinent terms and finish with subsequent authorities that add to, delete from, modify, or clarify the rule or parts of the rule through discussion and interpretation.

2. Otherwise, start with a watershed opinion

If there are no constitutional, statutory, or regulatory provisions on point, start with a much cited, much applied opinion that is cited as the source for the Borrowed Rule that is used by virtually every authority you have read on the topic. We refer to these as **watershed cases**. Subsequent authorities can and will modify the rule, and you will have to decide how to present the watershed case's rule and the three or four (or more) subsequent authorities that have changed the rule in some way, as shown in Examples 1-3 from Chapter 4.

3. Do not change the order or basic contents of the elements of a much borrowed rule.

A frequently borrowed rule or rule from a watershed case almost always will be presented the exact same way in most if not all of the authorities you are reading on the topic. It is not recommended that you change the order of the elements or change the wording of the elements of the rule when you present it as the rule in your writing. You don't want to cause the reader to wonder, did this person miss something, or did she copy this down wrong?

In your presentation of the rule, you may in some instances add an element to the three or four traditional elements of the rule, giving proper recognition to the traditional sources of the rule and the authority that has added an element (see Example 3 from Chapter 4), but in most circumstances it is best to present the rule in the traditional manner, and then write additional sentences showing the changes to the rule through the line of cases and authorities upon which you are relying. Refer to section F on Rule Synthesis below.

4. Do try to reconcile your authorities; do not formulate a rule with inherent contradictions.

Courts are not always neat and tidy about the rules they apply to resolve the cases before them, but you should strive to be neat and tidy with the authorities you have to work with. If a controlling case sticks out—bucks the normal rules—try to distinguish the authority to see if it can be relegated to the persuasive pile and dealt with in the explanation section, not the rule section. If this cannot be done, try to harmonize and reconcile the opinion with the rest of your authorities. Is the holding really contradictory compared to other opinions? Can you present the rule in a different way that takes into account the cases presenting the rule one way and the renegade case that presents it another way? If you are having a hard time harmonizing the case, you might simply have to present two rules—the rule from the other authorities and the rule from the individual case.

5. List interpretive rules and exceptions after the main rule

A handful of your cases may borrow the traditional borrowed rule, but they go on to state interpretive rules or exceptions to the rule. In these circumstances, you should present the traditional borrowed rule first, and then list the interpretive rules and exceptions afterwards.

An **interpretive rule** provides criteria to aid in the interpretation and application the rule itself. For example:

[**Rule**] Fraud requires proof of (1) a representation; (2) its falsity; (3) its materiality; (4) the speaker's knowledge of the falsity or his ignorance of the truth; (5) the hearer's reliance on the representation; (6) the hearer's ignorance of the falsity; (7) the hearer's right to rely; (8) the reasonableness of the hearer's reliance; and (9) proximately caused damages from the reliance. Coyote v. Runner, 345 W.2d 258, 259 (Apex 1978). [**Interpretive Rules**] Fraud is a disfavored cause of action. Id. Fraud will never be presumed. Bird v. Cat, 788 W.2d 890, 894 (Apex Ct. App. 1st Dist. 1990). Plaintiff must prove each element with clear and convincing evidence. Id.

These interpretive rules modify the way lawyers should look at the entire rule. Fraud is not the average cause of action. Fraud is different—it is harder to prove and harder to prevail on than most claims. Refer to the following example, based on Example 1 from Chapter 4:

[**Rule**] To prevail on a claim for injuries caused by a dog, a plaintiff must plead and prove: (1) ownership of the dog by the defendant; (2) causation of the injury by the dog; and (3) lack of provocation of the dog. Billy v. Tilly, 887 W.2d 234, 236 (Apex 1996); Lori v. Benji, 667 W.2d 234, 236 (Apex 1993). [**Interpretive Rule**] Dog bite liability is rooted in the area of negligence, and as such, a comparative negligence analysis applies in calculating the responsibility for a dog's attack. Id. at 569.

This interpretive rule tells us that dog bite liability is not based on strict liability or other theories of tort liability. It is a negligence-type claim, which informs lawyers that they can prove it and defend against it with the common tools used in negligence actions, including a comparative negligence analysis. Interpretive rules reflect that the cases discussing the overall rule have thrown in extra rules that modify how we all should interpret and apply the borrowed rule.

An **exception** to rule is just that; the opinion carves out a set of facts or circumstances and states that rule will not cover these facts or circumstances or it will work a different way in these facts or circumstances. For example:

[**Rule**] To prevail on a claim for injuries caused by a dog, a plaintiff must plead and prove: (1) ownership of the dog by the defendant; (2) causation of the injury by the dog; and (3) lack of provocation of the dog. Billy v. Tilly, 887 W.2d 234, 236 (Apex 1996); Lori v. Benji, 667 W.2d 234, 236 (Apex 1993). [**Exception**] The rule does not apply to police dogs when these dogs are acting in their ordinary law enforcement capacity. City of Dogpatch v. Mauledguy, 786 W.2d 345, 348 (Apex Ct. App. 1st Dist. 1996).

6. List sub-rules on elements of the rule in the TREATment of the individual element

Interpretive rules are to be distinguished from **sub-rules** that provide criteria for the interpretation and application of one element of a rule. There may be an interpretive rule that only applies to the sub-rule on one element. For example, we learn the following from Example 1 from Chapter 4:

[**Rule**] To prevail on a claim for injuries caused by a dog, a plaintiff must plead and prove: (1) ownership of the dog by the defendant; (2) causation of the injury by the dog; and (3) lack of provocation of the dog. Billy v. Tilly, 887 W.2d 234, 236 (Apex 1996); Lori v. Benji, 667 W.2d 234, 236 (Apex 1993).

[**Sub-rule on Ownership Element**] "The concept of 'ownership' of the dog is not limited to a person having actual possession of title to the animal, but includes a person who harbors or has control over a dog." Billy, 887 W.2d at 236.

[**Sub-rule on Provocation Element**] "Provocation requires an actual physical attack on the dog; verbal attacks do not count." Id. [**Interpretive Rule of the Sub-rule**] The burden of proof on plaintiff to show lack of provocation is a high one, and substantial evidence must be brought forth in order to bear the burden. Lefty v. Smartz, 553 W.2d 567, 568 (Apex 1987).

If the authority is stating a sub-rule as to a single element of the rule, and the element presents an issue that is to be covered in a separate TREATment, then the sub-rule would be presented in your rule section on that individual element, rather than in the rule section for the rule on the major issue. In the first example in this section, if you were going to do a separate TREATment of the ownership element, you would state the sub-rule on ownership from Billy ("The concept of 'ownership' of the dog is not limited to a person having actual possession of title to the animal, but includes a person who harbors or has control over a dog.") in the rule section of your TREATment of the ownership element.

7. **Do accept the possibility that two competing rules might exist.**

Rarely, but on occasion, two rules coexist and compete at the same time in the same jurisdiction. A line of controlling cases will follow the one rule, and a line of controlling cases will follow the other rule. This situation is unusual enough that you should reexamine your authorities to determine if you have found the secret entrance to your destination or simply stumbled into a blind alley:

   a. If the rules appear to be inconsistent, reexamine the facts of each case in the competing lines of authority. Can you reconcile the competing lines as being a rule with an exception to the rule for a particular fact pattern?
   b. Consider whether there are different public policies at work in the competing lines of authority. If there are, then you might have to refine your understanding of the issue. If a particular set of facts drives the application of one set of public policies and a different set of facts drives the application of another set of public policies, you should be able to predict the factual set in which your client's facts belong, and determine the correct policies and correct rule to apply to the client's situation.

If neither situation applies, then you have found the rare situation of two competing rules defined and applied in controlling authority of the same jurisdiction and hierarchy of judicial authority. When this happens, you must do your best to present both rules, and to analyze the law and apply both rules to your client's facts to predict the most likely outcome under each competing rule.

V. RULE SYNTHESIS

The rules above provide the basic criteria for rule formulation. If you have a statute or regulation that provides the exact wording of the rule on your issue, you should present that wording first and foremost in your rule section, followed by any further statements that explain, modify, or supplement the elements of the rule found in cases and other authorities that construe and apply the statute or rule. The same principle applies when you have a single wording of the rule, often the version laid down by a landmark, watershed case in the area, that is used consistently by most if not all of the authorities in your jurisdiction. You should present the traditional wording of the rule first, followed by any further explanation and modification of the rule found in later authorities.

However, when you have several controlling authorities (or the best authorities that you have) that do not agree on the wording of the applicable rule, you should try to synthesize the precedents into a coherent statement of the rule and its required elements. Supporting discussion and commentary about the rule can be presented separately, but the actual statement of the required elements of the rule should be made as cohesively as possible. An unsynthesized presentation of the rule can look sloppy and lazy.

An example is necessary to explain the distinction. Assume that you have three authorities on money had and received in Apex, which state the following in relevant part:

"The core of the claim of money had and received is a transfer of funds to the defendant, caused by the mistake of the plaintiff, and the defendant's retention of the funds is unjust. The historical origins of this claim were an action at law for assumpsit. In essence, it is a claim of restitution for unjust enrichment in the particular context of money transfers." First Federal Bank and Trust Co. v. Stevens, 678 W.2d 234, 237 (Apex 1988).

"Apex law of money had and received requires a transfer to the defendant and an unjust retention of the funds. It is permitted for the transferor to have made a mistake of fact, but not a mistake of law, in sending the funds to the defendant. If the defendant caused or contributed to the transferor's mistake of fact, this will mitigate in favor of a finding that the defendant's retention of the funds is unjust." Green Cross and Red Shield of Apex v. Carson, 688 W.2d 564, 566 (Apex Ct. App. 1st Dist. 1991).

"Historically, money had and received was a legal, not an equitable action, but the modern claim borrows the elements of unjust enrichment—an enrichment by transfer of funds, and that the enrichment is unjust. If the defendant is lawfully entitled to the amount of the transfer by virtue of a prior debt or account from the transferor, the retention of the funds is not unjust. It does not matter if the transferor did not plan to pay the debt or account until a later date, so long as the debt was due and owing." ATI Transnational Credit Corp. v. Adam's Asphalt Co., 778 W.2d 42, 44-45 (Apex Ct. App. 1st Dist. 1994).

An unsynthesized presentation of the rule (in a rule section) based on these three authorities might look something like this:

UNSYNTHESIZED RULE SECTION

Money had and received is a transfer of funds to the defendant, caused by the mistake of the plaintiff, and the defendant's retention of the funds is unjust. First Federal Bank and Trust Co. v. Stevens, 678 W.2d 234, 237 (Apex 1988). It is permitted for the transferor to have made a mistake of fact, but not a mistake of law, in sending the funds to the defendant. Green Cross and Red Shield of Apex v. Carson, 688 W.2d 564, 566 (Apex Ct. App. 1st Dist. 1991). If the defendant caused or contributed to the transferor's mistake of fact, this will mitigate in favor of a finding that the defendant's retention of the funds is unjust. Id.

If the defendant is lawfully entitled to the amount of the transfer by virtue of a prior debt or account from the transferor, the retention of the funds is not unjust. ATI Transnational Credit Corp. v. Adam's Asphalt Co., 778 W.2d 42, 44-45 (Apex Ct. App. 1st Dist. 1994). It does not matter if the transferor did not plan to pay the

---

> debt or account until a later date, so long as the debt was due at the time of the transfer. Id.
>
> Historically, money had and received was a legal, not an equitable action. Id. The origins of this claim were an action at law for assumpsit. First Federal Bank, 678 W.2d at 237. In essence, it is a claim of restitution for unjust enrichment in the particular context of money transfers—namely, an enrichment by transfer of funds, and that the enrichment is unjust. Id.; ATI, 778 W.2d at 45.

This example accurately reports the law, but in a largely undigested form. It may appear to some authors to be the safest way to state the rule—no one can accuse you of misstating the law—and others might think it is the most accurate way to present the law, since you did not change much of anything from what the authorities said about the law. But "safest" and "closest to the wording of the sources" is not always the best policy in rule formulation.

Remember that your task is not only to spit back the law to the reader, but to explain it in plain English and present it to the reader in the most concise and understandable way. The above example commits two sins that should not be committed by a good legal writer: it is too wordy, and it does not help the reader understand the law any better than if you simply handed her the photocopies of the three cases. A proper rule synthesis will take the rambling discourse on the law stated above and report it back in accurate, plain English, making the necessary connections and combinations of required elements so that the reader gains a broader understanding of the rule in much less time (and much less words) than if she pulled the cases and read the pages cited. This is a worthy goal of legal writing.

The following example shows a synthesis of the authorities, which should make the presentation of the rule more helpful to the reader:

SYNTHESIZED RULE SECTION

In order to prevail on a claim of money had and received, a plaintiff must prove: (1) a transfer of funds to the defendant, (2) that is the result of a mistake of fact but not of law, and (3) that has caused an unjust enrichment of the defendant. See First Federal Bank and Trust Co. v. Stevens, 678 W.2d 234, 237 (Apex 1988); ATI Transnational Credit Corp. v. Adam's Asphalt Co., 778 W.2d 42, 44-45 (Apex Ct. App. 1st Dist. 1994); Green Cross and Red Shield of Apex v. Carson, 688 W.2d 564, 566 (Apex Ct. App. 1st Dist. 1991).

If the defendant caused or contributed to the transferor's mistake of fact, this will mitigate in favor of a finding that the defendant's retention of the funds is unjust. Green Cross and Red Shield, 688 W.2d at 566. But if the defendant is lawfully entitled to the amount of the transfer by virtue of a debt or account from the transferor that is due, the retention of the funds is not unjust. ATI, 778 W.2d at 44-45.

The above example is not only shorter, more concise and direct, but it has made connections and linked parts of the authorities together in a way that the rote recitation of the first example did not. The second example helps the reader grasp the meaning of the rule faster and more completely than the first example. Note that "<u>see</u>" was used as a prefatory word for the authorities on the synthesized rule; no one case is the source of the exact wording and phrasing you used for the elements of the rule, so a signal is necessary, but the authorities directly support the synthesis of the rule you developed, so "<u>see</u>" is the proper signal.

Rule synthesis also can be employed in the situation where a standard wording of the rule exists (from a statute, rule, or landmark case), but later authorities have restated, redefined, or supplemented the elements of the rule. Remember that in these circumstances, the original version should be stated first, followed by a synthesis of the later authorities. In this way, the law is presented to the reader in the most efficient package.

Chapter 6

Organization of Legal Writing

This chapter presents the organizational format that will be used for analyzing a legal issue and reporting your conclusions in legal writing. The format discussed herein addresses the discussion of a single issue—it will be duplicated one or more times in each piece of writing to address each individual issue you are analyzing.[1] The format is derived from the rule-based reasoning syllogism[2] and it instructs you to introduce your <u>T</u>hesis on the issue in the form of a heading, provide the <u>R</u>ule or rules that address the issue, <u>E</u>xplain each rule and instruct the reader about how the rules are to be interpreted and applied, <u>A</u>pply the rules to your client's situation, and restate your <u>T</u>hesis as a conclusion. Thus, the format is referred to as **TREAT**.[3]

I. THESIS HEADING

The TREAT method begins when you have done all of the research and analysis of an issue and are ready to report your conclusions. Your discussion of an issue will begin with your position on the issue, called your thesis. The thesis almost always is written in one sentence, and it states what the issue is and how the issue should come out based on your analysis of the issue. In legal writing, you will start off your discussion of the issue by putting your thesis in a heading.

Presenting your thesis on the issue first brings to the front the most important part of the discussion: your answer to the legal question posed by the issue. Your readers will appreciate not having to wait for your answer. Putting your thesis on the issue in a heading that precedes the analysis and discussion of the issue further highlights this critical information for the benefit of the reader. When you consider that most of the writing you will do will discuss a number of issues in the same document, you can begin to understand that separating and highlighting your conclusions by use of thesis headings will help even

---

[1] Recall the definition of an "issue": An individual legal question implicated by a problem (a set of facts) that needs to be answered in order to render advice concerning the problem.

[2] Rule-Based Reasoning Syllogism: The answer is X because the authorities establish the rule that governs this situation, and the rule requires certain facts to be present, and these facts are present, so the application of the rule to the facts produces X result.

[3] TREAT is a refinement of the organizational scheme known as IRAC. <u>See</u> section VI of this chapter.

the busiest reader to pick up the most important parts of your discussion quickly and efficiently.

In the writing examples presented earlier in this text, you studied the situation of a client who owned a Doberman pinscher. Your client's dog encountered a girl as she was selling Girl Scout cookies, and the dog became agitated when the girl swung her bag of cookies at the dog's head. The dog apparently thought the girl was threatening it and it reacted by clamping its jaws onto her arm. Unfortunately, the girl and her mother got into it with the dog, and in the skirmish, the girl received several deep cuts on her arm. The case was analyzed under the mythical law of Apex, but for the purposes of this chapter, we will present the law as if you had done the research in Texas.

After completing your research and finding the rule that addresses the issue in Texas, and after analyzing your client's situation under the Texas rule, your conclusion is that your client, the dog owner, will be liable for the injuries inflicted on the woman's arm by the dog. When you write up your analysis, your thesis will be, "The dog owner will be liable for plaintiff's injuries."

When drafting the discussion of an issue, the thesis is stated as the heading of a section, and the paragraph that follows the heading will state the rule, as in the following example:

THESIS HEADING AND RULE SECTION:

1. <u>**The dog owner will be liable for plaintiff's dog bite injuries**</u>.

In Texas, a dog owner is liable for all injuries caused by his dog unless the dog is provoked by the victim. <u>Smithy v. Jonesy</u>, 123 S.W.2d 345, 347 (Tex. 1965); <u>Johnson v. Anderson</u>, 789 S.W.2d 234, 237 (Tex. App. 1989). The elements of a cause of action for dog-bite liability are therefore: (1) defendant's ownership of the dog, (2) injuries caused by the dog, and (3) lack of provocation of the dog by the plaintiff. <u>See</u> <u>Smithy</u>, 123 S.W.2d at 347.

Many practitioners, judges, or professors would prefer that you repeat or rephrase your thesis as the first sentence of the text in the section. This practice is particularly helpful if your thesis heading was a brief recitation of the points that are covered in the section rather than a more detailed summary of your conclusions. Restating your thesis as the first sentence of the section will benefit those readers who routinely skip reading the headings in a document. For example:

THESIS HEADING AND RULE SECTION:

1. <u>**The dog owner will be liable for plaintiff's dog bite injuries**</u>.

⸰ Defendant Jones, the dog owner, will be liable for all injuries caused to plaintiff by his dog because plaintiff did not provoke the dog. In Texas, a dog owner is liable for all injuries caused by his dog unless the dog is provoked by the victim. <u>Smithy v. Jonesy</u>, 123 S.W.2d 345, 347 (Tex. 1965); <u>Johnson v. Anderson</u>, 789 S.W.2d 234, 237 (Tex. App. 1989). The elements of a cause of action for dog-bite liability are therefore: (1) defendant's ownership of the dog, (2) injuries caused by the dog, and (3) lack of provocation of the dog by the plaintiff. <u>See</u> <u>Smithy</u>, 123 S.W.2d at 347.

II. RULE SECTION

A. Statement of legal principles and requirements that govern the issue

The rule section follows the thesis, and states the rule or rules that govern the legal issue. You will recall that a rule of law is a statement of the legal principles and requirements that govern the analysis of the legal issue at hand. Sometimes there is one rule that is followed by all the authorities in your jurisdiction. However, in other instances there will be authorities that state the rule in a slightly different way, or add a sentence or two describing the rule, or illuminate various nuances of the rule, or that add a new element or factor to the rule. In the previous two chapters, we discussed at length the process of finding and analyzing the authorities that define the rule of law that governs the legal issue at hand. We also discussed the process of synthesizing the various accounts of the rule into one coherent presentation of the rule.

The following chart should refresh your recollection about how to go about putting together the rule from multiple authorities and performing a "rule synthesis."

FORMULATING THE RULE (RULE SYNTHESIS)	
❶ Start with the highest and most recent controlling authority	◆ If you have a statute (or regulation), start with the statute ◆ If you have a watershed case that is controlling, start with that ◆ If your best authority is from the court of last resort, take the most recent opinion from that court, and start with that ◆ If these first three criteria do not apply, start with the most recent actual controlling authority that is on point ◆ Only if none of the above applies would you consider turning to non-controlling authority—primary or secondary ◆ Don't expect to use all of your authorities

❷ Reconcile differing statements or phrasings of the rule from controlling authorities, and attempt to synthesize the material into one coherent statement of the legal principles that govern the issue

❸ Write the rule first, interpretative rules second, and exceptions to the rule third

❹ Do not write a rule with inherent contradictions

❺ Do accept the <u>remote</u> possibility that two competing rules on the same issue might exist in the same jurisdiction

◆ DON'T change the wording of or paraphrase rules from statutes, administrative rules and regs, and watershed cases

◆ Unless a processed applied rule can be written smoothly and effectively in one sentence or phrase, write the rule first with modifications second

◆ Write interpretive sub-rules on elements of the rule in the section or sub-section of the discussion that discusses that element of the rule. Write exceptions to the sub-rules after you lay out the sub-rules themselves

◆ Check for ambiguity in the terms you have used to formulate the rule (even if some of these terms came from the authorities)

◆ When this happens, you may have to analyze the facts under both competing sets of rules

Your findings now have to be reported in the rule section. Occasionally, your rule section might be as small as one paragraph long, but frequently, you will wind up with two or more paragraphs if you have several accounts of the rule or more than one rule to present on the issue. The format of the rule section does not change whether you are talking about an elemental rule (a rule with required elements) or a rule with factors that must be evaluated or balanced.

B. Interpretative rules

The rule section also will present interpretive rules from primary and secondary authorities. Interpretive rules are actual statements from legal authorities that instruct lawyers and judges how to interpret or apply the rule on the issue at hand. They are not elements or factors of the rule, and they are not the same as the principles of interpretation and application that you will derive from a synthesis of the authorities presented in the explanation section, which are discussed in section III below. Instead, these are individual statements phrased in rule language that you will lift from the authorities that have discussed and applied the rule.

For example, in the hypothetical problem we have been working with, a case from your jurisdiction might characterize the rule on the claim for dog bite liability as a "disfavored cause of action," and state that "in order to prove liability for an animal bite, the plaintiff must prove each element of the claim with clear and convincing evidence." A secondary authority, such as a treatise on tort law, might explain that dog bite liability has moved from a point where "every dog was entitled to one unprovoked bite," to a point where "each attack by a dog, even the first, may give rise to a valid claim against the dog owner." These interpretative rules belong in the same section as the actual statement of the rule and its elements or factors, but you should state interpretive rules in one or more paragraphs after you have laid out the elements of the actual rule.

In our example, the rule on liability for dog attacks in Texas was stated the same way with the same three elements in each of the authorities you found in Texas, as quoted in the text box above. Adding interpretive rules for this rule would produce the following rule section:

THESIS HEADING AND RULE SECTION:

1. <u>The dog owner will be liable for plaintiff's dog bite injuries</u>.

In Texas, a dog owner is liable for all injuries caused by his dog unless the dog is provoked by the victim. <u>Smithy v. Jonesy</u>, 123 S.W.2d 345, 347 (Tex. 1965); <u>Johnson v. Anderson</u>, 789 S.W.2d 234, 237 (Tex. App. 1989). The elements of a cause of action for dog-bite liability are therefore: (1) defendant's ownership of the dog, (2) injuries caused by the dog, and (3) lack of provocation of the dog by the plaintiff. <u>See</u> <u>Smithy</u>, 123 S.W.2d at 347. The rule on dog bite liability has moved from a point where "every dog was entitled to one unprovoked bite," to a point where "each attack by a dog, even the first, may give rise to a valid claim against the dog owner." <u>Id.</u> A claim seeking to impose liability for a dog bite is a "disfavored cause of action," and "in order to prove liability, the plaintiff must prove each element of the claim with clear and convincing evidence." <u>Roberts v. Thomas</u>, 676 S.W.2d 34, 37 (Tex. 1979).

III. EXPLANATION SECTION AND EXPLANATORY SYNTHESIS

A. Purpose of the explanation section

In the explanation section, you will use some or all of the legal authorities you have found in your research to explain the rule and to show how the rule operates in various situations. This is the section that employs analogical reasoning. The goal of this section is to teach the reader the principles learned from earlier authorities that tell lawyers how to interpret and apply the rule. You will spell out the legal standards that govern the issue in the rule section. A law-trained reader can review the rules you lay out in the rule section and make an educated guess as to how these rules should work in actual situations, but this only will be a guess. Your job as the author of a piece of legal writing is to confirm or rebut that guess by explaining how the rules work in actual situations, which in most instances will require you to refer to the cases that have applied those rules to produce a real outcome. Consider the following:

THE GOAL OF THE EXPLANATION SECTION

The goal is to illustrate how the rule is to be interpreted and applied based on how the authorities have applied it in actual concrete factual settings, and on how commentators have interpreted the rule

- ◆ You are going beyond what the courts already have said about the rule in interpretive rules found in cases.
- ◆ You are presenting principles of interpretation that are supported by a careful reading of the cases
- ◆ You are doing the work of digesting and synthesizing the cases so the reader doesn't have to

Case-by-case presentations make the reader do most of the work and they are wasteful of space and time (i.e., the reader's attention span)

- ◆ Avoid case-by-case presentations even though they are easy to write, and sometimes fun to write
- ◆ Avoid them even though courts use them
- ◆ The only time to resort to a case-by-case presentation is when you have one or two cases that are so close to the facts that you want to cover them in great detail, or if you want to distinguish one or two troublesome cases in enough detail to make your point

---

The explanation section does not exist simply to provide titillating details from a number of cases to entertain the reader, and it does not exist to fill up the space from the end of your rule or sub-rule section to the beginning of your application section. Details from cases can be exciting, but the facts and details themselves do not teach the reader how the rule actually works. The explanation section exists to present principles of interpretation derived from cases and secondary authorities that will show the reader how a rule or sub-rule works in actual situations.

Lawyers and judges have a number of ways to go about this task. The common *unsynthesized* way used by many if not most lawyers and judges is to write a series of sentences and paragraphs describing the facts and holding of several cases. Typically, the author discusses one case at a time, devoting an entire paragraph to each case. At the end of it, the author hopes the reader has learned something from this list of factual details and holdings. What is learned often is up to the reader, because the typical author fails to continue on and write a paragraph or two summarizing what the cases teach us about how the rule works and drawing connections between cases that otherwise are factually different. In effect, the typical author simply is saying to the reader: "Here are a number of cases where the rule was applied and here is the outcome of those cases. You make sense out of it."

A case-by-case presentation is effective when you want to fully illustrate one or more cases that are exactly on point—they present the same facts and issues as your own case—to show how completely they should control your client's situation. Remember that American courts follow the common law system of precedent and stare decisis, so a prior case from a proper court that presents the exact same facts and issues as your case ought to control the outcome of your case. A detailed discussion of the facts and holdings of these key cases may be necessary and prudent for your analysis.

The second instance where a case-by-case presentation may be necessary is when you need to fully distinguish a potentially controlling authority that goes against your thesis. The process of distinguishing certain authorities may require a detailed discussion of the facts, issues, and holdings of the cases in order to separate them from your case.

In most instances, however, you will not have any positive or negative case that is on all fours with your case. You will have a number of helpful cases to which you can analogize your client's situation, and some that are not helpful, but none that is completely on all points with your case. In these situations, a synthesis of the authorities will aid the reader more than a recitation of one case after another.

In these circumstances, the case-by-case presentation method will fail you because your research does not uncover more than one or two cases on an element or factor of a rule. If you write an unsynthesized explanation section that only discusses one case, the reader will have very little chance of figuring out how the rule works in real life situations. For example, how do you know what "breaking" (an element of burglary) means? Well, you might have found one case in which a defendant broke a window and the court found that this was a breaking. Your explanation of this element might then lead the reader to believe that breaking means breaking a window. This conclusion is logical, but absolutely inaccurate.

B. Explanatory synthesis

THE PROCESS OF EXPLANATORY SYNTHESIS

❶ Read cases and look for common facts and common outcomes

◆ Group cases by facts
◆ Divide groups of cases by outcome

❷ Review the groups to find the factors or public policies that make the difference in the outcome

◆ Reconcile cases that have different outcomes; what policy or theme or factor determined the outcome in these cases
◆ Reconcile cases that have the same outcome on different facts; what common policy or theme or factors brought about the same outcome on different facts

---

❸ Write principles of interpretation that explain your findings

◆ Phrase your principles of interpretation in language that mimics interpretive rules

◆ Often you can use interpretive rules as principles that tie together multiple authorities; there is no requirement that you always have to come up with brand new principles

❹ Cite the cases that support your principles of interpretation with parentheticals that provide facts or other information about each case

◆ Parentheticals should contain enough information to illustrate how the individual case supports the general principle you have laid out

◆ Use shorthands and abbreviated phrases to save space

❺ When you draft the Application section, apply the principles of interpretation to your own facts; as a general rule, do not apply individual cases to your facts

◆ Applying principles to facts will make your analysis more convincing; you have spelled out the connections to be made between the authorities and then followed through and showed how the principles learned from a study of the authorities determines the outcome of the case at hand

◆ The exception to this rule is when you have one or two fabulous cases that are worthy of individual attention in the Explanation section; these should be discussed individually in the Application section, whether as support or to distinguish them

Explanatory synthesis takes the relevant authorities (those that have applied the rule in actual situations) and derives from them one or more principles of interpretation and application of the rule. These principles are derived from common factual elements, policies, or themes found in the cases and other authorities that are relevant to the interpretation of the rule. In its simplest form, explanatory synthesis requires you to try to identify a common element of earlier cases that is compared to the facts of your case to make the point that your case should enjoy the same outcome because your case shares this common element with the others, or that your case should have a different outcome, because it does not share this common element and thus is distinguishable.

For example, if all the prior dog bite cases in your jurisdiction in which the plaintiffs failed to recover involved adult victims who provoked the dog by striking it, and you have a client who is a dog injury victim but is a small child who accidentally fell against a dog, you could synthesize the earlier cases where plaintiffs did not prevail as "adult provoker" cases, and distinguish your own case because it involves a child who accidentally made contact with the dog, and a child should not be held to the same standard of care as an adult. This principle must be supported by the holdings of the cases, or by appropriate use of dicta from the cases. If the cases themselves anticipate the possibility that the provoker might be a small child who acts inadvertently and unintentionally, and the cases state that this would not have any bearing on the outcome, then your synthesis is unsupported by the authorities and you cannot assert it.

Optimally, however, you should strive to identify a policy or theme that underlies the earlier authorities and that resonates with and defines the applicable rule and the particular area of law in which the rule is found.

> A principle of interpretation that is derived from the central meaning, common ground, public policy, or theme behind a group of earlier cases where the rule was applied is probative of how the rule properly is to be interpreted and applied in cases in the present and future, such as your own. Furthermore, when you apply this principle to the facts of your client's case in the application section, the results will be more reliable than if you simply were to compare one earlier case at a time to the facts of the client's case.

> For example, if all the dog injury cases in your jurisdiction can be tied together with the theme that "the law provides a remedy for injuries suffered when the victim is acting peaceably and the dog is not," then use this as your explanation of the rule, followed by indicative reference to examples of how this theme is played out in the earlier authorities. This technique tells the reader how the rule has worked in your jurisdiction in the past, and how it should work again in the future. This is much more useful to the reader than simply writing a paragraph on each case, and concluding each paragraph with, "Once again, plaintiff recovered because the victim was acting peaceably, and the dog was not."

It is this kind of digested analysis of the cases that is missing from the average lawyer's explanation section, yet this is what is important to an understanding of how the rule works. Secondary authorities may state principles of interpretation and application directly—the authors of treatises, hornbooks, restatements, and law reviews go to great lengths to digest and make sense of the law for the reader—but judicial opinions often do not. The factual details and holdings from a group of individual cases do not in and of themselves define the category of situations that will satisfy the standards of the rule or a particular element or factor of the rule and what categories of situations will not. The factual details of cases often are exciting to write about, but your readers would just as soon have you cut to the chase and tell them the reasons why certain kinds of cases have satisfied the rule in the past and will again in the future, while others did not and will not.

The goal of the explanation section is to explain how the law works in several relevant indicative situations without making it appear that each case you discuss is a law unto itself. A line of precedents should not look like an obstacle course to get through before victory can be won. The cases to use in the explanation section are those that are most indicative of how the courts have applied the rule to facts that are relevant to the case at hand. The questions to ask yourself when drafting this section are, "Does this case add something new to my explanation of the rule?" and "Will my explanation be weaker if the reader does not know about this case?" If the answer to both questions is "no," leave the case out. Later chapters in this book will help you make the determination of which are the most important cases to discuss.

Where the individual facts of the authorities you are using are important, parentheticals can be used to guide the reader through some of the particulars of the facts, and you may be able to make use of the "compare . . . and . . . with . . . and" format of citation (see Chapter 9) to make the kind of connections you need to make to further reinforce how the rule or sub-rule works in various situations. When you explain how the rule works in the various situations represented by your cases, you should bring out the facts and circumstances that make the **positive cases** (the cases where the result is the same as what you predict your client's result will be in your thesis) sound more like your client's case than the **negative cases** (the cases where the result goes the other way from what you predict in your thesis). This technique is called analogizing to the good cases and distinguishing the bad cases. Synthesis aids this process because you can link together a number of positive authorities that stand for a proposition that supports your thesis, and you also can link together a number of negative authorities that do not support your thesis and show a common reason (facts, law, or policy) why each of them should not control the outcome of the instant case. If you do a good job of it, the reader is more likely to agree with your thesis.

C. Comparing unsynthesized and synthesized explanation sections

You might already know what *unsynthesized* explanation sections look like, because you can find them in many of the legal opinions you are reading in the case books for your other courses. An unsynthesized explanation section takes the reader on a historical walking tour of the cases that have interpreted the rule. We will attempt to show the difference between an unsynthesized explanation section and a synthesized section in the following examples.

Example 1:

An element of adverse possession is "exclusive possession" of the disputed land. The following cases explain how this element has been interpreted in Tennessee:

UNSYNTHESIZED EXPLANATION

In <u>Flowers</u>, the claimant cleared a road and cut down trees and used the land for his own purposes for ten years. He even built a fence, but the neighbors who owned the land pulled down the fence. The court held that the possession was exclusive anyway because the neighbors did not move back onto the land to use it after taking down the fence. <u>Flowers</u>, 979 S.W.2d at 470.

In <u>Conaway</u>, the claimant had no fence. He used the disputed land to build a shed and a horseshoe pit, and he put a little fountain on the land. He cut the grass and maintained the land and the improvement he had put on the land. His neighbor, who actually owned the land, came over and pitched horseshoes from time to time, and may have cut the grass once or twice in ten years, but these visits were sporadic. The claimant was the only one to make use of the land for ten years. The court held this to be exclusive. <u>Conaway</u>, 972 S.W.2d at 445.

In <u>Witt</u>, the claimant had a fence around the disputed land. Although the true owner of the land testified that he thought he could use the disputed land any time he wanted, the evidence revealed that the claimant was the only person who used the land. <u>Witt</u>, 845 S.W.2d at 667. Therefore, the claimant proved that his possession was "exclusive." <u>Id</u>.

This is how you could explain how this element has been interpreted and applied using a **synthesized** explanation section:

SYNTHESIZED EXPLANATION

Exclusive possession in Tennessee refers to the claimant being the exclusive user of the land rather than to the actions of the claimant in excluding people from coming on the land. <u>See</u> <u>Flowers</u>, 979 S.W.2d at 470 (claimants were the only ones to use the land for the ten year period); <u>Witt</u>, 845 S.W.2d at 667 (same); <u>Conaway</u>, 972 S.W.2d at 445 (claimants were the principal users of the land, because the true owner only made sporadic visits). Exclusive is used as an adjective to mean that the claimant is the only user, rather than as a verb meaning to exclude. <u>See generally</u> <u>Flowers</u>, 979 S.W.2d at 470; <u>Witt</u>, 845 S.W.2d at 667; <u>Conaway</u>, 972 S.W.2d at 445. Actions that might exclude others, such as fence building, do not determine whether a possession is exclusive. <u>Compare</u> <u>Witt</u>, 845 S.W.2d at 667 (claimant had a fence), <u>with</u> <u>Conaway</u>, 972 S.W.2d at 445 (claimant had no fence), <u>and</u> <u>Flowers</u>, 979 S.W.2d at 470 (claimant built a fence, but the owners tore it down). Total exclusion is not necessary, because the true owner can make sporadic visits to the land and still not defeat claimant's adverse possession claim. <u>See</u> <u>Conaway</u>, 972 S.W.2d at 445 (sporadic visits by the true owner to play horseshoes and cut the grass did not defeat the exclusive possession of claimant); <u>Flowers</u>, 979 S.W.2d at 470 (the owners' tearing down of claimant's fence did not defeat exclusive possession because the true owners still did not take over the parcel for their own use).

The difference between the two methods is that in the unsynthesized explanation section, the reader learns a lot of interesting details from the cases, but never hears about the underlying principles of interpretation of this element of the adverse possession rule that would help the law-trained reader apply this element to all future situations. The focus of the unsynthesized explanation section is on the cases, not on the principles or themes of interpretation that the cases support. A devoted law-trained reader may be able to ponder your history of the cases, and draw her own conclusions about the categories of situations that will satisfy the rule, and those that will not, but most readers would prefer you to take the time to think this through and present a complete analysis of how this element of the rule works.

The synthesized explanation section focuses on the principles of interpretation and application that can be discerned from the cases. This section resembles a small scale treatise on this particular element of the adverse possession rule. Factual details are presented when they are necessary to draw connections between cases and to distinguish positive cases from negative cases. A law-trained reader that reads this section will not have to wonder about the categories of situations that satisfy this element of the rule.

Example 2:

In Connecticut, the elements of money had and received are: (1) Receipt of money; (2) by mistake; (3) under circumstances that render the retention of the money unjust. The following cases explain the third element—whether retention of the money was unjust:

UNSYNTHESIZED EXPLANATION

In <u>First Federal Bank</u>, 678 N.E.2d at 237, defendant Stevens received an unexpected wire transfer from the plaintiff Bank. The court granted summary judgment to defendant Stevens allowing him to retain the funds because Stevens was entitled to the mistakenly transferred sum as an offset of a judgment Stevens had obtained against the Bank in an earlier lawsuit. The court held that the prior debt gave just cause for defendant to retain the funds. <u>Id.</u>

In <u>ATI</u>, 778 N.E.2d at 44-45, defendant Adam's had a potential claim against ATI, but no action had been filed and no judgment entered. Through a fortuitous mistake, Adam's received a wire transfer from ATI that was intended for Adam's replacement on a construction project. ATI immediately informed Adam's of the mistake, but Adam's refused to relinquish the funds. The court held that there was no justification for Adam's retention of the funds. <u>Id.</u>

<u>Blue Cross</u>, 688 N.E.2d at 566-68, shows the effect of time and laches on the unjust enrichment evaluation. Defendant Carson was a regular beneficiary of payments from Blue Cross for medical expenses. The case arose from a mistaken quarterly payment by Blue Cross of three *years* of benefits to Carson instead of three months. Blue Cross did not notice the mistake until a year later; by then, Carson had spent the money on his medical care and nursing home expenses. The court refused to order Carson to reimburse Blue Cross, because Carson had a valid expectation of indefinite quarterly payments from Blue Cross, and had changed his position drastically in reliance on his good faith belief that he was entitled to whatever payments he received from Blue Cross, no matter if they may have been larger or smaller than the average quarterly payment.

A **synthesized** approach to this explanation section would look like the following:

SYNTHESIZED EXPLANATION

Connecticut case law has demonstrated the importance of a present obligation from the transferor to the transferee in determining whether the transferee's retention of the funds is unjust. See First Federal Bank, 678 N.E.2d at 237 (present obligation; no unjust enrichment); ATI, 778 N.E.2d at 44-45 (no present obligation; unjust enrichment); Blue Cross, 688 N.E.2d at 566-68 (present obligation; no unjust enrichment). If there is an outstanding debt that is due between the transferor and the transferee, the fact that the transferor did not intend to pay the debt at the time of the transfer does not prevent the transferee from justly retaining the funds it fortuitously received. See First Federal Bank, 678 N.E.2d at 237 (present obligation sufficient to allow retention); ATI, 778 N.E.2d at 44-45 (no present obligation; retention was unjust). Even if the funds were not all due at the time of transfer, the expectation of receipt of funds through an existing account or payment scheme can render the retention just. See Blue Cross, 688 N.E.2d at 566-67 (finding was buttressed through transferor's laches that caused a change in transferee's circumstances).

As in example 1 above, the unsynthesized explanation section focuses on the cases themselves while the synthesized explanation section focuses on the principles of interpretation and application that can be derived from the cases. Note well that many of the individual facts from the cases are left out of the synthesized explanation section. Facts such as the horseshoe pit and shed in one adverse possession case and the wire transfers in two of the money had and received cases are only relevant if they tell the reader something about how the rule properly is applied and how the facts affected the outcome produced by the application. Since these facts did not affect the application of the rule and the outcome of this application, these facts were left out of the synthesized account. The facts about fences in the three adverse possession cases and the facts about debts and current obligations in the three money had and received cases were relevant to an understanding of how the rule works, so these facts were included in parentheticals in the synthesized version.

A synthesized method is shorter in terms of using up fewer pages out of your page limit than the unsynthesized method. But this result only is one reason to use explanatory synthesis, not the best reason. It is not just a time and space-saving device; it makes the reader's comprehension of the situation clearer and your analysis and conclusions stronger.

Explanatory synthesis also has a positive effect on the application section, discussed in section IV below. If the facts and policies of the cases are synthesized in this way, it makes it easier to compare the client's situation to the category of prior situations that satisfy the rule that are defined by the authorities. You will not write an application section that says, "As in Flowers, our claimant had a partial fence . . . Unlike in Witt, the fence did not go all the way around the disputed parcel . . .," which make it seem like the cases are the rule, rather than the cases standing as individual examples of situations where the rule was applied to produce a certain outcome. Your application section instead might state that, "Claimant and her predecessor in interest were the only persons to use the disputed parcel for fourteen years. Therefore, they will satisfy the exclusive possession requirement." Using the above example on money had and received, it would be simple to write an application section that states, "In our case, there was no outstanding debt or payment scheme to justify the defendant's retention of the funds," and thus to apply the rule to the client's facts in a short, straightforward manner.

D. Use of secondary authorities

The explanation section also may include discussion of secondary authorities—scholarly works that interpret or explain the law. These authorities cannot control the outcome of your case, but they can be used to help persuade the reader that you are on the right track with your thesis. Secondary authorities can be used as support for a principle that you are deriving from the cases in your jurisdiction. If you are joined by one or more scholars in drawing the conclusion that there is a relevant underlying theme that ties together most if not all of the prior cases, then reference to the work of these scholars will make your explanation section more persuasive than if you were to write your own personal thoughts on the same topic and present these thoughts by themselves.

An example of the use of secondary sources to explain a rule is shown in the following paragraph:

The underlying public policy behind the Texas rule is that persons "attacked by a domesticated animal when the person is acting peaceably and not directly threatening the animal" shall recover from the owner of the animals. See Chester A. Arthur, Texas Animal Laws 234 (1953). Although Professor Arthur was referring to the Roaming Livestock Damage Act, Tex. Agric. Code Ann. § 222.1234 (Vernon 1944), there is no practical difference between livestock that are roaming loose on the property and domestic animals, such as dogs, that are encountered on the property. See Arthur, supra, at 235. The law provides a remedy for injuries suffered when "the victim is acting peaceably and the dog is not." Mary M. McDermott, When a Best Friend Bites: Dog Bite Liability in Texas, 45 Tex. L. Rev. 122-23 (1979).

This paragraph discusses the policies at work in the situation that mitigate in favor of your thesis. We made a point of using secondary authorities that discuss these policies rather than just spinning them out of our own mind and recollection. It is important to support every statement about the law by referring to authority, even if you are talking about public policy.

Given the priority of primary controlling authority in legal analysis, in legal writing, you should discuss the cases from the applicable jurisdiction in your explanation section before you present secondary authorities that further support the principles of interpretation you have derived from these cases. The secondary authorities should be used to buttress the principles found in the controlling case law, not to supersede them.

E. Explanation of rules not found in cases

We have been focusing on rules that were found in cases, but you also will be writing about legal rules that come from constitutions, statutes, and administrative rules and regulations. The same process applies, because to explain the rule that is found in a constitution or statute or regulation, you still will use cases as examples of specific situations where that rule was applied and secondary authorities that explain how the rule should be interpreted. If the statute or regulation is fairly new and there are no reported cases where that statute or regulation was applied and no secondary sources explaining the rule, you will use the principles of statutory interpretation discussed in Chapter 5 and your own powers of legal rhetoric.

Consider the following two examples dealing with the fictional 1999 Nevada Pit Bull Control Law and its effect on your client's case. Assume that your client does own a pit bull terrier, but this dog was not the dog that caused the injury to the woman (you will recall that client's Doberman pinscher was involved in the incident). The statute provides in pertinent part:

> Pit bull terriers pose a significantly greater risk of danger to the public than other dogs. . . . There is no way to insure the safety of persons coming into contact with a pit bull whether or not the person provokes the dog. Therefore, an owner of a pit bull shall be strictly liable for all personal injuries caused to humans by his dog(s) regardless of whether the victim provoked the dog(s) or not.

In the absence of interpretive authorities, you might write a rule, explanation, and application section that would look like something like this:

Rule, explanation and application sections when there are no authorities interpreting the statute	In 1999, the Nevada Legislature passed the Pit Bull Control Law, Nev. Rev. Stat. § 222.5678 (1999), which provides in pertinent part that:
	Pit bull terriers pose a significantly greater risk of danger to the public than other dogs. . . . There is no way to insure the safety of persons coming into contact with a pit bull whether or not the person provokes the dog. Therefore, an owner of a pit bull shall be strictly liable for all personal injuries caused to humans by his dog(s) regardless of whether the victim provoked the dog(s) or not.
	No case or commentator has interpreted this section, and nothing in the legislative history sheds light on the meaning of this section of the statute. Although on its face, this section contains an ambiguity as to whether the owner of a pit bull is strictly liable for injuries caused by any of his dogs, pit bulls or others,

the statute otherwise is clear that the purpose of the provision is to protect the public from the special dangers presented by pit bulls. It defies the internal consistency of the statute to assert that the provision imposes strict liability on a dog owner simply because he owns a pit bull who had nothing to do with the injuries inflicted in the case at hand. Because plaintiff was injured by defendant's Doberman, not his pit bull, this statute will have no effect on this case and will not cause defendant to be strictly liable for plaintiff's injuries.

If there are authorities that have addressed the interpretation and application of the statute in ways that are relevant to your analysis, you would discuss these authorities in the following manner:

Rule, explanation and application sections when there are authorities interpreting the statute	In 1999, the Nevada Legislature passed the Pit Bull Control Law, Nev. Rev. Stat. § 222.5678 (1999), which provides in pertinent part that:
	Pit bull terriers pose a significantly greater risk of danger to the public than other dogs. . . . There is no way to insure the safety of persons coming into contact with a pit bull whether or not the person provokes the dog. Therefore, an owner of a pit bull shall be strictly liable for all personal injuries caused to humans by his dog(s) regardless of whether the victim provoked the dog(s) or not.
	Although on its face, the statute contains an ambiguity as to whether the owner of a pit bull is strictly liable for injuries caused by any of his dogs, pit bulls or others, the statute has been limited to attacks by pit bulls on humans. Chuy v. Taylor, 887 P.2d 246, 248 (Nev. 2000). A dog owner will not be strictly liable for an attack by one of his other dogs, a non-pit bull, simply because he owns a pit bull who had nothing to do with the injuries inflicted in the case at hand. See id.; Carlos R. Rivera, Current Developments in Nevada Law, 66 UNLV L. Rev. 322-23 (2000). Therefore, this statute will have no effect on this case and will not cause defendant to be strictly liable for plaintiff's injuries.

IV. APPLICATION SECTION

Application is the section where you apply the rule to your client's facts and show how the rule will work in your client's situation. If you are writing an informative objective work such as an office memorandum, you will explain how you think the client will fare based on your analysis of the law. If you are writing a partisan advocate's brief, you will use this section to argue exactly why your client wins when the law is applied to the facts.

In the application section, you must make the connection between your client's situation and the situations in the authorities you are relying on in support of your thesis. This section presents the second half of the analogical reasoning process that you began in the explanation section. The application section continues the practice of distinguishing bad cases from good cases so as to drive home your thesis. You must show that the negative authorities you discussed in the explanation section are different from your client's situation. If you relied on policy arguments, you must show how the client's situation furthers the policies you discussed in support of your thesis.

A typical, ***unsynthesized*** explanation section will produce an application section that looks like this:

APPLICATION SECTION FOLLOWING AN *UNSYNTHESIZED* EXPLANATION SECTION

In the instant case, there is no dispute that the defendant's dog attacked and caused injury to plaintiff, his neighbor, when she walked out of her apartment and bumped into the dog with her shopping bag. Thus, the first two elements of this cause of action are established. In reference to the third element, lack of provocation, plaintiff did nothing to present a serious threat to the dog, let alone strike the dog, in contrast to the plaintiff in <u>Smithy</u>. Plaintiff may have swung her shopping bag near the dog in a careless manner, but this is a far cry from the beating that the <u>Smithy</u> dog received before it attacked the victim in that case. Like the plaintiff in <u>Johnson</u>, the Scout was using a public hallway that led to the front door of the apartment building. According to <u>Johnson</u>, walking in a hallway is not a provocative action, and it certainly is no more provocative than mistakenly opening the wrong door of an apartment where the dog is found, as was the case in <u>Russell</u>.

Although the postman in <u>Johnson</u> was acting in the ordinary course of his daily employment duties, and plaintiff here was doing something outside of her ordinary employment activities, this should not be viewed as a legally significant difference precluding plaintiff from recovery. Recovery by plaintiff furthers the policy of allowing recovery where the victim was acting peaceably and the dog was not.

If you used explanatory synthesis to combine authorities in the explanation section, the application section will apply the principles of interpretation derived from the common facts or common theme of the earlier cases, rather than simply comparing the facts of the instant case first to one earlier case, then the next, then the next, and so on. You will explain how the common underlying theme is furthered by your interpretation of how the rule will apply in your case, or you will distinguish the earlier cases because of their common facts or policies that are not present in the instant case. Consider the following modified application section that follows a ***synthesized*** explanation section:

APPLICATION SECTION FOLLOWING A *SYNTHESIZED* EXPLANATION SECTION

In the instant case, there is no dispute that defendant's dog attacked and caused injury to plaintiff, his neighbor, when she walked out of her apartment and bumped into the dog with her shopping bag. Thus, the first two elements of this cause of action are established.

In reference to the third element, lack of provocation, the underlying theme of the Texas cases is that a plaintiff who is peaceably going about her business and is attacked by an aggressive dog will recover, while a plaintiff who picked a fight with the dog and caused injury to the dog first will not recover. Plaintiff did not pick a fight with defendant's dog. She did nothing to present a serious threat to the dog, let alone intentionally strike the dog. Plaintiff may have been careless in swinging her shopping bag near the dog, but that is a far cry from beating the dog. Recovery by the plaintiff furthers the policy of allowing recovery where the victim was acting peaceably and the dog was not.

This explanatory synthesis and application of synthesized principles only works if it is fair to link all of the prior cases together under the theme of "a plaintiff recovers when the plaintiff was acting peaceably and the dog was not." You cannot invent a common theme that is not present in the earlier cases, nor can you assume common facts that are not discussed in the cases. However, if you can discern a common set of facts and theme or policy that is important to the understanding of how the rule should work, it is helpful to your reader to point this out.

V. THESIS RESTATED AS A CONCLUSION

You should finish your discussion of an issue by restating your thesis as a conclusion. This is not the most critical part of the discussion, but we find that it makes a difference to the reader of legal writing to have that one sentence at the end that brings closure to the discussion.

The conclusion you make can be one sentence, and it can come at the end of the last paragraph of your application section. As an example, the thesis as conclusion line of the example we have been working with might be:

Therefore, defendant will be required to compensate plaintiff for her injuries in this case.

We do not intend to imply that the thesis restated as conclusion has to be a throwaway. It often is a single sentence, simply there to say this section is completed. But you can spend more time with a conclusion and use it to advance your argument one more step, or to make a smooth transition to the next topic. You only are limited by your own creativity.

VI. OTHER STRUCTURAL FORMATS

You may encounter in your studies a legal writing method of organization know as IRAC, pronounced "eye-rack," which stands for Issue - Rule - Application - Conclusion.

IRAC terminology		TREAT terminology	
Issue	Identifies the issue for the reader	Thesis	Identifies the issue for the reader and states your conclusion on the issue
Rule	States the legal principles that govern the issue	Rule	States the legal principles that govern the issue
	A good IRAC writer also will explain and illustrate how the rule works in actual situations	Explanation	Explains and illustrates how the rule works in actual situations
Application	Applies the rule to the facts of the case at hand	Application	Applies the rule to the facts of the case at hand
Conclusion	States your conclusion on the issue	Thesis restated as conclusion	Restates your conclusion on the issue

IRAC is taught in many legal writing courses, and there is nothing inherently wrong with the method as long as you are clear that the "Issue" item should state your position on the issue, which we call your thesis, and the "Rule" item should not only state the rules but explain them, and provide principles of how the rules should work in various situations based on a synthesis of earlier authorities. Some legal writing authors change the IRAC designation to IREAC for this reason.[4] If you do all of the above using IRAC or IREAC, you are essentially doing the same thing as we are telling you to do in the TREAT

---

[4] Another version of this format is CRAC, pronounced "see-rack" not "crack," which stands for Conclusion - Rule - Application - Conclusion. See Alan L. Dworsky, The Little Book of Legal Writing 105 (1992). This is even closer to the TREAT structure, because the Conclusion stated up front is supposed to be your thesis on the legal issue at hand. However, like IRAC, the CRAC form needs to be expanded so that it is clear that the concepts of explanation of the rule and how it works in various situations are part of your discussion.

format. We simply believe it is easier to remember to do all those things if they have their own reference letters.

VII. IDENTIFYING MULTIPLE ISSUES

We have been discussing the treatment of an individual issue within your client's case. The dog bite example with which we have been working boils down to one issue—whether the plaintiff provoked the dog. We mentioned in the application section the other two elements, but only so far as to point out that they are not in dispute, so there is no need to have a separate discussion of each element. We did not ignore them, because you must include in your writing some discussion of each required element or factor of the rule that applies to the case. But a single sentence is all the treatment these elements required.

In real life, this is an unusual position in which to be. More often than not, you will have more than one issue to write about. In the real world, a "client" (as defined earlier in this book to include the person or entity you are working for, which may include your more senior colleagues in the same law office) will come into your office with a problem, and you will have to identify what issues are implicated by the facts of the situation the client is in. Each problem that reaches your desk probably will raise more than one issue, and each issue will have at least one rule that applies to it. Each rule that applies can and often will have multiple elements or factors, each of which can present additional issues. An element or factor of a rule can have a sub-rule that has elements or factors, some of which will require separate treatment. It can get fairly complicated, but the TREAT format is flexible enough to accommodate that much complexity.

In order to determine the number of issues you have to treat, consider:

A. What are the separate legal questions you have to answer?

Most problems your client will bring to you will present more than one legal question to answer. If the client literally asks two questions, or one question that will involve the discussion of two unrelated legal issues—such as what separate causes of action might the plaintiff bring against the client based on the facts—then each question presents a major issue in your discussion. In an outline, the answers (theses) to these questions will appear as the major headings because you will state a thesis concerning each major issue as the heading of the discussion on that issue.

In the single issue discussion above, the major issue was, "Is the dog owner liable for plaintiff's injuries?" which was translated into the thesis heading, "The dog owner will be liable for plaintiff's dog bite injuries." If there were two or more possible claims that the plaintiff might bring against your client, your writing would have two or more major issues and major theses on these issues. For example, Roman I might be, "The dog owner will be liable to plaintiff under common law dog bite liability standards," Roman II might be, "The dog owner will be liable to plaintiff under a theory of negligence," and Roman III might be, "The dog owner will not be strictly liable to plaintiff under the Nevada Pit Bull Control Law." Each major issue must be handled in a separate TREAT discussion.

B. Which elements or factors of the rules and sub-rules of the rules are at issue?

A separate TREAT discussion is required to address each separate legal question, meaning each part of the problem that is in dispute and thus "at issue." If the rule that governs the issue at hand has one basic requirement, and thus one element, it may be handled in a single discussion of Thesis, Rule, Explanation, Application and Thesis as conclusion. If the rule has multiple elements or factors, but only one is in dispute, you also may discuss the entire rule in one TREAT discussion, as in our dog bite example above, where provocation was the only element of the rule that was in dispute. But if the rule itself presents multiple legal questions to answer, it will require more than one TREAT discussion. If the separate questions that must be answered are all based on elements or sub-parts of a single rule, we will refer to the treatments of those questions as sub-TREATs.

For example, if there was a serious question whether or not the defendant "owned" this Doberman pinscher within the meaning of the law—maybe it was a stray, and the defendant had just been feeding it each day out of the kindness of his heart—you would have a separate issue that would have to be answered in a separate sub-TREAT discussion, which would then be followed by the sub-TREAT discussion that addresses the issue of whether the plaintiff provoked the dog or not.

We emphasize that you must cover every element or factor of a rule in your discussion, but if the element or factor is established without question in your case because you are told that by the person assigning the project or because your opponent specifically admits it, the discussion of that element or factor does not require a full-blown TREAT format. A thesis or sub-thesis heading and one sentence can convey the required information:

> ### 1. Defendant is the owner of the dog.
>
> Defendant concedes that he is the owner of the dog that injured the plaintiff on August 12, 2005.

When multiple elements of a rule are in dispute and present a separate issue for sub-treatment, you should research cases and other authorities discussing that one element and show how that element works in various situations. That is how a sub-TREAT discussion is developed. In addition, a single element of a rule can present multiple issues for discussion, because the element may have a sub-rule that explains what that element means and how that element is to be applied, and the sub-rule itself may have multiple elements, each of which might be in dispute and require an answer. Since the questions suggested by the elements or sub-parts of a sub-rule are all based on the same sub-rule, we will refer to the treatments of these questions as sub-sub-TREATs. The same process occurs with a multi-factor rule that has at least one factor that has multiple sub-parts all of which raise separate issues to address.

VIII. STRUCTURING THE DISCUSSION OF MULTIPLE ISSUES

If you have multiple elements or factors at issue and sub-rules that present multiple issues to answer, you must organize your writing so that each part of the major rule or sub-rule is discussed in the TREAT format. In the case of a rule with multiple elements, a sub-TREAT on a single element will contain your Thesis on how that element will work in your client's case, any sub-Rule of law concerning that element, an Explanation of what that element means and how that element works in various situations, an Application of that element or the rule concerning that element to your client's situation, and your Thesis on that element restated as a conclusion.

Consider the following chart: if the rule on your major issue has multiple elements, and there is a sub-rule on each element of the rule on the major issue, and a sub-sub-rule on each element of the sub-rules on each element of the rule on the major issue, and all of these elements of the rule, sub-rules, and sub-sub-rules are in dispute and thus require discussion, you must layer your TREAT format to cover all the issues. The outline of the discussion of this major issue would take the following form:

I. THESIS on the Major Issue
   RULE on the Major Issue has two elements: A, B

   A. SUB-THESIS on Element A of the rule on the Major Issue
   SUB-RULE on Element A has two elements: 1, 2

      1. SUB-SUB-THESIS on Element 1 of the sub-rule on Element A
   SUB-SUB-RULE on Element 1 of the sub-rule on Element A
   EXPLANATION of sub-sub-rule on Element 1 of the sub-rule on Element A
   APPLICATION of sub-sub-rule on Element 1 of the sub-rule on Element A
   THESIS RESTATED as Conclusion on Element 1 of the sub-rule on Element A

      2. SUB-SUB-THESIS on Element 2 of the sub-rule on Element A
   SUB-SUB-RULE on Element 2 of the sub-rule on Element A
   EXPLANATION of sub-sub-rule on Element 2 of the sub-rule on Element A
   APPLICATION of sub-sub-rule on Element 2 of the sub-rule on Element A
   THESIS RESTATED as Conclusion on Element 2 of the sub-rule on Element A

   APPLICATION of the sub-rule on Element A
   THESIS RESTATED as Conclusion on Element A

   B. SUB-THESIS on Element B of the rule on the Major Issue
   SUB-RULE on Element B: Elements 1, 2, 3

      1. SUB-SUB-THESIS on Element 1 of the sub-rule on Element B
   SUB-SUB-RULE on Element 1 of the sub-rule on Element B
   EXPLANATION of sub-sub-rule on Element 1 of the sub-rule on Element B

> APPLICATION of sub-sub-rule on Element 1 of the sub-rule on Element B
> THESIS RESTATED as Conclusion on Element 1 of the sub-rule on Element B
>
> 2. SUB-SUB-THESIS on Element 2 of the sub-rule on Element B
> SUB-SUB-RULE on Element 2 of the sub-rule on Element B
> EXPLANATION of sub-sub-rule on Element 2 of the sub-rule on Element B
> APPLICATION of sub-sub-rule on Element 2 of the sub-rule on Element B
> THESIS RESTATED as Conclusion on Element 2 of the sub-rule on Element B
>
> 3. SUB-SUB-THESIS on Element 3 of the sub-rule on Element B
> SUB-SUB-RULE on Element 3 of the sub-rule on Element B
> EXPLANATION of sub-sub-rule on Element 3 of the sub-rule on Element B
> APPLICATION of sub-sub-rule on Element 3 of the sub-rule on Element B
> THESIS RESTATED as Conclusion on Element 3 of the sub-rule on Element B
>
> APPLICATION of the sub-rule on Element B
> THESIS restated as Conclusion on Element B
>
> APPLICATION of the rule on the Major Issue
> THESIS restated as Conclusion on the Major Issue

You will note that when a rule presents multiple issues, the sub-treatment of those issues takes the place of the explanation section of the rule. The same goes for a sub-sub-treatment of a sub-rule on an element of a major rule. You write the sub-sub-treatment as the explanation of the sub-rule and return to the sub-rule's treatment in the application section.

Chapter 7

The Office Memorandum and the Client Letter

In this chapter, we will examine the most common forms of objective, informative legal writing: office memoranda and client letters. These types of writing typically are assigned by your boss or a colleague who works in the same office with you. With an office memorandum, the facts and problems of the client about whom you will be writing typically will be relayed to you second hand; thus, you will have a static set of facts to work with as you research and draft the memo. You should expect that the audience for your work will be one or more law-trained readers, and this will affect how you draft the memo.

A client letter is a report of legal research and analysis that is intended for the eyes of the client, who may or may not be a law-trained reader. If you are certain that the only audience of your work will consist of law-trained readers, you can draft the client letter like an office memorandum. But a classic client letter is one that may be read by non-law-trained readers, which again will affect your composition of the letter.

I. FOCUSING ON THE READER OF THE OFFICE MEMO

An office memo, by definition, is going to be read by someone in your law office. This will be a legally trained reader. The reader will know basic concepts about the law in general, and will usually know something about the particular area of the law you are writing about. If the problem you are writing about is "money had and received"—the area of law dealing with persons who receive money by mistake and whether they have to return it—you should expect that the reader of your memo will know something about the law of restitution and unjust enrichment, of which money had and received is a particular sub-topic.

All of the readers of your memo may not be known to you at the time you write the memo. Certainly, if you get the assignment from a particular lawyer in your office, you can be sure that that lawyer is supposed to read it, but others who are working on the case that generated the research assignment will also read your memo, and you may not have met the whole team. The complete team may not be formed yet; others will be added to the case, and all of them will read your memorandum. The list does not end here, however, because your memo will go on file in your office, and someone months or years down the road will want to see what other people in the office have done on the topic of "money had and received," and they will dig up your memo. These possibilities should drive home to you the importance of writing with sufficient detail in the facts and other sections so that your work will be intelligible to many potential readers. It also should impress on you the need always to put your best work forward in every office memorandum you write, because months and years later fellow lawyers and clients of the firm who do not know you very well or at all will be getting their first impression of you and your legal skills from an office memo you wrote. As Woody Allen once said, "You don't get a second chance to make a first impression."

At some point, your memo may be shared with the client. Clients sometimes want to see the work product that they paid for, and others want to keep up on how the case is progressing and what their counsel are doing to progress it. At some point, your client will need to learn the good news or bad news concerning your research, and your office memorandum is a potential vehicle to carry that news. Although the client may not be a law-trained reader, we recommend that you still draft your office memoranda for a law-trained reader. The incidental risk that non-lawyer clients may get their hands on it is not enough for you to attempt the near-impossible task of trying to write the memo so that it is properly detailed and informative for the lawyer and yet easily understandable to the lay person. Write an executive summary or client letter to accompany the memo, instead. Of course, if you specifically are instructed to draft the memo for a non-law-trained client, do so, but that memorandum will be crafted in the manner of a client letter, not a typical office memoranda.

II. ATTENTION LEVELS OF THE LAW-TRAINED READER

You know that your work will be read by a law-trained reader, but you do not know how much time the reader is going to devote to your memo. Unfortunately, there is no way to know. A slightly more senior associate working on your case might devote a great deal of time to your work. A more senior lawyer, a partner in the firm for example, might devote just a little time or a lot of time to it. The lawyer-client may be so busy with other matters that they will only read the first two pages and say, "If it's important enough, they'll tell it to me in person."

Do you despair? Do you give up and go sell used cars? No! You learn that the most important page of your office memorandum is the first page. Front-load the important information so that even the busiest reader will get something out of your memo by reading only the first page.

The first page deals with the "issues" (also known as "questions presented") and your "conclusions" (sometimes referred to as "brief answers"). You should strive to make these sections informative by including relevant facts and details about the elements of the rules, as well as your conclusions about the application of the law to the facts. If the reader sees the issues you are writing about and hears about the rules and your conclusions, that reader will be well on her way to grasping your entire report just from the first page.

On the other hand, your brief answers still must be concise. You must be informative, but do not go overboard. Everyone can be informative if they take three pages to report a half page of information. You must respect your reader's time pressures and try to keep the issues and brief answers sections on the first page. Inform the reader of the issues, the rules, the most important facts, and all of your conclusions in terse, clearly written sections, with short, clean sentences and short paragraphs. The only reason to spill over on the second page is if you have more than two issues or questions to present, and therefore, three or more brief answers to write.

We will now focus on the structure of the office memorandum, the specific sections you will write, and the particular requirements of each section.

III. STRUCTURE OF THE OFFICE MEMORANDUM

There is one basic format for the office memorandum, although from place to place and office to office, the labels for the different sections will vary. Obviously, you should follow whatever form your law office prefers. We will present the classic form with the two sets of labels with which we are the most familiar.

Form 1: Issues and Conclusions

Section name:	What it looks like:
Caption	<div align="center">M E M O R A N D U M</div>
	TO: Recipient(s) Name(s)
	FROM: Your Name
	DATE: Date
	RE: Client Name or File Number or other Identifier
	SUBJECT: Brief Description of the Subject Matter of the Memo
Issues Presented	<div align="center">ISSUES</div> 1. Description of first issue, in the form of a Yes-No question [i.e., ends in a question mark]. 2. Description of second issue, in the form of a Yes-No question.
Conclusions	<div align="center">CONCLUSIONS</div> 1. Conclusion on the first issue. More detailed than the simple Thesis as Conclusion you will write at the end of the TREATment of the issue. 2. Conclusion on the second issue.
Facts	<div align="center">STATEMENT OF FACTS</div> One or more paragraphs laying out the factual background of the case.

Discussion	DISCUSSION
	Your TREATments of each issue, each TREAT being introduced by your Thesis headings.
[No Conclusion]	[In this format, you have already put your conclusion(s) up front, so there is no need to have a conclusion at the end.]

Form 2: Questions Presented and Brief Answers

Section name:	What it looks like:
Caption	MEMORANDUM
	TO: Recipient(s) Name(s)
	FROM: Your Name
	DATE: Date
	RE: Client Name or File Number or other Identifier
	SUBJECT: Brief Description of the Subject Matter of the Memo
Questions Presented	QUESTIONS PRESENTED
	1. Description of first issue, in the form of a Yes-No question.
	2. Description of second issue, in the form of a Yes-No question.
Brief Answers	BRIEF ANSWERS
	1. Brief Answer on the first issue. This is the same as the "Conclusion" section above, which is more detailed than the Thesis as Conclusion from your TREATment of the issue.
	2. Brief Answer on the second issue.
Facts	STATEMENT OF FACTS
	One or more paragraphs laying out the factual background of the case.
Discussion	DISCUSSION
	Your TREATments of each issue, each TREAT being introduced by your Thesis headings.

<table>
<tr><td>Conclusion</td><td>

CONCLUSION

Your conclusions on each issue. At the very least, this is a place to restate all of your Theses as Conclusions from each of your TREATments on your major issues (questions presented). It also is a place to raise other issues that should be researched and make recommendations on future actions by the client or the attorneys on the case.

</td></tr>
</table>

The content of the sections does not change even though the labels change. The main issues you will be writing about are expressed in the form of questions even if you call them "Issues" instead of "Questions Presented." The main difference in the forms is that one form leaves off a redundant conclusion. If you have a particular need for a separate conclusion—namely that you have other issues you want to suggest for further research or that you have recommendations for future action by the client or the lawyers—then you should try to use the format that includes a conclusion at the end. We usually find that we do not have anything new to say at the end of the memorandum, so we generally use the form that leaves off the conclusion at the end. Whatever your preference, it is important to remember not to save anything that is critically important to include in a conclusion at the end. It is the last thing people will read, and therefore, by definition, the section they are most likely to skip. If it is important, you should work it into the Brief Answers or at least into the Discussion.

IV. DRAFTING THE CAPTION

No mystery here. You need to identify the recipients, who the memo is from, and the date of the memo. If there are any "carbon copy" (CC) recipients, they would go in between the TO line and the FROM line. The DATE is very important, because it tells every reader that the research reflected in the memo stopped as of that date, so any developments in the law after that date will not be covered in the memo. If a reader comes across your memo two years after you wrote it, she should be on notice that the research most likely is out of date, and someone will need to follow up on the research to bring it up to date.

In most offices where we have worked, there was a client number and a matter number to go with the client name and the matter name, all of which we would stick on the RE line. Example:

RE: <u>Tom Jones/Groovin' Records v. Jones</u> (12679/57954)

The SUBJECT line tells the reader the topic of the memo. This should only be a few words, not a full blown thesis sentence on your issues. Example:

SUBJECT: Breach of "Time is of the Essence Clause" under Nevada Law

Some law offices will leave off either the RE line with the client information or the SUBJECT line, or they will use the RE line to state the subject of the memorandum and use a different description for the client and matter information. You should follow whatever is the preferred form for an office memorandum in the office where you are working, but in the absence of a preferred form, use the form we have presented.

Please note that the entries in the Caption are single spaced, but each entry is separated from the next by two spaces. Example:

M E M O R A N D U M

TO: Sandra Glib Gabber
           Xavier A. Bernstein

CC: A. Barney Stormer
           Miriam N. Haque

FROM: Sarah D. Lawyer

DATE: September 8, 2005

RE: <u>Tom Jones/Groovin' Records v. Jones</u> (12679/57954)

SUBJECT: Breach of "Time is of the Essence Clause" under Nevada Law

---

V. DRAFTING THE ISSUES OR QUESTIONS PRESENTED

The Issues section can be troublesome when you are starting out drafting office memoranda. Vague statements of the issue, such as "Should our client prevail?" are a waste of time; they tell the reader nothing. We recommend that you put factual information into the statement of the issues, and when you do so, borrow terminology from the rule that applies to the issue so that the reader is immediately informed as to what it is you researched and hears some of the operative terminology that she will see again in the Brief Answer and again in the rule sections of the memorandum. However, don't make the Issues section so detailed that it looks like you performed research with a microscope, zeroing in so specifically that the memo only can be used if another client came in with the exact same case. Your office will want to get more out of its research dollar than that.

The best way to write an Issue or Question Presented is to draft it in two parts: a phrase that identifies the relevant law and a phrase that identifies the legally significant facts. The most common formulation of the first phrase begins with a verb, such as "Does," "Is," "Can," "Do," or "Will." This phrase should contain key, relevant terms from the law that signal to the reader what the legal issue is. The second phrase begins with "when" or "where" and provides the most important facts from the case that ultimately will determine which way the issue will come out. Thus, a good question presented is structured as "[verb] + [legal issue] [where] + [legally significant facts].

You choice of words matters when you are presenting the key facts. Choose nouns and verbs that are found in the legal standards that you will discuss later in the rule section. In this way, you can introduce the pertinent terms from the law in the same phrase as the pertinent facts.

Compare the following statements of the Issue from the Dog Bite hypothetical we have worked with in previous chapters:

Example 1 - A useless statement of the issue. It tells the reader nothing:

ISSUE

1. Is Mr. Jones liable?

This is far too vague. It tells nothing about the actual issue that was researched and answered. It does not even mention that a dog was involved. Avoid this lazy format.

Example 2 - Still no good. It does not have enough details of the facts or the rule:

ISSUE

1. Is Mr. Jones liable when his dog bit the plaintiff?

Getting better, but this still is too vague. Who is Mr. Jones? Is he a party to a lawsuit? Who is the plaintiff? What happened? All of these questions could be answered here and now for the benefit of the reader, but you are forcing her to go to the Brief Answer section, or worse, to the Discussion section before the questions will be answered. You probably would not get fired for this type of drafting, but you can do much better.

Example 3 - USE THIS FORM:

ISSUE

1. Is defendant Jones liable when the dog he owned bit a girl scout who was selling cookies at the defendant's home and who did nothing to provoke the dog prior to the dog bite?

This is right on target. We know who is involved, a little of what happened, and we hear about "ownership" and "provocation," which are terms borrowed from the rule. This statement of the issue should suggest to the reader that provocation was a major part of the issue you researched. This is the best form to use.

Compare this form to the following:

Example 4 - This form uses incorrect terminology and distorts the issue:

ISSUE

1. Is defendant Jones liable when the dog he possessed mauled a girl scout who was selling cookies at the defendant's home and who did not rile up, excite, or anger the dog prior to the mauling?

This has sufficient detail and appears to state the issue, but the difference is that the author did not borrow the correct terminology from the rule in presenting the issue. Worse yet, the example makes it look like other words are the operative terms for dog bite liability. First of all, we are talking about dog "bite" liability, not dog "mauling." The legal standard is "ownership," not "possession" of a dog, and "provocation," not "riling up, exciting, or angering" a dog. Borrow the correct terms when stating the issue so that these terms will resonate later when the reader gets to the rule section.

You can go overboard with factual detail, as in the following example:

Example 5 - This form goes overboard with details:

ISSUE

1. Is our client, defendant Martin R. Jones, liable when his Doberman pinscher bit the plaintiff, a girl scout, when the girl scout had used public sidewalks, climbed up Jones' front stoop, rang the doorbell, and yelled, "Girl scout cookies," all prior to the dog's attack?

This is an over-share of information. You are giving the reader no incentive to look at your Brief Answer. She is expecting the Brief Answer to be "Yes" or "No," nothing more, based on all that you supplied in the Issue. You don't want to disappoint her when she gets to your Brief Answer and sees that it is a full paragraph.

This construction also makes it look as if the memo is so tied to the client's situation that it would not be useful for any future client who had a different set of facts. The reader might have doubts as to the usefulness of the memo if the dog in her case was a St. Bernard, or if the plaintiff crossed the lawn, or knocked on the door, or came to have a petition signed rather than to sell something. Excessive information in the Issue section does the work a disservice.

VI. DRAFTING THE BRIEF ANSWERS OR CONCLUSIONS

The most important part of your office memorandum is the Brief Answers section. This section comes very early in the memo, all on the first page if possible, based on the number of issues discussed in the memorandum. With this priority in placement, this section will get a lot of attention from the reader. Therefore, you should strive to make your Brief Answers useful and informative so that even the most casual reader who only reads the first page of your memo will get the most important information then and there.

The three things you must include in each Brief Answer or Conclusion are:

(1) a **summary of the rule** that applies to and answers the issue;
(2) the **most important facts** upon which the issue will turn; and
(3) **your conclusion**.

They will not necessarily be discussed in that order, but all parts must appear.

Because the Questions Presented or Issues are phrased in the form of a yes or no question, each Brief Answer should begin with the word "**yes**" or "**no**." Do not equivocate. Most of you will be paid a handsome sum for your legal analysis, so do not cheat the reader by starting your Brief Answer with a "probably," or "probably yes," or "maybe," or "It is uncertain, but the law is leaning toward no." If there is that much uncertainty in the law, or if the issue could go one way or the other depending on the establishment of a certain fact, **explain** the uncertainty or the fact that creates the two possible outcomes, but start off the section with a yes or no answer based on the most likely outcome.

After you have taken a stand, yes or no, on the Issue, go on to present a summary of the rule and the critical facts that will determine the issue. The most efficient way to do this is to discuss the relevant facts as they would fall in the context of an element of the applicable rule. If you are careful and skillful enough, you may be able to reveal the elements of the rule and the facts together in one sentence.

> ➤ *Example:* If the rule on money had and received is: (a) receipt of money (b) under circumstances that render the retention unjust, a good Brief Answer might contain the following phrase:
>
> > "Defendant received through a mistaken wire transfer money that he did not earn and to which he had no lawful entitlement, rendering his retention of the money unjust."

This is not easy, and it might be more trouble than it is worth to attempt to reveal the disputed elements and the facts in one sentence. If you are uncertain whether your formulation adequately reveals the rule that is being applied to resolve the issue, it certainly is fine to double up the rule and the factual statement in the Brief Answer, as in the following:

> ➤ *Example:* "The rule on money had and received is: (a) receipt of money (b) under circumstances that render the retention unjust. Defendant received through a mistaken wire transfer money that he did not earn and to which he had no lawful entitlement, rendering his retention of the money unjust."

We emphasize that if the rule is long, you should summarize the rule and the operative facts as briefly as possible. **Never quote** the entire borrowed or applied rule that the reader will find in the rule section of the TREATment of the Issue. If certain elements obviously are established, you do not need to summarize these elements. The facts you will use to present the rule only are those upon which the issue will turn. This section is supposed to be "brief," so you have to be selective in what facts to mention.

Finally, you must present your conclusion. If you have done a good job with the rule and the facts, the conclusion will follow easily. It does not hurt to finish your Brief Answer with the same sentence or phrase that you will use as your thesis heading on that issue.

Each Brief Answer, however informative, should not be longer than one paragraph. Our rule of thumb for paragraphs is two to five sentences and no more than one third of a page. This is all you should need for the Brief Answer on any issue. It requires practice to develop the skill to write so efficiently, but it is not any harder than trying to figure out the Rule Against Perpetuities in property class.

The Dog Bite example we have been working with might look like this:

QUESTION PRESENTED

1. Is defendant Jones liable when the dog he owned bit a girl scout who was selling cookies at the defendant's home and who did nothing to provoke the dog prior to the dog bite?

BRIEF ANSWER

1. Yes. Defendant owned the dog that bit the girl scout, so liability for a dog bite will turn on whether the girl was acting peacefully in a place where she had a lawful right to be, and whether she provoked the dog. The girl scout was acting peacefully on a public sidewalk where she had a lawful right to be. The girl did not strike or threaten the dog nor did anything else to provoke the attack. Therefore, defendant will be liable for his dog's attack on the plaintiff.

If the issue was liability for money had and received, the Question Presented and Brief Answer might look like this:

QUESTION PRESENTED

1. Is defendant Jones liable for money had and received when he received and retained an unanticipated wire transfer from Western Bank because of the Bank's mistake?

BRIEF ANSWER

1. Yes. Liability for money had and received requires a mistaken transfer the receipt of which amounts to an unjust enrichment. Western Bank mistakenly wired $100,000 to defendant Jones, and Jones is not entitled to retain the money. Jones is

---

> not lawfully entitled to receive and retain any amount of money from Western Bank. Because Jones received through a mistaken wire transfer money that he did not earn and to which he had no lawful entitlement, his retention of the money is unjust, and Jones is liable for money had and received.

VII. DRAFTING THE STATEMENT OF FACTS

The Statement of Facts is important for three reasons: first, it tells the uninformed reader what the background of the case was and the facts that were present that led to your conclusions. Anyone picking up your memo even years later will know what was going on in your case, and in combination with the law you present, should see why you reached your conclusions.

The second reason is that the Statement of Facts shows an informed reader what you, the author, knew at the time you wrote the memo. Very often, in the course of a legal matter, you learn the facts piece by piece as you go along; this is inevitable because of the process and practice of discovery in litigation or disclosure in other contexts. As a result, an office memorandum written early in the case often will be based on an incomplete and even erroneous understanding of the facts. If you have taken care to draft a good Statement of Facts, your informed reader later will be able to see the erroneous information you were working with, and mentally can correct it and evaluate if it affects your conclusions.

The third use is that the Statement of Facts should reveal what you, the author, thought were the most important facts in the case. Your research and analysis of the authorities should educate you as to what are the most relevant facts in your client's situation, and these are the ones you should bring out in the Statement of Facts. Your readers will expect that you have presented the most relevant facts in the Statement of Facts, so if a fact is discussed later in the Discussion section that did not appear in the Statement of Facts, they will either discount that fact's importance (giving you the benefit of a doubt as to why it was left out of the Statement of Facts), or they will discount the Statement of Facts you wrote, considering you now to have done a sloppy job.

With these three priorities in mind, you always should draft your Statement of Facts so as to provide a context for the case and to bring out all the relevant facts that determine the issues about which you are writing. Use the narrative reasoning skills we discussed in Chapter 2 to drive home your points by driving home the facts that will determine the issues.

> ➤ Although you do want to bring out all the relevant facts, it is not time to write a novel. You should strive to limit the Statement of Facts to one page or less. In a very complicated case, you might use between one and two pages. Be as concise as you can. In real life, office memoranda do not come with page limits, but you should respect the reader's time and attention span.
> ➤ You may face the difficult decision of whether to put in a fact that is not relevant to the law but is interesting. If you have the room (based on page limitations), include it. You want your memo to be memorable. But do not go overboard; too

many interesting tidbits will drown out the truly relevant facts that you need the reader to pick up.

We mentioned earlier that one of the audiences of your memo might be the client. If your boss intends to circulate your memo to the client, you will draft it with that fact in mind. However, some of the time you will not know ahead of time whether the memo will eventually make its way into the hands of a client. A client might read her legal bill and call up your boss demanding to see the memorandum that cost her $8,000, and your boss may speed it off to her, perhaps without even rereading and revising it to "sanitize" it for the client's eyes. Our advice is to be sympathetic to the client in the statement of facts, but do not say anything overtly critical or humorous about the client.

If the client took an action that will produce serious consequences under the law, describe the act and the consequences in a serious, professional way.

> *Example:*   "Allied's failed to retain the documents relating to its disposal of Agent Orange even after the special agent requested to see these documents."

"Allied terminated the contract after only six months, which is contrary to the specific provision in section 12(B) of the contract providing for a three year term."

Do not say: "The idiot client failed to retain the documents . . ."

"Allied's comptroller, Bill Smith, obviously doing drugs that week, terminated the contract after only six months . . ."

Do not editorialize in the memo.

> *Do not say:* "If you ask me, this conduct is unbelievable."

"Allied deserves to lose this case for what it tried to pull here."

Similarly, if you and your colleagues have pet names for the client and its managers, inside counsel, and officers, these never should be "memorialized" in writing.

Being sympathetic does not mean being a cheerleader. This kind of zeal should be reserved for your writing as an advocate. Remember that the office memorandum is an objective work, so present the facts, warts and all. If your client did something dirty or embarrassing and it is extremely relevant to the analysis under the law, state it. In most instances your office memoranda work product will not be turned over to the court or to your opponents, so it is generally safe to discuss sensitive matters. Naturally, you should discuss the matters in a serious, professional way. Do not abuse your license to discuss the dirt.

Do not talk about the law or its elements or the legal standards that govern the case in the Statement of Facts. There is a whole separate section devoted to the law called the "Discussion." The Statement of Facts is for facts only.

Leave out legal conclusions from your Statements of Facts. Draw your legal conclusions in the Discussion section.

> ➤ *Legal Conclusions:* "The doctor operated **negligently**."
>
>   "The truck driver was **reckless**."
>
>   "The transfer **unjustly enriched** Jones."

Factual conclusions are appropriate to state in the Statement of Facts. Factual conclusions are reasonable inferences drawn from the facts.

> ➤ *Factual Conclusions:* "The doctor performed the operation in **less than one third the time** normally allotted for the procedure by the hospital and the Texas Board of Healing Arts."
>
>   "The doctor's breath and his demeanor during the operation **suggested** to three witnesses in the operating room that he was **intoxicated**."
>
>   "The truck driver **accelerated** and attempted to drive around the railway barriers **at a high rate of speed**."
>
>   "Jones **had no debt or account** with the person who transferred the money to Jones when Jones was **not the intended recipient**."

Our example of a Statement of Facts for the girl scout Dog Bite case from Chapter 2 could be modified for inclusion in an office memorandum written by one of defendant's attorneys as follows:

STATEMENT OF FACTS

On April 7, 2005, at 11:30 a.m., plaintiff Sally Peterson, a Girl Scout, was walking with her mother, Janice Peterson, on defendant's street, going from door to door selling cookies. As she reached defendant's house, Sally walked from the public sidewalk up the front walkway and front stoop, and rang the doorbell. At this point she screamed, "Girl Scout cookies!" in a loud voice. Defendant's Doberman pinscher, Cuddles, was startled by the child's screams, and approached plaintiff on the front

---

stoop. Having no other means of restraint, the dog placed his mouth around plaintiff's arm. Plaintiff's mother was driven into a rage by this act, and set upon the dog, beating it across the eyes and snout with her large pocketbook and an umbrella she was carrying. In spite of this attack and in accordance with its training, the dog did not let go of the child's arm, and in the altercation, the mother pushed and pulled plaintiff so much that the dog's teeth were driven into and across plaintiff's arm, causing lacerations. A neighbor, Ralph Jones, eventually arrived at the scene and forced open Cuddle's jaws, freeing the plaintiff. Both Cuddles and Sally received stitches for the cuts they suffered in the incident.

The money had and received facts might look like this:

STATEMENT OF FACTS

At 9:02 a.m. on March 11, 2005, Western Bank wire transferred $100,000 to an account owned by defendant Hugo Jones. The money was intended to be transferred to an account of co-plaintiff Richard Shaft. Due to a typing error, two digits of the account number were transposed by a clerk of Western Bank, which caused the mistaken transfer. One hour after the transfer, Jones withdrew $100,000 from his account. Six hours after the transfer, the Bank notified Jones of the mistake and requested return of the funds. Jones refused. Jones is not a creditor of Bank or Shaft, nor is he the holder of any account with the Bank or Shaft that would entitle him to the $100,000.

VIII.   DRAFTING THE DISCUSSION SECTION

We already have discussed the mechanics of drafting the Discussion section in Chapter 6 and other chapters. This is the section where you TREAT each issue and sub-issue raised by the rule and its elements and their sub-rules. The examples we gave in Chapter 6 are equally applicable here:

DISCUSSION

I. DEFENDANT SMITH IS LIABLE FOR PLAINTIFF JONES'S DOG BITE INJURIES BECAUSE SMITH OWNED THE DOG AND JONES ACTED PEACEFULLY IN A LAWFUL PLACE AND DID NOTHING TO PRO- VOKE THE DOG.

In Apex, to prevail on a cause of action for injuries resulting from the attack of a dog, a plaintiff must prove: (1) defendant owned or harbored the dog; (2) plaintiff was peacefully conducting himself or herself at the time of the attack; (3) plaintiff was in a place where he or she had a lawful right to be; and (4) plaintiff did not provoke the dog into attacking. <u>Timmy v. Lassie</u>, 567 W.2d 123, 125 (Apex 1995); <u>Bobby v. Rin Tin Tin</u>, 569 W.2d 789, 791-92 (Apex Ct. App. 1st Dist. 1997).

A. <u>Smith admits that he owned the dog.</u>

Smith admits that he owned and harbored the dog that caused plaintiff's injuries. Therefore, this element is not disputed in this case.

B. <u>Jones was acting peacefully because she engaged in normal behavior and did not behave in a loud and boisterous manner near the dog</u>.

To be conducting oneself peacefully, one must be: (a) engaging in a normal day-to-day activity or business; and (b) not behaving in a loud and boisterous manner in close proximity to a strange dog. <u>Bobby</u>, 569 W.2d at 792. . . . [*etc.*]

There are some additional drafting points to explore:

A. It is important to use your <u>T</u>heses as headings in the Discussion section.

If your reader is not going to take the time to read your memo cover to cover, she at least may skim it and read the headings. If you use your <u>T</u>heses as headings, the reader will get the entire gist of your argument just by reading these headings.

Good <u>T</u>hesis headings contain a conclusion followed by the "because" part—the facts and legal principles that support the conclusion. A <u>T</u>hesis heading that only states the conclusion is only doing half the job.

> *Not good:* Smith will not be liable under the Illinois Dog Bite Statute for his dog's bite.

    Good: Smith will not be liable under the Illinois Dog Bite Statute for his dog's bite because Jones provoked the dog into attacking.

    Not good: Harris was not unjustly enriched when he received the Union Bank wire transfer by mistake.

    Good: Harris was not unjustly enriched when he received the Union Bank wire transfer by mistake because he had a preexisting debt with Union Bank that exceeded the amount of the transfer.

In each example above, the first <u>T</u>hesis heading only states a conclusion; it does not explain and support the conclusion by providing the facts and legal principles that establish the conclusion. The second <u>T</u>hesis heading in each pair provides the "because" part, and these headings will provide an effective summary of the discussion if the reader merely skims your <u>T</u>hesis headings.

B. Order your analysis in the same order that you listed the issues in the Questions Presented or Issues sections. Discuss elements of rules in the order that they are presented in the <u>R</u>ule section.

One of your most important goals in drafting the Discussion section is to avoid confusing the reader. You can confuse the reader by defeating her reasonable expectations. If you list three Questions Presented, the reader will expect these issues to come up in the Discussion section in the same order, one - two - three. If you list four elements of a rule, (1) - (2) - (3) - (4), the reader is going to expect you to discuss the elements in that order. If you deviate from this order, the reader can become confused and may start to wonder whether she missed something or if you left something out.

C. Use "roadmaps" whenever you think the reader will benefit from a little direction.

Your writing will be appreciated more by your readers if you keep them on the same page with you. If you simply follow the order in which the issues are presented and discuss the elements of a rule in the order in which they are listed, there is no need to give further directions. A roadmap is superfluous, because no reader is going to get lost. But if you insist on going out of order, use a **roadmap** sentence or paragraph that will explain the order to the reader ahead of time.

You can present the roadmap for the entire Discussion section right before your first thesis heading.

> ➤ *Example:* "In this memorandum, the issue of liability for breach will be discussed first, followed by the issue of the Statute of Frauds, and last, the issue of potential damages for breach."

The same roadmap device is used in a TREAT section when you want to skip elements or discuss them in a different order than they are presented in the rule. If you have several no-contest, no-dispute elements to dispose of, it can save space to use a roadmap to explain that they are not at issue and will not be discussed. This roadmap would come right after the last paragraph of the rule section on the major rule that governs the major issue.

➤ *Example:*

> ## I. DEFENDANT SMITH IS LIABLE FOR PLAINTIFF JONES'S DOG BITE INJURIES BECAUSE SMITH OWNED THE DOG AND JONES ACTED PEACEFULLY IN A LAWFUL PLACE AND DID NOTHING TO PROVOKE THE DOG.
>
> In Apex, to prevail on a cause of action for injuries resulting from the attack of a dog, a plaintiff must prove: (1) defendant owned or harbored the dog; (2) plaintiff was peacefully conducting himself or herself at the time of the attack; (3) plaintiff was in a place where he or she had a lawful right to be; and (4) plaintiff did not provoke the dog into attacking. <u>Timmy v. Lassie</u>, 567 W.2d 123, 125 (Apex 1995); <u>Bobby v. Rin Tin Tin</u>, 569 W.2d 789, 791-92 (Apex Ct. App. 1st Dist. 1997).

In this matter, the first element of ownership of the dog is not in dispute; defendant Smith admits that he owned the dog. The remaining elements will be discussed in the order that they are listed above.

D. Draft the Discussion at an appropriate level of detail and information for your known audience.

Your law school professors will strive to teach you many principles about many areas of the law, and you will learn more in preparation for the bar exam. How much an average lawyer will retain cannot be predicted, but in drafting an office memorandum, you should assume that your reader is very familiar with the basic law of contracts, torts, civil procedure, and property, and, depending on your office, probably is somewhat familiar with criminal law, evidence, income tax, constitutional law, and the other classic "bar exam" subjects. If the people assigning the work are specialists in the area—for example, you are researching a civil procedure issue for litigators or a tax issue for tax lawyers—you can assume that the readers will be up to speed on the basics. But no lawyer will know everything, which is why they asked you to do the research in the first place.

What this means is that you should draft your office memorandum at an appropriate level of detail for your audience. If you are researching a contract issue, there is no need to go back to the first week of contracts class and write about a contract requiring offer and acceptance, consideration, and lawful subject matter. You don't have to start at day one of torts when you have a negligence issue, either. But you should not assume that a complex area of the law such as securities law is readily understood by anyone other than a securities law expert. It may be necessary to lay a foundation to provide basic details about the fundamental principles of the area in which your issue resides, before tackling the TREATment of the actual issue you were asked to research.

E. Discuss collateral issues that have the potential to impact your main issues.

Very often as you are researching and analyzing your problem, you will stumble on collateral issues, not necessarily tied into the actual issues you were asked to research, but which are discussed in the authorities you are reading or which occur to you as you are writing. If the issue does not have the potential to impact your analysis of the assigned issues, you have the choice to ignore it or to take it up and resolve it in a separate TREATment. But if the issue does have the potential to impact the main issues, you should take up the issue and resolve it.

For example, in a breach of contract problem, you may have been asked to research the issue of whether the defendant had the proper mental capacity to contract in light of his mental illness, but you also may have been told that the defendant disputed that the signature on the contract was his own, even though several witnesses saw the defendant sign the document. The "signature issue" is collateral to the other issue on capacity; nothing about the signature necessarily affects the outcome of your analysis. You have the choice to take up and resolve the issue in your memo as a help to the attorneys who assigned the work, but in this instance, there is no real need to do it. The same does not hold true if the additional issue was that the defendant is understood to have been using recreational, non-prescription drugs at the time of the contracting. The use of recreational drugs has the potential to affect the person's mental state, making the latent mental illness more or less severe in the circumstances, so this issue should be resolved in the memo.[1]

IX. DRAFTING THE CONCLUSION

We already have touched on the main reasons you might decide to write a formal Conclusion at the end of your office memorandum. If you have discovered other issues that you want to suggest for further research (presumably collateral issues, or you should have taken them up in the memorandum itself), or if you have recommendations for future action by the client or the lawyers, then you may decide to draft a final Conclusion section. Some of you simply may want to restate your main points one more time. Whatever your incentive, remember not to save anything that is critically important to include in a Conclusion at the end. The Conclusion is the last thing people will read, and therefore, by definition, the section they are most likely to skip. If it is important, you should work it into the Brief Answers or at least into the Discussion.

---

[1] **Practice Tip:** Before you go off and spend a lot of time and the client's money researching and resolving a collateral issue, it is a good idea to inquire of the assigning attorneys whether this issue actually is being researched and analyzed by someone else, so that you do not duplicate their efforts. They will be impressed that you thought of it and asked, and the worst thing that will happen is that they will officially assign you the task of researching and writing the analysis of the issue.

X. CLIENT LETTERS

We have come across some legal writing texts that propose to assign the drafting of a client letter to law students as the first or second writing assignment, prior to assigning the drafting of an office memorandum. The thought apparently is that the client letter is a simpler, more rudimentary document to draft, and thus an appropriate subject for novices. This is far from the truth. Client letters are difficult to draft, and we would not want to draft one until after we already had completed an office memorandum on the same topic. We would want to be sure that we had completed the research and analysis and thought through it enough to write a coherent memorandum suitable for a law-trained reader. Then and only then would we turn to the crafting of a document that can be understood by a non-lawyer.

The client letter is targeted to a non-lawyer. You must take special care to discuss the legal issues in terms that can be understood by a non-legally trained reader. When a legal term of art must be used, such as "estoppel" or "res judicata," take the time to define these words in laymen's terms. Do not use the Black's Law Dictionary definition, because this is a dictionary written for lawyers and other legally-trained readers.

If a statute, rule, or regulation is involved, go ahead and cite the applicable terms. You must then explain the terms both in laymen's language and as the terms have been interpreted by later authorities.

Citation to and use of other types of legal authorities are thorny issues in client letters. Clients often realize that there are other sources for the law than legislation and administrative regulations. Most clients understand the general concept that a ruling from a court in a lawsuit can control other persons and situations beyond the parties in the lawsuit itself, but there rarely is a need to cite and explain a multitude of cases in the explanation and application sections of your report on the law. If one or two controlling cases are very close to your client's situation, you can take the time to explain the facts and holding of these cases, but no more than that. Rarely should you refer to secondary authority no matter what its relative weight and prestige.

Your client is going to be most interested in your conclusions. You should take special care to write them clearly and accurately. Do not hide behind vague or equivocal conclusions. Your client is not paying you to come up with a "probably" or a "maybe yes." If there is significant uncertainty as to the probable outcome, explain the source of the uncertainty, and discuss the most likely outcomes based on the most likely answers to the variables you have identified.

The format of a client letter need not be as formalized as an office memorandum. Most letters are drafted without topical or thesis headings and few would follow the TREAT format because the client most likely only needs to see the rules and the applications and your conclusions.

Sample client letters are provided after the sample office memoranda presented in the section below.

XII. SAMPLE OFFICE MEMORANDA

The pages that follow contain four complete examples of office memoranda. The first two are a "before" and "after" pair that illustrate the difference between a memorandum that does not follow the TREAT format and does not use explanatory synthesis, and a corrected version that does. The third and fourth examples are student work that illustrate good and bad aspects of legal writing in an office memorandum context. We have reproduced the actual memoranda with our comments interjected throughout. Our comments will appear as:

> This is our comment, inserted into the text of the example.

Please understand that these are samples of good work, not models. None of the examples is perfect. None of them provides you with a standard form for drafting an office memorandum. Do not try to cram your own writing into a straight jacket by trying to copy one of these samples.

We have attempted to correct all the citations in the examples so that they follow current citation rules.[2]

> These first two samples are a "before" and "after" set of memoranda. The "before" memo is a simple, three-page memo reporting on a single question: "Does the client have a claim against an online service for publishing erroneous stock information?" Although the author does communicate this conclusion, the author does not attempt to follow the TREAT format or use explanatory synthesis. This is the **"before"** memo:

MEMORANDUM

TO: Jane B. Nimble

CC: Marcus B. Quick
             Harry S. Moose, Jr.

FROM: Mary K. Smith

DATE: March 7, 1997

RE: ABC/USA-Online Matter

SUBJECT: Claim against USA-Online for Erroneous Reporting of Stock Price
             and Volume of Shares Traded

---

[2] In the few instances where there is a difference in citation form between the Bluebook and the ALWD Manual, we have corrected the citations for Bluebook form.

> The issue stated below is clear enough. The reader receives sufficient information about the facts and the straightforward legal issue that the memo discusses. Note that when there is a single issue, the heading is singular—ISSUE not ISSUES—and there is no need to number the issue.

ISSUE

Is USA-Online potentially liable to ABC & Co. ("ABC") for erroneous reporting of ABC's stock price and volume of shares traded?

> The conclusion below is adequate, because the issue is so straightforward. There is only one element of a rule to introduce to the reader: USA-Online has no duty to ABC. Again, with a single conclusion, the heading is singular: CONCLUSION.

CONCLUSION

No. There is no indication that USA-Online would be liable to ABC for erroneous reporting of this information because USA-Online does not owe a duty of care to plaintiff. There are a number of cases whose facts are close to those of ABC, and they uniformly hold that there is no cause of action against USA-Online.

> The facts section below is adequate because the facts of the case were very simple. This facts section is short and to-the-point, but it contains the facts the reader needs to know.

STATEMENT OF FACTS

ABC is one of thousands of companies whose stock information is picked up by USA-Online from Standard and Poor's reporting service and published on USA-Online's "Market Marker" web page. On March 1, 1997, USA-Online erroneously reported that ABC's stock price had dropped to 1/10th of its value and also reported that the volume of shares traded for the stock had increased tenfold. As a result, there was significant volume of trading in ABC's stock, which pushed its value down. When confronted with this information, USA-Online refused to correct the error immediately, but it promised to "take care of it within two to three business days." Eventually, it corrected the information three days after the erroneous reporting.

DISCUSSION

> Here is where things get interesting. The author wanted to report the findings of the research, which uncovered four cases that were on point, all of which agreed that the client had no claim. But the memo eliminates all semblance of order by jumping to a case-by-case account of these authorities. The reported findings are short enough that most readers would not get lost, but this is a dangerous practice. The discussion does not begin with a thesis heading, and it does not begin with a rule section. At most, it looks like an explanation section. In addition to not following the TREAT format, the explanation here is completely unsynthesized.

In <u>Daniel v. Dow Jones & Co.</u>, 137 Misc. 2d 94, 520 N.Y.S.2d 334 (N.Y. County 1987), the court held that a subscriber to Dow Jones' on-line financial news service had no cause of action against Dow Jones. The claim arose from Dow Jones' reporting of misleading financial information about a company, which the subscriber relied on to make a transaction, and lost money on the deal. The court emphasized that the news service had no duty of care toward the general public, including its subscribers, to make sure that the information was correct. Applying the principles of the Restatement (Second) of Torts § 552 (1987), the court found that plaintiff was not a member of a protected class of persons to whom specific information is provided for their guidance in a business transaction, and who reasonably rely on the information. In addition, the court noted that the on-line service was entitled to special protection under the First Amendment (and New York Constitutional law), and that liability would not be imposed absent proof of libel, defamation, or intentional conduct.

An earlier opinion, <u>Jaillet v. Cashman</u>, 139 N.E. 714 (N.Y. 1923), <u>aff'g</u>, 202 A.D. 805 (1st Dep't 1922), <u>aff'g</u>, 115 Misc. 383 (N.Y. County 1921), affirmed the dismissal of a complaint brought against Dow Jones for publishing erroneous business information on its news ticker service. Dow Jones erroneously reported that the U.S. Supreme Court had ruled that stock dividends were to be considered taxable income, when in fact just the opposite was true. Before the information was corrected, plaintiff sold his own stock and sold other stock "short" in reliance on the report. After the report was corrected, plaintiff lost money because the stocks rose instead of falling. The court likened the ticker service to a newspaper, and held that Dow Jones had no duty of care to plaintiff because they had no contractual or fiduciary relationship, and the conduct alleged did not amount to deceit, libel, slander, or other intentional misconduct.

In <u>Ginsburg v. Agora, Inc.</u>, 915 F. Supp. 733 (D. Md. 1995), the court followed these principles in finding that defendant, the publisher of an investment newsletter entitled "John Pugsley's Journal," was not liable to a subscriber who followed the author's specific advice to invest in the spread between the price of the 10-year T-note futures contract and the 10-year T-bond futures contract (the "NOB Spread"). Plaintiff followed the advice and lost $128,000. Three months later, defendant retracted its prior statement and advised against the investment strategy. The court rejected plaintiff's multiple claims brought under state and federal securities laws and the common law. The court cited Restatement § 552 and found that the newsletter was the same as a newspaper. Thus, it owed no duty to plaintiff even though he was one of only a small number of subscribers. The court also found that the paper was expressly intended to be used for making investment decisions.

In <u>Gutter v. Dow Jones</u>, 490 N.E.2d 898 (Ohio 1986), Dow Jones's Wall Street Journal newspaper made a typographical error and omitted a designation in certain information about a bond; it failed to print an "f" next to the bond listing to indicate that the bond was trading "flat." Plaintiff thought the bond was trading with interest and he bought it, suffering a loss as a result. The court followed the reasoning of <u>Jaillet</u>, <u>supra</u>, and found that the claim was defeated by (1) a lack of duty of care to plaintiff, and (2) First Amendment protections.

> The conclusion is short, but it has a purpose: the author wanted the client to understand that there was no claim and no apparent crack in the authorities that might allow a toehold for arguing that the law should be expanded or modified. The author wanted the client to understand that it had no claim, no way, no how; don't even try.

Therefore, there is no support for the type of claim ABC wants to bring. No case has suggested that the media has a duty to verify and ensure the correctness of the financial information it reports, and none of the authorities suggests that there is room for an argument that the law should be modified or extended.

M.K.S.

> This is the **"after"** memo. The initial sections (Issue, Conclusion, Facts) are the same. The difference is the Discussion section, where we have edited the memo so that it follows the TREAT format and uses explanatory synthesis.

MEMORANDUM

TO: Jane B. Nimble

CC: Marcus B. Quick
           Harry S. Moose, Jr.

FROM: Mary K. Smith

DATE: March 7, 1997

RE: ABC/USA-Online Matter

SUBJECT: Claim against USA-Online for Erroneous Reporting of Stock Price and
           Volume of Shares Traded

ISSUE

Is USA Online potentially liable to ABC & Co. ("ABC") for erroneous reporting of ABC's stock price and volume of shares traded?

CONCLUSION

No. There is no indication that USA-Online would be liable to ABC for erroneous reporting of this information, because USA-Online does not owe a duty of care to plaintiff. There are a number of cases with facts that are close to those of ABC, and they uniformly hold that there is no cause of action against USA-Online.

STATEMENT OF FACTS

ABC is one of thousands of companies whose stock information is picked up by USA-Online from Standard and Poor's reporting service and published on USA-Online's "Market Marker" web page. On March 1, 1997, USA-Online erroneously reported that ABC's stock price had dropped to 1/10th of its value and also erroneously reported that the volume of shares traded for the stock had increased tenfold. As a result, there was significant volume of trading in ABC's stock, which pushed its value down even further. When confronted with this information, USA-Online refused to correct the error immediately, but promised to "take care of it within two to three business days," and it corrected the information three days after the erroneous reporting.

DISCUSSION

I. USA-ONLINE WILL NOT BE LIABLE TO ABC FOR ERRONEOUS REPORTING OF ABC'S STOCK INFORMATION BECAUSE USA-ONLINE HAS NO DUTY TO ABC TO REPORT INFORMATION ACCURATELY.

> The first paragraph is the rule section. Note that the author laid out several interpretive rules.

To state a claim for negligence or breach of fiduciary duties, the defendant must have a duty to the plaintiff to use reasonable care in the performance of its actions. LeClercq v. Shapo, 798 N.E.2d 23, 26 (N.Y. 1996). A media outlet, whether it be a newspaper of general circulation or a specialized stock information service, does not owe a duty of care to the general public or to the companies whose stock information it reports to make sure that the information is reported accurately. Jaillet v. Cashman, 139 N.E. 714, 716 (N.Y. 1923), aff'g, 202 A.D. 805 (1st Dep't 1922), aff'g, 115 Misc. 383 (N.Y. County 1921); Daniel v. Dow Jones & Co., 137 Misc. 2d 94, 95, 520 N.Y.S.2d 334 (N.Y. County 1987); Ginsburg v. Agora, Inc., 915 F. Supp. 733 (D. Md. 1995). Only a member of a protected class who personally has received information for guidance in a business transaction may assert a claim if the provider gives erroneous information. Daniel, 137 Misc. 2d at 95; see Restatement (Second) of Torts § 552 (1987). A plaintiff will not be able to assert a claim for simple negligence, although he may be able to assert a claim if the news outlet is guilty of libel, defamation, or intentional conduct. Jaillet, 139 N.E. at 716; Daniel, 137 Misc. 2d at 95; but see Ginsburg, 915 F. Supp. at 734 (no cause of action for state or federal securities fraud).

> The second paragraph is the explanation section that now is drafted using explanatory synthesis.

A duty to take care as to the accuracy of reported financial information arises only if the plaintiff receives particular information from the defendant for his own personal guidance in a business transaction. See Jaillet, 139 N.E. at 716; Daniel, 137 Misc. 2d at 95; accord Gutter v. Dow Jones, 490 N.E.2d 898 (Ohio 1986). A duty of care will arise only if there is a contractual or fiduciary relationship between the plaintiff and the defendant. See Jaillet, 139 N.E. at 716 (Dow Jones's stock ticker service had no duty of care to plaintiff because it had no contractual or fiduciary relationship with the plaintiff); Daniel, 137 Misc. 2d at 95 (plaintiff was not a member of a protected class of persons to whom specific information was provided for their guidance in a business transaction); Ginsburg, 915 F. Supp. at 734 (publisher of John Pugsley's Journal had no duty to plaintiff even though he was one of only a small number of subscribers to the journal, and the journal expressly was intended to be used for making investment decisions); Gutter, 490 N.E.2d at 900 (Dow Jones's Wall Street Journal newspaper lacked a duty of care to a reader who relied on erroneously reported stock information); Restatement (Second) of Torts § 552. Otherwise, the First Amendment, U.S. Const. amend. I, and the public policy supporting a free and unfettered press favor denying members of the general public the right to sue a news outlet for erroneous publication of stock information. See Daniel, 137 Misc. 2d at 95 (on-line service was entitled to special protection under the Free Speech and Free Press provisions of the United States Constitution and the New York Constitution); Gutter, 490 N.E.2d at 900 (Dow Jones was entitled to First Amendment protections).

> The application section is the third paragraph. It is possible to write a direct and to-the-point section here because the explanation section was synthesized.

In the instant case, ABC had no contractual or fiduciary relationship with USA-Online, and ABC was not a member of a protected class of persons to whom specific information was provided for its guidance in a business transaction. ABC is one of thousands of companies whose stock information is picked up by USA-Online from Standard and Poor's reporting service and published on USA-Online's "Market Marker" web page. There is no allegation that USA-Online's conduct was anything but simple inadvertence or negligence. No allegation is made that USA-Online engaged in libel, defamation, or intentional conduct.

Therefore, there is no support for the type of claim ABC wants to bring. No case has suggested that the media has a duty to verify and ensure the correctness of the financial information it reports, and none of the authorities suggests that there is room for an argument that the law should be modified or extended.

M.K.S.

> The next two sample memoranda were drafted by our students. Each discusses the same legal issue in the same jurisdiction. Note the different approaches to the problem that each takes.

MEMORANDUM

TO: Professor Plum

FROM: Exam #; Section #

DATE: November 27, 2000

RE: Tunetaster/InYourFace.com Contract (C01234/17654)

SUBJECT: Tunetaster's avoidance of liability for breach of contract based on commercial frustration, an extension of impossibility of performance.

> The issue stated below is well crafted. The reader hears a significant number of facts and the author has crafted the recitation to match up neatly with the elements of the rule of commercial frustration.

ISSUE

Can Tunetaster.com, Inc. ("Tunetaster") be excused for breach of contract and avoid liability to InYourFace.com through the defense of commercial frustration after pleading guilty to charges and entering into a consent decree with the government, thereby nullifying its entire service or 95% of the activities of its service?

> This conclusion is concise and effective. The author's drafting is right on the money. This conclusion has details of facts, elements of the rule, and legal conclusions, all neatly presented in two sentences. One note: it is premature to use the term "prove" as in "Tunetaster will fail to prove" because the parties are not yet embroiled in a lawsuit and Tunetaster has had no chance to perform discovery and build up its case. Therefore, the author should state this conclusion more directly: "Tunetaster had control of its business practices and actions and will be deemed to have had control over the frustrating event."

CONCLUSION

No. Although the value of Tunetaster's performance will be totally or nearly totally destroyed by the guilty plea and signing of the consent decree, commercial frustration will not serve as a defense. Tunetaster will fail to prove that it did not have control of its business practices and actions that caused the frustrating event and that the action of the government was not foreseeable.

> This facts section below is not a biased, one-sided account favoring the client, Tunetaster. It presents all relevant facts that will affect the application of the rule. This is the correct method to use in an objective office memorandum. This section is drafted in a clear, concise, professional manner.

STATEMENT OF FACTS

Tunetaster.com, Inc., an on-line service provider, began service on January 7, 1999, allowing users of its free software to download music recordings in violation of the owners' copyrights. These unlicensed transfers are estimated to be 95% of Tunetaster's traffic.

In January 2000, Tunetaster entered into a three-year advertising contract with InYourFace.com to provide banner advertisements on Tunetaster's screens for similar recordings that are available to be downloaded through the Tunetaster service. The terms of the contract included a $10 million dollar up-front payment to Tunetaster for the first three-year term, and $0.05 for each click on a banner ad by a Tunetaster user.

The contract contains two key clauses. The first clause states, "Whereas, Tunetaster has been successful in attracting more than eight million users . . ." Contract between Tunetaster and InYourFace.com dated Jan. 2000 ("Contract") at 1. The second clause states, "The parties . . . shall not take action to frustrate the reasonable expectancies of the other party." Contract at 3. The Contract between Tunetaster and InYourFace.com does not contain a force majeure or "Act of God" clause.

On September 1, 2000, the government brought a criminal action against Tunetaster for unfair competition and anticompetitive practices and for aiding and abetting willful copyright violations. Tunetaster intends to plead guilty and enter into a consent decree. The effect of this action will nullify the entire Tunetaster service, or at least 95% of its activities. Illinois law applies to disputes arising from the Contract. Any action against Tunetaster concerning the contract likely will be brought in Lake County, Illinois, where Tunetaster has its principal place of business.

DISCUSSION

> The thesis heading on the main issue is short and barely gets the job done. We favor a thesis that gives more information—a conclusion and the "because" part—which includes facts and legal principles that lead up to the conclusion. A better thesis would have been: "Tunetaster will be held liable for breach of contract because it was in control of the circumstances that rendered its performance impossible."

I. TUNETASTER WILL BE HELD LIABLE FOR BREACH OF CONTRACT.

> As you will see, the rule section in this assignment was rather complicated. Three steps were needed to show the ultimate rule that applies to the main issue. These are presented in paragraphs 1-3.

As a general rule, where the parties to a contract, by their own conduct and positive undertaking, create or charge a duty upon themselves, they must abide by the contract and make the promise good; subsequent contingencies not provided against in the contract, which render performance impossible, do not bring the contract to an end. See Leonard v. Autocar Sales & Service Co., 64 N.E.2d 477, 479 (Ill. 1946); Farm Credit Bank of St. Louis v. Dorr, 620 N.E.2d 549, 554 (Ill. App. Ct. 5th Dist. 1993). Exceptions to this rule include when performance is rendered impossible by an act of God, or where performance is based on the continued existence of a particular person or thing, and the death or destruction of that thing occurs. See Leonard, 64 N.E.2d at 479; Farm Credit Bank, 620 N.E.2d at 554-55.

The doctrine of frustration is an extension of the latter exception. See Leonard, 64 N.E.2d at 479-80; American National Bank v. Richoz, 545 N.E.2d 550, 553 (Ill. App. Ct. 2nd Dist. 1989). It extends to contracts where the cessation of a condition or state of things has made performance impossible and the object frustrated. See Leonard, 64 N.E.2d at 480; American National, 545 N.E.2d at 553. Parties may avoid liability because the contract did not bind them to perform under such changed conditions. See Leonard, 64 N.E.2d at 480.

> The following paragraph uses rule synthesis. The author used rule synthesis to present the three elements of the rule because the traditional way to phrase the rule was with two elements (the first two listed here), even though more recent cases had modified the rule to add a third element. This version of the rule does not appear in any one of these authorities, but by analyzing and synthesizing the authorities, the author produced this rule which is wholly supported by each of the authorities cited by the author. Note the parenthetical after the Comdisco case that indicates that the case applies Illinois law. This added information bolsters the persuasive value of this out-of-state case.

The defense of commercial frustration will be applied only when the defendant has satisfied three rigorous tests: (1) the frustrating event was not reasonably foreseeable; (2) the value of the counterperformance has been totally or nearly totally destroyed by the event; (3) the frustrating event was not within control of the promisor. See Farm Credit Bank, 620 N.E.2d at 555-56; American National, 545 N.E.2d at 553; Greenlee Foundries, Inc. v. Kussel, 301 N.E.2d 106, 111 (Ill. App. Ct. 1st Dist. 1973); Comdisco Disaster Recovery Services, Inc. v. Money Management Systems, Inc., 789 F. Supp. 48, 53 (D. Mass. 1992) (applying Illinois law).

> This is the sub-TREAT on the first element. Again, we are not fond of this short thesis heading because it lacks the "because" part. A better heading would be: "Tunetaster reasonably could have foreseen the frustrating event because it will be charged with awareness of the threat of government action and changing market conditions."

A. Tunetaster reasonably could have foreseen the frustrating event.

The court reasonably must construe the parties' contract and determine whether the event which caused the impossibility might have been anticipated or guarded against in the contract. See Leonard, 64 N.E.2d at 480; Mouhelis v. Thomas, 419 N.E.2d 956, 959 (Ill. App. Ct. 2nd Dist. 1981). Whether the nonoccurrence of an event was a basic contract assumption is a question of foreseeability. See In re Corkey, 645 N.E.2d 1384, 1389 (Ill. App. Ct. 2nd Dist. 1995); Northern Illinois Gas Co. v. Energy Cooperative, Inc., 461 N.E.2d 1049, 1060 (Ill. App. Ct. 3rd Dist. 1984).

> The author starts the explanation section with the discussion of a single case. It sounds like we are on the road to an unsynthesized explanation section, but we are not. The author chose to highlight this one case because its facts and issues are extremely similar to the facts and issues of the client's case, and this case succinctly shows how the rule should work in the client's case.

In Farm Credit Bank, the appellants claimed that their purpose of the contract had been frustrated, causing an inability to perform loan obligations. The appellants argued that the unforeseeable, frustrating event was caused by the implementation of governmental policies which led to higher loan interest rates. The court held that the appellants' loan was a variable-rate loan, and that, therefore, the frustrating event was foreseeable. See 620 N.E.2d at 556.

> Now the author presents principles of interpretation and application derived from authorities using explanatory synthesis.

Changing market conditions and factors affecting the business environment that are common in a particular area of business cannot be claimed as unforeseeable events. See Northern, 461 N.E.2d at 1059 (court refused regulated public utility's claim that a government agency's refusal of a price increase request coupled with other market factors which damaged business were unforeseeable). Complicity with or actual involvement in the event that frustrates performance will prevent a party from being excused from performance. See Comdisco, 789 F. Supp. at 53 (defendant admitted that it helped bring about the acquisition that frustrated performance); Greenlee, 301 N.E.2d at 111-12 (defendants signed lease for property in an area known to them to be unstable, and after riots broke out, made an unsuccessful claim that the occurrence was unforeseeable).

A force majeure clause assigning risk in the event of a governmental ban will place the risk on the party specified if that event occurs. Compare Commonwealth Edison Co. v. Allied-General Nuclear Services, 731 F. Supp. 850, 853 (N.D. Ill. 1990) (force majeure clause in the contract assigned the risk of a governmental ban to the plaintiff, and the materialization of that expressed risk led to the plaintiff's liability), with M.A. Felman Co. v. WJOL, Inc., 243 N.E.2d 33, 39 (Ill. App. Ct. 3rd Dist. 1968) (mere reference to FCC regulations in a contract did not assign liability to a specific party or cause termination of the contract after the implementation of subsequent regulations). Clauses within a contract may indicate that a frustrating event is reasonably foreseeable. See Comdisco, 789 F. Supp. 48, 54 (because the contract anticipated the possibility of the plaintiff's need for protection from risk, the court held that the frustrating event was reasonably foreseeable); Commonwealth Edison, 731 F. Supp. at 853 (same).

> This application section applies the principles of interpretation that were presented above. It does not attempt to apply individual cases to the client's case because this author took the time to use explanatory synthesis in the explanation section. Now, in the application section, the author can apply synthesized principles about how the rule is to be interpreted and applied to the facts of the instant case.

Based on Tunetaster's entrance into the market, as well as its continued business activities and practices, Tunetaster reasonably should have been aware of the known government policies in that area of business, and that providing software which allows music to be downloaded, in violation of copyright laws, would lead to a legal inquiry and possible legal action. Further, the Contract indicates that the basic assumption is that Tunetaster's membership would continue based on its ability to provide software to download music, and that frustrating action should not be taken by either party. See Contract at 1 and 3. This indicates a need for protection from risk, against which Tunetaster could have protected itself within the contract. Therefore, Tunetaster reasonably could have foreseen the frustrating event.

> This is the sub-TREAT on the second element. Once again, the thesis heading lacks the "because" part as described above.

B. The value of Tunetaster's performance will be totally or nearly totally destroyed.

> This sub-rule section is not synthesized. The sub-rules here present three separate facets of the same general rule pertaining to this element. It reads like three interpretive rules strung together. A reader would presume that the authorities provided these principles separately as presented here, rather than providing one single version of the sub-rule. If this reader presumption is incorrect, the author should redraft this section.

The fact that performance has become inconvenient or accompanied with loss will not excuse performance. See Deibler v. Bernard Bros., Inc., 53 N.E.2d 450, 453 (Ill. 1944). To excuse performance, a party must show that he only can operate at such a severe loss that, if the performance is not excused, it would result in great injustice. See Northern, 461 N.E.2d at 1061. When performance of a contract becomes impossible because governmental laws or regulations are enacted that make such performance illegal, the non-performance may be excused. See Felman, 243 N.E.2d at 36.

> The explanation in the paragraph that follows is a good example of explanatory synthesis.

Governmental actions and restrictions that render a business less profitable and more difficult to carry on do not destroy performance. See Leonard, 64 N.E.2d at 481 (government's taking of a short-term period of a leasehold estate did not destroy the contract subject matter and does not effect the duty to pay rent); Deibler, 53 N.E.2d at 452 (car dealer defaulted in the paying of rent for dealership property, claiming that governmental restrictions on the sale and manufacturing of cars made performance more difficult). An increased cost of performance does not constitute a complete loss of performance value. See Northern, 461 N.E.2d at 1061 (appellant failed to show that higher oil prices and the government's refusal for a price increase caused performance to continue only at a loss). Though the value of business is made more difficult and less profitable after the occurrence of an event, this does not deem the value of performance destroyed. Compare Greenlee, 301 N.E.2d at 111 (court found that business could and did continue, though with some loss, after a riot occurred in the area), with Smith, 370 N.E.2d at 274 (destruction of the main store adjacent to the leased premises constituted commercial frustration, as the value and performance of the leased premises would have changed drastically).

In the present case, Tunetaster's service would be totally or nearly totally shut down by its guilty plea and signing of the consent decree. This would cause the value of Tunetaster's performance to be drastically changed because Tunetaster would be admitting that its method of performing InYourFace.com's contract was illegal. Tunetaster might be able to perform the contract, but its performance would be worthless to InYourFace and Tunetaster because only 5% of Tunetaster's users are expected to continue to use the service and 95% of prior members would not be exposed to the targeted advertisement banners of InYourFace.com. Therefore, the value of Tunetaster's performance would be totally or nearly totally destroyed.

C. Tunetaster had control over the frustrating event.

> This entire section is unsynthesized. Note the difference. It is difficult for the reader to determine if this is a long rule section or an explanation section, and if the latter, what the rules are that the author is trying to illustrate. The reader is treated to a random presentation of principles, and many of them appear to be interpretive rules. There is nothing that indicates to the reader that these authorities combine to state one or more concrete principles on how the concept of control over the frustrating event is to be interpreted and applied.

When a party by contract engages in an act, it is deemed that party's fault if he did not expressly provide against contingencies by or within the control of the party. See Deibler, 53 N.E.2d at 452-53. Illinois law will not apply the doctrine of frustration to excuse a party from its contractual obligations where that party contributed to, or had control over, the occurrence of the alleged frustrating event. See Comdisco, 789 F. Supp. at 53.

When performance of a contract becomes impossible because governmental laws or regulations make such performance illegal after the contract is entered into, the non-performance may be excused. See Felman, 243 N.E.2d at 36. However, such illegality must not have come about through the action of either of the parties to the contract. Id. at 36-37. Parties to a contract will be assumed to have known the law at the time of contract. See Warshawsky v. American Automotive Products Co., 138 N.E.2d 816, 818 (Ill. App. Ct. 1st Dist. 1956). If a failure to know the law is the reason for the frustration, the courts deem the error to be one of law and do not afford relief to the contracting parties. Id. The parties are presumed to know the law well enough to contract in light of the prevailing law, so if the contract turns out to be unprofitable because of the application of the laws that existed at the time of contracting, the frustrating event is deemed to have been controllable by the promisor. Id. See Comdisco, 789 F. Supp. at 53.

> This paragraph is the application for this section. The application lacks impact because it follows an unsynthesized rule or explanation section and there are no concrete principles to apply to the facts. The author is forced to apply the random concepts presented above, and this results in an application section that is not persuasive.

Tunetaster entered into a legal contract with InYourFace.com to provide advertisements on Tunetaster's screens. Tunetaster should have had knowledge of the law in regard to its method of performance and cannot claim that it did not after assuming the risk in the Contract. Tunetaster's guilty plea to the charges of the government, as well as the physical signing of the consent decree, would be an admission by Tunetaster that it broke the law, and brought about the frustrating event by its own actions. Therefore, the frustrating event was within the control of Tunetaster's avoidance of liability for breach of contract based on commercial frustration.

> These last two sentences are the application section and thesis restated as conclusion on the main issue. When the last sub-TREAT is concluded, the author returns to the main TREAT to finish it with these closing sections that complete the TREAT structure. These sentences are appropriate for this purpose.

In light of the facts that Tunetaster reasonably could have foreseen the frustrating event that destroyed the value of its business, and that Tunetaster had control over the frustrating event, Tunetaster will not be excused from performance. Tunetaster will be liable for breach of its contract with InYourFace.com.

MEMORANDUM

TO: Colonel Mustard

FROM: Exam #, Section #

DATE: November 27, 2000

RE: <u>Tunetaster/InYourFace.com Contract</u> (C01234/17654)

SUBJECT: Impossibility of Performance/Frustration of Contract under Illinois Law

> The issue section below provides a lot of information about the facts and key terms from the law that pertain to the issue in this case. It is well crafted.

ISSUE

Will the defense of commercial frustration excuse Tunetaster.com, Inc. ("Tunetaster") from breach of the contract with InYourFace.com ("IYF") if Tunetaster enters into a consent decree, when the government action was not foreseeable, the value of Tunetaster's user base to IYF will be destroyed by the consent decree, and Tunetaster has control over entering into the decree?

> The analysis in this conclusion is slightly different from the first sample memo, but the outcome is the same. This conclusion has details of the facts, the elements of the rule, and the legal conclusions on each element. It is clear, concise, and informative.

CONCLUSION

No. Tunetaster did not reasonably foresee the frustrating event, the government action resulting in a 95% decrease in its user base if Tunetaster enters into a consent decree. Entering into this consent decree will destroy the value of IYF's counterperformance by nullifying the user base. However, Tunetaster does have control over entering into the consent decree. If Tunetaster pleads guilty, the company is not using reasonable efforts to avoid the frustrating event. Therefore, Tunetaster will not be excused under the doctrine of commercial frustration.

> This statement of facts presents the relevant facts and provides enough detail so that the analysis and conclusions that follow make sense.

STATEMENT OF FACTS

Client Tunetaster is an on-line service like Napster that allows users of free Tunetaster software to copy MP3 files on other users' computers. Currently, about 95% of Tunetaster's users are copying music recordings in violation of the owners' copyrights. Since Tunetaster began its business on January 7, 1999, it has attracted tens of thousands of new users ever month, and as of September 2000, had over 13 million users. In January 2000, Tunetaster entered into a contract with IYF (the Contract, exhibit 1 to the Complaint) in which IYF provided banner advertisements on Tunetaster's screens. Users saw these banner ads while downloading music through Tunetaster. The initial contract term was three years. As part of the Contract, IYF paid Tunetaster $10 million upfront for the three-year term and a commission of $0.05 for each click on a banner ad by a Tunetaster user. While nothing in the Contract directly addresses whether Tunetaster was to maintain a set number of users or expand its user-base yearly, the Contract states:

> Whereas, Tunetaster has been successful in attracting more than eight million users and has increased its membership and rate of transfers each month of its existence;
>
> . . .
>
> The parties shall use their best efforts to perform the contract during the contract term, and shall not take action to frustrate the reasonable expectancies of the other party.

Contract ¶¶ 1, 3.

The U.S. Department of Justice began investigating Tunetaster on June 1, 2000, and brought a criminal action on September 1, 2000, for unfair competition and anticompetitive practices, and for aiding and abetting willful copyright violations under 17 U.S.C. § 506 (2000) and 18 U.S.C. § 2319. If Tunetaster enters into a consent decree, which will require it to block all transfers of copyrighted recordings, all or 95% of the service activities will cease to exist. Illinois law applies to disputes arising from the Contract. Any action against Tunetaster concerning the contract likely will be brought in Lake County, Illinois, where Tunetaster has its principal place of business.

DISCUSSION

> This author, too, is presenting short thesis headings that lack the "because" part. A better thesis would have been: "Tunetaster will not be excused for breach of contract under the doctrine of commercial frustration because it was in control of the circumstances that rendered its performance impossible."

I. TUNETASTER WILL NOT BE EXCUSED FOR BREACH OF CONTRACT UNDER THE DOCTRINE OF COMMERCIAL FRUSTRATION.

We are skipping the rule section and the first sub-TREAT to several sections that illustrate explanatory synthesis.

* * *

B. Tunetaster had control over the occurrence of the frustrating event.

> This is the sub-rule section on the element of control over the frustrating event.

In Illinois, a contractual duty will not be discharged if there are circumstances showing contributing fault on the part of the person subject to the duty. See Felbinger and Co. v. Traiforos, 394 N.E.2d 1283, 1289 (Ill. App. Ct. 1st Dist. 1979); Greenlee, 301 N.E.2d at 112.

> The following explanation section illustrates effective explanatory synthesis. Normally, you would synthesize more than two cases to support each principle, but the author was limited to the small number of Illinois cases that were on point.

Performance is not excused if it lies within the power of the promisor to remove the obstacle to performance. See Felbinger, 394 N.E.2d at 1289 (defendant's own default on mortgage made it impossible to pay commission on property sale); Comdisco, 789 F. Supp. at 53 (applying Illinois law) (party participated in acquisition of other company, and thus contributed in frustrating the contractual purpose).

A governmental decree forbidding a party to perform is a standard occasion for invoking the doctrine of commercial frustration. See First Nat'l Bank v. Atlantic Tele-Network Co., 946 F.2d 516, 521 (7th Cir. 1991) (applying Illinois law). The party invoking the defense must have made reasonable efforts to prevent occurrence of the frustrating event. Id. New York courts have not allowed this defense when there is a judicial order against the promisor unless the party vigorously challenged the event by diligent efforts. See Lowenschuss v. Kane, 520 F.2d at 265 (defense applied when promisor vigorously fought injunction in order to complete contractual transaction); Gen. Aniline & Film Corp. v. Bayer Co., 113 N.E.2d 844, 847 (N.Y. 1953) (where defendants did not challenge consent decree, defense lacked validity).

While Tunetaster did not know that the government would take this action, the company has control over whether or not they enter into a consent decree, which will cause nullification of their user base. By entering into this decree, Tunetaster would be making no effort to remove the obstacle to performance. While Tunetaster did not directly cause the occurrence, it is within the company's power to vigorously challenge the consent decree in court. Unless Tunetaster has no chance of winning its case against the government, or it would not be monetarily feasible to take the case to court, the company must use reasonable efforts to challenge the action. Furthermore, the contract states that the parties "shall use their best efforts to perform the contract, and shall not take action to frustrate the reasonable expectancies of the other party." Contract at ¶ 3. Without trying everything possible to avoid the consent decree, Tunetaster is not using its best efforts to prevent frustration of the contract. Therefore, if Tunetaster enters into the consent decree, the company had control over the occurrence of the frustrating event.

C. The value of IYF's counterperformance was destroyed.

The doctrine of commercial frustration applies when the expected value of performance to the injured party has been destroyed. See Smith, 370 N.E.2d at 274.

> This next paragraph is another good example of explanatory synthesis.

Even when it was physically possible for the injured party to perform, the court found the counter-performance was destroyed when the purpose or condition implied in the contract was changed drastically. Compare id. (when fire destroyed main building and adjacent building only suffered smoke damage, purpose of lease still was thwarted), with Comdisco, 789 F. Supp at 53 (applying Illinois law) (injured party still could benefit from contract because it still had full use of other party's contractual services). If the frustrating event merely makes performance less profitable, but performance still is possible, performance is not excused. See Greenlee, 301 N.E.2d at 111 (when company experienced small decrease in business due to rioting, defense not available); M.A. Felman Co. v. WJOL, Inc., 243 N.E.2d 33, 37 (Ill. App. Ct. 3rd Dist. 1968) (performance was made possible because advertiser paid damages so other party could buy advertising time rather than granting it free advertising time).

> This application paragraph is forceful and effective because it follows a synthesized explanation section and can apply concrete principles of how the rule is to interpreted and applied to the facts of the case. It applies principles, not individual cases.

In the instant case, IYF's counter-performance is placing advertisements on Tunetaster's service and paying commission per click on banner ads. If Tunetaster enters into the consent decree, keeping 95% of its users from frequenting its site, IYF still can advertise on the service, but IYF will receive little or no business. IYF's business with Tunetaster is not merely less profitable, but nearly destroyed. In addition, Tunetaster will receive little commission because few, if any, users will be clicking on IYF's banner ads. The purpose of the contract will change too drastically when Tunetaster's user base is nullified. Also, neither party has proposed an alternate method to maintain the existence of the user base. Therefore, the value of the counter-performance is totally or nearly totally destroyed.

> These last two sentences are the application section and thesis restated as conclusion on the main issue as required to complete the TREAT on the main issue.

As stated above, although the frustrating event was not reasonably foreseeable and the value of the contract will be destroyed by the event, Tunetaster will not be excused from performance under the doctrine of commercial frustration because it was in control of, and will in fact bring about, the frustrating event through its own actions. Thus, Tunetaster will be liable to InYourFace for breach of contract if it enters into the consent decree.

XIII. SAMPLE CLIENT LETTERS

The pages that follow contain two client letters. The first is a sample letter drafted to report the research in the first two sample memoranda provided above on liability of a stock news service for erroneous reporting, and the second is a sample letter drafted to report the research in the last two sample memoranda above on commercial frustration.

Sample 1 - Erroneous Reporting of Stock Information

LITIGIOUS, TEWE, DeMAXE L.L.P

March 14, 1997

Roger Bannister
ABC Widgets Corp.
1424 Progress Parkway
Seattle, WA 99999

Re: ABC v. USA-Online

Dear Roger,

Thank you for allowing us to advise you on your recent dispute with USA-Online. I am very sorry to report that there is no indication that USA-Online would be liable to ABC for erroneous reporting of your stock information earlier this month. The problem is the law does not impose a duty on USA-Online to get the information right, and ABC does not have a claim against USA-Online when they do not get it right. There are a number of cases with facts that are close to those of ABC, and they uniformly hold that publicly traded companies have no claim against stock news reporting services like USA-Online when these services make mistakes in reporting stock information.

USA-Online will be treated like any other member of the press that reports stock information. A media outlet, whether it be a newspaper of general circulation or a

---

specialized stock information service, does not owe a duty of care to the general public or to the companies whose stock information it reports to make sure that the information is reported accurately. Only someone who personally has received information for guidance in a business transaction may assert a claim if the provider gives erroneous information.

ABC had no contractual or fiduciary relationship with USA-Online, and ABC did not personally receive stock information from USA-Online for its guidance in a business transaction. ABC is one of thousands of companies whose stock information is picked up by USA-Online from Standard and Poor's reporting service and published on USA-Online's "Market Marker" web page.

We considered a number of theories, but there is nothing in the facts to indicate that USA-Online's conduct was anything but simple inadvertence or negligence, and the law absolves them from liability for simple inadvertence or negligence. Nothing in facts indicates that USA-Online engaged in libel or defamation, which would require us to prove that they intentionally or recklessly reported false information about ABC. We do not see any viable claim that ABC could assert against USA-Online.

I am sorry to bring you such bad news. Please feel free to call me to discuss this or any other matter.

Sincerely yours,

Candace Tewe

Sample 2 - Commercial Frustration

LESSIS MOORE P.C.

March 14, 2000

Martina Schenck
Tunetaster, Inc.
1517 Martin Luther King Blvd.
Santa Bonita, CA 91999

Re: Tunetaster/InYourFace Contract

Dear Martina,

It was a pleasure talking with you last month about the situation you are in with InYourFace (IYF) and the Justice Department action. As I predicted at our meeting, there is very little hope that your entry into the consent decree with the Justice

Department will release you from your obligations with IYF. Illinois law will not apply the doctrine of frustration to excuse a party from its contractual obligations where that party contributed to, or had control over, the occurrence of the alleged frustrating event. Our research confirms that your voluntary action to end the Justice Department case that will bring about the drastic reduction in your business cannot be used to escape your obligations under the contract. Companies cannot voluntarily cause the business loss and then walk away on the excuse that the business loss frustrates future performance of the contract.

When performance of a contract becomes impossible because governmental laws or regulations make such performance illegal after the contract is entered into, the non-performance may be excused. In fact, this is a classic justification for non-performance. However, such illegality must not have come about through the action of either of the parties to the contract. Parties to a contract will be assumed to have known the law at the time of contract. If a failure to know the law is the reason for the frustration, the courts deem the error to be one of law and do not afford relief to the contracting parties. The parties are presumed to know the law well enough to contract in light of the prevailing law, so if the contract turns out to be unprofitable because of the application of the laws that existed at the time of contracting, the frustrating event is deemed to have been controllable by the promisor. The law is clear on this point. We can find nothing in the facts that would release you from your obligations to IYF in the contract.

I am sorry that we cannot find a theory to enable you to escape from the contract, but we stand by our advice that entry into the consent decree is the best outcome for you in the circumstances. We would like to research your exposure to damages under the contract with IYF if you will give us approval to move on to this topic. Please feel free to call me to discuss this matter, and I look forward to seeing you at Thursday's board meeting.

Sincerely yours,

Louis B. Lessis

Chapter 8

Editing and Fine-Tuning Your Writing

I. STYLE ISSUES FOR THE OFFICE MEMORANDUM

A. Plain English

1. Avoid legalese

It is a common trap for a law student to read and absorb the ancient, old, and relatively dated authorities in her casebooks, and then turn around and try to recreate that stilted, wordy, Latin and French-infested verbiage in her own writing. Do not do it. The "plain English" revolution finally has overtaken the legal field, and you are advised to speak and write as plainly as possible, using ordinary words, leaving out the legalese ("said parcel," "null and void," "the party of the first part," "aforesaid," and many more), and the Latin and French *("Est ipsorum legislatorum tanquam viva vox," "Et de ceo se mettent en la pays")* as much as possible. The object of legal writing is not to use words and phrases that only could have been learned in law school; instead, you are to explain the issues and rules in common language as plainly as you can.

The exceptions to this rule are those Latin and French phrases that have been so ingrained in the law that they are now legal terms of art, and there is no way to express the concept they stand for in a concise manner except by using the Latin or French term. Examples: *res ipsa loquitur, res judicata, respondeat superior.* In these instances, use the phrase as the most efficient tool to express a complicated concept, not as a crutch to make your writing look more lawyerly.

2. Be concise

A less obvious form of legalese is a lawyer's tendency to use far too many words to express herself. Part of the goal of using plain English is to be readily understood, and to this end, you should strive to write as concisely as possible. Omit needless words in your writing. Rigorously examine each sentence and see if it can be made shorter. Break up long sentences with independent clauses into two or three short sentences. Paragraphs generally should contain no more than five sentences and be less than one third of a page in length.

3. Limit your use of the passive tense

The passive tense or passive voice involves the phrasing of a sentence so that the true object of the sentence comes first, followed by a form of the verb "to be" in front of the action verb of the sentence, and the true subject of the sentence comes last. Examples: "The house was searched by the police." "The plan was enforced by the committee." The active tense has the subject before the verb and the verb before the object, as in: "The police searched the house." "The committee enforced the plan."

One problem with the passive tense is that it is too easy to slough off the "subject" (sitting at the end, where the object usually goes) from the sentence, leaving the true subject unnamed. This sentence pattern makes the writing vague and indefinite. Examples: "The house was searched." "The plan was enforced." In each example, the reader does not know the true subject, the actor of the sentence—who searched the house? Who enforced the plan?

The second problem is that the object-verb-subject construction simply sounds weaker than the active voice. The active tense is punchier and makes the point quicker. The writer gives the subject proper emphasis, followed by the verb. Active voice pushes the reader through the piece smoothly and efficiently with each active sentence. Furthermore, a subject-verb-object construction tends to correspond more accurately to reader expectations. Readers generally expect sentences to unfold in this fashion, unless there is a good reason to be emphasizing the object instead of the subject of the sentence.

If your goal, however, is to de-emphasize the subject, then you intentionally can use the passive voice to draw attention **off** the subject. If you need to downplay the fact that your client let go of the wheel and sent his car out of control and hit the plaintiff and sent him flying twenty feet into the air, you can phrase this, "Defendant's Chevrolet went out of control. The plaintiff was hit and thrown twenty feet into the air." The reader is not focusing on your client and the fact that he may have caused both things to happen; all the reader is thinking about is the two occurrences of the car going out of control and the plaintiff being hit.

The last problem is that the passive tense is wordier than the active tense. "The police searched the house" is two words shorter than "The house was searched by the police." Not a huge difference, but when you are striving to make your writing more concise, you can save a handful of words just by rephrasing all of your passive sentences into active sentences.

B. Quotations

Much angst is wasted on the question of whether to quote or not to quote from your sources. We do not think this needs to be so troublesome for law students and attorneys. There are some obvious boundaries within which you will be safe if you follow a moderate level of quotation. The boundaries are as follows:

1. Never plagiarize

Plagiarism is the act of appropriating the writing or the ideas of another and passing them off as the product of one's own mind. See Black's Law Dictionary 1035 (5th ed. 1979). In the law, it is not so much the borrowing of language and ideas from legal sources that is troubling—you must rely on legal sources for the language and meaning of the law. Rather, the problem is the failure to attribute them by proper citation to the source from which you got them that is the problem. Failure to cite not only is an offense against ethics and intellectual honesty and, in some instances, a violation of the author's copyright, it actually is a terrible idea for your legal writing. Unless and until you become a famous authority on the law, few attorneys are going to be interested in what you personally say is the law or what ought to be the law if you fail to cite legal authorities to back up your statements. What they want to hear is what the sources say, and you must assure them that you are getting the information from proper sources by providing a citation to each authority you rely on in your analysis. If language is borrowed, with quotes around it or not, you must cite the source of the language. No one will be convinced by your analysis if you write statements about the law and legal principles without citing a source for each statement.

In the academic setting, the ban against plagiarism is strict because you are being graded on your own work. There is ample opportunity to copy from other students' papers or from treatises or law review articles and to pass off the analysis and information as your own. You certainly are gambling that the recipient of your work will not discover the source from which you are copying or will not notice the similarities in your work and others. This is a serious ethical violation, and you should not gamble your future livelihood on the chance that your professors will not discover the secret sources of your writing.

2. Do not quote so much that the quotes attempt to replace your own analysis of the issues.

The other extreme from quoting and citing too little is quoting too much. Students nervous about saying it right or getting the analysis right often err on the side of quoting everything they possibly can quote, so that their paper is nothing but a sea of quotation marks. These uncertain students must think, "If the courts or the legal scholars explained the rule in a certain way, who am I to differ." We have seen office memoranda completely extracted from a law review article or practice manual on the topic, where the article or manual actually was cited throughout the paper. This was a bold practice, but not very smart.

Heavy quotation often is unnecessary in the rule section, although it can be required in limited circumstances such as if your rules come from constitutions, statutes, or regulations. But if you find yourself writing nothing but quotes in the explanation section and even in the application section, stop. It is critical to provide your own legal analysis of the issues in the explanation and application sections, both to explain the rule and how it works in various situations, and to apply it to your client's facts. No matter how great the author of an authority was, that author was not looking at the law from your client's exact perspective, the way that you should. You are looking at a particular issue in the context of a particular set of facts and circumstances that will almost never be duplicated in any source that you might find on the law. Therefore, you must do the analysis on your own and only use quotations to highlight critical language from the most important explanations and interpretations of the rule from the best controlling authorities.

3. Proper quotation technique

It is proper to quote the applicable or pertinent terms of a rule of law in most circumstances. At times, it is very important to do so. You should quote the exact terms of a rule of law when:

(a)   the judicial orders and opinions from your jurisdiction all use the same wording of the rule;
(b)   the rule comes from a constitution, statute, or administrative regulation;
(c)   the rule contains certain required elements or terms of art that must be identified (for example, "proof beyond a reasonable doubt," "clear and convincing evidence"). In this last instance, only the terms of art need to be quoted.

In addition, if a source uses a short or pithy phrase or other language that captures your client's situation exactly, it is appropriate to quote it. We emphasize short and pithy. Beyond that, avoid using excessive and lengthy quotations from the cases.

4. When to use quotation marks

The law is different from most other disciplines. In many instances in legal writing, you can simply quote a single sentence directly from a source and provide a citation to the source and page number without using a set of quotation marks. We can only imagine that this practice gained acceptance because the alternative would be a paper littered with quotation marks. We sometimes get nervous when we intentionally quote a phrase from a case verbatim, so we use quotation marks in these circumstances. We also use them when we want to drive home that a certain court (usually the highest court in the applicable jurisdiction) has said something about the law that is very favorable to our client, and we do not want the reader to miss the fact that this is the court's own words, not ours. If you are quoting more than a single sentence, you must use quotation marks or the block quote format discussed in the sub-section below.

If you are struggling with a decision whether to use quotation marks, employ the "Seven-Word" rule.[1] This is a useful rule of thumb that says if you use seven of the exact words from the source in a row, you should put them in quotes. Legal scholarship does not

---

[1]   Some law schools impose a different word count that is less than seven words. Be sure to follow the rules of your school.

require this, and most attorneys do not follow it, but it can help you resolve your own personal internal debates on the topic.

5. The mechanics of quotation

Citation rules state that if your quotation is more than 50 words, block it off from the rest of the paragraph by double indenting the quoted material, single-spacing it, and leaving off the quotation marks. The citation to the source of the quote goes on the next unindented line of the paragraph, immediately following the quotation. If the quotation is less than 50 words, you should leave it in the body of the paragraph, use quotation marks if you have determined to do so, and do not change the spacing of the paragraph or lines containing the quotation; in other words, leave it in the same formatting as the rest of the paragraph in which it appears. The citation to the source of the quotation immediately follows the quote in the same paragraph.

➤ *Example:*

> In his landmark book on legal writing, Professor Murray stated:
>
> > The ALWD manual and Bluebook state that if your quotation is more than 50 words, block it off from the rest of the paragraph by double indenting the quoted material, and single-space it, and do not put quotation marks around it. If the quotation is less than 50 words, you should leave it in the body of the paragraph, use quotation marks if you have determined to do so, and don't change the spacing of the paragraph or lines where the quotation appears; in other words, leave it in the same formatting as the rest of the paragraph in which it appears.
>
> Michael D. Murray, <u>Legal Research and Writing</u> 112 (2002).
>
> Professor Murray recommends, "If you are struggling with a decision whether to use quotation marks, employ the 'Seven-Word' rule." <u>Id.</u> at 111.

Edit your quotations as much as possible. Only use the relevant, catchy words, or the required terms and standards of the rule in your quoted material. Ellipses (. . .) are used to show where you have left out irrelevant or unnecessary language from your source. Brackets [ ] are used to indicate a place where you have changed a word or a letter or punctuation from the quoted material so as to make it flow and fit in the context and syntax of your writing.

➤ *Examples:* "If [law students] are struggling with . . . whether or not to use quotation marks, [they should] employ the 'Seven-Word' rule."

"If you [have] struggl[ed] with [the] decision . . . to use quotation marks, employ the 'Seven-Word' rule" in the future.

If your ellipses and brackets clutter the material so much that it looks like military intelligence officers censored your work, consider phrasing the material the way you would like it to appear, and then write it up that way without quotes, but provide a correct citation to the source. The law allows this kind of freestyle quotation in most reasonable instances.

6. Quote accurately

Your readers must be able to rely upon your research. This will be true whether the document you are writing is an office memorandum or a court brief. You must check—and double check—and triple check—the accuracy of your quotes. Sometimes you will find that you have missed a word, or misspelled a word, or inserted words that were not in the original. Check also to be sure that your citations (the volume, reporter or other source, and page numbers) absolutely are correct.

C. Parentheticals

Parentheticals are used to tell one or two pieces of information about an authority in as *few* words as possible. They are not used to write a sentence or two summarizing the authority. Parentheticals in legal writing are drafted without reference to normal rules of grammar and punctuation; thus you can say exactly what you want to say in the shortest possible words.

➤ *Example:* Martin v. Lewis, 234 W.2d 456, 458 (Apex Ct. App. 1st Dist. 1958) (summary judgment on fraud claim denied); Smith v. Wesson, 568 S.W.2d 345, 347 (Tex. 1978) (police search held unconstitutional).

The only time a citation is used inside a parenthetical is when you are indicating that one case is citing or quoting another, as in:

➤ *Example:* Estate of Able v. Cain, 992 W.2d at 567 (citing Saul v. David, 912 W.2d 234, 236 (Apex 1994) (en banc)).

There also are acceptable short cuts that can be used in parentheticals, such as "(same)," which means that the fact or information stated in the previous parenthetical applies equally to the next authority you are citing, so you put a (same) parenthetical after the next authority.

➤ *Example:* Martin v. Lewis, 234 W.2d 456, 458 (Apex Ct. App. 1st Dist. 1958) (summary judgment on fraud claim denied); Smith v. Wesson, 568

S.W.2d 345, 347 (Tex. 1978) (police search held unconstitutional); <u>Enfield v. Remington</u>, 498 S.W.2d 357, 367 (Tex. 1968) (same).

Parentheticals can be used in combination with brackets to make an entire section shorter. Compare the efficiency of the following examples:

➢ *Not good:* <u>Smith v. Jones</u> involved a breach of bailment duties. In <u>Smith</u>, the court stated "Roscoe Smith owed a duty of care to Wally Jones when Alex Tuttle took charge of Mr. Jones' property." 12 W.2d at 24. In that case, Roscoe Smith was the plaintiff, Alex Tuttle was his agent, and Wally Jones was the defendant. <u>Tommy v. Armour</u> was another breach of bailment duties case, and the court again held that plaintiff owed a duty of care to defendant when plaintiff's agent took charge of defendant's property. 10 W.2d at 45.

➢ *Good:* The court held that "[plaintiff] owed a duty of care to [defendant] when [plaintiff's agent] took charge of [defendant's] property." <u>Smith v. Jones</u>, 12 W.2d at 24 (breach of bailment duties case). <u>See</u> <u>Tommy v. Armour</u>, 10 W.2d at 45 (same).

D. Discuss dicta correctly so as not to trick the reader into thinking it is holding from a case.

Dicta from a court opinion, particularly an opinion from a court of the applicable hierarchy of judicial authority, can be very important to your analysis, and you will find many occasions to discuss dicta in your writing. However, it is important to remember that dicta is not controlling, and you cannot pass it off as holding when you include it in your office memorandum or other legal writing. The goal is to discuss dicta in such a way that the reader will not be led to believe that what you are talking about is holding.

1. Obvious and not so obvious ways to discuss a court's holding

It might be easiest to look at the ways you would describe a court's holding in a case; then you can try ***not*** to sound like these when you are referring to dicta. The following are obvious ways to discuss a court's holding in your writing:

➢ *Holding:* "The court held that . . ."

"The court concluded that . . ."

"The case stands for the proposition that . . ."

"The plaintiff prevailed because . . ."

"The outcome of the case was . . . because . . ."

"The court found that . . . [legal conclusion]"

In the last example, if what you fill in the blank is a **legal conclusion**, a statement regarding the law, then the sentence communicates that the legal conclusion the court found is part of the holding of the case. If it is a **fact** that the court found (for example, "The court found that plaintiff had three children"), then the sentence does not communicate a legal holding but instead a factual finding. Because factual findings and legal conclusions can be tricky to differentiate on a quick read through, you should avoid using the phrase "the court found . . ." except in the instance where the court was the finder of fact and you need to report the facts that were found by the court.

In addition to the above, there are some non-obvious ways to say "this is holding," as in the following:

➤ *Holding:*   All Oregon loggers are required by law to equip their saws with a chain brake. <u>Lefty v. Stihl Chainsaw Co.</u>, 114 P.2d 23, 26 (Or. 1962).

This sentence and citation do not use the words "held," "holding," "concluded," "found," etc., but when you state a rule or a principle of law and follow it with a citation without further comment or explanation, you are telling the reader that the case you are citing **held** this point.

Another non-obvious discussion of holding is the following:

➤ *Holding:*   The court discussed the fact that in Oregon, all loggers must equip their saws with a chain brake. <u>Lefty</u>, 114 P.2d at 25.

In this example, you used some supposedly neutral word like "discussed," and even threw in the word "fact," but the sentence says "holding" just as clearly as the other examples. Don't get hung up on magic words like "discussed" or "mentioned" or "noted," because in the right context they can communicate "holding" as easily as other more direct words.

2. How do you avoid saying "holding"?

To avoid communicating that something from a case is holding when it is really dicta, you must discuss the material in such a way that it is clear that it is dicta, but still has importance—and you should explain the importance. You may use such expressions as:

➤ "The court stated . . ."

"The <u>Finley</u> case discussed . . ."

"The Supreme Court in <u>Jones</u> noted . . ."

"Judge Breyer mentioned . . ."

These words (stated, discussed, noted, mentioned) are not magical talismans to dispel the evil implication of holding, but they can get you in the right frame of mind to discuss the issue and the importance of the issue without spelling it out as holding. If you are skating on thin ice (and you know it), throw in a reference as to why you think this is or may be dicta:

> ➤ *Examples:* "Although the case did not turn on this issue, the court found that . . . [your dicta issue]"
>
> "The court noted that . . .[dicta issue], but did not resolve the dispute on this basis."
>
> "The court noted the defendant's argument that . . . [your dicta issue], and indicated that this position had merit, although it was not necessary to reach the issue in this case."

3. Avoid using the word "dicta" in your writing.

The examples in the section above communicate to the reader that the information is not necessarily holding, but none of them use the word "dicta." It is important to avoid using the term "dicta" in your writing; for example, do not say, "The court, in dicta, stated that . . ." or "The [issue] was discussed in the case, although it was dicta." The reason for this is that the word "dicta" has a negative impact on a reader's attention span. Many readers will immediately turn off their attention to the item when they see the word "dicta," even though, if they seriously thought about it, they would realize that the item might still be important.

Some readers also believe that if you single out something in your writing as "dicta," you are intentionally trying to tell them that you think the issue is a big nothing, of no importance or relevance to the case, and a waste of time. One judge of a United States District Court where one of the authors practiced would often correct a party who had started to discuss something that she was describing as "dicta" by telling her, "That's not dicta, that's important!"—the implication was that if it really were dicta, it would not be important. We believe some readers who see the word "dicta" in a section of your work will skip over the whole discussion of the issue. Therefore, avoid turning off these readers, and ban the word "dicta" from your writing.

E. Formality of language

Legal writing must be professional and it must sound that way. You should not be loose with your language and should not attempt to inject humor or "hipness" into your writing by using slang or colloquialisms. There is too much at stake in legal matters to be cavalier about language.

The following rules apply generally to all legal writing, including office memoranda:

1. Do not use slang and colloquialisms.

Slang is sloppy and unprofessional. There is nothing to be gained by using it in legal writing. Even though many attorneys like to be "folksy" in person,[2] this "folksiness" should not slip over into legal writing. Professional legal writing is not read aloud to the client or to the court. Therefore, a masterful use of the vernacular is wasted on these audiences.

In this book, you will find several examples of colloquial speech used deliberately to set a more casual tone. This is not appropriate in the legal work you will produce for your clients. The following examples, although extreme, should indicate the kind of language we are talking about.

➤ *Bad:*   It don't sit right under the law. The judge won't cotton to it.

  Good: The position is erroneous, and the judge is not likely to accept it.

  Bad: Defendants were kin folk. They went pub-crawling and got plastered.

  Good: Defendants were related to each other as first cousins. They went to several pubs and became intoxicated.

Some folksy words almost have a term of art status. For example, we would not abandon the term "good old boy" from our legal vocabulary to describe this type of person, especially if someone refers to another person (or to himself) in this way. However, we would abandon the terms "bubba" or "redneck" or "trailer park trash," because they carry a more derogatory connotation and are unprofessional.

2. Avoid slash constructions unless that is the actual word, phrase, or address that you are quoting or referring to.

A common legal shortcut or shortcoming is to create new words by placing two words on either side of a slash.

➤ *Bad examples:* Bob was a teacher/researcher.

                The scope of the committee is research/analysis.

                We formed a discovery/deposition/motion-practice team.

---

[2]   Some lawyers, or more likely their parents or grandparents, may still be watching reruns of "Matlock" and think that this is how a lawyer should sound when trying a case.

This is awkward English, and it should be avoided. It does not take up that much more space to use "and" in these circumstances.

The phrase "and/or" is a particular favorite of legal writers.

> *Bad examples:* The court of appeals will reverse and/or remand the case back to the trial court.
>
> The rule states plagiarism is punishable by death and/or a fine of $50,000.

If the actual text you are quoting has the phrase "and/or" in it, then by all means quote it that way. But in most instances, "and/or" can be replaced by "or," or sometimes by "and," depending on the grammatical meaning of your sentence. In those instances that you believe "or" does not complete the idea, use the construction "_____ or _____ or both." Example: "The rule states plagiarism is punishable by death or a fine of $50,000 or both." This construction is preferable to the "and/or" phrasing.

Some words and phrases always have slashes. For example: "http://www.geocities.com/Athens/Oracle/9080/." If the word you are quoting or referring to necessarily has a slash, you should use the slash form in your writing.

3. Avoid contractions but do use shorthand words and phrases.

In this book, you might find that we have employed a contraction from time to time. Do not be misled by this. Contractions are considered improper in actual, legal work product, and you should avoid them.

However, it is perfectly fine to use shorthand words and abbreviations of parties, institutions and agencies, acts and statutes, once you have correctly identified them in your work.

> *Example:* The Securities Exchange Commission ("SEC") refused to apply the Securities Act of 1933 ("'33 Act") to the post-sale use of the Section 14 "red herring" prospectus ("prospectus") by McDonnell Douglas Corporation ("MDC"). The SEC said that MDC satisfied the requirements of the '33 Act by providing an updated prospectus to each buyer.

4. Do not use symbols except where required.

Avoid using symbols (&, @, #) in your writing unless the symbol is part of a rule, statute, the name of a company or firm, or an email address. Examples: 14 U.S.C. § 123, 13 Apex Comp. Stat. Ann. ¶ 3-307, Williams & Connelly, farnsworthea@slu.edu. If you want to say "number 13," write out the word "number," do not write "#13."

The description of money is a particular exception to the rule. If you are referring to a rounded sum, like one hundred dollars, it is appropriate to write "one hundred dollars," or "$100." Do not write the decimal points, "$100.00." If, however, the sum has dollars and cents in it, use numerals and a dollar sign, for example, "$101.32," rather than writing that sum out in words.

If you are drafting a legal document such as a will, a check, a settlement agreement, or a contract, follow the practices of your office. In these instances, a word phrase followed by redundant numerals in parentheses may still be used, as long as your office follows this old, awkward methodology. Example: one hundred one dollars and thirty-two cents ($101.32).

5. Avoid first-person and second-person references.

It is common in oral conversations with your colleagues and clients, and even with your opponents, judges, and court personnel, to use first and second person references, such as: "We are moving to dismiss." "I have an objection." "Our case is strong." "My research shows that no case controls this issue." "You should settle this case early." Avoid this practice when you are composing your legal writing. It is a simple matter of formality: writing must be more formal than our spoken communications.[3]

Do not try to be clever and use "this writer" or "this author," instead of the forbidden first person reference; these substitutes are still first person references that must be avoided. Instead, always refer to your side by using your client's name, or by the customary shorthand reference to your client used in your office.

➢ *Correct:*   "Boeing can argue . . ."

 Incorrect: "We can argue . . ."

Not only is this the preferred phrasing, it actually is more accurate, because **parties** make arguments and take positions and bring motions, not their counsel. When referring to the other party in litigation, call them by their name, or their party designation (plaintiff or defendant), or other shorthand reference, and attribute all actions and statements to the party, not the attorney, on the other side.

➢ *Correct:*   "Defendant W.R. Grace failed to file its answer on time."

 Incorrect: "Ms. Smith failed to file an answer on time." [if Ms. Smith is the party's attorney]

---

[3] An obvious exception to this rule is the client letter, which is much more informal that the office memorandum and the court brief, and most often will use first and second person references such as: "Our research indicates . . . ." "You should not terminate the contract . . . ." "We would like to examine your files on . . . ."

6. Do not use rhetorical questions.

It is mystifying why law students and lawyers alike enjoy rhetorical questions. They are a cheap argumentative device akin to a temporary "straw man" argument that is erected for a moment just so that you can smash it to bits in the next breath. If the point you are making is obvious, simply state it in a concise way and move on. Phrasing your point as a rhetorical question does not make the point more obvious. If your reader is inclined to disagree with the point you are making, she will answer your rhetorical the opposite way from your intended answer, and you will have squandered space in your paper that you could have used to convince her that you are right. So, are you going to use rhetorical questions from now on?

7. Write out dates

In legal writing, you should write out dates in the American English form of Month-Day, Year, as in "August 31, 1998." Do not write "5/4/98" or "Aug. 31, 1998" or "31 August 1998." Many people outside the United States would read "5/4/98" as "April 5, 1998," not "May 4, 1998." You can avoid this confusion by sticking to the Month-Day, Year formulation.

The commas shown in the phrase "On August 31, 1998, Jones went to . . ." are required. You can leave the commas out only if you leave out the "day": "In August 1998 Jones went to . . ." is correct.

F. Internal consistency and parallelism

Proper legal writing is internally consistent. It promotes clarity to use the same names or terms to refer to the same parties, persons, and objects throughout your work. For example, compare the following:

> ➤ *Good:* The Chevy truck went through the intersection. The truck then ploughed into the Ford station wagon. The station wagon was wrecked.

> *Bad:* The truck went through the intersection. The Chevy then ploughed into the Ford. The vehicle was wrecked.

The principle of parallelism also applies to verb tenses, articles, and pronouns. Verb tenses, articles, and pronouns must match the subject throughout a paragraph and section of a paper. If you have inserted a quotation into a paragraph, you must check to see if you need to change the tense and verb endings of your quotation to match the tense and subjects of your sentence where the quote appears. Use brackets where necessary. For example:

> *Good:*   Mr. Cleaver maintained in his deposition that his duty had been fulfilled when he "[took] over Clark Enterprises and [paid] off [his] debt to Wayans." Cleaver Dep. at 13, line 10.

Bad: Mr. Cleaver maintained in his deposition that his duty had been fulfilled when "I am taking over Clark Enterprises and paying off my debt to Wayans." Cleaver Dep. at 13, line 10.

It is easier for readers to follow your writing if the sentence format and order of words also follow parallel forms. Compare the following:

> *Good:*   The rule has three criteria. The first criterion is . . .

The second criterion is . . .

Finally, the third criterion is . . .

Bad: The rule has three criteria. The first criterion is . . .

Secondly, we have to consider the factor of . . .

As for the last element, . . .

G. Sexist language

Women make up at least half of the graduating classes from law schools, anywhere from 30 to 40 percent of the practicing bar, and represent a growing percentage of judges and corporate counsel. There is no excuse for writing with sexist, male-dominated language in legal contexts. All judges, clients, and attorneys are not men, and there is no justification for exclusively using the pronouns "he" "him" "his" or "himself" in generic references to these persons and positions.

Our own method to avoid sexist language is to use feminine pronouns in reference to lawyers, judges, and clients as often as we feel comfortable doing so. Other methods are to use the combinations "he or she," "him or her," "herself or himself" in the construction of your sentences, although this can become tiresome if it appears too frequently. To avoid tiring out the reader with these inclusive combinations, you can simply rephrase a number of your sentences. Instead of saying, "An attorney must carefully account for his or her client's funds," say "An attorney must carefully account for client funds." Substituting the indefinite "their" for "his or her" is grammatically inappropriate; it is better to restate the sentence and leave out the possessive pronoun altogether.

H. References to cases and courts

In your first year of law school and beyond, you will be writing a great deal about judicial orders and opinions. There are special considerations involved in such references to cases and courts that do not always come naturally.

Be precise in describing what the court did: the court **granted** or **denied** a motion, **sustained** or **overruled** an objection to evidence, **accepted** or **rejected** an argument or position, **held** an issue of law, and **found** a fact.

Do not attribute emotions to courts. Courts don't feel, so do not say, "The court felt that Jones was wrong."

Always use the **past tense** to describe what the court said or did in a case you are using as authority. The case is done; it is in the past. It is not happening right now or in the future, so the past tense is the only appropriate tense. For example, state "The <u>Jones</u> court held that Smith provoked the dog" not "The <u>Jones</u> court holds that Smith provoked the dog."[4]

The court is singular, no matter how many judges sat and heard the case or joined in the opinion. The court is a thing, not a person. Therefore, when using a pronoun to refer to the court, use "it" not "they."

There are several ways to refer to the case you are currently involved in. You can say "the case at hand," "the instant case," "the case at bar," or simply "this case" as long as it is clear that you mean the case currently before the court. Whichever form you like the best, use it consistently in your writing.[5] Do not use "the case at hand" in one paragraph and "the instant case" in another and "the case at bar" in another; your object never should be to keep the reader guessing.

I. Citation to authority

1. The Golden Rule

Chapter 9 of this book is devoted to mechanics of citation. We are not going to talk about the many rules about mechanics in this short section. Instead, we only will discuss the Golden Rule of citation:

The Golden Rule of Citation

Whenever you make a statement about the law in your Discussion section, you *must* provide a citation to authority.

---

[4] Contrast this with constitutions, statutes, and regulations, which are on the books and exist in the present tense. You should state: "U.S. Const. amend XIV provides . . ." not "provided."

[5] Author Murray's personal favorite is "the instant case" because it reminds him of instant coffee, and he likes coffee. Author DeSanctis also likes coffee, but she drinks decaf.

That is the rule, and it is an absolute rule, not just a rule of thumb. Any legal proposition—defined as any statement of the law or about the law, a rule of law, the holding of a case, or a legal principle, whether collateral to your discussion or directly on point—*must* have a citation to legal authority. **Every time** you end a sentence in the Discussion section, check to see if it contains a legal proposition (as defined here). If so, put a citation to authority.

The use of the words "Discussion section" here is not accidental; you do not need citations to authority in your Questions Presented and Brief Answers sections. These sections would become far too crowded and lengthy if you cited authorities in them. Citation to *factual* sources in your Statement of Facts, however, is appropriate.

2. Jump cites must be provided

Citations must include the exact page where the material you are citing appears, which is called a "jump cite" or "pinpoint cite" or "pin cite." In the example, <u>Shorty v. Lefty</u>, 823 W.2d 234, 237 (Apex 1990), the reference to page "237" is the jump cite, meaning the page of the case where the material you are referring to appears. When you are citing an authority to explain the rule, or facts, or other parts of your discussion, you must provide a jump cite. Do not be lazy and simply cite the first page of the authority and send your reader off to find the material somewhere in that authority.

3. Cite all the sources you need, but do not string cite

Citations must reflect all of the sources you need to compose the rule or discussion for which you are providing a cite. When you present a legal rule or part of a rule that comes from several cases, cite to all of them.

On the other hand, do not over-cite. The only proper place to cite a long string of cases is in the explanation section when you are presenting a thorough explanatory synthesis. String citations (<u>Case 1</u>, <u>Case 2</u>, <u>Case 3</u>, <u>Case 4</u>, etc.; *ad nauseam*) in the rule section are unnecessary. They do not necessarily signal the reader that you did superior research and therefore found more cases than the average attorney; rather, it speaks to the fact that you do not know how to discern the rank and weight of your authorities and did not bother to cite only the very best. String citations are particularly tiresome to a reader who is going to look up all of the cases you cite, and if that reader is a law clerk who has the judge's ear, you may make an enemy in a place you did not need one.

There are a limited number of circumstance when you should consider using a string of citations in the rule section:

➢ The first is when it is critical to show that a great number of courts (and cases) have come out in favor of your position. This might be necessary if the position you are asserting is controversial or counterintuitive. It also might be necessary if you are relying on persuasive authority only, and you think the home court reading your argument may have a hard time swallowing it.

➤ The second is when you promise the reader that multiple authorities support your proposition. If you state that five states have held the same legal proposition, you now must cite five authorities.

➤ The third is when the second or third citation bolsters the value of the entire string of authorities. An example of this is when you cite an older case from the highest court of the applicable jurisdiction, and wish to follow it up with one or more cites to more recent controlling cases:

> Kent v. Olson, 24 W.2d 237, 246 (Apex 1924); Wayne v. Gordon, 323 W.2d 776, 779 (Apex 1960); Powerpuff Girls, Inc. v. Yugio Masters, Inc., 989 W.2d 34, 38 (Apex Ct. App. 1st Dist. 2005).

The citation to the 2005 controlling authority tells the reader that this proposition of law still is alive and well in your jurisdiction.

Otherwise, if you have controlling authorities that all say the same thing and all are from the same general time period, **cite no more than three** of these redundant cases for the point on which they all agree. Of course, pick the three best cases in terms of facts and outcome that support your position.

J. Tone: humor and excessive emotion is out; vivid and engaging work is in

The law is too serious of a business for humor. People will win and lose real money and will face a potential criminal sentence of weeks, months, and years of real time on the basis of what you do for them. If just one person fails to appreciate your joke (your client, your opponent, the judge, etc.), then you have done a disservice to your client.

We use humor all the time in this book and in the classes we teach. A light approach is fine in a textbook or in the classroom. But do not carry this mirthful spirit into your legal writing. You should always write as though you were already a lawyer and had a real client that will suffer real consequences from what you do.

This is not to say leave out all vivid, descriptive, and even clever language from your writing. Clever language used sparingly can be effective and is acceptable. You can turn a clever phrase, but do it to make a point, to drive something home, and to make an impression that might last a bit longer; never do it just to be funny.

We have used the following in actual briefs filed with the court:

➤ *Examples:* "Defendant is not asking the court to reinvent the deal." [Used in reference to the allegation that the court should rewrite the agreement between the parties].

"Wal-Mart put the brakes on the auto insurance marketing plan."

These examples were not screamingly funny, but we think they were acceptable.

Do not show anger or other excessive emotion in your writing. No one wants to read a lawyer's vicious sniping at the other side, or a long, sorrowful recitation of the equities of the situation. It is not professional. You might lose your cool in person, but you should not do it in writing. Compare the following:

> *Bad:*   "Plaintiff's counsel lies and cheats the court by asserting this farcical position."

  Better: "Plaintiff's position is completely erroneous."

  Best: "Plaintiff's position is erroneous." or "There is no merit to plaintiff's position."

We are not advocating that you should strive to be bland and never should get agitated or forceful about your position. You can be forthright. You can be direct. You can show that you feel strongly about the equities. However, do not do so by bleeding your sympathy and sorrow all over the page or burning the very words off the paper with scorching prose. For example:

> *Bad:*   "This imprisonment cries out to heaven! Petitioner screams, 'Give me liberty or give me death!' but the Court is deaf to his plea."

  Good: "The principles of law and equity demand that petitioner be released. There is no other just result."

II. FINE TUNING WITH ALTERNATIVE MODIFICATIONS OF THE TREAT FORMAT

We have designed the TREAT format to be versatile enough to cover most situations in which you will communicate your findings on the law in writing. The format allows for the TREATment of as many major issues as you need to discuss in a writing, and within each TREATment of a major issue, it allows for the sub-TREATment of as many sub-issues and sub-sub-issues as are presented by your major issues.

The basic format presents the TREATment of major issues one before the other—the first major issue before the second, and the second before the third, and so on. Occasionally, this structure becomes awkward or ineffective because one major issue encompasses another major issue within its discussion. For example, a procedural issue, such whether or not a motion for preliminary injunction should be granted, may require the analysis of a major substantive issue, namely the likelihood of success on the merits.[6] Instead of

---

[6] The factors considered for the issuance of a preliminary injunction are: (1) the probability that the moving party will succeed on the merits; (2) the threat of irreparable harm to the moving party; (3) the balance of hardships between the moving party and the non-moving party; and (4) the public interest. <u>See</u> <u>United Indus. Corp. v. Clorox Co.</u>, 140 F.3d 1175, 1178-79 (8th Cir. 1998); <u>Dataphase Sys. v. C L Sys., Inc.</u>, 640 F.2d 109, 114 (8th Cir. 1981) (en banc).

TREATing the issue of the right to a preliminary injunction before the TREATment of the substantive issue as you would in the traditional TREAT structure, it makes sense to discuss the substantive issue in the middle of the TREATment of the preliminary injunction issue, namely, in the sub-TREATment of the "success on the merits" element.

For example, if the substantive issue was whether the movant will prevail on a claim of money had and received, and the procedural issue was whether the movant can obtain an injunction to prevent the defendant from further transferring the funds, the traditional TREAT organization would look something like this:

I. JONES BANK WILL PREVAIL ON ITS CLAIM OF MONEY HAD AND RECEIVED BECAUSE THE MISTAKEN RECIPIENT HAD NO RIGHT TO RETAIN THE FUNDS

   A. Smith Co. received the funds from Jones Bank.
   B. The transfer occurred by mistake.
   C. It is unjust for Smith Co. to retain the funds.

II. JONES BANK WILL BE ABLE TO OBTAIN A PRELIMINARY INJUNCTION AGAINST FURTHER TRANSFER OF THE FUNDS BY SMITH CO.

   A. As discussed above, Jones Bank will succeed on the merits.
   B. There is a significant threat of irreparable harm to Jones Bank.
   C. The balance of hardships between Jones Bank and Smith Co. favors Jones Bank.
   D. Granting the injunction is in the public's interest.

This format can be improved by discussing the substantive issue in the TREATment of the procedural issue:

I. JONES BANK WILL BE ABLE TO OBTAIN A PRELIMINARY INJUNCTION AGAINST FURTHER TRANSFER OF THE FUNDS BY SMITH CO.

   A. Jones Bank will succeed on the merits of its claim of money had and received because Smith Co. received fund by mistake and had no right to retain the funds.

      1. Smith Co. received the funds from Jones Bank.
      2. The transfer occurred by mistake.
      3. It is unjust for Smith Co. to retain the funds because Smith Co. had not prior account or debt from Jones Bank.

    B. <u>There is a significant threat of irreparable harm to Jones Bank because the money was intended for a time-sensitive transaction with SwissBank.</u>

    C. <u>The balance of hardships between Jones Bank and Smith Co. favors Jones Bank.</u>

    D. <u>Granting the injunction is in the public's interest.</u>

This alternative format will improve the discussion of a procedural rule that incorporates one or more substantive issues into its analysis; it will not work with procedural rules that merely provide a legal standard for the court to award or deny relief. In addition to the rule for the issuance of a preliminary injunction discussed above, the rules for the certification of a class action,[7] and for mandatory joinder of parties,[8] are good candidates for the alternative format, because each rule contains internal substantive law issues that must be discussed before the outcome of the analysis of the procedural rule can be completed. The same is not true for procedural rules such as the rule for the granting of a motion to dismiss for failure to state a claim,[9] or for the award of summary judgment.[10] Even though the discussion of these motions will involve substantive issues, there is little to be gained by attempting to discuss the substantive issues within the same TREATment of the procedural rule. The procedural rule can be discussed first, followed separately by the substantive issues in the traditional TREAT format. Alternatively, the procedural rule can be combined with the discussion of the substantive issues, as in the following examples:

---

[7] One or more members of a class may sue or be sued as representative parties on behalf of all only if: (1) the class is so numerous that joinder of all members is impracticable; (2) there are questions of law or fact common to the class; (3) the claims or defenses of the representative parties are typical of the claims or defenses of the class; and (4) the representative parties will fairly and adequately protect the interests of the class. Fed. R. Civ. P. 23(a).

[8] A person who is subject to service of process and whose joinder will not deprive the court of jurisdiction over the subject matter of the action shall be joined as a party in the action if: (1) in the person's absence complete relief cannot be accorded among those already parties; or (2) the person claims an interest relating to the subject of the action and is so situated that the disposition of the action in the person's absence may (i) as a practical matter impair or impede the person's ability to protect that interest or (ii) leave any of the persons already parties subject to a substantial risk of incurring double, multiple, or otherwise inconsistent obligations by reason of the claimed interest. . . . Fed. R Civ. P. 19(a).

[9] Under Fed. R. Civ. P. 12(b)(6), a complaint should not be dismissed for failure to state a claim unless it appears beyond doubt that the plaintiff can prove no set of facts in support of his claim which would entitle him to relief. <u>Conley v. Gibson</u>, 355 U.S. 41, 45-46 (1957).

[10] [Summary] judgment sought shall be rendered forthwith if the pleadings, depositions, answers to interrogatories, and admissions on file, together with the affidavits, if any, show that there is no genuine issue as to any material fact and that the moving party is entitled to a judgment as a matter of law. Fed. R. Civ. P. 56(c).

Example 1—Summary judgment issue combined with substantive law issue:

I. JONES BANK IS ENTITLED TO SUMMARY JUDGMENT ON COUNT III (MONEY HAD AND RECEIVED) BECAUSE THERE IS NO DISPUTE OVER THE FACT THAT THE MISTAKEN RECIPIENT HAD NO RIGHT TO RETAIN THE FUNDS

   A. There is no dispute concerning the facts that Smith Co. received the funds as a result of Jones Bank's mistake.
   B. Jones Bank is entitled to judgment as a matter of law on Count III because there is no legal or equitable justification for Smith Co. to retain the funds transferred by Jones Bank.

Example 2—Motion to dismiss issue combined with substantive law issue:

I. SMITH CO.'S MOTION TO DISMISS JONES BANK'S COMPLAINT FOR FAILURE TO STATE A CLAIM MUST BE DENIED BECAUSE THE COMPLAINT ALLEGES A PRIMA FACIE CASE OF MISTAKEN TRANSFER.

   A. Jones Bank has alleged the requisite elements of money had and received.

      1. Notice pleading is sufficient in federal court.
      2. Jones Bank alleged a transfer, by mistake, and Smith Co.'s retention is unjust.

   B. The factual allegations stated in the complaint are sufficient to state a cause of action upon which relief may be granted.

III. EDITING TIPS

A. Write early, rewrite often

The mantra of great authors is that there is no such thing as good writing, only good rewriting. Editing and rewriting takes time, and you cannot do a good job if you do not leave yourself the time. The mere act of writing forces you to get organized in your thinking and your argument. Whenever you sit down and actually write a draft of the work, the drafting process will reveal defects, gaps, quirks, and problems in your research or analysis. It may change your mind about your legal conclusions. Therefore, leave time for this to occur. The Sunday before the Monday the paper is due is too late.

Rewrites have a similar function to get the argument in order, correct mistakes, fill in the gaps, beef up the weak areas, and prune the bushy areas. There is a law of diminishing returns at play here; the eighth rewrite will not fix as many errors as the third, but given that each rewrite can improve the work, it is worth doing as many rewrites as you can.

B. Employ more than one editing and proofreading technique

There is more than one way to edit and proofread your own work. Simply reading through your work from start to finish is one way, but you probably have observed that you still miss typographical errors and other spelling, citation, and grammatical errors using this method. The problem is that your brain becomes accustomed to the passages you have written and skips ahead, saving time but not actually reading each word and sentence. In order to avoid your brain's built in capacity to skim text, you should try reading your work backwards, word for word and then sentence by sentence. Although this technique is painful, it will succeed in interrupting your brain's inherent text skipping capacity, and you will be able to read your text word for word. Another technique is to create a paper mask that only allows you to see a few words of text at a time, and then use it to read your paper slowly, word for word. Denying your brain the sight of familiar words in familiar sequence helps to slow it down so that you can look harder at the actual text.

When you are editing and rewriting for general flow and readability, consider reading the text out loud to yourself. This often causes you to stumble and trip right over the portions of your text that need clarification or simplification. Reading out loud also forces your brain to look at each word so that you can read it (reading and recitation being two different activities for your brain, and the latter activity forces your brain to slow down and actually perform the former activity).

C. Stay objective

Editing is a good time to test the objectivity of your work. An office memorandum is supposed to be an objective, fair treatment of the pros and the cons of the client's situation. You may have gotten carried away with the client's cause and have taken her side too much. Editing is a time to reexamine your work and make sure that you have treated both sides (yours and the Devil's) fairly. Your readers (bosses, clients, other colleagues) really do want the right answer, not the answer that you know they want to hear. If you need encouragement in giving the hard, but correct answer, remember your ethical duties to the client, and remember that lawyers get sued for malpractice more and more these days if your "popular" but inaccurate advice gets the client in trouble.

D. Track the language of the authorities when applying the rule to your facts

The principle of parallelism uses the wording of the factors, elements, and legal standards from the cases, statutes, and court rules when applying them to your facts in the application section. If the standard is "wrongful abuse," describe the client's situation using the terms "wrongful" and "abuse." If the authorities use the terms "prompt disclosure," describe whether the client was "prompt" in making a "disclosure." Do not use synonyms ("improper behavior," "tortious abuse," "rapidly informed," "immediately reported") just to be different and creative. The reader may miss the connection and not get the point you are making.

E. Be as definite as you can be

We always tell our students that someone is counting on you to get the correct answer, and that they may be paying you a lot of money for this purpose. Do not make it appear as if you gave up halfway through by reporting your answer as a "maybe yes," or "probably no." The major answers you give in your work (the brief answer, and each <u>T</u>hesis you write) should be definite. The brief answer should start with a yes or no, not a "maybe yes," or "probably no." Take your best shot based on your analysis of the law. If you think there absolutely is no way to make a definitive yes or no answer to the question you wrote in the issue section, then you should go back and rephrase your issue so that you can give a yes or no answer.

Of course, from time to time, your explanation of your conclusions and the analysis of the application of the rule to your facts will run into the inherent uncertainties of the law. Here, you should try to be as precise as possible in explaining yourself, but where you must express a lack of certainty, pinpoint the **precise source** of the uncertainty. If it is that one case that cannot be effectively distinguished, explain that. If a point turns on whether a court will accept or reject a certain argument or make a certain application of the law to your facts, explain that and explain what happens if the court goes either way. But start your brief answer with a yes or no and then proceed to explain the source of the uncertainty.

F. Statement of facts: how much is too much?

When pruning your statement of facts, consider this test: (1) Am I going to mention this fact again in my discussion section? (2) Am I going to use it to analogize my case to another case or distinguish my case from a contrary authority? (3) Am I going to use this fact in meeting or discussing the application of an element? or (4) Is this fact necessary to explain the client's situation, and if the fact is not present, will the uninformed reader still understand the situation? If **none** of the above apply, consider jettisoning the fact.

G. Editing the discussion section

1. Side issues, interesting questions

We assume you will not be spending a lot of time (and space) writing about topics that are not part of the assignment. Do not do it. No one will get brownie points for pointing out the most side issues that may affect the case as a whole, rather than resolving the research topic at hand. Remember: the presumption is that you should answer any legal question that you raise in your office memo. This should give you pause to raise too many interesting questions.

2. Redundancy is bad

Repeating yourself is a vice. It does not pay to say the same thing two or three times. I'll say it again, ...

Lawyers are prone to redundancy. Many must think, if I say it twice, that is twice as good. This idea may exist because repetition is a good technique in oral advocacy—but save it for that context. You may think you are driving home a point, like we just tried to do in the paragraph above, but more often than not you are driving someone insane.

We are not saying that you should not make your point clearly, or that you shouldn't explain yourself fully even if that takes two or three sentences on one point. You should explain the same point or the same conclusion in a different way **if** there is something to be revealed through that second exposition. Clarification of legal principles is no easy task; don't make it harder by trying to adhere to some rule of **no** repetitions ever. Repeating things two or three times is no good if the second and third times do not shed new light on the principles you are explaining.

3. Too many authorities?

It does not pay to cite dozens of authorities if you cannot synthesize them properly or discuss any of them in enough detail to make your point and explain your conclusions. Do not drown out the best controlling and persuasive authorities in a sea of "also rans." If you have strong cases, explain them. If there are many others, cite them once and leave them be—don't try to explain all of them. Use parentheticals to give a few key facts or points from these other cases that support your argument. A fascinated reader will look up these other cases and get the benefit of them if she wants them.

Chapter 9

Legal Citation

Part I. The ALWD Citation Manual

GENERAL RULES

The ALWD Citation Manual was created in 1999 by the Association of Legal Writing Directors as an alternative to The Bluebook. It is published by Aspen Publishers and currently is in its second edition.

The ALWD Manual (or, "ALWD") was designed as a "Restatement" of current citation practices and was created by legal writing professionals as a straightforward method for standardizing and teaching legal citation. ALWD was prepared primarily in response to two major criticisms about The Bluebook. One common criticism is that The Bluebook was written primarily for journal editors, not practitioners, and thus focuses on largely arcane, irrelevant rules and examples that attorneys simply do not need in practice. As a result, The Bluebook can be challenging to learn. The "Practitioners' Notes" at the front of The Bluebook (17th edition and earlier) were quite limited, especially as compared to the rules in the rest of the text. Determining citation rules for the vast majority of the documents that attorneys use in practice—legal memoranda and court documents—thus could require considerable ambiguity resolution and guess-work, whereas the directions for journal editors working on article footnotes are painfully detailed and complex.

A second common complaint about The Bluebook is that each new edition typically has included unpredictable and puzzling rule changes that many people maintain are motivated purely by the need of the students at the Ivy League law schools publishing it to create a new edition.

The saga continues. The Bluebook **18th edition** will be published in the fall of 2005. In some respects, it responds to the concerns that ALWD addressed. In particular, the "Bluepages" (which replace the Practitioners' Notes) provide "easy-to-comprehend instructions for the everyday citations needs" of law students, practitioners, law clerks, and other legal professionals: essentially a synopsis of all of the rules most commonly used in practice. In addition, several formerly ambiguous rules have been clarified, and two rules have been completely rewritten to bring them up-to-date with current practice. Rule 18 (covering electronic sources) has been completely revamped to account for the growing popularity of citation to Internet sources; and Rule 21 has been redone to correspond to majority citation conventions in foreign and international legal fields. About a dozen or so other rules and many of the tables have been expanded, updated, or otherwise modified.

Despite the intense disagreement over which manual is better and why, there are actually very few citation differences for practitioners between the ALWD Manual and The Bluebook. Both manuals essentially teach the same basic system of citation, though they do so in different ways and with a few disparities at the margins. You should recognize, moreover, that there are other variations to this citation system. Some law school journals have their own citation rules (Chicago and Texas are two examples); West and Lexis use their own variations; and some law firms and courts deviate from the basic rules as well. As a result and regardless of whether you learn legal citation via The ALWD Manual or The Bluebook, your goal should be to understand legal citation principals in general—and to remember to consult local rules or conventions for specific requirements that neither manual addresses.

The headings in the remainder of this chapter corresponded to each of The ALWD Manual's seven parts. We highlight the most important information from each Part and, where applicable, note the differences between ALWD and The Bluebook (referenced below as "BB"). This chapter is not a substitute for reading The ALWD Manual; indeed, as is the case with any manual, you must actually use it in order to master it.

I. CITATION SENTENCES AND CITATION CLAUSES

There are two basic ways to incorporate a citation into a legal document. If the source relates to the entire textual sentence, then the citation should follow as its own "sentence." If, however, the source relates only to part of the sentence, then it will be incorporated as a clause, set off from the text it concerns with commas (ALWD R. 43).

In terms of typeface, most legal citations are presented in a combination of ordinary type and either *italics* or <u>underlining</u>. These typeface apply regardless of the type of document in which the citation appears (law review vs. court document) and regardless of where the citation appears within that document (in text or in a footnote).[1]

It usually does not matter whether you choose italics or underlining, though ALWD does appear to express a preference for italics (*see* ALWD Rules 1, 12). Whichever you choose, be consistent throughout your document! Do not use a combination of italics and underlining.

Appropriate citation material to italicize or underline includes:

- Case names
- Titles of most documents
- Introductory signals
- Internal cross-references (*supra* and *infra*)
- Prior and subsequent history
- The short form *id.*

---

[1] This rule differs from the BB rule for law review citation form which requires different fonts for different types of documents and placement of sources (*see* BB R. 2). The ALWD rule is the same as the BB rule for practitioner's documents as described in part II of this chapter.

A. Citation sentence

A citation sentence is used when you are citing authority after a period that ends a complete sentence. The citation sentence starts with a capital letter, and ends with a period:

> The standard is one of gross negligence. *Hallam v. Jones*, 118 S.W.2d 222, 224 (Mo. 1947).

Multiple cases and other authorities in a citation sentence are separated by semi-colons:

> The standard is one of gross negligence. Mo. Rev. Stat. § 232.12 (1986); *Hallam v. Jones*, 118 S.W.2d 222, 224 (Mo. 1947); *Jones v. Carmichael*, 446 S.W.2d 333, 335 (Mo. App. E. Dist. 1987).

B. Citation clauses

When a citation supports only part of a sentence, the citation is inserted in the sentence, set off by commas before and after. This is referred to as a citation clause:

> The Illinois Dog Bite Statute, 510 Ill. Comp. Stat. 5/16 (1996), defines a dog-owner's liability for a dog bite.

Multiple authorities supporting a clause are separated by semi-colons, but the whole citation clause is set apart by commas as above. A citation clause does not necessarily start with a capital letter—it only does if you are citing an authority without any introductory phrase, and the authority starts with a capital letter. A sentence citation which supports the second clause can follow at the end of the second clause, after the period that ends the sentence, as in the following example:

> Dog bite liability requires a lack of provocation, either intentional or unintentional, *see* 510 Ill. Comp. Stat. 5/16 (1996); *Beckert v. Risberg*, 210 N.E.2d 207, 208 (Ill. 1965); *Nelson v. Lewis*, 344 N.E.2d 268, 270 (Ill. App. 5th Dist. 1976), but provocation can be offset if the dog's attack is particularly vicious and disproportionate to the provocation. *Nelson*, 344 N.E.2d at 271.

As a general matter, within a citation sentence or citation clause, cite the highest and most recent controlling authorities first, followed by lesser and earlier authorities in order of their weight. This order of presentation is important.

Correct: A dog owner is liable for all injuries caused by his dog unless the dog is provoked by the victim. *Smithy v. Jonesy*, 123 S.W.2d 345, 347 (Mo. 1965); *Johnson v. Anderson*, 789 S.W.2d 234, 237 (Mo. App. E. Dist. 1989); *Son v. Anders*, 780 S.W.2d 134, 137 (Mo. App. E. Dist. 1980).

Incorrect: A dog owner is liable for all injuries caused by his dog unless the dog is provoked by the victim. *Johnson v. Anderson*, 789 S.W.2d 234, 237 (Mo. App. E. Dist. 1989); *Son v. Anders*, 780 S.W.2d 134, 137 (Mo. App. E. Dist. 1980); *Smithy v. Jonesy*, 123 S.W.2d 345, 347 (Mo. 1965).

In certain circumstances, you will be presenting a large number of authorities that are not controlling and may be of equal importance. When you are in this situation, the order of authorities cited according to ALWD is:

1. Constitutions
2. Statutes
3. Treaties and other international agreements
4. Cases, in the order of:
   a. U.S. Supreme Court
   b. Federal appellate courts
   c. Federal trial courts (including bankruptcy courts)
   d. Judicial Panel on Multidistrict Litigation
   e. Federal claims courts, military courts, tax courts
   f. Administrative agencies
   g. State courts (by state, in alphabetical order, and then by level of court within a state, highest to lowest)
   h. Foreign courts
   i. International courts (ICJ, PCIJ, arbitral panels)
5. Legislative history materials
6. Administrative and executive materials
7. Records, briefs, pleadings of litigants
8. Secondary sources, in the order of:
   a. Restatements
   b. Books and treatises
   c. Law review articles
   d. Annotations (for example, American Law Reports)
   e. Magazine and newspaper articles
   f. Unpublished materials

Within a particular category (for example, federal appellate court or district court cases), the materials should be listed in the order described in ALWD Rule 45.4. The following rules are of particular note:

U.S. Court of Appeals cases should be ordered first by court (1st, 2d, 3d, etc) and then in reverse chronological order.

U.S. District Court cases are ordered first alphabetically and then in reverse chronological order.[2]

---

[2]   BB Rule 1.4 specifies a slightly different order. *See* part II of this chapter.

II. INTRODUCTORY PHRASES (ALWD R. 44)

Either a citation sentence or a citation clause can be preceded by an introductory word or phrase. When the word or phrase begins a citation sentence, it is capitalized. Otherwise it is not.

The entire introductory word or phrase is either underlined or italicized whether or not the source that follows it is underlined or italicized. The signal should be separated from the rest of the citation with one space—do not include any punctuation between the signal and the rest of the citation (ALWD R. 44.6).

Each phrase connotes something different about the authority that follows it:

[No introductory phrase]	Connotes that the authority contains (states) the exact or nearly the exact phrase or sentence for which you are citing the authority (*i.e.*, the words you use are 99% the same as in the source). You may have changed the verb tense or dropped a minor word or two (this, than, the, etc.), but otherwise, one turning to the authority would find that statement in the authority at the page or section to which you are citing. This form is used whether or not you actually put quotation marks around the statement.
	If the statement is a legal proposition or conclusion (as opposed to a fact or something other than a statement about the law), this form also connotes that the statement is part of the holding of the case.
See	Connotes that the authority contains the idea and the concept for which you are citing the authority, but the exact words will not be found in the authority. The authority must directly support your statement. You would still cite to a particular page or section of the authority where the idea or concept is stated.
See also	Connotes that the authority contains related or additional information or material that supports the proposition for which the authority is cited, but the exact statement (concept or idea) is not found in the authority. A parenthetical should be used to explain why or how the material supports the proposition. For example:
	The *Erie* doctrine confuses the issue of choice of law. *Masters v. Johnson*, 55 Ohio App. 23, 24

(1987); *see also Hill v. Williams*, 766 P.2d 433, 444 (Okla. 1978) (*Erie* confuses most issues of conflict of laws, including forum selection).

Accord   When you have two or more authorities that clearly support the statement or proposition for which you are citing them, but the actual statement only is found in one of the authorities, use *accord* to preface the other citations. For example:

> A doctor must use reasonably prudent methods to detect viral agents. Mo. Rev. Stat. § 516.132.2 (1999); *accord Smith v. Jones*, 755 S.W.2d 232, 240 (Mo. App. E. Dist. 1996); *Janes v. Roth*, 432 N.E.2d 222, 223 (Ill. App. 5th Dist. 1986).

Cf.   Connotes that the cited authority states a different proposition from the main proposition for which the citation is given, but the second proposition is sufficiently analogous as to lend support to the main proposition. A parenthetical or other explanation should be used to explain the relevance. For example:

> Architects must take reasonable care to choose a design that will preclude subsidence of the building. *Cf. Cliff v. Hector*, 239 S.E.2d 235, 237 (S.C. App. 1st Dist. 1975) (civil engineer required to take reasonable care to choose non-subsiding design); *Uriah v. Heap*, 236 S.E.2d 457, 459 (S.C. App. 1st Dist. 1973) (same, building contractor).

Compare . . . [and] . . . with   Used to express that a comparison of one or more cases with one or more other cases will reveal something about the way the law works in this area. Again, a parenthetical explanation should be used to drive the point home even more. Note well that in this citation form commas separate the authorities, not semi-colons. For example:

> If the damages are nominal, a defamation claim will be dismissed. *Compare Norton v. Cramden*, 432 Vt. 234 (1990) (nominal damages of fifteen dollars, claim dismissed), *and Ricardo v. Mertz*, 335 Vt. 245 (1982) (nominal damages of two dollars,

claim dismissed), *with Scooby v. Shaggy*, 553 Vt. 987 (1997) (damages of $150,000, claim not dismissed), *and Hadji v. Quest*, 288 Vt. 256 (1978) (damages of $75,000, claim not dismissed), *and Van Dyke v. Petry*, 228 Vt. 667 (1975) (damages of $55,000, claim not dismissed).

E.g. (See, e.g.)[3]

Introduces authorities that support the proposition stated. The concept and general proposition would be found in the cited authorities, but not necessarily the exact word or phrase you are stating. Unlike *see* or *see also*, the phrase "*e.g.*" is used if you are stating a rather general legal proposition and wish to suggest that there are many authorities that hold this, and the listed authorities are a representative sample. If the listed authorities actually do not state the exact proposition for which you are citing them, but support it nonetheless, use "*see, e.g.*" instead.

But see (But see, e.g. But cf.)

If you are citing an authority contrary to the proposition stated, you would use *but see* in situations where you would use see or no introductory phrase, and *but see, e.g.* if you are listing several contrary authorities that go against the proposition. Use *but cf.* if the contrary authority is not directly on point, but sufficiently analogous to cause concern; a parenthetical should be used to explain the state of things. For example:

> Most states have adopted the UCC Sales provisions. *But see* La. Rev. Stat. Ann. § 355.1 (West 1988). In the majority of states, statute of frauds requires contracts for goods over $500 in value to be in writing. *But cf. Goodman v. Du Bois*, 235 La. 468, 469 (1986) (civil code requires writing only for specific purpose contracts, or for land sales).

See generally

The most nebulous of introductory phrases, *see generally* is used to introduce background or other relevant

---

[3] Note that the BB requires a comma at the end of this signal. *E.g., See, e.g.,* or *But see, e.g.,* all are to end in commas according to BB R. 1.2.

material—often secondary sources—that are helpful to an understanding of the issues.

III. SHORTHAND DEVICES FOR REPEAT CITATIONS (ALWD 10, 11)

ALWD Rule 11 provides a basic introduction to the concept of "full citations" and "short forms." A full citation includes each component required for the particular source she is citing and gives readers all the information they would need to locate that source in a library. The full citation format for each specific source will require slightly different components, which are identified and discussed in connection with specific source materials later in the manual (Rules 12-42). The first time a source is cited—in any type of legal document—you must use the full citation format for that kind of source. Thereafter, you may rely on a "short form," which omits some of the required information in a full citation but still enables a reader to identify and locate the source. Acceptable short forms also vary depending on type of source; where the short form occurs in relation to the full citation; and whether the source is cited in text or in a footnote.

Id.

One short form that nearly all legal citations share, however, is "*Id.*," which is short for "idem" and means "the same." *Id.* replaces as much of the immediately preceding citation as is identical with the current one. In other words, if you cite:

Unumb v. Murray, 191 F.3d 285, 286 (D.C. Cir. 2005),

and want to refer the reader to the same case at a different page in the very next citation, then you would write for the next citation:

Id. at 287.

If I wanted to refer the reader to exactly the same case at exactly the same page, I would just write:

Id.

because the entire preceding citation contains exactly the same information that I need—even the page number is the same.

Supra and *infra*

Supra ("above") and *infra* ("below") (ALWD R. 10) are internal cross-references; they are signals that refer readers to other parts of the same document. They most commonly are used in footnotes. They do not refer readers to outside sources. Use *supra* to refer to material that appears earlier in your paper and *infra* to refer to material that will appear later. For example:

---

[17] *Supra* n. 10.

[18] *Infra* text accompanying n. 50.

There is also a second use of *supra*—not as an internal cross-reference, but as a short citation for certain types of sources (ALWD R. 11.4). This use of *supra* functions more like *id.*. It can only be used after a source has been cited once in full format. But, unlike *id.*, it cannot be used for all sources. It is typically used for sources cited by author name, such as books, law review articles and web sites. Do not use *supra* to refer to cases, statutes, constitutions, regulations and other legislative materials. And, of course, do not use *supra* to refer back to the immediately preceding authority—*id.* is the appropriate short form there.

CASES

I. STYLE OF THE CASE (ALWD R. 12)

The names of the first named parties on each side become the style of the case; they are separated by a "v." and underlined or italicized:

Smith v. Jones   not   *Smith, Bradley, and Tom v. Jones, Microsoft, Inc., Jones Brothers Constr. Co., and Mayfair Hotel Co.*

A. Certain words are omitted

Omit the parties' first names (unless they are part of a company name):

Smith v. Jones   not   *Roger Smith v. Percy Jones*

But *Roger L. Smith, Inc. v. Percy Jones and Co.* is correct because these are company names.

Titles, offices, before or after the party's name (for example, Mr., Mrs., Dr., M.D., PhD, Commander, General, Surgeon General of the United States) are omitted unless the person is sued only by her title, and her actual name does not appear in the case style:

Brit v. Mayor of Santa Monica [if the Mayor is not sued in her own name]

Brit v. McDonald   [if Mayor McDonald is sued under her own name]

But not *Brit v. McDonald, Mayor of Santa Monica,* and not *Dr. Brit, M.D. v. Ms. McDonald*

B. Use ALWD standard abbreviations

Abbreviations may be used in legal citations for common sources, such as legal periodicals, case names, and court names. ALWD presents tables of standard abbreviations in Rule 2 and in Appendices 3, 4 and 5. If a word does not appear in one of those tables, it should not be abbreviated.[4]

In general, single capital letters must be grouped together, but any other combination of two or more letters to be set apart from single capitals or other combinations by a space. For example, the following abbreviations are correct:

S.D.N.Y.
E.D. Va.
F. Supp.
Cal. App.

Ordinals, such as 2d and 3d, are treated as one capital letter, and can be grouped together with other single capital letters, as in the following examples:

F.2d
N.Y.3d

But if the ordinal follows a cluster of two or more letters, it must stand alone:

F. Supp. 2d
Cal. Rptr. 4th

---

[4] ALWD eliminates the use of apostrophes in abbreviations of names and titles in the style of the case. So, for example, the BB recommends as abbreviations: ass'n, dep't, gov't, and int'l. ALWD changes these to: assn., dept., govt., and intl.. This does not apply to case history terms, such as "aff'd," "rev'd," which still use apostrophes in ALWD and BB (see T.8).

Abbreviate company, party, and other names in case styles according to Appendix 3:

> Consolidated becomes Consol.
> Enterprise becomes Enter.
> Industry, industries, industrial become Indus.
> South is S.
> East is E.

Federal court names are abbreviated according to Appendix 4; state court abbreviations can be developed using a combination of Appendix 1 and Rule 2, or by looking up abbreviations for each individual word in Appendix 3.

> Appellate Division is App. Div.
> Commonwealth Court is Commw. Ct.
> Superior Court is Super. Ct.

When abbreviating state names, follow the rules in Appendix 1. Note that the correct abbreviation for a state is not always the U.S. Postal Service abbreviation. For example:

> Ala.
> Del.
> Miss.
> N.M.
> Alaska
> Iowa
> Idaho
> Utah

Abbreviations for case history terms[5] are found in rule 12.8:

> aff'd
> rev'd
> cert. denied
> rev'd on other grounds

As are official terms for actions that are not abbreviated:

> appeal denied
> vacated
> modifying
> mandamus denied

---

[5] Apostrophes are used in many of these abbreviations in ALWD and BB.

II. REQUIRED INFORMATION FOR CASES

Each case citation must tell four pieces of information: (1) the case name; (2) where you find the case; (3) the court; (4) the year of the case. But this information may be conveyed in as many as nine components:

(1) Case name
(2) Reporter volume
(3) Reporter abbreviation
(4) First page of case
(5) Jump cite (Pinpoint cite or Pin cite) page
(6) Court abbreviation
(7) Date of opinion
(8) Subsequent history designation
(9) Subsequent history citation

Here is an example (the first as it might appear in a legal document, the second broken down to label the nine components listed above:

Gettysburg Morning Post v. Hallam, 144 A.2d 25, 45-46 (Pa. 1966), *rev'd*, 378 U.S. 250 (1967).

(1) *Gettysburg Morning Post v. Hallam*, (2) 144 (3) A.2d (4) 25, (5) 45-46 ((6) Pa. (7) 1966), (8) *rev'd*, (9) 378 U.S. 250 (1967).

A. Page spans and jump cites (pinpoint cites or pin cites)

If you are referring to a particular part of the case (and you should be in most instances), you must provide a jump cite (also known as a pinpoint cite or pin cite) that refers the reader to the specific page or pages of the opinion that support your proposition. To create a jump cite, put a comma after the page number where the case begins and then cite the page(s) where the material appears. More than one page can be referenced. If the material is on separate pages, cite them separately: 23, 24, 29, 35.

If the material carries over from one page to another, you should indicate the page span. ALWD gives writers a choice on how to present a page span. You may retain all digits or drop repetitive digits and retain two on the right-had side of the span. Thus, ALWD permits either of the following examples.

125-126
125-26

If you are referring to material on the first page of a case, you must repeat the first page number:

Presley v. Jackson, 833 S.W.2d 222, 222 (Tenn. 1996).

B. Court information

A case citation must include the abbreviation for the court that decided the case (in parentheses preceding the date). Abbreviations are listed in Appendices 1 and 4.

When citing a federal case, information about the state or about the court division is omitted. Thus, it is **incorrect** to write:

(7th Cir. Ill. 1980)
(D.N.J. Newark Div. 1997)

However, when citing a state case, you must include available information about departments, districts or divisions at the appellate or trial court level because this information is necessary to determine whether or not the cases is controlling or how persuasive a non-controlling authority might be in the case at hand. Appendix 1 contains much of the necessary information, and the ALWD web site (www.alwd.org) also contains charts that explain how the states' appellate courts are divided.[6]

Capulet v. Montague, 500 N.E.2d 180 (Ill. App. 1st Dist. 1998).

If the court that wrote the opinion is obvious from one of the reporters you are citing (for example, a reporter with the state's initials is presumed to report the cases of the highest court in the state; a reporter with the state's initials and "App." added on is presumed to report the decisions of the state's intermediate level appellate court), then you need not put the court designation in the parentheses with the year. However, you still need to note the division or department deciding the case.

Constance v. Reader, 234 N.Y.2d 245 (1965).

[Reader presumes from the N.Y. reporter citation that the case is from the N.Y. Court of Appeals, the highest court in New York].

Irving v. Bissell, 546 N.Y.S.2d 180 (App. Div. 4th Dept. 1988).

[Reader presumes N.Y. from the reporter citation, but the citation is not to a case from the state's highest court, and thus the reader requires information about the division of the appellate court that decided the case].

---

[6] A further difference between ALWD and the BB is that the BB indicates parenthetical references to appellate courts using a Ct. in the parentheses, while ALWD does not. In the BB, the California Court of Appeal is Cal. Ct. App. while in ALWD it is Cal. App. In the BB, the Illinois Appellate Court is Ill. App. Ct. while in ALWD it is Ill. App.

Sometimes an official reporter with the state's initials reports more than just the highest court's cases. If so, you must supply additional information to correct the reader's erroneous presumption, but only as much as is necessary to identify the court:

> *Roth v. Vidal*, 665 Idaho 456, 458 (App. 1st Dist. 1987).

> not   *Roth v. Vidal*, 665 Idaho 456, 458 (Idaho App. 1st Dist. 1987).

III. SUBSEQUENT HISTORY

Subsequent history codes must be used if there is relevant subsequent history to a case (for example, *appeal dismissed, aff'd, rev'd on other grounds, mandamus denied*, etc. See ALWD R. 12.8(a)). Examples:

> *Rogers v. Hammerstein*, 388 F.2d 345, 366 (2d Cir. 1958), *aff'd*, 354 U.S. 578 (1959).

The denial of a writ of certiorari (cert. denied) or the denial of other discretionary appeals from a court of last resort with selective jurisdiction should not be included unless the denial occurred less than two years ago or if "the denial is particularly relevant" (*See* ALWD Sidebar 12.6). A citation that has no subsequent history information represents that there have been no relevant legal proceedings in the case occurring after the cited opinion.

If the year of the original opinion is the same as the year of the subsequent opinion(s), you only put the year in parentheses after the last citation. In the following example, all of these opinions would be from 1996:

> *Apple Computer v. Gates*, 789 P.2d 876, 878 (Wash. App. 1st Dist.), *reh'g denied*, 791 P.2d 345 (Wash. App. 1st Dist.), *appeal dismissed*, 792 P.2d 579 (Wash. 1996).

IV. PARENTHETICALS (ALWD R. 12.11)

Parentheticals are used to provide useful explanatory information that will help the reader understand the significance of a case or the lack thereof. For example, parentheticals can be used for providing some details of the facts that show why you are citing it, or some clarification of the holding if this might not be clear from what preceded the citation, or to clear up a possible misconception about the case not obvious from a naked cite; for example, "Hey reader, this was a plurality opinion, not a majority opinion." Examples:

> *Jones v. Clinton*, 156 F.3d 678, 681 (8th Cir. 1999) (court indicated that defendant lied).

> *Marshall v. Brennan*, 477 U.S. 345 (1969) (per curiam).

Punctuation and complete sentences usually are avoided in parentheticals in order to save space. An exception exists if you actually quote a whole phrase or sentence from the case. Compare this example with the first example above:

> *Jones v. Clinton*, 156 F.3d 678, 681 (8th Cir. 1999) ("We find that the defendant lied to the country.").

If you are citing non-majority opinions, they are noted with their author:

> *Tex v. Texas Horn Co.*, 357 Ark. 456, 468 (1948) (Simpson, J., dissenting).

Multiple parentheticals are possible. Please separate each parenthetical with a space:

> *Marshall v. Brennan*, 477 U.S. 345, 349 (1969) (per curiam) (noting that the "clear and convincing evidence" standard applied).

V. SHORT FORMS FOR CASES

The long form of a citation need only be given once in any document; in fact, it is bad form to present it more than once. People will think you are citing a different case and got the citation wrong. In addition to the form used for all authorities (*id.*), with cases, you should use the plaintiff's name (or a short recognizable part of the name if the name is long, as in the case of a corporation) along with the volume-reporter-page number, or one of the other approved forms listed below when you are doing a repeat cite in a situation where *id.* cannot be used:

Full cite: *Alexander v. Jones*, 432 N.W.2d 356 (Wash. 1988).

Proper short forms: *Alexander*, 432 N.W.2d at 358-59.
In *Alexander*, the court dismissed the suit. 432 N.W.2d at 358-59.

Full cite: *Speedy Drydock and Transfer Co., Inc. v. Bosley*, 517 S.W.2d 425 (Mo. App. E. Dist. 1978).

Proper short forms: *Speedy Drydock*, 517 S.W.2d at 426.
Speedy Drydock is the only case to apply the cruel and unusual standard. 517 S.W.2d at 426.

The following forms are **incorrect**:

> *Alexander* at 358.

> *Speedy Drydock, id.* at 426.

If the plaintiff's name is too common (or shows up too many times in cases you are going to cite), use the defendant's name instead:

> *United States v. Calandra* should be shortened to *Calandra*
> *Smith v. Netanyahu* should be *Netanyahu*
> *Commissioner v. Mitchell* should be *Mitchell*
>
> *Shalala v. Harris* should be *Harris* [This would be the case if Donna Shalala is the Commissioner of Health and Human Services, and so is a plaintiff in 9 out of the 10 cases you are citing in your Social Security case.]

VI. CITATION FORMS FOR OTHER AUTHORITIES

STATUTES AND CODES

The typical citation to a federal statute contains five or six components, depending on whether the code is official or unofficial (ALWD R. 14).

(1) Title or volume number where the statute appears;
(2) Abbreviated name of the code;
(3) Section symbol;
(4) The section number of the statute; and
(5) The year the code was published (not the year the statute was enacted or became effective).

When you are citing a statutory section, use the official version of the statute. Do not cite the annotated or other unofficial versions. Of course, if you are citing some commentary or notes or committee reports or interpretative information on the statute that is not found in the official version, certainly cite to the annotated version or wherever the material appears. If you are citing to an unofficial code, then you must include an additional item: the Publisher's name in parentheses prior to the date.

If you never learned how to do a § sign on your computer, write "sec." instead. For example, Mo. Rev. Stat. sec. 400.2-201 (1986). If a ¶ symbol is involved, and you cannot make the ¶ symbol, write "para." instead. More than one section is expressed by §§ or "secs." More than one paragraph is expressed by ¶¶ or "paras."

You are free to use the official or the popular name of the statute in your citation sentence or clause:

> Securities Act of 1933, 15 U.S.C. §§ 77a-77aa (1994).
> Labor Management Relations (Taft-Hartley) Act § 301(a), 29 U.S.C. § 185(a) (1988).

Note the spacing in the following examples—the § sign stands for the word section so there is a single space before and after the § sign.

Federal:

      Official: 30 U.S.C. § 523 (1988).

      Annotated: 30 U.S.C.A. § 523 (West 1995).

Illinois:

      Official: 510 Ill. Comp. Stat. 5/16 (1996).

      Annotated: 510 Ill. Comp. Stat. Ann. 5/16 (West 1995).

New York:

The annotated versions of the statutes published by McKinney and Consolidated Laws Service are official. A third unannotated form published by Gould also is official; go figure New York would be so lax. The form of the citation is stranger still:

    N.Y. [subject matter abbrev.] Law § x (publisher 19xx).

    As in: N.Y. Gen. Constr. Law § 456 (McKinney 1989).
            N.Y. Mun. Home Rule Law § 77(a) (Consol. 1990).

CONSTITUTIONS

Under ALWD R. 13, a constitution is cited by the abbreviated name of the country or state followed by the word "Const.," followed by the abbreviated name of the section, article, or amendment, and none of it is underlined or italicized:

U.S. Const. amend IV.
Ariz. Const. art. 2, sec. 6.

RULES

Rules of procedure and evidence are abbreviated as shown in ALWD R. 17 and are not underlined:

Fed. R. Evid. 401.
Fed. R. Civ. P. 23.
Fed. R. App. P. 4(a).

Under ALWD R. 19, administrative rules and regulations are cited to the Code of Federal Regulations (CFR), if possible, and to the Federal Register or other source if not found in CFR. A typical citation contains: (1) the volume number; (2) the abbreviation C.F.R.; (3) the section sign and section number (called the pinpoint reference); and (4) the year of publication of the most recent edition of the C.F.R.

28 C.F.R. § 637.7 (1990).

You can add the name of the regulation:

Barge Overnight Locking Regulations, 85 C.F.R. § 251.1 (1990).

RESTATEMENTS, TREATISES, and OTHER BOOKS

ALWD R. 27 states that restatements should be italicized (or underlined),[7] so you would cite them as:

Restatement (Second) of Torts § 23 (1977).

Other books, treatises and non-periodic materials are governed by Rules 22, 24, (A.L.R.s), 25 (dictionaries) and 26 (encyclopedias), and generally will be cited with: (1) author's full name, followed by a comma; (2) title of the book or topic name (italicized or underlined); (3) pinpoint references (including volume, section and page(s) that you are citing); (4) translator (if any); (5) in parentheses, the edition number (if any); and (6) the publisher; and (7) the year of publication. For example:

E. Allen Farnsworth, *Contracts* 345, 346-48 (110th ed. West 2000).
76 Am. Jur. 2d *Trusts* §§ 1-4 (1992 & Supp. 2001).

Depending on the type of source you want to cite, you should refer to the specific ALWD rule governing it, because some of the information can vary.

LAW REVIEW ARTICLES

Finally, ALWD R. 23 covers legal and other periodicals, such as law reviews. The form is: (1) author's full name, followed by a comma; (2) the title of the article (italicized or underlined), followed by a comma; (3) the volume number of the law review; (4) the abbreviated name of the law review (Appendix 5 for specific abbreviations and spacing);

---

[7]   This differs from the BB—The BB notes that Restatements are not to be underlined or italicized (<u>see</u> B6.1.3 and Rule 12.8).

(5) page number where the article begin, followed by the pinpoint page(s) you are citing; and (6) year of publication. For example:

> Christy H. DeSanctis, *The ALWD Citation Manual is Fun*, 99 Colum. L. Rev. 23, 26 (1999).

Part II. The Bluebook (A Uniform System of Citation)

GENERAL RULES

The Bluebook was created by the law review boards of several Ivy League law schools; in the fall of 2005, it will be published in its 18th edition. The vast majority of the American legal community currently follows the Bluebook's citation rules, so there is no getting around the arduous task of learning these forms. If you don't learn them, your writing will look sloppy, unprofessional, and worst of all, incorrect.

Though the Bluebook was created primarily for use in law review articles, the most recent edition (the 18th) goes much further toward bridging the citation gap between scholarly publications and documents used by practitioners. The white-colored pages, which comprise the bulk of the book, still provide forms and examples geared mainly toward authors of law review articles. However, several rules specifically explain the difference between law review citations and citations in other legal documents (see, e.g., R.2), which is a helpful new feature of the 18th edition. In addition, the Bluebook now includes forty pages at the front that are directed specifically toward authors of legal office memoranda and court briefs. These blue-colored pages – called, appropriately, the "Bluepages" – provide an introduction to basic legal citation principles for law students and practicing attorneys. They are a much-expanded version of what were previously known as "Practitioner's Notes" and essentially constitute a summary of the 13 rules most commonly used in legal practice. Following the Bluepages (cited herein as "B#") are two practitioner-directed "Tables." BT.1 suggests abbreviations for words most commonly found in the title of court documents; BT.2 references the "Local Rules" in force in various state and federal courts – which *always* take precedence over the Bluebook. Additional tables containing information about different jurisdictions and publications are found at the back of the manual.

The forms used as examples throughout this section of this Chapter follow the forms noted in the Bluepages and in all respects comply with the Bluebook 18th edition, so you can rely on our examples when drafting your office memoranda and court briefs.

I. CITATION SENTENCES AND CITATION CLAUSES

Citations to authority are phrased in two ways: citation clauses and citation sentences. See Bluebook Rule 1.1 (hereinafter "BB ___"). Titles and styles of cases and many other authorities are to be underlined or italicized (but not both). In any example in the BB section of this chapter where you see underlining, the underlined portion of the citation could have been italicized. <u>See</u> B2 (p. 4). A choice to italicize or underline must be followed consistently in your document; you cannot switch from italicizing to underlining within the same document.

A. Citation sentence

A citation sentence is used when you are citing authority after a period that ends a complete sentence. The citation sentence starts with a capital letter, and ends with a period:

> The standard is one of gross negligence. <u>Smith v. Jones</u>, 118 S.W.2d 222, 224 (Mo. 1947).

Multiple cases and other authorities in a citation sentence are separated by semi-colons:

> The standard is one of gross negligence. Mo. Rev. Stat. § 232.12 (1986); <u>Smith v. Jones</u>, 118 S.W.2d 222, 224 (Mo. 1947); <u>Jones v. Carmichael</u>, 446 S.W.2d 333, 335 (Mo. Ct. App. E. Dist. 1987).

B. Citation clauses

When a citation supports only part of a sentence, the citation is inserted in the sentence, set off by commas before and after. This is referred to as a citation clause:

> The Illinois Dog Bite Statute, 510 Ill. Comp. Stat. 5/16 (1996), defines a dog-owner's liability for a dog bite.

Multiple authorities supporting a clause are separated by semi-colons, but the whole citation clause is set apart by commas as above. A citation clause does not necessarily start with a capital letter—it only does if you are citing an authority without any introductory phrase, and the authority starts with a capital letter. A sentence citation which supports the second clause can follow at the end of the second clause, after the period that ends the sentence, as in the following example:

> Dog bite liability requires a lack of provocation, either intentional or unintentional, <u>see</u> 510 Ill. Comp. Stat. 5/16 (1996); <u>Beckert v. Risberg</u>, 210 N.E.2d 207, 208 (Ill. 1965); <u>Nelson v. Lewis</u>, 344 N.E.2d 268, 270 (Ill. Ct. App. 5th Dist. 1976), but provocation can be offset if the dog's attack is particularly vicious and disproportionate to the provocation. <u>Nelson</u>, 344 N.E.2d at 271.

Within a citation sentence or citation clause, cite the highest and most recent control-ling authorities first, followed by lesser and earlier authorities in order of their weight. This order of presentation is most important.

Correct: A dog owner is liable for all injuries caused by his dog unless the dog is provoked by the victim. <u>Smithy v. Jonesy</u>, 123 S.W.2d 345, 347 (Mo. 1965); <u>Johnson v. Anderson</u>, 789 S.W.2d 234, 237 (Mo. Ct. App. E. Dist. 1989); <u>Son v. Anders</u>, 780 S.W.2d 134, 137 (Mo. Ct. App. E. Dist. 1980).

Incorrect: A dog owner is liable for all injuries caused by his dog unless the dog is provoked by the victim. <u>Johnson v. Anderson</u>, 789 S.W.2d 234, 237 (Mo. Ct. App. E. Dist. 1989); <u>Son v. Anders</u>, 780 S.W.2d 134, 137 (Mo. Ct. App. E. Dist. 1980); <u>Smithy v. Jonesy</u>, 123 S.W.2d 345, 347 (Mo. 1965).

In certain circumstances, you will be presenting a large number of authorities that are not controlling and may be of equal importance. This happens frequently in law review articles, and remember that the Bluebook was designed to be a citation manual for law review articles. When you are in this situation, the order of authorities cited according to BB 1.4 is:

1. Constitutions and other foundational documents
2. Statutes
3. Treaties and other international agreements
4. Cases, in the order of:

<u>Federal</u>
a. U.S. Supreme Court
b. Courts of Appeals
c. Court of Claims, Court of Customs and Patent Appeals, and bankruptcy appellate panels
d. District courts, Judicial Panel on Multidistrict Litigation, Court of International Trade
e. District bankruptcy courts and Railroad Reorganization Court
f. Court of Federal Claims, Court of Appeals for the Armed Forces, and Tax Court
g. Administrative agencies (alphabetically by agency)

<u>State</u>
h. Courts (alphabetically by state, and then by level of court within a state, highest to lowest)
i. Administrative agencies (alphabetically by state and then by agency within each state)

Foreign
j. Courts (alphabetically by jurisdiction and then by rank within each jurisdiction)
k. Agencies (alphabetically by jurisdiction and then by agency within each jurisdiction)

International
l. International Court of Justice, Permanent Court of International Justice
m. Other international tribunals and arbital panels (alphabetically by name)

5. Legislative materials
6. Administrative and executive materials
7. Resolutions, regulations, and decisions of intergovernmental organizations
8. Records, briefs, pleadings of litigants
9. Secondary sources, in the order of:

    a. Uniform codes, model codes, and restatements
    b. Books and pamphlets
    c. Law review articles and works in journals
    d. Book reviews not written by students
    e. Student-written journal articles and book reviews
    f. Annotations (for example, American Law Reports)
    g. Magazine and newspaper articles
    h. Working papers
    i. Unpublished materials
    j. Electronic sources

Within a category of cases (for example, federal appellate court cases), the materials are listed in reverse chronological order (most recent first, and so on). If the year is the same, then list them in alphabetical order. For some of the other categories (constitutions, statutes) see BB 1.4 for the specific ordering rules (which generally follow a federal-state-foreign format).

II. INTRODUCTORY PHRASES (BB 4.1)

Either a citation sentence or a citation clause can be preceded by an introductory word or phrase. When the word or phrase begins a citation sentence, it is capitalized. Otherwise it is not.

The entire introductory word or phrase is underlined or italicized in practitioner's formatting. Each phrase connotes something different about the authority that follows it:

[No introductory phrase]	Connotes that the authority contains (states) the exact or nearly the exact phrase or sentence for which you are citing the authority (i.e., the words you use are 99% the

same as in the source). You may have changed the verb tense or dropped a minor word or two (this, than, the, etc.), but otherwise, one turning to the authority would find that statement in the authority at the page or section to which you are citing. This form is used whether or not you actually put quotation marks around the statement.

If the statement is a legal proposition or conclusion (as opposed to a fact or something other than a statement about the law), this form also connotes that the statement is part of the holding of the case.

<u>See</u>

Connotes that the authority contains the idea and the concept for which you are citing the authority, but the exact words will not be found in the authority. The authority must directly support your statement. You still would cite to a particular page or section of the authority where the idea or concept is stated.

<u>See also</u>

Connotes that the authority contains related or additional information or material that supports the proposition for which the authority is cited, but the exact statement (concept or idea) is not found in the authority. A parenthetical (<u>see</u> BB 1.5) should be used to explain why or how the material supports the proposition. For example:

> The <u>Erie</u> doctrine confuses the issue of choice of law. <u>Masters v. Johnson</u>, 55 Ohio App. 23, 24 (1987); <u>see also</u> <u>Hill v. Williams</u>, 766 P.2d 433, 444 (Okla. 1978) (<u>Erie</u> confuses most issues of conflict of laws, including forum selection).

<u>Accord</u>

When you have two or more authorities that clearly support the statement or proposition for which you are citing them, but the actual statement only is found in one of the authorities, use <u>accord</u> to preface the other citations. For example:

> A doctor must use reasonably prudent methods to detect viral agents. Mo. Rev. Stat. § 516.132.2; <u>accord</u> <u>Smith v. Jones</u>, 455 S.W.2d 232, 240 (Mo.

Ct. App. E. Dist. 1986); <u>Janes v. Roth</u>, 432 N.E.2d 222, 223 (Ill. App. Ct. 5th Dist. 1976).

<u>Cf.</u>

Connotes that the cited authority states a different proposition from the main proposition for which the citation is given, but the second proposition is sufficiently analogous as to lend support to the main proposition. A parenthetical or other explanation should be used to explain the relevance. For example:

> Architects must take reasonable care to choose a design that will preclude subsidence of the building. <u>Cf.</u> <u>Cliff v. Hector</u>, 239 S.E.2d 235, 237 (S.C. Ct. App. 1st Dist. 1975) (civil engineer required to take reasonable care to choose non-subsiding design); <u>Uriah v. Heap</u>, 236 S.E.2d 457, 459 (S.C. Ct. App. 1st Dist. 1973) (same, building contractor).

<u>Compare</u> . . . [<u>and</u>] . . . <u>with</u>

Used to express that a comparison of one or more cases with one or more other cases will reveal something about the way the law works in this area. Again, a parenthetical explanation should be used to drive the point home even more. **Note well** that in this citation form **commas** separate the authorities, not semi-colons. For example:

> If the damages are nominal, a defamation claim will be dismissed. <u>Compare</u> <u>Norton v. Cramden</u>, 432 Vt. 234 (1990) (nominal damages of fifteen dollars, claim dismissed), <u>and</u> <u>Ricardo v. Mertz</u>, 335 Vt. 245 (1982) (nominal damages of two dollars, claim dismissed), <u>with</u> <u>Scooby v. Shaggy</u>, 553 Vt. 987 (1997) (damages of $150,000, claim not dismissed), <u>and</u> <u>Hadji v. Quest</u>, 288 Vt. 256 (1978) (damages of $75,000, claim not dismissed), <u>and</u> <u>Van Dyke v. Petry</u>, 228 Vt. 667 (1975) (damages of $55,000, claim not dismissed).

<u>E.g.</u>, (<u>See, e.g.</u>,)

Introduces authorities that support the proposition stated. The concept and general proposition would be found in the cited authorities, but not necessarily the exact word or phrase you are stating. Note the comma that is required at the end of this signal. Unlike <u>see</u> or <u>see also</u>, the phrase "<u>e.g.</u>," is used if you are stating a rather general legal proposition and wish to suggest that there are many authorities that hold this, and the listed authorities are a representative sample. If the listed authorities actually do not state the exact proposition for which you are citing them, but support it nonetheless, use "<u>see, e.g.</u>," instead (and put commas after each word in this signal).

<u>But see</u> (<u>But see, e.g.</u>, <u>But cf.</u>)   If you are citing an authority contrary to the proposition stated, you would use <u>but see</u> in situations where you would use <u>see</u> or no introductory phrase, and <u>but see, e.g.</u>, if you are listing several contrary authorities that go against the proposition. Use <u>but cf.</u> if the contrary authority is not directly on point, but sufficiently analogous to cause concern; a parenthetical should be used to explain the state of things. For example:

> Most states have adopted the UCC Sales provisions. <u>But see</u> La. Rev. Stat. Ann. § 355.1 (West 1988). In the majority of states, statute of frauds requires contracts for goods over $500 in value to be in writing. <u>But cf.</u> <u>Goodman v. Du Bois</u>, 235 La. 468, 469 (1986) (civil code requires writing only for specific purpose contracts, or for land sales).

<u>See generally</u>   The most nebulous of introductory phrases, <u>see generally</u> is used to introduce background or other relevant material—often secondary sources—that are helpful to an understanding of the issues.

III. SHORTHAND DEVICES FOR REPEAT CITATIONS (BB 10.9 and B5.2)

When you cite the same authority more than once, you do not have to keep writing the full citation form (also called the "long form") for the work over and over again. You can use the following to make short work of repeat citations:

<u>Id.</u>   Use as a shorthand to recite the exact same authority that you just previously cited, with no other authorities in between. Of course, a page number or section number might change. For example:

Red is used for anger. <u>Ida v. Ona</u>, 123 U.S. 234, 238 (1923). Blue is for peace. <u>Id.</u> Purple is for sorrow. <u>Id.</u> at 239.

The UCC statute of frauds requires a writing. Mo. Rev. Stat. § 400.2-201. The writing is necessary if the goods cost $500 or more. <u>Id.</u> However, the damages will still be limited to the costs to cover. <u>Id.</u> § 400.2-701 *et seq.*

You cannot use <u>id.</u> after a citation containing more than one authority. <u>Id.</u> can only refer back to a single author-ity, and you cannot use it to refer back to the authority last cited if that authority was paired with others. The following examples are *incorrect*:

Incorrect form   *The Erie doctrine confuses the issue of choice of law. <u>Masters v. Johnson</u>, 55 N.E.2d 23, 24 (Ill. 1957); <u>Hill v. Wil-liams</u>, 766 P.2d 433, 444 (Okla. 1978). It also confuses the law of forum selec-tion. <u>Id.</u>*

[Cannot use <u>id.</u> here because preceding ci-tation sentence had two cases in it. <u>Id.</u> can-not be used to refer back to both, nor does it refer back to the last one cited.][8]

Incorrect form   *Illinois is a comparative negligence state. <u>Ricardo v. McGillicutty</u>, 345 N.E.2d 789, 791 (Ill. 1967); <u>Arnez v. Ball</u>, 788 N.E.2d 654, 656 (Ill. App. Ct. 1988). Plaintiff's percentage of fault reduces the verdict, even if plaintiff's fault exceeds 50 percent. <u>Arnez</u>, id. at 657.*

[Specifying which of the two preceding cases you are referring back to does not

---

[8]   Note, however, that sources identified in explanatory parentheticals, explanatory phrases, or sub-sequent history are ignored for purposes of this rule (<u>see</u> B5.2).

> **help—it still is bad citation form to use id. here.**]

Instead, you must use a different short form for the multiple authorities or whichever one of them you want to cite to. These examples are **CORRECT**:

> The Erie doctrine confuses the issue of choice of law. Masters v. Johnson, 55 N.E.2d 23, 24 (Ill. 1957); Hill v. Williams, 766 P.2d 433, 444 (Okla. 1978). It also confuses the law of forum selection. Masters, 55 N.E.2d at 24; Hill, 766 P.2d at 444.

> Illinois is a comparative negligence state. Ricardo v. McGillicutty, 345 N.E.2d 789, 791 (Ill. 1967); Arnez v. Ball, 788 N.E.2d 654, 656 (Ill. App. Ct. 5th Dist. 1988). Plaintiff's percentage of fault reduces the verdict, even if plaintiff's fault exceeds 50 percent. Arnez, 788 N.E.2d at 657.

A few wrinkles to the id. rule are worth noting. First, when citing cases **in law review footnotes**, the "5 footnote rule" applies to **any short form citation**. This means that a short form (including id.) is appropriate only to refer back to a case in one of the **preceding 5 footnotes**. If you are attempting to refer back to a case cited prior to that, you must use a full citation. **The same rule does not apply to citations in practitioners' documents – only to law review footnotes** (BB 10.9(a)).

Second, when id. refers to a **different opinion** in the same case, a parenthetical is required. In other words, if you have been citing to a majority opinion for several citations, use of id. is appropriate; however, if you then shift to citing a concurring opinion, you must include a parenthetical so indicating (BB 10.9(b)(I)).

Third, for cases in which a parallel citation is required, the id. form looks slightly different (to avoid confusion):

Terrenzoni v. Cosgrove, 500 Pa. 105, 110, 240 A.2d 540, 545 (1968).

becomes: Id. at 111, 240 A.2d at 546.

Supra

According to BB 4.2, <u>supra</u> refers to an earlier cited **book, treatise, or other volume,** when it is not the immediately preceding authority. (If it is the immediately preceding authority, you use <u>id.</u>). Even when the source was first cited in a footnote, you no longer reference the footnote number with <u>supra</u> in the current edition of the Bluebook. For example, if you cited Laurence Tribe's treatise, <u>Constitutional Law,</u> earlier in your work in footnote 2, you can use the following form to cite it again later on:

> Tribe, <u>supra</u>, at 335-36.
> (not Tribe, <u>supra</u> n. 2, at 335-36).

<u>Supra</u> is no longer used to refer to a previously cited case, statute or rule because they each have their own forms.

Infra

<u>Infra</u> is not used as an introductory phrase for citations to legal authority. <u>Infra</u> is used to direct attention to sections or footnotes or other portions of the text that come later in the same document. When used in this way, <u>infra</u> usually follows the word <u>see</u>.

> <u>See</u> <u>infra</u> Part IV.
> <u>Infra</u> pp. 10-11.
> <u>See</u> sources cited <u>infra</u> note 7.

<u>Supra</u> also can be used in this informal way to refer back to a preceding section of the text.

> <u>See</u> <u>supra</u> part IV.
> <u>Supra</u> pp. 10-11.

CASES

I. STYLE OF THE CASE (BB 10)

The names of the first named parties on each side become the style of the case; they are separated by a "v." and underlined or italicized:

<u>Smith v. Jones</u>   not   <u>Smith, Bradley, and Tom v. Jones, Microsoft, Inc., Jones Brothers Constr. Co., and Mayfair Hotel Co.</u>

A. Certain words are omitted

Omit the parties' first names (unless they are part of a company name):

<u>Smith v. Jones</u>   not   <u>Roger Smith v. Percy Jones</u>

But <u>Roger L. Smith, Inc. v. Percy Jones and Co.</u> is correct because these are company names.

Titles, offices, before or after the party's name (for example, Mr., Mrs., Dr., M.D., PhD, Commander, General, Surgeon General of the United States) are omitted unless the person is sued only by her title, and her actual name does not appear in the case style:

<u>Brit v. Mayor of Santa Monica</u>   [if the Mayor is not sued in her own name]

<u>Brit v. McDonald</u>   [if Mayor McDonald is sued under her own name]

But not <u>Brit v. McDonald, Mayor of Santa Monica</u> and not <u>Dr. Brit, M.D. v. Ms. McDonald</u>

B.   Use Bluebook standard abbreviations

The Bluebook requires you to abbreviate certain words in very definite, specified ways. In general, the Bluebook requires single capital letters to be grouped together, but any other combination of two or more letters to be set apart from single capitals or other combinations by a space. For example, the following abbreviations are **correct**:

S.D.N.Y.
E.D. Mo.
F. Supp.
Ill. App. Ct.

Ordinals, such as 2d and 3d, are treated as one capital letter, and can be grouped together with other single capital letters, as in the following examples:

F.2d
N.Y.3d

But if the ordinal follows a cluster of two or more letters, it must stand alone:

Ill. App. 3d
F. Supp. 2d
Cal. Rptr. 4th

Various rules and tables in the Bluebook provide other abbreviations:

In the relation of, on behalf of, become: **ex rel.** (BB 10.2.1(b))

Petition of, In the matter of, In re the Will of, In re the Estate of, become: **In re** (BB 10.2.1(b))

Abbreviate company, party, and other names in case styles according to BB Table T.6:

Consolidated becomes Consol.
Enterprise becomes Enter.
Industry, industries, industrial become Indus.
South is S.
East is E.

Court names are abbreviated according to BB Table T.7. [Note the spacing]:

Appellate Division is App. Div.
Commonwealth Court is Commw. Ct.
Superior Court is Super. Ct.
Judicial Panel on Multidistrict Litigation is J.P.M.L.

Case history terms' abbreviations and non-abbreviations are found in BB Table T.8. Guess what the following abbreviations refer to:

aff'd
rev'd
cert. denied
rev'd on other grounds

There also are official non-abbreviations, as follows:

appeal denied
vacated
modifying
mandamus denied

Follow the rules for state's abbreviations and non-abbreviations in BB Table T.10. The Bluebook *rarely* uses the U.S. Postal Service abbreviation. For example:

> Ala.
> Del.
> Miss.
> N.M.

But see

> Alaska
> Iowa
> Idaho
> Ohio
> Utah

Abbreviate other terms according to Bluebook standard abbreviations in BB Tables T.6-T.16.

II. REQUIRED INFORMATION FOR CASES (BB 10.1)

Each citation must tell four pieces of information: (1) the case name; (2) where you find the case; (3) the court; (4) the year of the case.

In a typical citation the style (parties' names) is followed by a comma (the comma is not underlined or italicized), then the volume number of the source of the case, then the abbreviation for the volume or reporter, then the page number where the case begins. Then comes the parentheses with the court code and year. For example:

> Presley v. Jackson, 833 S.W.2d 222 (Tenn. 1996).

If you are referring to a particular part of the case (and whenever possible you should be referring to a particular part of the case), you must provide a **jump cite** (also known as a **pinpoint cite** or **pin cite**) that refers the reader to the specific page or pages of the opinion that support your proposition. To create a jump cite, put a comma after the page number where the case begins and then cite the page(s) where the material appears. More than one page can be referenced. If the material is on separate pages, cite them separately: 23, 24, 29, 35. If the material carries over from one page to another, indicate this in this way: 23-24, 35-37. If the second page number is a three or four digit number, reduce it to a two digit number, unless it follows a two digit number: 137-38, 205-06, 1078-79, 99-101. The following forms are all **correct**:

> Presley v. Jackson, 833 S.W.2d 222, 225 (Tenn. 1996).
> Presley v. Jackson, 833 S.W.2d 222, 226-27 (Tenn. 1996).
> Presley v. Jackson, 833 S.W.2d 222, 225-26, 228, 230 (Tenn. 1996).

If you are referring to material on the first page of a case, you must repeat the first page number:

Presley v. Jackson, 833 S.W.2d 222, 222 (Tenn. 1996).

The court codes for each United States jurisdiction are listed in BB Table T.1. Study these well, and **note the spacing** of these codes. The codes for foreign jurisdictions are in BB Table T.2.

If the court that wrote the opinion is obvious from one of the reporters you are citing (for example, a reporter with the state's initials is presumed to report the cases of the highest court in the state; a reporter with the state's initials and "App." added on is presumed to report the decisions of the state's intermediate level appellate court), then you should not put the court designation in the parentheses with the year. The following forms are **correct**:

Constance v. Reader, 234 N.Y.2d 245, 247, 456 N.E.2d 234, 236, 565 N.Y.S.2d 238, 239 (1965).

[Reader presumes from the N.Y. reporter citation that the case is from the N.Y. Court of Appeals, the highest court in New York].

Will v. Smith, 345 Ill. App. 2d 235, 237 (5th Dist. 1989).

[Reader presumes from the Ill. App. citation that the case is from the Illinois Appellate Court, the intermediate level appellate court in Illinois].

Sometimes an official reporter with the state's initials reports more than just the highest court's cases. If so, you must supply additional information to correct the reader's erroneous presumption, but only as much as is necessary to identify the court:

Roth v. Vidal, 665 Idaho 456, 458 (Ct. App. 1st Dist. 1987).

not Roth v. Vidal, 665 Idaho 456, 458 (Idaho Ct. App. 1st Dist. 1987).

Note: The 1st Dist. in the parentheses in the example above is an example of a district or division identifier that is used if the case you are citing has the potential to be controlling authority. You use it to show the reader whether or not the case actually is of the proper district or circuit to be controlling. The Bluebook tells you to include reference to the district, department, or division of an intermediate level appellate court if the information is "of particular relevance." (See BB 10.4, p. 90.) We interpret "of particular relevance" to mean controlling or not controlling. In the example above, the lawsuit would have been governed by Idaho law, and filed somewhere in Idaho, so that a certain district of the Idaho Court of Appeals would be controlling. If there is no way that the case you are citing is controlling (for example, if the case you are citing is not an Idaho case), you do not use the district or division identifier.

If you are preparing a document (pleading, motion, memorandum) that will be filed with a state court and you are citing a case from a state court in the same state where you are litigating, you must consult the local rules of the court to determine if the local rules require you to provide a fifth piece of information: a parallel citation to the state's official reporter, if any. This *only* applies to documents that will be filed with the court, and *only* if the local rules of the court require you to provide a parallel citation. It does not apply to office memoranda even if you are writing a memo and you know that your case has been filed in a certain state court, and you are about to cite a case from a court of the same state.

Examples of this for the states of Illinois and New York, are shown below:

Illinois:

Supreme Court:	Ann v. Joann, 222 Ill. 2d 333, 444 N.E.2d 555 (1990).
	[the form to use if you are writing a document that will be filed in a court in Illinois whose local rules require you to provide a parallel citation]
	Ann v. Joann, 444 N.E.2d 555 (Ill. 1990).
	[the form to use if you are not writing a document that will be filed in a court in Illinois, or if the local rules do not require you to provide a parallel citation]
Appeals Court:	Bill v. Jeff, 322 Ill. App. 3d 554, 677 N.E.2d 776 (1st Dist. 1988).
	[form for an Illinois court if the local rules require you to provide a parallel citation]
	Bill v. Jeff, 677 N.E.2d 776 (Ill. App. Ct. 1st Dist. 1988).
	[form other than to an Illinois court or if the local rules do not require you to provide a parallel citation]
New York:	(especially note the spacing here):
Court of Appeals:	Van Halen v. Death Row Records, 522 N.Y.2d 333, 454 N.E.2d 545, 778 N.Y.S.2d 889 (1990).

[if you are writing to a court in N.Y. and if the local rules require you to provide a parallel citation. Note the **two** parallel citations]

Van Halen v. Death Row Records, 454 N.E.2d 545 (N.Y. 1990).

[if you are not writing to a court in N.Y. or if the local rules do not require you to provide a parallel citation]

If you are citing to a Court of Appeals case before 1848, note that the name of the highest court may not have been the Court of Appeals—check out BB at pp. 220-221.

Supreme Court, App. Div.:   Cash v. Sun Records, 822 A.D.2d 554, 877 N.Y.S.2d 886 (1st Dep't 1988).

[to N.Y. court whose local rules require parallel citations]

Cash v. Sun Records, 877 N.Y.S.2d 886 (App. Div. 1st Dep't 1988).

[other than to N.Y. court or if the local rules do not require you to provide a parallel citation]

Although the BB may appear to contradict itself, follow the above and leave out the N.Y. from the parentheses when citing an appellate division case from N.Y.S.2d. We find direct support for this conclusion on page 90 of the Bluebook (BB 10.4). Note that if your case is before 1896, it may be from a different volume or court than noted above.

Trial courts: Ross v. Motown Records, 677 Misc. 2d 668, 677 N.Y.S.2d 887 (Sup. Ct. Queens County 1988).

[writing to a N.Y. court whose local rules require a parallel citation. This is a cite to a Supreme Court case][9]

---

[9] Here, you are identifying the specific court in the parentheses, because it is "of particular relevance" to the reader. In a multi-level trial court system like New York's, it is relevant to show what level of court is cited and what county it is from because it may affect the persuasive value of the opinion. BB 10.4, p. 90.

In re Gill, 344 Misc. 2d 853, 456 N.Y.S.2d 891 (Sur. Ct. Duchess County 1975).

[to a N.Y. court requiring parallel citations, citing a Surrogate's court case]

Ross v. Motown Records, 677 N.Y.S.2d 887 (Sup. Ct. Queens County 1988).

[not writing to N.Y. court or if the local rules do not require you to provide a parallel citation]

III. SUBSEQUENT HISTORY

Subsequent history codes must be used if there is relevant subsequent history to a case (for example, appeal dismissed, aff'd, rev'd on other grounds, mandamus denied, etc. - BB Table T.8). Example:

Rogers v. Hammerstein, 388 F.2d 345, 366 (2d Cir. 1958), aff'd, 354 U.S. 578 (1959).

The denial of a writ of certiorari (cert. denied) or the denial of other discretionary appeals should not be included under BB 10.7.1 unless the denial occurred less than two years ago or if "the denial is particularly relevant."

A citation that has no subsequent history information represents that there have been no relevant legal proceedings in the case occurring after the cited opinion.

If the year of the original opinion is the same as the year of the subsequent opinion(s), you only put the year in parentheses after the last citation. In the following example, all of these opinions would be from 1996:

Apple Computer v. Gates, 789 P.2d 876, 878 (Wash. Ct. App. 1st Dist.), reh'g denied, 791 P.2d 345 (Wash. Ct. App. 1st Dist.), appeal dismissed, 792 P.2d 579 (Wash. 1996).

IV. PARENTHETICALS (BB 10.6)

Parentheticals are used to provide useful explanatory information that will help the reader understand the significance of a case or the lack thereof. For example, parentheticals can be used for providing some details of the facts that show why you are citing it, or some clarification of the holding if this might not be clear from what preceded the citation, or to clear up a possible misconception about the case not obvious from a naked cite; for example, "Hey reader, this was a plurality opinion, not a majority opinion." Examples:

Jones v. Clinton, 156 F.3d 678, 681 (8th Cir. 1999) (court indicated that defendant lied).

Marshall v. Brennan, 477 U.S. 345 (1969) (per curiam).

Punctuation and complete sentences are usually avoided in parentheticals in order to save space. An exception exists if you actually quote a whole phrase or sentence from the case. Compare this example with the first example above:

Jones v. Clinton, 156 F.3d 678, 681 (8th Cir. 1999) ("We find that the defendant lied to the country.").

If you are citing non-majority opinions, they are noted with their author:

Tex v. Texas Horn Co., 357 Ark. 456, 468 (1948) (Simpson, J., dissenting).

Multiple parentheticals are possible. Please separate each parenthetical with a space:

Marshall v. Brennan, 477 U.S. 345, 349 (1969) (per curiam) (noting that the "clear and convincing evidence" standard applied).

V. SHORT FORMS FOR CASES (BB 10.9 and B5.2. Please also re-read what we wrote above in connection with use of short forms generally.)

The long form of a citation need only be given once in any document; in fact, it is bad form to present it more than once. People will think you are citing a different case and got the citation wrong. In addition to the form used for all authorities (id.), with cases, you should use the plaintiff's name (or a short recognizable part of the name if the name is long, as in the case of a corporation) along with the volume-reporter-page number, or one of the other approved forms listed below when you are doing a repeat cite in a situation where id. cannot be used:

Full cite: Alexander v. Jones, 432 S.W.2d 356 (Mo. 1988).

Proper short forms: Alexander, 432 S.W.2d at 358-59.

In Alexander, the court dismissed the suit. 432 S.W.2d at 358-59.

Full cite: Speedy Drydock and Transfer Co., Inc. v. Bosley, 517 S.W.2d 425 (Mo. Ct. App. E. Dist. 1978).

Proper short forms: Speedy Drydock, 517 S.W.2d at 426.
Speedy Drydock is the only case to apply the cruel and unusual standard. 517 S.W.2d at 426.

The following forms are *incorrect*:

> <u>Alexander</u> at 358.
> <u>Speedy Drydock</u>, <u>id.</u> at 426.

If the plaintiff's name is too common (or shows up too many times in cases you are going to cite), use the defendant's name instead:

> <u>United States v. Calandra</u> should be shortened to <u>Calandra</u>
> <u>Smith v. Netanyahu</u> should be <u>Netanyahu</u>
> <u>Commissioner v. Mitchell</u> should be <u>Mitchell</u>
>
> <u>Shalala v. Harris</u> should be <u>Harris</u>
>
> > [This would be the case if Donna Shalala is the Commissioner of Health and Human Services, and so is a plaintiff in 9 out of the 10 cases you are citing in your Social Security case.]

VI. CITATION FORMS FOR OTHER AUTHORITIES

STATUTES AND CODES

The Bluebook devotes a whole chapter to the topic of citing statutes (BB 12), but a lot of that is devoted to obscure citation forms that do not come up much in practice. The typical citation to a statute contains: (1) the title or volume number where the statute appears; (2) the abbreviated name of the code; (3) the section number of the statute; (4) the year the code was published (not the year the statute was enacted or became effective).

Some state statutes put the code name first, then the volume and section number. You should follow whatever order is listed in BB Table T.1.

When you are citing a statutory section, use the official version of the statute. Do not cite the annotated or other unofficial versions. Of course, if you are citing some commentary or notes or committee reports or interpretative information on the statute that is not found in the official version, certainly cite to the annotated version or wherever the material appears.

If you never learned how to do a § sign on your computer, write "sec." instead. For example, Mo. Rev. Stat. sec. 400.2-201 (1986). If a ¶ symbol is involved, and you cannot make the ¶ symbol, write "para." instead. More than one section is expressed by §§ or "secs."[10] More than one paragraph is expressed by ¶¶ or "paras."

---

[10] <u>See</u> BB 12.9(b) and 6.2(c) for additional information on the use of the word "section" versus the section sign "§."

You are free to use the official or the popular name of the statute in your citation sentence or clause:

Securities Act of 1933, 15 U.S.C. §§ 77a-77aa (1994).

Labor Management Relations (Taft-Hartley) Act § 301(a), 29 U.S.C. § 185(a) (1988).

Note the spacing in the following examples—the § sign stands for the word section so there is a single space before and after the § sign.

Federal:

Official: 30 U.S.C. § 523 (1988).

Annotated: 30 U.S.C.A. § 523 (1995).

Illinois:

Official: 510 Ill. Comp. Stat. 5/16 (1996).

Annotated: 510 Ill. Comp. Stat. Ann. 5/16 (West 1995).

New York:

The annotated versions of the statutes published by McKinney and Consolidated Laws Service are official. A third unannotated form published by Gould also is official. The form of the citation is stranger still:

N.Y. [subject matter abbrev.] Law § x (publisher 19xx).

As in: N.Y. Gen. Constr. Law § 456 (McKinney 1989).

N.Y. Mun. Home Rule Law § 77(a) (Consol. 1990).

N.Y. C.P.L.R. 8209 (Gould 1991).

[Note the lack of a section symbol in the C.P.L.R. cite—Bluebook Table T.1, p. 222 tells you to leave it out.]

CONSTITUTIONS

Under BB 11, a constitution is cited by the abbreviated name of the country or state followed by the word "Const.," followed by the abbreviated name of the section, article, or amendment, and none of it is underlined or italicized:

U.S. Const. amend IV.
Ariz. Const. art. 2, sec. 6.

[Note well where the commas appear and do not appear in these examples.]

RULES

Rules of procedure and evidence are abbreviated as shown in BB 12.8.3 and are not underlined:

Fed. R. Evid. 401.
Fed. R. Civ. P. 23.
Fed. R. App. P. 4(a).

Under BB 14.2, administrative rules and regulations are cited to the Code of Federal Regulations (CFR), if possible, and to the Federal Register or other source if not found in CFR. A typical citation contains: (1) the volume number; (2) the abbreviation C.F.R.; (3) the section number; (4) the year of publication of the most recent edition of the C.F.R.

28 C.F.R. § 637.7 (1990).

You may include the name of the regulation:

Barge Overnight Locking Regulations, 85 C.F.R. § 251.1 (1990).

RESTATEMENTS, TREATISES, and OTHER BOOKS

Bluepages rule 6.1.3 and BB R. 12.8 provide that restatements are not underlined, so you would cite them as:

Restatement (Second) of Torts § 23 cmt. a, illus. 2 (1977).

Under BB 15, other books and treatises are to be cited with: (1) volume number (if any); (2) author's full name, followed by a comma; (3) title of the book (underlined or italicized); (4) page(s) or section number(s) that you are citing; (5) parentheses with edition number (if any); and (6) year of publication. For example:

2 Michael D. Murray, <u>Federal Practice as I Practice It</u> § 10.2 (4th ed. 1999).

E. Allen Farnsworth, <u>Contracts</u> 345, 346-48 (110th ed. 2000).

LAW REVIEW ARTICLES

Under BB 16, the form for citing law review articles is: (1) author's full name, followed by a comma; (2) the title of the article (underlined or italicized), followed by a comma; (3) the volume number of the law review; (4) the abbreviated name of the law review (check BB Table T.13 for spacing and abbreviations); (5) page number where the article appears, followed by the page(s) you are citing; and (6) year of publication. For example:

Christy H. DeSanctis, <u>The Bluebook is Fun</u>, 108 Colum. L. Rev. 19, 25 (2005).

Chapter 10

Introduction to Legal Research and Printed Sources of the Law

Part II of this book will address the process of legal research and will examine in detail the printed sources for the law and the most popular computerized and online sources. This chapter introduces the process of legal research to answer specific legal questions and the major categories of printed source materials used in legal research.

THE PROCESS OF LEGAL RESEARCH

I. INITIAL ASSESSMENT OF THE PROBLEM

Every research project starts with a problem. Your client, who at this moment may be your boss or a more senior colleague in the office, tells you a story—a set of facts that describe a certain situation—and the client thinks legal research will be necessary to answer one or more questions suggested by the fact situation. Your first job is to assess the problem so as to identify the issues—the specific legal questions that need to be answered—then to determine if additional facts are needed from the client or other sources, and finally to put together a plan of action to find the legal sources necessary to answer the questions.

A. Determining what is at issue

Your first question should be, "Do I know what is at issue in this problem?" If you can answer this question at the outset because the facts immediately suggest to you specific legal questions in specific areas of the law, then you can move on to the tasks of gathering additional facts (if needed), and planning out your research to answer the questions. You are in the comfortable position of knowing one or more areas of the law well enough to take a fact pattern, to know what areas and topics within the areas are implicated by the facts, and to formulate specific questions to answer based on the facts.

However, the specific questions to answer may not occur to you while you are reading or listening to the facts. You may have an idea about which areas of the law are implicated by the problem (e.g., this sounds like a fraud case, or this probably is a copyright case), but you will not necessarily know enough about these areas of the law and their fundamental background principles, claims, defenses, and policies to be able to determine the specific legal questions you need to answer. You may not even know the general areas of the law implicated by the problem. Assuming the "client" cannot shed any light on this (or has left the assignment in your in-box and cannot be reached), you will need to do background research into the law.

B. Background research into the area of law

If you do not know what areas of law are implicated by the problem, let alone specific legal questions to answer, you will have to start your research broadly. You have facts, so start with the facts. Look up some of the words from the operative facts in a legal dictionary or legal encyclopedia. Legal dictionaries, like <u>Black's Law Dictionary</u>, define legal terms of art and many other words that appear in legal settings. The definition of a simple word from your facts, such as "privacy" or "signature" or "title" (in reference to property), may point the way to several areas of law that should be investigated in order to zero in on the actual issues you will need to answer.

Legal encyclopedias, such as <u>Corpus Juris Secundum</u> and <u>American Jurisprudence</u> attempt to present the entire law of a certain jurisdiction (<u>Corpus Juris Secundum</u> and <u>American Jurisprudence</u> target the whole United States) in a topic by topic outline format. An encyclopedia's scope is extremely broad, but the depth of its coverage of any given topic necessarily is limited. At most, you will learn the black letter law concerning the various claims, defenses, issues, and policies that are at work in the area. The indices to the encyclopedia will point you to various legal areas for background investigation into the law. You can start in the index with a few key words like those above—privacy, signature, title—and the index will tell you what areas of the law might be implicated by these facts.

When you have a background resource, you will read it to answer the following questions:

◆ What are the major issues in this area of the law, both old and new?
◆ What are the kinds of claims, injuries, damages, causes of action, and defenses that are brought or claimed or asserted in this area?
◆ What constitutional issues are implicated (if any)?
◆ Are there statutes, rules, or administrative regulations that typically are found in this area?

The information you find in a dictionary or encyclopedia may help you get your feet wet, but you may exhaust what they have to say on your matter without determining the actual issues that are implicated by your facts. You will have to go deeper, to hornbooks, treatises, and practice guides.

Treatises are books or binders written by one or more legal scholars and are devoted to a scholarly presentation and discussion of the law in a specific area, such as torts, contracts, insurance law, class actions, or securities regulation. They often are written in several volumes, if not dozens of volumes, as in the case of Wright and Miller's <u>Federal Practice and Procedure</u>. The level of discussion tends to be intense, and it is targeted to legal scholars and lawyers, but law students generally can figure out what's going on through careful reading and re-reading. Hornbooks are a one volume treatise on a certain area of the law, such as Farnsworth's <u>Contracts</u>, and are specifically designed for use by law students and lawyers alike. Hornbooks will try to cover the same type of information as a treatise, but they necessarily are constrained by their one-volume page limit in the depth to which they can discuss each topic and subtopic of the law.

Practice guides, with titles such as <u>Rhode Island Products Liability Handbook</u> or <u>California Practice Guide: Family Law</u>, are specifically written for practicing attorneys, and out of respect for the time pressures of this audience, they attempt to present the most important information needed by practitioners in the area in a succinct manner, without going into great detail of discussion or explanation of all the nuances of the legal area and its major topics and subtopics. Because they take such a direct approach, practice guides can be perfectly adequate to supply your need for general background information on the issues, causes of action, defenses, constitutional and statutory treatment, and policies of the area of the law, but in other instances you will need a more thorough source, and you will look for a treatise.

Annotated law reports have an important function in finding relevant cases on specific legal topics, and they can be written in a similar style as an encyclopedia, although each annotation is narrowly focused, and there is not necessarily an annotation covering every topic you would like to investigate. Annotations are designed to collect and report cases and other primary authorities on the specific topics they discuss, rather than to analyze or critique the law of the area. In that annotations specifically are designed for use as a case finder, they are less useful than a treatise or practice guide in teaching you a broad foundation of legal principles and black letter law in a given legal area, although they can be very useful if you are looking for citations to relevant cases from multiple jurisdictions.

Law review articles probably are not a good place to get grounded in an area of law. The typical well-written article is a narrowly focused work with incredibly detailed analysis. Compared to an encyclopedia, a typical law review article is an inch wide and a mile thick. Instead of delving into such deep waters at the start of your analysis of a problem, you should start out with more reasonable resources, such as encyclopedias or practice guides, and move on to a treatise.

Law school casebooks are not particularly useful for gaining a foundation in a specific area of the law in a reasonable period of time. There is nothing wrong with consulting a casebook on the topic, but these texts primarily are designed to teach law in a certain methodical way, case by case, showing examples of the development of the law and highlights of the big issues, so that a law student can learn to think about the law in general and this area of the law in particular. Cases are chosen because of what they say and how they demonstrate the historical and intellectual development of the law, not necessarily because they represent the prevailing authority in any jurisdiction. This organization is not conducive to quickly identifying your questions about the topic.

Avoid commercial study aids—Nutshells, Gilbert's, Emmanuel's and the like—when you are taking on a legal problem in preparation for research. These study aids are meant to help you learn an entire course of study in the law, and although they are quicker to consult than a casebook, they will not point you to all of the issues implicated by an actual legal problem that exists in an actual jurisdiction and is governed by that jurisdiction's law. Encyclopedias, practice guides, and treatises do not take that much longer to consult, and they will provide you with more complete information to set you off on your research task.

All of the background authorities discussed above will cite cases, and it is a good idea to start reading the cases from your jurisdiction as you come across them to see examples of how the overall rules work in specific situations. Aside from that, in the background research stage, there is no real need to pick up a digest and actually use its descriptive word index to identify digest topics relating to your facts and then to use these digest topics to find listings of cases in your area. This will soon be your task when you get down to actual research, but at this point, you are just trying to identify the issues.

At the end of your self-guided introduction to an area of law, you will need to return to your facts and determine the specific questions that are presented by these facts. If you still cannot do this, return to the background material. You might also discover a need for additional factual information from your client or other sources.

C. Background research into the facts

After becoming grounded in a new area of the law, you may determine that your boss or the client did not give you enough factual information to address the issues intelligently. Go back and ask them for more information. Assuming that they have disclosed all the information that currently is available to them, you may have to perform your research with what you already know or, with certain kinds of factual information, you can turn to alternative sources of information.

As a college graduate with a bachelor's or higher degree in one or more academic disciplines, you no doubt are aware of many sources of factual information, whether it be informational, archival, technological, statistical, historical, or geographical. Libraries of the general and specific kind are obvious places to turn if you need technological information about the field that your client is involved in so that you can understand the facts of the legal sources you will be studying. You may need geographic information about the place involved in the facts—What is there? What does it look like? You may need historical information about your client's situation—What led up to this situation? Has this problem been going on before my client got involved? Has this problem come up before and been resolved in a certain way? Other more specialized information is kept in various depositories. You might need, for example, archived information of the local Recorder of Deeds' office regarding a piece of real estate, or statistics from the local Department of Health.

D. Background information of the "how to do it" kind

When you leave the friendly confines of law school and move on to practice, you may soon find yourself in need of "how to do it" information in a new area of the law. For example, your client is a creditor of a personal estate, but you don't know how to intervene in the probate case or file an adversarial claim against the estate. Your client may be in a domestic relations case where a guardian needs to be appointed, but you have no idea how to go about getting a guardian appointed. Or your client has a claim against a bankrupt debtor, but you have no idea how to prepare and file a proof of claim. "How to" sources include:

1. Your colleagues, and other lawyers you know

Your colleagues and other attorneys can be the shortest, most direct path to this practical information. Ask people who have done it before, and hopefully they can teach you to avoid the mistakes and pitfalls of the area. As a law student, you most likely do not have knowledgeable colleagues that you can consult even if the professor would let you do this on a law school assignment, so you will need to try other avenues.

2. Practice guides and practice-oriented continuing legal education (CLE) materials

Practice guides and CLE materials are drafted for practitioners. They are written to assist practitioners who already practice in the area of law covered by the guide and those who are new to the area. Because they are so practice-oriented, these guides will provide you with "how to do it" information about drafting a demand, or raising defenses, or preparing a claim in that area of the law. Sample pleadings, discovery, contracts, wills, and other documents often will be provided as models from which to work. Law students should be careful to follow whatever model is provided by their professor rather than one found in a guide book, but if none is presented, the guides can show you rudimentary forms for many legal documents.

3. The agency or court

If you are making your first foray into the Division of Family Services, the Probate Court, or the Bankruptcy Court, do not be intimidated about calling up the agency or court and asking, "How do I do something?" You may have to call several times to get the right person to answer your questions, but they often can tell you what you need to know and provide you with the right forms to use.

4. Pleading and practice form books

Speaking of forms, if that really is all you need, there are books devoted to this topic. Form books are particularly useful for somewhat obscure practice areas like admiralty law—if you are told, for example, that you have to go "arrest" a ship, you will need certain forms of pleadings and documents to accomplish this. The first time you have a case in one of these areas you will be feeling your way along in darkness, and form books at least can shed some light on the paperwork involved in the process.

II. PLANNING YOUR RESEARCH

After formulating the questions you must answer, you must develop a plan for finding the sources to answer each issue. You should divide your plan into categories—how are you going to find:

◆ Primary controlling authorities
◆ Primary persuasive authorities
◆ Secondary authorities
◆ Sources for checking and validating your authorities.

It is advisable to write up a plan of action for your research and follow it. Write down the sources you will use and the order in which you will use them. Leave space in your plan outline to make notes on what you checked and what you found.

Writing a plan makes you focus on the task at hand. It forces you to get organized. It reveals gaps in your plan when you finish jotting it down and have a look at what you came up with. And it will keep you honest—your written plan will remind you to do the job properly, as you planned it, so that you can check off all the items and complete the plan.

Keep a good record of every item (every individual authority) that you find, including what it says and the citation of the authority and page number where you found the material. This will save you hours of frustration in the future when you cannot find the same book on the shelf, or the library is closed, or you cannot quite remember the name of the case that said something crucial about a certain element of a legal rule.

A well prepared record of the findings also can be used as a skeletal outline of your written work product, which you later can flesh out and turn into a proper treatment of the issues. For example, as you research, you probably will learn that there are a certain number of required elements for the rule on the issue, and two or three exceptions to the rule, and a number of defenses to the rule. Writing down this information about the rule in your notes will create a skeleton outline of the rule section of your written product. As you find authorities that provide the sub-rules, factors, policies, considerations, or simply provide explanation or clarification of any of the items in the outline, you can fill in the information as a rough outline of the explanation sections of the treatments of the main issue and the elements of the rule. Then, when you stop, you will have a fairly complete skeletal outline of the actual work product you will draft. If you can fill in the skeletal outline on a computer as you go along, your conversion of the skeletal outline to a fully detailed outline or even the actual paper will be even easier.[1]

---

[1] This method saves time in the long run, but there is an up front investment of time (and the client's money) that might not be justified if the project is sufficiently simple or the deadline is drastically short or the client cannot or does not want to pay you for this level of work. A good example is if the client (or your boss) just wants an oral answer to the question and tells you not to spend more than four or five hours on it. Don't worry about a carefully prepared research plan that you will methodically fill in to create a skeleton outline of your work product. Just go and find the authorities.

III. PERFORMING THE RESEARCH USING PRINTED SOURCES OF THE LAW

A. Determining the scope of the research

In the real world outside of law school, the research plan you devise will depend in part on the time allotted or money allocated to the project by you, your boss, the client, or the court. You cannot always adopt a "leave no stone unturned" plan in which you will try to completely exhaust every possible source for the law. Sometimes the deadline set by your boss or the court is too short for that; other times, the client simply cannot or will not afford that level of research. You may find that this is particularly true where electronic research (Westlaw or Lexis) is involved. So time and money are important factors in actual law practice.

Another factor is your knowledge of the area of the law. If you know the area well, you will not have to look for authorities in as many places and you can zero in on the sources you know are likely to lead you directly to the answer. When you are familiar with the area, you will feel more confident when you think you have found the right answer so that you can stop your research. The converse is true when you are less familiar with the area of law—you will need to look to more sources to find authorities and you may not be as confident when are trying to decide whether you should stop your research.

B. Legal research sources

We briefly mentioned several of the sources you will use in your actual legal research. By way of further introduction, we will describe these and other sources in this section.

SOURCES FOR PRIMARY AUTHORITIES: CASES

Reporters

Reporters, such as the Federal Reporter, New York Miscellaneous Reports, and Missouri Cases, actually contain the opinions and orders of courts that you will study in order to determine the law. However, you will not be able find all of the relevant cases just by pulling reporters off the shelves. Each volume of the reporter series will contain mini-digests and tables of cases and other reference information, but it is much more beneficial to use other "case finder" resources to locate the citations to the cases you should research, and then to look them up in the reporters.

Digests

Digests are the first and foremost "case finder" resource. Digests contain lists of excerpts from cases (West Group's digests are lists of headnotes from the cases West has published) organized by key words from these cases, and by various legal concepts, short phrases, and terms of art. You start your research by breaking down your issues into key words and legal concepts, and then refer to the digest index to determine under which digest topics to look for cases. One of the nicest things about digests is that they are organized by region (national, regional, or state), or jurisdiction (federal vs. an individual state) or subject matter (e.g., bankruptcy, military law) so that you can zero in on the best cases for your problem.

Annotated Law Reports

Annotated Law Reports (ALR) are a "case finder" resource made up of reports called "annotations" on certain specific legal topics, with dozens and dozens of citations to cases in that area. Often the publication of an annotation on a given topic is prompted by the issuance of an important case in the area, or by the emergence of a conflict between courts or jurisdictions regarding a certain area of the law. The reports really are just text written so as to have a place to hang all the footnotes citing to the cases; there rarely is any synthesis of these authorities attempted in the reports, and unlike a treatise or law review article, you generally will not find a thesis or even the author's point of view on the law. As a result, ALRs do not carry much weight as secondary persuasive authorities. This should not trouble you, however, because you most often will refer to an ALR annotation to get the current law in a specific area and to find the prevailing authorities that support the current law, not to cite the annotation as authority in and of itself. Because the law moves on and the cases become dated and sometimes are overturned or superseded by more recent authorities, annotations are updated or superseded from time to time.

Encyclopedias and Practice Guides

We have placed encyclopedias and practice guides together not because they are similar in nature but because we have adequately described them above. Encyclopedias and practice guides primarily are used as background material to obtain an initial footing in an unfamiliar area of the law. Either source can be used to find cases, but unless the encyclopedia is drafted for your particular jurisdiction, reference to cases from your jurisdiction will be accidental at best. A general encyclopedia is a good background resource, but it is not the right place to pin down the prevailing authorities in any one jurisdiction. Practitioners and judges alike sometimes cite the national encyclopedias, Corpus Juris Secundum and American Jurisprudence, for basic black letter principles of an area of the law, but reliance on these sources as legal authority should be suspended when you have primary authorities or stronger secondary authorities to cite, as discussed in Chapter 5 above.

Practice guides generally are written for one jurisdiction, so it is easier to find relevant law cited in them. But the mission of practice guides is to provide a background in the law and certain "how to" information about the practice area, not to provide an up to the minute account of the prevailing authorities in the area. Thus, they generally are not cited as secondary authority unless there is a drastic lack of other authority on the issue you are researching.

We did not include dictionaries in the heading above. This is because you should never hope to find a relevant case from your jurisdiction cited in the definition of any given legal word relating to the issues you are researching.

SOURCES FOR PRIMARY AUTHORITIES: STATUTES

Statutory Compilations, Annotated and Unannotated

You can find references to statutes in any of the legal sources we have discussed above and in the secondary sources described below. If, however, you want to start out your research by looking for a statute, the place to turn is the index of your local statutory compilation or state code. There, legal words and concepts are listed that refer you to statutory headings and citations that pertain to the specific topics that have been covered by statutes in your jurisdiction. You will peruse this list of statutory headings to see if your issue is covered by one or more statutory sections.

The same process applies whether you are working with annotated or unannotated versions of the statutes. Annotated versions simply add excerpts and citations to cases and other authorities that have applied and interpreted the statutory section you are researching. The annotations are roughly organized like a mini-digest on the topic of the particular statutory section at hand, and like digests, they are very important case finding tools.

SOURCES OF SECONDARY AUTHORITY

Treatises and Restatements

Treatises and restatements are both a secondary persuasive authority on the law itself, and a case finding tool. Treatises and restatements of the law generally are written with a national scope of reference, so the authors borrow from the law of many jurisdictions to find, explain, and critique the most common principles of the law on any given legal topic. They will also point out notable exceptions and innovations in the law from the jurisdictions where they are found. Treatises and restatements cite authority in support of their discussion of the law, so they are wonderful sources for primary persuasive authorities on the topics you are researching. Among these citations, you probably will find citations to one or more cases from your jurisdiction, but this is not enough to begin to exhaust the potentially controlling authorities on your issue.

The value of treatises to legal research is three-fold. First, as a source of background information in an area, they can be invaluable. Second, many treatises and all of the restatements of the law promulgated by the American Law Institute, although secondary authority, have iron-clad reputations leading to a very high persuasive value when used to support other authorities from your jurisdiction and elsewhere. You cannot contradict controlling authority with a treatise or restatement, but when the two agree, citing a treatise or restatement in support of your discussion is well worth the time and effort. Third, reference to treatises also is a useful check on your own formulation of the rules and elements of the rules on a given topic. When we check a restatement or major treatise and find a different rule stated than the one we have formulated on a given issue, we are given pause, and will go back and recheck our own primary authorities to make sure we have analyzed them correctly.

Law Review Articles and Legal Periodical Indices

Law review articles are an important secondary persuasive authority, and are excellent sources for primary persuasive authorities and other secondary authorities on the very particular topics that the articles discuss. Occasionally, they can be a useful tool for finding controlling authorities if the article focuses on the law in your jurisdiction. In most instances, however, law review articles will review the law from a variety of jurisdictions, and references to your jurisdiction's law will be hit or miss.

An index to legal periodicals is used to locate law review articles and other publications that discuss your topic. These indices are organized by topic, which generally are key words, terms of art, and short phrases used in the articles themselves, and the indices present a listing of the titles and citations to the articles and publications.

SOURCES TO CHECK THE VIABILITY OF YOUR AUTHORITIES

Shepard's Citations and KeyCite

The primary and indispensable printed sources to check the viability of your authorities are the various volumes and series of Shepard's Citations. Shepard's Citations volumes are organized by jurisdiction or subject matter, and within a given set of volumes, they list each case and certain other authorities issued or promulgated by that jurisdiction (or with that subject matter) and after each listing, they cite every case that has cited the authority. Furthermore, they code the citations to indicate which headnotes of the case were referenced in the citing authority, and whether the authority "treated" the opinion in some legally significant way (such as to overrule, reverse, question, criticize, or follow the opinion). Thus, you can look up the listing for your authority, and scan the citations to see if your authority has been reversed or criticized or has some other subsequent history that would be important to your analysis of the authority.

Shepard's is now available on-line as a companion service on Lexis or as a stand alone on-line service. Westlaw's computer assisted legal research service has developed an authority checking and verification product known as KeyCite which performs the same function as Shepard's Citations.

Pocket Parts and Supplements

Most digests, ALRs, treatises, and other hardbound sources provide a means to keep the material in the volumes up to date, and thus, reliable. Pocket parts are often inserted into the back of the volumes, or supplemental softbound volumes or hardbound volumes are printed and shelved with the volumes. These updates report new developments in the law or additional sources of information that have been enacted or handed down since the publication of the main volume. A researcher always should check for pocket parts or supplemental volumes when performing research to make sure that the material you are looking at is current and accurate.

IV. REACHING YOUR GOAL AND KNOWING WHEN YOU ARE FINISHED

Chapter 19 discusses the topic of research planning and determining when you have completed your research in greater depth than this section. At some point in your research, you will find that all of the new authorities you are finding are citing the authorities you already have found. At this point, the following criteria may be used to determine if you are finished with your research:

(1) If you have found several (3-5) controlling authorities that agree with each other as to the legal issue at hand, and they are recent enough in time not to give you pause (within the last thirty years for a highest court/highest controlling authority and ten years for an intermediate level appellate court/second highest controlling authority is a good rule of thumb here);

(2) If you also found several good persuasive authorities that support your controlling authorities, including a treatise or other secondary authority that supports your findings;

(3) If you have reconciled or distinguished all contrary controlling authorities and any important persuasive authorities; and

(4) If you do not have any nagging questions that you know should be answered before you move on to writing;

Then you are finished.

This is only a rule of thumb. It is not going to hold true in every research problem you will encounter in law school or in actual practice. But having some guidelines is better than having none.

Chapter 11

Federal and State Reporters of Cases

Your law school experience so far most likely has been filled with judicial opinions. The case method of teaching the law remains overwhelmingly popular in the first year curriculum of law schools. In legal research, cases can define the law on any given topic by creating and advancing the law though the Common Law process of *stare decisis*, and by interpreting and modifying the law that is created through the other primary sources, legislation, and administrative rules and regulations. Reporters, such as the Federal Reporter, New York Miscellaneous Reports, and Kentucky Reports, contain the opinions and orders of courts that you will study in order to determine the law.

You cannot talk about the reporting of cases in the United States without talking about West Publishing Company, or as it is currently known, Thomson West. West publishes a report of the vast majority of cases that are issued in the United States. Along with the West publications, there are some states that have their own official reporter for the cases issued by the state's highest court or all of the courts in the state.

This chapter discusses reporters and the elements of reported cases, and examines in detail the system for reporting cases used by West, including West's National Reporter system for state and federal cases.

I. CASE REPORTERS AND ELEMENTS OF REPORTED OPINIONS

A. Case reports and reporters

Reporters are compilations of cases, most often organized by jurisdiction (e.g., New York Reports, Illinois Reports, Federal Reporter), or by geography (North Eastern Reporter, South Western Reporter), or by subject matter (e.g., Federal Securities Law Reporter; Employment Decisions, Federal Rules Decisions), or by year, or by some combination of the these categories (e.g., year and subject matter).

B. "Unpublished" cases

As we explained earlier in Chapter 5, if a case is not published in an official outlet for a jurisdiction's cases—the official reporter for the jurisdiction or a supplemental or regional reporter—then the case is referred to as "unpublished." Chapter 5 discussed how unpublished opinions have diminished precedential value as legal authority.

You will find unpublished opinions in the form of: (1) slip opinions, which are separate looseleaf pages put out by the court itself and picked up by attorneys, law firms, judge's chambers, and law offices; or (2) computerized versions of court opinions found in databases through computer assisted legal research. The primary on-line legal research providers, Lexis and Westlaw, pick up slip opinions and other copies of a court's opinions as they are issued by the court and they make them available on their on-line research databases regardless of whether the cases eventually will be put into a reporter. Occasionally, you can find unpublished opinions in loose-leaf publications on specific legal topics, such as the Securities Law Reporter, and the BNA Labor Law Reports. Although not published in an official outlet, these opinions are more readily available, even to lawyers who do not use computer-assisted legal research, and therefore, they carry more weight than other officially "unpublished" material unless the local rules of your jurisdiction specifically declare that commercially published cases still are "unpublished" and may not be used in official legal documents in that jurisdiction.

C. State trial level court opinions

Opinions from state trial level courts generally are not published. There are exceptions, including trial level cases from New York, Pennsylvania, Virginia, and Ohio, that are regularly published in reporters. In contrast, in the federal system, many opinions of the U.S. District Courts are published, and those that are published are found in the Federal Supplement reporter or the Federal Rules Decisions.

D. Appellate level court opinions

Most state and federal reporters are devoted to publishing the reports of appellate level courts. These courts can issue controlling authority, so it is particularly important for researchers to make themselves aware of the cases that the appellate courts of the applicable jurisdiction have issued on the topic of the research.

On occasion, appellate court judges decide not to publish a certain opinion. There are various reasons why this decision is made, such as: (1) the judges think the case does not involve significantly new legal principles and the law on this topic needs no further explanation or elucidation from the facts and issues involved in the case at hand; (2) the judges have determined to write a more cursory opinion in the case, often referred to as a *per curiam* opinion, which would be incomplete as a precedent if lawyers tried to use it in the future; (3) the judges have decided only to publish opinions that are highly topical or highly significant; or (4) the judges have decided to publish opinions only where they are making new law—changing, adding to, overruling, or modifying the law in some way.

E. Reporting in two or more different reporters

Parallel reporting of cases is common in the United States. By publishing the same cases in a variety of outlets, the publishers attempt to make them available to a wider circle of researchers. For example, New York Court of Appeals opinions are reported in three different reporters—The New York Reports, the New York Supplement Reporter, and the North Eastern Reporter. U.S. Supreme Court cases are reported in the United States Reports, the Supreme Court Reporter, and the Lawyer's Edition Reporter.

F. Elements of reported opinions

1. The title (also called the caption or style) of the case.

The parties' names are featured in the report of a judicial opinion, usually written as Plaintiff's Name v. Defendant's Name. Other forms are:

In re Party's Name

State ex rel. Jay Nixon, Attorney General, v. Defendant

Ex Parte Party's Name

Plaintiff #1's Name v. Defendant #1's Name [where there are multiple plaintiffs and multiple defendants]

2. The citation

Very often a citation to the case is given at the beginning of the case, and sometimes the report also gives the citation of the case in a different reporter—a "parallel citation." The citation is a shorthand reference to the reporter(s) where the case is found:

N.Y.; N.Y.2d—	New York Reports; New York Reports, Second Series
F.; F.2d; F.3d—	Federal Reporter; Federal Reporter, Second Series; Federal Reporter, Third Series

The citation gives the volume number first, then the shorthand for the reporter, then the page number where the case begins:

212 N.E.2d 43	Citation for a case in volume 212 of the North Eastern Reporter, Second Series beginning at p. 43.
788 F. Supp. 239	Citation for a case in volume 788 of the Federal Supplement Reporter beginning at p. 239.

Further information is required when you are citing the case in legal writing. Although the citations and parallel citations given in a reporter are useful, they do not necessarily correspond to proper Bluebook or ALWD Manual citation forms. In fact, much of the time they are wrong. Refer to Chapter 9 for more information.

3. The court

A report of an opinion always discloses the court that issued the opinion. The level of court and the court's place within or without the applicable hierarchy of judicial authority will be of particular importance to any researcher.

4. Docket number

Usually, the report gives the docket number of the case. The docket number is the number assigned to the case by the clerk's office of the court where the case was filed. The combination of numbers and letters tells the informed reader certain information about the case, such as:

4:98-CV-455-DJS	In the U.S. District Court for the Eastern District of Missouri, these numbers tell you the case was filed in the Eastern Division, it was filed in 1998, it was the 455th civil case filed in 1998, and it was assigned to Judge Donald J. Stohr.
696-2487, Division 5	In the Missouri Circuit Court for the 22nd Judicial Circuit, these numbers tell you that this case was filed in St. Louis City in 1996, it was the 2,487th case filed that year, and that it was assigned to Division 5 of the court.

5. Date of the decision and opinion

As discussed in Chapter 5, the dates of the opinions are very important to the ranking of the authorities as legal precedent. More recent authority generally is stronger than earlier authority, all else being equal.

6. Synopsis (a/k/a prefatory statement, heading, summary)

Sometimes the first text printed in a case report is a short paragraph summarizing the case, informing the reader which party prevailed in the case, and giving a little background information about the facts and issues involved in the case. If this paragraph appears before the judge's name, then it is **not** part of the actual opinion. The publisher of the case reporter wrote it and inserted it into the report of the case. The publisher is giving the reader a brief introduction to the case, which is helpful for the reader to use to orient herself. **However, because it is not part of the actual opinion, you should not cite to it.** It is also advisable to read the synopsis critically and not simply rely on what it says about the case because every once in a while the publishers of these summaries have been known to get the information about the issues or the holding of the case wrong.

If a paragraph summarizing the case appears below the judge's name in the body of the opinion, then it is part of the opinion, and you can cite to it and rely on what it says. In these instances, it should be called an introductory section rather than a synopsis, heading, or summary.

7. Headnotes and syllabi

Reporters published by West all have headnotes. Other publishers also write syllabi or headnotes at the start of their opinions. Headnotes and syllabi are short paragraphs that break out the individual legal principles that were discussed in the case. They can serve as thumbnail sketches of some or all of the legal issues that were taken up by the court in the opinion and what the court said about them.

Headnotes and syllabi are always printed before the judge's name and before the body of the opinion, so they are **not** part of the actual opinion. **Therefore, you should not cite to them, and as with synopses and summaries, you should read them critically and not automatically rely on what they say about the legal principles discussed in the case.** Headnotes and syllabi are the creation of the editorial staff of the publisher, not the court that issued the opinion, and the publisher may have interpreted the case incorrectly.

West's headnotes not only give a thumbnail sketch of the various issues involved in a single case, but the headnotes themselves are collected and republished in other volumes called **digests** (also published by West), where they are categorized and organized by the general area of law, sub-topic in that area, and specific issue or "key words" within the area of law. Thus, these digests are a great resource to find cases that are on point for your legal research. Digests will be discussed further in Chapter 12.

8. Names of counsel

The names of the attorneys who represented the parties in the case sometimes are printed in the case.

9. Facts

Rarely is there a separate "statement of facts" section identified as such in an opinion. It is customary for the court to discuss the facts up front, first thing, but this fact section simply will be the first three or four paragraphs of the body of the opinion, with no obvious separation from the rest of the opinion. The court can bring up and discuss new facts at any time in the case, and a careful reader will watch out for these new facts. The facts discussed are part of the opinion, and you can cite to them and rely on them in your analysis just like any other part of the opinion.

10. Opinions of the court and separate opinions of judges

The author of the opinion is printed just above the body of the opinion. With multi-judge courts, there are a number of possible combinations of judges who sign off on the opinion or who write their own opinion in the case:

Unanimous opinion	Every judge votes the same way.
En banc opinion	The whole court or a large number of judges on the court sat to hear the case—Note well that only a majority of the judges on the court, not all of the judges, have to agree in order for the opinion to be called an *en banc* opinion with the additional force and weight that this designation carries.
Majority opinion	A numeric majority of the judges that heard the case—2 out of 3, 3 out of 5, 5 out of 9, 7 out of 12—agreed with the opinion.
Plurality opinion	There was no single opinion commanding a numeric majority, but one opinion (the plurality opinion) got more votes than any other separate opinion, and a majority of the judges or justices agreed with the outcome reflected in that opinion although not with its rationale. For example, in the U.S. Supreme Court with its nine justices, a plurality opinion might have received four votes, two other judges might have concurred in the result, and there may have been one or more dissenting opinions, none of which received as many as four votes.
Concurring opinion	One or more judges agree with the end result of a majority or plurality opinion, but the judges want to express different reasons as to why they think this result should be reached.
Dissenting opinion	One or more judges do not agree with the majority opinion or the plurality opinion, and they write separately to express how they think the case should be resolved.
Per Curiam opinion	An opinion of the entire panel in which no particular judge of the panel is identified as the "author." Often it is more cursory and less detailed in its discussion of the facts and the law than other opinions of the court, and often the judges will withhold it from official publication.

11. Decision—the judgment, order, or decree

The judgment declares who won and who lost. It will order or award relief to one or more parties, or it will affirm, reverse, or remand the case at hand.

G. Official and unofficial reporters

Every jurisdiction has at least one "official" reporter for the jurisdiction's judicial opinions that are to be published, whether they be from the jurisdiction's appellate courts or trial level courts or both. Some jurisdictions have several "unofficial" reporters where the same opinions (and sometimes others) also can be published. To make matters worse, some jurisdictions used to have an official reporter, and then they abandoned it, and some previously unofficial reporter became the only reporter of that jurisdiction's case, and thus was transformed into the "official reporter."

New York and Illinois have an "official" reporter—the New York Reports and the Illinois Reports. They have an unofficial reporter, West's regional reporter encompassing these two states, the North Eastern Reporter. In addition, they each have a second unofficial reporter, West's New York Supplement reporter and the Illinois Decisions reporter.

Missouri falls into the category of states that used to have an "official" reporter—the Missouri Reports for the Missouri Supreme Court's cases— but it is now defunct, and the Missouri Supreme Court's cases are published in West's regional reporter encompassing Missouri, called the South Western Reporter. Thus, the South Western Reporter now is Missouri's "official" reporter.

The Bluebook tells you which reporters are "official" and which are "unofficial" for each of the states. When you are writing something to a court in a state, the Bluebook requires you to follow local rules, which often require you to cite to the "official" reporter in that state and to provide a parallel citation to each of the unofficial reporters (if any exist in that state, and if the case is found therein). Otherwise, when referring to a state's opinions in a memorandum or in a document prepared for a lawsuit pending in a different state, you can cite to an unofficial reporter—usually the West regional reporter for that state.

II. FEDERAL COURT REPORTS

The following section discusses the reporters of **federal cases** and the official citation form for each of the reporters.

A. United States Supreme Court cases

1. Official Reporter:	The United States Reports (U.S.)
2. Unofficial Reporters:	Supreme Court Reporter (S. Ct.)
	Lawyer's Edition Reporter (L. Ed., L. Ed. 2d)
3. Other:	United States Law Week (U.S.L.W.) unofficial, advance reports of cases

The earlier official volumes of the U.S. Supreme Court cases (up to 1874) were organized and identified by the name of the reporter who collected the cases and published them in volumes; e.g., Cranch, Black, Wallace. Later they were re-organized into volumes 1-90 of the U.S. Reports, but the official citation to these cases still includes the reporter's name. For example:

14 U.S. (1 Wheat.) 15, 18 (1816)

5 U.S. (1 Cranch) 101, 104-05 (1801)

The Bluebook requires you to cite to the United States reports (U.S.) if the case is published therein. If it is not yet in the U.S. Reports (it does take a year or more for the Government Printing Office to get each volume organized and published) then you cite to the case in other volumes in this order of preference: cite to the Supreme Court Reporter (S. Ct.) first, but if it is not in there, cite to the Lawyer's Edition (L. Ed., L. Ed. 2d), and if not even there, then cite to the U.S. Law Week (U.S.L.W.).

B. Federal court of appeals cases

The opinions of the United States Courts of Appeals (1881-present) are reported in one official reporter—the **Federal Reporter (F., F.2d, F.3d)**. There are no unofficial reporters, but some are "unpublished" and found only as slip opinions or on Lexis and Westlaw. The citation forms look like this:

Greenbaum v. Greenhaw, 112 F.3d 234, 235 (8th Cir. 1998) [regular citation]

Murray v. Griggs, No. 97-2346-EDM, ___ F.3d ___, 1998 WL 12567, at *4 (8th Cir. Nov. 23, 1998) [Note the docket number and the long form of the date. This citation indicates that the case will be published in the Federal Reporter eventually, but it hasn't made it there yet—for now, you can find it on Westlaw, and you are referring to page *4 of the opinion]

Kelley v. Underwood, No. 95-1234-WDM, 1996 WL 12778, at *5 (8th Cir. Jan. 14, 1996) [This indicates that the case was not and will not be published in the Federal Reporter—but you can find it on Westlaw, and the citation is to p. *5 of the case]

Goldman v. Weinberger, No. 95 Civ. 1245, slip op. at 5 (9th Cir. Jun. 22, 1996) [The case only exists as a slip opinion—here you are citing to page 5 of the slip opinion]

Earlier U.S. Courts of Appeals' opinions (1789-1880) were compiled and published in volumes called **Federal Cases (F. Cas.)**, arranged not by year but alphabetically. There are tables to help you locate cases when you only know the year and one party for example. Each case is numbered sequentially, and the proper citation to these cases includes the sequential number as follows:

Delrich v. Pittsburgh, 18 F. Cas. 598, 602 (C.C.W.D. Pa. 1859) (No. 10,444).

C. Federal district court cases

The opinions of the United States District Courts (1932-present), to the extent they are published, are reported in one official reporter—the **Federal Supplement** (**F. Supp.,** **F. Supp. 2d**). Note the space between the F. and the Supp. in the citation short form. There are no unofficial reporters, but many opinions are unreported and found as slip opinions or on Lexis and Westlaw.

Baum v. Green, 998 F. Supp. 134, 138-39 (E.D. Mo. 1997) [regular citation]

DeSanctis v. Gruggs, No. 4:97-CV-2346-DJS, ___ F. Supp. ___, 1998 WL 18367, at *2 (N.D.N.C. Nov. 23, 1998) [Note the docket number and the long form of the date. This citation indicates that the case will be published in the Federal Supplement eventually, but it hasn't made it there yet—for now, you can find it on Westlaw, and you are citing to page *2 of the opinion]

Kelley v. Underwood, No. 95CV1234WS, 1996 WL 17998, at *3 (S.D. Ill. Jan. 14, 1996) [This indicates that the case was not and will not be published in the Federal Supplement—but you can find it on Westlaw, and *3 is the page number you are referring to]

Vermeil v. The St. Louis Rams Football Club, No. 695 Civ. 1245, slip op. at 5 (W.D. Mo. Jun. 24, 1996) [The case only exists as a slip opinion—here you are citing to page 5 of the slip opinion]

Earlier opinions (pre-1932) of the U.S. District Courts, to the extent they were published, were published in the Federal Reporter. Certain U.S. District Court cases that construe, interpret and apply the Federal Rules of Civil Procedure (Fed. R. Civ. P.) and the Federal Rules of Criminal Procedure (Fed. R. Crim. P.) are reported in the **Federal Rules Decisions** (**F.R.D.**). Cases reported in the Federal Rules Decisions are not reported in the Federal Supplement volumes. The reason that the Federal Rules Decisions exists is that federal trial level courts are the only courts that deal with the Federal Rules of Civil and Criminal Procedure on a day-to-day basis (because these rules have to do with litigation and trials), so they have much more occasion to interpret and apply these rules and their opinions on the rules carry more weight than the average U.S. District Court opinion. A citation to the Federal Rules Decisions appears as follows:

Dole v. Clinton, 188 F.R.D. 144, 152 (N.D. Cal. 1997)

D. Other volumes for federal cases

1. **Military Justice Reporter (M.J.)** - reports appeals from military court martials.

2. **Bankruptcy Reporter (B.R.)** - reports bankruptcy law decisions from the U.S. Bankruptcy Courts and the U.S. District Courts and reprints certain U.S. Supreme Court and U.S. Court of Appeals' decisions on bankruptcy law.

3. **Federal Claims Reporter (Fed. Cl.)** - reports opinions from the U.S. Claims Court which is a trial level federal court that hears claims against the United States, usually arising from a government contract.

III. STATE COURT REPORTS, WEST'S NATIONAL REPORTER SYSTEM, AND REGIONAL REPORTERS

A. State court cases

The following are examples of reporters for state cases, and their proper citation form:

1. Official reporters

An official reporter is the reporter specifically designated by the state to report the state's cases. There may be an official reporter for each level of court in the state, or one reporter that reports all the appellate courts in the state.

Example: New York Reports (N.Y., N.Y.2d) – reports New York Court of Appeals cases.

N.Y. Appellate Division Reports (A.D., A.D.2d) – reports New York Supreme Court Appellate Division cases.

Illinois Reports (Ill., Ill. 2d) – reports Illinois Supreme Court cases.

Illinois Appellate Court Reports (Ill. App., Ill. App. 2d) – reports Illinois Appellate Court cases.

Idaho Reports (Idaho) – reports both Idaho Supreme Court and Idaho Court of Appeals cases.

If the state's name (e.g., Alaska or Idaho) or a two, three or four letter abbreviation for the state (e.g., Kan., Mass., Md., Mich.) is given by itself as the shorthand for a reporter, it reports the state's highest court's opinions. Idaho, Kan., Mass., Md., Mich. are the abbreviations for the official reporters of the courts of last resort in Idaho, Kansas, Massachusetts, Maryland, and Michigan. In some instances, as with Idaho above, this reporter also will report intermediate level appellate court cases.

If an "App." is put next to the state's short abbreviation, this becomes the abbreviation for a reporter that reports the state's intermediate level appellate court's opinions. E.g., Cal. App., Cal. App. 2d—reports the California Court of Appeal's opinions.

2. Regional reporters—official and unofficial

West's Regional Reporters have divided the country into unusual geographical regions. Illinois is in the region covered by the North Eastern Reporter (N.E., N.E.2d), Kentucky and Missouri are in the region covered by the South Western Reporter (S.W., S.W.2d), Iowa is in the region covered by the North Western Reporter (N.W., N.W.2d), and Kansas is in the region covered by the Pacific Reporter (P., P.2d). West's regional reporters generally are unofficial reporters of state court cases, but many exceptions exist. For example, the South Western Reporter is the official reporter of Missouri's cases, but it is an unofficial reporter of Arkansas's cases.

When citing a case that is reported in a regional reporter, you must tell the reader where the opinion originated. This information is enclosed in parentheses before the year of the opinion. Similar rules apply for short abbreviations as with official reporters above—if the abbreviation for the state is given by itself, it stands for the state's highest court. If some version of "App." appears next to it, it stands for the intermediate level appellate court. For example:

> Bell v. Jar, 887 So. 2d 334 (Ala. 1992) [highest level court in Alabama—the Alabama Supreme Court]

> Hoe v. Rake, 788 S.W.2d 332 (Mo. Ct. App. E. Dist. 1992) [intermediate level appellate court—the Missouri Court of Appeals, Eastern District]

> Johns v. Con Edison Corp., 45 N.E.2d 23 (N.Y. 1951) [highest level court in New York—the New York Court of Appeals]

> Rivera v. C.B.C., Inc., 324 N.E.2d 479 (N.Y. App. Div. 3d Dep't 1963) [intermediate level appellate court—the New York Appellate Division, Third Department]

3. West's state-specific publications

Some states have a special West reporter devoted solely to that state's cases. As you might guess, the states with the biggest population and the most potential for lawsuits get this treatment. Examples:

New York Supplement (N.Y.S., N.Y.S.2d. N.Y.S.3d)

Illinois Decisions (Ill. Dec.)

California Reporter (Cal. Rptr., Cal. Rptr. 2d. Cal. Rptr. 3d)

4. West's reprint editions of one state's cases

As a convenience to practitioners with more limited budgets, West often will reprint one state's cases that are taken out of the regional reporter where these cases originally were published. These volumes are given a name on the spine, such as "Colorado Cases," or "Texas Cases," but these are not a separate state-specific reporter, as discussed in the section above. These volumes maintain the same volume and page numbers as the regional reporters where the cases originally were published, so you would cite to the regional reporter as if that is the volume where you found the particular case you are researching. For example, when citing a Colorado case that you found in "Colorado Cases," you still would cite the volume and page number from Pacific Reporter where the case originally was published, not the "Colorado Cases" reprint reporter. **Do not attempt to cite the reprint volume, not even as a parallel citation.**

5. Topical, subject matter reporters

There are private publishers other than West that publish (or in most cases, republish) cases that deal with a single specific area of the law. Practitioners of that area of the law may subscribe to the reporters so that they can keep a more limited number of volumes on their shelves that still will contain the cases they will need to turn to time and time again. Examples of these reporters and their citation forms are as follows:

The Blue Sky Law Reports (Blue Sky L. Rep.) (CCH)—reports state securities law cases. [Note: the separate parentheses in the citation that gives the shorthand for the private publisher, Commerce Clearing House].

Environmental Reporter Cases (Env't Rep. Cas.) (BNA)—prints environmental law case. [BNA indicates a private publisher, the Bureau of National Affairs].

B. The National Reporter System

The Supreme Court Reporter, Federal Reporter, Federal Supplement, and all the regional reporters make up West's National Reporter System. West collects and publishes all fifty states' opinions and the federal courts' opinions in various reporter series, all following the West model of annotating and categorizing the opinions.

Each reporter in the system follows the West model for reporting cases, and has the following components:

1. **Introduction, synopsis**—all West cases have this introductory section at the start of each case. It is written by West, not the court, and it is not part of the opinion and should not be cited. Occasionally, the editors who draft these sections get the information wrong. They may erroneously report who won, or misstate the outcome of certain issues, so you always should double-check the opinion itself before using any information found in the synopsis.

2. **Headnotes (a/k/a Key Notes)**—West writes headnotes for the various issues of law that are taken up by the opinion. Lists of headnotes from cases are categorized and compiled into digests based on topical key numbers. You can research in the digests for specific topics and key numbers to find cases that have discussed that specific legal issue. Again, these headnotes are not part of the opinion, so do not cite to them. As with the synopsis, headnotes can report things erroneously, so always check the information against the text of the opinion itself.

3. **Advance sheets**—West prints preliminary editions of their case reports in paper-back form, and they print these volumes soon after the cases are issued and far in advance of the cases' publication in "official" government operated reporters. The cases reported in the advance sheets already are assigned their permanent volume and page number, which does not change when they are put in a hard-bound edition of the West reporter. Your cites to a West advance sheet still will be accurate when the cases in the advance sheets are converted to a hardbound volume.

4. **Reference Aids**—West generates Tables of Cases, cross-references to the official reporters' citations, statutes construed, rules construed, a mini-digest just for each reporter volume, lists of judges for each court reported in the volume, and many more reference aids. The advance sheets also have "Judicial Highlights" and "Congressional and Administrative Highlights" which are reports of recent cases and recently enacted laws and administrative rules and regulations.

Chapter 12

Case Finders and Verification Sources: Digests, Annotated Law Reports, and Shepard's Citations

This chapter discusses the primary tools used to find cases: section I discusses digests and section II discusses annotated law reports. Section III discusses Shepard's Citations, a tool primarily used for checking and verifying that your cases still are good law, and secondarily used to find other relevant cases that have cited your cases.

I. DIGESTS

A. Finding cases on point using digests

1. Catch words, concepts from legal issues

When you are given a legal problem and you set off to use a digest to find cases that discuss this legal problem, the first thing to do is to break your problem down into catch words, legal concepts, or brief phrases that summarize the legal issues (legal questions) implicated by your problem. The gateway to the digests is their indices, and the indices are organized into alphabetical lists of key words, brief phrases, and legal concepts.

For example, if the problem you are given is the following: A hunter with a rifle runs into someone's home in pursuit of a running deer and trips and falls and discharges his weapon killing a housewife, then the first thing to do it to break the problem down into concepts, catch words, and brief phrases:

> Hunting and Negligence with hunting;

> Weapons, Guns, Rifles and Negligence with guns; weapons in household or indoors; accidental discharge of weapon; accidental shooting;

> Trespassing and Negligence while trespassing; liability for damage or injury to property owner

What did we leave out?—deer; pursuit/hot pursuit of quarry; running with guns; tripping; housewife. Maybe the first couple (deer, hot pursuit, running with guns) might turn up a case or two, but probably not. Use your discretion. The latter words and concepts (tripping, housewife) are probably dead ends. Experience will help you make the determination of what to look up and what to leave out.

2. Look up these words, concepts and phrases in your digest's indices

Digests themselves are organized by catch words (key words), concepts, and short phrases. They present cases dealing with those catch words, concepts and phrases. The indices to the digests, called a descriptive word index, lists and cross-references these and other related key words, concepts and short phrases. Even if you do not come up with the exact key word from your problem, you often will find a cross-reference that leads you to the correct term. E.g., "gun" will cross-reference you to "weapons;" "dog" will cross-reference you to "animals;" "hunting" will cross-reference you to "negligence–sports and recreation."

The other nice thing about digests is that they are organized by region (national, regional, or state) or jurisdiction (federal vs. state) or subject matter (bankruptcy, military law) so that you can zero in on the best cases for your problem.

3. If you run short, search more broadly, think of synonyms

If you cannot find cases using the most promising words and concepts, broaden your inquiry into these other areas. Read all the "Hunting" headnotes. Read further in the "Weapons, Guns" headnotes. Think of synonyms for your initial words and concepts and search for them.

B. West's digests—key number system

West is the King of Digests, just like they are the King of Case Law. Common features of West digests are:

1. Legal situations are divided into seven major categories:
   Persons
   Property
   Contracts
   Torts
   Crimes
   Remedies
   Government
2. Categories are subdivided into more than 415 topics which are arranged in one alphabetical sequence and are numbered.

   Example: 95. Contracts

Each topic is subdivided into specific sub-topics—words, concepts, phrases, and assigned a **key number**. This is written as the topic followed by the Key symbol (⌦) followed by the key number.

Example: Contracts ⌦ 23 = Qualified or conditional acceptance of offer

Contracts ⌦ 88 = Presumptions and burden of proof

These key numbers correspond to the same sub-topic (word, concept, phrase, issue) in every digest published by West. The sub-topics in turn correspond to the headnotes you find at the beginning of every case published by West. If you find a good headnote in a case, you can get the key number off that headnote and go to any West digest and look up other potentially relevant cases that contain that same sub-topic identified by the key number.

On Westlaw, the topic name (e.g., Contracts) is replaced by its number (95) and the key symbol (⌦) is replaced by the letter "k"

Example: 95k23 = Contracts—Qualified or conditional acceptance of offer

95k88 = Contracts—Presumptions and burden of proof

C.   How do you find what topics and key numbers to look up

Common features of West's Key Number System used to find topics and key numbers and thereafter to find relevant cases include:

Descriptive Word Index	When you look up a word or short phrase from your issues, this index will show you sub-topics and key numbers associated with your word or short phrase.
Topic Outlines, Analysis	Each topical section of the digest (e.g., Contracts; Weapons; Racketeer Influenced and Corrupt Organizations) begins with a listing of the subjects covered by that topic and the subjects that are excluded and handled elsewhere. Therefore, you will know if you are looking in the right topical section. Following that is a detailed outline of the sub-topics and key numbers covered under the general topic at hand.
Table of Cases	If you know the name of a case on point, you can look it up here and find the key numbers associated with that case; then you can look up these key numbers in the

digest to find other cases on point. Previously, these tables were organized using the plaintiff's name only, but more recently, digests have created parallel entries for each case which are arranged according to the defendant's name; e.g., "Wade, Roe v." will be listed in addition to "Roe v. Wade."

Defendant-Plaintiff Table

Some digest volumes still have these. They were used to find the full name of a case on point where you only knew the defendant's name. More recently, these volumes have been rendered obsolete because digest tables of cases have started creating parallel entries for each case which are arranged according to the defendant's name, as described in the entry above.

Words and Phrases

Special volume presenting words and phrases from cases (i.e., words and phrases that are judicially defined), and listing a case or two that have these words or phrases in them. From there, you look up the cases in a Table of Cases, or find the case itself, and from there find out the headnotes associated with the case. Note: not every digest series has these volumes. The American Digest Series (Decennial Digests, General Digests) and the Regional Digests don't have them.

Popular Name Tables

Within a digest or by themselves, these tables point you to the correct name of cases that have developed a more popular name, such as the "Right to Die" case (<u>Cruzan v. Director, Missouri Dep't of Health</u>), or the "Abortion Rights" case (<u>Roe v. Wade</u>). Again, not every digest series prints these.

Key Number

If you already know a key number, you can look up other cases having head notes with that same key number.

Advance Pamphlet and Pocket Parts

Don't forget to look for the most recent cases in the digest's advance pamphlet volumes and pocket parts.

Advance Sheets (Reporters)

Remember the advance sheets for each West reporter? They have a mini-digest covering the headnote abstracts for the cases reported in the advance sheets. They come out as frequently as weekly.

D. West's digest series

1. West's United States Supreme Court Digest

Provides access to U.S. Supreme Court decisions back to 1790. Listings are by subject and case name.

2. Federal Practice Digest

A series of five successive series of digests which cover decisions of the federal court system. U.S. Supreme Court cases are listed first, then the U.S. Court of Appeals cases by order of circuit, then the U.S. District Court cases are listed alphabetically by state and district within the state (e.g., California district court cases are listed before Colorado district court cases, and Northern District of California cases before Southern District of California cases). The series runs as follows:

Federal Digest, cases through 1938

Modern Federal Practice, 1939-1960

Federal Practice Digest 2d, 1961-Nov. 1975

Federal Practice Digest 3d, Dec. 1975-1983[1]

Federal Practice Digest 4th, 1984 forward[1]

3. Regional digests

West publishes 7 regional reporters but only 4 regional digests: Atlantic, Southern, Northwestern, and Pacific Digests.

Regional digests include cases for each of the states in the region. Headnotes under a key number are arranged alphabetically by state.

4. State digests

West publishes a state digest for 47 states. They have more comprehensive coverage than regional digests—they include the cases from the state's courts and cases from federal courts that arise from the state or involve the law of the state (e.g., The Florida Digest

---

[1] There was some unusual compilation of headnotes of cases from Dec. 1975 to Dec. 1983—some were categorized in the Fed. Prac. Digest 3d and some in the Fed. Prac. Digest 4th, so to locate cases from this period you should refer to both the 3d and the 4th series of the Fed. Prac. Digest.

includes U.S. Supreme Court and U.S. Court of Appeals, Eleventh Circuit cases that arise from Florida or involve Florida law).

5. American Digest System

Modestly described as the "Master Index to all the Case Law of our Country," this is West's attempt to beat the world to digest all recent opinions. There are three components—Century Edition, Decennial Digests, and General Digests.

a. Century Edition Digest 1658-1896

Since the National Reporter System did not exist during this period, there were no key numbers. Volumes 21-25 of the 1st Decennial Digest has a Table of Cases from this period and an index can be found at the end of vol. 50 of the Century Edition Digest.

b. Decennial Digests 1897-2001

Issued every ten years. (Since 1981, they are issued in two parts every 5 years). Each series contains a Table of Cases, Descriptive Word Index, List of Subjects included and excluded at the start of each topical section. The 2nd and 3rd Decennial key numbers are cross-referenced to section numbers in the Century Digest.

c. General Digests 2001-Present (in progress)

Because Decennial Digests are not supplemented or updated, General Digest volumes contain the latest headnotes in all West Reporters. They are arranged by topic; each volume has a table of key numbers covered in the volume. You will not find things fast enough looking volume by volume, however, so a cumulative table of topics covered in the preceding ten volumes is included in each 10th volume.

6. Specialized digests

West publishes digests for two of the special federal reporters it publishes, and on two other topics: Bankruptcy Digest, Military Justice Digest, U.S. Federal Claims Digest, Education Law Digest, U.S. Merit Systems Protection Board Digest. As suggested by the title, these digests are focused on particular kinds of cases.

E. Other digests

West does not have a monopoly on the digest business (yet). Lawyer's Edition had its own U.S. Supreme Court digest series. Now it is owned by West, so who knows what the future of these volumes will be.

Looseleaf services and private reporting services (BNA, CCH) sometimes have digests to accompany their looseleaf publications. American Law Reports has its own digest series.

II. ANNOTATED LAW REPORTS

A. What are annotations and annotated law reports

Annotations are articles that collect cases on a single legal topic. Arguably, they are prompted by a new and interesting case—perhaps even a watershed case with groundbreaking effect—in a certain area of the law. The case is reprinted in the reports along with annotations and commentary that summarize, collect cases, and provide the background and legal context for the case and the specific area of the law involved in the case. Hence the name, "annotation."

Annotations are often drafted to address a point of legal ambiguity or controversy (at least one that arguably exists at the time of their publication). An editor will take on an issue which, due to a court decision, legislation, or some other "legal event," has become unsettled, or when one that was unsettled becomes settled.

Annotations are somewhat similar to a case comment in a law review, but generally they are written more objectively. The purpose of the annotated law report is not to assert a point of view but to collect cases and present a useful outline and summary of the law on a certain, specific topic. Thus, they can be more useful to the practitioner who may not want to wade through someone's thesis and argument in a law review article.

Annotations are very specific. You will not always find one on the topic you want. An annotation on a related topic may be of some use to you, but the best annotations are those that hit your issue on all fours.

B. What are annotations used for

Annotations are another way to find and collect cases on your topic of interest. They are also a secondary source of the law, but only middling in terms of persuasiveness. Like a treatise, hornbook, or legal encyclopedia, they can provide you with a basic grounding in a specific area of the law so that you can understand a problem that your client has brought to you or your law office. Again, they are so specific that at times you cannot always find one that serves your particular need. But when you do, they can really give a great deal of relevant law that is directly on point.

C. Who writes them

Editors at the publishing company or freelance editors write annotations. One author per annotation is the norm. The author is a lawyer, but you probably will not know who she is or how good a lawyer she is. Therefore, don't bet the client's farm on what you find in an annotation.

Use a great deal of caution when you are thinking of citing an annotation. They are a secondary source of law and carry some weight with the judges and lawyers who like them, but they are middling in persuasiveness at best. Be aware that not everyone likes them or uses them, and you probably will not know a particular judge's likes and dislikes ahead of time. On the other hand, if your boss at the law office likes them, by all means use them to please her!

D. American Law Reports—the granddaddy of them all

American Law Reports (A.L.R.) are synonymous in some peoples' minds with annotated law reports, and this generalization is not that far from the truth. A.L.R. dominates the field of annotated law reports. That the abbreviation is the same for both is no accident.

It used to be that A.L.R. was published by Lawyers Cooperative Publishing Company (The Supreme Court Lawyer's Edition reporter people), and Lawyers Coop. was a major competitor to West and its digests. West did not like this, however, so they bought the company. Now West publishes A.L.R. under the Lawyer's Coop. name, and they have made moves to more closely tie A.L.R.s to their key note driven system.

1. Function of A.L.R.s

Many lawyers use A.L.R.s as a primary resource, in place of digests. Others use them as a tertiary resource, a last ditch effort to find cases that they cannot find anywhere else. Probably neither practice is the best way to make use of them. A.L.R.s are more than merely a "case finding index," although this is one of their functions. Annotation editors try to collect all of the relevant judicial opinions, statutory and regulatory law—in theory, all the relevant law—then analyze and organize it into a useful commentary. The editors look to all jurisdictions, state and federal, wherever relevant law may be found, and attempt to present it to the researcher in a logical, coherent fashion. Thus, A.L.R.s should be viewed and optimally used as complement to digests and other case-finding resources.

2. Limitations of A.L.R.s

Do not be seduced by the attractiveness of the A.L.R. package. There are certain things that A.L.R.s do well, but there are several things they do *not* do:

- They do not "answer" the legal question, but organize relevant authority around and about that issue so that the researcher can efficiently investigate, analyze and eventually draft the writing that answers the question at hand.
- They are not jurisdiction specific—so you will have to sort through a lot of information to find relevant and controlling authorities from your jurisdiction, and you will probably have to do follow-up research based on the controlling and persuasive authorities you do find. (This is probably their single, most important draw-back.)

◆ They are not written like a proper office memorandum. They have an outline, but it is not the kind of outline we have been discussing in this book to draft a proper office memorandum. Some uninformed individuals might consider an A.L.R. annotation to be a good "paper." Not so. Besides constituting plagiarism, that belief misapprehends the annotations' purpose, which is to assemble the relevant law so that the researcher can get quickly to important and relevant information—the issues and cases that define the client's problem. They will not give you or your client an answer, just resources toward the answer.

◆ A.L.R.s are focused on narrow, specific legal issues, particularly those that are troublesome and unsettled, rather than on general catch words, phrases and key number concepts like West's digests are. It is often hit or miss with A.L.R.s, whereas digests will almost always find you something relevant to work with.

3. How to find relevant A.L.R.s

You can locate A.L.R.s with the A.L.R. Index, periodically republished (and check for pocket parts), and with intervening "Quick Index" supplements that fill in between re-publications of the General Index.

Lawyers Cooperative also maintains a "digest" for A.L.R.s (and the Lawyers's Edition Supreme Court reporter) which is supposed to provide subject matter/topical access to A.L.R. annotations.

4. A.L.R. series

First series of A.L.R.—1919 to 1948

Second series (A.L.R. 2d)—1948 to 1965

Third series (A.L.R. 3d)—1965 to 1980

Fourth series (A.L.R. 4th) —1980 to 1992

Fifth series (A.L.R. 5th)—1992 to present (ongoing).

A.L.R. Federal (A.L.R. Fed.)—1969 to present (ongoing). Limited to federal questions. As a result, federal issues are not covered in the last part of the A.L.R. 3d and 4th and 5th.

5. Updating older A.L.R.s

As you can see, the A.L.R. series has been going on for quite some time, and many of the annotations your will find in your research will be crusty with age. Fortunately, A.L.R.s have several updating resources:

◆ A.L.R. 3rd, 4th, and 5th and A.L.R. Fed. are updated by pocket parts.

◆ A.L.R. 2d are updated by a separate hard-bound publication, called the "Later Case Service," which usually is shelved with the A.L.R. 2d. Then someone realized that a hard-bound volume would itself quickly go out of date. Whoops! So, the Later Case Service got its own pocket parts.

◆ Don't worry about the first series of A.L.R.—they are too old to fuss over. For the antiquarian in the group, the series is updated with paperback books which are not published for each volume and are not cumulative—in other words, you have fish through all of them. Then there are something referred to as Blue Book of Supplemental Decisions, in seven volumes.

6. Verifying the accuracy of A.L.R.s

Aside from the usual "shelf-life" problems addressed above, sometimes the law changes drastically and rapidly. An annotation can go bad if it is not refrigerated. The freon for this refrigeration is the "Annotation History Table," which is found in the very back of the Annotations' General Index (currently in six volumes, usually shelved at the end of all the A.L.R.s). The history table tells you if an entirely new annotation was written to replace or "supersede" an earlier one. It will also tell you if a second annotation was written to amend or "supplement" an earlier one.

The Annotation History Table is organized by its respective A.L.R. series, then by customary citation form for each annotation. If your annotation is not listed, then it has not been superseded or supplemented (but check the **index's** own pocket part to be sure!). If it is listed, there will be a reference to the supplementing or superseding A.L.R. annotation.

III. THE WONDERFUL WORLD OF SHEPARD'S CITATIONS

A. Frank to the rescue!

In 1873, Frank Shepard said, "We all worry about whether these cases we are relying on are getting overturned, criticized, followed, or just ignored and abandoned; someone should keep track of this." Someone (probably Frank's wife) said, "Frank - put your money where your mouth is. You keep track of them! If you do a good job, they'll name a verb after you."

And he did. Frank set about to compile volumes that list all the cases that cite other cases, and he encoded the list to show if the citing case did damage to the original case. He did such a bang-up job that, just as his wife predicted, we use the verb "to shepardize" to refer to process of verifying our cases in honor of old Frank.

B. What can you accomplish with Shepard's Citations

1. Finding the parallel citations to cases.

They are listed first in the Shepard's listing for the case.

2. Trying to find out if the case is still "good law."

1. Shepard's can be used to find the direct history of the case.

Shepard's will tell you if a case has been reversed or overruled or modified by a later decision of a court higher up in the same chain of judicial authority.

2. Shepard's can also be used to find most (hopefully all) of the indirect history of the case.

If a subsequent case has cited the case at which you are looking, it will be listed in Shepard's. If the case treated the opinion in a certain way (criticized, followed, explained, distinguished, limited, and others) or your case was cited in a dissent from the listed case, this will be coded in the list. Therefore, if a case expressly overturns or abrogates your case (by name), it will show up in Shepard's.

3. What are these codes used in Shepard's

Shepard's uses the following codes to explain how a listed case affects the case you are shepardizing:

a	affirmed (<u>i.e.</u>, the listed case affirms the case you are shepardizing)
c	criticized
d	distinguished
e	explained
f	followed
h	harmonized (the listed case differs from your case, but reconciles the differences between itself and your case)
j	dissenting opinion (a dissenting opinion cites the case you are shepardizing)
L	limited (listed case restricts the application of your case to specific, limited circumstances)
m	modified
o	overruled
p	parallel (this code means the listed case describes the case you are shepardizing as "on all fours" with it; it finds your case directly on point in all respects)
q	questioned
r	reversed
S	superseded (as opposed to lowercase "s", which means the listed case is the "same case" as the case you are shepardizing)
v	vacated

The codes appear prior to the Shepard's citation for the citing case. <u>E.g.</u>, the listing "f 939P2d894" means the case found at 939 P.2d 894 follows the opinion you are shepardizing. The listing "d 345FS616" means the case at 345 F. Supp. 616 distinguishes the case you are shepardizing. You don't know on what basis the court distinguished your case, or whether this is significant to your potential use of the case; it only alerts you that a later case has distinguished it.

As shown in the example above, "d 345FS616," Shepard's uses its own, non-Bluebook abbreviation for certain reporters. There is a table of such abbreviations at the beginning of each volume of Shepard's.

4. Can Shepard's miss negative subsequent history?

Every case stands for one or more points of law—the holding of the case involves at least one issue of law. If a subsequent case overturns the **law** applied by your case by reversing, criticizing, limiting, or modifying one or more of the authorities upon which your case is relying for the law in the area, then the case you are researching may no longer be a good authority. The underpinning of your case may have been cut away. But this fact will not show up in Shepard's unless the subsequent case cites your case, and it may not. Therefore, just because your case checks out in Shepard's with a clean bill of health, it does not mean the law the case stands for (and therefore, the case itself) is still good law.

5. How do you compensate for this?

Rarely will you have only one case in an area of law to shepardize, so when you shepardize the rest of your cases, the odds improve that any drastic changes wrought by subsequent cases will show up in the history of one or more of the cases you have found and are planning to rely on. Thus, you will be tipped off to a significant change in the law. Also, you will do other kinds of research—in digests, annotations, law reviews, treatises, perhaps even encyclopedias and legal periodicals—and any significant change in the law should be covered in those volumes. These kind of things are not kept a secret; however, do not live under the delusion that a clean check in Shepard's means the case is good as gold.

6. Should the codes alone be enough to cause you to doubt a case?

The little codes Shepard's uses are useful in flagging cases, but you must still read the cases. Maybe the subsequent case only overturned part of the opinion you want to use, leaving the part you like as "good law." Maybe it modified the case, but this modification does not affect your issue. Codes like "distinguished," "explained" don't tell you much— read the cases to find out what's going on.

Reliance on the codes alone one way or the other is fraught with peril. The Shepard's people have been known to be wrong—they may list a case as "criticizing" your case, but when you read the case, you find that it does not criticize the case; it does not lay a glove on you.

C. Trying to find other cases using "one good case" with Shepard's

Shepard's can be a tool to find other relevant cases (and A.L.R. annotations, and law review articles)—namely those that cite the good cases you have already found and are shepardizing. And of course the same can be said for the bad cases you found—don't ignore them. Shepardize them to find other bad cases that you need to distinguish and handle.

This works even if you only have one good headnote from a case—Shepard's will list (and code) the particular cases that have cited your case for the proposition stated in each of the headnotes found in your case.

Example: f 797FS^{2}245

This is a Shepard's reference for a subsequent case found at 797 F. Supp. 245, that "follows" your case (i.e., adopts and applies the legal reasoning and legal rule of the case) and cites the case for the proposition found in headnote 2 of the case.

D. Shepard's for non-cases

Shepard's also exist for A.L.R. annotations, and for statutes, rules, administrative regulations, and constitutional provisions from the states and the federal system (e.g., Shepard's for the Code of Federal Regulations (C.F.R.), Federal Rules of Civil Procedure (Fed. R. Civ. P.), Internal Revenue code and certain IRS documentation, procedures and opinions). Shepard's are there for some "major" law reviews and the restatements of the law, and there are even Shepard's for patents, copyrights and trademarks.

Some Shepard's cover one particular subject matter (e.g., Bankruptcy, Banking, Corporations, Criminal, Energy, Immigration, Labor, Occupational Safety and Health (OSHA), Insurance, Medical Malpractice, Partnership, Products Liability, Professional Conduct, Tax, Uniform Commercial Code (U.C.C.)).

A useful companion volume to Shepard's is <u>Shepard's Acts & Cases by Popular Names, Federal & State</u>. This references all state and federal laws by their "short title," a title that is featured with almost every statute and act (e.g., Securities Act of 1933, Securities Exchange Act of 1934, Clean Air Act). Citations are provided to the state statutes and session laws, federal statutes (U.S. Code), and federal Statutes at Large. The case part lists some famous (or notorious) cases by their popular names (The "Right to Life" case; the "Flag Burning Case").

E. Which Shepard's do you use

Shepard's comes in many forms:

<u>State specific citators</u>, which provide the official and parallel citations of citing cases from the state where the case arose (and only that one state).

Regional citators, for each of West's regional reporters, which give the regional reporter citations for each citing case, including cases from state and federal courts other than those in the state where the case arose.

Federal citators (for the Federal Reporter or the Federal Supplement) if you have a federal case; these will scour the nation for federal and state cases citing the federal case.

All Shepard's list A.L.R.s and law reviews (local ones, and the twenty or so "major" ones that Shepard's likes).

F. Updating Shepard's

Updating Shepard's Citations volumes can be tedious because the printed volumes are not cumulative. They do not repeat information previously printed by them. If your case is old, you will need to pull two or more hard bound volumes to run the history of your case.

Shepard's does not use pocket parts to update their volumes; instead, there are soft-bound supplements and supplements to supplements. Hence, when you are running a history, each successive volume of Shepard's Citations must be consulted, from the "old" bound volumes to the "newer" bound volumes, through the interim paperback cumulations, to the most recent paperback update.

Shepard's does, however, give you a hint as to what volumes are needed to run a complete history of a certain case: the cover of the most recent supplement will tell you which volumes to consult in order to get up to the minute coverage. Thus, you will not have to search through a bunch of soft cover volumes that have been superseded and outdated that your librarian hasn't gotten around to throwing away yet.

G. Shepard's and KeyCite on-line

The only real competition to Shepard's is through computer assisted legal research. There are no printed substitutes for Shepard's. If you are unplugged, Frank's books are the only game in town.

Once you are on-line, you have some choices. Westlaw's KeyCite service is designed to replace Shepard's. KeyCite collects all the direct subsequent history that Shepard's collected, and (West claims) even the *indirect* negative history; if a case trashes a group of cases that all have the same holding or rely on common authority, or if one case in the line of subsequent history gets negative treatment, West says KeyCite will pick up on such indirect attacks even if the authority you are checking is not actually cited in the later case. Shepard's does not do this for you (yet), so West may have the edge. Shepard's is available as a stand alone on-line service and is now a companion feature on Lexis's on-line service.

The great thing about KeyCite and Shepard's on-line is that the reports you pull up when you check a citation are cumulative and comprehensive; you do not have to run the same cite through multiple databases in the same way that you have to pull multiple Shepard's volumes off the shelves in order to check one citation. Thus, using the on-line version of these cite checking services, although fee based, may actually save your client money. What you pay for the on-line service may well be offset by the time saved in not having to pull and pour over multiple volumes in order to check each cite (and time is money).

Westlaw's Insta-Cite service and Lexis' Auto-Cite service used to do many of the same "is this still good law" functions as Shepard's and also strove to pick up on cases that change the law without citing the particular case, so they were even more useful at times than Shepard's. But each service is being phased out. KeyCite is designed to replace Insta-Cite, while Lexis has partnered with Shepard's. In other words, if you are on-line, you can run Shepard's checks on Lexis or KeyCite checks on Westlaw from the comfort of your computer terminal (for a fee).

Chapter 13

Secondary Sources of the Law: Encyclopedias, Treatises, Law Reviews, and Periodicals

I. ENCYCLOPEDIAS

A. A few words about anything and everything; in depth information on nothing

Remember the adage: a general practitioner knows nothing about everything; a specialist knows everything about nothing. Encyclopedias are general practitioners in the world of legal research.

Lawyer's Cooperative put a more favorable spin on this: encyclopedias (like their <u>American Jurisprudence</u> product) are useful for their *breadth* of information; annotations (like their A.L.R. product) are useful for their *depth* of information.

B. When to use encyclopedias

Someday you may need a quick introduction to an area of the law. That is all you'll get, but it is necessary sometimes to gather the big picture and read about the big issues and the most basic black letter law about an area of the law. Encyclopedias will point you to some indicative cases on the topic. They are not the best source to find cases, but they can give you a head start on finding relevant authorities that will introduce you to headnotes and key numbers that can be used to expand your research.

Encyclopedias are an official source of law—secondary source, of course—so you can cite to them. Many judges are fond of citing them. Encyclopedias generally are reliable and well regarded for the basic, black-letter law concepts they state. But a **major** treatise that is devoted to the legal topic at hand still will carry more weight in terms of persuasiveness to the extent that the same information is found in both sources. And if the concept is so basic that it shows up in an encyclopedia, it should be found in one or more controlling or potentially controlling primary authorities, which are by far the best source for the information.

C. Main examples

1. Corpus Juris Secundum (C.J.S)

West's entry into the encyclopedia market is Corpus Juris Secundum (C.J.S.). West originally described C.J.S. as: "A complete restatement of the entire American law as developed by all reported cases." West has recently (last 15 years) back-peddled and now calls it: "A contemporary statement of American law as derived from reported cases and legislation." More selective, less comprehensive.

a. How do you find information on your topic?

In order to find information in an encyclopedia, use a words and phrases index, just like a digest (West's digests refer you directly to sections of C.J.S., too), or just pull out the volume listing your topic (the volumes are arranged alphabetically by topic names) and read the section on your topic or look a the section's index.

b. Can you cite to C.J.S.?

As a secondary source of law, you can cite to C.J.S., but it is definitely not a hot source, and later on you may be interrogated by your boss about why you could not find anything better. As stated above, if what you are citing is so basic that it will appear in an encyclopedia, then it should appear in some controlling primary authority (a case or statute or rule from your jurisdiction), so go find such a controlling authority. That is the better practice. If you cannot find one, cite a primary source of law as persuasive authority (and maybe throw in a cite to C.J.S. for good measure). If you still cannot find a good non-controlling, persuasive case, something is wrong—you or C.J.S. Look at the cases C.J.S. cites—maybe they are as old as the hills. You will have to decide then if C.J.S. still is good law and still accurate.

2. American Jurisprudence Second (Am. Jur. 2d)

Lawyer's Cooperative's entry into the encyclopedia market is American Jurisprudence (Am. Jur.), now in its second edition. Am. Jur. was the scrappy contender who challenged West's dominance, only to decide that they couldn't beat 'em, so they joined 'em. What will happen to American Jurisprudence now that West has bought it out? Who knows. The authors' own observations are that West intends to move forward with Am. Jur. while C.J.S. may be on the road to discontinuation.

Is Am. Jur. Better than C.J.S.? Am. Jur. is comparable to C.J.S. in many relevant particulars, such as how to find topics and volumes on your topic, but Am. Jur. has been regarded as a better done, more authoritative source on the law than C.J.S. Many people find it highly reliable and persuasive—the same people who like A.L.R.s, no doubt. Therefore, cite to it a little more freely than C.J.S. (Again, nothing beats a primary controlling authority that says the same thing as Am. Jur., so don't get lazy—find one!).

3. Am. Jur. Proof of Facts; Am. Jur. Trials; Am. Jur. Legal Forms and Pleading and Practice Forms

American Jurisprudence has some other volumes especially devoted to litigation that cover the proof of facts and trials of certain claims in certain areas of the law, and useful legal forms. Many people rave about these volumes. They are probably beyond the scope of what you have to do for this class, but definitely have a look at them if you go on to Trial Practice, Civil Practice, or a clinic.[1]

4. State encyclopedias

State encyclopedias, such as Illinois Jurisprudence, serve a similar function as the national encyclopedias but with a dominant or exclusive focus on the law of one state. West has published several state encyclopedias. Virginia, West Virginia, Georgia, and Tennessee have encyclopedias that are not published by West.

II. TREATISES AND HORNBOOKS vs. PRACTICE GUIDES AND CLE PUBLICATIONS

Treatises come in various shapes and sizes. Some are in binders, some are bound. Some are multi-volume, while others, especially the hornbook variety, are one volume. There are different categories of treatises, namely

1. Critical treatises;
2. Interpretive treatises;
3. Expository treatises; and
4. Student hornbooks.

The common feature of treatises is that each is painstakingly researched and drafted, they usually are written by a legal scholar who has business writing in the treatise's area of study, and the work should command a decent amount of respect among lawyers and judges, such that citation to the treatise is welcome. Treatises all are secondary authorities, but they can be very high up on the scale of secondary persuasive authorities.

---

[1] **Practice tip:** Always read the explanatory text and any introductory notes to the forms in legal form books and practice guides before you make use of them. Often these notes will tell you how to address each of the provisions of the form, and will confirm or deny that a certain form is the correct form for your client's needs.

Do not be confused by the quasi-treatises created by practitioners for use by other practitioners. They more particularly may be identified as:

1. Lawyers' practice guides and desktop reference books for state-specific or specialized areas of practice;
2. Continuing Legal Education (CLE)-type books from the American Law Institute and the American Bar Association (ALI-ABA), Practicing Law Institute (PLI), local bar associations, and many more.

These works might be painstakingly researched and drafted, but not always. The author might be a true expert in the area, or not—many practice guide chapters and CLE publications are ghost-written by junior associates at law firms, who then find their work published under the name of a senior partner of the firm. We've seen this happen; in fact, we've been the ghost-writing victims. In any event, these publications never carry the same weight as a classic treatise or hornbook. When we refer to "treatises" in the remaining portion of this chapter, we are referring to categories 1 through 4 on the preceding page, not these last two categories. We will refer to the last two categories as "practice guides" and "CLE publications."

A. Citation to treatises—gold mine or fool's gold?

Previously, we addressed the value of treatises. In general, the name of the game is prestige, reputation, general reliability, and acceptance in the field. Some treatises are as good as gold, and you should feel free to cite them. Others may look like gold but you'd be panning for pyrite instead. If you are not sure about the reputation of a given treatise, ask your law professors or colleagues about the reputation of the work. You do not want to be relying heavily on a work that largely is discredited.

Hornbooks, generally speaking, have good authors and state reliable black letter law. But almost every author of a hornbook will have a separate "major," multi-volume treatise on the same topic, and this would be the better authority to cite. If the language you like only is found in the hornbook, go ahead and cite it, but if it appears in both, cite the "major" treatise by the same author.

Try not to rely on a practice guide or desk reference, especially one that is state specific and has a title like "Michigan Practice Guide" or "Nevada Civil Practice Manual." These are best left for background information, not as authority you would cite in a memo or brief. The only safe use of such authority is to add weight to an otherwise shaky citation to primary authority or to another secondary authority. Rarely should you cite one by itself for any significant legal proposition. As hinted above, some treatises look and feel like a desk reference, so you need to be sure where the work you are looking at falls. Ask your law professors and colleagues if you are wondering.

Regarding CLE publications, some of these titles can be useful, but **only** when there simply is no other legal authority on point—no cases, no digest or encyclopedia references, no law review articles, no A.L.R.s They can be and often are the most cutting edge source on emerging areas of the law, but this is the **only** time you should think about citing them. Do not use them if the information can be found in other, "traditional" sources of the law. And be careful to use a reputable compiler of CLE materials—ALI-ABA, PLI, National Institute of Trial Advocacy ("NITA") are more reliable than state or local bar associations or other local legal associations. Finally, even if it was the only thing on earth on point, you still should hesitate to cite a CLE publication in a brief submitted to a court.

You may have noted that we did not list student help books and commercial outlines in the above lists—West's Nutshells, Gilbert's, Emmanuel's, Casenote Legal Briefs, Black Letter Law series, Shell Out the Last $25 in Your Spending Money series, Read This Instead of the Casebook series, and more titles every year. There is good reason for this: Don't ever cite a Nutshells or Gilbert's or Emmanuel's or the ilk in any legal writing, particularly in your legal research and writing class and when you get to the actual practice of law. You would become a laughing stock of legendary proportion.

We cannot even mention laypersons' legal guides—"How to do your own living will," "Do-it-yourself legal forms," "Reader's Digest Legal Guide," and computer programs such as "Willpower™"— in the same breath as the first three categories. Never, never, never think of using them for any purpose in law school or the practice of law.

B. How do you use treatises

Treatises are similar no matter what the field—law, psychology of child development, microbiology, stamp collecting, etc. Read the table of contents or the index, and any other tables that orient you to the pages you want to read.

C. Updating

The process of updating treatises varies: some are looseleaf and readily and frequently are updated. Some get pocket parts. Some are simply not supposed to go out of style (but, like those plaid golf pants your uncle bought in 1978, tragically they do). If the treatise analyzes an area of law that changes rapidly, such as employment law or securities law, and if the work is not updated with insert pages, supplemental volumes, or pocket parts, you should be very leery of using it.

III. RESTATEMENTS—NOT YOUR ORDINARY TREATISE

The American Law Institute ("ALI") was formed to clean up the law. All the best legal minds were invited. They decided to "restate" the law of certain areas in a comprehensive, highly reliable, and highly authoritative way. The aim was to create something so authoritative that even the Common Law would be brought into line—and they would be called the "Restatements of the Law." And to a large extent, they succeeded.

In general, restatements are highly authoritative—equal to the **best** treatises and almost equal to primary controlling authority when you use them in the explanation and application sections of your work. If you think a primary controlling authority says something contrary to a restatement, you should have another look at the primary authority—make sure you are reading it right, and make sure it is good law and not on its way out. We did say "almost" equal, because nothing beats primary controlling authority.

Restatements are highly reliable, largely due to the stature of the people appointed as "reporters" of the restatements, and the peer review, comment, revising, and redrafting procedures that the restatements undergo before they are finally completed.

Note, however, that some restatements are "progressive" in nature (some of the second and the third series of restatements especially), trying to advocate what the law should be, rather than simply restating what it is. This is a problem, because your state may not buy into the particular theory espoused in the particular restatement section you are examining. Be careful. Just because you find an answer to a legal question in a restatement does not mean you are finished. You must check to make sure your jurisdiction follows this provision of the restatement, and if it does, whether it has modified, explained, limited, expanded, or done something else with it. You must always answer the question, how does this section of the restatement work in this state?

IV. UNIFORM LAWS

Uniform Laws are a model for legislation—a statutory regime on a topic—that are drafted so that each state can have a chance to adopt the same form of statute on this topic. Uniform laws are drafted and redrafted, commented on and criticized by legal scholars, so that they are highly tuned and authoritative models for passage in all 50 states. Major examples are The Uniform Commercial Code, the Uniform Fraudulent Transfer Act, and the Model Penal Code.

Because of their "uniform" nature, the interpretations of a provision of a uniform law by one state is more often than not held to be very persuasive in other states. This factor is an added boost to the persuasive authority of a court in a sister state.

V. LAW REVIEWS, LAW JOURNALS

A. This can be complicated

You rarely will appreciate how complex, how troublesome, how many issues (old, present, and emerging issues) are involved, and simply what is at stake in an area of law until you read a law review article on that subject. Reading (and writing) law review articles often is a humbling experience. A good law review article takes months to research and write.

The authors of law review articles—law professors, practitioners, judges, and law students—strive to plumb the depths of an area of law and present a detailed exposition of the old and new problems, issues, and simply stated, what is going on in an area. There is a drive to print articles on current and emerging topics; you will not find too many recent articles on negligence of railroad operators, unless there recently was some new development in the law of this area.

B. More than you can shake a stick at

Over the last seventy years, the law review and law journal printing business has boomed. It used to be one journal per school—The Harvard Law Review, The Yale Law Journal, The Washington University Law Quarterly. Then things got topical, more focused, and you have the Columbia Journal of Transnational Law, Richmond Journal of Law and Technology, Iowa State Hog Farming Law Review (planned for 2006). At last count, Harvard had ten journals.

C. The table of contents is easy to find

The table of contents of individual copies of a law review is printed on the cover of the booklet. As indicated by these tables of contents, the featured works found in law reviews and law journals fall into several categories:

1. Articles—the full-blown exposition on an area of law with topical current events interest. Written most often by a law professor, but sometimes by a practitioner, judge, or other expert.
2. Notes—student articles, similar to the above. Sometimes referring to an student article about a recent case, rule, or statute and what it does to the law in a given area.
3. Comments—written by students, law professors or practitioners, they are less than a full article, and often comment on a recently controversial, disputed area of the law. Sometimes they refer to a short article about a recent change (case, rule, statute) in the law, so the definition intersects with Notes above.
4. Commentary (Essays, Correspondence)—talking heads compete, saying "this is what the law should be," and pick apart each others' opinions.
5. Symposium issue—an issue devoted to one theme or devoted to reprinting of the speeches and presentations of a major conference at the law school.

D. Are you supposed to be impressed?

Yes, law review articles can be truly impressive, full of information, incredibly well researched, and stunning in their conclusions, but . . . **should you cite to them?**

Law reviews, in general, are high on the list of persuasive secondary authorities. Of course, as secondary authorities, no law review article will substitute for primary legal authority, and certainly not for primary controlling legal authority.

The persuasive value of any given article depends first on the author—famous names in the law get attention and respect. The best author is a nationally known and recognized figure in the area of law in which the article is written. If a famous mind steps out of their area of expertise to write—Professor John Coffee leaves securities and mergers and acquisitions law and decides to do a piece on Irish criminal law— the article still is valuable, but not as amazing as the situation where the expert writes on a topic within their expertise.

The value depends little on the law review or law journal itself—the prestigious scholars will often leave their prestigious schools with prestigious law reviews and publish somewhere else, and they should get the same attention and respect no matter where they are writing. In a crunch, sometimes the school itself will rub a little respect on to a journal and all of its articles (i.e., why would Harvard think it could get away with ten journals).

As with all secondary authorities, if garbage went in, garbage will go out. It matters a great deal if an individual article is well researched, well reasoned, well written, and simply that it makes sense. Even Arthur Miller makes mistakes, and some of them get published.

F. Compared to other secondary authorities, where do law review articles rank?

Subject to the criteria above, law reviews generally are much better authority than an A.L.R. But they are not necessarily better than a treatise. Major, multi-volume treatises (like Wright & Miller, <u>Federal Practice and Procedure</u>) carry more weight, mainly because these important treatises must stand the test of time before they become accepted and admired. So an old way of thinking that stands up for years can tip the scales more than a fresh perspective on a hot topic. Of course, a good law review article is better than a mediocre treatise.

Law reviews are better than an encyclopedia in terms of persuasive authority. They are, of course, used for a different purpose than encyclopedias. Specifically, you will not use a law review article primarily for finding cases, although this can be an incidental benefit of a well researched article.

G. Finding law review articles

If you are trying to locate law review articles by hand (i.e., without using a computer), the first place to look is the current Index of Legal Periodicals. It is organized like most indices we have been mentioning in this book. Your law school reference librarian can help you out with this resource the first time you go on a search.

Far simpler and quicker than the indices are the law review databases available on-line on Westlaw, Lexis, and the Internet. Westlaw and Lexis each let you search for articles by word or phrase or topic or author. You can search the entire database or more focused databases defined by type of publication, subject matter, geography, or date, or a combination of these factors.

VI. OTHER PERIODICALS

Just as practice guides and desk reference works can masquerade as a treatise, bar journals and legal magazines can be similar to law reviews in appearance, but as a rule, they are not as detailed, comprehensive, or authoritative as a law review. They contain nuts and bolts, practice-oriented material. Thus, they only are as authoritative as the average practice guide or CLE publication. Rank these lower than treatises and A.L.R.S.

Legal newspapers, newsletters, and special interest publications—on topics such as international law, elder law, law and economics—once again rarely are as detailed, comprehensive, or authoritative as a law review. Thus, they are not as authoritative as true law review articles. Use them as you would a CLE publication, unless you notice that the author of the work is a superstar.

Chapter 14

Court Rules, Local Rules, and Loose-leaf Services

I. COURT RULES

This section of this chapter examines the federal rules of procedure and evidence that apply in federal court.

A. Federal rules of "general" application

The following rules are of general application in the federal courts:

Federal Rules of Civil Procedure (cited as Fed. R. Civ. P., first promulgated in 1938): These rules instruct litigants in how to proceed in civil cases in federal court. The rules cover timing issues, content and construction of pleadings, parties and joinder issues, discovery standards and methods of discovery, trials, post-trial motions, judgments, and other issues of procedure. The official version of the rules is found in the Appendix to Title 28 of the U.S. Code.

Federal Rules of Criminal Procedure (cited as Fed. R. Crim. P., first promulgated in 1946): These rules instruct litigants in how to conduct a criminal case in federal court. The official version of the rules is found in the Appendix to Title 18 of the U.S. Code, along with the Federal Sentencing Guidelines and the Rules for Conducting Trial of Misdemeanors before U.S. Magistrate Judges.

Federal Rules of Appellate Procedure (cited as Fed. R. App. P., first promulgated in 1968): These rules instruct litigants in how to conduct an appeal in federal appellate courts. The official version of the rules is found in the Appendix to Title 28 of the U.S. Code.

Federal Rules of Evidence (cited as Fed. R. Evid., first promulgated in 1975): These are the rules regarding the relevance, admissibility, foundation and capacity, and requirements of evidence and witnesses in civil and criminal trials in federal court. The official version of the rules is found in the Appendix to Title 28 of the U.S. Code.

B. Sources regarding the federal rules of general application

Appendix to Title 28 of the United States Code—As mentioned above, the unannotated, official versions of the Federal Rules of Civil Procedure, the Federal Rules of Appellate Procedure, and the Federal Rules of Evidence are printed in the Appendix to Title 28 of the United States Code. Also included are the Judicial Conference Advisory Committee Notes ("Advisory Committee Notes"), which are contemporaneous constructions and explanations of the rules by the general committee responsible for recommending changes and additions to the rules.

U.S.C.A., U.S.C.S.—Annotated versions of the rules and Advisory Committee Notes are found in the United States Code Annotated (West) and the United States Code Service (West, formerly Lawyers Coop). As with the code itself, U.S.C.A. promises that its annotations contain comprehensive coverage of all cases citing a rule or rules, while U.S.C.S. promises selective, theoretically more relevant annotations to cases that actually say something important about a rule or rules. The **U.S.C.A.** also prints "Practice Commentaries" on certain rules; e.g., Fed. R. Civ. P. 45. These notes are useful to the practitioner, but are not as persuasive as the Advisory Committee Notes when used as an interpretative authority.

Federal Procedure, Lawyers Edition (West, formerly Lawyers Coop)—Contains all the federal rules of general application and the Advisory Committee Notes on the rules. Other volumes include the local rules for all the circuit courts of appeals, and the local rules for all the district courts in the country.

Federal Rules Service (West, formerly Lawyers Coop)—Collects and prints the federal rules of general application, and publishes cases interpreting the federal rules, including cases that are otherwise unpublished in the Federal Reporter, Federal Supplement, or Federal Rules Decisions (but are generally found on Westlaw and Lexis). Parts of the series include the **Federal Rules Service reporter** (for the cases), **Federal Rules Digest** (classifying the cases reported in digest form), **Federal Court Local Rules**, and **Finding Aids volumes** (which are considered useful in locating the information you need from the other volumes in the set).

Federal Rules of Evidence Series (West, formerly Lawyers Coop)—Similar to the Federal Rules Service, it publishes cases interpreting the Federal Rules of Evidence, including cases that are otherwise unpublished in the Federal Reporter, Federal Supplement, or Federal Rules Decisions (but are generally found on Westlaw and Lexis). It also has a **Reporter** series, **Digest**, and **Finding Aids volumes** devoted to the Federal Rules of Evidence.

Federal Rules Decisions (F.R.D.) (West)—A reporter series that publishes federal cases that interpret the federal rules of general application. Cases reported in these volumes are not reported in Federal Supplement or Federal Reporter. They also print updates and amendments to the rules, and some drafting "legislative" history, judiciary committee and Federal Judicial Center reports, and general commentary on the rules.

West's Rules Pamphlets—West yearly puts out very useful pamphlets of the major federal rules of general application for civil cases and criminal cases. The civil volume is called **Federal Civil Judicial Procedure and Rules**, and it contains the Federal Rules of Civil Procedure, Appellate Procedure, and Evidence, Rules of the Judicial Panel on Multi-District Litigation, Rules of the U.S. Supreme Court, the U.S. Constitution, and portions of the text of Title 28 of the U.S. Code. The criminal volume is called **Federal Criminal Code and Rules**, and it contains the Federal Rules of Criminal Procedure, Appellate Procedure, and Evidence, the Rules of the U.S. Supreme Court, the complete text of Title 18 of the U.S. Code, which lays out most federal crimes, and portions of Titles 15, 21, 26, 28, 31, 41, and 46 of the U.S. Code that contain other federal criminal laws.

West has an interesting way of updating its rules pamphlets—if a yearly pamphlet goes out of date during the year (unexpectedly or not), West will "quickly" issue a little paste-in pocket part and try to get it out to all of its customers who bought the yearly pamphlet. Various reasons that might cause this to happen are that a large number of new rules are promulgated, or several old rules are significantly amended, or some other important development occurs. Routine or minor changes to a few rules or the addition of only a small number of rules will not prompt this kind of treatment.

Westlaw and Lexis—the full text of the rules of general application and the Advisory Committee Notes, and even some drafting "legislative" history, are found online. For example, on Westlaw, you can search the following databases:

> **US-RULES**—Federal Rules of general application are found in the US-RULES database. It contains the text of all the rules, Advisory Committee Notes, and Practice Commentaries. These databases are taken from the U.S.C.A., so they are automatically annotated. You can limit your search using the citation (ci) field; e.g., if you only want rules from the Fed. R. Civ. P., you can put "ci(frcp)" in your search.

> **US-ORDERS**—Federal Orders are found in the US-ORDERS database. An "orders" database contains the amendments and additions to the rules in the "Rules" databases occurring between publication of the official text of the rules. The amendments are often promulgated by an administrative order of a court (e.g., the U.S. Supreme Court), hence the name for the database. The US-ORDERS database also contains commentary and reports issued by the Judi-

cial Conference Advisory Committee and its Standing Committees on the Rules, or from the Federal Judicial Center, that pertain to certain rules.

RULES-ALL—Local Federal Court Rules for all states are found in the RULES-ALL database.

xx-RULES—Local Federal Court Rules and state court rules for a particular state are identified by state abbreviation xx-RULES; <u>e.g.</u>, MO-RULES. The database will include all districts within the state; <u>e.g.</u>, MO-RULES contains the rules for the Western District of Missouri and the Eastern District of Missouri and any local rules for federal bankruptcy and tax courts in those districts. This database also includes all the rules of procedure for state courts, <u>e.g.</u>, MO-RULES contains the Missouri Supreme Court Rules, and the local rules for the individual state courts, such as the Local Rules for the Missouri Circuit Court, 22nd Judicial Circuit, St. Louis City. Again, they are based on West's products for the state, so they automatically are annotated.

ORDERS-ALL—Local Federal Court Orders for all States are found in the ORDERS-ALL database. It is an "orders" database, as described above.

xx-ORDERS—Local Federal Court Orders by State are in the xx-ORDERS database; <u>e.g.</u>, IL-ORDERS

FBKR-RULES—a database containing the Federal Bankruptcy Rules from Title 11 of the U.S. Code.

FCJ-RULES—Federal Criminal Justice rules are found in the FCJ-RULES database. These include the Federal Rules of Criminal Procedure; the Rules for Misdemeanor Trials before U.S. Magistrates; and Habeas Corpus rules for actions under 28 U.S.C. §§ 2854 and 2855.

FINT-RULES—Federal International Law Rules for the Court of International Trade and other international proceedings.

FMRT- RULES—Federal Maritime Law rules, used for maritime actions in federal courts, but please note that this does not include Local Rules for Admiralty Cases in the various district courts in the U.S.

FMIL-RULES—Federal Military Law rules for military appellate courts.

FSEC-RULES—Federal Securities Law - Rules, used for administrative actions and requests involving the Securities Exchange Commission.

FTX-RULES—Federal Taxation rules are general rules for tax court matters, found in Title 26 of the U.S. Code, but there may be local tax court rules to look for in the xx-RULES database.

US-RULESCOMM—Federal Rules of Practice & Procedure Advisory Committee Minutes. These are the minutes of the standing committees on the various rules which are charged with drafting and amending the federal rules, and who advise and report to the Judicial Conference Advisory Committee. Coverage begins in 1992 and 1993. You can limit your search to committee minutes on one set of rules using the citation (ci) field; e.g., if you only want minutes of the committee on the Fed. R. Civ. P., you can add "ci(frcp)" to your search.

FPP—Wright and Miller's treatise, Federal Practice & Procedure, can be searched at FPP.

C. Other federal rules

Certain rules pertain to specific types (subject matter) of actions.

Bankruptcy: Rules for conducting actions in the United States Bankruptcy Court are found in Title 11 of the U.S. Code.

Taxation: Rules of Practice and Procedure for the United States Tax Court are found in Title 26 of U.S. Code (the Internal Revenue Code).

International Trade: Rules of procedure in the United States Court of International Trade are found in the Appendix to Title 28 of the U.S. Code.

The Appendix to Title 28 also includes certain "local rules" for particular courts; e.g., the Rules of the Supreme Court of the United States, Rules of the United States Court of Federal Claims, the General Rules of the Temporary Emergency Court of Appeals of the United States.

D. Secondary sources for commentary, interpretation of rules

The **Judicial Advisory Committee Notes** that are printed following the text of each rule in the U.S. Code, U.S.C.A., U.S.C.S., each West pamphlet, and most every other volume on the rules, are a secondary persuasive authority, and are considered to be highly persuasive. They are not "drafting history" per se; you would cite to the Advisory Committee Notes as a contemporaneous construction and explanation of what the rules mean, rather than evidence of drafter's intent.

The **Practice Commentaries** for certain rules that are printed in some of West's publications and on Westlaw are the same type of commentary and construction of the rules from a practical viewpoint, but are less persuasive than the Advisory Committee Notes above.

We've talked about **Wright & Miller's** Federal Practice and Procedure (West), before. It is very useful, and now it is on-line in Westlaw's FPP database. Its competitors include: Moore's Federal Practice (Matthew Bender), Federal Litigation Guide (Matthew Bender), West's Federal Practice Manual (West), Federal Procedure, Lawyers Edition (West, formerly Lawyers Coop), Cyclopedia of Federal Procedure (West, formerly Lawyers Coop).

Weinstein's Evidence is a good volume on evidence in general and the Federal Rules of Evidence in particular.

II. FEDERAL AND STATE COURT LOCAL RULES

Court Copies—The first place to get a copy of the local rules is the court itself. Very often the courts give them away, or charge a nominal fee for the paper. These copies should be considered an official version of the rules, but always ask if there are any **administrative orders** issued by the court (see Court Orders above) that have modified the rules or procedures of the court since the publication of the set of rules they are giving out. These administrative orders are usually available in slip copy form at the clerk's office if you ask for them.

West Pamphlets—West yearly puts out very useful pamphlets of local rules of state and federal courts identified by the state's name; e.g., **New Jersey Court Rules**, **Washington Court Rules**. They are a companion to the federal general rules pamphlets discussed above. The local rules of the federal courts in the state typically are included, as are the state's general rules of procedure for state courts in the state. Periodically, the local rules of each of the state trial courts (e.g., Local Rules of the 22nd Judicial Circuit, St. Louis City) will be printed, but not every year. The pamphlets are sometimes updated during the year with a paste-in pocket part, if the rules incur very significant changes.

By way of example, we are including the table of contents of the Local Rules for the U.S. District Court for the Eastern District of Missouri so that you can look at the kinds of matters that are covered in the rules.

Local Rules for U.S. District Court, Eastern District of Missouri

TABLE OF CONTENTS

FEDERAL RULE REFERENCE - LOCAL RULE NUMBER

I.   **Scope of Local Rules**

Federal - Local
1 - 1.01   Title and Citation
81 - 1.02   Application and Numbering of Local Rules

86 - 1.03   Effective Date
86 - 1.04   Relationship to Prior Rules and Actions Pending on Effective
                 Date
6 - 1.05   Modification of Time Limits
1 - 1.06   Judge Defined

II.   Commencement of Actions

Federal - Local

5 - 2.01   Files and Filings
3 - 2.02   Papers to be Filed in Civil Cases
81 - 2.03   Cases Removed to the District Court
38 - 2.04   Demand for Jury Trial
3 - 2.05   In Forma Pauperis
45 - 2.06   Pro Se Actions
3 - 2.07   Divisional Venue
40 - 2.08   Assignment of Actions and Matters

III.   Disclosure and Discovery

Federal - Local

26 - 3.01   Federal Rule of Civil Procedure 26(a)(1)
26 - 3.02   Filing of Discovery and Disclosure Materials
33 - 3.03   Interrogatories
37 - 3.04   Motions Concerning Disclosure and Discovery
12CR - 3.05   Disclosure and Motions in Criminal Cases

IV.   Motions

Federal - Local

7 - 4.01   Motions and Memoranda
78 - 4.02   Oral Argument or Testimony Regarding Civil Motions
42 - 4.03   Motions to Consolidate
7 - 4.04   Communication with the Court
7 - 4.05   Submission of Motion Package

V.   Differentiated Case Management

Federal - Local

16 - 5.01   Case Management Tracks
3 - 5.02   Track Information Statements
16 - 5.03   Rule 16 Scheduling Conference
16 - 5.04   Case Management Orders

VI.   Alternative Dispute Resolution

Federal - Local

16 - 6.01	Mediation and Early Neutral Evaluation
16 - 6.02	Referral to Alternative Dispute Resolution
16 - 6.03	Neutrals
16 - 6.04	Communications Concerning Alternative Dispute Resolution
16 - 6.05	Reporting Requirements

VII.   Trials

Federal - Local

47 - 7.01	Jurors and Juries
83 - 7.02	Trial Exhibits

VIII.   Judgments

Federal - Local

41 - 8.01	Dismissal for Failure to Prosecute
54 - 8.02	Motions for Attorney's Fees
54 - 8.03	Bill of Costs
41 - 8.04	Assessment of Jury Costs

XI.   Special Proceedings

Federal - Local

81 - 9.01	Bankruptcy Court Matters
56 - 9.02	Social Security Appeals
58CR - 9.03	Petty Offenses
71A - 9.04	Condemnation Cases

X.   Admiralty Cases

Federal - Local

9 - 10.01	Scope of Admiralty Rules
9 - 10.02	Actions in Rem, Special Provisions
9 - 10.03	Actions in Rem and Quasi in Rem, General Provisions

XI.   United States Magistrate Judges

Federal - Local

73 - 11.01	General Authority of United States Magistrate Judges

XII.   Attorneys

Federal - Local

83 - 12.01	Attorney Admissions

83 - 12.02	Attorney Discipline
83 - 12.03	Attorney Admission Fee Non-Appropriated Fund
83 - 12.04	Former Law Clerks
83 - 12.05	Law Student Practice
83 - 12.06	Appointed Counsel's Fees and Expenses in Civil Cases
83 - 12.07	Attorney's Obligations Regarding Appeal

XIII. **Miscellaneous Provisions**

Federal - Local

32CR - 13.01	Probation and Pretrial Services Records
83 - 13.02	Use of Photographic and Recording Equipment
46CR - 13.03	Surety on Criminal Bonds
67 - 13.04	Deposit of Funds with the Court
83 - 13.05	Pleadings and Documents Filed Under Seal

III. STATE GENERAL RULES OF PROCEDURE

The states' general rules of procedure are often found in the official state statutes, but <u>not</u> always. For example, you will not find the Missouri Supreme Court Rules anywhere in the Missouri Revised Statutes.

You will almost always find the state rules in the annotated version of the state statutes; <u>e.g.</u>, you will find the **Missouri Supreme Court Rules** printed in **Vernon's Annotated Missouri Statutes** (West), and in pamphlet editions such as **Missouri Court Rules** discussed above. Naturally, the annotated statutes will provide annotations to the rules. The pamphlet editions (<u>e.g.</u>, Missouri Court Rules) do not have annotations.

IV. DRAFTING REPORTS ("LEGISLATIVE HISTORY") OF THE FEDERAL RULES

Records of the U.S. Judicial Conference: Committees on Rules of Practice and Procedure (Congressional Information Service)—CIS, the legislative history maven, has collected the records of the committees drafting the rules. Ultimately the rules are approved and promulgated by order of the United States Supreme Court.

As noted above, the Advisory Committee Notes are not really drafting history and are not considered to be evidence of the drafter's intent. Instead, they are a contemporaneous construction of the rules, but are held to be very persuasive.

Federal Rules Service; Federal Rules Decisions—these volumes will print various reports and commentary that precede the promulgation of rules or are contemporaneous with the rules. If the report is from a member of the drafting committee, or the committee itself, or from a Supreme Court justice who voted on the rule, it can be used like "legislative history." <u>E.g.</u>, a Supreme Court justice might write a piece on a new federal rule and what it means, which is akin to a legislative subcommittee/committee report or conference committee report on legislation, because it is a discussion of the meaning of the rule from a person who actually voted on the rule.

Drafting History of the Federal Rules of Criminal Procedure—volumes devoted to the drafting history of the Federal Rules of Criminal Procedure.

Federal Rules of Evidence: Legislative Histories and Related Documents—volumes devoted to the legislative and drafting history of the Federal rules of Evidence.

V. CITATOR SERVICES

Shepard's has several volumes which attempt to track the cases citing the rules—**Federal Rules Citations; United States Citations-Statutes, Shepard's Citations** for the various states; **Shepard's Federal Law Citations in Selected Law Reviews.**

The U.S.C.A., U.S.C.S., and other volumes track cases citing the rules, but they do not sort them in terms of positive or negative treatment. If a rule drastically is reinterpreted by a case in your jurisdiction, you will have to search through the entire annotations list to find it.

On-line, Westlaw's rules databases are based on U.S.C.A. and the companion state volumes, like Vernon's Annotated Missouri Statutes, so you will get annotations to the cases citing the rule.

LOOSE-LEAF SERVICES

I. WHY ARE LOOSE-LEAF SERVICES CREATED?

A. To keep things current.

Loose-leaf service are generally binders or newsletters whose goal is to keep practitioners up to speed in a specific area of the law. They are especially useful for areas that have a lot of administrative law, and in which the law (rules, regulations, legal standards) change frequently. <u>E.g.</u>, employment law, labor law, tax law, securities law.

B. Information overload!

If the rules, regs, opinion letters, service bulletins, and other material comes out thick and fast in your area of the law, you cannot always rely on your own skills (or your partners', associates', or librarian's skills) in staying abreast of what the law is in a heavily regulated and active area. You subscribe to a loose-leaf service instead, and rely on it (the publisher and its team of editors and researchers) to do the leg work for you so that you can browse an executive summary or pick up an index and go right to the material that answers your legal questions.

The services strive to **collect** resources, **edit and organize** the information, and especially perform **indexing** of the material. This is what you pay for in a loose-leaf service.

The full text of cases, laws, rules, and regulations, and significant legislative history information often are reported in the volumes. Tables of cases, statutes, regulations, and cross-references to the same are popular, too. Often reports and editorials will accompany each release, and summarize and alert you to new developments reported therein so that you can tell at a glance if you need to dig into a periodic release of information. They are increasingly found on Westlaw and Lexis. E.g., almost all BNA publications are on Lexis and Westlaw, and a few of the CCH titles.

II. TYPES OF LOOSE-LEAF SERVICE

Newsletters

Binders with Interfiled Pages

Combination of the Two

A regular newsletter will produce reports and information about the area of law on a periodic basis (weekly, bi-weekly, monthly, etc.). Contents include new court cases, new administrative rules and regulations, opinion letters, previews of upcoming law, editorial comments, recent state and federal developments, and more. You can browse through the publication each period, or wait until you have an issue and go to an index and see what transpired since the last time you looked at this particular area.

Binders with interfiled pages collect and organize the law in one place for you. When the law changes, the publisher issues new pages to replace the ones that have become outdated—reporting the new laws, new rules and regs that now apply, taking out the old ones that have been superseded or abrogated, giving notice of new cases, bulletins, opinion letters, and other interpretations that have come down.

The updating can be periodic (e.g., weekly, monthly), or done on an "as-needed" basis. The updating is done by a team of researchers and editors at the publisher (e.g., Federal Securities Law Reporter, Copyright Law Reporter, Antitrust & Trade Regulation Report) or is handled by one particular author or editor and his or her researchers (e.g., Newberg on Class Actions, Moore's Federal Practice). These latter volumes are often referred to as "**treatises**," although they operate just like any other loose-leaf publication.

III. PUBLISHERS

Commerce Clearing House (CCH) and Bureau of National Affairs (BNA) are the primary contenders. Matthew Bender, Research Institute of America (RIA), West, Aspen, LEXIS Law Publishing are in the game to a lesser extent.

Chapter 15

Constitutions and Federal, State, and Municipal Legislation

CONSTITUTIONS

I. THE CONSTITUTION OF THE UNITED STATES OF AMERICA

We the people, in order to form a more perfect union . . . etc.

The United States Constitution is the foundation of the federal law in the United States and a regulator of state laws. The Constitution is a "living" document—meaning that the prevailing view of scholars of constitutional interpretation is that the U.S. Constitution is not a static text, but is meant to be interpreted and applied in light of current conditions in the country.

"Framers' Intent," a phrase referring to the interpretations, intentions, and aspirations of the drafters of the Constitution as to their work product, plays an important role in untangling thorny ambiguities in the text of the Constitution in a way not seen with ordinary legislation. People would rather pick the brain of James Madison than any 21st Century Supreme Court justice on the meaning and application of the Constitution.

The primary interpreter of the Constitution is the United States Supreme Court. This leads to some pretty heady case law. This area of the law gets very interesting, because the opinions of the Court are so detailed and complex, and the people writing them have such distinct personalities and persuasions. You often get multiple dissents and pluralities, and a jumble of opinions in cases that are hard to reconcile. The complex and high caliber problems of constitutional law attract some high-powered scholars, so the commentary written on the Constitution is as weighty and fruitful as the opinions that are the subject of this commentary.

II. PRIMARY SOURCES FOR RESEARCHING AND INTERPRETING THE CONSTITUTION

Locating cases is a primary goal, and the usual suppliers (from West) lead you to them.

A. Annotated constitutional law materials

1. United States Code Annotated, Constitution of the United States Annotated

These volumes are part of West's United States Code Annotated (U.S.C.A.). Each article, section, and clause of the Constitution is annotated in the Notes of Decisions section with every case that cites the clause or section, cross-referenced to digest topics and encyclopedia sections. There also is a good index. (Remember West's promise: We'll be comprehensive so you can be, too.)

2. United States Code Service, Constitution

The one-time competitor to West (Lawyers Cooperative) produced this volume, which also has annotations and a useful index. It also is cross-referenced to a lot of other former Lawyer's Cooperative products, such as ALRs.

3. The Constitution of the United States of America (Library of Congress Edition)

The Congressional Research Service of the Library of Congress has put together a nice set of volumes with the text of each article, section, and clause, and it includes analysis and commentary by the editorial staff. In the commentary, important U.S. Supreme Court cases are cited and discussed, and references are made to the proceedings of the Constitutional Convention, and to various dissenting opinions of justices and other materials. Tables include:

- Proposed amendments pending before the states;
- Proposed amendments not ratified by the states (the Equal Rights Amendment, for example);
- Acts of Congress held unconstitutional in whole or in part;
- State constitutional provisions and state statutes held unconstitutional in whole or in part;
- Local ordinances held unconstitutional;
- U.S. Supreme Court decisions overruled by subsequent Supreme Court decisions.

This set is held to be a useful starting point for research into any constitutional law problem.

4. Digests

Various digests exist to lead you to cases on constitutional law topics: U.S. Supreme Court Digest (West); Digest of the United States Supreme Court Reports, Lawyers Edition (LEXIS Law Pub.). The Federal Digest and Federal Practice Digest in its various editions (3rd, 4th etc.) includes citations to U.S. Supreme Court cases.

5. ALR annotations

A.L.R. Federal and A.L.R. 1st, 2nd, 3rd, 4th, and 5th series may contain law report annotations on constitutional law issues.

6. Shepard's

United States Citations and state units cover cases citing and interpreting the Constitution.

B. On-line access

Of course, you can get to the text, annotations, cases, and a lot of the commentary in treatises and law reviews on-line with Lexis and Westlaw. Lexis has the United States Code and the United States Code Service. Westlaw has the U.S.C.A..

III. SECONDARY SOURCES FOR INTERPRETATION

There are voluminous writings on every significant topic of constitutional law. This area attracts the best legal minds. In that this area of law is complex, and the opinions of the Supreme Court are highly complicated and often confusing from the multiple opinions, pluralities, concurrences, and so forth, and because it is widely believed that a proper interpretation includes reference to background and historical information from the framing of the Constitution, secondary persuasive sources are very important to this area, and they should be looked to more routinely than in other areas of the law.

A. Collections of commentary and bibliographies

Constitutional law is rich in its collections of commentary and other secondary sources. The Encyclopedia of the American Constitution contains 2,100 articles collected for the Bicentennial. There also was some bibliographic collecting. The Founder's Constitution contains five volumes of documents that bear on the text and drafting of the Constitution. A Comprehensive Bibliography of American Constitutional and Legal History, 1896-1979 is a multi-volume bibliography of resources, while The Constitution of the United States: A Guide and Bibliography to Current Scholarly Research is a good one volume work collecting authorities.
　　Constitutional Law Dictionary is more than a dictionary, it collects cases, too.

B. Leading treatises on constitutional law

The following are generally considered to be highly authoritative works on constitutional law issues: Ronald Rotunda and John Nowak's Treatise on Constitutional Law:

Substance and Procedure; Laurence Tribe's one volume American Constitutional Law; Chester Antieau's Modern Constitutional Law. Naturally, if your constitutional law professor has other favorites, or criticizes one or more of these authors, follow your professor's guidance while in her course.

C. Framers' intent and founding fathers' information

It can be a chore to find and interpret the source material for framers' intent, but the following volumes can help: Documents Illustrative of the Formation of the Union of the American States (Library of Congress Leg. Ref. Serv.); Documentary History of the Constitution of the United States of America, 1786-1870 (Library of Congress Leg. Ref. Serv.); The Federalist—essays and papers of some of the primary drafters, Madison, Jay, and Hamilton. Sometimes referred to as the Federalist Papers. Some of these resources are online—Westlaw's dial-up service's BICENT database contains the above three sources.

D. The Constitutional Convention

If you find a need to look at the actual debates and proceedings of the Constitutional Convention, try the following: Records of the Federal Constitution of 1787; Elliot's Debates (The Debates, Resolutions, and Other Proceedings in Convention, on the Adoption of the Federal Constitution (1827)); Documentary History of the Ratification of the Constitution.

V. STATE CONSTITUTIONS

The official version of a state constitution generally is printed in the state's official statutes. West and a few others supply annotations in their annotated version of the state statutes. Columbia University School of Law's Legislative Drafting Research Fund has collected texts of the 50 state constitutions in the Constitutions of the United States: National and State volumes. This also has a companion set of volumes called Index Digest of State Constitutions, which reports the various constitutional provisions from the states on a collection of topics for comparative purposes. State Constitutional Conventions, Commissions and Amendments (microfiche collection) gathers documents and information from the conventions that established the state constitutions.

FEDERAL LEGISLATION

I. HOW FEDERAL LAWS ARE MADE

> "All Legislative Powers herein granted shall be vested in a Congress of the United States, which shall consist of a Senate and House of Representatives."

U.S. Const. art. I, § 1.

A. Forms of congressional action[1]

The work of Congress is initiated by the introduction of a proposal in one of four principal forms: the bill, the joint resolution, the concurrent resolution, and the simple resolution.

1. Bills

A bill is the form used for most legislation, whether permanent or temporary, general or special, public or private. A bill originating in the House of Representatives is designated by the letters "H.R.," signifying "House of Representatives," followed by a number that it retains throughout all its parliamentary stages. Bills introduced in the Senate get an "S.," followed by a number. Bills are presented to the President for action when approved in identical form by both the House of Representatives and the Senate.

2. Joint resolutions

Joint resolutions may originate either in the House of Representatives or in the Senate. There is little practical difference between a bill and a joint resolution. Both are subject to the same procedure, except for a joint resolution proposing an amendment to the Constitution. On approval of such a resolution by two-thirds of both the House and Senate, it is sent directly to the Administrator of General Services for submission to the individual states for ratification. It is not presented to the President for approval. A joint resolution originating in the House of Representatives is designated "H.J.Res.," followed by its individual number. Joint resolutions become law in the same manner as bills.

3. Concurrent resolutions

Matters affecting the operations of both the House of Representatives and Senate are usually initiated by means of concurrent resolutions. A concurrent resolution originating in the House of Representatives is designated "H.Con.Res.," followed by its individual number. On approval by both the House of Representatives and Senate, they are signed by the Clerk of the House and the Secretary of the Senate. They are not presented to the president for action.

4. Simple resolutions

A matter concerning the operation of either the House of Representatives or Senate alone is initiated by a simple resolution. A resolution affecting the House of Representatives

---

[1] This section is largely drawn from the U.S. House of Representative Information Resources, and the publication "How Our Laws Are Made," reported at http://thomas.loc.gov/home/lawsmade.bysec (last visited Jan. 22, 1999).

is designated "H.Res.," followed by its number. They are not presented to the President for action.

B. Introduction and referral to committee

Any Member in the House of Representatives may introduce a bill at any time while the House is in session by simply placing it in the "hopper" provided for this purpose at the side of the Clerk's desk in the House Chamber. The sponsor's signature must appear on the bill. A public bill may have an unlimited number of co-sponsoring Members. The bill is assigned its legislative number by the Clerk and referred to the appropriate committee by the Speaker, with the assistance of the Parliamentarian. The bill is then printed in its introduced form, which you can read in Bill Text. If a bill was introduced today, summary information about it can be found in Bill Status Today.

An important phase of the legislative process is the action taken by committees. It is during committee action that the most intense consideration is given to the proposed measures; this is also the time when the people are given their opportunity to be heard. Each piece of legislation is referred to the committee that has jurisdiction over the area affected by the measure.

C. Consideration by committee—public hearings and markup sessions

Usually the first step in this process is a public hearing, where the committee members hear witnesses representing various viewpoints on the measure. Each committee makes public the date, place, and subject of any hearing it conducts. The Committee Meetings scheduled for today are available along with other House Schedules. Public announcements are also published in the Daily Digest portion of the Congressional Record.

A transcript of the testimony taken at a hearing is made available for inspection in the committee office, and frequently the complete transcript is printed and distributed by the committee.

After hearings are completed, the bill is considered in a session that is popularly known as the "mark-up" session. Members of the committee study the viewpoints presented in detail. Amendments may be offered to the bill, and the committee members vote to accept or reject these changes.

This process can take place at either the subcommittee level or the full committee level, or at both. Hearings and markup sessions are status steps noted in the Legislative Action portion of Bill Status.

D. Committee action

At the conclusion of deliberation, a vote of committee or subcommittee members is taken to determine what action to take on the measure. It can be reported, with or without amendment, or tabled, which means no further action on it will occur. If the committee has approved extensive amendments, they may decide to report a new bill incorporating all the amendments. This is known as a "clean bill," which will have a new number. Votes in committee can be found in Committee Votes.

If the committee votes to report a bill, the Committee Report is written. This report describes the purpose and scope of the measure and the reasons for recommended approval. House Report numbers are prefixed with "H. Rep." and then a number indicating the Congress (for example, H. Rep.105-279, referring to a House Report from the 105th Congress).

E. House floor consideration

Consideration of a measure by the full House can be a simple or very complex operation. In general, a measure is ready for consideration by the full House after it has been reported by a committee. Under certain circumstances, it may be brought to the floor directly. The consideration of a measure may be governed by a "rule." A rule is itself a simple resolution, which must be passed by the House, that sets out the particulars of debate for a specific bill—how much time will allowed for debate, whether amendments can be offered, and other matters. Debate time for a measure is normally divided between proponents and opponents. Each side yields time to those Members who wish to speak on the bill. When amendments are offered, these are also debated and voted upon. If the House is in session today, you can see a summary of Current House Floor Proceedings. After all debate is concluded and amendments decided upon, the House is ready to vote on final passage. In some cases, a vote to "recommit" the bill to committee is requested. This is usually an effort by opponents to change some portion or to table the measure. If the attempt to recommit fails, a vote on final passage is ordered.

F. Resolving differences

After a measure passes in the House, it goes to the Senate for consideration. A bill must pass both bodies in the same form before it can be presented to the President for signature into law. If the Senate changes the language of the measure, it must return to the House for concurrence or additional changes. This back-and-forth negotiation may occur on the House floor, with the House accepting or rejecting Senate amendments or the complete Senate text. Often a conference committee will be appointed with both House and Senate members. This group will resolve the differences in committee and report the identical measure back to both bodies for a vote. Conference committees also issue reports outlining the final version of the bill.

G. Final steps

When either house orders the third reading of a bill, it simultaneously orders the **engrossment** of the bill. This is a formal reprinting of the bill in the final form that the bill will take before voting takes place in each chamber. (In earlier days, the final version was written up in large script, hence the term "engrossment.")

Votes on final passage, as well as all other votes in the House, may be taken by the electronic voting system which registers each individual Member's response. These votes are referred to as Yea/Nay votes or recorded votes, and are available in House Votes by Bill number, roll call vote number, or words describing the reason for the vote. Votes in the House may also be by voice vote, and no record of individual responses is available. After a measure has been passed in identical form by both the House and Senate, it is considered **"enrolled,"** and the **enrolled version** of the bill represents the official legislative enactment of the bill.

Presentation occurs when the enrolled version of the bill is sent to the President, who may sign the measure into law, veto it and return it to Congress, let it become law without signature, or, at the end of a session, pocket-veto it.

II. PUBLICATION OF FEDERAL LAWS[2]

A. Slip Laws — Statutes-at-Large — United States Code

One of the important steps in the enactment of a valid law is the requirement that it shall be made known to the people who are to be bound by it. If the President approves a bill, or allows it to become law without signing it, the original enrolled bill is sent from the White House to the Archivist of the United States for publication. If a bill is passed by both houses of Congress over the objections of the President, the body that last overrides the veto transmits it. It is then assigned a public law number, and paginated for the Statutes at Large volume covering that session of Congress.

The public and private law numbers run in sequence starting anew at the beginning of each Congress and, since 1957, they have been prefixed for ready identification by the number of the Congress. For example, the first public law of the 105th Congress is designated Public Law 105-1 and the first private law of the 105th Congress is designated Private Law 105-1. Subsequent laws of this Congress also will contain the same prefix designator—the second public law passed by the 105th Congress is designated Public Law 105-2, and so on.

B. Slip laws

The first official publication of the statute is in the form generally known as the "slip law." In this form, each law is published separately as an unbound pamphlet. The heading indicates the public or private law number, the date of approval, and the bill number. The heading of a slip law for a public law also indicates the United States Statutes at Large

---

[2] This section is drawn from the U.S. House of Representatives Information Resources, http://thomas.loc.gov/home/lawsmade.bysec/publication.html (last visited Jan. 22, 1999).

citation. If the statute has been passed over the veto of the President, or has become law without the President's signature because he did not return it with objections, an appropriate statement is inserted instead of the usual notation of approval.

The Office of the Federal Register, National Archives and Records Administration prepares the slip laws and provides marginal editorial notes giving the citations to laws mentioned in the text and other explanatory details. The marginal notes also give the United States Code classifications, enabling the reader immediately to determine where the statute will appear in the Code. Each slip law also includes an informative guide to the legislative history of the law consisting of the committee report number, the name of the committee in each house, as well as the date of consideration and passage in each house, with a reference to the Congressional Record by volume, year, and date. A reference to presidential statements relating to the approval of a bill or the veto of a bill when the veto was overridden and the bill becomes law is included in the legislative history as a citation to the Weekly Compilation of Presidential Documents.

Copies of the slip laws are delivered to the document rooms of both houses where they are available to officials and the public. They may also be obtained by annual subscription or individual purchase from the Government Printing Office and are available in electronic form for computer access. Section 113 of title 1 of the United States Code provides that slip laws are competent evidence in all the federal and state courts, tribunals, and public offices.

C. Statutes at Large

The United States Statutes at Large, prepared by the Office of the Federal Register, National Archives and Records Administration, provide a permanent collection of the laws of each session of Congress in bound volumes. Each volume contains a complete index and a table of contents. The volumes from 1956 through 1976 each contain a table of earlier laws affected. These tables were cumulated for 1956-1970 and supplemented for 1971-1975 in pamphlet form and discontinued in 1976. The 1963 through 1974 volumes also contain a most useful table showing the legislative history of each law in the volume. This latter table was not included in subsequent volumes because the legislative histories have appeared at the end of each law since 1975. There are also extensive marginal notes referring to laws in earlier volumes and to earlier and later matters in the same volume.

Under the provisions of a statute originally enacted in 1895, the version of the laws printed in the Statutes at Large is **legal evidence** of the terms and requirements of federal statutory law and will be accepted as **proof positive** of those laws in any court in the United States.

The Statutes at Large are a chronological arrangement of the laws exactly as they have been enacted. The fifth law passed by a Congress is printed immediately before the sixth law passed, regardless of the content of these laws. There is no attempt to arrange the laws according to their subject matter or to show the present status of an earlier law that has been amended on one or more occasions. The code of laws serves that purpose.

D. United States Code

The United States Code contains a consolidation and codification of the general and permanent laws of the United States arranged according to subject matter under 50 title headings (*see below*). It sets out the current status of the laws, as amended, without repeating all the language of the amendatory acts except where necessary for that purpose. The Code is declared to be **prima facie** evidence of those laws, meaning that the words viewed in the U.S. Code are held to be the terms of the law unless someone comes forward to rebut the U.S. Code version by reference to the Statutes at Large or the Slip Law version of the law. Its purpose is to present the laws in a concise and usable form without requiring recourse to the many volumes of the Statutes at Large containing the individual amendments.

The Code is prepared by the Law Revision Counsel of the House of Representatives. New editions are published every six years and cumulative supplements are published after the conclusion of each regular session of the Congress. The Code is also available in electronic form for computer access.

Twenty-two of the 50 titles have been revised and enacted into positive law, and two have been eliminated by consolidation with other titles. Titles that have been revised and enacted into positive law are referred to as **codified reenactments**, and they achieve the same status as the laws printed in the Statutes at Large; in other words, the U.S. Code text of a codified reenactment is legal evidence of the law and the courts will receive the text as proof positive of the terms of those laws. Eventually, all the titles will be revised and enacted into positive law. At that point, they will be updated by direct amendment.

E.   The 50 titles of the United States Code

The Code is divided into 50 titles by subject matter. Each title is divided into sections. Sections within a title may be grouped together as subtitles, chapters, subchapters, parts, subparts, or divisions. Titles may also have appendices which may be divided into sections, rules, or forms.

The subjects covered by the 50 titles of the U.S. Code[3] are:

1. General Provisions
2. The Congress
3. The President
4. Flag and Seal, Seat of Government, and the States
5. Government Organization and Employees
6. Surety Bonds (repealed by the enactment of Title 31)
7. Agriculture

---

[3] Law Revision Counsel, U.S. House of Representatives, http://www.legal.gsa.gov/fedfra1g.html (last visited Jan. 7, 1999).

8. Aliens and Nationality
9. Arbitration
10. Armed Forces
11. Bankruptcy
12. Banks and Banking
13. Census
14. Coast Guard
15. Commerce and Trade
16. Conservation
17. Copyrights
18. Crimes and Criminal Procedure
19. Customs Duties
20. Education
21. Food and Drugs
22. Foreign Relations and Intercourse
23. Highways
24. Hospitals and Asylums
25. Indians
26. Internal Revenue Code
27. Intoxicating Liquors
28. Judiciary and Judicial Procedure
29. Labor
30. Mineral Lands and Mining
31. Money and Finance
32. National Guard
33. Navigation and Navigable Waters
34. Navy (eliminated by the enactment of Title 10)
35. Patents
36. Patriotic Societies and Observations
37. Pay and Allowances of the Uniformed Services
38. Veterans' Benefits
39. Postal Service
40. Public Buildings, Property, and Works
41. Public Contracts
42. The Public Health and Welfare
43. Public Lands
44. Public Printing and Documents
45. Railroads
46. Shipping
47. Telegraphs, Telephones, and Radiotelegraphs
48. Territories and Insular Possessions
49. Transportation
50. War and National Defense

III. RESEARCHING FEDERAL STATUTORY LAW

A. United States Statutes at Large

The Statutes at Large has the exact language and form passed by Congress, and so it is the official law of the land. If other versions (other codifications) differ, they are in error and the Statutes at Large control. The Statutes at Large has three main parts: Public Laws, Private Laws, and Treaties.

1. Public laws

Public laws are the most important to this course of study and to your future research (until you get into an area where treaties are equally important, such as international law or intellectual property law). Public laws are further codified into the United States Code (U.S.C.) and commercial codifications, such as the United States Code Annotated by West (U.S.C.A.), and the United States Code Service (West, formerly Lawyers Cooperative) (U.S.C.S.). Public Laws are applicable to everyone in the U.S.A. They are referenced as:

P.L. 95-123 or Pub. L. 95-123.

As discussed above, this reference represents the "123rd" public law enacted by the 95th Congress, and it will be found in numerical (and thus chronological) order within the Statutes at Large, first by the Congress (95th) and then by the sequential enactment number (123). P.L. 95-123 follows P.L. 95-122 and precedes P.L. 95-124.

The Statutes at Large are cited as "Stat." e.g., 92 Stat. 1020. *This is the official citation form* for the Statutes at Large and the laws found therein, although when researching, either the Public Law number (P.L.) or the Statutes at Large (Stat.) citation will enable you to locate Public Laws in the Statutes at Large.

2. Private laws

Private Laws affect only single individuals or small groups, mainly in the areas of: (1) immigration and naturalization; and (2) personal claims involving the government, e.g., regarding the timeliness of a Tort Claims action against the United States. If Congress determined to make a U.S. citizen of Winston Churchill or a Cuban refugee such as Elian Gonzales, they would do it by passing a private law.

3. Treaties

Treaties have the same importance and legal effect as the laws passed by Congress according to the U.S. Const. art. VI, cl. 2 (". . . all Treaties made, or which shall be made, under the Authority of the United States, shall be the supreme Law of the Land . . .") although they do not require the approval of the House of Representatives. Article II, § 2, cl. 2 of the United States Constitution gives the President the power, "with the Advice and Consent of the Senate," to make treaties, if approved by a two-thirds majority of the Senate quorum voting. In addition to the Statutes at Large, treaties are found in several reporter series, such as United States Treaties (U.S.T.), and Treaties and other International Acts Series (T.I.A.S.).

B. Early publication of new laws and amendments to existing laws

The Statutes at Large and the United States Code both are published by the Government Printing Office. Thus, they are three to five years (Stat.) and twelve to twenty-four months (U.S.C.) behind the date of enactment of the laws they publish. There is also a delay with the two commercial services, U.S.C.S. and U.S.C.A., although it is only a few weeks delay in most instances.

1. U.S.C.C.A.N.

When you need more timely information, West publishes the United States Code, Congressional & Administrative News (U.S.C.C.A.N.), an unofficial news publication. It is a respected source, but it is not an official source of the law—cite to it only when the law or amendment is not yet reported in one of the commercial services, U.S.C.A. or U.S.C.S. U.S.C.C.A.N. does not publish every law or amendment, only the more prominent and important ones (often the ones you will be looking for), and it gets them to press quicker than the other services. (U.S.C.C.A.N. also is a source of legislative history, which is discussed in the next chapter).

2. U.S.C.S. Advance Service

There is a companion service to the U.S.C.S., the United States Code Service Advance Service, which tries to get out new legislation within two to three weeks of passage. They use the Public Law Number for organization and issue a paper bound supplement.

3. Slip Laws, U.S. Law Week, Westlaw, and Lexis

The fastest print publication is by Slip Laws, although done by the Government Printing Office, they are distributed to subscribers such as law libraries within days or a week or so of passage. U.S. Law Week (U.S.L.W.) also gets to print quickly, although only the most important or controversial acts (cutting edge, newsworthy, etc.) are published here.

Fastest of all is Westlaw and Lexis, which contain databases for tracking proposed legislation and providing the text of each draft version as it progresses through the legislative process. Thus, if a bill becomes law, the final version immediately is available. Note, however, that because of the ability to track each version as it progresses, any search you run will pull up multiple versions of the same bill. What you are looking for is the official version passed by both houses, which is referred to as the **"enrolled" version.**

C. Codifications and subject organization

The Statutes at Large are chronological—a law is passed and printed in the volume for the 95th Congress; the 96th Congress amends it—the amendment shows up in the volume for that Congress. Other laws were passed on the same topic by the 88th, 90th, 91st and 93rd Congresses—these laws are found in the volumes for those Congresses. Nothing in the Statutes at Large cross-references or compiles the ongoing results of all this legislation. This is where the codification services enter the picture.

1. United States Code

Upon enactment, Public Laws are sent to the Congressional Office of Law Revision Counsel, who breaks the law down into its component parts and assigns the parts to the fifty titles and subsections of the U.S. Code.

While the Statutes at Large represents the official version of the laws actually voted upon and passed by the Congress, the U.S.C. is held to be "presumptively" official because it is a reorganization of the official version. Thus, the U.S.C. is presumed to be a correct statement of the law and may be cited. However, if there exists a difference between the Code and the Statutes at Large, the Statutes at Large controls and must be cited. Accordingly, the U.S.C. must be used with caution, and where a U.S.C. provision's express wording is crucial to your case or legal analysis, the prudent lawyer will always confirm that wording in the Statutes at Large.

However, if the title of the U.S. Code you are looking at is marked with an asterisk (*), this indicates that Congress has passed into positive law the "codified" versions of the law as found in the United States Code. Thus, the codified version in the U.S. Code is no longer simply presumptively correct, it becomes the <u>official</u> version, and the Statutes at Large version no longer controls (or, more accurately, the codified re-enactment takes its place among the Statutes at Large, thereby supplanting the original enactment). This has been done to 22 titles of the U.S. Code. So pay attention to asterisks! Note, however, that subsequent amendments to the codified re-enactments printed in the U.S. Code are simply "presumptively correct" even though they are printed in the same volume of the U.S. Code as the official text—that is, until Congress goes ahead and re-enacts the codified amendments into positive law.

The United States Code began in 1926 and is re-issued every six (6) years. It is updated by supplements during intervening years. It contains only the law, historical notes, and commentaries on the law.

2. West's United States Code Annotated

West's United States Code Annotated ("U.S.C.A.") is organized exactly like and uses the same referencing system as the United States Code; e.g., 17 U.S.C. § 101 (the U.S. Code version), is found in the U.S.C.A. at 17 U.S.C.A. § 101. U.S.C.A. prints the same text (you hope), historical notes and commentaries found in the U.S.C. itself, along with additional information added by West editors; <u>e.g.</u>, law review references, C.F.R. elaboration, and annotations—brief quotes from and abstracts of cases that cite the statutory section at hand, which can help you find relevant cases that construe and apply the statute. West prints an annotation for *every* case that mentions a U.S. Code provision, so many of the cases will be redundant (they all say the same thing), but you can expect comprehensive coverage, and easily can skip to your jurisdiction's cases in the list of annotations. Annotations are subdivided by specific issues and topics from the area of law of the statutory section you are researching.

Special volumes annotate the United States Constitution, and the entire U.S.C.A. has a thorough index, including a "Popular Names Table," which references codified enactments by their "short titles." It has annual "pocket parts" to keep it current.

The U.S.C.A.'s main shortcoming is that is relies on the language of the U.S.C. itself, and the U.S.C. is only presumptively correct. If the U.S.C. codifiers commit "sins of omission and commission," West will replicate these errors. (Of course, West's typesetters and editors can make transcription errors of their own, too). Sometimes the U.S.C.A. will note an error in the language from the "official version," or annotations from cases will note an error, but this is not always the case.

The Bluebook requires citation to the U.S. Code (U.S.C.) for the codified version of a federal statute, not the U.S.C.A. If the U.S. Code is inconsistent with the Statutes at Large, citation must be to the Statutes at Large.

3. United States Code Service

In the same manner as the U.S.C.A., the United States Code Service ("U.S.C.S.") prints the law so as to be consistent with the U.S. Code, so if you want to find 17 U.S.C. § 101 in the U.S.C.S. you look for 17 U.S.C.S. § 101. The U.S.C.S. includes everything that is in the U.S.C., plus law review and C.F.R. references (not necessarily the same ones found in U.S.C.A.), and "annotations" referencing case law construing each code provision. There is a General Index and Popular Names Table, and the volumes are kept current with pocket parts.

There are two differences between the U.S.C.A. and the U.S.C.S.: before creating annotations, the publisher of U.S.C.S. tries to weed out inapposite, redundant, and irrelevant cases that happen to cite the code. As a result, there usually are fewer case references in the U.S.C.S. than in the U.S.C.A., but you supposedly receive greater assurance of their relevance. If you trust the editors' discretion, you might zero in on truly relevant cases more quickly with U.S.C.S., but if you want to see the universe of cases citing the statute, stick to U.S.C.A. Time might make that decision for you.

A second, very important difference between U.S.C.S. and U.S.C.A. is that U.S.C.S. does not follow the U.S.C.'s wording. Instead, U.S.C.S. editors check its wording against the Statutes at Large and, to the extent a deviation is found, they include the official wording and highlight that passage, bringing it to the researcher's attention.

The United States Code Service includes other features that assist legal researchers. Following the U.S.C.S.'s general presentation and general index, U.S.C.S. offers separate annotated renditions of the Federal Rules of Civil Procedure, Criminal Procedure, Appellate Procedure, Administrative Procedure, U.S. Supreme Court Rules & Procedure, Federal Circuit Court Local Rules, Federal Sentencing Guidelines, and others. On the topic of regulatory law, the U.S.C.S. has an "Index & Finding Aids to Code and Federal Regulations," which cross-references U.S.C.S. provisions and the C.F.R. rules and regulations promulgated from the statutory provision, and vice versa—you can move from the statute to the regulatory law or from the regulatory law back to the statute.

STATE AND MUNICIPAL LEGISLATION

I. SESSION LAWS

In the same manner as the federal government, state legislatures enact laws that are published in chronological order (in order of the date of passage of the laws) in volumes identified by the session of the legislature wherein the law was passed (akin to the U.S. Statutes at Large). Hence the term "Session Laws."

II. CODIFICATIONS OF STATE LAWS

In that a yearly or bi-yearly report of the statutes passed in the chronological order of passage is not very useful to the researcher for finding all of the laws on a given topic, states codify their statutes in volumes referred to as the state **code** or **laws** or **statutes**, often with a descriptive reference such as **compiled**, **revised**, or **consolidated**. E.g., Missouri Revised Statutes; Illinois Compiled Statutes; Idaho Official Code; General Statutes of Connecticut; General Laws of the Commonwealth of Massachusetts.

The codes generally provide:

- Text of the state constitution (and sometimes the federal constitution);
- Text of the statutes themselves in the "proper" codified subject matter area;
- Historical notes (including a list of prior enactments of law on the same topic);
- Indices (to find the laws you should be looking at);
- Official commentary on the statute or the section at hand (this is unusual);
- Tables for referencing rules, administrative law relationships, cross-references to related sections and statutes, bill numbers that became session laws, popular names of legislation, etc. (this is common, and very useful);
- Court rules (the Mississippi Rules of Civil Procedure, etc.)

The official laws of the state are updated in the ordinary ways with pocket parts or pamphlets, supplements (often soft-bound), and replacement volumes.

III. ANNOTATED STATUTES

The usefulness of annotations to cases that carry out, interpret, or construe the statutes is not lost on the states (and West Publishing). You will find an annotated version of each state's laws. Sometimes the annotated version is the "official" version (or the only version) of the state statutes (e.g., New York), so check the Bluebook. Pocket-parts, pamphlets, and supplements are the preferred methods for updating annotated statutes.

IV. ON-LINE SERVICES

Westlaw and Lexis are sources for each state's unannotated *or* official statutes (e.g., CA-ST on Westlaw), and almost all states' annotated statutes (e.g., CA-ST-ANN on Westlaw). Recent session laws for several states also can be found on Westlaw and Lexis. Indeed, these will be the most up-to-date versions of the statutes and session laws available. Note that the unannotated library will not necessarily be the "official" statutes. Many times on Westlaw, the xx-ST database does not get you the official state statutes—it gets you the text of the statutes as printed in one of West's annotated versions of the state statutes, but Westlaw withholds showing you the annotations. If you simply hate to read annotations, there you go.

If you want the official statutes, many states have a web site where you can access their official state statutes and sometimes their recent session laws. State bar associations often duplicate this service providing the same information and other links to state legislative material.

IV. MULTIPLE STATES SOURCES

Often, you will have the most success finding the statutory laws of multiple jurisdictions (or all 50 states) on a given subject in a topical publication of the loose-leaf variety, brought to you by private publishers such as Bureau of National Affairs (BNA), Commerce Clearing House (CCH), and others. For instance, if you want the laws of all fifty states on securities fraud (similar to federal Rule 10b-5), you could check out one of CCH's volumes on Blue Sky Law (the term coined for state securities laws), or Securities Litigation. If you want multiple states' laws on sexual harassment in the workplace, you could check out one of BNA's volumes on employment discrimination.

V. MUNICIPAL LAW

A local public library or local law library most likely is the best or only place to look for local ordinances. Finding city codes or even publications of local ordinances on-line often is a hit or miss process, but some of you may be lucky enough to live (or study, or both) in a city that has reported its information on the Internet. For example, the St. Louis Public Library has created a searchable web site for the City of St. Louis Charter, Revised Code, Ordinances (starting in 1991), and even Alderman Meeting minutes (i.e., legislative history) starting in May 1998 (the library probably has paper copies of earlier minutes available for examination, but not on-line), all at the SL Public Library web site: www.slpl.lib.mo.us/cco/index.htm.

Finding cases that interpret these laws is even harder. You always can search on Westlaw or Lexis in a general state law database for the hits on the terms or the reference number/citation of a local ordinance. But very few "annotated" municipal codes exist. State digests sometimes devote attention to cases that interpret a municipal charter or local ordinance. You can search the annual index to the volumes, or search on-line (if the state digest is on-line).

Shepard's State Citations tracks cases that interpret municipal laws. There is a separate set of volumes called Shepard's Ordinance Law Annotations that annotate cases that construe municipal ordinances on broadly defined topics and specifically defined sub-topics from any number of jurisdictions (cities). Thus, you can find cases from a variety of states that construe the same type of ordinance, and offer these findings as persuasive evidence of how to interpret your own local ordinance.

Chapter 16

Legislative History

I. WHAT IS LEGISLATIVE HISTORY?

Legislative history is a term used to designate the documents and materials that contain the historical and background information generated while a bill or other legislative action is on its way to becoming a law. It includes draft versions of the bill, redrafts, testimony at various hearings on the bill, committee reports, studies, legislative floor debates, executive messages, and other materials generated in this process.

II. FOR WHAT PURPOSES IS LEGISLATIVE HISTORY USED?

Legislative history is used to monitor the progress of a bill or other action to determine its status (prior to enactment into law), and to determine "legislative intent"—trying to figure out what the legislature meant when they wrote or rewrote the bill (and eventually the law) a certain way. This is used to further argue an interpretation of the law or to attempt to resolve ambiguities created by the words of a statute.

As a bill is amended and rewritten during the legislative process, each version is reprinted. The theory behind the usefulness of legislative history is that these progressive additions, deletions, and alterations in the language are direct evidence of deliberate thinking on the part of the legislators who contributed to the creation of the law. For example:

> If a bill originally stated that dog-owners were to be excluded from its coverage, but this exclusion was written out of the bill just prior to enactment into law, one could argue persuasively that the legislature intended to include dog-owners within the coverage of the statute.

> If a legal standard in the law was originally phrased as "actual knowledge," and the bill was later amended in this section to state a standard of "actual or constructive knowledge," one could argue that the legislature intended the standard of knowledge to be lower, and certainly not the same as "actual knowledge."

The reports generated by committees and conferences, and the floor debates where questions about the statute and explanations of the meaning of the terms are discussed, are also taken to be evidence of legislative intent. For example:

If the sponsor of a bill told the House of Representatives in a speech on the floor of the House that the law would definitely encompass dog-owners in its scope, and nothing else in the debate contradicts this statement, one could argue that the representatives understood the law to cover dog-owners when they voted on the law.

III. LEGISLATIVE HISTORY AS LEGAL AUTHORITY

Legislative history is *not* a source of the law and it is never to be considered primary controlling authority. The terms of the statute itself are the only primary, potentially controlling legal authority regarding the law created by the statute.

However, legislative history is not simply commentary. It is not simply a secondary persuasive authority, such as a treatise or law review, that discusses the meaning of a statute. It is evidence of legislative intent prior to the fact of enactment that goes beyond the realm of interpretations by third-parties after the fact. Thus, in most instances, it carries more persuasive weight than even the commentary and interpretation of a great legal scholar.

As the goal of statutory interpretation always is to determine the meaning of the statutory text, oftentimes evidence of the authors of that text is relevant and helpful to finding the meaning of difficult or ambiguous terms. In a situation where one particular piece of legislative history directly answers a question or resolves an ambiguity in the absence of other pieces of legislative history that produce contrary inferences, then the use of the uncontroverted legislative history to discern the meaning of the text seems imminently prudent and appropriate.

However, there is a basic tension created by an attempt to use legislative history in litigation or other legal fora: as discussed above, there is a long-standing and strongly supported school of thought that believes that statutes should be interpreted on the basis of the terms of the statute alone. The rules of construction discussed in Chapter 5 aid the process of reading and applying the text, but it is the text that should govern the meaning of the statute. Ambiguities in statutory language are to be resolved textually (the logical meaning of the terms used in the statute) and contextually (the logical meaning of the statute as a whole and its meaning in the context of the existing law on the topic), not by resorting to evidence of the drafters' intent. But advocates are not always pleased with the way the terms of a statute are likely to be read and applied. Their clients may be on the short end of that equation. So, it is common for good advocates to search for support for a beneficial interpretation amidst the legislative history.

Courts often (but not always) are a willing audience for this kind of evidence of legislative intent, because the process of reading and interpreting the complicated terms of a statute can be uncomfortable. Judges want reassurance that they are not making a huge mistake. The bottom line is that advocates will keep digging for it and thrusting it under the courts' noses, and the courts will keep reading it and writing opinions that adopt arguments for interpretation that rely on legislative history. So, the study of legislative history is here to stay.

IV. WHAT DOCUMENTS AND MATERIALS MAKE UP LEGISLATIVE HISTORY?

A legislative history is made up of two components: the first is the chronology of events for the legislation in question—whether and when the bill was introduced, referred to committee or subcommittee, reported out, debated, sent to conference, voted on, and signed into law. The second component is the documents and testimony that were produced during the course of the chronology. In order to find out about these two components, it is necessary to understand the process by which legislation is enacted. (See Chapter 15, above).

The cornerstone of a legislative history is the bill number and the subsequent Public Law number. Bills are numbered sequentially in the order they are introduced. If they fail to be enacted in a given Congress, but are reintroduced in a subsequent Congress, their number will change with each new Congress.

As a bill progresses through the legislative process, it may generate several different kinds of documents. Note well that not every bill generates the same number and type of legislative history documents—it all depends on how complicated or troublesome the legislation was or how it was handled by the two chambers prior to enactment.

After a bill is introduced and numbered, it is assigned to a committee. Committees produce four different types of documents: Committee Prints, Committee Documents, Hearings, and Reports.

Committee Prints are compiled by the administrative staff of a Congressional committee as background for the committee members. They contain statistical data and background information and may be reproduced from such sources as the Congressional Research Service.

Committee Documents are sent to the committee by administrative agencies or the executive branch. Generally, they contain facts and information regarding the subject matter of the bill.

Hearings come in two forms: legislative committee hearings to receive testimony in support of (or against) bills currently before the House of Representatives or Senate, and investigative hearings on important issues which are not the subject of pending legislation, but which may lead to legislation in the future.

Committee Reports are written by the members of the committee and contain recommendations on why the bill should be passed. The report usually contains the text of the bill, an analysis of its content and meaning, and the committee's rationale for its recommendations. There may also be a minority statement if there was a disagreement among the committee members. Of all the documents to come out of committee, the Committee Report generally is considered to be the most important in establishing legislative intent, because it contains the legislators' own words and contemporaneous construction of the meaning of the legislation and it is intended to guide the thinking of the entire legislature on the meaning of the legislation.

At this point, the reported bill is sent back to the appropriate chamber for consideration. Floor debates along with amendments and votes on the legislation are contained in the **Congressional Record**.

Floor debates are considered to be another source of direct evidence of legislative intent, again because they are the legislators' own words. However, please note that the actual record of any given debate may be called into question because each Congressman can amend and edit the record of their remarks on the floor before the final version is recorded in the Congressional Record, and she even can submit prepared remarks and statements into the Record that were never actually delivered to the members of the chamber, and no one knows whether any legislator other than the author knew anything about the remarks. (Since March 1978, such inserted remarks are preceded and closed in the Congressional Record by a bullet (•), so that the researcher can know the material was not actually delivered to the chamber.)

If a conference is required to reconcile different versions of a bill that were debated and approved in the Senate and the House, a conference report may be generated. Note: no transcript or record of the proceedings of the conference committee is made, so the report generally is all you have to go on.

Conference Reports, even more than Committee Reports, are held to be important in establishing legislative intent, because they contain a contemporaneous construction and explanation of the meaning of the legislation from representatives of both chambers prior to the final consideration of the legislation by the two chambers. The conference report will appear in one the following formats: (a) In two parts consisting of the text of the agreed language of the bill and a discussion known as the "Joint Explanation of the Conferees." (b) Only the text of the sections where compromise was needed. Researchers also should be aware of the following facts regarding Conference Reports:

1. After the conference report is officially filed it goes to the House and Senate for debate. Technically, once on the floor it cannot be amended. However, legislators occasionally are able to manipulate the rules to their favor and make amendments.
2. The conference report always is printed in the Congressional Record in the House section.
3. Usually, researchers will be able to obtain a copy of a conference report from the House or Senate Document Room. However, if the conference report has generated a lot of interest (such as the Tax Reform Act of 1986) it will be sold by the GPO.
4. Specialized commercial services such as CCH or Prentice-Hall will reprint conference reports relevant to their subject matter in their various loose-leaf volumes on the topic of the statute.
5. The conference report will be cited as "H. Rept.", not as "H. Conf. Rept." If the Senate requested a printing of conference report it will be cited as "S. Rept." One may also see a citation to both a House and Senate conference reports. Such reports are identical and only one version need be obtained.

After each chamber of Congress has agreed upon the final version of a bill, the enrolled bill is sent to the President for signature, and if signed, it becomes a law and is published as a Slip Law.

V. HOW TO COMPILE A LEGISLATIVE HISTORY

You need to know at least one of the following things before you can start your legislative history:

Bill number and date introduced; or

Public Law number and date enacted.

You can find these numbers and names in several places (this is not a complete list):

1. "Bill Tracking Reports" available on Westlaw or Lexis in the resource areas for federal or state legislation.
2. CIS Legislative History volumes, index of subjects and names.
3. CCH Congressional Index. The "Enactments" section gives bill number for public laws and public law numbers for bills.
4. Statutes at Large and the U.S. Code Congressional & Administrative News (U.S.C.C.A.N.) are arranged by public law number, and list bill number and short title for each public law. The United States Code Service also issues monthly pamphlets with new public laws.
5. Congressional Record Index. The subject index gives bill numbers, and the "History of Bills and Resolutions", arranged by bill number, gives public law numbers for enacted bills. The table of "History of Bills Enacted into Public Law" in the Daily Digest, arranged by public law number, gives bill numbers for each public law. Beginning with 1985, the Congressional Record and Daily Digest can also be searched on Lexis and Westlaw.
6. United States Code Annotated (U.S.C.A.) and United States Code Service (U.S.C.S.). The public law number and date of enactment are given in "history notes" following each U.S. Code section.
7. If you know the name of the act, the "Popular Name Table" in the U.S.C., U.S.C.S., and U.S.C.A. will give you the public law number. Shepard's Acts and Cases by Popular Name gives the public law number and date enacted.
8. The Congressional Quarterly Weekly Report (CQ) has a weekly status table of major legislation. It is particularly good for tracking complex legislation such as appropriations bills. The annual Congressional Quarterly Almanac (Law Reference) gives a summary legislative history for public laws.

A. Compiled legislative histories

Using a compiled legislative history (a legislative history already researched and compiled by an outside organization) is one of the best time-saving devices you ever will encounter in your legal career. The following sources provide you with comprehensive histories for some important legislative enactments:

On-line: Arnold and Porter's Compiled Legislative Histories for Selected Laws on Westlaw.

Westlaw contains the compiled legislative histories of a dozen or more major pieces of legislation, including several important civil rights and discrimination laws from the 1960's and 70's. These were compiled by the Arnold and Porter law firm.

Books: Nancy P. Johnson, <u>Sources of Compiled Legislative Histories</u> (2000)

Bernard Reams, <u>Federal Legislative Histories: An Annotated Bibliography and Index to Officially Published Sources</u> (1994)

When you have the name of the act and the public law number, check the library catalog (or a reference librarian) to find out if the law library has a compiled legislative history for your law. The two most widely used bibliographies of compiled legislative histories are Nancy P. Johnson, <u>Sources of Compiled Legislative Histories</u> (Fred B. Rothman 1979, William S. Hein 2000) (updated biennially by looseleaf inserts), and Bernard Reams, <u>Federal Legislative Histories: An Annotated Bibliography and Index to Officially Published Sources</u> (1994).

If your library does not have a published history, use the guidelines below to compile your own. The set of steps outlined here is only one of several methods of compiling a legislative history.

B. To do a legislative history of a bill passed in 1970 to the present

◆   Westlaw or Lexis

If you can afford to, use the fee-based on-line services. All federal and many of the states' legislation is tracked, and federal committee reports, records of amendments, and floor debates from the Congressional Record are available to you in each service's legislation databases. The coverage does not go back in time forever, but it should be useful for collecting legislative history documents for legislation enacted within the last fifteen to twenty years.

◆   Thomas - the Library of Congress legislative website

A free resource is the "Thomas" Library of Congress website (thomas.loc.gov). Thomas collects many of the legislative history materials for fairly recent legislation (passed since 1995)[1], but its coverage may expand in the future.

---

[1]   Thomas's coverage includes: House and Senate Committee Reports (1995 – present); Bills (1989–present); Public Laws by public law number (1973–present); Bill Summary & Status (1973–present); Congressional Record (1989–present); Index to the Congressional Record (1995–present).

If you are stuck in the books, or if your statute is fairly old (pre-1995) use:

◆ Congressional Information Service's CIS Index and CIS Abstracts and the annual CIS Legislative History volumes.

There is a CIS Index for the U.S. Serial Set (committee reports), U.S. Congressional Committee Hearings, and U.S. Congressional Committee Prints (covering the years 1833 to 1969). The <u>Congressional Information Service</u>'s Digest of Public General Bills and Resolutions began in 1936 and allows you to trace a bill from the public law number. The Monthly Catalog goes back to 1896 and covers documents published by the United States printing office.

<u>Congressional Information Service</u>'s Legislative History volumes provide the following:

A. Beginning with 1984, the Legislative History volume contains histories of every public law: complete citations, with abstracts, of every public law, plus related hearings, reports, committee prints, bills, debates, plus bibliographic references, without citations, to related bills.

B. From 1970 to 1983, the Legislative History section appeared in the back of the annual <u>Abstracts</u> volume and contained only citations to documents, with references to the abstracts elsewhere in the volume.

C. CIS gives only the dates of debates. To find the page number of debates in the Congressional Record, use the Congressional Record Index. The "History of Bills and Resolutions" in the annual index volume lists all the pages where a bill is mentioned or debated. (For sessions of Congress after 1981, there is not yet an annual Congressional Record Index; rather, there are only biweekly indexes. Each index gives the complete history of bills acted upon during the two weeks covered.)

C. To do a legislative history of any bill introduced before 1970

1. To find committee reports and documents:

Use the CIS U.S. Serial Set Index. The subject/key word index gives complete titles of reports and documents, lists the type of report (Senate report, House report, etc.), Congress, session and the Serial Set volume number where reports are bound. There is a complete numerical listing and schedule of Serial Set volumes that is more comprehensive than the Government Printing Office's own Numerical Lists. For the years 1893-1940, you can also use the Document Catalog. Each volume is a catalog of government publications issued during one Congress. Entries are listed under subject, personal author, issuing agency or committee, and sometimes title. Complete bibliographical information, including serial set volume numbers, is provided for Reports and Documents. The Document Catalog is still useful, but it is less inclusive than the various CIS indexes, with respect to Congressional documents.

2. To find committee hearings:

Use the CIS US Congressional Committee Hearings Index. This set also is published by the Congressional Information Service, and it provides complete citations and brief abstracts for hearings from 1833 to 1969. The Senate Library Index of Congressional Committee Hearings & Supplements and Shelf-list of Congressional Committee Hearings is useful for looking up hearings before 1979, but in general, both should be considered superseded by the CIS indices. Alternatively, you may try to find the information in the Document Catalog and the Monthly Catalog. There is also the CIS Unpublished Senate Committee Hearings Index. The index currently covers 1823 through 1964, but the material will be supplemented. Copies of these hearings are available on microfiche from CIS.

3. To find committee prints:

The best source is the CIS US Congressional Committee Prints Index. This companion to the Hearings Index also provides a detailed subject and name index, and a brief abstract of each print. You also can use the Monthly Catalog and the Documents Catalog to identify earlier prints.

4. To find floor debates:

If you are on-line, search the Congressional Record on Westlaw or Lexis. If you are limited to books, use the Congressional Record Index. The "History of Bills and Resolutions" in the annual index volume lists all the pages where a bill is mentioned or debated.

STATE LEGISLATIVE HISTORY

Lexis and Westlaw track many states' legislation, but they do not routinely collect legislative history documents. The best practice is to visit a law library in the state (or view the law library's web page) or to call a reference librarian at a major law school in the state or at the state's legislature or court of last resort to find out how to research the state's legislative history. It also is possible to go to the state legislature's web site or the state bar association's web site and see if the information is present on the Internet.

Not every state collects and retains legislative history. In some states, there is no record of legislation other than a record of the bills introduced and amendments made to the bills prior to the bills' passage. In other states, audio recordings of floor debates or committee proceedings are made and retained, but access to the recordings and the ability to make copies of the recordings is not guaranteed in each of these states. Therefore, an inquiry to a knowledgeable law librarian in the state is the first and best step to finding out whether and how to perform research into the legislative history of the state's laws.

Chapter 17

Federal Regulatory and Administrative Law

I. WHY REGULATORY AND ADMINISTRATIVE FUNCTIONS ARE DELEGATED BY CONGRESS AND THE EXECUTIVE BRANCH

Congressmen and other legislators and government officials realize they cannot regulate every area of conduct in the modern world by passing new laws or amending old ones. They do not have the time, certain areas are too complex and detailed with minutia to allow effective legislative drafting, and certain areas are simply beyond the expertise of Congressmen to regulate.

Thus, the power to regulate certain areas is delegated to administrative and regulatory agencies and commissions. Congress can choose an existing agency to take on the task, or provide for the creation and funding of an entirely new agency or commission.

The delegation itself occurs through a broadly worded **statute** setting out the intention to regulate an area, along with a specific reference to implementation by regulations, and specific delegation to an agency or commission (or providing for the creation of same). The Executive Branch (the President, the Cabinet Departments of government) can also delegate this rule-making and regulatory authority to agencies through an **Executive Order**.

Executive and judicial powers often are delegated to the agency—thus, the power to make rules and regulations often coincides with the power to adjudicate disputes arising under the laws that the agency is charged with executing and administrating. For example, the Securities Exchange Commission can prosecute and adjudicate claims and charges (administrative actions) under the federal securities laws as well as promulgate rules for the conduct of the securities business. The SEC also reviews applications and grants or withholds permission for certain actions that are undertaken in the business, such as an initial public offering by a formerly privately held business.

II. TYPES OF ADMINISTRATIVE LAW

This chapter focuses on federal administrative rules and regulations, but there are other forms of administrative law:

1. **Orders**—reports of disposition and resolution of agency matters;
2. **Licenses and permits, certificates**, and other forms of permission or qualification;

3. **Advisory Opinions**—a report and advice concerning what the agency would do with a hypothetical situation. Often persons request the issuance of such an opinion so that they can see what the agency would do with their case. Agency opinions are considered to be a reliable and persuasive source for predicting the agency's behavior, but they are not binding on the agency and they are not binding on courts considering the same issue of law;

4. **No-Action Letters**—specific to certain areas, such as securities regulation, these are opinions of the agency on a specific set of facts indicating that the agency will not take any action against the party requesting the No-Action Letter. The party requesting the letter can rely on the promise of no action. Others may attempt to use the No-Action Letter as persuasive authority in a subsequent agency action or a court proceeding as proof that the law should be enforced the same way in similar situations (akin to Advisory Opinions, above), but the letters are not binding on the agency in other parties' cases and they are not binding on the courts;

5. **Decisions**—reports of the agency's rulings in an administrative and regulatory action concerning a party accused of violating the rules and regulations of the agency. These decisions arise through adjudicatory functions. The actual prosecution by the agency is separate from the adjudication, the latter function being performed by special boards of review, administrative law judges, hearing examiners, or other officers, so that the same persons are not prosecutor, judge, and jury. These decisions are used as precedent in later cases, and are considered highly persuasive although they are not binding on the agency or the courts.

III. THE FEDERAL REGISTER

Once authority to regulate is delegated, the agencies charged with rule-making responsibilities are empowered to institute rules—also called "regulations"—which have the full force and effect of law on the public as if Congress itself had enacted them. The agency must implement their regulations in the proper fashion; *i.e.*, in accordance with the Administrative Procedures Act, 5 U.S.C. §§ 553 *et seq.* and §§ 701 *et seq.*

The Administrative Procedures Act provides that administrative rules must follow certain procedures for public notice of their proposal, namely, issuance of "proposed rules," with opportunity for public comment and input and, ultimately, publication as a "Final Rule" for all to see. To this end, the Federal Register ("Fed. Reg.") was established. It is published daily by the Government Printing Office each day that the federal government is in operation. The Federal Register is the vehicle by which the public is notified that certain rules or regulations, or modifications of the same are under consideration, and where the public gets actual notice of applicable rules.

Each issue of the Federal Register may contain:

- Table of Contents listing the agencies reporting in the issue and page references to the various items associated with these agencies;
- CFR Parts Affected in this Issue (see Updating, below);

- Presidential Documents;
- Proposed Rules—allowing the public to comment on same;
- Notices—reports other than rules, regulations and proposed rules; e.g., grant application deadlines, filing of petitions and applications;
- Sunshine Act Meetings;
- Unified Agenda of Federal Regulations—by virtue of the Regulatory Flexibility Act, in April and October the agencies publish an agenda of the regulatory actions they are proposing and developing. Rules appear in four groups: (1) Prerule stage; (2) Proposed Rule stage; (3) Final Rule stage; (4) Completed Actions;
- Reader Aids—phone numbers of who to contact for info; a **cumulative table of CFR Parts affected during the month**; parallel table of Fed. Reg. pages for the month; bills of Congress that recently have become law; and, on Mondays, a CFR Checklist of the CFR Parts;
- Special Sections—for publication of agency documents.

While the Federal Register is a nice open forum for comment and criticism, you would have to read the Federal Register every day to hope to stay on top of the rules in your area of the law and to find out if they were changed in some way; i.e., were they amended or modified, superseded, or withdrawn. The Federal Register works like the Statutes at Large— it is a chronological, newspaper-like presentation of federal regulations, daily issue after issue piled one upon the other in an increasing flood of rules and regs—and you have heard how hard it is to stay on top of federal legislation just by reading the chronological output in the Statutes at Large.

Accessing the Federal Register has gotten a whole lot simpler since 1994 when the U.S. Government Printing Office (GPO) put a searchable version of the Federal Register on-line on its web site: http://www.gpoaccess.gov. The GPO will allow you to search the Federal Register (1994 forward) and the current edition of the Code of Federal Regulations (discussed below) *for free.* The GPO calls this "browsing" but it works like a regular Internet search. The results are sorted statistically by number of occurrences and proximity of your search terms.

Outside cyberspace, the Federal Register has a monthly index (the **Federal Register Index**), updated cumulatively each month, so that the December issue basically is an annual index of the year's rules and regulations. It lists rules alphabetically by agency rather than by subject matter, so you have to be up on which agency would be handling your topic.

Congressional Information Service publishes a **CIS Federal Register Index** starting in 1984, issued weekly in loose-leaf form, with monthly cumulative indices and permanent semi-annual bound volumes. It has subject matter organization as well as cross-indexing by name, CFR sections affected, federal agency docket numbers, and a Calendar of Effective Dates and Comment Deadlines.

IV. CODE OF FEDERAL REGULATIONS

The "Code of Federal Regulations" (C.F.R.) was created to present a "codification" of the rules and regulations promulgated by the federal administrative agencies. C.F.R.

annually publishes only those rules and regulations that are in full force and effect at the time of its publication, and it is published (or re-published) in full once each year. Modified and withdrawn regulations are removed and the new ones or modified versions are published. Also omitted from the C.F.R. is all the "legislative/rule-making history" information that preceded the final rule's publication, but which was printed in Federal Register. Perhaps most importantly, the C.F.R. reorganizes the Federal Register's provisions into a subject organization.

In the same sense that Congressional hearings and reports and floor debates may be critical in construing a statute's meaning, the "regulatory" or "rule-making" history may be critical in divining a regulation's meaning and intent. The discussions, "preambles," interim reports, alternative suggestions, and other information remain buried in the Federal Register, and a researcher may need to dig them out to fully understand a provision. Fortunately, both the C.F.R. and Federal Register provide useful "history" paragraphs with each provision that assist in this mining process.

The C.F.R.'s subject matter organization <u>roughly</u> parallels the subjects used in the United States Code. For example, Title 26 of the U.S. Code deals with federal taxation and the Internal Revenue Code and, similarly, 26 C.F.R. concerns the Internal Revenue Service and I.R.S. Regulations; Title 18 of the U.S. Code concerns the federal penal code and Code of Criminal Procedure and, similarly, 18 C.F.R. concerns the Justice Department and its operations and policies. But the parallelism between the respective subjects or "Titles" is not complete; <u>e.g.</u>, 17 C.F.R. deals with Commodities and Securities Regulation (which is Title 15 of the U.S.C.), not with copyright (Title 17 of the U.S. Code). Only 28 of the C.F.R.'s titles are the same as the U.S. Code's.

Within each C.F.R., the organization of the sections and subsections bears no similarity to the organization of the sections of the parallel U.S. Code titles, although they sometimes parallel the original legislation's organization (the organization found in the Statutes at Large) before the law was codified in the U.S. Code; <u>e.g.</u>, Section 10(b) of the statutory text of the Securities Exchange Act of 1934 is implemented by 17 C.F.R. § 240.10b, while the codification of Section 10(b) is found at 15 U.S.C. § 78j.

A. C.F.R.'s organization

The C.F.R. is re-published annually, each time dropping out any regulation that has been withdrawn, or updating old provisions that were amended since the last C.F.R. edition. But the C.F.R. is published in four parts—one quarter of the text is published each calendar quarter. The first quarter (CFR Titles 1-16) is published on January 1st, the second quarter (CFR Titles 17-27) on April 1st, the third quarter (CFR Titles 28-41) on July 1st, and the last quarter (CFR Titles 42-50) on October 1st. Each quarterly set changes the color of the binding as the year passes, and the colors used change each year.

Whenever using a C.F.R. volume, check its cover to see when that volume originated—that's when your "updating" problem will begin (<u>see</u> Subsection D below*).

B. Locating relevant and current C.F.R. provisions on-line

1. Westlaw and Lexis

The Westlaw and Lexis CFR databases can be searched for regulations using key words (search terms). If you are in a statutory database, you can use the links to CFR sections listed in the annotations.

2. Internet

The U.S. Government Printing Office will allow you to search the current edition of the C.F.R. for free at its web site: http://www.gpoaccess.gov. As mentioned above, the site is searchable—the GPO calls it "browsing"—but it works like a regular Internet search. The results are sorted statistically by number of occurrences and proximity of your search terms.

Congressional Universe's web service contains the Federal Register from 1980 forward, and the current C.F.R., searchable for a fee (unless you use your academic license, or go through your local law library's system). The LEGI-SLATE service can be accessed on the Internet and you can search for Federal Register and C.F.R. provisions. It is a fee based service. Counterpoint Publishing's web service contains the Federal Register from 1993 forward, and the current C.F.R.—both are searchable for a fee.

C. Locating relevant and current C.F.R. provisions by the book

The C.F.R. is indexed, but the index is nearly useless. The problem is the C.F.R. Index's subjects are determined by the literal nomenclature (titles) of the rules and regulations themselves, not by logical legal topics and subtopics. This is not how we (the average researchers) normally think of the law, and it is directly contrary to the methodology used by digests, encyclopedias, and dictionaries, and most legal indices. We should have no reason to expect that we can guess how all the relevant regulations for our area are going to be described. If there happens to be a rule or regulation with a title that matches what you are looking for, you will find it in the C.F.R. index; but if you are searching for a topic not found in any title or description of a rule or regulation, you are out of luck. Therefore, almost any method of identifying relevant C.F.R. provisions is superior to the C.F.R. index.

Instead, use the implementing statutory authority that authorized and delegated the area. Annotated statutes, such as West's United States Code Annotated ("U.S.C.A.") and former Lawyers Coop's United States Code Service ("U.S.C.S.") annotate the U.S. Code provisions with references to regulations that those U.S. Code provisions spawn.

In addition, you can find regulations because they are discussed and cited in case law, law review articles, treatises, loose-leaf services and other specialty publications. The reference to relevant C.F.R. provisions is general case law or journal databases is more hit or miss—not the start and end of good research into the applicable regulatory law—but you sometimes "hit" on a cite to a regulation in a case or law review article when you were not thinking about the C.F.R. or possible regulations at all. However, it will usually be more effective to consult a good treatise or set of loose-leaf volumes devoted to the area you are researching, because these will specifically focus on the regulations in the area.

D. Updating C.F.R. provisions

Subsequent to any C.F.R. volume's publication, the government has continued to operate, and any given C.F.R. provision may have been changed or withdrawn since its most recent publication. This is reflected in the Federal Register, so you will need to check the Federal Register for any changes.

To understand how C.F.R. updating is accomplished, first examine an issue of the Federal Register. In the front, you will find a short list of "C.F.R. Parts Affected in this Issue." That's only good for the one, daily issue. But Federal Register Publishes a separate volume (housed with the C.F.R.'s) called "**List of CFR Sections Affected**" (abbreviated "**LSA**"), a cumulative list of C.F.R. provisions "affected" in some way in periods beginning with the last publication of the C.F.R. volume for your section under study, and ending with the LSA issue's month. (E.g., if your section of the C.F.R. was last published in the C.F.R. on October 1, 1998, and you are looking at an LSA volume dated March 1999, the LSA volume will list changes from Oct. 1, 1998 to March 31, 1999.) The issue of LSA will be an "annual" accumulation of changes for the titles of the C.F.R. published one year before the publication date of the LSA in December, March, June, and September; e.g., the March issue of LSA will cumulate the year's changes for CFR titles 17-27. You must also check the latest Fed. Reg. issues following the publication date of the latest applicable LSA volume up to the date you are doing your research for the **cumulative tables of CFR Parts affected that month**.

The GPO web site (http://www.gpoaccess.gov) provides many of the resources needed to update federal regulations: Federal Register from 1994 to the present; CFR from 1996 to the present; LSA from 1986 to the present (note that the search or browse feature only is available from 1997 to the present). You also may use Westlaw's or Lexis's CFR databases to update regulations.

Shepard's Code of Federal Regulations Citations provides citations to specific regulations by C.F.R. citation, and you can thereby find out if the regulation is still in force. You also can locate cases where that particular provision was at issue, as well as law review and A.L.R. annotation references.

Chapter 18

Computer Assisted Legal Research

Loosely speaking, computer assisted legal research (CALR) is anything that has to do with legal research for which you would use a computer, including on-line services, the Internet (World Wide Web), CD-Roms, intranet, and networked files and collections. Part I of this chapter focuses on the two most popular, most reliable, and yes, most expensive on-line service providers, Westlaw and Lexis. Part II discusses computer assisted legal research using other resources found on the Internet and World Wide Web.

PART I. COMPUTER ASSISTED LEGAL RESEARCH USING WESTLAW AND LEXIS

I. ON-LINE SERVICES

Westlaw and Lexis are fee-based, meaning that you pay for the service by the hour, or by the search, or by certain package and flat-rate deals, but you never use them for free once you leave law school and lose your student academic license. Westlaw and Lexis are databases of legal sources (electronic libraries) that require you to inquire and correctly identify the authorities for which you are looking. They are not intelligent machines; they will not anticipate what you really want to find when you are asking for the wrong thing, although they will suggest additional sources (databases) you did not ask to search in if the service thinks these sources are relevant. Nevertheless, all of this driven by the searches you construct, so you must draft your searches correctly and completely.

II. DO THEY REPLACE LAW LIBRARIES?

The answer to the question, "Do Westlaw and Lexis replace traditional law libraries?" is a definite "Yes" and "No." Yes, the majority of what you will need to practice law, both primary and secondary authorities, is found on-line today. You will in most cases be able to handle any given research project from start to finish without walking into a law library. The databases in Westlaw and Lexis put vast resources at your fingertips. Add to that the ever expanding Internet and World Wide Web resources, and you may never feel a need to leave your terminal to render your advice to your client.

But that does not mean the computer replaces the law library altogether. There is a definite need for having printed resources and law libraries. Even in the new millennium, many law offices do not provide access to Lexis and Westlaw or forbid their attorneys from using it except in very limited circumstances. They or their clientele either cannot or will not afford the luxury of these pricey on-line services. In a more substantive comparison, many sources are easier to search in books than on-line.

A good example of this is statutes. Many researchers find it is easier to identify the entire codified statutory regime that governs a topic in an annotated volume of the statutes rather than in an on-line statutory database. The organization and structure of the statutory regime is more obviously reflected in the books. Treatises likewise are easier to research in books than on-line, because the basic tools of a table of contents and index are not as wieldy in their on-line incarnations.

If you asked the question that heads this section to a random sampling of attorneys and legal professionals, you would get a variety of answers and more and less strong emotional responses depending on the age of the persons you questioned. There is an inverse correlation between a person's age and the extent to which she believes on-line resources can replace printed resources. You also will get a different response from managing partners and billing partners at law firms. The main reason for their evaluation of the services is that even if they believe that computers can completely replace printed materials, the economics of the situation still dictate the practice and performance of research both on-line and with printed materials.

Law libraries are overhead costs for a law firm. Most firms do not charge clients directly for the upkeep of their law libraries, except in so far as they are an overhead cost that impacts the rates that the firm sets for billable hours. But there can be a cost to the client for the inefficiency of researching solely in printed materials, because the inefficiency drives up the billable hours charged to the client for the research. This must be balanced against the costs of using the on-line services, which most often are directly charged to the client or they are eaten by the firm. These charges can sometimes look shocking on a legal bill, and cause the billing partners to blanch and demand pointless explanations from CALR-happy associates in the manner of: "Why did this take so much time to research?"

There is a partial solution in the form of block purchase plans and flat-rate, unlimited usage plans at law firms, which can turn the on-line service into an overhead cost. More entrepreneurial firms will pay a flat fee but still will bill the clients for the minutes of on-line service used at the hourly rate the firm *would have* paid had they not had a flat rate plan, thus turning the on-line services into profit centers.

III. BEFORE YOU LOG ON: PLANNING YOUR RESEARCH

Think of on-line services as vacuum cleaners in your client's pocket. The longer you leave them on, the more money they suck out of your client. Wasting this resource is bad for your client, your firm and you.

The first time to think hard about your research is not after you log-on but before. Get out the old analog equipment – the pad and paper. Work over your research. Break it down, figure out what you are looking for.

A. Initial assessment of the problem

Ask yourself the following (and demand answers) before your plunge into the service databases:

1. Do you know what legal issues are suggested by the problem? Do you know which area(s) of law the problem implicates?
2. Do you already have a pretty good understanding of this area of the law? Do you already know the background, the big picture issues, the policies, claims, and defenses of this area?

If not, the place to learn is not on-line at your client's expense. Do some background research in the books and get yourself grounded in the issues, the basic law, the policies and so forth.

B. Write down a plan for each issue you have to research

A research plan will save you a lot of time and your client a lot of money in the long run. The plan lays out the issues you are researching and how you are going to research these issues. You need to identify places to search, as well as the searches you will run while you are on-line.

Divide your plan into categories: How are you going to find:

1. Primary Authorities, both controlling and persuasive: cases, statutes, rules.
2. Secondary Authorities: treatises, restatements, law reviews, and others.

Instead of books, reporters, and folders in the library, you are going to be searching databases. Write down the databases you will search and the order in which you will use them. (See section IV. DATABASES below). Then write down the initial searches you want to run (the "queries").

As you progress, keep a log of what you have searched with brief notes of what you are getting. A log confirms that you followed your plan and it keeps you honest. It is a record of the materials you found, how you found them, the databases you were searching, and what inquiries you were using. In case you misplace the printouts of the results of your research, your log can reconstruct the project. The web based versions of the services may keep track of your last 50 or so searches, but your log will be more helpful in keeping track of your strategies, your failures, as well as your findings.

IV. DATABASES

Each on-line service provider maintains its legal sources in databases. Westlaw calls them "Databases," while Lexis calls them "Sources." Databases are divided up by jurisdiction or topic or both, and by types of primary authorities (cases vs. statutes), and secondary authorities (texts and treatises, restatements, periodicals, law reviews, newspapers) that are found in the database.

The following are examples of different databases that can be searched on Westlaw:

WESTLAW DATABASE	SCOPE
ALLCASES	All state and federal cases. (i.e., all levels of the state courts, US Supreme Court, US Courts of Appeals for all the circuits, all district courts)
ALLFEDS	All federal cases (US Supreme Court, courts of appeals for all the circuits, all district courts) post 1945
-OLD e.g., ALLFEDS-OLD	Added on to the end of certain databases, it retrieves older cases, usually pre-1945
SCT	US Supreme Court cases post 1945
CTA	Court of Appeals cases from all circuits
CTAx	Court of Appeals cases from x Circuit (substitute the number of the circuit for the x; use DC for the D.C. Circuit)
e.g., CTA2	Cases from the US Court of Appeals for the Second Circuit
ALLSTATES	All state court cases from all published levels of the state courts
xx-CS	All state court cases from xx State (substitute the postal abbreviation for the state for the xx)
e.g., MO-CS	All Missouri state court cases
xx-CS-ALL	All state and federal cases associated with xx State (xx is postal abbrev. for the state)
e.g., IL-CS-ALL	All Illinois state cases, and federal cases from the US Supreme Court, the Seventh Circuit and all district courts in Illinois
FEDx-ALL	Federal court cases from one circuit (x is the number of the circuit, or DC for D.C. circuit); US Supreme Court, the circuit court identified, and all district courts within that circuit
e.g., FED8-ALL	Federal court cases associated with the Eighth Circuit (US Supreme Court, Eighth Circuit, and district courts in Missouri, Arkansas, Iowa, Minnesota, North and South Dakota, and Nebraska
CTAx-ALL	All state and federal courts associated with (x) circuit

<u>e.g.</u> CTA8-ALL	Cases from the state and federal courts of the Eighth Circuit (US Supreme Court, Eighth Circuit, and district court and state court cases from Missouri, Arkansas, Iowa, Minnesota, North and South Dakota and Nebraska
xx-ST	Unannotated statutes from xx State
<u>e.g.</u>, MI-ST	Unannotated version of Michigan Statutes
xx-ST-ANN	Annotated version of xx State's statutes
<u>e.g.</u>, NJ-ST-ANN	Annotated version of New Jersey Statutes
TP-ALL	All texts and periodicals combined
JLR	All law journals, law reviews, law publications, and bar journals combined
TEXTS	All texts and treatises combined
STLULJ	Saint Louis University Law Journal

V. BOOLEAN SEARCHING: FORMULATING YOUR SEARCH REQUESTS

You will be searching the full text of the documents (<u>e.g.</u>, cases) in a database for key words. You have the ability to tell the on-line service to search for logical connections between words, so that your results are more logical. You want to draft a query that is more likely to bring up relevant, apposite authorities rather than inapposite, unhelpful authorities.

For example, you want to find dog-bite cases in Illinois. If you search and ask for every case in Illinois that has to do with dogs <u>or</u> bites, you'll get a ton of cases—every civil and criminal case that has a canine actor or involving a dog in some way, and every case with a bite, whether from man or beast. But if you only search for dog within three words of bite (dog /3 bite), you will retrieve a lot fewer cases that are much more likely to be useful to you.

A. Key words, catch phrases, and concepts from legal issues

The first thing to do is to break your problem down into key words, catch phrases, legal concepts, and terms of art that summarize the legal issues (legal questions) implicated by your problem.

Suppose a client comes in with this problem:

> Your client is a hunter who was hunting with a high-powered rifle and ran into someone's home in pursuit of a running deer. He tripped and fell and discharged his weapon, killing a housewife.

Break the problem down into concepts, catch words, and brief phrases. This exercise is similar to when you were preparing to dive into a descriptive word index in a digest or encyclopedia or other source. Your goal is to choose words or short phrases that should definitely be found in authorities that will discuss the law that governs your problem. The word combination you come up with only has to appear once in the authority for it to be selected and displayed by the service. It remains for you to read the authority to see if it really is on point – in other words, if the reference to your word combination was relevant to your problem or simply accidental.

We chose the following initial list of terms from the problem:

hunting, gun, home or house, discharge or shooting or killing

What did we leave out? – deer; pursuit/hot pursuit of quarry; running with guns; tripping; housewife. Why? Because I thought it more unlikely that relevant cases would contain these terms. If you require Westlaw or Lexis to search for infrequently appearing terms, you will severely limit the number of matches in your results and may miss relevant cases.

B. Think synonyms

Always write down a number of synonyms for your search words. Synonyms expand the possible words an authority could contain and thus allow broader results from your search:

hunting, stalking, chasing, sport

weapon, gun, rifle, pistol, bullet

home, house, household, indoors

shoot, shot, shooting, accident, discharge, "went off," fire, killed

negligence, negligent, liable, culpable

C. Terms and connectors: what logical connections between the terms do you want

Logical connectors refer to the spatial (in a grammatical sense) relationship between the terms for which you have decided to search, whether it be within a few words of each other, within the same sentence, before or after certain other terms in the same paragraph, or simply within the same document.

1. Connectors

When phrasing search queries, the same connectors will work in Westlaw and Lexis except as noted:

/x	Within x number of words, before or after.

dog /3 bite	Will pull up any document where the word "dog" shows up three words ahead of or behind the word "bite."

In Lexis, you also can write this "w/x" – dog w/3 bite.

+x	Precedes by no more than x words.

dog +2 bite	Will get you documents where "dog" precedes the word "bite" by no more than two words.

In Lexis, you can write this "pre/x" – dog pre/2 bite.

/s	Within the same sentence, before or after. A sentence is any string of words ending in a period, no matter how long or how many commas or semicolons are in it. Each headnote in a West publication is one sentence.

dog /s bite	Will pull up any document in which "dog" appears in the same sentence as "bite."

+s	Precedes in the same sentence.

dog +s bite	Will get you documents where "dog" precedes the word "bite" in the same sentence.

/p	Within the same paragraph. A paragraph is any string of sentences divided by a hard return, no matter how long.

dog /p bite	Pulls up any document in which "dog" appears in the same paragraph as "bite."

+p	Precedes in the same paragraph.

dog +p bite	Will get you documents where "dog" precedes the word "bite" in the same paragraph. Not a very useful distinction.

        &   Within the same document.

dog & bite	Pulls up any document in which "dog" appears in the same document as "bite." Lots of cases.

Lexis makes you write out the word "and" – dog and bite.

%   But not in the same document as.

dog % bite	Will pull up all cases with the word "dog" in them as long as the word "bite" is NOT also in the same document. If you want cases about dog breeds, dog shows, dog meat, or sales of dogs, and do not want to read any dog bite cases, you might use this.
RICO % Puerto	Gets you racketeering cases under the federal RICO statute without getting you every published case from Puerto Rico (But you will not get any RICO cases that are from Puerto Rico).

Lexis has an even nicer feature: not w/x. If you use this, you can specify cases with a certain word but not if it is within x words of another word.

dog not w/3 bite	In Lexis, this will get "dog" cases as long as the word appears further than three words from "bite" somewhere in the document, but "bite" can otherwise appear in the document. Less exclusive.

2. Expanders and alternative forms

If you want to search for multiple words and synonyms as advised above, you need to express the concept of "or."

(a space)   In Westlaw, a space in your search query automatically means "or."

dog canine w/3 bite biting chomp crunch scratch harm maul

Means:	dog or canine within three words of bite or biting or chomp or crunch or scratch or harm or maul

Lexis does not recognize spaces as "or" connectors. You must type the word "or" to express "or" – dog or canine w/3 bite or biting or chomp or crunch or scratch or harm or maul

*	The asterisk is an expander that replaces a character in a word. This is useful if you are not sure of the spelling. It is also useful to use at the end of words to express multiple possible endings. You cannot use it at the beginning of a word. The number of * you chose limits the number of characters the service will add to your term: ** allows the service to add two characters; *** allows the service to add three.

wom*n	Will find both woman and women.
bath****	Will find bath, bathe, bathroom, bathing, bathmat, etc., but not bathtowel or bathhouse.
bank***	Will find bank, banks, banker, bankers, banking, etc., but not bankrupt, bankruptcy, etc.

NOTE: The asterisk is also useful to confuse Westlaw into letting you search for words that Westlaw thinks are too common to be searched (that is the error message you will get) and ordinarily will not let you proceed with a query that has such words in it such as "after" or "before" or "from." You can fool Westlaw by writing "af*er" "bef*re" and "fr*m" and Westlaw will let you search for these words.

!	The exclamation point is a universal expander used at the end of a string of letters to allow searches for any possible endings.

bank!	Will find bank, banks, banker, bankers, banking, bankrupt, bankruptcy, bankroll, banknote, etc.

3. Plurals and possessive forms

Normally, Westlaw and Lexis assume that you want the plurals and possessive forms of all the words you search, so they automatically pull up documents with the plurals and possessives in them. "Dog" will get you "dogs" and "dog's" and "dogs,'" and "plaintiff" will get you "plaintiffs," "plaintiff's," and "plaintiffs.'" Unusual plurals (women, mice, geese, indices, memoranda, etc.) are *not* picked up, so search for them in addition to your singular terms. The same goes for unusual singulars (datum, criterion, alumnus, etc.), and possessives (my, mine, his). If you *only* want the singular or the plural of a word, you could try using but not (%) to exclude the form you do not want. e.g., procedure % procedures. You potentially would exclude a lot of documents that you really do want. In Lexis, you have to take different unusual measures that your trainer can fill you in on.

4. Acronyms, abbreviations, and compound words

Search for single-letter abbreviated words and acronyms in this way:

R.I.C.O.	Will get you RICO, R I C O, R. I. C. O., and R.I.C.O.
F.R.C.P.	Will get you FRCP, F R C P, F. R. C. P., and F.R.C.P.

Search for potentially compounded words with a hyphen in between:

whistle-blower	Will get you: whistleblower, whistle blower, and whistle-blower.
dog-catcher	Will get you: dogcatcher, dog catcher, and dog-catcher.

5. Phrases

In Westlaw, put phrases in quotes – Westlaw will pull up both exact matches and some nearly exact matches:

"beyond a reasonable doubt"	Will also get you "beyond reasonable doubt" or "beyond the reasonable doubt."

You can still use an expander if you are not sure of the spelling or if you think multiple endings are possible:

"res ipsa loquit*r"	Will get you "res ipsa loquitor" and "res ipsa loquitur."
"wheels of justice grind exceedingly fine!"	Will find the phrase no matter if it ends in "fine" or "finely" in various documents.

In Lexis, the system does not think of spaces as "or" connectors, so you do not need quotation marks for phrases:

res ipsa loquit*r	Still gets you "res ipsa loquitor" and "res ipsa loquitur."

D. Putting it all together—use expanders and connectors to make a better search

Using the connectors and the expanders allows you to search for synonyms and varying forms:

Example: hunt! stalk! chas*** sport /p weapon gun rifle pistol bullet /s home house household indoors /s shoot! shot accident! discharge "went off" fir*** kill*** /p neglig! liab! culpab!

E.   Revise and re-search again and again

If you get too many (50+) cases the first time you run the search, revise your search, tighten up the connectors, drop some of the expanders, or leave out some of the alternative terms you first used:

> hunt! chas*** /8 weapon gun rifle /s home house household indoors /10 shoot! shot accident! discharge "went off" fir*** kill*** /p neglig! liab! culpab!

Try this again and again until you get a reasonable number of documents to look at. If you have the opposite problem, no case or too few (fewer than five?), expand your query, make broader connectors and add synonyms:

> hunt! stalk! chas*** sport & weapon gun rifle pistol bullet /50 home house household indoors /50 shoot! shot accident! discharge "went off" fir*** kill*** & neglig! liab! culpab!

F. Advanced searching: fields, date restrictions, locate and focus

1. Field and segment searching

Field searching is an excellent way of limiting the number of cases you might otherwise pull up in a search. You can search one part of a document, known in Westlaw as a "Field" and in Lexis as a "segment" (e.g., just the synopsis that starts off the case, just the title or style of the case, or just the headnotes).

In Westlaw, if you want to search certain parts of the document, you can code your searches as follows:

co   Searches the court field—what the name of the court is. You put what you are looking for in parentheses.

> co(nj)   searches for courts having a connection to New Jersey

sy	Searches only the synopsis field — the West summary at the beginning of the case.

	sy(neglig!)	searches the synopsis for forms of the term "negligence" "negligent" etc.

he	Searches the headnotes for a term.

	he(copyright)	searches the headnotes for the term "copyright"

to	Searches the Topic field from the West list of topics from the digest series.

ti	Title or style of the case, the parties.

	ti(roe & wade)	searches for titles of cases with Roe and Wade in them
	ti(roe +s wade)	searches for titles where Roe precedes Wade

You can use them in combination by separating with a comma:

	to,he,sy(neglig!)	searches the Topic, Headnotes, and Synopsis fields for variations on the term "negligence"

There are quite a few more fields—consult your Westlaw materials or ask your Westlaw representative. Lexis has a similar concept called "Segments" which are searched in similar fashion.

2. Date restrictions

Often you only will want to pull up cases before or after a certain date, or within a certain range of dates:

da	A date restriction. You can limit to a single date or before or after a given date. In combination, you can set a range of dates. (You must use a four-digit year due to Y2K compliance.)

	da(after 01/01/1998) da(aft 01/01/1998) da(> 01/01/1998)	You only will get cases after Jan. 1, 1998

da(before 01/01/1988)	You only will get cases before Jan.
da(bef 01/01/1988)	1, 1988
da(< 01/01/1988)	
da(1997)	You only will get cases from 1997
da(>01/01/80) & da(<01/01/90)	You only will get cases from the 1980's

Date restrictions and field searches are added to a search query with an &:

dog +2 bite & co,sy(il) & da(aft 01/01/1965)

Lexis includes fill-in-the-blank boxes on their main query screen asking you if you want to add date restrictions to your search.

3. Searching for particular headnotes (keynotes)

On Westlaw, the topic name of a keynote (e.g., Contracts) is replaced by its number on the master list of key note topics (95), and the key symbol (⊶) is replaced by the letter "k"

95k23	Will get you cases with that headnote (keynote) number in it, Contracts: Qualified or conditional acceptance of offer
95k88	Will get you cases with the headnote, Contracts: Presumptions and burden of proof

You can search for all notes under one topic:

to(95)	Either form will get you contracts cases.
to(contracts)	

If you want to search a particular topic for terms within a headnote:

to(95) /p (breach /2 implied /3 covenant /4 good faith fair dealing)

Gets you all cases with a contracts headnote that contains the terms "breach of covenant of good or faith or fair or dealing"

4. Locate (or focus)

Once you have your search results, and you really want to zero in on the most important cases, you can run a search within a search on Westlaw (called "Locate") or on Lexis (called "Focus"). You would formulate a Locate query in the same way as a regular search query, with terms and connectors, fields, dates, headnotes, and any other search addition:

95k125 & date(>07/15/1988)   Would zero in on documents within your search results that contain Contracts headnotes with key number 125, and are dated after July 15, 1988.

VI. NATURAL LANGUAGE SEARCHING

In an effort to dumb down the requirements to search the on-line services, both Westlaw and Lexis came up with a simplified method referred to as "Natural Language" searching. Westlaw calls is WIN: Westlaw is Natural™ or simply "Natural Language," and Lexis calls it FREESTYLE™ searching. You simply enter a sentence that sums up your research topic without regard to logic or synonyms or connections, and Westlaw finds you cases that have as many of those words in it as it can. The service assumes each word is connected by an "and" (&) connector. The service ignores certain words (an, but, the, etc.). Results are limited to twenty (or however many you tell it to get), and results are sorted by statistical relevance (unless you tell it to sort by some other way); e.g., the more times your terms appear in a document and the closer proximity they appear to each other in the document bumps the document up on the list of results. Basically, it works like many Internet search engines—Google and Excite, for example.

Is a hunter liable when he accidentally shoots someone in their home

The service probably will ignore "is, a, when, he, in, their" and sort the cases that have hits on the remaining words. There are several reasons why you generally should avoid Natural Language searching:

A. It is not logical enough.

You are doing legal research, not surfing the net for recreation. You are not just trying to find twenty odd cases having several of your search terms in them; you are trying to find *all* of the relevant, timely, controlling authorities. You can make a much more accurate search with Boolean logic connectors and the methods described above.

B. It does not find synonyms.

If an important controlling authority from your jurisdiction (or worse yet, a line of controlling authorities) expressed the law in slightly different terms than you put in your natural search, you are out of luck.

C. You cannot be certain you have exhausted the field.

With just "and" (&) as the connection, you will not want to run searches such as "dog bite." You can run twenty different natural language searches, but that is wasting your time. You can do a better search with terms and connectors the first time. Just spend a few more minutes coming up with a good list of search words and synonyms and create a search with logic connectors.

VII. KEYCITE™ AND SHEPARD'S™ CITATIONS

As mentioned in Chapter 11, two kinder, more useful citation checking services exist on-line. Lexis has Shepard's™ On-line, a computer version of the printed volumes, and Westlaw has the KeyCite™ service. With both, you simply input the citation you are checking, and the service runs it through all the proper databases and comes up with a single comprehensive report.

With Shepard's on-line, there is no searching for cites in one volume, then a more recent volume, then the most recent supplement, as there is with Shepard's in book form. You even can preset what kinds of information you want and in what order you want it to appear in the report—only negative authority, or only positive authority that cites headnotes 3 and 6, or only cases where the case was followed, and many other combinations. It is truly more efficient than the book version, but it does take a while on-line to cite-check an entire memorandum or brief.

KeyCite presents a report of citations with negative and positive citations cited separately, and the citations are listed in the order of "level of treatment." Each citing authority is ranked with a set of stars to indicate the extent that it discusses the case you are checking:

**** four stars ("Examines")	means the citing authority really talks a great deal about the case, often in a page or more of the case
*** three stars ("Discusses")	means the citing authority cites and discusses the case, usually in more than a paragraph but less than a full page
** two stars ("Cites")	means the citing authority cites the case but only has a short discussion, usually in less than a full paragraph or footnote
* one star ("Mentioned")	means the citing authority only cites it in passing, usually in a string cite, with no significant discussion of the case.

As with Shepard's on-line, there are ways to predetermine the kind of citation references you will get in the report, and how they are organized.

Flagging symbols are used by each on-line service to warn you of developments in the subsequent history of an authority. Westlaw uses little flags, Lexis uses little highway road signs.

Red Flag; Red Stop Sign	The case is bad law, meaning it has been reversed, overturned, abrogated, or severely criticized by a proper authority on at least one legal issue. (You should check to see which issue was overturned.)
Yellow Flag; Yellow Caution Sign	The case has some negative history, usually criticism from a later court, but the on-line service still thinks it is good law.

Other symbols are used to show non-detrimental subsequent history:

Blue H (Westlaw); Green + (Lexis)	The case has subsequent history, such as a later opinion in the same case, or the opinion was affirmed, or certiorari was denied, or some other neutral or positive history has occurred.
Green C (Westlaw); Blue A (Lexis)	The case has been cited neutrally or favorably by other authorities.

Part II. COMPUTER ASSISTED LEGAL RESEARCH USING THE INTERNET AND WORLD WIDE WEB

I. COMPARISON OF THE ON-LINE FEE BASED SERVICES AND FREE INTERNET SERVICES

In order to appreciate the transition from computer assisted legal research using fee-based services to research using the free resources and services of the Internet, you must consider the benefits of the former services and compare them to the detriments of the latter.

Westlaw and Lexis offer the following:

◆ High price - high expectations.

No one will argue with you if you assert that Westlaw and Lexis are expensive. But you get a reliable, high quality product for your money. The price you pay begs high expectations for foolproof research assistance, and Westlaw and Lexis both fulfill these expectations.

◆ Reputations that are tested by tens of thousands of users.

Nearly every attorney in the United States has used Westlaw and Lexis. Thousands, if not tens of thousands of attorneys use the services every day. If there ever were to be a glitch in the services (beyond the usual frustration of getting hang-ups and slow service at times) or in their coverage of legal information, it would be revealed by thousands of users and corrected as soon as possible.

◆ Westlaw and Lexis are in stiff competition with each other.

At this point in time, there is not that big a difference between Westlaw and Lexis, and both services have an enormous incentive to keep it that way. Each would like to gain an edge, but it is more important for each to maintain parity in the legal information arms race. The customer benefits from this life and death competition, because services are kept fresh, new databases are added all the time, existing coverage is extended, and material is updated and kept current, all so that customers are kept satisfied.

◆ Westlaw and Lexis constantly are updated and kept current.

As mentioned in the previous section, neither fee-based service can afford to let the other gain an edge in current materials, so each service keeps their databases as up to date as possible. What this means is that statutes are available the moment that they are passed into law, cases are added to the databases within hours or at least within a day or two of their issuance, and databases constantly are expanded and kept current.

◆ Now available on the Internet.

Westlaw and Lexis are now available on the Internet, so it is easier than ever to access them wherever you are in the world.

Now compare the above factors to the free resources and services of the Internet and World Wide Web:

◆ The Internet is free.

It's true, you cannot beat the price.

◆ Reputation?

The sites discussed in part II of this chapter have some history and track record to them. They generally are admired for the accuracy and usefulness of their information, but when you replace a profit-making incentive and a life or death struggle to survive (Westlaw and Lexis) with an altruistic desire to do well and benefit all mankind (most Internet sites), you do not necessarily get the very best service. Sometimes you get what you pay for.

There is very little peer review from practicing lawyers concerning Internet legal research sites unless you want to go far out of your way to find out what some Internet gazetteers or reference librarians are saying about a site. The average attorney will not want to spend time tracking down the dirt on each site before she uses it and relies on it Even if a few sites are investigated thoroughly, there is no guaranty that they will stay accurate and up to date.

◆ Competition? Quality control?

There is no real competition between the services that provide free legal information on the Internet. It is true that some sites, such as Findlaw.com., do accept advertising. These sites might hope to raise advertising revenue based on the number of hits, so market forces have some role, but the scale of attraction of new users vs. potential loss of users if your site has or develops some shortcomings is so small in comparison to the battle between Westlaw and Lexis that it does not propel too many web management decisions. Most sites just exist to provide information with no real hope of making any money in the process. Many sites want to excel in the accuracy and coverage of their information as a matter of academic or institutional pride, but there is little to be done to regulate the quality of sites that do not share this zeal for excellence. A few sporadic visitors checking out the free merchandise are not going to police a site's content, accuracy, and up-to-dateness.

◆ You can put ANYTHING on the Internet

Probably the most alarming fact about the Internet is that anyone can post "legal" information on the Internet and World Wide Web and make it available to anyone searching for legal information. Whether or not the publisher makes an effort to publicize it, sooner or later search engines will find it and catalog it, and it will show up in searches. No one regulates the posting of information on the web. No one controls it. No official body reviews it for quality, content, and accuracy. No one guarantees that the legal or factual information on sites is good enough to use to render legal advice to clients under a **legal malpractice** standard.

Speaking of malpractice, consider the fact that lawyers, judges, and bar disciplinary people all know that lawyers use Westlaw or Lexis, and that it is a perfectly acceptable and reliable way to do legal research. Using these systems in a reasonable manner will not get you into trouble. In fact, refusing to use them may be more problematic in some situations than using them too much, because a disgruntled client may assert that you failed to do proper research when you avoided these modern, up-to-the minute research tools.

◆ You cannot count on proper updating and maintenance of sites.

Updating of sites and keeping them current is a real problem for many websites. It takes an enormous amount of time and effort to update all of your pages. The bigger and better a legal site gets, the more it needs to be updated to keep it great. Westlaw and Lexis make that investment of time and effort. Does Cornell Law Library or the federal Government Printing Office have the resources or time to do it as well?

II. WHY WOULD YOU USE THE INTERNET FOR LEGAL RESEARCH

◆ You have to.

❏ No other alternatives.

If you have no Westlaw or Lexis password, and your firm will not allow you to get one and will not allow you to go to a public or court library and use the services for a fee, then you are stuck. You will use the Internet.

❏ Economic factors.

Law students will not want to hear this, but at some law offices, even in the new millennium, the firm's managers or the firm's clients preclude you from using the on-line fee-based services, or severely limit their use. Their services cost so much that managers faint at the bills, and clients choke on them. It is not uncommon for a client to impose a rule that all Westlaw or Lexis research must be pre-approved by the billing partner for the client.

◆ What you have to research can be done equally well or better on the Internet than on Westlaw-Lexis

There are some situations, described below, when you will have a problem that can be solved as effectively using the Internet as with Westlaw or Lexis. In those limited circumstances, go forth and surf the net, but be careful not to confuse the average legal issue with those rare issues that can be answered using the Internet as the sole research tool.

III. APPROPRIATE USES OF THE INTERNET AS A TOOL FOR LEGAL RESEARCH

◆ Background information.

You always can use the Internet as a starting point to get your feet wet in a research project and not rack up extra fees for the client. You can find certain primary and secondary legal sources, factual information, and background information to move you to an understanding of the issues and policies before you dive in to do the direct research to address the problem at hand.

◆ The Internet can be used as the primary tool for legal research in the following instances:

❏ When you are looking for a particular item.

If what you need to find is one particular thing, such as a case, a statutory provision, or a federal administrative regulation, and you know what it is called, and you know what it will look like, so that when you pull it up you will know you found it, then the Internet is every bit as effective as Westlaw or Lexis. Findlaw.com. for example, is a perfectly effective way to get an electronic copy of a case whose cite you know.

❏ When you already have a very good idea what the answer to your research problem is, and you are researching merely to confirm what you already know.

We told you in the preface that knowing the answer ahead of time is a rare luxury for a lawyer, and we meant it. When it happens that you have become familiar with the correct answer to a certain kind of legal problem, but you would like to browse a few sources to make sure your memory is not playing tricks on you, using the Internet for this limited purpose is fairly safe.

❏ When it does not really matter what you find, as long as you find something.

There are situations in legal practice where gathering a small but representative sample of authorities will suffice to address the problem at hand. In the middle of trial, you do not need to find all fifty cases in your jurisdiction that say that proof of collateral sources of compensation such as insurance coverage generally is inadmissible in a personal injury case. All you need is one or two cases to remind the judge of the law and to convince her that you are not making this up. When you are drafting a brief, and you want to state an undisputable black letter law proposition, and you simply want to find one case from your jurisdiction that has said this proposition, using the Internet to track down a case is perfectly fine.

◆ The Internet <u>should not</u> be used as the primary tool for legal research in the following instances:

❑ When you are researching a problem for a client that requires you to find and interpret all of the relevant and applicable law in your jurisdiction in order to render correct, reliable, legal advice.

If a client is counting on you to find and analyze all of the relevant authorities in order to render correct legal advice, you should not step to the plate and try to hit a hardball with a whiffle ball bat. You might get the bat in just the right position, and one time out of a thousand you will connect and knock the ball out of the park, but the odds are against you. Unfortunately, most of the time, this will be the kind of research problem you will be faced with.

❑ When you need to verify and confirm that the authorities you are using still are good law.

If one of the main shortcomings of the Internet is that it is not kept up-to-date and not verified for accuracy, then you should never rely on Internet sites to ensure that the authorities you are using still are good law. Go to the Shepard's books or beg the billing partner or the client to let you use Keycite or Shepard's On-line.

❑ When you really need the answer to the problem quickly.

Westlaw and Lexis will give you a reliable response instantly if you know what questions to ask and where to ask them. No one Internet site can provide you with the complete picture on the average legal issue, so in order to use the Internet more reliably, you must try different sites and cross-check the information you are finding to give yourself a better chance of seeing 90% of the relevant authorities. If we all had enough time to browse twenty sites to make sure we were reading every kind of authority that is accessible on the Internet, then we would significantly reduce the odds of making a huge mistake. But this requires a great deal of time, and time truly is money to a practicing attorney. In fact, almost every time you use the Internet instead of Westlaw or Lexis, you are trading increased research time for cheaper research tools. You might have come out ahead if you simply paid the fee for Westlaw or Lexis and got a reliable answer in much less time.

IV. RESOURCES FOR LEGAL RESEARCH ON THE INTERNET

The remainder of this chapter discusses the most commonly used and most often recommended legal research sites on the Internet. We have tried to point out the things that each site does well. If all you want is a single authority that states a certain proposition, many of these sites will work for you. This is especially true if you already know the citation for the document you seek. However, as discussed above, if you are trying to perform research to answer a client's legal question when you do not already know the answer, there is no single site that gets the job done for every kind of problem. Only by using a combination of sites will you hope to come close to a reliable answer.

A. Directory sites and legal search engines

It is safer to run a used bookstore than an information desk. Directory services collect lists of legal information sites and catalog them for searching. If you follow up on a list item and get burned, do not blame the directory service. There is no promise that the directories will be complete, although they grow every week. The search engines provided below will pull up results, but it is up to you to sort through them and to decide whether the materials offer reliable information.

1. Findlaw (www.findlaw.com)
Search engine: lawcrawler.findlaw.com

Findlaw is a directory of legal topics and links to legal information. It has topical information on dozens of areas of the law and also contains links to legal news. In short, the site contains everything from commentary on recent U.S. Supreme Court cases to information about how to find a lawyer in your area. The site contains federal and state materials, including statutes and cases. Its search engine allows searching of the Findlaw site or a large group of legal-related sited that Findlaw has collected. However, the search engine does not support full Boolean logic searches, and it can be difficult to narrow a research inquiry to find exactly what you are looking for. We have found this site to be particularly useful in finding Supreme Court cases—which you can find by citation or by scrolling through cases decided in a particular term.

2. Cornell Legal Information Institute (www.law.cornell.edu)

This site contains texts of various federal materials, including the Constitution, various sections of the U.S. Code (without annotations), the Federal Rules of Evidence and Civil Procedure, as well as model laws including the UCC. It also contains selected Supreme Court opinions and maintains links to various topical areas. Like Findlaw, this site does not support full Boolean searches. The Court Options menu, though, is useful and allows searching of U.S. Supreme Court cases, Courts of Appeals cases (by Circuit), and New York state cases. Selected other states can be searched through links to state sites. The links to state sites can be useful, but be aware that many states have limited date availability (and go back only to the mid-1990s).

3. LexisONE (www. lexisone.com)
Search engine: search.lexisone.com

LexisONE is billed as a resource center for small law firms. It allows searches for all U.S. Supreme Court cases and other federal and state cases from 1996 forward. If you know a citation for a case from 1996 forward, you can Lexsee (find) the case immediately and download for free.

Significantly, LexisONE also allows pay-as-you-go access to the full Lexis-Nexis service, with plans starting as low as $25 per day and $32 per week. You also can check cites in a document for $4 per cite so, for small firms filing fewer briefs, it may be worth it.

Its search engines supposedly support searches of the free case law data bases and legal websites collected by LexisONE and, in this respect, you may be able to limit a search and scope of hits reasonably. But our tests using the service were not satisfactory (as compared to searches done through the full Lexis-Nexis database).

B. Web sites that contain good links to legal resources

The following web site are ones that we have found particularly useful for their lists of links to other legal sources, e.g., to sites that have information on specific practice areas.

1. ABA Legal Technology Resource Center
(www.lawtechnology.org/lawlink/home)

The ABA site contains links to various online resources, including federal, state and international materials.

2. American Law Sources Online (www.lawsource.com/also)

American Law Sources contains general links to other websites containing legal and government-related materials for the United States, Canada and Mexico.

3. CataLaw (http://www.catalaw.com)

Like the name suggests, this site is a catalog of links to free legal resources on the internet, organized by legal topic and region.

4. Heiros Gamos (www.hg.org)

HG contains links to various federal and state materials, as well as topical information on over 70 specific practice areas. Significantly, it also contains links to law journals as well as other legal periodicals.

5. Internet Legal Resource Guide (www.ilrg.com)

This site can be useful if you are looking for forms, as it contains a categorized index of legal resources, including links to legal forms.

6. Law.com Dictionary (dictionary.law.com)

A good site if you are looking up the definition of a legal term of art.

7. LLRX (www.llrx.com)

This site is particularly useful for legal technology news, web research guides, and links to the same.

8. Megalaw (www.megalaw.com)

Megalaw is a directory of annotated legal topics and contains subject indices with links to legal sources. It has a particularly thorough listing of legal links.

9. Virtual Chase (www.virtualchase.com)

Virtual Chase is a law-firm supported site that contains a list of annotated links and a good summary of current legal issues in the news.

C. Sites for federal court opinions, statutes and regulations

As we have noted above, several free search engines enable users to download legal opinions at no cost—and this can be particularly useful if a supervisor asks you to read a leading case in an area or summarize a particular ruling. But often, it is difficult to find cases without a name or a citation and when you do not know what case or cases is controlling in a particular area.

Good resources for finding a case or statute for which you know the name or citation, or for finding one or two cases on a proposition of black-letter law include:

1. Cornell Law School's Legal Information Institute (www.law.cornell.edu)

As noted above, the Court Opinions menu on this site allows searching for U.S. Supreme Court and other federal cases. The site also is one of the first to announce cases that are granted certiorari, and it can be useful if you are tracking the development of a particular case.

In addition, you can search and review the entire U.S. Code on the Cornell site, and you can also search individual titles of the code—a great resource if you know what section you are looking for and want to get a lay of the land.

2. U.S. Supreme Court (www.supremecourtus.gov)

The Supreme Court's own web site gives you access to recent slip opinions (from the last year or so) and other information about its operation. You can hear recordings of U.S. Supreme Court arguments in RealAudio® format on oyez.nwu.edu.

3. Individual federal court sites

Most Federal Circuit courts (and many district courts) now publish their cases online. These are generally made available soon after a decision has been handed down, but coverage going back several years is limited. In addition, these sites have links to the various court rules, which are important anytime you are filing a brief in any of these courts.

- 1st Circuit: http://www.ca1.uscourts.gov
- 2nd Circuit: http://www.ca2.uscourts.gov
- 3rd Circuit: http://www.ca3.uscourts.gov
- 4th Circuit: http://www.ca4.uscourts.gov
- 5th Circuit: http://www.ca5.uscourts.gov
- 6th Circuit: http://www.ca6.uscourts.gov
- 7th Circuit: http://www.ca7.uscourts.gov
- 8th Circuit: http://www.ca8.uscourts.gov
- 9th Circuit: http://www.ca9.uscourts.gov
- 10th Circuit: http://www.kscourts.org/ca10
- 11th Circuit: http://www.ca11.uscourts.gov/opinions.htm
- D.C. Circuit: http://www.cadc.uscourts.gov
- Federal Circuit: http://www.fedcir.gov

4. Government Printing Office (www.gpoaccess.gov)

The GPO web site is an excellent source for obtaining sections of the U.S. Code (current edition), the Code of Federal Regulations (1996-present), the Federal Register (1994-present), bills (1993-present), and the Congressional Record (1994-present). The site is searchable. Search results tend to be overbroad, but if you are patient, you easily can find the section that you are looking for—especially if you have know key words in the title or terms of art that can limit your results.

5. FirstGov (www.firstgov.gov)

This site is a relatively good portal with links to useful federal government sites.

D. Sites for state court cases and regulations

Courts.net (www.courts.net)

This site contains links to all of the state court sites where opinions are catalogued. In addition, most state statutes, constitutions, and legislative materials are housed on individual state sites, so this can be a good place to start if you are looking for a particular source relating to state law. Coverage is limited—most state sites contain materials dating back only to the mid-1990s.

E. Federal legislative history

The Thomas site, Library of Congress (thomas.loc.gov)

The Internet is becoming one of the best sources for finding federal legislative documents—if you are searching for a statute enacted after 1995. The Library of Congress maintains an enormously useful and user-friendly site called "Thomas" that enables access to full texts of congressional documents, including past and current bills and actions taken on them.

House and Senate reports can be searched by word or phrase, report number, bill number, or committee. Alternatively, you can browse listings of recent bills for reports on point. In addition, you can limit your search to the particular type of report you are seeking—whether it be a House Report, Senate Report, Conference Report, or report of a joint committee. Coverage dates back to 1995.

Individual bills can be searched by word or phrase or by bill number. You can limit your search to bills that have received floor action, bills that have been enrolled, or to House or Senate bills. Coverage dates back to 1989.

You also can search the Congressional Record—dating back to 1989. You can search it by work or phrase, by Member of Congress, or by date or date range. This can be a particularly useful way to find legislative history, especially if you know the sponsor of a bill or the members of a committee that worked on it. You can limit your search by section of the Congressional Record—House, Senate, Extension of Remarks, and Daily Digest—or by date, date range, or member name.

Thomas also enables you to search the index to the Congressional Record back to 1995. Page references for index terms and bill numbers are linked to the full text of the Congressional Record.

Public laws dating back to 1973 are summarized and indexed on Thomas by public law number. You can find information on bill sponsors and floor actions, and you can uncover detailed legislative summaries of each bill. Short and popular titles of bills are also revealed.

F. Administrative agency opinions

You can search for decisions of federal administrative agencies on the University of Virginia's Administrative Agency Opinion site (www.law.virgina.edu/admindec), or you can check the individual agency's web site for similar information. For example, the Federal Election Commission (www.fec.gov) catalogues its opinions, and these can be searched relatively easily with key words. Other agencies maintain similar sites.

G. More mainstream search engines

Several more mainstream search engines may also be useful for finding legal information, though finding applicable, controlling precedent via a general search engine can be like finding a needle in a haystack.

1. Google (www.google.com)

Google, as you may already know, is huge, fast, and reliable. Google's "advanced search" options allows you to narrow your results, but it does not support logical connectors between terms other than AND, OR, and BUT NOT so it can be difficult to pinpoint what you are looking for. Google Uncle Sam (www.google.com/unclesam) limits your search to U.S. Government sites that Google has collected.

2. Alta Vista (www.altavista.com)

Alta Vista is one of the largest search engines, but it is not particularly fast. Unlike Google, Alta Vista allows you to use an additional logical connector, "NEAR," in the advanced search mode. The authors have, however, found Google to be more reliable and to generate more on point documents, despite this fact.

3. Fast (www.alltheweb.com)

An alternative to Google that operates much the same way (i.e., without connectors besides AND, OR and BUT NOT) and it is, like its name says, relatively fast.

Chapter 19

Strategies for Research and Determining When You are Finished

By way of summary of the research strategies first introduced in Chapter 10, we will repeat the stages of planning for research and the execution of the plan.

I. INITIAL ASSESSMENT OF THE PROBLEM

Your first job is to assess the problem so as to identify the issues—the specific legal questions that need to be answered—and then to determine if additional facts are needed from the client or other sources, and then to put together a plan of action to find the legal sources necessary to answer the questions.

A. What is at issue?

You may have an idea about which areas of the law are implicated by the problem (e.g., this sounds like a fraud case, or this is probably a copyright case), but you will not necessarily know enough about these areas and their fundamental background principles, claims, defenses, and policies to be able to determine the specific legal questions you will need to answer. You may not even know the general areas of the law implicated by the problem. Assuming the assigning attorney or the client cannot shed any light on this, you will need to do background research into the law.

B. Background research into the area of law

When you have a background resource, you will read it to answer the following questions:

- What are the major issues in this area of the law, both old and new?
- What are the kinds of claims, injuries, damages, causes of action, or defenses that are brought or claimed or asserted in this area?
- What constitutional issues are implicated (if any)?
- Are there statutes, rules, or administrative regulations that typically are found in this area?

The information that you find in a dictionary or encyclopedia may help you get your feet wet, but you may exhaust what they have to say on your matter without determining the actual issues that are implicated by your facts. You will have to go deeper, to hornbooks, treatises, and practice guides.

At the end of your crash course in the area of law, you need to be able to return to your set of facts and determine the specific questions that are presented by these facts. If you cannot do this, return to the background material. You might also discover a need for additional factual information.

C. Background research into the facts

If you determine that your boss or the client did not give you enough factual information to answer the issues intelligently, go back and ask for more information. Assuming the well is dry, or the professor who assigned the work will not tell you anything else, you will perform your research with what you already know, or turn to alternative sources of factual information.

D. Background information of the "how to do it" kind

The background information you need may be simply "how do you do it" information in this area of the law. "How to" sources include your colleagues and other attorneys (in real life, not law school), practice guides and CLE materials, the actual agency or court involved, or pleading and practice form books.

II. PLANNING YOUR RESEARCH

After formulating the questions you must answer, you must come up with a plan for finding the sources to answer each issue. You should divide your plan into categories—how are you going to find:

◆ Primary controlling authorities
◆ Primary persuasive authorities
◆ Secondary authorities
◆ Sources for checking and validating your authorities.

It is advisable actually to write up a plan of action and follow it. Write down the sources you will use and the order in which you will use them. Leave space in your plan outline to make notes on what you checked. Keep a good record of every item (every individual authority) that you find, including what it says and the citation and page number. This last piece of advice will save you hours of frustration in the future when you cannot find the same book on the shelf, or the library is closed, or you cannot quite remember the name of the case that said something crucial about a certain element of a legal rule.

A well prepared record of the findings also can be used as a skeleton outline of your written work product, which you later can flesh out and turn into a proper TREATment of the issues. For example, as you research, you probably will learn that there are X number of required elements for the issue, and 2 or 3 exceptions to the rule, and X number of defenses to the rule. Writing them down in your notes on what you are finding will create a skeleton outline of the Rule section of your written work product. As you find authorities that provide the sub-rules, factors, policies, considerations, or simply provide explanation or clarification of any of the items in the outline, you can fill in the information in the proper sections of the TREATment of the main issue and elements as you proceed along in your research. Then, when you stop, you will have a fairly complete skeleton outline of the actual work product you will draft. If you can fill in the skeleton outline on a laptop computer as you go along, even better.

III. PERFORMING THE RESEARCH

A. What determines the scope of the research

You cannot always adopt a "leave no stone unturned" plan in which you will try to completely exhaust every possible source for the law. Sometimes the deadline set by your boss or the court is too short for that; other times, the client simply cannot or will not afford that level of research. So time and money are important factors in actual law practice.

Another factor is your knowledge of the area of the law. If you know the area well, you will not have to look for authorities in as many places, and you can zero in on the sources you know are likely to lead you directly to the answer. When you are familiar with the area, you will feel more confident when you think you have found the right answer and can stop. The converse is true when you are less familiar with the area of law—you will need to look to more sources to find authorities and may not be as confident that you are done with the research.

B. Sample research plans

There is no perfect research plan, but some plans are better than others. If you have endless amounts of time and no money issues to constrain you, you could spend weeks and often months researching almost any issue of law. The more time you spend, the more likely it is that you will find, review, and analyze every important source on the law in the area. But no one—no law student, no law professor, and certainly no practitioner—has unlimited time for research. Accordingly, the advice below is directed toward helping you put together a *practical* research plan, not a perfect plan. The sample plans here will guide you through the steps of your research and refer you to the sources you should consult along the way. By following an appropriate plan for the time frame (or money constraints) of your situation, you will allow yourself the greatest opportunity to find all of the relevant authorities and not miss something important.

Research is broader than writing. Every plan described below will ask you to look at a greater number of authorities than you will wind up writing about in your office memorandum or court brief. You must read broadly and check and recheck your findings in a variety of ways in order to determine what the law is; then you present it in writing using the most authoritative, most telling, and most indicative authorities.

The plans are organized by the amount of time or money with which you have to work. The first four plans assume that no statute or rule or regulation is involved in the determination of the issue; the fifth plan addresses a statutory or regulatory research issue.

1. **Plan 1**—When you have lots of time (and expense is not an issue), whether or not you are familiar with this area of law. [More than 5 days to 1-2 months research plan].
   a. You can be as thorough as you want. Start with the restatement, and then a top notch treatise. Then move on to an ALR or two.
   b. Read the cases cited, especially those from your jurisdiction. Use the digests to find even more cases. Shepardize or KeyCite your cases to find even more cases, and read them; then Shepardize or KeyCite the new cases.
   c. Move on to a different treatise (if there is one), and perhaps a third treatise. Make sure you are arriving at the correct rules of law regarding your issue by cross-checking with more than one treatise authority. Note that even here, you are not attempting to read the treatise or restatement cover to cover. This would be virtually impossible. You are looking at the applicable sections or chapters that cover your topic.
   d. Read several law review articles on point. Note any current developments, emerging issues, and changes in the law. Read the articles critically, and attempt to distinguish the author's "take" on the law—her views, criticisms, recommendations, and predictions—from the actual prevailing legal principles discussed in the article. You should be most interested in the latter.
   e. Read a recent CLE publication on this topic to make sure you have the most up-to-date information about the law—the breaking news stories, the most recent developments. Of course, you also have been checking the pocket parts, supplements, and advance sheets of the reporters, treatises, and ALRs as you go along.
   f. Shepardize or KeyCite your cases again. Check the good cases and the bad cases. Read every citing authority.
   g. Re-read your best authorities one more time. Be sure you understand them and get all of your notes and citations (and page numbers) in order.
   h. If you've got the money to spend—yours or your client's—make copies of every authority (<u>i.e.</u>, the whole case, or the relevant pages of the treatise, restatement, law review or ALR) that you think you might use to write up your results; both the authorities that go your way and the authorities that do not.
2. **Plan 2**—When you cannot or do not want to spend much time, but you are well familiar with this area of the law. [2-5 day research plan].

    a. Go for the jugular—try first to find controlling primary authorities.

        i. Digests—Look for cases on point. You may get the answer right there, right now.

        ii. Treatises or restatement—Quickly consult a treatise or restatement as a check to make sure your results are in line with established authority.

        iii. CLE publications, ALRs, or law review articles?—Maybe, just to make sure there has not been a significant new change in the law in the last few months.

        iv. Other secondary sources?—Probably not.

    b. Verify and validate your authorities with Shepard's or KeyCite.

3. **Plan 3**—You cannot or do not want to spend much time, but you are NOT familiar with this area of the law.

    This is a conundrum. You need the time but you do not have the time.

    a. If the issue is money, not time per se, consider doing the background research described above as non-billed time.

    b. If the issue really is time—"I only have X days to do this"—reverse the plan so that you at least read the restatement or a treatise first, and then hit the digests. In this way, you have a better chance of figuring out the big picture— all the issues and defenses and constitutional problems, etc.—before zeroing in on individual cases.

    c. Do not fail to verify your sources with Shepard's or KeyCite—you will not do anyone any good if you report bad law to them.

4. **Plan 4**—No time at all, whether or not you are familiar with this area of law. [A few hours to 1 day plan]

    a. Cases first and foremost—use the digests, find cases, and Shepardize or KeyCite them to find more cases (as well as to make sure they still are good law).

    b. Squeeze in one good treatise or the restatement just to make sure you have not missed the big picture and left out a crucial area of the law in your analysis.

Of course, the fourth plan is risky. You can miss important things by moving so fast, especially if you were not that familiar with the area of law to begin with. But you do not always have the luxury of checking and rechecking a broad range of authorities. Do what you can in an intelligent manner. And always Shepardize or KeyCite your good and bad authorities.

5. **Plan 5**—When a Statute, Rule, or Administrative Regulation is involved [An addition to one of the plans above]

    a. When a statute or rule or regulation applies, you must start with the statute, rule, or regulation in your research. Read what it says.

    b. Review an annotated version of the statute or rule—this will show you cases citing the statute or rule, and it will note cases that add, change, explain, modify, or distinguish the statute or rule. Read the cases.

  c. Research the administrative regulations, the sub-regulations and administrative rules that implement the regulations, and "official" and unofficial interpretations by administrative and executive entities charged with implementing the regulation (the agency itself, the attorney general, a regulatory body or commission).

  d. If there appear to be divergent opinions in the authorities you are reading about the meaning or application of certain provisions of the statute or regulation, then research the legislative history of the statute or drafting and ratification history of the rule or regulation.

  e. Then move on to the cases, treatises, restatements, ALRs, law reviews as provided in the plans above.

IV. HOW DO YOU KNOW WHEN YOU ARE FINISHED?

Follow this rule of thumb for determining when you are finished with your research:

 (1) If you have found several (3-5) controlling authorities that agree with each other as to the legal issue at hand, and they are recent enough in time not to give you pause (a good rule of thumb is within the last thirty years for a highest court/ highest controlling authority and ten years for an intermediate level appellate court/second highest controlling authority);

 (2) If you also found several good persuasive authorities that support your controlling authorities, including a treatise or other secondary authority that supports your findings;

 (3) If you have reconciled or distinguished all contrary controlling authorities and any important persuasive authorities; and

 (4) If you do not have any nagging questions that you know should be answered before you move on to writing;

Then you are finished.

  This is only a rule of thumb. It is not going to hold true in every research problem you will encounter in law school or in actual practice. But having some guidelines is better than having none.

  One guideline for applying the rule of thumb is to look to see if the sources you are finding all start to agree with each other and all wind up citing each other, and you no longer are finding new authorities in your searches. If your on-line searches fail to turn up new authorities and your searches in secondary authorities are referring you to sources that you already have read, then you should be finished. You still will have to read and analyze the authorities you found, but you will not need to keep searching for more authorities to add to your collection. By the same token, if each new search turns up new and unfamiliar authorities, you most likely are not finished.

  Each item in the rule of thumb can be further explored, as follows:

A. Several recent controlling authorities that agree

1. Finding paydirt!

It is a lovely thing to start your research and find a bunch of recent controlling authorities that agree on the topic at hand. If they include a statute and several recent cases from the highest authority in the jurisdiction, you are in heaven. Unfortunately, it will not always be this way.

2. Not finding anything?

You will not always find a highest court/highest level authority case on point, or you will not find one from the last thirty years. That is okay; it happens from time to time. You may not even find an intermediate level appellate opinion on point. That is rare, but it happens once in a while. Keep looking for controlling authorities. Try new sources, try new ideas, new research terms and topics, but realize that occasionally there simply is no really good controlling authority on point.

3. How do you "keep looking?"

The key to good research is to think broadly and to think synonyms. Broad thinking will allow you to examine the issue in a number of lights, to recast it several times, and eventually to expand on the topics and subjects that you will search under.

Synonyms are the key to proper coverage in research. We cannot use clairvoyance to figure out exactly how West Group or other compilers, editors, and authors have categorized the sources you need to find to answer the question. So, you must think of several ways to say the same thing—several subjects, topics and subtopics—in other words, synonyms, so that they will collect all the authorities on point. Sometimes this is an easy call, and sometimes the first topic/subject/subtopic you search under produces paydirt, but not always.

If you need more incentive, this process remains critical when you turn to the computer to do your research. You will need to come up with many synonyms for search terms in order to hit on all the correct authorities. So get good at it now, because it is not just for books, and it will not get any easier later.

4. Old cases are not by definition bad cases.

Do not make up your mind ahead of time that you simply will not write about—will not even cite—any case that is "too old." Sometimes "old" is the only game in town.

When we talk about using and writing about "old" authorities, we assume that you have researched well enough to satisfy yourself that there are no other, more recent controlling authorities of the same or higher level court that cover the same area. If there are, then the current, prevailing authorities control, not the old cases. But if "old" cases are the only cases around, proceed with the old cases.

The question always is: "Is it still good law?" This depends on what the law has done since that case came down. Ask the following questions:

◆ Is anyone still citing the case for this proposition or for any proposition? Or is it an abandoned derelict on the waters of the law?

◆ Has the case been abandoned and rejected directly or indirectly by more recent authorities? (i.e., no one is citing it, and other cases with different legal rules and standards are covering this area of the law now.)

◆ Are the newer cases (perhaps only from the intermediate level court) simply talking a different language (different policies, factors, elements, standards) from that in the earlier case? Has the law moved beyond the old case?

◆ Has the area of law changed by way of statute or rule since the case was handed down?

5. Why controlling authorities are of paramount importance.

Controlling authorities are of paramount importance for the obvious reason that they will control the outcome of the issue at hand. You cannot ignore a controlling authority—if it is duplicative of other equally or more recent controlling authorities, you may wind up not writing about it, but you must take it into account in formulating your answer to the research topic. If it is contrary to your other authorities, you must try to reconcile it or distinguish it, and if it cannot be reconciled or distinguished, you must think about changing your "answer" to the legal question you are researching so that this case can work its way into the mix. If it simply cannot work with the other authorities, you have one of those **rare** situations where you have to hedge a little on what the law is.

6. Statutes and rules are controlling.

Statutes and regulations from the applicable jurisdiction are controlling, but rarely will they be the last word on a topic. Statutes and rules are written with a view to the law on the topic that already exits—to the extent that they do not change the existing law (the rules, sub-rules, legal standards, factors, policies and so forth), then the earlier law (common law and statutory/rule-based law) continues to have effect and importance.

7. A whole new regime?

Occasionally, a statute or a whole new set of laws—a new legal regime—is passed to wipe the entire slate clean and to start a new set of laws on a given topic. The Employee Retirement Income Security Act (ERISA) and the Racketeer Influenced and Corrupt Organizations Act (RICO) are examples of this. But this genesis effect lasts until the first court gets a case under the new legal regime; then the court interprets the law, and its opinion becomes part of the law; and the next court interprets the law, and the law has been advanced—at least clarified, perhaps modified, perhaps expanded or diminished. Thus, you must always look for the cases on the topic you are researching, even if it largely is a "statutory" issue.

8. What are "statutory" research issues?

How do you know when to look for a statute? There is no hard and fast rule, but the following are several ways of getting to the right answer.

If the area of the law is one that traditionally is regulated by statute (and by the time you graduate, you should have a basic understanding of this kind of area), then you should start looking in the index to the statutes in your jurisdiction for sections that cover your topic. For example, the following areas of state law are traditionally regulated by statute:

Employment (by statutes, rules, and regulations)

Domestic relations

Trusts, estates, wills, intestate succession

Evidence (by rule, rather than statute)

Procedures for legal process and litigation (by statutes or rules)

Criminal law

Public health and safety (building codes, zoning, traffic)

Taxation (by statutes and regulations)

Government—at the state, county, municipal, and local level

Products liability and product safety

Statutes of limitations

Securities, negotiable instruments, checks, promissory notes, etc. (by statutes, rules, and regulations)

Banks, banking, loans and lending, debtor and creditor

Landlord - tenant

Sales of goods (by the UCC, for instance)

There are more, but this is a good list to start with. If you are not sure, it never hurts to just start with the index to the statutes. If you do not find anything, you can move on.

Almost all federal questions are based on a statute or federal administrative rule or regulation. There is very little federal common law. So, if you have a case governed by federal law (not a diversity action—that most likely is governed by state law), then start looking for the federal statute(s) on point.

Secondary sources, especially ones that are focused on your jurisdiction, often will discuss statutes and rules that apply to the topic. This is another good place to start if you are not sure if a statute is involved. Do not ignore state practice guides just because you may never cite them in your final memorandum.

Look at the cases and other authorities you are reading—if they mention a statute, then look it up, and see what's going on. It may turn out to be merely incidental to the problem, but you will never know unless you look it up.

B. Several good, recent, persuasive authorities

There are several possible reasons why you would want to find recent, persuasive authorities:

1. Reality check

If you found several controlling authorities already, you may only want to examine a few persuasive authorities to make sure your research has not slipped off the deep end— that you have not stumbled into a little dead-end of the law and missed the boulevard that you were supposed to follow to the answer. A treatise or other broadly written, comprehensive work can do that. Cases from other jurisdictions can reveal that your jurisdiction's law is followed elsewhere (or not).

2. Comfort level

Finding a decent treatise that agrees with your findings is a comfort. An ALR or even a law review article can do the trick, too, but it is harder to find one on point. Other materials (CLE publications, practice guides) can be used to make sure your findings are up to date and not out of line with recent trends.

3. Good authority for big picture, policy issues

As discussed above, secondary sources have many uses other than as authority for briefs. You may want these broader, "big picture" references to make sure you have the lay of the land.

4. More analogous facts

Looking for cases as persuasive authority is a good way to find a case that is closer to the facts of your own case than any of the controlling cases from your own jurisdiction. These cases will confirm that the law is applied to your client's situation to produce the results you are reporting, whether or not the actual case is binding authority.

C. Reconciling/distinguishing authority

What more needs to be said? You have to reconcile or distinguish controlling authority, as mentioned above. It is a good idea to try to reconcile or distinguish persuasive authority, too, but especially if the authority is "impressive"—a major treatise in the area; a recent case from the highest court of a major state that has reason to handle this area of the law a lot; something written by a highly respected author in this area; anything else receiving high marks as persuasive authority, but which goes against your findings.

D. Nagging questions?

Your own mind will sometimes tell you you are not finished. You still wonder if you should follow up on the legal factor discussed in several of the cases. Should I go research this standard discussed in the cases to see exactly what it means? Should I go and see what this case (or related rule or statute) says? There is no absolute yes or no answer here; you will have to decide if it is worth it. But your conscience may be indicating to you that you should head back to the library.

Chapter 20

Adversarial Legal Writing

Part III of this text deals with **advocacy** in legal writing and oral communication. The lessons to be learned in this section involve how to satisfy your ethical duty to represent your client effectively in a contested matter. A contested matter is any legal matter in which the interests of the parties differ. This might be anything from litigation in a court, to a purchase and sale transaction, to a corporate deal, or to a license application to a governmental regulatory body. Contested matters are the most typical legal situations in which you will be representing a client. In contested matters, you often must communicate with an opponent and a third-party decision-maker, such as a court or an arbitrator, in addition to communicating with your client and your supervisors and colleagues at your law office. The examples and chapters below focus on litigation at the trial level and appellate level, but the considerations raised throughout this section apply in any contested matter.

This chapter will focus on the difference between objective legal writing and adversarial legal writing and will examine issues and considerations for writing in an adversarial context. Chapter 21 will focus on the general requirements of pretrial motions in court, and Chapters 22 and 23 will zero in on the particular requirements of motions to dismiss and motions for summary judgment. Chapter 24 will look at appellate advocacy and the general requirements for appeals and writs, and the topic of standards of review. Chapter 25 will focus on the structure and content of appellate briefs, and Chapter 26 will examine the art of oral advocacy at the pretrial, trial, and appellate levels of litigation. Chapter 27 will look beyond your first year legal writing experience to moot court and to actual practice situations in which collaborative legal writing will be the norm.

I. DIFFERENCES BETWEEN OBJECTIVE AND ADVERSARIAL LEGAL WRITING

Objectivity is required in order to render appropriate legal advice to your colleagues and clients. The office memorandum as the paradigm of objective, informative legal writing is designed to be read by people who are working for the client and are presumed to be friendly to the client or who at least owe a duty to the client to keep its confidences. Office memoranda must reflect a critical appraisal of the client's situation, and not just engage in cheerleading to pump up the team. An internal office memorandum must be informative of the good and bad facts of the case and present the blemishes along with the beauty marks of the client's legal position.

Adversarial legal writing is different. It is not the opposite of objective writing—it is an honest and truthful presentation of the merits of the client's case that is crafted so that it supports the client's position and **only** the client's position in the best possible way. A good advocate does not abandon her objectivity concerning the blemishes and beauty marks of her client's legal position when she is evaluating her client's case. But the work product of an advocate emphasizes the strong points and does its best to mitigate the effects of the bad points. Adversarial writing takes sides and advocates for one outcome— the outcome favoring the client.

Adversarial legal writing does not engage in fraud or obfuscation about the facts and law concerning the matter—nothing can be gained from lying and cheating except defeat and disbarment. The briefs and memoranda that you will file with the court and serve on your opponents will not lie about the facts and misstate the law. Rather, you must use your skill to present the facts and argue the law in a way that best favors your client. The facts that support your client will be front and center, and negative facts will be explained and defused. The applicable law will not be distorted or outright misstated by you, but to the extent that the statutes, cases, and other authorities allow you to emphasize and interpret the law in a way that better supports your client's position, it is your job as an advocate to make the most of these opportunities.

Lawyers wear several hats in contested matters. They are an officer of the court, bound to uphold the law and promote justice. Attorneys who lie and cheat about the facts and the law certainly violate this duty. Lawyers also must be counselors, seeking the best pathway to the best outcome for the client, whether that means cooperation and concession or more aggressive action. Attorneys whose motto is to fight every case to the bitter end violate this obligation. Lastly, lawyers must be advocates who play a role in the adversarial legal system of the United States by promoting the interests of their client at every stage of the matter in order to allow the court to reach a just result. Proper adversarial legal writing is one of your duties as an advocate.

II. THE NATURE OF THE ADVERSARIAL SYSTEM

Anglo-American legal tradition and, in particular, the American legal system has as its fundamental underpinning the theory that a judge and jury are better able to do justice and resolve disputes when the parties to the suit each are represented by advocates who present a biased, one-sided argument in favor of their clients. The adversarial system depends on its participants approaching litigation and dispute resolution as a high stakes contest in which your client can win or lose something that is significant, and in which every player in the process expects you to promote your client's position and not promote your opponent's position. There are other models for justice and dispute resolution in the world, but this is the American way.

III. STRATEGIES AND GOALS FOR ZEALOUS REPRESENTATION IN THE ADVERSARIAL CONTEXT

A. Follow the fifteen minute rule and write clearly and concisely

Supreme Court Justice Ruth Bader Ginsburg has commented that brief writers before the United States Supreme Court make two mistakes: first, they do not write clearly and concisely, and second, they do not write with their audience—the U.S. Supreme Court, with its current composition of judges—in mind.[1] In the words of Justice Ginsburg, "Every sentence in a brief should be written so that the judge would never feel the need to read the sentence twice."[2] That is a high standard to meet.

Judges everywhere believe that they have more than enough cases to work on and too much material to read and digest in any given case. They will not tolerate complex, cumbersome, redundant, and overly verbose writing in briefs and memoranda to the court. Justice Ginsburg promised her audience that if a brief writer failed to follow her advice, and she felt bogged down in a work, she would skip back to the summary of argument and forget the rest of the brief, or hand it off to one of her law clerks to digest and encapsulate for her.[3] That kind of reception is not your goal as an advocate. If a judge on the highest court in this country with one of the smallest caseloads believes this, imagine the attitude of the typical judge with hundreds more cases pending on his docket when he receives your complex, prolix work. A judge is not going to suffer through this kind of work for very long.

In response to this judicial attitude, we advocate following the **Fifteen Minute Rule**:

FIFTEEN MINUTE RULE

Write so that you can prove your argument
to the reader in fifteen minutes.

There is nothing magical about fifteen minutes—and no guarantee that you will even get that much attention from a judge. But if you draft and edit your work so that a busy judge can capture the best parts of your entire position and argument on a given motion or appeal in fifteen minutes or less, you will have served your client and the court very well.

There are several ways to accomplish this in writing:

◆ Front load your best material. Write an introduction to your brief that tells the court enough facts, law, and argument that you can convince the judge that your client should prevail, all in roughly half a page of text;
◆ Use the statement of facts to advocate your position;
◆ Use meaningful, argumentative thesis headings throughout the discussion or argument section;
◆ Draft the discussion or argument section in as clear, concise, and direct a manner as is possible;

---

[1] Comments delivered during "A Conversation with Justice Ruth Bader Ginsburg," at the Annual Meeting of the Association of American Law Schools, Washington D.C. (Jan. 8, 2000).

[2] Id.

[3] Id.

◆ Use the conclusion solely to request your relief, not to summarize or rehash your arguments and not to make a new point in support of your case.

These topics all will be discussed at greater length in the next chapter.

B. Know your audience and write with your audience in mind

This is a general principle of legal writing, but reaching this goal is even more difficult in a litigation context. With objective writing, you will tend to know your immediate audience very well, whether they be your colleagues or your clients, because you will have worked with them for some time, or at least you will have access to people who know them well and can tell you pointers on how to draft your work to better satisfy them. With litigation, you often are writing to a judge before whom you have never appeared prior to this case, and with whom no one in your office has had much experience. At the appellate level, depending on the shuffle of panels and assignment of cases in your jurisdiction, you may never get two of the same judges on a panel more than two or three times in your career. All of this leads to uncertainty in knowing exactly who your audience is.

Simply living with the uncertainty as inevitable kismet is not good enough. You should make calls to people who have tried any number of cases (even one) before the judge. Private civil litigators may not have as much exposure as prosecutors, public defenders, and criminal defense attorneys whose case loads often give them a better chance of seeing the same judge repeatedly over the course of several years, so do not neglect them when you are gathering your information.

Use your on-line resources to read everything that your judge has written in the area of law of your case. Westlaw allows you to search the judge field (ju) for opinions written by a particular judge, and Lexis allows you to search the OPINIONBY segment for the same purpose. Justice Ginsburg is disgruntled because of all the courts and judges in the land, the sitting members of the United States Supreme Court have the most well documented track record of any court in the nation. Every opinion, concurrence, and dissent written by the members of the court is well documented, and the oral arguments before the court are recorded on audio tape and text, so that the personal style of each justice during the arguments can be reviewed. In spite of this, Justice Ginsburg bemoans that many litigants write and argue as if their client and their friends at the firm were their only audience, and that they simply are preaching to their own choir.[4]

C. Concede facts and give up arguments when it will benefit your client to do so; do not concede when it will not

Let us disabuse you of the notion that we think lawyers should never concede facts or abandon arguments. Not so. The value of a concession depends on the stage of the dispute

---

[4] Comments of Justice Ruth Bader Ginsburg, <u>supra</u> note 1.

and the nature of the dispute. Early in a contested matter, it may not benefit your client to reveal all the facts your client knows to your opponents until you discover what your opponents know and what their version of the facts is. On the other hand, early in the dispute may be a good time to reveal or stipulate to certain facts because it will save your client the time and energy in responding to discovery of those facts. Almost every relevant fact, good or bad, will be disclosed in the course of litigation, but litigation is not the only option nor is it often the best option for a client in a contested matter. Mediation or negotiation are far superior to litigation for the proper resolution of many contested matters, and management of facts is required for you properly to advocate for your client in these proceedings.

Certain concessions simply are against your client's interest no matter what the stage of the dispute. If you are representing a defendant (the accused party), be especially careful about conceding facts that have any bearing on liability or damages in a case. If you are representing a plaintiff (the aggrieved party), do not concede facts that may lead to an affirmative defense or avoidance for your opponent. Your evaluation of the facts must be long-sighted.

In litigation, give up a legal argument if it advances your cause with the court. Do not brief an argument if the chances that it will make you look foolish and obstinate are greater than the chances that any legal decision maker will agree with the argument and rule in your favor. Your best argument will look better if it is not seen in the vicinity of two other terrible arguments. Judges never make their decisions based on the number of arguments you raised.

On the other hand, do not arbitrarily limit the number of arguments you will make. Do not get stuck on one complicated argument, putting all your eggs in one basket, when you also can raise one or two less complicated arguments in addition to the complex argument. Leave your options open, as discussed below.

D. Know the facts and the law, and know your options

You cannot help your client if you do not learn the facts of your client's case. In order to know which facts are likely to be important, you have to know the law. Naturally, knowing the law and the facts is required if you are going to give advice and represent your client in any way or shape or form.

A doctor would not prescribe medicine without listening to the patient's symptoms first and determining what illnesses might be present and what side-effects might affect the patient if they take a certain medication. Similarly, a lawyer who does not know the facts and the law sooner or later will take an action that is directly against her client's interests.

Knowing the facts and the law also will enable you to know your options. If you do not know your options you will miss something important. If you do not know the facts or law, you could inadvertently close off one or more of your options and eliminate otherwise perfectly acceptable forms of relief for your client.

One of the main problems with lawyers is not that they do not know the law, but that they are too busy to be prepared. They do not take the time to figure out what they are doing or should be doing in a case. They lose sight of the big picture or never see it in the first place, and chase leads down one rabbit trail of facts or law after another without taking the time to think the case through, forming decisions on what needs to be done, planning the tactics and strategies that will get the job done, and then doing it.

The law is **not** one of the disciplines where 90% of the battle is just showing up. You must be prepared for the setting in which you are about to engage your lawyering skills. If it is the motion to dismiss stage, think about what you are doing with the motion or opposing the motion—What does it mean to bring (or defend) this motion? What are you trying to accomplish? What is the effect of this course of action as opposed to others? If it is the summary judgment stage, ask the same questions. What you can and should do at these stages differs, so think about it and make sure you are aware of what you are doing. You may not always win your motions or win the case just by being prepared, but you certainly will lose more motions and cases (and clients) if you are not prepared.

Chapter 21

Pretrial Motions

The period in litigation after a case is filed in a court and before the case actually goes to trial before a fact-finder is called the "pretrial" period. This is the time to raise defenses against claims, and investigate the facts of the case through the process of discovery. In the pretrial period, a party may make a formal request for the court to do something for it—it requests relief from the court—and these requests are called "motions" because the party is acting "to move" the court for relief. Motions cover any type of request for relief, from the relatively mundane request for an extension of time, all the way to the dramatic dispositive motions—motions to dismiss and motions for summary judgment—in which a party asks the court to throw the opponent's case out of court or to grant the party judgment in the case as a matter of law.

I. STRUCTURE OF PRETRIAL MOTIONS AND MEMORANDA IN SUPPORT

Motion practice is initiated by a party (called the "movant") when it files the motion with the court, which is then followed by the opponent's filing of a response or opposition, and often then followed by the movant's filing of a reply to the opposition. In some jurisdictions, the motion itself will be drafted so as to contain all the legal and factual support it needs. In many other jurisdictions, the document that bears the title of "motion" merely makes the specific request for relief from the court, and a separate document called a "memorandum in support of the motion"[1] contains all of the legal and factual support for the motion.

The requirements, if any, for a motion to be accompanied by a separate "memorandum in support of the motion" will be identified and defined in the local rules of the court where you are litigating. Responses or oppositions to motions[2] and replies to responses or oppositions typically include all of the factual and legal support in the same document; there is no separate document to file to accompany the memorandum in opposition or reply.

---

[1] In various jurisdictions, this document may be called "suggestions in support," "points and authorities in support," or "brief in support" of the motion. You must pay attention to the local rules and not become too attached to one particular name for this type of litigation document.

[2] Depending on the local rules, the document may be titled "response," "opposition," "memorandum in opposition," "suggestions in response," or "points and authorities in opposition" to the motion.

In the section below, we have outlined the structure of the document that will lay out the legal arguments of the movant in support of the motion, whether it is included in the motion or in a separately filed document. We will refer to this document from now on as the "**memorandum in support.**" The structure outlined below for responses or oppositions to motions applies to the document that presents the opponent's legal and factual support for its opposition to the motion, and we will refer to this document as the "**memorandum in opposition.**" The third structure outlined below applies to the document that presents the movant's further legal and factual support for its motion in response to the opposition to the motion; we will refer to this simply as the "**reply.**"

A. The structure of the memorandum in support

A typical pretrial memorandum in support, no matter what kind of relief it seeks, will have the following sections:

> **Caption**
> **Title**
> **Pre-Introduction**
> **Introduction**
> **Statement of Facts**
> **Argument**
> **Conclusion**

Each section will be discussed in detail below.

B. The structure of the memorandum in opposition

The structure of the document that opposes the motion is the same:

> **Caption**
> **Title**
> **Pre-Introduction** (however, it may be unnecessary, as discussed below)
> **Introduction**
> **Statement of Facts**
> **Argument**
> **Conclusion**

C. The structure of the reply

The reply has the following format:

Caption
Title
Introduction
Argument
Conclusion

You will leave out the pre-introduction because the court by now knows what the motion is, and you most often will leave out the statement of facts, unless you need to clarify or correct something your opponent put in its version of the facts.

II. THE CAPTION, TITLE, AND PRE-INTRODUCTION

The caption identifies the court, the parties, and the docket number for the case. Often the judge's name is listed, too. How this information is to be arranged varies from jurisdiction to jurisdiction, but a typical structure is shown in the examples below.

The title is straightforward—it should introduce the party filing the memorandum and the purpose of the memorandum. For example: Defendant Smith's Memorandum in Support of Motion to Dismiss Plaintiff's Complaint for Lack of Personal Jurisdiction, or Plaintiff Arch Communicator's Memorandum in Support of Motion for Summary Judgment.

The pre-introduction is our term to refer to the first one or two sentences of the motion that come right after the caption and title of the motion. This section is used solely to tell the court what the motion is and the relief that is sought. Once again, this section is straightforward—you should identify yourself (the movant) and identify the party against whom the motion is brought. Usually, you will be moving the court under the auspices of a certain rule of procedure, so cite the rule in the pre-introduction. Then state the relief sought, and move on to the introduction. Unlike the sections that follow the pre-introduction (the introduction, statement of facts, argument, and conclusion), the pre-introduction has no heading of its own.

What do all of these look like? Here is an example:

CAPTION	UNITED STATES DISTRICT COURT SOUTHERN DISTRICT OF NEW YORK

	GEORGIE BOLLING, a Minor, by)
	his father and next friend, Robert)
	Bolling,)
	  Plaintiff,)
	)
	  v.) No. 97-2345-TRW
	)
	ALDEN HALL HISTORICAL SITE,)
	and ELLIOTT STIRLING,)
	)
	  Defendants.)

TITLE	DEFENDANTS ALDEN HALL AND STIRLING'S MEMORANDUM IN SUPPORT OF MOTION TO DISMISS FOR FAILURE TO STATE A CLAIM
PRE- INTRODUCTION	Defendants Alden Hall Historical Site ("Alden Hall") and Elliott Stirling ("Stirling") move this Court pursuant to Fed. R. Civ. P. 12(b)(6) to dismiss the complaint brought by Plaintiff Georgie Bolling ("Plaintiff") for failure to state a cause of action upon which relief may be granted.

Opponents do not necessarily have to put a pre-introduction into their memorandum in opposition. Remember that the opposition follows the motion and memorandum in support, so the court has had the opportunity to become familiar with the motion and is likely to read the movant's papers before looking at the opposition papers. If the title of the opposition is sufficiently detailed to identify the party opposing the motion, the movant's name, and the nature of the motion that is opposed, then the opponent does not need to write a pre-introduction that simply would repeat the information.

➤ *Properly detailed title:* Plaintiff Van Pelt's Memorandum in Opposition to Defendant Brown's 28 U.S.C. § 1404 Motion to Transfer
➤ *But not this:* Plaintiff's Memorandum in Opposition to Motion to Transfer

The same principle applies to the reply—at this point the court should be very familiar with the motion, so a properly drafted title to the reply that identifies the movant, the opponent, and the motion will preclude the necessity of a pre-introduction.

➤ *Properly detailed title:* Defendant Brown's Reply to Plaintiff Van Pelt's Opposition to Brown's 28 U.S.C. § 1404 Motion to Transfer

III. THE INTRODUCTION

The introduction follows the pre-introduction. It has a heading ("Introduction"). It is the most important section of the motion.

A. The objective of the introduction

The introduction has a simple objective, but one that takes all of your accumulated skill and experience to accomplish. You must grab the court's attention and try to win the motion in the introduction. If you can draft an introduction that meets this end, you will be well on your way to a successful career in litigation or other adversarial contexts.

The movant and opponent obviously have different interests, but the objective to be obtained in the introduction is similar: win the motion. Therefore, the parties will state:

Movant: Why the motion at hand is necessary, and why I prevail.

Opponent: Why the motion at hand is improper (untimely, unnecessary, or scandalous), and even if it's not one of the above, why I should prevail.

B. The importance of the introduction

Remember that in the law, first things matter the most, and the attention span of your audience always will be limited. Therefore, the introduction—the first substantive section of the motion or opposition—is critical. You must place your best facts and the best points of your legal argument before the judge as soon as you can. This means that you should not be cagey in the introduction. Do everything you can to present your best points to the court and win the motion in the introduction.

C. The drafting of the introduction

1. Movant's introduction

> **Movant's introduction must include:**
>
> • Background facts (from movant's perspective)
> • Movant's theme of the case and of the motion
> • Key operative facts upon which the motion turns
> • Snapshot of the law on the motion
> • Movant's conclusions (why the client prevails)

As movant, you must present enough of the background facts to tell the court what is going on, but only facts favorable to your client's position.

> *Example*: This lawsuit represents Van Pelt's attempt to spread the blame for her own negligence. Van Pelt's unauthorized modification of Brown's treadmill caused it to malfunction, killing one of Van Pelt's employees. In spite of the fact that the treadmill was in perfect working order when it was delivered to Brown's shipper and when it arrived at Van Pelt's health club as acknowledged by Van Pelt on the shipping receipt, Van Pelt has sued Brown for strict liability for design defect and failure to warn.

The filing of a pretrial motion may provide the first occasion for the court to take notice of a pending lawsuit and open the court file and read about the case. Courts generally do not read complaints or answers as they are filed, and most often will wait for a reason to read up on a case before they will invest that kind of time. The filing of a motion provides that reason. The court may start with the motion papers themselves, as these papers may be sitting on top in the court file (a typical system for filing material in a court file is by reverse chronological order with the most recently filed material sitting on top in the file). Therefore, movant has a strong incentive to tell the background of the case early in its memorandum in support as this may be the court's first introduction to the case.

The next task is to tell the facts that are most important to the motion at hand, and give a snapshot of the law that applies. Remember: this is just the introduction. Only tell as much of the law as is necessary to drive home your conclusions, and only discuss the elements of the rule that turn the case in your favor. Drive home the one or two best facts that further your argument. Then plug in your conclusions. They should be obvious from what you wrote leading up to the conclusions. Your conclusion is that the client must prevail, and the client's position should appear as ironclad as a tank and as righteous as scripture.

> When discussing the law and your legal conclusions in the introduction, you should try to make each sentence perform two or three tasks; give a conclusion and the "because" part— the facts and the principles of the law that lead to the conclusion.

> *Example:* {**conclusion**} Personal jurisdiction over the defendant Brown is improper because the {**legal principles**} Due Process clause requires minimum contacts with the forum state and {**facts**} Brown's two visits to the state were for charity purposes unrelated to any business activity conducted by Brown. {**conclusion**} Brown did not form any substantial connection to Pennsylvania because {**facts**} his two visits to the state were volunteer appearances for fund raising, amounting to less than six hours in the state, and thus were {**legal standards, conclusion**} random and fortuitous contacts. {**conclusion**} The visits were not connected to this lawsuit because {**facts**} the suit arises from Brown's sales of exercise equipment to plaintiff Van Pelt which were {**legal principles, facts, and conclusion**} transacted in Ohio where the sales agreements were signed and the contracts were formed.

Limit your citations to authority to the barest minimum. The default rule is not to cite *any* authority in the introduction. Most of the time, you will not have anything you need to cite in the introduction, but a short reference to the one statute, rule, or regulation that governs and controls the outcome, or to the very most important and strongest controlling cases that favor your position (no more than one or two) can be appropriate. This section has to flow, and long form citations clutter it up too much.

> ➤ *Example:* Personal jurisdiction over defendant Brown is improper because the Due Process clause requires minimum contacts with the forum state and Brown's two visits to the state were for charity purposes unrelated to any business activity conducted by Brown.
> ➤ *Do not write*: Personal jurisdiction over defendant Brown is improper because the Due Process clause, U.S. Const. amend. XIV, sec. 1, requires minimum contacts with the forum state, Int'l Boot Co. v. Texas, 323 U.S. 123, 128 (1945); Hanover Trust Co. v. Blatt, 456 U.S. 678, 682 (1967), and Brown's two visits to the state were for charity purposes unrelated to any business activity conducted by Brown. See Affidavit of Derek Brown dated July 14, 2005, ¶ 4 (attached hereto as exhibit 1).

Do not apologize for bringing the motion (unless you already have brought two such motions in the case; at that point, you should explain the need for a third). There are certain conventions in legal drafting ("praying" for or "respectfully requesting" relief; "respectfully submitting" your motion) that are proper, formal writing, but they are not intended to be an apology. If you are forced to bring repetitive motions (such as in a discovery context), explain why your opponent forced you to bring the latest motion.

> ➤ *Example:* Defendant Brown moves this court to compel the production of the medical reports of two of plaintiff Van Pelt's doctors. This is the third such motion to compel brought by Brown to obtain Van Pelt's complete medical records because Van Pelt persists in refusing to turn over the reports. In Van Pelt's deposition, she made reference to three treating physicians who attended her at Woodstock Hospital—Doctors Linus Pauling, Ludwig Schroeder, and Patty Peppermint. Only Doctor Pauling's report has been disclosed to Brown. Brown is entitled to the reports of all physicians who treated her for the injuries at issue in this matter.

The remaining components of an introduction are the themes—a theme for the case and a theme for the motion. A properly drafted theme for the case will be a single sentence or short phrase that sums up the client's position on the merits of the case that will resonate with the court and convince it that your client's position has merit and is worthy of careful attention. Think marketing message, not dissertation.[3] Your goal is for the court

---

[3] Do marketing messages work? Try and identify the companies that are associated with these slogans: "It's the real thing." "Just do it." "You're in good hands." "The king of beers." If you identified at least two of these companies just by their slogan, the marketing agencies are doing their job.

to start to think of the case as a whole in a light that favors your client. Naturally, the sound bite you draft will resonate more completely if you back it up with background facts that support your theory of the case.

> *Example*: {**theme of the case**} This lawsuit represents Van Pelt's attempt to spread the blame for her own negligence. {**supporting facts**} Van Pelt's unauthorized modification of Brown's treadmill caused it to malfunction killing one of Van Pelt's employees. In spite of the fact that the treadmill was in perfect working order when it was delivered to Brown's shipper and when it arrived at Van Pelt's health club as acknowledged by Van Pelt on the shipping receipt, Van Pelt has sued Brown for strict liability for design defect and failure to warn.

A properly drafted theme for the motion will cause the court to be receptive to all of your arguments and to sympathize with your client's facts and circumstances.

> *Example:* {**theme of the motion**} There is no legal justification for Van Pelt to file this lawsuit in Pennsylvania. The only explanation for this choice of forum is that Van Pelt wishes to harass Brown by attempting to force him to litigate in a distant forum. {**supporting facts**} Although the sales agreement between Van Pelt and Brown were signed in Brown's place of business in Ohio and Van Pelt took delivery of the goods in Ohio through a shipping agent of her choice (Federal Express), Van Pelt sued Brown in Pennsylvania where she resides.

2. Opponent's introduction

Opponent's introduction must include:
• Background Facts (from opponent's perspective)
• Opponent's theme of the case and of the motion
• Key operative facts upon which the motion turns
• Snapshot of the law on the motion
• Opponent's conclusions (why the client prevails)

Opponents must take on the motion and the memorandum in support and turn it back on the movant. As indicated above, the requirements for the introduction are the same for the opponent as they were for the movant. Opponents must try to win the motion, and the introduction is the first step.

Opponents have more choices to make in responding to a motion. If you actually have a decent argument or even the better of the argument on the motion—the facts and the law actually support your side, not the movant's—then you can take the motion head-on, and argue point by point why the movant is erroneous on the facts, the law, or the conclusions. At the end, you argue that the client should win, and your position is ironclad scripture (not to mix metaphors or anything). This is the most satisfying option.

If, as an opponent, you have a difficult position on the merits, you should examine procedural issues regarding the timing of the motion or the propriety of movant's decision to bring this motion at this stage of the case as a whole. If laches have set in—you are in a much worse position now than if this motion had been brought a month ago—then you should argue laches in defense against the motion. If the motion is the second or third in a row by the movant, you are entitled to point out whether the second or third motion is necessary or question whether movant simply is trying to delay the case and frustrate the opponent. Courts are sensitive to tactical behavior, and if there is clear evidence that movant is being tactical, it may benefit you to raise this in your defense to the motion.

D. Themes in the introduction

Both the movant and the opponent should try to sell their theme for the case and for the motion at hand in the introduction. A theme for the case or for the motion is the summation of the strengths of the case that is designed to help the court grasp the facts and equities of the case, but in a way that favors the litigant's client. A theme should be able to be summed up in a tag line—your pitch to the court in a marketing sense. A theme that catches on with the court can help you play up your strengths and play down your weaknesses. If you make a connection with the trial judge, every time she picks up the court file of your case she will be humming your theme song ("This is the case where the woman modified the treadmill and killed her employee and now is trying to spread the blame.").

You must adopt a theme that ties in with the facts and your legal argument. Do not forget that although you may be writing an introduction to an initial procedural motion, it could be the first document the court or law clerk looks at in regard to the entire case, so you want to get them thinking about the case in the correct way (your client's way).

Themes vary from case to case. Some popular themes and variations on these themes are:

- **You've got to live by your word.** A man's word is his bond. What good is a person (or a company) if they cannot live up to their word. Holding people to their word is the foundation of contract law.
- **Misuse of power.** Big, aggressive bully of a corporation vs. smart, little, under-financed corporation (your client). Big government agency against the little guy (your client).
- **Getting what you deserve.** Getting exactly what you bargained for. Getting what is fair for a victim in your situation. Getting what is right, in spite of what a contract or a rigid legal stipulation says you should get. A case of an innovative, cutting edge competitor (your client) vs. slip-shod, rip-off upstart company.
- **Cheating, taking what you don't deserve.** Overreaching. Sponging off. Unjust enrichment. Taking unfair advantage of a fortuitous situation. Ducking important rules or regulations.

- **Placing blame on the correct party.** Innocent, diligent bystander (your client) vs. careless and highly culpable opponents.
- **Dishonesty.** Deceit. Hiding important facts. Failing to disclose material information. Your opponent lied about many things in the past. This lawsuit is just the latest example of lying.
- **Sloppiness.** Opponents are sloppy. Look how sloppy they are about the facts and authorities in the motion. Look at their own business practices. Their whole case is sloppy—you'll never get the complete, straight story from them.
- **Laches.** Opponents have brought the suit too late—we've changed our position in reliance on their acting one way, and now they sue to go the other way. This motion is the same thing—too little, too late, and we are put in a bad position by their bringing it at this stage of the case.

Be careful not to pick an offensive theme. Do not start with the American vs. foreigner theme unless you like dancing on thin ice. Do not rely on themes such as, "She was just a hysterical woman" or "He was just a typical good old boy," unless you desire to potentially offend half the jury and the judge.

Lying is a theme you have to think twice about, because it is unpopular with judges and juries. Be careful about trying to say, "The other side is bunch of liars. This latest motion is just a new pack of lies." Judges and juries do not want to assume that people lie all the time. If you are going to use this theme, you must have concrete evidence of deception on more than one occasion, and tread lightly.

This advice goes double for accusations against other lawyers in briefs and in oral argument. Do not call another lawyer a liar in front of a judge unless you have ironclad proof of the lie. Even then, be careful and only accuse as far as you need to go. Use non-confrontational language: "His statement simply was not true" instead of "He lied to me." It makes for a very tense and unpleasant situation when attorneys start pointing the finger at each other over their truthfulness. Ad hominem attacks are much more likely to turn the court against you rather than help you prevail on the motion.

E. Length of the introduction

Most introductions will be at least a half a page, and some will be as long as a full page. Filling in details of the background of the case, the facts, the theme, and the legal principles that lead up to your conclusions will take some space; nevertheless, you should limit yourself to one page of text or less because you do not want to overwhelm the reader with information. The introduction is supposed to be an introduction, not the entire memorandum.

F. Sample introductions

Here are some examples of introductions from a dog bite case. Hopefully, you will be able to see the strategies at work and the themes that each side has adopted for their side of the case.

The "objective" facts of the case are as follows:

A small boy, Georgie Bolling, was with his father, Robert Bolling, touring an outdoor historic site walking from building to building. They saw one more building farther off to the side and headed for it. No fences or rope blocked off the house. There was one sign buried halfway in a snow bank. By the time they got close enough to see what the sign said—"Private Property - Keep Out"— the two were approached by a dog, roaming loose. The dog was friendly and playful. The boy decided to surprise his father by throwing a snowball at him. The father saw it and ducked, and the snowball hit the dog, spraying it with powdery snow. The dog attacked the boy, and had to be dragged off of him. The boy received 120 stitches and multiple bruises in the altercation. The boy and his father sued the historical site and the dog's owner, Elliott Stirling, for damages for the attack. The defendant moves to dismiss the complaint for failure to state a claim.

Example 1 – Defendant's perspective

UNITED STATES DISTRICT COURT
SOUTHERN DISTRICT OF NEW YORK

GEORGIE BOLLING, a Minor, by	)	
his father and next friend, Robert	)	
Bolling,	)	
Plaintiff,	)	
	)	
v.	)	No. 05-2345-TRW
	)	
ALDEN HALL HISTORICAL SITE, and	)	
ELLIOTT STIRLING,	)	
	)	
Defendants.	)	

DEFENDANTS' MEMORANDUM IN SUPPORT OF MOTION TO DISMISS FOR FAILURE TO STATE A CLAIM

Defendants Alden Hall Historical Site ("Alden Hall") and Elliott Stirling ("Stirling") move this Court pursuant to Fed. R. Civ. P. 12(b)(6) to dismiss the complaint brought by Plaintiff Georgie Bolling ("Plaintiff") for failure to state a cause of action upon which relief may be granted.

INTRODUCTION

Plaintiff's action to recover for a dog bite is barred because he provoked the dog. On February 1, 2005, Plaintiff was trespassing on private property adjacent to the galleries and display areas of the Alden Hall Historical Site museum. Plaintiff admits that he provoked Stirling's dog into a defensive action by spraying the dog with snow. Complaint, ¶ 8. Although he was not trying to hit the dog with a snowball, New York law declares that inadvertent provocation of a dog precludes an action arising from the dog's bite as surely as intentional provocation. The dog acted in accordance with its training as a guard dog and reacted to Plaintiff's act by subduing Plaintiff, which in the process resulted in Plaintiff receiving lacerations on his arm. Even though Plaintiff admits that the dog was sprayed by snow and that he provoked it in this manner, Plaintiff still brings this complaint seeking damages not only from the dog's owner but also from Alden Hall, the adjacent property owner. Under controlling authority of this state, provocation of the dog is a complete bar to recovery and mandates the dismissal of this complaint as against Alden Hall and Stirling.

Example 2 – Plaintiff's Perspective:

UNITED STATES DISTRICT COURT
SOUTHERN DISTRICT OF NEW YORK

GEORGIE BOLLING, a Minor, by his father and next friend, Robert Bolling,	)))	
Plaintiff,	))	
v.	))	No. 05-2345-TRW
ALDEN HALL HISTORICAL SITE, and ELLIOTT STIRLING,	)))	
Defendants.	)	

PLAINTIFF'S RESPONSE TO DEFENDANTS ALDEN HALL AND STIRLING'S FED. R. CIV. P. 12(b)(6) MOTION TO DISMISS FOR FAILURE TO STATE A CLAIM

INTRODUCTION

Defendants Elliott Stirling ("Stirling") and Alden Hall Historical Site ("Alden Hall") have taken the position that they can give a vicious dog free rein to roam a public place where it might injure small children. Stirling's dog's attack on Plaintiff Georgie Bolling ("Georgie") on February 1, 2005, in which Georgie had his arm ripped so badly that it required 120 stitches, was not "provoked" by Georgie as that term has been defined in New York case law. The attack was vicious and disproportionate to the accidental dusting of snow that the dog experienced when it got in the middle of Georgie and his father's snowball game. The fact that the dog was loose and menacing patrons of the museum as they attempted to keep to the public walkways and go about their business touring the museum points directly to the liability of both defendants. The defendants failed to provide proper signage warning of the dog and failed to provide proper boundaries to prevent patrons such as Georgie from accidentally straying onto private property. Plaintiff's complaint states all the elements required for recovery under the New York "Dog Bite" statute, N.Y. Dog Bite Law § 516, and defendants' motion to dismiss for failure to state a claim must be denied.

IV. THE STATEMENT OF FACTS

The statement of facts is not first in order of appearance and is not first in order of importance (the introduction occupies that place in each instance), but it is an important section that many lawyers fail to use properly. The most mundane thing to be accomplished in the statement of facts is to tell a little more of the background of the case, especially if this is the first substantive motion and it is filed early in the litigation, and to tell the facts that are necessary to resolve the motion. This is where most advocates stop. But you should go further in making this section count in favor of your client.

A. Drafting the statement of facts

1. Advocacy through narrative reasoning and story telling

You should always try to advocate you client's case in every section of the motion, and the facts are no exception. Every chance that you get to write a "Background" or "Statement of Facts" section is a chance to tell your client's story—the good (your client), the bad (your opponent) and the ugly (what your opponent did).

The style of argumentation that you should employ in the facts is narrative reasoning. It is a story told through a succession of events, facts building upon other facts, that clearly adds up to the conclusion you want the reader to reach—BUT—and this is a huge "but"— you do not state the conclusion in this section if, as is most often the case, it is a legal conclusion.

The key to a successful statement of facts is being able to state the same relevant facts as your opponent ought to state, but in a manner that tends to favor your client. You will not succeed by hiding key facts; your opponent will bring them out and you will look the worse for having tried to sweep them under the rug. Instead, talk about the material facts of the case, good and bad, but emphasize the good, and put the bad in terms that mitigate their effect on your client's position.

There are various techniques for emphasizing good facts and downplaying bad facts. Facts you want to emphasize always will have a greater impact if you phrase them in the active tense. Facts you want to deemphasize sometimes can be mitigated by phrasing them in the passive tense. The passive tense also takes the focus off of the true subject of the sentence (the actor or instigator), and if your client is the actor and instigator and she did something undesirable, it will help to draw the focus off of her.

Evaluate the words you use, especially your verbs, adjectives, and adverbs. "Letting someone go" or "laying off someone" is a fairly neutral way of expressing a reduction in force (as is the term "reduction in force"); "firing" someone is not neutral at all. "Coming into contact" with something does not paint much of a mental picture; "smashing" into it paints a picture with sound effects. Consider the following examples that work from a single set of facts, but paint two widely divergent pictures:

Example 1 - Common Facts: Client Jones was going 60 m.p.h. in a 45 m.p.h. zone on his way to his therapist, a doctor of psychology. He was late. The road was wet. A poodle came out from behind a parked car and moved into the road in front of him. Jones swerved, his car slid out of control, and he hit a parked car owned by plaintiff.

Plaintiff's Version: Defendant was late for an appointment with his psycho-therapist and was speeding at 60 m.p.h. on rain slick pavement in a 45 m.p.h. zone. A poodle walked into the path of Defendant's speeding car, and Defendant swerved and sent his car spinning out of control. Defendant then smashed his car into the back of plaintiff Smith's parked car.

Defendant's Version: Mr. Jones was proceeding to an important appointment. A dog jumped out in front of him taking him completely by surprise. In an effort to avoid hitting the dog, he turned the wheel quickly but the car slid on the damp pavement and came into contact with the plaintiff's car.

> *Comment: Plaintiff's version makes us think Jones might be unbalanced, perhaps mentally ill. Plaintiff emphasizes the speed and the lateness factor. The road sounds dangerous—rain slick. The facts about Jones' reaction to the dog all are phrased in the active tense—Jones swerved, he sent the car out of control, he hit the other car. And not just hit it, he smashed into it.*

> *Defendant Jones does not ignore all of the events of that day and pretend that he was somewhere else. Jones deals with the same facts, but we hear them in terms that allow us to give Jones a little credit. Jones gives a plausible reason for his haste. Damp pavement is a much better adjective for wetness than rain-slick. The dog took Jones completely by surprise. What happened next is phrased in the passive tense, taking some of the heat off of Jones. The result is plaintiff's car was hit, but "coming into contact" certainly is not as auditory as "smashing" (with metal and glass flying).*

Example 2 - Common Facts: ABC Corp. laid off thirteen workers in a reduction in force (RIF). ABC used a business productivity formula. Six of the workers who were laid off were over the age of 40, four of these were women. Four more who were laid off were minorities, two of whom were women. Mr. Smith, a white male age 37, made the final decision of whom to lay off.

Plaintiff's Version: ABC's most recent RIF was spearheaded by Cliff Smith, a white male. Smith targeted women, minorities, and workers whose age was over 40 for ten of his thirteen cuts. When he fired six elderly workers, he made sure four of them were women, and when he singled out four minorities for firing, he made sure half of them were women. Smith used a formula that ensured that these people could be disposed of with the excuse of increasing productivity.

Defendant's Version: ABC was forced by competitive economic factors to lay off thirteen workers. A formula was used based on a worker's years of service, evaluation grades, and amount of contract revenue generated in the last five years. The thirteen lowest performing workers were laid off.

> *Comment: Isn't "spearheaded" a wonderful word for plaintiff? It is a perfectly common word in daily parlance, but in a fact pattern involving a reduction in force, it suggests that Smith carried off someone's head on a spear. Plaintiff's statement of facts is drafted entirely in the active voice, because plaintiff wants the reader to focus on a particular person (Smith) doing these things. The mention of an "excuse" is a polite and formal way of suggesting subterfuge—an artiface. Plaintiff would have liked to have used the word "pretext" or "pretextual" but these are legal conclusions, and legal conclusions do not belong in the statement of facts as discussed in the section below.*
>
> *Defendant's section is drafted in the passive voice so that the reader does not focus on who did these actions. It also is short; it suggests that this was a routine procedure, done at dozens of companies across the country each day, and there is not much more to say about it than that.*

2. Legal conclusions vs. factual conclusions

Legal conclusions do not belong in the statement of facts section. They stick out like a sore thumb. Judges get exercised about legal conclusions in the facts because when they find them, it looks like the author is trying to cheat, starting her argument too early and in the wrong section. Judges tend to think that statement of facts should be objective, not argumentative, and you only will irritate them by stating legal conclusions right under their nose in the facts section. The statement of facts can advance your argument—that is the whole point we have been trying to communicate above—but it cannot do it in a sloppy, careless manner by stating obvious legal conclusions along with the facts.

In order to carry out the objective of advancing your client's cause in the statement of facts but not stating legal conclusions, you must understand the distinction between legal and factual conclusions. Factual conclusions that are reasonable, logical inferences drawn from the facts generally are fine to insert in the statement of facts. Consider the following examples:

> *Factual Conclusions:*   The car ***was going fast*** on the wet road.
>
> The accident happened ***when there still was enough light to see.***
>
> The doctor had ***followed the standard procedures*** at the hospital for learning a new surgical procedure before she attempted to do it herself.
>
> Smith used a formula that ensured that these people could be disposed of with the ***excuse*** of increasing productivity.

What you need to avoid is legal conclusions:

> *Legal Conclusions:*   The driver was ***reckless*** for driving at that speed.
>
> The accident was ***caused*** by the defendant.
>
> The doctor was ***not negligent*** in attempting to perform the procedure she had just learned.
>
> Smith used a formula that ensured that these people could be disposed of under the ***pretext*** of increasing productivity.

You do not need to state legal conclusions in the statement of facts; if you tell an engaging story and emphasize the right facts and draw appropriate inferences and factual conclusions, every law trained reader will know where you are going and they will fill in the legal conclusions. Even if they do not, they are one page turn away from reading your legal conclusions in the proper place for them—the argument section.

B. Limits on drafting the facts – style and good taste

There are rules of style and decorum that we have discussed before and which clearly apply in this setting.

> ➤ Do not go overboard with emotion. It is unprofessional, and will turn the court against you.
>
> > *Acceptable:* After being fired by ABC Corp., plaintiff Smith was forced to take two jobs to support her two daughters. As a single mother living far away from

all of her relations, she had no other choice. Smith became ill from stress and exhaustion, and was hospitalized for two days in May 2005 with chest pains and irregular heart beats.

> *Do not say:* Defendant ABC Corp. was not satisfied with destroying plaintiff's dreams of lifetime employment at the company; the company threw this poor, struggling single mother out into the street, abandoning her in her time of need just as her worthless lover had abandoned her seven years earlier. ABC Corp. caused Smith's heart attack and put her in the hospital just as surely as if they had injected her with adrenaline and electrified her chest. They broke her heart, plain and simple.

If you are a plaintiff, give a fair account of the injuries, using compelling terms. Do not overstate the injuries in a blatant attempt to draw sympathy or outrage. Do not give gruesome, gratuitously revolting statements of the facts.

> *Example:* If the broken machinery almost ripped your client's arm off, say so: Plaintiff's arm was caught in the machine and nearly ripped off of his body.

> *Do not say:* The machine acted with murderous efficiency to rip plaintiff from stem to stern.

A fair account of the injuries by a plaintiff is not a stump speech to inflame the listeners. If the facts are grisly—a sex crime or violent act against a child, for example—tell the story completely, but remember to write it as a professional. Think network evening news, not Jerry Springer. Write it like the New York Times would, not like a "National-Midnight-Star" rag sheet (to borrow a clever name from Second City Television) would. Be clear and compelling, but do not put on a tear-jerker or freak show:

> *Acceptable:* Plaintiff Kruger's arm was caught in the machine and nearly ripped off of his body. Kruger described the pain to a paramedic as "excruciating." In a matter of seconds, he lost complete use of his arm.

> *Do not say:* Plaintiff's screams rang out as the machine slowly, horribly tore his flesh. Blood spurted from his arm and coated the machine, dripping down to form a large puddle on the floor. Words cannot describe the sounds of a man having his arm ripped from his body and the scene of gore as the jaws of a murderous machine try to tear a limb from its shoulder.

Defendants have no incentive to dwell overly long on plaintiffs' injuries. Try to downplay them as best as possible, but move on quickly.

Example: The machine caused several lacerations to plaintiff's arm resulting in loss of its functionality. However, plaintiff experienced a quick recovery and regained nearly complete functionality of his arm within six weeks of the incident.

➤ Do not give unnecessary detail because you will wear the court out. You should not have to spend more than a page or at most two pages on the statement of facts for the average pretrial motion.

Good: Defendant Jones was late for an appointment with his psycho-therapist and was speeding at 60 m.p.h. on rain slick pavement in a 45 m.p.h. zone. A poodle walked into the path of Defendant's speeding car, and Defendant swerved and sent his car spinning out of control. Defendant then smashed his car into the back of plaintiff Smith's parked car.

Not this: Defendant Jones was running approximately eight minutes late for his appointment with his psycho-therapist, Dr. Will Shrinker. He went speeding along on his way to Dr. Shrinker's office on Mulberry Lane, a mixed business and residential street with a 45 m.p.h. speed limit. He was traveling at an average speed of 60 m.p.h. as confirmed by a passive police monitoring unit on Mulberry Lane that Jones passed by; his speed also was generally confirmed by two eye witnesses at the scene, Mrs. Vera Stigmatism and Mr. Esau Nothing. At some point soon after passing by the monitoring unit, a poodle walked out into the path of Defendant's speeding car. Defendant took action immediately. He swerved the car to the left, and sent his car spinning out of control. There is no indication that he was able to regain control of the car. Jones' car spun out of control for more than two seconds, again, as confirmed by Mrs. Stigmatism and Mr. Nothing. Defendant then smashed his car into the back of plaintiff Smith's parked car. No one witnessed the actions of the poodle after Jones swerved away from it, but the poodle was unharmed in the incident.

These details may be interesting, but it is unlikely that they will have any effect on the average pretrial motion. Remember, a motion represents only a tiny part of a much bigger case, and if these details are not relevant for the particular purpose of the motion at hand, leave them out. They will wear out your reader and squander her attention span.

➤ Do use descriptive terms for facts, verbs, adjectives, and adverbs borrowed from the case law and authorities to describe the facts (i.e., employ parallelism). For example:

Example: If the facts described in the authorities for proper conduct is "proactive measures to prevent infection," state in the facts that your client "undertook the following proactive measures to prevent infection by viral agents."

Do not say: The client undertook "safety measures," "infection control protocol," or "strenuous action to curb infection."

➤ If the term is a legal conclusion, however, avoid stating it using the conclusory term. This would be the equivalent of writing a legal conclusion in the facts section. Simply report the action:

> *Example:* If the legal standard requires a finding of lack of provocation, do not simply state that: "Plaintiff did not provoke the dog in any way." This is a legal conclusion. Instead, say: "Plaintiff did not bother the dog, or anger, or threaten, or intimidate, or rile up the dog in any way." Even an adjective like "provocative" carries a legal conclusion, so be careful of such words.

> If "immediate notification" of the injury is the operative legal standard, you can probably get away with stating that your client "immediately notified the plaintiff of the injury at 11:23 a.m." But this is a bit conclusory, and it might offend some judges. To be on the safe side, avoid the legal terms of art, but state what happened in explicit terms: "Within fourteen minutes of the incident, defendant informed plaintiff of the injury."

➤ Do not be redundant, unless the point that you are making *is* the number of times your opponent did the same bad thing.

C. Do you cite authority in the statement of facts?

Cites to legal authority will be unnecessary because you are not going to be making statements about the law in the facts section. But citation to **factual authority** to back up your statements in the **statement of facts** is required. Do it whenever you cite a certain fact for the first time.

> *Example:* Brown's two visits to the state were for charity purposes unrelated to any business activity conducted by Brown. See Affidavit of Derek Brown dated July 14, 2005, ¶ 4 (attached hereto as exhibit 1) ("Brown Aff."). Van Pelt did not attend either of the visits. Complaint ¶¶ 3-5. The charity visits had nothing to do with Brown's sales of exercise equipment to Van Pelt. Brown Aff. ¶ 6. Neither visit lasted longer than three hours, putting the total time that Brown spent in Pennsylvania at less than six hours. Id.[4]

---

[4] As illustrated in the example, id. is a proper shorthand for referring back to the immediately preceding factual authority. Other shorthand phrases should be defined for the benefit of the reader, as shown in the example: Affidavit of Derek Brown dated July 14, 2005, ¶ 4 ("Brown Aff.").

Later, in the argument section, you do not need to keep citing back to the authority each time you discuss that fact.

D. In what order do you have to present the facts?

Choose whichever order is the most compelling for your argument, but with one strong piece of advice: if chronological order works, use it. It is the easiest to follow. People expect it. It makes them happy.

If a chronological presentation does nothing for your client, use a topical or thematic presentation of the facts. In a contract case, you might first talk about the contract terms, then how the parties first got together on the deal, pre-negotiation actions, then the negotiation, then the post-contracting activities, or you might talk about the three main components of the contract, and how each one was negotiated and performed. In a personal injury case, you might first talk about the accident and the injury (your client's involvement) then about the facts leading up to the injury (the causation facts).

You might use a client-oriented presentation. In a patent infringement or unfair trade practices case you might first talk about your client, its history, its business; then the development of the client's product; then the competitor and its product (which may have been earlier in time). Always tell the facts with the client's interest and client's point of view in mind.

E. Sample statement of facts

Consider the following examples:

Example 1: Introduction and Statement of Facts from Defendants' Motion to Dismiss in the Bolling v. Stirling and Alden Hall case:

UNITED STATES DISTRICT COURT
SOUTHERN DISTRICT OF NEW YORK

GEORGIE BOLLING, a Minor, by his father and next friend, Robert Bolling,	))))	
Plaintiff,	))	
v.	))	No. 05-2345-TRW
ALDEN HALL HISTORICAL SITE, and ELLIOTT STIRLING,	)))	
Defendants.	)	

DEFENDANTS' MEMORANDUM IN SUPPORT OF MOTION TO DISMISS FOR FAILURE TO STATE A CLAIM

Defendants Alden Hall Historical Site ("Alden Hall") and Elliott Stirling ("Stirling") move this Court pursuant to Fed. R. Civ. P. 12(b)(6) to dismiss the complaint brought by Plaintiff Georgie Bolling ("Plaintiff") for failure to state a cause of action upon which relief may be granted.

INTRODUCTION

Plaintiff's action to recover for a dog bite is barred because he provoked the dog. On February 1, 2005, Plaintiff was trespassing on private property adjacent to the galleries and display areas of the Alden Hall Historical Site museum. Plaintiff admits that he provoked Stirling's dog into a defensive action by spraying the dog with snow. Complaint, ¶ 8. Although he was not trying to hit the dog with a snowball, New York law declares that inadvertent provocation of a dog precludes an action arising from the dog's bite as surely as intentional provocation. The dog acted in accordance with its training as a guard dog and reacted to Plaintiff's act by subduing Plaintiff, which in the process resulted in Plaintiff receiving lacerations on his arm. Even though Plaintiff admits that the dog was sprayed by snow and that he provoked it in this manner, Plaintiff still brings this complaint seeking damages not only from the dog's owner but also from Alden Hall, the adjacent property owner. Under controlling authority of this state, provocation of the dog is a complete bar to recovery and mandates the dismissal of this complaint as against Alden Hall and Stirling.

STATEMENT OF FACTS

On February 1, 2005, Plaintiff and his father toured the grounds of Alden Hall. Complaint, ¶ 4. They did not stay on the tour route, and instead approached a building (Stirling's private residence) that was set off from the rest of the museum buildings. See Complaint, ¶¶ 4-5. Plaintiff saw a sign that indicated that he and his father were standing on private property and which advised them to "Keep Out." Id. ¶ 6. Plaintiff claims that the remaining portion of the sign, which advised them of the presence of Stirling's dog, was covered by snow and not visible. Id. Nevertheless, Plaintiff and his father ignored the sign and proceeded directly to the house that they now knew was private property. Id. ¶ 7. Shortly thereafter, Stirling's dog, Pebbles, greeted the two. Id. ¶ 8. Pebbles did not attack the two, but approached them in a friendly manner. Id. At this point, Plaintiff and his father started a snowball fight in which Plaintiff missed a throw at his father and wound up hitting the dog with a snowball, spraying the dog with snow. See Affidavit of Elliot Stirling dated June 3, 2005, ¶ 7. The dog reacted to the attack by an uninvited guest according to his training as a guard dog and engaged Plaintiff to subdue him. See id. This involves restraining the arm of the attacker with the only means available to a dog, his mouth. Id.

Plaintiff apparently struggled with the dog and received several cuts on his arm. See Complaint, ¶ 9.

The two most important facts in this case, which Plaintiff must concede, are that Plaintiff strayed off the public pathways and did not return to them when he and his father saw the warning sign, see Complaint ¶¶ 4-5, and that Plaintiff angered the dog by spraying it with snow. See Complaint, ¶¶ 7-8.

Example 2: same example, but from plaintiff's perspective.

UNITED STATES DISTRICT COURT
SOUTHERN DISTRICT OF NEW YORK

GEORGIE BOLLING, a Minor, by his father and next friend, Robert Bolling,	))))	
Plaintiff,	))	
v.	))	No. 05-2345-TRW
ALDEN HALL HISTORICAL SITE, and ELLIOTT STIRLING,	)))	
Defendants.	))	

**PLAINTIFF'S RESPONSE TO DEFENDANTS ALDEN HALL AND
STIRLING'S FED. R. CIV. P. 12(b)(6) MOTION TO DISMISS FOR
FAILURE TO STATE A CLAIM**

INTRODUCTION

Defendants Elliott Stirling ("Stirling") and Alden Hall Historical Site ("Alden Hall") have taken the position that they can give a vicious dog free rein to roam a public place where it might injure small children. Stirling's dog's attack on Plaintiff Georgie Bolling ("Georgie") on February 1, 2005, in which Georgie had his arm ripped so badly that it required 120 stitches, was not "provoked" by Georgie as that term has been defined in New York case law. The attack was vicious and disproportionate to the accidental dusting of snow that the dog experienced when it got in the middle of Georgie and his father's snowball game. The fact that the dog was loose and menacing patrons of the museum as they attempted to keep to the public walkways and go about their business touring the museum points directly to the liability of both defendants. The defendants failed to provide proper signage warning of the dog and failed to provide proper boundaries to prevent patrons such as Georgie from accidentally straying onto private property. Plaintiff's complaint states all the elements required for recovery under the New York "Dog Bite" statute, N.Y. Dog Bite Law § 516, and defendants' motion to dismiss for failure to state a claim must be denied.

STATEMENT OF FACTS

As stated in the Complaint, ¶¶ 4-9, the incident on February 1, 1998, involved a vicious attack by a German Shepard guard dog on a small boy, Georgie Bolling. Georgie and his father were following a tour route and keeping to the public walkways, which led them to a building which looked the same as all the other museum buildings. Id. ¶ 4. Nothing fenced in, blocked off, or otherwise demarcated this building and its surroundings from the rest of the public tour area. Id. By the time the two stumbled upon a sign partially sticking up out of the snow that informed them that they had managed to get onto someone's private property, Georgie and his father were already face to face with defendant Stirling's guard dog. Id. ¶ 5. Nothing about the dog seemed threatening at first, so the two proceeded along the public walkway to the house to ask if there was any more to see on the tour. See id. ¶ 6.

Georgie, as a typical seven year old might do, thought it would be amusing to start a friendly snowball game with his father in the yard. See Complaint, ¶ 7. Georgie never intended to involve the dog in the game and aimed his first snowball at his father. See id. The snowball somehow missed, and the dog was accidentally sprayed with the light powdery snow. See id. ¶ 8. (This accidental dusting with snow is what the defendants refer to as "direct provocation" for a vicious attack. Defendants' Memorandum in Support of Motion to Dismiss at 2, 4).

The guard dog's reaction to the snow dusting he received was completely unexpected and violent: the dog jumped on Georgie and ripped into his arm with vicious force. See Complaint, ¶ 9. The cuts he inflicted were deep and the German Shepard had to be dragged off of his victim by Georgie's father. Id. Georgie's father managed to pick Georgie up and flee from the scene, chased by the guard dog who continued to menace the two. Id. He ran several hundred feet until two museum employees could assist his escape by grabbing and restraining the dog. Id. After Georgie was rushed to the hospital emergency room, the doctors needed 120 stitches to close up the wounds inflicted by the German Shepard. See Affidavit of Walt Pacquin dated June 4, 2005, ¶ 3.

V. ARGUMENT

The argument section roughly parallels the discussion section of the office memorandum, but, as you probably already have guessed, it is not drafted in the same manner as the discussion section of an objective, informative legal memorandum. The argument must be as persuasive, well-reasoned, and credible as any office memorandum, but it must be completely one-sided in favor of the client.

You may think, "The law is what it is," but that thought implies that the law always is concrete and black and white. Not so. The black letter law legal principles in any given area usually are not the rules over which you will be litigating. The law at the margins of every area of law (and they often are broad margins) is fluid, changing, painted in shades of gray, not necessarily well-defined, and sometimes even inconsistent. In many cases, it will take all of your skill as an interpreter and analyst of legal sources to take the raw material of the law and find a way to present it in such a way that the client's position looks reasonable, logical, and downright righteous under the law. But at least you often will have a good supply of paint and canvas that the authors of the legal sources have provided to you.

A. Goal for the argument

The argument has one goal: to enable the client to win the motion. It is not intended to present an in depth exposition on the general area of law presented by the motion. It is not intended to inform the court of the interesting and difficult aspects of the specific area of the law that governs the motion. It is not meant directly to educate the court about the pros and cons of a decision on the motion; the only message you should send is that the only proper outcome is ruling in your client's favor, but there are many negatives associated with not ruling in your client's favor. It is argument. It is not education.

Do not read this to mean that the goal of the argument section is to misrepresent or distort the true meaning and effect of the controlling law in your jurisdiction. Nowhere do we advocate lying and cheating about the law. Our rule for the argument section is as follows:

THE RULE FOR THE ARGUMENT SECTION:

Advocacy requires a client-oriented, persuasive rendering of the correct legal standards that govern the motion.

Every part of this rule deserves explanation and emphasis.

1. Client oriented

You are going to show why the client should prevail using controlling and persuasive legal authorities in a way that supports your arguments. It is a one-sided presentation. You will make the argument that your client should win.

2. Persuasive

No one wins an argument just by shouting the loudest. Your skills of legal exposition and creativity will be tested as never before when you have to take on a difficult assignment in a difficult area of law and present the law in such a way that any reader will be able to understand your points and be convinced that your client's position is sound. Naturally, your ultimate goal is to convince one person, the judge, that your position is not just sound, but in fact correct.

3. Correct legal standards—no cheating!

If we are being redundant, we apologize, but we want to be exceedingly clear that the proper and ethical methodology of an advocate is not to lie and cheat about the law. You must present a correct interpretation of the law, albeit not necessarily every case that has been handed down in this area, and not every sentence about the rules from the authorities in the area.

If the law does not support you, either do not make the argument (best idea) or present your argument with an explanation that it depends on a change in the law. Never misrepresent the law to the court.

4. Movant's advice

Movants should follow this advice: **Movants should never bring a motion for which there is no legal support.** If you are the Movant, you should not even wonder about stretching or distorting the law because you should not bring a motion for which there is no legal support.

5. Opponent's advice

If you are the opponent and you have a decent argument on the merits, then pursue it first and foremost. This is the best practice. But if the movant has done her job correctly, chances are that the law does not support your client's position. You still have a number of choices:

a. Be open and discuss the law as it is, but argue for a change

In every opposition, you will do you best to argue against the Movant's position, and attempt to distinguish Movant's authorities, but if the controlling law is against you, the most forthright and sometimes effective course to follow is to admit the controlling law is negative and against your client, but argue that the law should be changed or interpreted differently so that your client can win. You will not win this way very often, but you might keep the client happy because you fought the good fight, and you will impress the court a great deal with your candor. Naturally, the more effort you put into the task of finding primary and secondary persuasive authorities that are favorable to you client, and support for the policies you will assert are furthered by a change in the law, the more likely it is that you will prevail.

Note well that we only are talking about a situation where the **controlling** authority in your jurisdiction is against you, or there is no controlling authority and all of the persuasive authority you can find goes against you. If it is merely a situation where there is some good and some troublesome authority, you should not be approaching the court in a defensive posture, but rather doing your best to present the best law to the court, and trying hard to distinguish and downplay the negative authority.

b. Change the issues, and argue a legal position that you can defend

No one said you have to stick to the issues that the movant thought were important for the motion. If the substance of the motion (the merits) are bad for your client, argue procedural reasons for the denial of motion. Evaluate whether it is possible for you to argue that the motion is improper, against the rules, untimely, unnecessary, violates laches, and then, and only then, get into the merits. You might argue that the motion is described as or argues XYZ, but the movant really should be bringing PDQ motion or making a PDQ argument, and you proceed to explain that your client wins under a PDQ analysis. This is the method of the skilled litigator, to turn a sow's ear of a motion into a silk purse.

We explained this tactic more thoroughly above in the section on the introduction, and if you get the impression that we really like this option, you are right. This option turns the tables on the movant so that you can argue your own points. Not only do you increase your chances of actually winning, but the movant will have to use up his reply brief addressing your points rather than furthering hers.

B. Structure – TREAT format

The TREAT format applies to the drafting of the argument section—argumentative Thesis headings, Rule section, Explanation of the positive and negative authorities, Application to the client's situation, and Thesis restated as a Conclusion. Because the argument has to further the client's cause in winning the motion, the following considerations apply that are different from or in addition to the requirements for the discussion section of the office memorandum:

1. Argumentative thesis headings

One of the reasons that we stress the importance of the introduction is that it gets the important information to the reader in the shortest possible time, so that even if she only reads the first page of your motion, she will have the chance to hear the most important parts of your entire argument on the motion. The same thing applies to the drafting of the headings that will divide up your argument section—make them useful, argumentative, and informative, so that even if your reader merely skims through your motion, she still will have the opportunity to see each point (each conclusion) of your argument.

A good thesis heading not only reveals a conclusion but provides the "because" part—the legal principles and facts that lead up to the conclusion. For example, the following are good argumentative Thesis headings:

➤ **Examples of proper thesis headings in the argument**

A. Bolling did nothing to provoke the dog prior to the attack because he did not directly attack or threaten the dog as required under New York law.

B. Bolling was acting peacefully in a place where he had a lawful right to be because he walked on a public sidewalk at Alden Hall without causing any noisy disturbance.

C. Provocation does not bar Bolling's recovery because the dog's attack on Bolling was vicious and disproportionate to the dusting of snow the Dog received from Bolling.

The following are **not** good headings:

A. Lack of Provocation
B. Bolling was acting peacefully in a place where he had a lawful right to be.
C. The dog's attack was disproportionate.

These last three examples do not suggest enough of the facts and principles of the law to make the headings useful, and the first of these three does not even tell the author's conclusion about the topic. Do not waste a heading by writing something like these. Let your headings be a quick summary of your argument if read one right after the other.

2. Forming a favorable rule for the rule section

The law is not static, and neither does your expression of the law have to be static. There are many ways to express legal rules and to characterize how the rules work and how they ought to be interpreted and applied. This section reviews these methods.

There is one hard and fast rule for the rule section of your motion: you must cite and discuss all applicable constitutional provisions, statutes, or administrative regulations. If a constitutional, statutory, or administrative provision is on point, it is controlling and must be presented. There is no way around it. You at least must cite it, and you should go so far as to quote the pertinent, applicable language (or sections or sub-parts) from the statute or rule.

Beyond the citation and excerpting of the applicable terms of constitutional, statutory, or administrative provisions, you have many opportunities to express what the law means in a way that favors your client. Cite and discuss cases that construe (alter, modify, extend, etc.) the statute or rule, and any administrative law authorities (administrative rules and regulations) that interpret and implement the legislation.

If the rule is determined largely by case law in the absence of a statute or rule or as a progression of the law after the passage of the statute or rule, you must focus on deriving the best rule for your client using the best authorities available. This is the hardest advice to communicate tangibly, because we can describe the goal and give a few pointers, but the actual task of taking a body of undigested law and pulling from it the best authorities and the best language as to the rule and facts from each of these authorities is something that you simply will have to do for yourself. What is a good use and what is a great use of authorities will vary from assignment to assignment.

➤ *The rule reads:* Plaintiff's choice of forum is a factor in the determination of a transfer of venue motion but it is not a conclusive factor.

> *Example 1 - Favoring transfer:* Plaintiff's choice of forum never has been given conclusive weight in the venue transfer analysis. [CITES]. It merely is one of many factors for the court to consider. [CITES].

> *Example 2 - Opposing transfer:* In determining a transfer of venue motion, the court must give regard to the plaintiff's choice of forum. [CITES]. Each court is mandated to consider the effect of denying plaintiff her choice of forum, and most courts give it priority in the order of discussion of the issues. [CITES].

Both of these characterizations of the rule are accurate, but one tends to favor transfer and the other does not. "Priority" in the second example refers to the fact that in most cases, the issue of protecting plaintiff's choice of forum is discussed first, but the word has positive connotations beyond the simple expression of the order of discussion. In both examples, it may be necessary to use the prefatory word "<u>see</u>" in front of the citations to authority if you are drawing a direct inference supported by the authorities rather than repeating exactly what the authorities say.

➤ *The rules read:* Claimants must demonstrate a likelihood of confusion between the trademark and the allegedly infringing mark. Courts are to use a "reasonable viewer" standard.

> *Example 1 - Favoring claimant:* Plaintiff need only show that there is a likelihood of confusion by a reasonable viewer when the infringing mark is compared to the original trademark. [CITES]. Plaintiff need not prove actual confusion among a particular group of viewers, but only a "reasonable viewer." [CITES].

> *Example 2 - Opposing claimant:* Plaintiff bears the burden of proving that there is a likelihood of confusion not among a learned consumer or a devoted user of its products, but among a random group of "reasonable viewers." [CITES]. It is not enough to show that devoted users would recognize the similarity. [CITES].

The characterization of the rule in example 2 simply sounds harder to meet. It lays out the same principles of the law as the first example, but it does so in a way that expresses that the burden on the claimant is onerous. This phrasing helps to oppose the claimant.

The following chart should refresh your recollection about how to go about putting together the rule from multiple authorities, performing a "rule synthesis," and putting it into the Rule section of an objective work. Naturally, start with controlling authority.

Formulate the Rule (Rule Synthesis)

❶ Start with the highest and most recent controlling authority	◆ If you have a statute (or regulation), start with the statute.
	◆ If you have a watershed case that is controlling, start with that.
	◆ If your best authority is from the court of last resort, take the most recent opinion from that court, and start with that.
	◆ If these first three criteria do not apply, start with the most recent actual controlling authority that is on point.
	◆ Only if none of the above applies would you consider turning to non-controlling authority—primary or secondary.
	◆ Don't expect to use all of your authorities.
❷ Reconcile differing statements or phrasings of the rule from controlling authorities, and attempt to synthesize the material into one coherent statement of the legal principles that govern the issue	◆ DON'T change the wording of or paraphrase rules from statutes, administrative rules and regs, and watershed cases.
	◆ Unless a processed applied rule can be written smoothly and effectively in one sentence or phrase, write the rule first with modifications second.
❸ Write the rule first, interpretative rules second, and exceptions to the rule third	◆ Write interpretive sub-rules on elements of the rule in the section or sub-TREAT discussion that discusses that element of the rule. Write exceptions to the sub-rules after you lay out the sub-rules themselves.
❹ Do not write a rule with inherent contradictions	◆ Check for ambiguity in the terms you have used to formulate the rule (even if some of these terms came from the authorities).
❺ Do accept the <u>remote</u> possibility that two competing rules on the same issue might exist in the same jurisdiction	◆ When this happens, you may have to analyze the facts under both competing sets of rules.

Try to find a common, underlying rule of law that governs the issue at hand that can properly be derived from or traced to controlling authority. Examine the ways that the rule has been recited in the various controlling authorities. Then draft the rule section compiling the best words and standards from the authorities in the form of a rule synthesis with terms that tends to favor your client's legal position. You must be fair, but you most often will have leeway to craft the rules in a light that is more favorable to your client than a random selection of principles and interpretive rules found in cases.

The style and formatting advice for how office memoranda should be drafted generally applies, but remember that the goal in a motion is to present the law in the best possible light for your client. Explore the authorities for the best possible rendition of the legal standards that govern the issue. A rule synthesis may help you avoid a sticky wording of the rule on the issue that shows up in some but not all of the authorities. Naturally, if the rule comes from a statute or administrative rule, you are stuck with the official wording, but you still can look for later interpretive authorities that may have explained the rule in ways that are kinder to the client. Even if you refuse to do a rule synthesis, and decide to present the legal principles seriatim, start with the rules and standards that most favor your client's situation, and finish with those the client has the most problems with, but still can manage to meet.

3. Use interpretive rules that support the client's case

Look for interpretive rules and sub-rules that help the client's cause. If the rule is from a statute or administrative rule, these interpretive rulings may be the only friendly rendition of the legal standards that you will find in favor of your client. Do not cite incidental interpretive rules that do not help the client's cause; leave that to your opponent, if she is on the ball. Only cite interpretive rules that support your client's facts and your theory of the case.

> *Example:* Your client combined a photograph of a famous celebrity who was on trial for murder with the famous photograph of Lee Harvey Oswald holding the mail order rifle that he allegedly used to assassinate President John F. Kennedy so that it appears that the celebrity is holding the famous rifle in the famous Oswald pose. The celebrity sued your client for violation of his right of publicity. One defense is to show that the use is a parody. In your jurisdiction, in order to prove a parody defense, you must show that the original image was transformed in such a way that it is obvious that there are two works present—an original image of the celebrity and a new image that is directly critical of the celebrity.

In your rule section that discusses this parody requirement, you have the choice of using the following interpretive rules for parody that appear in various controlling authorities of the applicable jurisdiction:

Good interpretive rule: "The creator of the new work must add value to the old work."

This is good because your client did add value to the work through her artistic additions. The new work is clever and comments on the celebrity through use of artistic symbolism.

Better interpretive rule: "It must be obvious that there are two works evident from examination of the alleged parody—an older image of the celebrity, and a new image with new content, meaning, and expression that is critical of the celebrity. It is not enough if the creator of the images intends to criticize the celebrity if the meaning of the altered image is not evident from looking at the altered image itself."

This is even better than the above example because it is closer to your client's facts. Your client's work reveals two well known original images and a third image—the combined image—and it will be obvious to anyone familiar with the two original images that the client's image has new content, meaning, and expression achieved by putting the celebrity into the position of a famous assassin. This effect needs no explanation from your client; it is obvious from looking at her work.

Not good interpretive rules: "The value of the new work may be established by showing that the application of artistic skill transformed the work into a unique new work that does not depend on the celebrity's image for its value. It also may be shown by the fact that the artist is so famous that his work is far more valuable for his having created it than any mundane image of the celebrity created by an unknown artist."

Although these interpretive rules would not necessarily be fatal to your client's situation, they are not that helpful. Remember, you have a choice in what interpretive rules to bring out, and the first rule here seems to fit the situation of a painter or sculptor—or even a cartoonist—better than an artist like your client who combines photographs for expressive effect. Would the average person viewing your client's works see the application of valuable artistic skill, or just cleverness? The second rule may not suit your client at all if your client is not a famous artist whose works are of obvious value even to a casual follower of the arts (such as most judges and some jurors). Therefore, you should avoid bringing out both of these interpretive rules in your rule section.

4. Use of explanatory synthesis in the explanation section

In the explanation section, you should use explanatory synthesis to explain how the rule works in real life situations in the most compact and powerful manner. The following chart reveals the principles and methodology of drafting the explanation section and using explanatory synthesis:

Explain the Rule (Explanatory Synthesis)

Goals of the Explanation Section	
The goal is to explain how the rule is to be interpreted and applied based on how the authorities have applied it in actual concrete factual settings, and on how commentators have interpreted the rule	◆ You are going beyond what the courts already have said about the rule in interpretive rules found in cases ◆ You are presenting principles of interpretation that are supported by a careful reading of the cases ◆ You are doing the work of digesting and synthesizing the cases so the reader doesn't have to
Case-by-case presentations make the reader do most of the work and they are wasteful of space and time (i.e., the reader's attention span)	◆ Avoid case-by-case presentations even though they are easy to write, and sometimes fun to write ◆ Avoid case-by-case-presentations even though courts use them ◆ The only time to resort to a case-by-case presentation is when you have one or two cases that are so close to the facts that you want to cover them in great detail, or if you want to distinguish one or two troublesome cases in enough detail to make your point
The Process of Explanatory Synthesis	
❶ Read cases and look for common facts and common outcomes ❷ Review the groups to find the factors or public policies that make the difference in the outcome	◆ Group cases by facts ◆ Divide groups of cases by outcome ◆ Reconcile cases that have different outcomes; what policy or theme or factor determined the outcome in these cases ◆ Reconcile cases that have the same outcome on different facts; what common policy or theme or factors brought about the same outcome on different facts
❸ Write principles of interpretation that explain your findings	◆ Phrase your principles of interpretation in language that mimics interpretive rules

❹ Cite the cases that support your principles of interpretation with parentheticals that provide facts or other information about each case

❺ When you draft the Application section, apply the principles of interpretation to your own facts; as a general rule, do not apply individual cases to your facts

◆ Often you can use interpretive rules as principles that tie together multiple authorities; there is no requirement that you always have to come up with brand new principles

◆ Parentheticals should contain enough information to illustrate how the individual case supports the general principle you have laid out

◆ Use shorthands and abbreviated phrases to save space

◆ Applying principles to facts will make your analysis more convincing; you have spelled out the connections to be made between the authorities and then followed through and showed how the principles learned from a study of the authorities determines the outcome of the case at hand

◆ The exception to this rule is when you have one or two fabulous cases that are worthy of individual attention in the Explanation section; these should be discussed individually in the Application section, whether as support or to distinguish them

You cannot waste the reader's time in an adversarial matter. Judges will not take the time to read five or more paragraphs of facts from cases that have applied the rule. You only should discuss as much of the facts from the authorities as is necessary to explain your application of the law to the client's facts. In explanatory synthesis, you can do that through the use of parentheticals and other devices that shorten the discussion (e.g., conclusory, declarative statements of the critical importance of the authorities, followed by a cite to multiple authorities, or use of the "Compare . . . with . . ." citation method). Even if you decide it is necessary to expound on the facts of one particular controlling case, because it is *the* case on this topic in the applicable jurisdiction, you should limit yourself to an exposition of those facts to which you are going to draw an analogy or distinction. The necessity to provide any explanation of the authorities that discuss a rule will depend on the procedural versus substantive nature of the rule (see discussion of procedural vs. substantive arguments below), and the importance of the rule to the motion at hand.

5. Movant's anticipation and handling of negative authority

If you have a number of good **controlling** authorities, the fact that there are a number of negative **persuasive** authorities out there is of little concern to anyone. Occasionally, the movant will have a situation where nothing but favorable authority exists on the motion you are drafting— you cannot find a single authority that goes against your client's position. Enjoy that feeling as long as you can, because it is fleeting. Just as often, you will have a body of good authorities that favor your client's position and some bad authorities that go against the client in one way or the other. One of the toughest jobs of the movant is to decide how much negative authority on the law to anticipate and handle (distinguish, explain) in the opening motion. It is tough because your space always is limited, and you do not want to do such a good job raising and discussing negative authorities that you write your opponent's brief for her.

We will assume first of all that you do have some controlling authorities in favor of your position. Always cover your positive controlling authorities first in the explanation section—you do not want to start off in a defensive posture. Then, the best advice we can give is to try to save space at the end of each explanation section to discuss any significant potentially controlling negative authorities. "Significant" means they are close enough to the facts of your situation that you are given pause when you read them, and they are recent enough that you cannot easily argue (if called upon to do so, probably in the reply brief you will file) that the law has changed and moved on from these older sources. It pays to have the first word on these negative potentially controlling authorities, and it is far less likely that you will be educating the other side about cases that they would not otherwise find in their research (and even if the opponent would have missed them, the court probably will not).

If you do not have any controlling authority in favor of your position, then you **must** show why there is no controlling authority that goes directly against your position (or you should not be bringing the motion in the first place). In the explanation section, you first must discuss your positive persuasive authorities, and then distinguish any negative potentially controlling and negative persuasive authorities.

The principles of "explanatory synthesis" discussed above apply with equal force in distinguishing negative authority in the explanation section. If there are several negative cases, try to group them on the basis of common facts and common holding and discuss them as a group. Thus, you can distinguish the whole group in one fell swoop, and de-emphasize the impact of the number of cases. If there is no way to group them on the basis of facts and holding, you still should try to find a common thread of legal argument or public policy that characterizes them. If you can refute and distinguish the logical underpinning of the cases, you can more easily convince the court that the entire group of cases should be rejected because they all rely on the same logical foundation.

If there is no negative potentially controlling authority, you have more leeway in determining how much negative persuasive authority to anticipate and distinguish. Be careful not to raise and explain too much negative persuasive authority and thus help your opponent write her brief in opposition. The scope of persuasive authority is far ranging, and if you are the kind of diligent and thorough researcher that we hope you will be after reading this book, you may be finding a lot more negative persuasive authority that your opponent and the court will not bother to look for. Remember, too, that you will have a reply brief in which to address anything that your opponent finds that she puts to good use against you.

So, what kind of persuasive authority should you incorporate? We would limit it to primary persuasive authorities (cases, primarily) that are from the proper jurisdiction.

> ➤ *Example:* In a case in the New York Supreme Court for New York County that is governed by New York law, your case is controlled by the decisions of the 1st Department of the Supreme Court, Appellate Division. Cases that are not from the proper hierarchy of judicial authority are not controlling (e.g., cases from the 2nd, 3rd, or 4th Departments of the Supreme Court, Appellate Division), but these may be regarded as highly persuasive

> ➤ *Example:* In a federal question case in the United States District Court for the District of Massachusetts, only decisions from the United States Court of Appeals for the First Circuit control. The decisions of the other United States Courts of Appeals (e.g., from the Second through the Eleventh Circuits and the D.C. and Federal Circuits in between) are not controlling, but should be regarded has highly persuasive.

These authorities are highly persuasive because of the law they apply, and even if they are not even potentially controlling, they can carry the day and deserve your attention to distinguish and explain them.

We would not go out of our way to address other kinds of primary or secondary persuasive authority unless it has an extremely high stature—for example, Wright and Miller on Federal Practice and Procedure, a restatement of the law, a judicial superstar—and the discussion is close enough to your situation to cause you to sweat.

Lastly, let us advise you that if you have nothing with which to distinguish persuasive authority or no explanation that ameliorates the effect of the authority, it is best ***not*** to raise it at all. You are drawing a lot of attention to a persuasive authority when you anticipate it in your opening brief, and if you only make a half-hearted attempt to distinguish the authority, it will stand out like a beacon for your opponent and the court to notice. Remember, we are talking about a motion and memorandum of law drafted for the adversarial system, and if you do not cover something, it is your opponent's job to raise it and cover it. Always try to distinguish an authority that is more likely than not to be controlling, but beyond that, avoid doing your opponent's work for her.

6. Opponent's handling of negative authority

The opponent has little choice in this matter—you must attempt to distinguish and explain all of the potentially controlling and strong persuasive authority that the movant has thrown at you. It is a terrible error not to address all of the potentially controlling authority in your opposition. Beyond that, we would strive to say something positive about the primary persuasive authority upon which movant relies, and do as much as you can to counteract the negative secondary persuasive authority.

C. How much of a TREAT to give – procedural vs. substantive issues and counter-arguments

1. Procedural versus substantive

The procedural-substantive distinction will often help you to make a determination about whether to draft a complete TREAT of an individual issue in your motion—especially, whether to draft a full blown explanation section to explain the rule on the issue and how it works in various factual situations. The simplest way to determine whether or not an issue is more procedural than substantive is to see if the governing rule comes from a court rule of procedure, such as the Federal Rules of Civil Procedure. For example, if you have one issue to brief in the motion that is simply "What are the standards necessary for granting summary judgment in *any* case," then you are dealing with a procedural rule, Fed. R. Civ. P. 56, and what it and the authorities that interpret it say about the award of summary judgment in any federal civil litigation.

Generally, the rules of procedure deal with topics relating to the propriety of the case being in a court (e.g., subject matter jurisdiction), a person being before the court (personal jurisdiction, service of process, and venue), the content of pleadings and papers and addition or amendment of claims and defenses, timeliness issues (timing of filings and statutory limitations periods), whether complete relief is possible between the parties (joinder of claims or parties, third-party practice), discovery matters, evidence, and whether and how a party gets to do something in the case (including motions, scheduling, stays, trials, and relief from judgment).

In contrast, a substantive issue involves the parties' rights and defenses, including claims and causes of action and the elements of same, affirmative defenses and avoidances and the elements of same, damages and remedies, and the actual substantive right to certain relief, such as the substantive law that determines whether a complaint has stated a claim upon which relief may be granted, whether the actual claims or defenses asserted in the parties' pleadings are subject to summary judgment, and whether a party is entitled to a new trial or judgment as a matter of law on one or more of its actual claims.

If you determine that an issue is purely procedural, you may consider the following when deciding how much of a TREAT and explanation to give the issue:

1. If you are citing an authority solely for a legal standard on procedure that it discusses, it is most likely unnecessary to discuss the facts of the authority. Many of the rules on procedure come from statutes and "rules," such as the Federal Rules of Civil Procedure, that have no facts. But aside from that, the facts of a case that states a useful legal standard or interpretive or explanatory rule on a procedural issue may not be important or illustrative to your argument.

2. If you are making an argument that the procedural rules should be applied in a certain way to the client's facts, then you will want to analogize to other cases where the rule was also applied to similar facts, and you will need to draft an explanation section. Often in a motion to dismiss for lack of personal jurisdiction, venue, subject matter jurisdiction, or violation of the statute of limitations, you will need to compare and analogize your client's facts to facts in similar cases in order to make a compelling argument on the procedural point.

The courts tend to be less consistent on purely procedural (who gets to do what and when and how) determinations than on substantive determinations. You will often find cases going either way. This fact may be attributed in large part to the appellate standard of review on procedural points, which generally grants a great deal of discretion to the trial court to make whatever procedural decisions it feels appropriate in the case before it. In the face of this body of potentially inconsistent authority, you still must discuss and apply or distinguish all potentially controlling authority on purely procedural points, but any persuasive authorities that go against your client's position on these points generally can be ignored. Cite the good persuasive authority on procedure and leave the rest out. Of course, if the "bad" persuasive authority is a powerhouse (some super-judge, a great treatise such as Wright & Miller, etc.), then you still might take the time to explain it away, but it is not required. Maybe wait and see if your opponent tries to make a lot of hay with it.

2. Anticipating counter-arguments

Anticipation of an opponent's defenses and counter-arguments on a motion is something a movant must worry about—movants have the choice. An opponent has to respond to the movant's arguments one way or the other. But devoting an entire TREAT section to laying out and refuting an opponent's counter-argument is a substantial investment of precious space in your motion, and you should be wary of attempting this maneuver.

In general, the same principles apply here as determine when to cite and distinguish negative authority: if the opponent's argument is fairly obvious and the negative authorities are almost certainly going to be found by your opponent, then it is a good idea to try to have the first word and set the right spin on the argument. If the opponent's argument is not particularly strong, or the authorities are fairly obscure and not easily found and interpreted, then you have much less incentive to take them up and try to refute them.

The problem is that you never want to do your opponent's work for her. Do not develop and discuss a contrary argument so well that your opponent will easily take up your discussion and do a good job briefing the counter-argument in her opposition brief. Your discussion and counter-analysis on the topic may provide more fodder for her brief than anything the opponent could develop in support of the argument on her own. Thus, if you are fairly certain that your opponent will not even think of an argument or will present it in a most unconvincing way, do not discuss the issues and points of the contrary argument ahead of time. Of course, if your opponent is a top-flight lawyer who will not miss the issues and arguments that are present in the case, then you should feel free to do as thorough a counter-analysis as you can afford to, in light of the available space for the argument.

One additional piece of advice: do not set up a straw man argument and attribute it to the opponent in one breath just so that you can tear it to pieces in the next. Do not try to reduce a rational argument to a ridiculous and frivolous position that no one would actually assert. Straw man arguments are a cheap rhetorical device that will never carry much weight with the court, and will instead make you look ridiculous for attempting this maneuver. Give fair credit to a serious counter-argument and then do the best job you can to refute it.

However, when you have decided to anticipate and refute a serious counter-argument, you should still limit your citations to negative authority in the counter-analysis. Although we are being a bit redundant, this bears repeating. When you are spinning out an argument that belongs to your opponent, you should never present it with all the cases you found in support of that argument. If there are potentially controlling authorities, discuss and distinguish only the most recent authorities. If it is an argument that will rely on persuasive authorities, discuss only a few of the weakest, most easily refuted persuasive authorities. Make the house look so shabby that even your opponent will be embarrassed to live in it.

D. How many issues do you TREAT in a given motion?

Even though we anticipate that our readers will be wondering how many TREATs are necessary in a motion, we still feel a little foolish by raising this question here—the answer is necessarily dependent on the individual problem you were assigned and the substance of the motion that relates to the problem. A single motion may present several issues to brief, some procedural and others substantive, each of which might deserve its own TREAT, and the Rule that governs each issue may have multiple elements, each of which deserves its own sub-TREAT. Your ability to identify the issues from the problem (the facts) that were told to you, and your ability to unpack these issues and add new issues based on your research into the law that applies to the problem, is the key ability that your entire law school education is attempting to develop in you.

The following example is illustrative of the process. A motion to dismiss for lack of personal jurisdiction under Fed. R. Civ. P. 12(b)(2) might assert that defendant has no minimum contacts with the jurisdiction and no "hook" or nexus with the jurisdiction under the state "Long Arm" statute. The various TREATs necessary to answer the question might be broken down as follows:

ARGUMENT

Rule Section – this **procedural** rule does not require a full TREAT. The second sentence merely is a roadmap or "umbrella" section for the rest of the motion.	Fed R. Civ. P. 12(b)(2) provides: " . . ." This action must be dismissed because plaintiff cannot obtain personal jurisdiction over defendant in this forum under either the state Long Arm statute, and any attempted exercise of jurisdiction would violate the requirements of the Due Process clause of the United States Constitution.
Thesis on first substantive Issue	**I. PLAINTIFF FAILS TO SHOW DEFENDANT'S CONNECTION TO THE FORUM UNDER THE WISCONSIN "LONG ARM" STATUTE**
Rule Section – this is a substantive rule, so a full TREAT with sub-TREATs is necessary.	A federal court sitting in diversity must evaluate the propriety of the exercise of personal jurisdiction over the defendant under both the local state "Long Arm" statute and the requirements of the Due Process clause of the United States Constitution. <u>Tough v. Easy</u>, 123 F.3d 456, 458 (7th Cir. 1998). The Wisconsin "Long Arm" statute, Wis. Stat. § 1000.01 ("Long Arm Statute"), provides for service of process and the exercise of jurisdiction over an out-of-state defendant when the defendant has performed one or more of the following acts in the State of Wisconsin: (a) made a contract in the state; (b) conducted business in the state; . . .
Sub-Thesis regarding second substantive Issue	**A. Defendant did not make a contract in Wisconsin because the sales orders between the parties were entered into in Illinois.**
Sub-Rule, Explanation, Application and Thesis-Conclusion on second Issue. This is a sub-TREAT of the first prong of the Long Arm Statute	In order to satisfy the "making of a contract" prong of the Long Arm Statute, plaintiff must show that defendant . . . Making a contract means . . . <u>Parker v. Brothers</u>, 567 N.W.2d 987, 989 (Wis. 1973) (sales order issued from Illinois so contract was made in Illinois); <u>Clifford v. Eisle</u>, . . . The instant case presents the same exact situation as in <u>Parker</u> and <u>Clifford</u> and the other sales order cases discussed above. Defendant did not . . . Therefore, plaintiff fails to satisfy the first prong of the Long Arm Statute.

Sub-Thesis regarding third substantive Issue	**B. Defendant did not transact business in Wisconsin because transaction of business requires a party's physical presence, and mere communication of business information by electronic media is insufficient.**
Sub-Rule, Explanation, Application and Thesis-Conclusion on third Issue. This is a sub-TREAT of the second prong of the Long Arm Statute	In order to satisfy the "transaction of business" prong of the Long Arm Statute, plaintiff must show that defendant . . . Transaction of business includes . . . Trivial v. Pursuit Co., 897 N.W.2d 487, 488 (Wis. 1993) (yearly visits to distributors in Wisconsin was transaction of business in Wisconsin); Alfred v. Wayne, . . . Unlike in Trivial and Alfred and the other "doing business" cases discussed above, in the instant case, defendant never stepped foot in the jurisdiction, and only communicated over the Internet and through telephone conversations. . . . Therefore, plaintiff fails to satisfy the second prong of the Long Arm Statute. Because plaintiff cannot show defendant's nexus with the forum under either prong of the statute, this action must be dismissed.
Thesis regarding fourth substantive Issue	**II. EXERCISE OF JURISDICTION OVER THE DEFENDANT VIOLATES THE "MINIMUM CONTACTS" REQUIREMENT OF THE DUE PROCESS CLAUSE.**
Rule, Explanation, Application and Thesis-Conclusion on fourth Issue	Even if jurisdiction were proper under the Wisconsin Long Arm Statute, plaintiff still cannot show that jurisdiction would be proper under the Due Process clause of the United States Constitution . . . Due process requires a showing of minimum contacts . . . In the instant case, defendant has never stepped foot in Wisconsin, and . . . Therefore, the exercise of personal jurisdiction over defendant would violate the Due Process clause, and this action must be dismissed for lack of personal jurisdiction.

VI. THE CONCLUSION SECTION

Some lawyers mix up the introduction and the conclusion—they often confuse the benefits of a strong beginning to their argument with a strong ending. Ideally, you could do both— a reader who was entranced by your rhetoric would follow your brief to the end and receive a strong, satisfying summation that reemphasizes all points raised in the brief and caps them off with a zinger to send the happy reader on her way. However, in actuality, your reader will not necessarily get to your last page. Therefore, a strong beginning is much more important than a strong ending. Focus your efforts there.

What is left for the conclusion of a pretrial motion? You tell the court exactly what you want the court to do, and then sign your name. It is important to get this right— you really do not want the court to have to guess about what you want it to do.

Examples of perfectly good conclusions to pretrial motions:

CONCLUSION

For the reasons stated herein, this Court should dismiss plaintiff's Petition for failure to state a claim upon which relief can be granted.

CONCLUSION

For the reasons stated above, plaintiff Jones respectfully requests the Court to deny defendant Smith's motion to dismiss or in the alternative, to stay this action.

Powerful stuff, no? You might have a lot to ask the court to do, so this section might get more complicated (and interesting). Consider the following conclusion of a motion for preliminary injunction in a trademark infringement case:

CONCLUSION

WHEREFORE, for the reasons stated above, plaintiff respectfully requests the Court to:

(a) issue an order temporarily enjoining defendant and all of its agents, employees, and contractors from the creation, display, distribution, and sale of the "Bart Simpson" mark T-shirts and products described in ¶¶ 6-9 of the Complaint filed herewith this day;

(b) issue an order temporarily enjoining defendant and all of its agents, employees, and contractors from all advertising involving the "Bart Simpson" mark described and defined in ¶¶ 6-7 of the Complaint, and specifically requiring defendant to cancel, suspend, and withdraw all print ads described in ¶ 10 of the Complaint,

---

> all radio promotions described in ¶ 11 of the Complaint, and all web pages of the internet web site at http://www.gocrazyfolks.com displaying or describing "Bart Simpson" T-shirts and products described in ¶ 12 of the Complaint;
>
> (c) issue an order temporarily enjoining defendant from the creation, display, distribution, sale, and advertising of any other and additional works (including derivative works) displaying or using the "Bart Simpson" mark described and defined in ¶¶ 6-7 of the Complaint.

VII. FORMATTING A TRIAL LEVEL BRIEF

Sometimes local rules require a certain kind of formatting. Follow the local rules. In the absence of such rules, we recommend the following:

A. The caption, title, all headings, the signature block, and all footnotes are single-spaced. Everything else is double-spaced.

B. All text should be in the same font style, e.g., Times Roman, CG Times, Courier, or other professional looking font. Footnote text should be the same size as the regular text, or no more than one point smaller than the regular text; i.e., if the regular text is 12 point, the footnote text should be 12 point or 11 point, but no smaller.

C. One inch margins on all four sides are recommended.

D. Page numbers should be at the bottom center of each page from page 2 to the end.

E. Major headings for divisions of the brief are in bold, all caps, centered, and underlined. For example:

<u>INTRODUCTION</u>
<u>STATEMENT OF FACTS</u>
<u>ARGUMENT</u>
<u>CONCLUSION</u>

F. Major headings for the Argument are in bold, all caps, and preceded by an uppercase Roman number (I, II, III, etc.), and begin at the left margin. The text of the heading is indented from the Roman number.

G. Secondary headings in the Argument are in bold, underlined, lowercase (or title case – initial letter of each significant word capitalized), preceded by an uppercase letter (A, B, C, etc.), and are indented five spaces from the left margin. The text is indented from the letter.

H. Tertiary headings are in bold, lowercase or title case, not underlined, preceded by an Arabic number (1, 2, 3, etc.), and are indented ten spaces. The text is indented from the number.

I. Quaternary headings are in lowercase, underlined, not bolded, preceded by a lowercase letter (a, b, c, etc.), and are indented fifteen spaces, with the text indented from the letter.

J. Further headings would be lowercase, not bolded or underlined, preceded alternatively by lowercase Roman numbers (i, ii, iii, etc.), or Arabic numbers in parentheses ((1), (2), (3), etc.), or other numbering of your own devising, and indented five additional spaces per level.

This looks like this:

Progression of Headings for Pretrial Motion:

<u>ARGUMENT</u>

I. **PLAINTIFF FAILS TO ALLEGE A CAUSE OF ACTION FOR FRAUDULENT MISREPRESENTATION.**

    A. **<u>Plaintiff fails to allege that the representation was material.</u>**

        1. **The representation did not impact either part of the contract implementation plan.**

            a. <u>Part I of the plan was completed.</u>

                i. The time table for Part I was met.

                    (1) Groundbreaking occurred on schedule.

If you need to go further, what you do is up to you. This many levels of headings is almost never necessary, but if you get a little crazy, you have a format to refer to.

VIII. STYLE ISSUES OF MOTIONS

A. Tone and formality

A motion must be formal in tone. Your audience usually is a judge or other legal decision maker (arbitrator, mediator, rule-making committee, etc.), and she rarely is impressed with levity or informality in writing. The same general rules regarding formality and tone that apply in the case of office memoranda also apply and with additional force in the case of court briefs. By way of review, these rules are:

1. Do not use slang.
2. Do not use colloquialisms.
3. Avoid first-person and second person references – I, my, you, your, etc. A party asserts arguments or makes motions, not the attorneys, no matter if you are referring to your own side or the opposition.

4. Avoid slash constructions (Bob was a teacher/researcher) unless that is the actual word, phrase, or address that you are quoting or referring to.

5. Do not use contractions.

6. It is fine to use shorthand words and abbreviations of parties, institutions and agencies, acts and statutes, once you have correctly identified them in your work.

> *Example:* The Securities Exchange Commission ("SEC") refused to apply the provisions of the Securities Act of 1933 ("'33 Act") to the post-sale use of the Section 14 red herring prospectus ("prospectus") by McDonnell Douglas Corporation ("MDC"). The SEC said that MDC satisfied the requirements of the '33 Act by providing an updated prospectus to each buyer.

7. Do not use symbols (&, @, #) unless the symbol is part of a rule, statute, or an email address; e.g., 14 U.S.C. § 123, 13 Lab. L. Ann. ¶ 3-307, goldmanr@slu.edu.

8. Avoid the use of humor. This is not to say leave out all vivid, descriptive, and even clever language from your writing. Clever language used sparingly can be effective and is acceptable. You can turn a clever phrase, but do it to make a point, to drive something home, to make an impression that might last a bit longer; never do it just to be funny.

9. As with the statement of facts, do not show anger or other excessive emotion in your argument. No one wants to read a lawyer's vicious sniping at the other side, or a long, sorrowful recitation of the equities of the situation. It is not professional. You might lose your cool in person in the heat of argument, but you should not do it in writing. This is not to say be bland, dull, and never get assertive or forceful about your position. You can be forthright! You can be direct! You can show that you feel strongly about the equities! But not by bleeding your sympathy and sorrow all over the page or burning the very words off the paper with scorching prose.

B. Footnotes

Footnotes are a luxury in court briefs—do not abuse the privilege. Yes, they are single-spaced, and the text can be smaller in font size if you want to test your readers' eyes and irritate them, and as a result, you can fit more in them per square inch than regular text. But avoid devilish temptations and use them correctly.

Often there are local rules which force you to use footnotes in very limited ways: for example, no legal argument can be asserted in footnotes; no legal authority may be cited or discussed in footnotes; and other such rules. But even if these rules are not present, you should never try to put a significant part of your argument in footnotes for the following reasons:

1. It looks bad.

The courts (and writing instructors) create page limits for a reason: they do not want to read excessive material. If you cheat them by loading up the word count with huge footnotes, they will resent it.

2. Some people never read footnotes.

Footnotes are a distraction that some readers purposefully avoid. If you put something important in a footnote, it is lost to these people forever.

3. Footnotes are a nuisance.

Even if the judge or other reader does read footnotes, if you constantly pull her attention away from the regular text and down into footnotes she will be irritated.

So, what do you use footnotes for?

1. Side issues that deserve brief attention

If you have a minor, non-dispositive issue, not related to other issues as a stepping-stone issue or sub-issue, and you think it should be raised and discussed, but you are certain that it does not deserve its own TREAT, than you may raise it and discuss it briefly in a footnote. Again, err on the side of *not* relegating issues to footnotes until you have the confidence won from years of experience because an issue buried in a footnote may be missed completely by some of your readers.

2. Additional facts of some interest to the analysis

In the argument section, you might consider raising additional facts that have some interest value to the analysis, but which were not raised in the statement of facts. A proper citation to support for the facts is necessary.

As suggested by our warnings above, you should never relegate key facts upon which the case might turn to footnotes. We also point out that this is really only an option for the argument or Discussion section, because you should avoid using footnotes in the statement of facts.

3. Tertiary legal support for the argument

This is an area rife for abuse, so be careful. If you have a bit of persuasive primary or secondary authority that helps the cause but is not a show-stopper, and there is no critical reason for it to be discussed in the regular text, you might raise it in a footnote. In order not to appear to be violating the page limitation, you should use this option not more than two or three times in any motion.

Never use a footnote as a place to squeeze important controlling authority or any other vital part of the support for your argument. Do not use footnotes as a place to create or continue a string-cite of redundant authority—these are abuses of the page limit that will only serve to anger your reader.

C. Parentheticals

The rules on usage of parentheticals in adversarial legal writing largely are the same as with office memoranda. You can use them as a helpful way of presenting information in shorthand form, if the information is properly presented in shorthand form. The whole process of explanatory synthesis impresses on you the task of making sure you learn how to write clear, concise parentheticals to illustrate how your cases support the principles you are laying out. Parentheticals also are used in citations to indicate additional information about the authority.

> ➤ *Appropriate uses:*   Parody requires transformation. <u>Smith</u>, 12 F.3d at 34 (Johnson, J. concurring) (addition of text transformed original image into parody); <u>Jones</u>, 11 F.3d at 567 (citing <u>Hardy</u>, 123 F.2d at 45) (artistic interpretation created new meaning and message of parody).

Beyond these uses in citations and explanatory syntheses, do not attempt to use parentheticals in plain text simply as a space saving device. They do not substitute for a proper explanation of information from the facts or holding of a case when this information cannot be summarized in a few words or a short phrase. In addition, they should not be used as a way of presenting facts or other information in a brief without regard to the niceties of grammar, and thereby saving on space (<u>i.e.</u>, because in a parenthetical, you can leave out articles and connectors and "non-essential" terms). Abuse of this rule simply is another way of cheating on page limits and it is regarded with similar disdain.

> ➤ *Questionable uses:*   Parody requires transformation which creates new content, meaning or expression (parodies add: text, transforming images, commentary, ridicule, messages) so that the new work is shown to comment on the original and not supersede the objects of the original (parodies avoid drudgery of coming up with something fresh). <u>Smith</u>, 12 F.3d at 34; <u>Jones</u>, 11 F.3d at 567; <u>Hardy</u>, 123 F.2d at 45.

IX. FINISHING THE MEMORANDUM IN SUPPORT

A. Cite-checking

Cite-checking is an absolute **must** for anything you submit to a court. If you cite a case that is bad law, your opponent is afforded a great opportunity to embarrass you in front of the court, and you and your client will look very bad.

B. Proof-reading

Some of you may be allergic to proof-reading your own work. Take an antihistamine. The appearance of your work will affect what the reader thinks of your work (and you as a lawyer), whether consciously or unconsciously. Sloppy writing equals sloppy research equals sloppy lawyering equals sloppy lawyer with a sloppy case. You do not want to create such a negative perception for you, your client, and perhaps even your law firm. It is important to take the time to proof-read, and if you do not know how to, you had better learn.

Please note that using the **spell-checker** on your word processing program will not be sufficient. Your spell-checker is not going to catch "form" when you meant "from," "statue" when you meant "statute," "pubic" when you meant "public." It will not know that you meant to put "your" not "you," or "there" not "their." A spell-checker also might suggest changes to legal words that you actually spelled correctly; it may tell you to use "tortuous" when you actually mean "tortious" (in relation to a tort). Spell-checkers have their limits, and their limits require you to proof-read on your own.

There is more than one way to proof-read. The most effective way we have found is to read your writing backwards, starting at the end and reading it backwards word by word and then sentence by sentence. Reversing the reading forces you to read each word and each sentence slowly, and you will catch a lot more typographical and spelling and citation errors at this speed. This can be a painful chore, but the results are excellent.

Another method is to read the work out loud to yourself or to have someone else read it out loud to you. Not only will you or your friend catch some errors in this way, you also are likely to find awkward passages and words that do not flow easily which you can then go back and rework to improve your phrasing.

C. Editing

A much repeated adage in writing is that, "There is no such thing as good writing; only good rewriting." The first drafts of your memorandum in support will not be perfect. You must allow yourself the time to correct mistakes, clear up rough patches that destroy the flow of the work, tighten up the sentences, and improve the wording.

Editing often is needed just to get the memorandum within the page limits. Page limits are not just for legal writing classes. Every court in which we've practiced has had page limitations on motions and memoranda in support. Beyond page limits is the general rule that a pre-trial motion needs to be direct and to the point. Terse writing is more effective. Flabby writing makes the reader spend more time than she wants on your brief. This is a sin committed more often by the so called "premiere" law firms, because they allow their attorneys the time to crank out huge documents, and they have clients that can afford to pay the huge legal fees racked up when an attorney writes a massive volume of material in a brief. Do not perpetuate this trend. If you can say it very well in five or six pages, do not turn in fifteen.

The skill of what to cut out and what to leave in is the sum and substance of legal advocacy and legal writing. Naturally, the same criteria as to what to put in your brief apply when you are considering what you should take out. The practice of this skill is a lifetime devotion.

Chapter 22

Motions to Dismiss

A motion to dismiss may be brought at various stages in a litigation, but it is most commonly filed early in the pretrial proceedings, after the complaint has been filed but before defendant has filed any other motion or pleading. The motion argues that one or more or all of the claims raised by plaintiff in its complaint should be dismissed from the case.

If all of the claims asserted in the complaint are dismissed, the action is dismissed, and plaintiff can appeal the dismissal. Otherwise, plaintiff has to start over with a new complaint, or the same complaint in a new forum (if the forum was the reason for the dismissal), and plaintiff hopes the statute of limitations has not run by this point or that he might take advantage of a procedural "savings clause."

If fewer than all of the claims are dismissed, the litigation continues as to the remaining claims. Plaintiff either has to forego the dismissed claims or try to amend the complaint to reassert the claims for relief in a new and hopefully non-objectionable form, or refile the same claims in a different forum (if the forum was the problem, and if the statute of limitations has not run, and if plaintiff is willing to carry on two litigations against the same defendant at the same time). Otherwise, plaintiff has to wait for a final judgment on the remaining claims and then appeal the dismissal of these initial claims at that time.

I. INITIAL PRETRIAL MOTION FOR DEFENDANT

As mentioned above, the most typical time for a defendant to file a motion to dismiss is as the initial action by the defendant in response to the filing of the complaint. The motion is filed in lieu of answering the complaint or petition. You certainly do not need to file a motion to dismiss, and grounds for the motion will not exist in very many cases. In federal court, a motion to dismiss is governed by Rule 12(b), Fed. R. Civ. P., and its various subsections.

Plaintiff can assert a motion to dismiss a counterclaim if the plaintiff is a counterclaim defendant. It might be asserted by a cross-claim defendant (a co-defendant or co-plaintiff in the case) to dismiss a cross-claim, or by a third-party defendant to dismiss a third-party claim. Rule 12(b) governs these situations as well.

II. MOTION TO DISMISS FOR LACK OF JURISDICTION OVER THE SUBJECT MATTER - FED. R. CIV. P. 12(b)(1)

The first subsection under Rule 12(b) deals with a motion that argues that the court has no subject matter jurisdiction because:

➤ there is no diversity or not enough amount in controversy under 28 U.S.C. § 1332;
➤ there is no federal question presented by the complaint under 28 U.S.C. § 1331, or
➤ the specific subject matter of the action belongs in a different forum (e.g., a bankruptcy action that should have been brought in a United States Bankruptcy Court).

Certain allegations may overlap other subsections of Rule 12(b), such as an argument that one or more claims are not ripe, or are moot, or the complaint does not present a valid case or controversy, all of which also can be challenged under Fed. R. Civ. P. 12(b)(6).

The motion attacks some defect in the complaint itself, so the movant *might* state that the allegations of the complaint are presumed true (taken at face value) for purposes of the motion if the problem is not what plaintiff alleges to be the grounds for subject matter jurisdiction, but rather an allegation such as that claims themselves are not ripe or are moot or do not present a case or controversy. However, more often than not, the problem will be that the complaint erroneously alleges facts and makes improper factual and legal conclusions in support of subject matter jurisdiction, and movant must challenge and refute these erroneous grounds by bringing out the "correct" facts and conclusions regarding subject matter jurisdiction. In these instances, movant *cannot* assume the facts pleaded in the complaint to be true for purposes of the motion or for any other purpose—it would be a fatal error to do so.

If new operative facts regarding subject matter jurisdiction are alleged or attempted to be proved by the movant, then the opponent of the motion may request an extension of time to address the new facts, and perhaps to take discovery of the support for the new facts. There is no guaranty that movant will be afforded the time or granted the right to take discovery on subject matter jurisdiction. If the Rule 12(b)(1) motion is pled in conjunction with a Rule 12(b)(6) motion (see below), and new facts are alleged, the court has the option to convert the proceedings to a summary judgment motion under Fed. R. Civ. P. 56, and discovery more often will be afforded to the opponent of the motion to dismiss.

III. MOTION TO DISMISS FOR LACK OF JURISDICTION OVER THE PERSON - FED. R. CIV. P. 12(b)(2)

A Rule 12(b)(2) motion argues that the court has no jurisdiction over the person of the defendant(s) because:

➤ they are not present in the jurisdiction (don't reside there, aren't subject to service of process there, and cannot be found there in person or through a proper agent);
➤ they are not properly haled into the court under the applicable state Long Arm statute (the Long Arm statute of the state where the court is located); or
➤ they cannot properly or reasonably be haled into the court under the Due Process Clause of the U.S. Constitution, and the related doctrines of "minimum contacts" and "traditional notions of fair play and substantial justice."

Any facts alleged in the complaint that have any bearing on personal jurisdiction over the defendant **cannot** be presumed to be true by movant for purposes of the motion. In most cases, plaintiff will have alleged facts in support of the assertion of personal jurisdiction over the defendant, and defendant cannot buy into these erroneous allegations. The defendant movant must assert and prove the "correct" facts regarding personal jurisdiction in the motion. So, movant should strike the phrase "presume the facts alleged in the complaint to be true for purposes of the motion" from any 12(b)(2) template; you never will use this phrase.

The appropriate way to introduce new jurisdictional facts is to allege them in the motion supported by an attached affidavit or declaration under penalty of perjury from a knowledgeable person (usually your client). Not everyone does it the appropriate way, and not every judge requires you to do it the appropriate way, but we encourage you to do the right thing.

Both sides have the right to ask for discovery regarding jurisdictional facts. Neither side is guaranteed the right to such discovery, but the judge is hard-pressed not to grant it in many cases, especially if both sides ask for it. It is more likely to be granted to the opponent if the movant introduces and attempts to prove new jurisdictional facts in its motion to dismiss, and the opponent claims that it needs to explore them.

If the movant introduces new facts by affidavit or declaration, and the opponent (the plaintiff) responds by alleging still more facts by affidavit or declaration in support of personal jurisdiction, the case can degenerate into a big swearing match.[1] Judges do not like to make decisions on the basis of who swears the best or the most (this is called "trial by affidavit"), so a swearing match probably favors the opponent of the motion. In other words, the judge will probably deny the motion, perhaps without prejudice to try it again later, and leave the case as it is on the basis of the original facts alleged by plaintiff in support of jurisdiction. If this happens, defendant must be careful not to waive its argument by filing an answer or other pleading that fails to assert the same objections and challenges to personal jurisdiction—if you fail to object, defects in personal jurisdiction are deemed waived.

The judge might entertain a fact-finding hearing on personal jurisdiction, after which it will find the "true" facts and determine whether the exercise of personal jurisdiction is indeed proper. The testimony of witnesses and documents and other items that tend to prove such facts might be taken into evidence at such a hearing. Even if you wind up in a grand swearing match with your opponent or in a prolonged and expensive hearing on personal jurisdiction, the motion still is worth bringing because if you fail to assert your objections to defects in personal jurisdiction, the objections you might have had are deemed waived.

---

[1] "Swearing match" refers to the fact that the person making the affidavit (called the affiant) or the declaration (called the declarant) swears under penalty of perjury that the facts stated in the affidavit or declaration are true.

IV. MOTION TO DISMISS FOR IMPROPER VENUE - FED. R. CIV. P. 12(b)(3)

The 12(b)(3) motion argues that the venue is improper because:

➤ it fails to satisfy the requirements of 28 U.S.C. § 1391 or the applicable venue statute;
➤ there was a forum selection clause that required the case to be brought in a different venue; or
➤ plaintiff is mistaken in its facts alleged in support of its choice of venue.

If the motion to dismiss for lack of venue is granted, the plaintiff still can pick up the pieces and file the suit in an appropriate venue, as long as the statute of limitations has not run.

A 12(b)(3) motion is commonly brought in conjunction with a 28 U.S.C. § 1404 motion and a 28 U.S.C. § 1406 motion. A 1404 motion is for transfer to a more convenient venue—more convenient to the defendant, to be sure, but justified either because of a forum selection clause or under a *forum non conveniens* argument. Section 1406 provides that if the court finds that venue is improper, the court can transfer the case to an appropriate venue, rather than dismissing the suit outright.

As with a Rule 12(b)(2) motion, movant **cannot** presume the facts alleged in the complaint in support of venue to be true for purposes of the motion. It would be fatal to do so. The appropriate way to introduce new and "correct" venue facts is to allege them in the motion supported by an attached affidavit or declaration under penalty of perjury from a knowledgeable person.

Both sides have the right to ask for discovery regarding venue facts, but neither side is guaranteed the right to such discovery. Venue generally is given a back seat to personal jurisdiction issues, and judges may forego the delay simply by denying discovery or by denying the motion to dismiss.

V. MOTION TO DISMISS FOR INSUFFICIENCY OF PROCESS OR SERVICE OF PROCESS - FED. R. CIV. P. 12(b)(4),(5)

A deficiency in "the process" means something was wrong with the papers themselves—erroneous or insufficient or incomplete information in the summons, complaint, or return of service. A defect in service of process means that the way the papers were served or the person upon whom they were served is improper. Examples of this would be service by publication when personal service was required, or service on a five-year-old friend of the son of the defendant rather than on the defendant, or service on a receptionist in the building lobby and not on a proper officer or agent of a corporate defendant.

A party filing a motion to dismiss for improper process or service of process rarely succeeds in obtaining a dismissal; 90% of the time the judge is just going to grant the plaintiff additional time for service and issue an additional summons[2] so that the plaintiff perform service correctly. If delay is your primary goal, then you might go ahead and file this motion. You should be aware that modern rules often shift the costs of opposing the motion or the cost of additional service of process back onto you if your motion is found to be erroneous.

VI. MOTION TO DISMISS FOR FAILURE TO STATE A CLAIM UPON WHICH RELIEF MAY BE GRANTED - FED. R. CIV. P. 12(b)(6)

This is the granddaddy of them all—a real show-stopper. The paradigm motion argues, "Even if everything plaintiff alleges were true, under the law applicable to this case, plaintiff cannot recover under any of its claims against defendant." This is a pretrial motion you really can sink your teeth into.

Since you have waited patiently though the other five subsections of Rule 12(b), we will now tell you that **this is the motion** in which movant should assume that all facts pleaded in the complaint are true and correct for purposes of the motion. This is the best strategy, because if movant does not make this assumption, or if new operative facts regarding the claims or defenses are alleged or attempted to be proved by the movant, then the court can reject the motion, or convert the motion to a Fed. R. Civ. P. 56 summary judgment motion. In the latter case, the court generally will grant an extension of time to the party opposing the motion so as to allow it time to gather facts in opposition to the movant's new facts. Discovery may be granted to either or both sides, and delay of the proceedings will result.

Note well that the assumption should be drafted to state only "that all facts pleaded in the complaint are true and correct **for purposes of the motion**." You do not assume the complaint and its claims to be true and correct for any other purpose, and you don't want to create the impression (true or not) that you are admitting the facts. So, be careful to use the proper wording of the presumption.

---

[2] Referred to in various jurisdictions as an alias summons (the second summons issued) or pluries summons (the third and any subsequently issued summons).

VII. FORMAT OF MOTIONS TO DISMISS AND THE OPPOSITION TO THE SAME

As with most motions, motions to dismiss generally have the following sections:

[PRE-INTRODUCTION]
<u>INTRODUCTION</u>
<u>STATEMENT OF FACTS</u>
<u>ARGUMENT</u>
<u>CONCLUSION</u>

The Pre-introduction identifies the motion before the court. The Introduction, as always, is the most critical section, and you need to draft a short, persuasive summary of your argument. Discuss the facts, law, and legal conclusions that tell the court why you should win.

Unless you are writing a 12(b)(6) motion, you should draft the Statement of Facts so that your client's position looks strong. In a 12(b)(6) motion, however, you customarily presume the plaintiff's complaint to be true for purposes of the motion, so you are limited in what you can do with the facts. Reorder and reword the plaintiff's rendition of the facts, but don't change the actual facts or introduce new facts unless you are prepared to face a quick denial of the motion or conversion of the proceedings to a drawn-out, expensive summary judgment motion context.

On a motion to dismiss for lack of subject matter jurisdiction, or personal jurisdiction, or venue, you can introduce and discuss new facts supporting your position. Factual conclusions are permitted, but you should draw the necessary jurisdictional or venue-related *legal* conclusions in your discussion section, not in the Facts. Be wary of the potential creation of a swearing match on the jurisdictional facts.

The Argument (or Discussion) is drafted in the usual way as discussed in Chapter 21. The Conclusion also is the same—one sentence telling the court what you want it to do.

The opposition to a motion to dismiss follows the same format. You will attempt to refute any new facts alleged, and rebut any legal arguments raised against your complaint and your choice of forum. Dig in your heels—it's your complaint, and your choice of forum. Don't blow it.

You do not have to slavishly follow the points alleged by the movant in the order raised by the movant—raise your best points in opposition first, followed by the next best and so on. If you have additional points that support your complaint that movant did not address, be sure to throw them in. Make your opponent sweat through its reply brief.

VIII.   SAMPLE MOTIONS

Sample 1 - Memorandum in Support of Motion to Dismiss

UNITED STATES DISTRICT COURT
CENTRAL DISTRICT OF CALIFORNIA
SOUTHERN DIVISION

GLOBAL STUDIOS,	)	
	)	
Plaintiff,	)	
v.	)	No. SA CV 01-9999 AHS
	)	
KINGSTON UNIVERSITY	)	
ELECTRONIC FREEDOM	)	
FRONTIER, LARRY MULLEN,	)	
LISA ROGERS, MEGHAN MORELY,	)	
and CHRIS HANSEN,	)	
	)	
Defendants.	)	

MEMORANDUM IN SUPPORT OF DEFENDANTS' MOTION TO DISMISS FOR LACK OF PERSONAL JURISDICTION

Defendants Kingston University Electronic Freedom Frontier, Larry Mullen, Lisa Rogers, Meghan Morely, and Chris Hansen (collectively referred to as "KUEFF") move this Court pursuant to Fed. R. Civ. P. 12(b)(2), to dismiss this action for lack of personal jurisdiction.

> One of the goals of movants' introduction is to slant the reader's thinking about the case as a whole. The introduction below does a good job of this. The movant wants to communicate a theme and tell its side of the story concerning the case as a whole (the first two sentences below) as well as its points on the motion (the rest of the section). The issues of the case as a whole are covered just far enough to leave the proper taste in the reader's mouth. Then the section gets down to business laying out the facts, law, and policies relevant to the motion at hand.

INTRODUCTION

Global Studios is suing KUEFF to abolish its constitutional right to post newsworthy information concerning the CSS/DeCSS controversy. Global Studios must believe that a news organization cannot report on DVD duplication without being subject to suit in California.

KUEFF moves to dismiss the suit for lack of personal jurisdiction. None of its members have been to California since the organization was founded. Less than one percent of the hits on the web site have been from users in California. No commercial activity takes place on the web site and the level of interactivity is miniscule; therefore, the organization has not purposefully availed itself of the privilege of conducting activities in California. Also, it would be totally unreasonable to require four college students to defend themselves across the country against a corporation like Global Studios. KUEFF's contacts with California do not satisfy the "minimum contacts" and "fair and substantial justice" required by the California Long-Arm statute, Cal. Civ. Proc. Code § 410.10 (West 2001), and the state and federal constitutional "due process" standards, Cal. Const. art. 1, § 7; U.S. Const. amend. XIV.

The statement of facts below brings out facts that are relevant to the motion, but it is too objective. It lacks the kind of advocacy we want to see in a facts section in a ligation brief that employs narrative reasoning to drive home the movants' points. This one sounds like a newspaper article, and lacks a point of view. The use of terms such as "the organization" depersonalizes the author's clients and disassociates the movants from the memo they have presented in support of their motion. The reader may wonder, "What disembodied observer wrote this?" It is better to write the facts from the clients' point of view. Compare this presentation of facts with the punchy, calculated, and effective presentation of the same facts in the Introduction of this memorandum in support: "None of its members have been to California since the organization was founded. Less than one percent of the hits on the web site have been from users in California. No commercial activity takes place on the web site and the level of interactivity is miniscule." Don't repeat yourself word for word, but maintain the same calculated selection and presentation of facts in both sections.

STATEMENT OF FACTS

DeCSS is software that can be downloaded and used to unscramble the protection program known as Content Scramble System (CSS) so DVDs can then be duplicated. Since March 2001, Kingston University in Troy, New York, has hosted a web site of a nonprofit student organization known as Kingston University Electronic Freedom Frontier (KUEFF).

> We object to authors who over-abbreviate their abbreviated short forms, such as "T.S. Dec." Give more information, such as "Sensor Dec."

See Declaration of Tracy Sensor dated Jan. 4, 2002, at ¶ 2 ("T.S. Dec."). The organization regularly posts news on its web site regarding issues of free speech on the Internet. See Declaration of Larry Mullen dated Jan. 8, 2002, at ¶ 2 ("L.M. Dec."). KUEFF's personnel and everything associated with its activities are located in New York. See L.M. Dec. at ¶ 4.

In September 2001, the organization began reporting on the CSS/DeCSS controversy. See T.S. Dec. at ¶ 3. The names and addresses of several web sites that provide DeCSS for downloading were mentioned in passing. See T.S. Dec. at ¶ 3. None of the addresses were hyperlinked. See L.M. Dec. at ¶ 3. KUEFF did nothing to encourage readers in California to visit these sites or download the software. See Complaint, Exhibit 1 ("Exhibit 1").

The organization's only contact with people in California has been through emails, the majority of which consist of information about KUEFF and news previously reported on

> Instead of simply saying, "Hey, we took two donations," the author should have undercut this negative fact by pointing out that the donations amounted to less than $100, and at least one of the donations was orchestrated by one of plaintiff's attorneys. This smacks of entrapment, and entrapment would help the movants' cause, rather than leave the court thinking, "They took money from California residents."

the web site. See L.M. Dec. at ¶ 6. There is evidence of only two donations being made via email, one by an attorney representing the plaintiff and another by the plaintiff's witness. See Declaration of Zachary Schulman dated Jan. 7, 2002, at ¶ 5; Declaration of Melanie Smead dated Jan. 12, 2002, at ¶ 5 ("M.S. Dec"). No contracts or sales have been made with anyone in California. There is no evidence that any hits from California led to installation of DeCSS. M.S. Dec. at ¶ 3.

ARGUMENT

> Thesis headings can provide the reader with a useful summary of the points of your argument, but only if you make them meaningful. The heading below only presents half of the information—the conclusion. Add to this the "because" part—the facts and legal principles that support the conclusion. Then your reader has the complete picture. A better heading would be: "THE ACTION MUST BE DISMISSED FOR LACK OF PERSONAL JURISDICTION BECAUSE NONE OF THE DEFENDANTS WERE PRESENT IN CALIFORNIA AND NONE OF THEM DID BUSINESS IN CALIFORNIA."

I. THE ACTION MUST BE DISMISSED FOR LACK OF PERSONAL JURISDICTION

> Observe how elegantly this rule section is drafted. There are a lot of rules to get through in the personal jurisdiction analysis, and this author is conserving space and the reader's attention span by laying them out succinctly without sacrificing the flow of the text.

Fed. R. Civ. P. 12(b)(2) provides that the defendant may make a motion to dismiss for "lack of jurisdiction over the person." This case has been brought before the United States District Court, Central District California. Therefore, the personal jurisdiction laws of California are applied.

> The author needs a cite for that last proposition.

The California Long Arm provision, Cal. Civ. Proc. Code § 410.10, states, "a court of this state may exercise jurisdiction on any basis not inconsistent with the Constitution of this state or of the United States." According to Cal. Const. art. 1, § 7 and U.S. Const. amend. XIV, "a person may not be deprived of life, liberty, or property without due process of the law."

Due process requires that a defendant, if not present in the state, "have certain minimum contacts with it such that the maintenance of the suit does not offend traditional notions of fair play and substantial justice." <u>Cybersell, Inc. v. Cybersell, Inc.</u>, 130 F.3d 414, 415 (9th Cir. 1997) (citing <u>International Shoe Co. v. Washington</u>, 326 U.S. 310, 316 (1945)).

Personal jurisdiction may be founded on either general jurisdiction or specific jurisdiction. <u>Panavision Int'l, L.P. v. Toeppen</u>, 141 F.3d 1316, 1320 (9th Cir. 1998). General jurisdiction exists when a defendant is domiciled in the forum state or when the defendant's activities there are "substantial" or "continuous and systematic." <u>Panavision</u>, 141 F.3d at 1320 (citing <u>Helicopteros Nacionales de Colombia, S.A. v. Hall</u>, 466 U.S. 408, 414-16 (1984)).

> Note the roadmap in the next two sentences. This direction is succinct but it keeps the reader informed as to the author's progression through this analysis.

Nothing in the complaint suggests that general jurisdiction is being asserted. Therefore, this motion will address the absence of specific jurisdiction over the defendants.

> The author created a sub-section A without writing any sub-section B. This is unnecessary, and a rookie mistake. Either set up the rule section under the main TREAT so that there does not need to be any sub-TREATs, or set it up so that there are at least two sub-TREATs. This memo was primed to have two major sections—long arm and due process, and due process is ready made for three sub-sections: purposeful availment, arising out of, and fairness. You can even break down purposeful availment into the sliding scale test and the effects test. We assume the author did not break up this memo into these parts because he felt short on space under the page limits and wanted to avoid using so many thesis headings, but some readers may become confused and alarmed if there is a subsection A and no subsection B.
>
> The heading of sub-section A lacks the "because" part. A better heading would be: "The court does not have specific jurisdiction over KUEFF because KUEFF was not present and did not do business in California and did not purposefully avail itself of California."

A. <u>The court does not have specific jurisdiction over KUEFF under the California Long-Arm statute.</u>

Courts use a three-part test to determine whether specific jurisdiction should be exercised:

(1) The nonresident defendant must do some act or consummate some transaction with the forum or perform some act by which he purposefully avails himself of the privilege of conducting activities in the forum, thereby invoking benefits and protections of its laws; (2) the claim must be one which arises out of or results from the defendant's forum-related activities; and (3) exercise of jurisdiction must be reasonable.

Panavision, 141 F.3d at 1320.

1. KUEFF did not purposefully avail itself.

Under the "sliding scale" approach, the likelihood that personal jurisdiction will be exercised is proportionate to the nature and quality of commercial activity conducted over the Internet. See Cybersell, 130 F.3d at 419 (citing Zippo Mfg. Co. v. Zippo Dot Com, Inc., 952 F. Supp. 1119, 1124 (W.D. Pa. 1997)).

At opposite ends of the scale are "passive" and "active" web sites; the middle consists of "interactive" sites where the user can exchange information with the defendant site. Callaway Golf Corp. v. Royal Canadian Golf Ass'n, 125 F. Supp. 2d 1194, 1200 (C.D. Cal. 2000).

> The author makes use of explanatory synthesis in the following explanation paragraph, but the paragraph is limited to one proposition that synthesizes two cases. The author should not have limited himself to two cases when there are dozens of cases available that illustrate these propositions. The author also should not limit the authority cited to district court cases when there are court of appeals cases that illustrate the proposition.

Specific jurisdiction primarily is exercised over "interactive" web sites when products, not advertisements or promotions, are sold. Compare S. Morantz v. Hang & Shine Ultrasonics, Inc., 79 F. Supp. 2d 537, 539 (E.D. Pa. 1999) (applying federal Due Process clause) (sale of promotional materials to forum residents via its web site too "fortuitous and random" to warrant exercise of jurisdiction); with Stomp, Inc. v. NeatO, LLC, 61 F. Supp. 2d 1074, 1077 (C.D. Cal. 1999) (specific jurisdiction appropriate over web site dedicated to sale of products on-line).

> The author commits an egregious error in the next sentence because the author states that "courts" have refused something, and then only cites only one case. Do not promise multiple cases and then deliver one case. A synthesis of cases would have been better here, but at least satisfy what you promise to the reader.

Courts have refused to recognize contacts manufactured by the plaintiff. <u>Millennium Enterprises, Inc. v. Millennium Music, L.P.</u>, 33 F. Supp. 2d 907, 911 (D. Or. 1999) (no personal jurisdiction where the only sales in California motivated by the plaintiff's interest in the lawsuit).

KUEFF operates a relatively "interactive" web site that allows users to email directly to the organization. However, unlike the site in <u>Stomp</u> that was established for the purpose of transacting Internet sales, KUEFF's site does not offer products for purchase. The only commercial activity on KUEFF's site has consisted of donations that were more akin to promotional transactions than product sales. And even if deemed substantial commercial activity, the donations may be disregarded as having been manufactured by the plaintiff.

> The section that follows sounds like a new rule section. This is confusing because the last paragraph above obviously was an application section. The reader cannot tell whether this is a new rule section because the author did not start a new sub-TREAT. Flipping from an application to a new rule section within the same sub-TREAT is confusing and unwelcome. The author should have started a new sub-TREAT here.

Under the "effects test," personal jurisdiction in a tort case is predicated on (1) intentional actions that are (2) expressly aimed at the forum state, and (3) cause harm, the brunt of which is suffered—and which the defendant knows is likely to be suffered—in the forum state. <u>Callaway</u>, 125 F. Supp. 2d at 1200.

> Again, the synthesis that follows contains only two cases. There was no dearth of authority on this proposition. The purpose of the explanation is to illustrate how the rule works, and the comparison of two cases is extremely limited in its illustrative power.

Believing a corporate defendant might be located in California or "foreseeing" an article might cause harm in California does not satisfy the "effects test." <u>Compare Callaway</u>, 125 F. Supp. 2d at 1200 (no personal jurisdiction where defendant did not know plaintiff had its principal place of business in California and was unaware the effects would be felt in California), <u>with</u> <u>Pavlovich v. Superior Court,</u> 109 Cal. Rptr. 2d 909, 918 (Ct. App. 6th Dist. 2001), *petition for review granted*, 36 P.3d 625 (Cal. Dec. 12, 2001) ("effects test" satisfied where defendant knowingly and intentionally caused harm in California).

The "effects test" should not apply to a strict liability intellectual property case because plaintiff never will have to prove that the defendants intentionally caused harm in California. However, assuming the effects test does apply, the plaintiff fails to meet the three prongs. The only intentional action committed by KUEFF was news reporting. Unlike

Pavlovich, KUEFF had no idea their site would be used as a directory to DeCSS sites, nor did they know Global Studios would suffer in California.

> This next sub-TREAT is short because the author is willing to concede this point. We agree completely. Movants have no business arguing about this element just for the sake of argument.

2. Global Studios claim arises out of KUEFF's forum-related activities.

KUEFF does not contest the assertion that to the extent plaintiff has been injured by defendant's commercial activity on its web site, plaintiff would not have suffered the alleged injuries "but for" defendant's activity. KUEFF does not contest the assertion that the cause of action alleged by plaintiff, if valid, arises out of KUEFF's forum-related activities.

3. Exercising personal jurisdiction over KUEFF in California would be unreasonable.

> We have skipped to the conclusion of the memorandum in support.

* * *

CONCLUSION

In light of the above, KUEFF respectfully requests the court to dismiss the complaint for lack of personal jurisdiction.

Sample 2 - Memorandum in Opposition to Motion to Dismiss

UNITED STATES DISTRICT COURT
CENTRAL DISTRICT OF CALIFORNIA
SOUTHERN DIVISION

GLOBAL STUDIOS,	)	
	)	
Plaintiff,	)	
	)	No. SA CV 01-9999 AHS
v.	)	
	)	
KINGSTON UNIVERSITY	)	
ELECTRONIC FREEDOM	)	
FRONTIER, LARRY MULLEN,	)	
LISA ROGERS, MEGHAN MORELY,	)	
and CHRIS HANSEN,	)	
	)	
Defendants.	)	

**PLAINTIFF'S MEMORANDUM IN OPPOSITION TO DEFENDANTS'
FED. R. CIV. P. 12(b)(2) MOTION TO DISMISS FOR LACK OF
PERSONAL JURISDICTION**

> The opponent chose to forego a pre-introduction sentence. This is fine because she communicated all of the required information in the title of this memorandum.

INTRODUCTION

Defendants have asserted that they can enable the theft of Plaintiff's property in California, Plaintiff's home state, yet evade responsibility for the resulting damage because their contacts with that forum were directed over the Internet. Plaintiff serves the public by writing motion pictures to Digital Versatile Disks (DVDs). Defendants, through their

> This introduction is hard hitting and does a good job steering the reader to the opponent's point of view, but it does go a tiny bit overboard. No one would agree that the movie industry "serves the public" by cranking out R-rated DVDs. Otherwise, this section efficiently presents the relevant facts, issues, law, and the policies from the opponent's perspective in a section that flows well.

website, provide access to a means by which Plaintiff's copyrighted material may be stripped from those DVDs. Through maintenance of a continuously accessible website, direction of explicit emails intended to and actually causing injury to Plaintiff, and solicitation and receipt of donations to support their cause, Defendants have purposefully availed themselves of the privileges of conducting activities in California. Plaintiff's suit arises from these contacts, and reasonableness dictates that Plaintiff's and California's interests in attaining jurisdiction over Defendants be obliged. Therefore, assertion of jurisdiction meets the due process requirements of both the California and United States Constitutions and comports with the California Long-Arm statute.

> The facts section below is right on the money. The author has set the stage for his arguments by assembling and emphasizing the most crucial and beneficial facts in a crisply drafted section. This is fine work.

STATEMENT OF FACTS

The viability of Plaintiff's business hinges on the protection of its copyrighted material stored on DVDs, which is provided by a computer program known as Content Scramble System ("CSS"). See Complaint, ¶¶ 10-11. Defendants provide access to a computer program known as DeCSS, the only function of which is to decrypt CSS and allow the pirating of material stored on DVDs. See Complaint, ¶¶ 10-13. Plaintiff filed a complaint with this Court to restrain Defendants from undermining its copyrights and ruining its business. See generally Complaint.

Plaintiff operates its business in California. See Complaint, ¶ 1. Although Defendants have no physical presence in that state, their website is easily accessible to California residents through the Internet, as evidenced by the eighty-five hits the site has received from California viewers. Declaration of Tracy Sensor dated Jan. 4, 2002, at ¶ 5 ("Sensor Dec."). Bolded headings featured on Defendants' website include "Contact us," followed by an invitation to "Subscribe to the newsletter by email, [and] exchange information," and "Donations," followed by a request for credit card information and an assurance that the donations are tax-deductible. See Complaint, Exhibit 1. The first heading has resulted in seven emails from California residents and fifteen reply emails from Defendants, at least two of which accommodated requests for information regarding how DeCSS can be obtained. Declaration of Larry Mullen dated Jan. 8, 2002, at ¶ 6 ("Mullen Dec."). The second heading has induced donations from at least two California residents. Mullen Dec. at ¶ 7. Furthermore, on at least thirty occasions, California residents have downloaded usable copies of DeCSS using only the information on Defendants' website. Declaration of Melanie Smead dated Jan. 12, 2002, at ¶ 3 ("Smead Dec."); Declaration of Zachary Schulman dated Jan. 7, 2002, at ¶ 3 ("Schulman Dec.").

ARGUMENT

> Although the motion to dismiss rule is a procedural rule that can be covered in a one-sentence rule section, as this author did below, this section would be more effective if the author were to write a roadmap to guide the reader to the two major substantive arguments on long arm jurisdiction and due process that immediately follow the procedural rule.

Defendants bring a motion to dismiss Plaintiff's action for "lack of jurisdiction over the person" under Fed. R. Civ. P. 12(b)(2).

> We hope by now it will come as no surprise when we point out that the thesis headings in this memorandum in opposition lack the "because" part. The heading below and those that follow it will not summarize the opponent's points in opposition because they only present a conclusion and do not include the facts and legal principles that support the conclusion.

I. THE CALIFORNIA LONG-ARM STATUTE CONVEYS PERSONAL JURISDICTION OVER DEFENDANTS.

> There were a lot of important rules to present to the reader in this rule section, and the author really did a nice job getting them out in a concise manner. The section flows well in spite of the compacted exposition.

Cal. Civ. Proc. Code sec. 410.10 provides that "A court of this state may exercise jurisdiction on any basis not inconsistent with the Constitution of this state or of the United States." The due process clause of each constitution prohibits the state from "depriving any person of life, liberty, or property, without due process of law." Cal. Const. art. 1, sec. 7; U.S. Const. amend. XIV. Thus, the limits of the state long-arm statute are co-extensive with the limits of federal due process. See Panavision Int. L.P. v. Toeppen, 114 F.3d 1316, 1320 (9th Cir. 1998).

Federal due process permits personal jurisdiction over a defendant in any state with which the defendant has certain minimum contacts, which can be established through contacts that give rise to specific or general jurisdiction. See Helicopteros Nacionales de Columbia, S.A. v. Hall, 466 U.S. 408, 414 (1984). In the present case, Plaintiff claims only specific jurisdiction.

> In text, as opposed to citations, use "Ninth" Circuit not "9th" Circuit.

The 9th Circuit applies a three-prong test to establish specific jurisdiction:

> Specific jurisdiction exists if (1) the defendant(s) has performed some act or consummated some transaction within the forum or otherwise purposefully availed himself of the privileges of conducting activities in the forum, thereby invoking the benefits and protections of state law, (2) the claim arises out of or results from the defendant's forum-related activities, and (3) the exercise of jurisdiction is reasonable.

> The cite to <u>Bancroft</u> below should be a long form cite because this is first appearance of the case in this memorandum. Be careful that when you edit your work you don't delete the first long form cite and wind up using a short form cite the first time the case appears.

See <u>Bancroft</u>, 223 F.3d at 1086; <u>Cybersell, Inc. v. Cybersell, Inc</u>, 130 F.3d 414, 416 (9th Cir. 1997). This memorandum in opposition will address each basis for specific jurisdiction in the order presented above.

A. <u>Defendants purposefully availed themselves of the privileges of conducting activities in California.</u>

> This is the first sub-TREAT of the paper. The author is following the TREAT format to the letter. This makes these complicated arguments more easily understandable to the reader, even if she is not up to speed on jurisdictional issues.

When a defendant's contacts occur over the Internet, purposeful availment is established by measuring the quality and nature of the commercial activity conducted by the defendant over the Internet on a sliding scale to determine if minimum contacts exist. <u>See</u> <u>Cybersell</u>, 130 F.3d at 419; <u>Zippo Mfg. Co. v. Zippo Dot Com, Inc.</u>, 952 F. Supp. 1119, 1124 (W.D. Pa. 1997).

> The author's use of explanatory synthesis in the following explanation section is excellent. He makes his points clearly and uses a lot of authority in a small amount of space. This furthers his arguments very effectively. Our one criticism is that the author uses too many persuasive authorities early in the section when he could have used controlling authorities from the United States Court of Appeals for the Ninth Circuit.

In addition to the mere capacity for interactivity of a defendant's website, actual transactions between the defendant and residents of the forum are required to establish purposeful availment. <u>Compare</u> <u>Digital Control, Inc. v. Boretronics, Inc.</u>, 161 F. Supp. 2d 1183, 1187 (W.D. Wash. 2001) (regardless of nature of website, no purposeful availment until defendant faces and makes choice to dive into forum), <u>with</u> <u>Tech Heads, Inc. v. Desktop Serv. Ctr.</u>, 105 F. Supp. 2d 1142, 1150-51 (D. Ore. 2000) (transaction with forum resident through website was critical to establishing purposeful availment), <u>and</u> <u>Heroes, Inc. v. Heroes Found.</u>, 958 F. Supp. 1, 5 (D.D.C. 1996) (solicitation and receipt of donations through website constituted actual transactions with forum residents and was critical to finding purposeful availment).

It is the quality, not the quantity of transactions that is relevant. <u>See</u> <u>Tech Heads</u>, 105 F. Supp. 2d at 1150 (proper jurisdiction when defendant's contacts with forum included one Internet transaction); <u>Stomp, Inc. v. Neato, L.L.C.</u>, 61 F. Supp. 2d 1074, 1078 (C.D. Cal. 1999) (proper jurisdiction when defendant's contacts with forum were two sales induced by plaintiff).

Although typically reserved for tort cases, the "effects test" has been used as an alternative method to establish purposeful availment in some intellectual property actions. <u>Compare</u> <u>Panavision</u>, 141 F.3d at 1321-22 (effects test appropriate because defendant's registration of plaintiff's trademarks as domain name was akin to a tort), <u>with</u> <u>Cybersell</u>, 130 F.3d at 420 (effects test inapplicable because defendant's posting of a passive website not akin to a tort). Purposeful availment is established through the effects test by showing that a defendant's foreign act was expressly aimed at and had effect in the forum state. <u>See</u> <u>Calder v. Jones</u>, 465 U.S. 783, 791 (1984); <u>Bancroft</u>, 223 F.3d at 1087. Because jurisdiction cannot be predicated on acts with merely foreseeable consequences, the express aiming element requires that the defendant engage in wrongful conduct aimed at entities known

> The author's use of <u>id.</u> in the next citation is improper. <u>Id.</u> only can be used to refer back to a single authority. It cannot follow a citation to two authorities.

to the defendant to be forum residents. <u>Id.</u>

Plaintiffs have two opportunities to prove purposeful availment: either the effects test or the sliding scale analysis will suffice, and if one test is satisfied, the court need not consider the other. <u>See</u> <u>Cybersell</u>, 130 F.3d at 417 (effects test inapplicable, inquiry moved on to sliding scale analysis); <u>Tech Heads</u>, 105 F. Supp. 2d at 1148 (effects test applied but not met, minimum contacts shown by sliding scale test); <u>Bancroft</u>, 223 F.3d at 1088 (purposeful availment analysis ceased when effects test was met).

> Because this application section follows a synthesized explanation section, the author can apply principles of how the law is to interpreted and applied rather than applying cases.

In the present case, the motion picture industry is the exclusive major proponent of the DVD format. Thus, Defendants have expressly targeted Plaintiff, as a member of that industry, by providing access to DeCSS. Defendant's activity is tort-like, causing an injury to Plaintiff in California. Because Defendants' activity has injured Plaintiff in California by enabling at least thirty downloads of DeCSS in that forum, the effects test is both applicable and satisfied.

Even without the effects test, Defendants' minimum contacts with California are shown through the sliding scale analysis. Defendants' activity was facilitated by their website, the interactive nature of which is indicated by the invitations to subscribe to a newsletter, exchange information, and make donations. The emails regarding how to obtain DeCSS sent to known California residents, and the online receipt of donations (privileged as exemptions under California law) from residents, provide the actual transactions with the

> There is no thesis restated as a conclusion in this section, and the argument ends rather abruptly. It always is a good idea to write a thesis restated as conclusion sentence to let the reader know that you are finished with the argument and are moving on to a new point.

forum required to show purposeful availment.

B. Plaintiff's claim arises out of Defendants' forum-related activities.

> This section is amazingly short because there is little to say about this element of the rule, and Defendants conceded the point in the sample memorandum in support provided above.

As Plaintiff's suit would not have arisen but for Defendant's contacts with California, this prong is satisfied. See Bancroft, 223 F.3d at 1088; Panavision, 141 F.3d at 1322.

C. Assertion of specific jurisdiction over Defendants is reasonable.

> Once again, we are skipping the last section.

* * *

CONCLUSION

For the reasons stated above, Plaintiff respectfully requests the court to deny Defendants' motion to dismiss for lack of personal jurisdiction.

Chapter 23

Motions for Summary Judgment

A motion for summary judgment is the ultimate pretrial dispositive motion. After discovery is completed, after all the evidence is uncovered in the case, you are going to challenge your opponent's claims or defenses and state that the facts are clear and the law provides that you are entitled to judgment right here, right now, on one or more or all of your opponent's claims or defenses.

I. FEDERAL RULE OF CIVIL PROCEDURE 56(c)

Federal Rule of Civil Procedure 56(c) governs summary judgment motions in federal court. It states in relevant part:

> The judgment sought shall be rendered forthwith if the pleadings, depositions, answers to interrogatories, and admissions on file, together with the affidavits, if any, show that there is no genuine issue as to any material fact and that the moving party is entitled to a judgment as a matter of law. A summary judgment, interlocutory in character, may be rendered on the issue of liability alone although there is a genuine issue as to the amount of damages.

Many aspects of this complicated rule deserve closer attention.

A. Material facts

The key to the consideration of whether a case (or an issue in a case) is appropriate for summary judgment is an analysis of whether the issue can be resolved as a matter of law without regard to any disputed material fact. You can have disputes over facts, just not material facts. Material facts are those that affect or potentially affect the outcome of the case (or the issue at hand) on the merits.

> *Example:* In a litigation involving the performance of a contract to create a metal sculpture, in which defendant asserts that he lacked the mental capacity to understand the terms of the contract because of his intoxication on the day of the contracting, you probably could have a dispute over the metal content of the sculpture—did it contain titanium or not?— and it would not affect a motion for summary judgment on defendant's defenses to the contract.

435

You could not have a dispute over the number of drinks defendant had before he signed the contract or what his blood alcohol level was on that day because those facts potentially would affect the analysis of his defenses on the merits.

If the dispute over the facts does not affect the outcome (e.g., no matter who is right on the facts, the outcome from those facts would be the same), then the dispute need not defeat summary judgment.

> ➤ *Example:*   If the common law marriage requirement in your state is "cohabitation for over a year," and plaintiff argues that the two lived together for seven years, while defendant argues that it was only five years, these two versions of the facts both meet the one-year requirement, so there is no need to withhold summary judgment because of this dispute.

B. Genuine dispute

The dispute over the facts must be genuine. A party's assertion of the facts (or the meaning of the facts) must be plausible and defensible. You cannot defeat summary judgment just by coming up with some outlandish version or interpretation of the facts that your client is willing to swear to in an affidavit or declaration. (Clients generally will do what you tell them to, and courts know that!) A manifestly frivolous position on the facts will not defeat summary judgment.

The party's position on the facts should not be directly inconsistent with the position it asserted before litigation was initiated or directly contrary to the position asserted earlier in the same litigation. In other words, you should not be allowed to defeat summary judgment simply by contradicting everything you said earlier in the case.

Note that the rule speaks of "pleadings, depositions, answers to interrogatories, and admissions on file, together with the affidavits," as proof of the facts that demonstrate "that there is no genuine issue as to any material fact and that the moving party is entitled to a judgment as a matter of law." Thus, the court looks to the complete record on the facts to determine if there is a genuine dispute. If your client is going to assert that there is a genuine dispute as to the facts, you had better get your story straight early, and repeat it consistently in the case, or it will appear that you are changing factual horses in midstream just for the sake of defeating the summary judgment motion and prolonging the litigation. This tactic should fail.

The affidavits and declarations offered in support of summary judgment must be asserted in good faith, and the witness must be competent (e.g., the witness swearing must have first-hand information of the facts and be able to testify to the same at trial), and not be asserted solely for the purpose of delaying and prolonging the litigation by defeating a valid summary judgment motion. If the judge thinks that you and your client are cooking up affidavits just to confuse the facts and to defeat summary judgment through false factual disputes, you and your client can be sanctioned.

C. The burden shifts

Initially, the movant bears the burden to show that there is no genuine dispute as to any material fact, and that he or she is entitled to judgment as a matter of law. Once that burden is met, however, the burden shifts to the opponent to produce concrete evidence to show that there is a genuine material factual dispute or that judgment is not proper as a matter of law. In other words, if movant presents a properly supported motion with affidavits or declarations showing that there is no dispute, the opponent cannot simply rest on its pleadings and the arguments of its counsel, but must come forth with affidavits and declarations and factual support of its own to show a genuine dispute as to material facts.

D. Judgment must be appropriate as a matter of law

The court must be able to determine from the undisputed facts that judgment is appropriate as a matter of law in favor of one of the parties. Although the movant meets her burden as to the facts, the motion will be denied if the law does not support the movant's position.

Even if the parties think the undisputed facts are complete enough to determine who should win, the court must make the ultimate determination, so even cross-motions for summary judgment can both be denied. The court may disagree and find that there is a genuine dispute over one or more material facts, or the parties failed to raise and stipulate to enough facts to make a determination in the case, or the court may decide that the law is not clear enough to make a decision at this stage before trial.

II. CROSS-MOTIONS FOR SUMMARY JUDGMENT

Occasionally, the local rules require the parties to submit their dispute to the trial court on cross-motions for summary judgment,[1] or the court may request the parties to file cross-motions on some or all of the issues in the case, or the parties may agree to stipulate to a set of facts and submit the case or issues in the case on cross-motions for summary judgment (and the parties hope that they have stipulated to enough facts to determine the issues of the motion). As indicated above, the filing of cross-motions is no guarantee that one of the motions will be granted if the court thinks there are not enough facts in the record to make a determination on the issues.

---

[1] For example, the Local Rules of the U.S. District Court for the Eastern District of Missouri require all appeals from the denial of Social Security benefits to be submitted on cross-motions for summary judgment.

III. STRUCTURE AND FORMAT OF A SUMMARY JUDGMENT MOTION AND OPPOSITION

Like other pretrial motions, a summary judgment motion has the following:

[PRE-INTRODUCTION]
<u>INTRODUCTION</u>
<u>STATEMENT OF FACTS</u>
<u>ARGUMENT</u>
<u>CONCLUSION</u>

In a summary judgment motion, the movant has a strong incentive not to create the appearance of factual disputes. Therefore, if you are the movant, you should not draft the statement of facts in a way that changes the logical meaning of the stipulated facts or the facts that are established in the record. You must exercise good judgment. You have the choice of which facts to highlight by placing them prominently in the section and by phrasing them in the active voice, and which facts to downplay by placing them in obscure locations and by phrasing them in the passive voice. But you should not draw controversial inferences from the stipulated or established facts. There is no room for emotional, argumentative, conclusory rhetoric in the statement of facts of a summary judgment motion. Save that for your discussion of the law and the equities in the case. If you go too far in drafting a statement of facts section that sounds magnificently favorable to your client, you may defeat the whole purpose of summary judgment by making it sound like there is a factual dispute in the case.

The opponent of summary judgment has no incentive to follow the rules stated above. If you are the opponent, you still are bound by the rules of style and good taste, but it is in your favor to create the appearance of a factual dispute, so draft the statement of facts in a way that highlights everything that favors your client.

If you have stipulated with your opponent as to the relevant facts and submitted the same to the court, then you need not offer additional proof in form of "pleadings, depositions, answers to interrogatories, and admissions on file, together with the affidavits (and declarations), if any." If there is no stipulation, then you must support each fact you assert as material and undisputed with the type of proof listed.

An opponent may be asserting its own right to judgment as a matter of law on undisputed facts in a cross motion for summary judgment—"Plaintiff agrees that the facts are not in dispute, and there is no reason for a trial, but plaintiff prevails under the applicable law." Otherwise, the opponent either has to prove that there is a genuine material fact dispute in the case precluding summary judgment, or that movant's arguments about the law are erroneous, whether or not the opponent is also seeking summary judgment at this stage.

We have alluded to what you should ***not*** do to try to defeat summary judgment: do not try to cook up a bunch of bogus affidavits that your hapless client will no doubt endorse. Do not attempt to change factual positions 180 degrees in mid-stream. Do not go back on what you have been stating are the facts and the law since the case began. None of these tactics will do you any good. In addition, do not sit on your complaint and rest on the arguments of counsel and expect the court to give you the benefit of a doubt. If your opponent has made a credible case, then prove up a genuine material factual dispute, and refute the opponent's legal arguments. This is one motion where the court probably will not do your thinking for you.

IV. SAMPLE MOTIONS

Sample 1: Memorandum in Support of Motion for Summary Judgment

---

UNITED STATES DISTRICT COURT
CENTRAL DISTRICT OF CALIFORNIA
SOUTHERN DIVISION

GLOBAL STUDIOS,	)	
	)	
Plaintiff,	)	
	)	No. SA CV 01-9999 AHS
v.	)	
	)	
KINGSTON UNIVERSITY	)	
ELECTRONIC FREEDOM	)	
FRONTIER, LARRY MULLEN,	)	
LISA ROGERS, MEGHAN MORELY,	)	
and CHRIS HANSEN,	)	
	)	
Defendants.	)	

MEMORANDUM IN SUPPORT OF DEFENDANTS' MOTION FOR SUMMARY JUDGMENT

Defendants move this Court pursuant to Fed. R. Civ. P. 56(c) for summary judgment in favor of Defendants on Plaintiff's complaint.

> Movants seeking summary judgment need a hard-hitting introduction, and the introduction that follows gets the job done. It really grabs the reader's attention and brings the whole case into focus. The issues, the facts, the law, and the policies are all introduced in a powerful set of sentences.

INTRODUCTION

As evidenced by the filing of its original complaint, Plaintiff asserts that it is entitled to obstruct the flow of information and ideas from Defendants to the public merely because it does not condone the message of Defendants' communications. Plaintiff's attempt to suppress Defendants' First Amendment right to free speech compels this motion. Plaintiff engages in the motion picture industry by translating motion pictures to digital versatile disks (DVDs). Defendants are members of a student group that operates an informational website featuring an online student newspaper. Along with several other unrelated stories, Defendants recently reported news and information regarding the debate over the use of DeCSS, a computer program that allows users to copy DVD movies. To provide a complete report to the public, Defendants referred to, in plain text without the prefix "www.", the names of a small number of DeCSS-provider sites. Defendants did not create DeCSS, nor did they post DeCSS, or provide a hyperlink to any website containing DeCSS, on their website. Defendants' right to report news and information on their website regarding the DeCSS debate is guaranteed by the First Amendment to the United States Constitution. Although the Government has a substantial interest in protecting copyrights from unauthorized circumvention, the Digital Millennium Copyright Act ("DMCA") is not narrowly tailored to serve this interest because it imposes overbroad speech restrictions that do not withstand constitutional scrutiny. Even if the DMCA is not overbroad, it is unconstitutional as applied to Defendants to the extent that it prevents them from reporting news and information in plain text on their website.

> This statement of facts emphasizes the facts that are the most beneficial for the defendants. For example, it emphasizes that the defendants are students and they are acting as members of the press, which are good facts for the judge to be dwelling on as she reads the motion.

STATEMENT OF FACTS

Plaintiff operates in the motion picture industry by producing and selling motion pictures on the DVD format, which are encoded by a program called Content System Scramble

("CSS"). Stipulation of Facts ("Stip."), ¶ 1, 7. Defendants are members of a student organization that publishes an informational website containing an online newspaper. Id. ¶¶ 2, 9. In this newspaper, Defendants regularly report technology-related stories and events. See Complaint, Exhibit 1. One story reported by Defendants was the debate over the use of DeCSS, a program which bypasses CSS and allows users to copy DVDs. Stip. ¶¶ 8, 10.

In the process of reporting the DeCSS debate, Defendants referred, in plain text, to the names of a small number of websites where DeCSS reportedly was available. See Complaint, Exhibit 1. At no time was the object code or source code for DeCSS available on any part of Defendants' website. Stip. ¶ 12. Furthermore, none of the references to reported DeCSS provider sites included the prefix "www." nor were any of them hotlinked or hyperlinked to those sites. Id. ¶¶ 11, 12.

> We recommend that you start off your summary judgment memorandum with the summary judgment standards. We do not mind the heading chosen for this section because the section should be limited to the presentation of a procedural rule and its interpretive rules, and this heading reveals that information. The placement of this section is faithful to the TREAT format. The reader may not need the refresher, but at least it lets the reader know you are up to speed on things. The first sentence of this section is important because it establishes which jurisdiction's law applies to the case for both substantive and procedural issues.

ARGUMENT

I. LEGAL STANDARDS FOR SUMMARY JUDGMENT.

When a federal court decides a case involving a federal question, federal procedural law is applied. See Benny v. Pipes, 799 F.2d 489, 493 (9th Cir. 1986). Under Rule 56(c) of the Fed. R. Civ. P., summary judgment is permitted if there is "no genuine issue as to any material fact, and the moving party is entitled to judgment as a matter of law." See Anderson v. Liberty Lobby, Inc., 477 U.S. 242, 247-48 (1986); Fazio v. City and County of San Francisco, 125 F.3d 1328, 1331 (9th Cir. 1997). The moving party bears the initial burden of demonstrating the absence of a genuine issue of material fact for trial by showing that there is a lack of evidence to support the non-moving party's case. See Matsushita Elec. Indus. Co. v. Zenith Radio Corp., 475 U.S. 574, 587 (1986). Once the moving party has met its initial burden, the non-moving party must introduce significant probative evidence tending to support the complaint. See Celotex Corp. v. Catrett, 477 U.S. 317, 323 (1986). In the present case, Plaintiff and Defendants have stipulated to all the material facts, and Defendants are entitled to summary judgment as a matter of law.

> Here, the reader jumps into the first substantive rule section. This section really belongs under thesis heading II below. Putting part of the rule section here jumps the gun and steps out of the TREAT format, and it might cause some readers to miss some of movants' most important rules, because they might routinely skip the summary judgment standards section and head for the first substantive argument.

In 17 U.S.C. § 1201(a)(2)(A) (1998), the DMCA provides that:

> No person shall manufacture, import, offer to the public, provide, or otherwise traffic in any technology, product, service, device, component, or part thereof, that is primarily designed or produced for the purpose of circumventing a technological measure that effectively controls access to a work protected under this title.

> The author may be correct about what this next sentence says, but we would quote the second trafficking provision. Statutory rules are too important to gloss over like this.

17 U.S.C. § 1201(b)(1)(A) differs slightly from § 1201(a)(2)(A), but in the instant case the distinction is irrelevant because only the sections' shared language is at issue.

II. THE DMCA DOES NOT SURVIVE A FACIAL CHALLENGE BECAUSE IT IS UNCONSTITUTIONALLY OVERBROAD.

> When you take the trafficking provisions out of this rule section, it becomes a section on the constitutional law issues of the case. This is a nicely drafted section that weaves many explanatory and interpretive rules into the discussion. First Amendment jurisprudence is rich with such rules, and this author makes good use of favorable authorities to set the right public policy tone for the motion. Our one criticism is that the author could have used explanatory synthesis to support all of these points without making the section much longer.

The First Amendment to the United States Constitution states that "Congress shall make no law . . . abridging the freedom of speech or of the press." U.S. Const. amend. I. First Amendment protection of speech does not turn on the popularity or social utility of the ideas and beliefs which it conveys. See New York Times Co. v. Sullivan, 376 U.S. 254, 270 (1964). The freedom of the press is a fundamental personal right that extends to every medium which acts as a vehicle of information. See Branzburg v. Hayes, 408 U.S. 665,

703 (1972). The Internet is one such medium, constituting a vast public forum entitled to full First Amendment protection. See Reno v. A.C.L.U., 521 U.S. 844, 868-70 (1997).

> The insertion of the next paragraph into the rule section is effective as it introduces the first step of a rule based reasoning syllogism that is separate from the syllogism developed by the other paragraphs of this rule section. The other paragraphs of this rule section are devoted to the standards and public policies of the First Amendment. This paragraph introduces a rule defining newspapers. Movants' legal strategy is to characterize its web site as a newspaper. If the internet is a big newspaper (step one), it will be easier for movants' web site to be characterized as a newspaper or part of a newspaper (step two). Movants have found a way to insert rules for two arguments into one rule section without disrupting the flow of the section. It is a shame that movants do not attempt to apply these rules to their own facts.

The Internet is rapidly evolving into a universal newspaper. See Religious Tech. Ctr v. Lerma, 908 F. Supp. 1353 (E.D. Va. 1995). Newspapers constitute important forums for the dissemination of information and expression of opinions and are devoted entirely to expressive activity. See San Diego Comm. Against Registration and the Draft v. Governing Bd. of Grossmont Union High School Dist., 790 F.2d 1471, 1476 (9th Cir. 1985).

When speech restrictions supporting government interests and First Amendment freedoms collide, the risk of non-persuasion rests with the government and not the speaker. See United States v. Playboy Ent. Group, Inc., 529 U.S. 803, 818 (2000). The appropriate level of constitutional scrutiny to be applied to a statute is determined by whether the speech restrictions it imposes are content-based or content-neutral. See City of Erie v. Pap's A.M., 529 U.S. 277, 289 (2000); Turner Broad. Sys., Inc. v. F.C.C., 512 U.S. 622, 642 (1994). A statute is overbroad under the First Amendment if it causes substantially impermissible applications relative to the law's legitimate sweep. See New York v. Ferber, 458 U.S. 747, 771 (1982).

> Movants' first substantive argument begins in sub-section A. Movant has several ways to argue this motion, and starts with the hardest argument first (proving that the DMCA is a content-based restriction on speech). This is a bold move, but it makes the most sense here because it does not sound convincing to start with the argument in subsection B (DMCA is content neutral and subject to "intermediate scrutiny" analysis) and move to a much harder point (if not content neutral, the DMCA is content based and subject to the much harder standard of "strict scrutiny").

A. The DMCA imposes content-based restrictions on speech, which are unconstitutional because they do not satisfy the strict scrutiny standard.

Content-based restrictions on speech are aimed at stifling speech on account of the message it conveys. See Turner 512 U.S. at 642. A restriction is content-neutral if it is justified without reference to the content of speech. See Hill v. Colorado, 530 U.S. 703, 720 (2000).

> This explanation section uses explanatory synthesis very well, but it appears that the author thought that she only could synthesize two cases for each point, which of course is not true. There are many First Amendment cases on point the author could have used to make broader illustrations.

In the First Amendment context, the government's purpose for regulating expressive activity is the controlling consideration in determining if the regulation is content-based or neutral. Compare Boos v. Barry, 485 U.S. 312, 321 (1988) (ban on use of signs to criticize foreign government within certain distance of embassy was attempt to regulate direct impact of message on listeners and was content based), with Renton v. Playtime Theatres, Inc., 475 U.S. 41, 48 (1986) (restriction on placement of adult theater aimed at controlling secondary effects of theater on neighborhood was justified without reference to content of theater's speech).

> Movants are using authorities well in this rule section. They prove that content based restrictions "stifle" speech (see above) and are "presumptively unconstitutional" (see below). These are points that movants want the court to be thinking about as the court evaluates this motion. Although the initial task is to convince the court to find that the DMCA is in fact content based, it doesn't hurt to set the proper tone about content based restrictions in general as movants are doing in this section.

Content-based restrictions are presumptively unconstitutional. See Free Speech Coalition v. Reno, 198 F.3d 1083, 1091 (9th Cir. 1999); Crawford v. Lungren, 96 F.3d 380, 384 (9th Cir. 1996). To defeat this presumption, content-based restrictions must meet a standard of strict scrutiny, which requires that they be narrowly tailored to serve a compelling government interest and employ the least restrictive means possible to serve that interest. See Playboy, 529 U.S. at 813; Sable Communications of California, Inc. v. F.C.C., 492 U.S. 115, 126 (1989).

Statutes placing content-based restrictions on speech conveyed through the Internet, although serving substantial government interests, have been susceptible to overbreadth defects and routinely are struck down. See Reno, 521 U.S. at 875 (content-based federal statute prohibiting communication of indecent material to minors through Internet unduly burdened protected speech of adults and was overbroad); <u>Free Speech Coalition v. Reno</u>, 198 F.3d 1083, 1095 (9th Cir. 1999) (statute failed strict scrutiny because it prohibited protected expression of non-minors and thus was not narrowly tailored).

If a less restrictive means of meeting the government's interest could be at least as effective in serving that interest, the restriction in question does not satisfy strict scrutiny. <u>See</u> <u>Playboy</u>, 529 U.S. at 815 (statute invalidated because targeted blocking of sexually explicit material was less restrictive means of serving government's interest); <u>Sable</u>, 492 U.S. at 130-31 (feasibility of technological means to control minors' access to sexually explicit phone messages provided less restrictive means of serving government's interest).

> Here is where the rubber meets the road: the Second Circuit found the DMCA to be content neutral, not content based. Movants have to convince this court to ignore that persuasive authority.

The anti-trafficking provisions of the DMCA at issue in the present case were recently analyzed in <u>Corley v. Universal City Studios, Inc.</u>, 273 F.3d 429 (2nd Cir. 2001). In that case, the court held that the DMCA was content-neutral, and that it was not unconstitutional because it passed intermediate scrutiny. <u>Id</u>. at 456-58. <u>Corley</u>'s interpretation of the DMCA was erroneous.

Like the defendants in <u>Corley</u>, Defendants in the present case report information to the public regarding the DeCSS debate. The right to communicate this information is ensured by the First Amendment and is not contingent upon government approval. However, the DMCA inhibits this right by restricting Defendants on account of the government's disagreement with its message. The DMCA seeks to prevent Defendants' speech solely because Defendants are talking about DeCSS as opposed to any other non-encryption related computer program. Thus, the DMCA is content-based, and Plaintiff cannot overcome the presumption against the constitutionality of content-based restrictions. As was conceded in <u>Corley</u>, the government has alternative means of serving its interest in preventing unauthorized access to copyrighted materials, which are less speech-restrictive than the blanket prohibitions of the DMCA. <u>Id</u>. at 455. Thus, similar to the statutes in <u>Reno</u> and <u>Free Speech Coalition</u>, the DMCA impermissibly hampers a substantial amount of protected speech and is overbroad.

B. Even if the DMCA is content-neutral, it does not constitute a reasonable time, place, or manner restriction and is thus unconstitutional.

> We are not thrilled with this rule section. It is not obvious that the DMCA is a time, place, manner restriction, so this rule section should have presented rules defining general content neutral restrictions first, and then explained that

> time, place, manner restrictions are a sub-set of the broader group of content neutral restrictions, and devoted its time to proving that the DMCA fits the definition. Instead, this section starts with a veiled presumption that the DMCA is a time, place, manner restriction and spends most of its time explaining the effect of its being a content neutral restriction. Movants have made it harder to persuade the court that the DMCA fits the general definition of a content neutral restriction when they start out with an erroneous presumption that its status is established.

A time, place, or manner restriction of speech is constitutional if it is content neutral, is narrowly tailored to serve a significant government interest, and leaves open ample alternative channels for communication of the information. See Ward v. Rock Against Racism, 491 U.S. 781, 799 (1989); Alameda Books, Inc. v. City of Los Angeles, 222 F.3d 719, 722 (9th Cir. 2000). This analysis of time, place, or manner restrictions varies little, if at all, from an analysis driven by the intermediate scrutiny standard announced in United States v. O'Brien, 391 U.S. 367, 376 (1968). See Clark v. Cmty. for Creative Non-Violence, 468 U.S. 288, 299 (1984).

A restriction meets the intermediate scrutiny standard if it furthers a substantial government interest unrelated to the suppression of free expression, and the incidental restriction on speech is no greater than is essential to further that interest. See O'Brien, 391 U.S. at 376. Interpreting the last element of this analysis, courts have allowed an incidental restriction on speech only to the extent that it does not burden substantially more speech than is necessary to further the relevant government interest. See Turner, 512 U.S. at 662; Ward, 491 U.S. at 799.

> Movants have shifted to explanation now. It is deceptive to start a new section with the word "However," but it is clear that the next two paragraphs employ explanatory synthesis and function as an explanation section.

However, the intermediate level of scrutiny is not satisfied if the regulation provides only ineffective or remote support for the government's purpose. See Lorillard Tobacco Co. v. Reiley, 533 U.S. 525 (2001) (statute forbidding placement of any advertisement for tobacco products lower than five feet from floor did not sufficiently serve government interest of preventing minors from using tobacco); Bolger v. Youngs Drug Products Corp., 463 U.S. 60 (1983) (statute prohibiting unsolicited mailing of contraceptive advertisements did not satisfy intermediate scrutiny test merely because such mailings were potentially offensive).

Restrictions are not narrowly tailored for purposes of intermediate scrutiny if they fail to leave open ample alternative channels of communication of the information. Compare Young v. Am. Mini Theaters, Inc. 427 U.S. 50, 54 (1976) (restriction on place where adult films could be displayed was upheld because it did not ban the form of expression altogether), with Schad v. Mount Ephraim, 452 U.S. 61, 70 (1981) (purported content-neutral restriction struck down because it imposed total ban on adult theaters).

> Proper use of explanatory synthesis makes for crisp, effective application sections, such as this one.

In the present case, the government has a substantial interest in preventing unauthorized access to copyrighted materials. However, the DMCA is not narrowly tailored to serving that interest because it leaves open no reasonable alternative means for Defendants to communicate their message. The DMCA closes off to Defendants the entire medium of expression offered by the Internet, and in so doing burdens substantially more speech than is necessary to serve the government's interest. As was mentioned above, the DMCA prohibits every means by which Defendants might communicate their message through that medium.

> The second paragraph of this application section is a little unusual, because it sounds like a new explanation section is beginning. But, in fact, the author is making clever use of Corley, the one authority that is closest on the facts to the case at hand, even though this case goes against movants' position in the instant case. Movants' use of Corley and the legislative history cited here is effective, and it is not too distracting in the application section even though it might have been included in the explanation section.

The trial court in Corley was aware of the likelihood that the DMCA burdens substantially more speech than is necessary to serve the government's interest, so the court modified the O'Brien standard to limit the DMCA's linking prohibition. See Corley, 273 F.3d at 456. The trial court's concern with the overbreadth of the DMCA also is evident in its discussion of the legislative history of the DMCA, as there was disagreement in the history over whether the House Commerce Committee's version of the statute, which was written to cure substantial overbreadth defects in the original version, adequately balanced copyright protection with First Amendment rights. See H.R. Rep. No. 105-586 (additional views of Reps. Klug and Boucher). This judicial and Congressional concern further

> There is no thesis restated as a conclusion in this section. Indeed, this section ends too abruptly. At least one sentence is missing that would conclude the thought expressed in this paragraph, such as, "Therefore, the DMCA fails intermediate scrutiny for failing to leave open ample alternate channels for Defendant's communication."

indicates demonstrates the overbreadth of the DMCA.

III. EVEN IF THE DMCA IS NOT FACIALLY OVERBROAD, IT IS UNCONSTITUTIONAL AS APPLIED TO PLAINTIFF.

> If you are keeping score, this is movants' third major argument. This one deviates from the TREAT format in that this section lacks a coherent rule section, explanation section, and application section. Rules are evident, and application is evident, but the structure is blended. Nevertheless, this section does make a positive impact on the reader in a small amount of space.

Trafficking in circumvention devices on the Internet may take the form of linking. See Corley, 273 F.3d at 456; DVD Copy Control Ass'n v. McLaughlin, No. CV 786804, 2000 WL 48512 at *4 (Cal. Super. Ct. Jan. 18, 2000). Linking is defined as the programming of a particular point on a screen to transfer the user to another web page when the point, called a hyperlink, is clicked. See Universal City Studios, Inc. v. Remeirdes, 111 F. Supp. 2d 321, 324 (S.D.N.Y. 1998), aff'd sub nom Corley, 273 F.3d at 456.

The DeCSS debate underpinning the present case has surfaced in court before, and there is disagreement on how to interpret the First Amendment rights of persons linking to DeCSS-provider sites. Compare McLaughlin, 2000 WL 48512 at *4 (links are the mainstay of the Internet, and a website owner cannot be held liable for the content of the sites to which it links), and DVD Copy Control Ass'n v. Bunner, 113 Cal. Rptr. 2d 338, 340 (Ct. App. 6th Dist. 2001) (review granted) (injunction prohibiting posting, and linking by inference, of DeCSS on website violated defendant's First Amendment rights), with Corley, 273 F.3d at 456 (linking prohibition is justified because it pertains only to non-speech component of hyperlink).

The court in Corley, analyzing this issue in the context of the DMCA, held that linking to DeCSS provider sites constituted offering DeCSS to the public or providing or otherwise trafficking in DeCSS in violation of the DMCA. See Corley, 273 F.3d at 455-58. However, Corley is distinguishable from the present case in two fundamental respects. First, the holding of Corley relied upon that court's finding that the statute was content-neutral because the DMCA regulates only the non-speech, functional component of hyperlinks. Id. at 456-58.

In contrast, the website maintained by Defendants in the present case contains only plain, non-hyperlinked textual references to the names of a small number of DeCSS-provider sites. This plain text contains no functional component. If a viewer were to click on one of these references, nothing would happen. Furthermore, Defendants chose not to attach the prefix "www." to the names of the DeCSS-provider sites. Thus, even if a visitor to Defendants' website were to "cut and paste" one of the these names into the URL text box and then instruct the computer to find the site, the viewer would be transported nowhere. It can be inferred that the lack of functionality of plain text was the source of the <u>Corley</u> court's apparent unwillingness to extend its linking prohibition to a plain text, non-hyperlinked list of DeCSS-provider sites. <u>See</u> David A. Peteys, <u>The Freedom to Link?</u>, 25 Seattle U. L. Rev. 287, 334 (2001).

The second distinction between <u>Corley</u> and the present case is that the defendants in <u>Corley</u>, by posting DeCSS on their own website and then creating several links to DeCSS-provider sites (an act of self-styled "electronic civil disobedience"), acted for the express purpose of disseminating DeCSS. <u>See</u> <u>Corley</u>, 273 F.3d at 442. By contrast, the Defendants in the instant case used plain text from which the prefix "www." was excluded. This confirms that Defendants' intent in using these references was merely to convey information as part of their report on the DeCSS debate, and was not to encourage the dissemination of DeCSS.

Further weakening the precedential value of <u>Corley</u> is that court's initial pronouncement that, due to the novelty of applying First Amendment law in the digital age, the court was subscribing to an evolutionary approach, favoring a narrow holding to allow the law to mature on a case-by-case basis. <u>Id</u>. at 445. These fundamental distinctions between <u>Corley</u> and the present case, along with the express admonition of that court that its holding be treated narrowly, evidence the fact that the DMCA cannot be extended to cover the activity of Defendants in the present case.

CONCLUSION

For the reasons stated above, Defendants respectfully request the Court to grant their motion for summary judgment on Plaintiff's complaint.

Sample 2: Memorandum in Opposition to Motion for Summary Judgment

---

UNITED STATES DISTRICT COURT
CENTRAL DISTRICT OF CALIFORNIA
SOUTHERN DIVISION

GLOBAL STUDIOS,	)	
	)	
Plaintiff,	)	
v.	)	
	)	
KINGSTON UNIVERSITY	)	No. SA CV 01-9999 AHS
ELECTRONIC FREEDOM	)	
FRONTIER, an unincorporated association,	)	
LARRY MULLEN, LISA ROGERS	)	
MEGHAN MORELY, and CHRIS	)	
HANSEN,	)	
Defendants.	)	

PLAINTIFF'S MEMORANDUM IN OPPOSITION TO DEFENDANTS' MOTION FOR SUMMARY JUDGMENT

Plaintiff Global Studios, in opposition to Defendants' Motion for Summary Judgment, states as follows:

> The introduction below is engaging and informative. It works in the applicable legal standards by its inclusion of key legal terms ("trafficking," "functional speech," "least restrictive means," "government interest"), and introduces the public policy theme of the case through terms such as "piracy" and "hackers."

INTRODUCTION

Defendants are members of an organization dedicated to circumventing technological access control measures and promoting piracy on the World Wide Web. The organization, masking its illegal activity in free speech rhetoric, wants the court to believe Internet trafficking cannot constitutionally be punished. However, the Defendants' web site provides hackers with instantaneous access to instruments like DeCSS that are used to bypass CSS, copy the content of DVDs, and play the duplicates on unlicensed devices. By prohibiting trafficking, the Digital Millennium Copyright Act ("DMCA") is targeting the "functional" aspect of speech and is not burdening more speech than necessary. The prohibitions are the least restrictive means of advancing the government's interest in preventing DVD duplication and copyright infringement. If hacker sites are not prevented from linking users to this software, the motion picture, music, and publishing industry will be in grave danger. Defendants' Motion for Summary Judgment should not be granted as a matter of law.

> This facts section is effective because it uses loaded terms ("hackers," "instantaneously . . . access the decryption sites," and "pirates") and advances the cause of the plaintiff by telling a very pro-plaintiff story.

STATEMENT OF FACTS

Defendants operate a web site "dedicated to maintaining a free and open electronic frontier." Complaint, Exhibit 1. The organization is funded through donations by hackers and people looking to circumvent various copyright laws. Declaration of Melanie Smead dated Jan. 12, 2002, ¶ 4 ("M.S. Dec"). Defendants' site provides a directory of web addresses where DeCSS is downloadable. See Stipulation of Facts ¶ 9 ("Stip."). The addresses are listed so a user instantaneously can access the decryption sites by pasting the addresses into the locator box of an Internet browser and adding the prefix www. See Stip. ¶ 5. All references to these sites have been made with knowledge of their content. See Stip. ¶ 10. In fact, through several e-mail conversations, members of the defendants' organization directed hackers to sites where the software was located. Complaint, Exhibit 1. DeCSS allows pirates to copy the content of DVDs and to distribute the duplicates throughout the world without making payments to the lawful owners, like Global Studios. See Stip ¶ 8.

> It is a good idea to start off a summary judgment memorandum with the summary judgment standards even if you are opposing the motion. The reader will know you are up to speed on the law.

ARGUMENT

I. SUMMARY JUDGMENT STANDARDS

When federal law applies, a federal court will apply federal procedural law. New SD, Inc. v. Rockwell Int'l Corp., 79 F.3d 953, 955 (9th Cir. 1996). Under Rule 56(c), Fed. R. Civ. P., summary judgment is appropriate only if there is no genuine issue of material fact and the moving party is entitled to judgment as a matter of law. Anderson v. Liberty Lobby, Inc., 477 U.S. 242, 247 (1986). The moving party bears the burden of demonstrating the absence of a genuine issue of material fact. Celotex Corp. v. Catrett, 477 U.S.

317, 323 (1986). This burden will not be satisfied by the mere existence of a scintilla of evidence in support of the movant's position; there must be evidence on which the jury could reasonably find for the movant. <u>Anderson</u>, 477 U.S. at 266. All evidence must be construed in the light most favorable to the non-moving party. <u>Gardner v. Nike, Inc.</u>, 279 F.3d 774, 777 (9th Cir. 2002). If the movant has met this burden, the non-moving party must then set forth facts showing that there is a genuine issue for trial. Fed. R. Civ. P. 56(e). A genuine issue exists when the evidence is such that a reasonable jury could find for the non-movant. <u>K. Villiariamo v. Aloha Island Air, Inc.</u>, 281 F.3d 1054, 1060 (9th Cir. 2002).

> This next sentence is important. You should inform the court whether you are going to challenge movant's rendition of the facts and the law, or just the law.

Plaintiff and the Defendants have entered into a stipulation of facts; however, there are genuine issues of fact that remain in this matter, and Defendants are not entitled to summary judgment as a matter of law.

> This first substantive TREAT section lays out the major rules. Remember to organize your rules in the proper order of authority, stating constitutional rules first, then statutory rules, then rules created by cases, including interpretive rules.

II. DEFENDANTS' MOTION FOR SUMMARY JUDGMENT SHOULD BE DENIED BECAUSE THE DMCA IS CONSTITUTIONAL ON ITS FACE

According to U.S. Const. amend. I, "Congress shall make no law . . . abridging the freedom of speech, or of the press." One of the "trafficking" provisions of the DMCA, 17 U.S.C. § 1201(a)(2) (1998), states:

> No person shall . . . offer to the public, provide, or otherwise traffic in any technology, product, service, device, component, or part thereof, that— (A) is primarily designed or produced for the purpose of circumventing a technological measure that effectively controls access to a work protected under this title;

Another provision, 17 U.S.C. § 1201(b)(1) (1998), states:

> No person shall . . . offer to the public, provide, or otherwise traffic in any technology, product, service, device, component, or part thereof, that—(A) is primarily designed or produced for the purpose of circumventing protection afforded by a technological measure that effectively protects a right of a copyright owner under this title in a work or a portion thereof.

The courts have a duty to insulate all individuals from the "chilling effect" upon First Amendment freedoms generated by vagueness and overbreadth. <u>Walker v. City of Birmingham</u>, 388 U.S. 307, 345 (1967).

> This next section starts with a useful roadmap sentence, then succinctly disposes of several issues in reduced TREAT discussions. This was an efficient use of space because none of these issues were dispositive, but each deserves at least this much attention.

This memorandum briefly will discuss Defendants' likely claim that their web site is a newspaper, followed by an analysis of the constitutionality of the DMCA provisions. Plaintiff concedes that the Internet is a public forum. <u>Planned Parenthood of the Columbia/Williamette Inc. v. Am. Coalition of Life Activists</u>, 244 F.3d 1007, 1019 (9th Cir. 2000). A "newspaper" is a medium for the dissemination of news of passing events printed and distributed at short but regular intervals. <u>United States v. Kelly</u>, 328 F.2d 227, 234 (6th Cir. 1964). A newspaper contains a broad range of news on all subjects and activities and is not limited to any specific subject matter. 17 U.S.C.A. § 202.3 6(f)(2) (2002). Defendants' web site does not meet this definition because it reports exclusively on Internet free speech issues.

Even if considered a newspaper, Defendants' web site would not be entitled to heightened protection from the provisions of the DMCA. Laws of general application do not offend the First Amendment simply because their enforcement against the press has incidental effects on its ability to report the news. <u>Cohen v. Cowles Media Co.</u>, 501 U.S. 663, 669 (1991). The press may not publish copyrighted material without obeying the copyright laws; it has no special privilege to invade the rights and liberties of others. <u>Id</u>.

> Now, we are getting into the meat of the argument. The short, crisp initial paragraphs make this section flow very well. Remember that you need not try to cram the entire rule section into one paragraph. This memorandum in opposition breaks the rules into several paragraphs, and it works very well.

A. Sections 1201 (a)(2) and (b)(1) of the DMCA are content-neutral regulations that are constitutional on their face.

> Notice how the opponent starts with a general definition of content neutral regulations and moves on to explain the definition and apply it to the facts of this case. Compare this to movants' sub-section II(B) above that presumes that the DMCA is a time, place, manner restriction and spends

> most of its time discussing the effect of its being a content
> neutral regulation. Of the two, the opponent's discussion of
> this topic is much more effective.

Restrictions targeting the "functional" aspect of expressive activity are "content-neutral." United States v. O'Brien, 391 U.S. 367, 377 (1968). The principle inquiry in determining content-neutrality is whether the government has adopted regulation of speech because of disagreement with the message it conveys. Ward v. Rock Against Racism, 491 U.S. 781, 791 (1989). The purpose of a content-neutral restriction can be justified without reference to the content of the message; however, the mere assertion of a content-neutral purpose may not be enough to save a law which, on its face, discriminates based on content. Turner Broadcasting Sys., Inc. v. F.C.C., 512 U.S. 622, 643 (1994).

Expressive activity, whether oral or written or symbolized by conduct, may be subject to reasonable time, place, and manner restrictions. Clark v. Cmty. for Creative Non-Violence, 468 U.S. 288, 293 (1984). Such restrictions are permissible so long as they are content-neutral, are narrowly tailored to serve a significant government interest, and leave open ample alternative channels of communication. Madsen v. Women's Health Center, 512 U.S. 753, 791 (1994).

A content-neutral regulation of expressive conduct that burdens speech incidentally will be sustained if it furthers an important governmental interest that is unrelated to the suppression of free expression and the incidental restriction on alleged First Amendment freedoms is no greater than is essential to the furtherance of that interest. O'Brien, 391 U.S. at 377.

To satisfy this intermediate scrutiny standard, a regulation need not be the least speech-restrictive means of advancing the government's interests. Turner Broadcasting Sys., Inc., 512 U.S. at 642-43. The means chosen just cannot burden substantially more speech than necessary to further the government's legitimate interest. Id. at 662.

> Here, the author makes a seamless transition to the ex-
> planation section. The author's use of explanatory synthesis
> is natural and informative.

Courts find that a regulation is content-neutral when people can determine whether the regulation applies to them without looking at the content of the speech. Compare Sable Communications v. F.C.C., 492 U.S. 115, 119 (1989) (prohibition on indecent interstate commercial telephone messages was not content-neutral because applicability depended on the content of the speech); with Ward, 491 U.S. at 791 (1989) (sound amplification guideline is content-neutral because it has nothing to do with content of the noise); and Clark, 468 U.S. at 294 (prohibition on sleeping in Lafayette park content-neutral because it does not consider the message presented).

Whether time, place, or manner restrictions meet the requirement of narrow tailoring depends on how effectively the government interest would be achieved in their absence. See United States v. Albertini, 472 U.S. 675, 689 (1985) (legislation making it unlawful for person to reenter military base after being barred was narrowly tailored where purpose of protecting government property would be achieved less effectively in its absence); Clark, 468 U.S. at 297 (prohibition on sleeping in Lafayette Park no greater than necessary because park would be exposed to more harm without the restriction). However, courts will not permit regulations that prevent a person from all reasonable or effective methods of communicating a particular message. See Frisby v. Schultz, 487 U.S. 474, 483 (1988) (ordinance banning picketing in front of a residence constitutional on its face because it allowed other means of communication such as telephone or mail contact with residents); Grayned v. City of Rockford, 408 U.S. 104, 111-12 (1972) (provisions that forbid noisy or diversionary activity that disrupts normal school activity left open ample alternative of peaceful picketing).

A burden on speech is no greater than essential under the O'Brien standard so long as the provisions are proportionally related to the end the legislation was designed to serve. See Council of Los Angeles v. Taxpayers of Vincent, 466 U.S. 789, 808-810 (1984) (complete prohibition of all signs on public property was necessary because the targeted "evil," visual blight, rendered each sign "evil"); Turner Broadcasting Sys., 520 U.S. at 215-16 (modest effects on free speech in the telecommunications industry permissible where burden imposed by the must-carry provisions was congruent to the benefits they afford).

The Supreme Court recognizes that the time, place, and manner test is essentially no different than the O'Brien test, which applies to regulations that incidentally burden speech. See Madsen, 512 U.S. at 791 (1994) (recognizing that the difference between the standards is too subtle for the Court to describe, yet acknowledging the O'Brien test is stricter); Ward, 491 U.S. at 798 (conceding that there is little, if any, difference between the tests).

> After doing a careful job synthesizing cases in the explanation section, the opponent can make the following application section short and to-the-point, which makes it all the more powerful and useful to the reader.

The DMCA "trafficking" provisions are content-neutral on their face because they can be justified without regard to the content of the trafficker's speech. Congress's purpose in enacting these provisions was to counter the threat of devices that enable pirates to reproduce and distribute DVDs at no cost. See H.R. Rep. No. 105-551. pt. 2, at 25 (1998). The content of the trafficker's message was irrelevant to the government's purpose. Congress has a significant interest in protecting the motion picture industry from copyright infringement. The growth of DeCSS on the Internet creates copyright problems, reduces DVD sales, and counters the utility of CSS.

Whether the regulations are assessed under the time, place, and manner test or the O'Brien test makes little difference. The statute is constitutional under both. Preventing copyright infringement is done most effectively by targeting people providing circumvention devices. Absent the DMCA, like the ordinance in Clark, the government's interest would not be effectively achieved. Also, ample alternatives for communication exist. Those who wish to promote DeCSS may speak in the print media, on the radio, or in many other contexts. They just cannot offer the DeCSS to the public. Each provision of the statute is directed at protecting the motion picture industry, which in light of developments such as the Internet and "Napster," has become such a substantial and compelling government interest that any incidental burdens on

> There is no thesis restated as a conclusion here. It would be useful to draft a summary of the many points made in this long sub-TREAT, such as, "The DMCA is content neutral because it regulates conduct, not speech, and it is narrowly tailored to further the substantial government interest of protecting the property of the DVD producing industry; therefore, it is constitution under the intermediate scrutiny analysis."

speech created by the DMCA are likely to be minimal in relation to this interest.

> This next section presents an alternative argument. The law in this area lays out several avenues movants can follow to victory, and the opponent must address and refute each one. For the opponent, the argument in sub-section A is far superior to the argument in sub-section B, so the opponent chose to defend the easier position (content neutral—intermediate scrutiny) first and the harder position (content based—strict scrutiny) second.

B. Even if the regulations are content-based, they still are constitutional.

Even if the DMCA is a content based restriction, it still passes muster under the First Amendment. Under the strict scrutiny test, content-based restrictions on speech are permissible if they serve compelling state interests by the least restrictive means available. Sable Communications, 492 U.S. at 126.

When an alternative is available that would effectively further the government's interest without being so burdensome on speech, a content-based restriction is unconstitutionally overbroad. Compare Reno v. A.C.L.U., 521 U.S. 844, 879 (1997) (legislation prohibiting "patently offensive" communications from transmission through interactive computer service to minors deemed unconstitutional because exceptions for messages with educational value could be made); and Sable Communications, 492 U.S. at 128 (prohibition of indecent dial-a-porn messages unconstitutional because credit card and scrambling rules represented a "feasible and effective" way to serve the government's compelling interest in protecting children); with Denver Area Educ. Telecomm. Consortium, Inc. v. F.C.C., 518 U.S. 727, 747 (1996) (provision permitting cable operator to prohibit patently offensive or indecent materials is constitutional because effective alternatives would require an all-out ban on such materials in order to advance the government's interest in protecting children).

The regulations proscribed by the DMCA are the least restrictive means to protect the motion picture industry from copyright infringement. The Defendants may propose exceptions for educational purposes. While a protection scheme with educational exceptions would be less restrictive, it would be ineffective in furthering the government interest in protecting the motion picture industry. The majority of people who obtain DeCSS are not going to use it for educational purposes, but many would be happy to pretend that their piracy was undertaken for these purposes. By allowing such exceptions, the courts would be opening the gates for DVD duplication, defeating the purpose of regulation.

> Once again, there is no thesis restated as conclusion at the end of this sub-TREAT. By switching the last sentence with the second-to-last sentence, and rephrasing the second-to-last sentence to read, "By allowing the exceptions proposed by Defendants, the courts would be opening the gates for DVD duplication, defeating the purpose of regulation," the opponent could have had a perfectly appropriate thesis restated as conclusion at the end of this section.

Unlike those in <u>Sable Communications</u>, the alternatives here are not feasible and effective.

III. DEFENDANTS' MOTION FOR SUMMARY JUDGMENT SHOULD BE DENIED BECAUSE THE DMCA PROVISIONS ARE CONSTITUTIONAL AS APPLIED TO THE DEFENDANTS

> The last section of the opponent's memorandum refutes yet another alternative avenue that is open to the movant. We will skip it and move to the conclusion.

* * *

<u>CONCLUSION</u>

In light of the above, Global Studios respectfully requests the court to deny Defendants' motion for summary judgment.

Chapter 24

Appellate Advocacy: Appeals, Writs, Standards of Review

This chapter discusses appeals and appellate advocacy. It examines the appellate process, types of appeals and appellate writs that exist, the timing of the various types of appeals, and the concept of standard of review. Lastly, it will discuss the procedures for the compilation and use of the record on appeal.

I. INTRODUCTION TO THE APPELLATE PROCESS

An appeal is the action taken by the non-prevailing or aggrieved litigant in a litigation or other adversarial matter. The appeal is made to a higher level court, usually a court of appeals or the court of last resort, but sometimes a trial level court can hear an appeal from an administrative agency, arbitral body, or a lower level trial court (for example, a federal bankruptcy court, federal tax court, or a state associate circuit court or magistrate court). The non-prevailing party takes an appeal when it believes that errors were committed during the course of the litigation by the judge, and sometimes by the jury. The errors assigned might involve the interpretation of the governing law, the application of the law to the facts, the finding of facts, or a procedural ruling before or during trial. The non-prevailing party will look for any way possible to reverse the outcome.

A. It is hard to win on appeal.

It is important to note that no matter what court you are in, it is very difficult to win on appeal. Most appeals fail, and in some jurisdictions, the vast majority of appeals fail. It is difficult to convince a higher court to overturn the determinations and actions of a lower court. Therefore, the first job of an advocate in a situation presenting a potential appeal is to counsel your client that most appeals fail, and that statistically there is a better than even chance (or worse) that her appeal will fail. Then you can review the potential errors that might be asserted in the appeal and see if there are grounds to reverse the lower court that make the risk worth taking.

B. Quality is much better than quantity.

When evaluating the possible errors committed by the lower court, quality is far more important than quantity. In other words, you will do much better if there is one horrible, unforgivable error you can point to, rather than a dozen somewhat troublesome errors that might be raised. Appellate courts are sensitive to the tactic of certain litigators to throw up as many assertions of error as they can think of, hoping that one will stick and cause the case to be overturned. This is a tactic of desperation, not of effective advocacy. A quantity of "also ran" errors or legal arguments on the errors also can drown out the effectiveness of any of the better allegations and arguments you may have. So, the second piece of advice we will give is to limit yourself to the most important and egregious errors and arguments in support of reversal and assert as few of these as possible.

II. TYPES OF APPEALS AND APPELLATE WRITS

A. Appeal after a final judgment

The normal channel of appeal is from a final judgment entered in the lower court. 28 U.S.C. § 1291; Fed. R. App. P. 4. Everyone has the right to take this kind of appeal, once. Timing is critical: the appeal must be made within a certain period of time after the final judgment in the case is "entered," and entered can mean "issued" (signed by the trial judge) or entered on the docket, so be sure to check and be certain what it means in your jurisdiction. If you are late, the appeals court is deprived of jurisdiction. See United States v. Robinson, 361 U.S. 220 (1960); Fed. R. App. P. 3, Advisory Committee Notes to 1967 adoption. The court cannot simply excuse your mistake.

The "notice of appeal" required to be filed by Fed. R. App. P. 3 and 4 is important. It triggers the appeal and identifies what exactly it is that you are appealing from—a summary judgment or other order disposing of some issues and claims earlier in the case, a verdict and judgment after trial, the granting or denial of a post-trial motion, or all or some of the above. It is not necessarily sufficient or accurate simply to state that you appeal from the final judgment in the case.

Although each litigant is entitled to one appeal as of right, it still must be noted that few of these appeals succeed. You may get in the door easily enough, but you may soon be walking out that same door empty-handed. There are ways to try to improve your odds: pick your appeals carefully, only challenge the most important errors, and only raise the strongest legal arguments in support of reversal. Beyond that, follow the advice on the drafting of briefs and the planning, preparation for, and execution of oral argument that will be discussed in the next two chapters.

B. Interlocutory appeals

The next type of appeal in order of frequency (going down the scale to remedies that are less frequently available) is the interlocutory appeal, which in federal court is governed by 28 U.S.C. § 1292. "Interlocutory" means that the appeal happens prior to a final judgment in the case. A final judgment is one that disposes of *all* claims of *all* the parties in the case, damages and all. That can take a while, especially in a multi-party, multi-claim case, and litigants do not necessarily want to go that far and spend that much money just to have someone take an appeal from the final judgment and show that certain interlocutory decisions were wrong, and then the case has to be done over. So, if a legal issue is resolved by the trial court in the middle of a case, not as part of the final disposition of all of the claims and defenses, and that determination of the issue will or may have a tremendous effect on one party's or both parties' prosecution of the case from that point forward, one or more parties might ask the trial court, "May we please find out what the appellate court thinks about this issue before we go further in this case?"

Both sides may have an interest in taking the interlocutory appeal. While the side that lost the point might feel totally handcuffed or crippled by the decision, the other side might think they got a good ruling but are not sure it will hold up on the appeal from a final judgment in the case, thus creating the potential that any judgment in the case will be overturned later on. A reversed judgment and a new trial would not be a good use of the client's litigation budget. So, although it is unusual for the party that prevailed on the point to join in the request for an interlocutory appeal, it is not unheard of, or the prevailing party might simply fail to oppose the request very strenuously.

All the party or parties can do is ask; no one has a right to an interlocutory appeal. Whether you get an interlocutory appeal may depend as much on the personality and background experiences of the trial judge (both in private practice and on the bench) as it does on your authority supporting the request. Some trial judges are neutral to the request, or they at least respect the argument that a lot of time and money could be wasted if the appeal is not granted. Other trial judges hate delay, or have been disappointed in the past by an interlocutory appeal that dragged one of the judge's case out for years and years, making the judge decidedly unfriendly to the request.

In any event, even if the trial judge approves the request and certifies the point of law for interlocutory appeal, the appeals court still can say, "No," under Fed. R. App. P. 5. This happens less often than a trial judge's actually agreeing to an interlocutory appeal, so once you are over the hurdle of the trial court's certification, the court of appeals part of the process should not cause you to lose too much more sleep.

C. Extraordinary writs – writs of mandamus, writs of prohibition

The most extraordinary way to obtain review of a lower court's determination is to petition the appeals court to issue a prerogative writ quashing or reversing the lower court's action. The writs most commonly requested in general civil practice are the writs of mandamus and writs of prohibition.[1] They are called "extraordinary" because it is an extraor-

---

[1] Other writs are the Writ of Habeas Corpus, demanding the production of some person from captivity or confinement, Writ of Quo Warranto, addressed to quash a continuing exercise of unlawful authority, and Writ of Certiorari, which literally refers to a higher court's order to a lower court to produce a certified copy of the record in a case for review of the proceedings, but has come to refer to any higher court's, but especially the United State's Supreme Court's, exercise of discretionary jurisdiction to review the determinations of a lower court or adjudicatory body.

dinary event when one of these requests is granted. The action of the lower court must be extraordinarily bad, the evidence of the errors and the legal support used to make the challenge must be extraordinarily strong, and the appellate court must be extraordinarily moved by your petition in order to entertain the writ. It is a grave task to chastise the actions of a lower court judge in this way, and the writ will not lightly be granted.

There is no specific time frame in which to bring the request for the writ—you can make the petition "as needed" in a case whenever the court performs an unlawful act or exceeds its powers in an unlawful manner. You should of course resist the temptation to request a writ except when faced with the most egregious mistakes of a judge. The judge you challenge is made aware of your request for the issuance of the writ and may take this challenge to her judicial action as a personal attack on her abilities and good judgment. This perception is unfortunate for at least two reasons: the chilling effect of the desire not to step on the judge's toes probably keeps attorneys from filing a petition for a writ in cases where the issuance of the writ might be warranted, and when an attorney is driven to make the request in good faith, there is a very real possibility that the attorney's future relationship with the judge who was "brought up on a writ" by the attorney may suffer in the instant case or others, whether or not the writ is actually issued.

"Mandamus," which literally can be translated as, "We command," is directed to a judge who has undertaken an illegal action or failed to take a required action, or has taken away rights of a party in an unlawful way. See Black's Law Dictionary 866 (5th ed. 1979); Bryan A. Garner, A Dictionary of Modern Legal Usage 546 (2d ed. 1995); David Mellinkoff, Mellinkoff's Dictionary of American Legal Usage 395-96 (1992). It basically is directed to cure an abuse of judicial power—a refusal to do the right thing for a party, or an insistence on doing the wrong thing. The writ, if granted, commands the inferior judge to restore the rights, perform the required duty, do the right thing, or undo the unlawful act.

"Prohibition" is directed to a judge who has exceeded his or her lawful authority and jurisdiction. Traditionally, it was intended to stop a judge from usurping jurisdiction (i.e., control) over an action or a party or the subject matter of a suit that was beyond the court's jurisdiction. Black's Law Dictionary at 1091; Garner, supra at 700-01; Mellinkoff, supra at 513.

In different jurisdictions, the meaning of the two writs has become blurred, see, e.g., Fed. R. App. P. 21(a)(1); Ill. S. Ct. Rule 381, or it may be more precise to say that the terms sometimes are used as if they were interchangeable. "Prohibition" might be used to cure a number of abuses in one jurisdiction, but in another jurisdiction the same abuses would be cured by "mandamus." Research the law and local practice of your jurisdiction to determine which writ is appropriate. At present, the differences between the two writs largely are academic.

Because the two writs are extraordinary, a litigant needs very good justification for the granting of the writ. You must strive to find the clearest authority that says what the judge did is absolutely wrong *and* reversible error. The best authority to cite is a case from the immediately higher appellate court or the highest court of the applicable jurisdiction that issues a writ of mandamus or prohibition to curb the **same** conduct that the judge did in your case. Next best is an opinion from one of these courts granting the writ in a similar situation. Next best after that is an opinion describing the conduct as reversible error. If you have to go outside your own line of judicial authority for support, generally speaking, the chances that the writ will be issued are much diminished. If you can come up with four or five examples from other appellate courts where the writ was issued to quash the same action when taken by judges in different jurisdictions, you may squeak by with that, but citation to controlling authority is far superior.

In federal court, under the Federal Rules of Appellate Procedure, Rule 21, the writ process involves the following: the aggrieved litigant in the United States District Court petitions the United States Court of Appeals to issue the writ. The legal document it files is called a petition for a writ of mandamus or prohibition. If the Court of Appeals does not believe the petition is meritorious, it will deny the writ, with or without detailed explanation. But if the Court of Appeals believes that the petition has merit, it will order the nominal respondent—the **district court judge**—to respond. While this is the technical form, the true substance is that the opponent of the petitioner responds in the judge's stead and raises the arguments in support of the judge's action that the judge presumably would raise. The district court judge theoretically could file her own response. After this round of briefing, if the appeals court still agrees with the petitioner's charges, it will issue the writ.

If the petitioner fails and the writ is denied at the initial stage or the second stage, you can continue to go up the appellate chain of command until you exhaust all avenues for appeal. For example, in the U.S. Court of Appeals, you can petition the U.S. Supreme Court for a Writ of Certiorari, U.S. S. Ct. Rules 10, 11, or for a Writ of Mandamus, U.S. S. Ct. Rule 20.

Some jurisdictions do not regard these writs with as much disfavor as others. In some states, writs of prohibition and mandamus are sought and granted more often than in the federal courts. The writs still are regarded as *extraordinary* and are rarely granted, but they are not as infrequent as a solar eclipse, which is a fairly accurate description of the frequency of the issuance of writs of mandamus in most United States Courts of Appeals.

III. STANDARDS OF REVIEW

Even before your appeal is pending before a court of appeals, an important concept to consider is the standard of review that the court must exercise when evaluating your various allegations of error and grounds for reversal. The standard of review instructs the court of appeals in how much deference to give the determinations of the court or adjudicatory entity below. The standard may allow for no deference, a great deal of deference, or an incredible amount of deference.

The standard of review can have a tremendous impact on the chances of success of an appeal. The difference between an issue on appeal case that is governed by a *de novo* standard, which is essentially no deference to the court below, as opposed to an issue governed by a clearly erroneous standard, which is a great deal of deference, is the difference between an appeal that may have a decent chance and one that may have a snowball's chance in hell. Thus, the issue of the appropriate standard of review must be examined before you take the appeal, and you should counsel your client about the chances for success based on your evaluation of the proper standard of review.

The standard of review is determined by the type of issue that is being asserted on appeal. In that there may be several issues raised in any given appeal, there may be several applicable standards of review that must be anticipated in evaluating and briefing the arguments on appeal. The standards discussed in this chapter generally apply in many jurisdictions, but you must research the law of your own jurisdiction to be sure, because standards do change from jurisdiction to jurisdiction. The types of issues that might arise on appeal and their corresponding standards of review are as follows:

A. Determinations of law – *"de novo"* standard of review

If you are appealing from the lower court's determination of a pure issue of law—what the law is or what the law means, the elements or legal standards that apply, the actual law that applies under a conflict of laws analysis, and other questions of law—then the standard of review is *de novo*. This is the best standard of review for an appellant, because it means that the court of appeals gets to revisit the issue from start to finish and make its own determination of what the answer should be. In essence, no deference to the lower court's determination is required. *De novo* review means that the court of appeals decides the issue as if the lower court had never even taken it up.

An appellant can make the same legal arguments in favor of its interpretation of the law that were made to and rejected by the lower court. Naturally, if the arguments failed once, you should go back to the research table and satisfy yourself that you are presenting the strongest possible argument on the law. Point out the specific areas where the lower court's reasoning and analysis went astray. It will do no good to remind the appeals court that they get to take a fresh look at the issue if you present the same failed arguments and do nothing to rebut the lower court's reasoning in the matter.

B. Determinations of fact by the jury standard of review

On the opposite end of the scale from *de novo* review is the standard of review that applies to review of the findings of fact made by a jury. The Seventh Amendment of the United States Constitution protects a jury verdict from attack by an appellate court: "no fact tried by a jury shall be otherwise re-examined in any court of the United States, than according to the rules of the common law." U.S. Const. amend. VII. The standard of review requires a showing that the jury's findings are not reasonable and are completely against the evidence when viewed in a light that most favors the jury verdict. See, e.g., Bykowicz v. Pulte Home Corp., 950 F.2d 1046, 1050 (5th Cir. 1992); United States v. Dozal-Bencomo, 952 F.2d 1246, 1250 (10th Cir. 1991). If any reasonable inferences can be drawn from the evidence to support the jury's findings, the jury's decision will be upheld. See Bykowicz, 950 F.2d at 1050; Dozal-Bencomo, 952 F.2d at 1250.

In a real and practical sense, there are good reasons for this standard: if a litigant could readily overturn a jury's findings, it would deny his opponent the right to a trial by jury and replace it with trial by appellate court, in which the litigant would be armed only with a transcript of the testimony of the witnesses and boxes of exhibits. The second reason is that the appellate court cannot sit in the same position as the jury in watching the witnesses and evidence and being able to evaluate their credibility from moment to moment in the course of their testimony. Nothing at the present level of technology and procedures for the creation of the record can duplicate the benefits of actually being at the trial. Thus, the appeals court will rarely if ever substitute their impressions and evaluations of the evidence for the jury's based solely on the appellate court's cold reading of the trial transcript and review of the documents and exhibits, divorced as it is from the actual introduction and use of this evidence at trial. The appellant will almost never succeed in challenging the jury's findings under this legal standard, and an appeal will almost always be a waste of the client's time and money.

C. Determinations of fact by the trial court in a bench trial – "clearly erroneous" standard of review

Nearly as onerous for an appellant is the standard of review of determinations of fact made by the trial court in a bench trial. The standard of review is "clearly erroneous"—the trial court's findings will not be set aside unless they are clearly erroneous, giving due regard to the trial court's opportunity to judge the credibility of witnesses. Fed. R. Civ. P. 52(a); United States v. Oregon State Med. Assoc., 343 U.S. 326, 332 (1952). This, again, is a great deal of deference, and it is warranted because of the inability of the appeals court to revisit the trial and judge the credibility of the witnesses and the impact and value of each piece of evidence as it was introduced and used in the proceedings.

D. Mixed questions of law and fact standards of review

The real trouble comes with mixed questions of law and fact—should they be treated like a determination of law, and given little or no deference under a *de novo* standard, or are they more like a determination of fact, and given a great deal of deference under a clearly erroneous standard? If the issue is a finding of historical fact, such as "Defendant was driving at a rate of 55 miles an hour," it is governed by the clearly erroneous standard. But if there is a fact conclusion and an application of the law to the facts so as to make a legal determination, such as "Defendant's driving at 55 miles per hour was reckless," then the issue is more complicated. The court had to make a legal determination of the applicable legal standard (recklessness), and a factual determination of the defendant's rate of speed (55 m.p.h.), in order to make the ultimate determination of whether the legal standard was satisfied by the facts found by the court (defendant was reckless when he drove at 55 m.p.h.). It is the incorporation of these factual and legal determinations to make the ultimate determination challenged on appeal that creates the controversy.

Courts can be split on what is more factual and what is more legal, so a litigant must research the standards in her own jurisdiction to evaluate the problem and be ready to present arguments to demand a favorable standard. There is room for advocacy in this area. If the courts of appeals in the jurisdiction tend to resolve these issues in favor of a finding that a *de novo* standard of review applies, appellant should strive to draft her issues presented so that they sound like issues of law or mixed issues of law and fact, so that they can enjoy the benefits of a *de novo* standard. But if these mixed law and fact determinations are treated like fact determinations, the appellant must be prepared for an uphill climb and must counsel her client accordingly.

E. Review of trial court's rulings on proceedings before and during the trial – "abuse of discretion" standard of review

A trial court makes a great deal of determinations in the course of a litigation, any one of which might cause discomfort to one side or the other, and might be challenged on appeal. The trial court might have to decide whether an amendment to the pleadings will be allowed, whether one party will receive an extension of time, whether certain types of discovery may be had or whether certain categories of information will be subject to discovery. All such decisions are reviewed under an "abuse of discretion" standard, meaning that unless the trial court abused its discretion in making the determination or failed to exercise its discretion at all, the ruling will stand.

The breadth of the discretion afforded to the trial court will vary from issue to issue, and from jurisdiction to jurisdiction. If the matter is one that clearly relates to the operation and proper administration of the court, such as granting an extension of time or allowing additional pages beyond the page limits for motions imposed by local rules, the matter will not be overturned even if the court of appeals thinks the trial judge's decision was ill advised and erroneous. The trial judge has the right to be wrong on these determinations. On the other hand, if the determination has a more profound impact on the outcome and merits of the case, such as the denial of an amendment to the complaint or the denial of the right to conduct additional discovery after new evidence has been uncovered in a case, then the trial court is afforded less discretion, and the decision will more readily be overturned on appeal.

A trial court's demonstrated ignorance of the applicable legal standards for the decision or of available options for the decision can be interpreted as an abuse of discretion or the failure to exercise discretion, and be overturned. Just because the trial court appeared to exercise discretion in a matter does not mean that the court had any discretion to exercise under the applicable legal standards, and so the purported exercise of discretion in and of itself may be an abuse of discretion. Careful research and analysis of the authorities in the local jurisdiction on the particular issue that is being challenged are required before an appellant can properly define the discretion afforded and determine whether it may have been abused.

F. Trial court's evidentiary determinations – "abuse of discretion" standard but the discretion is more limited

A trial court's determinations regarding the admissibility and exclusion of evidence and witnesses is subject to an abuse of discretion standard, United States v. Abel, 469 U.S. 45, 54-55 (1984), but in light of the fact that these decisions are so closely tied to the litigants' ability to prove their case or establish their defenses, the discretion afforded is scrutinized more carefully by the appeals court and tends to be more limited than other determinations made in the course of a trial. See, e.g., United States v. 68.94 Acres, 918 F.2d 389, 392, 395-96 (3rd Cir. 1990). If the trial court applied the wrong legal evidentiary standard or if the court makes an erroneous application of the proper standard to the evidence in the case, the appeals court may find that the trial court abused its discretion and overturn the decision. See id. The appeals court does not completely second guess the trial court as it might in *de novo* review, but it will substitute its judgment for the trial court on legal and mixed law and fact determinations where "a substantial right of the party" is clearly affected by the determination. Id. at 396.

If the trial court merely excludes evidence or witnesses that were not listed in pretrial materials, or were not disclosed to the opponent at the proper time in the litigation, or are otherwise offered in violation of a local rule or pretrial order, these evidentiary rulings will generally be held to be within the "broad discretion" of the trial court and affirmed. See id. at 396-97; Jansen v. Aaron Process Equip. Co., 149 F.3d 603, 609 (7th Cir. 1998).

IV. THE RECORD ON APPEAL

Part of the appeals process is the compilation and reference to the record of the proceedings in the court below, referred to as the "record on appeal." The record on appeal actually can mean three different things: (1) the district court's record, comprising everything that was filed in the district court, plus the trial transcript and docket entries ("district court record"); (2) the record actually transmitted to the court of appeals, which consists of some but not all of the district court record ("transmitted record"); or (3) a further distilled version of the transmitted record provided by the parties to the court of appeals in the form of a joint appendix or record excerpts ("excerpted record").

The transmitted record is prepared or supervised (monitored) in its preparation by the parties. Primary responsibility lies with the appellant, but either side has an interest in the process. The court of appeals would like the parties to get along enough to compile and submit one joint appendix of the proceedings below. That is not always possible, and either side may feel the need to present its own version of the record or submit additional portions not submitted by the other side. If these portions wind up playing a critical part in the court of appeals' review, it will have to sort out the mess and make a determination of what is the actual record.

A. What is the "real record" on appeal – district court record or transmitted record?

Prior to 1967, there was no question that the transmitted record was the "real" record; nothing else mattered. If you left something out of the transmitted record that you later decided you wanted to use, you were sunk. The support for the argument you wanted to make was lost to you. The Federal Rules of Appellate Procedure, Rule 10, sought to eliminate this trap by providing that the entire district court record constituted the record on appeal regardless of what was transmitted to the court of appeals. In other words, as a matter of law the district court's record now constitutes the record on appeal.

As a matter of reality, however, the court of appeals will rarely look beyond the transmitted record. Unless you properly supplement the transmitted record (see below), it will avail you little to argue that the court of appeals may consider something in the district court record that you forgot to include in the transmitted record. The court of appeals is likely to dismiss such an argument with a terse remark about how a party waives or abandons any argument that it fails to support by including the relevant parts of the district court's record in the transmitted record. As a practical matter, the transmitted record becomes the real record on appeal.

B. Supplementing the transmitted record

However, if a party realizes that it inadvertently omitted something from the transmitted record, it may move to supplement the transmitted record. If the court of appeals has not yet considered the case on its merits, the court is likely to grant such a motion. Thus, the district court record remains a reservoir from which the parties may select items for inclusion in the transmitted record throughout most of the appeal.

C. What the transmitted record contains

The transmitted record on appeal contains three types of materials selected by the parties: (1) the court reporter's transcript of the trial, which includes the parties' statements and oral arguments and objections, the judge's statements and rulings and instructions to the jury, the testimony of the witnesses, and the record of the admission of evidence in the case; (2) the pleadings, motions, and other filings from the clerk's office case file; and (3) the actual exhibits. The district clerk's certified copy of docket entries is also part of the transmitted record, but the district court clerk sends that up as soon as the notice of appeal is filed, so that counsel have nothing further to do with it. The court of appeals may order additions to the district court record for materials that were considered by the district court but not included in its record.

D. Appellant's and appellee's duties regarding the record

Appellant's duty is to "monitor" the preparation of the record; appellee's duty is to make sure nothing is left out that can support the trial court's decision. While the appellant has an incentive to make sure the record gets done on time (i.e., appellant must order the transcript and see to it that the file was sent), the appellant only wants to be sure to get the parts of the record sent up that can support an argument that the trial court erred. Appellee needs all the material that could support the trial court's decision. So, appellee must pay attention to what is being sent up.

Chapter 25

Appellate Briefs

I. THE IMPORTANCE OF ADVOCACY IN WRITING IN THE APPELLATE CONTEXT

The appeals process calls for the highest degree of advocacy in writing. As discussed in the previous chapter, most appeals involve an uphill fight, and in many cases the chances of success are dismal. To have a fighting chance, an advocate must pay close attention to the drafting and editing of her briefs.

Oral argument is a wonderful exercise, and we will devote an entire chapter to the examination of the skills and preparation needed to make the most of your time at the podium. But we must point out that of the many appellate court judges we have talked to or heard speak on this topic, the vast majority of these jurists find the briefs filed by the parties to play a greater role than the oral arguments in helping the judges make up their minds as to who should prevail in an appeal. All judges report that oral arguments are helpful, and occasionally these fifteen to thirty minute sessions of intense discussion and questioning of the issues can turn a judge around or convince a fence-sitter to jump to one side or the other. But no one discounts the critical importance of good appellate briefs.

Appellate courts have to look at cases from two perspectives: the rights and equities of the parties before them on the appeal and the effect that their ruling will have on the body of law in the area and on all future litigants in their jurisdiction. Advocates must be sensitive to these dual pressures and not over-emphasize the individual rights and equities of their clients to the exclusion of the bigger picture and the impact of these same arguments on future parties. Policy arguments play a greater role in advocacy the higher you go up the appellate chain because a court of last resort has the power to make the ultimate determination of the public policy that will be embodied in the case law of the jurisdiction. Appellate courts at any level will inquire into the implications of the arguments raised by the parties at oral argument, but you can set the stage for the argument by briefing these policy issues in your appellate briefs.

II. WHAT BRIEFS ARE ALLOWED?

In an interlocutory appeal or regular appeal pursuant to Fed. R. App. P. 28(a)-(c), the parties to the appeal are allowed the following briefs:

❑ Appellant's brief,[1]
❑ Appellee's brief,[2] and
❑ Appellant's reply brief[3] (optional).

With cross appeals, the party who appealed first is considered the appellant. Fed. R. App. P. 28(h). If both parties appealed on the same day, the plaintiff is treated as the appellant unless the parties otherwise agree or the court otherwise orders. Id. In a cross-appeal, the appellee's brief combines an answer to the first appeal with appellee's opening arguments on the cross appeal. Id. The second section of the brief that asserts appellee's cross appeal should not contain arguments that are properly addressed to the opponent's arguments on its appeal—these arguments should be kept in the answering part of the brief. Otherwise, it confuses the issues. Appellant then combines in one brief its answer to appellee's cross appeal and any reply on appellant's appeal. Id., Rule 28(c). Appellee concludes, if it chooses, with a reply to appellant's answering brief on the cross appeal. Id.

Extraordinary writs require a petition for the writ, and an answer that may be filed by some or all of the respondents, if the court of appeals orders respondents to answer. Fed. R. App. P. 21. Nothing in Rule 21 provides for a reply brief. Id. The petition serves the function of an opening brief by an appellant, although the internal structure is more like a trial level brief, as discussed in the next section.

III. STRUCTURE OF APPELLATE BRIEFS AND APPELLATE WRITS

A. Structure of writs of mandamus and prohibition

A petition for a writ is organized like a trial-level brief, with one critical addition: you must clearly state the grounds for the issuance of the writ up front in the introduction or, better yet, create a brand new section that will precede the introduction called "**Grounds for the Issuance of the Writ.**" Sometimes the general rules of procedure or the local rules of the court require additional sections to be drafted. See Fed. R. App. P. 21(a)(2)(B); Il. S. Ct. R. 381; Mo. S. Ct. R. 94.03.

Do not pull any punches here. You are not going to succeed if you hide the grounds for the issuance of the writ in the argument section. You need to get the court's attention early and show why the writ must be issued, using primary controlling authority. If that kind of authority does not exist, your chances of getting the writ issued are virtually nonexistent, but do your best with what you have to work with.

---

[1] In different jurisdictions, this brief might be called Appellant's Opening Brief, or Petitioner's Brief, or Petitioner's Brief on the Merits.

[2] In different jurisdictions, this might be called Appellant's Answering Brief, or Appellant's Response, or Appellant's Brief in Response, or Respondent's Brief, or Respondent's Brief on the Merits.

[3] In different jurisdictions, this might be called Petitioner's Reply Brief.

B. Structure of interlocutory appellate briefs

Interlocutory appellate briefs are organized the same way as the briefs in a regular appeal after final judgment. Of course, in the statement of the case or proceedings below sections, you should point out that the trial court certified the issue you are appealing for interlocutory appeal. Other than that, the briefs will look the same.

C. Structure of appellate briefs in the U.S. Supreme Court

The local rules of the court in which you are practicing will specify what sections you will need to include in your briefs. As an indicative example of these requirements, we will discuss each of the sections of the brief that are required by the United States Supreme Court Rules in the order required by those rules. Rule 24.1 of the U.S. Supreme Court Rules requires the following sections of a brief and it requires them to be presented in this order:

- ❑ Caption
- ❑ Questions Presented for Review (or Issues Presented, Points of Error, Points Relied On, Points on Review)
- ❑ Parties to the Proceeding
- ❑ Table of Contents
- ❑ Table of Authorities
- ❑ Opinions and Judgments Entered in the Case (or Opinions Below)
- ❑ Statement of Jurisdiction
- ❑ Constitutional, Treaty, Statutory, and Administrative Law Provisions
- ❑ Statement of the Case (or Statement of Facts and Proceedings Below)
- ❑ Summary of the Argument
- ❑ Argument
- ❑ Conclusion
- ❑ Appendices (or Addenda)

The rules of other appellate courts might require you to draft other sections, such as:

- ❑ Standard of Review
- ❑ Statement of Facts (if not included in the Statement of the Case above)

Each of these sections deserves closer attention, as follows:

1. Caption (on the Cover)

Appellate briefs are bound, meaning they have a stiff, card-stock cover and backing. The caption appears on the cover, and it generally takes up the entire cover of each appellate brief. The caption names the court, the docket number, the parties, the party submitting the brief, and the title of the brief. Typically the caption also will identify the court from which the appeal is taken and sometimes the name of the judge below, and the identity of the attorneys that produced the brief.

Drafting a caption should not be too much trouble. If you have never seen what the formatting of this information looks like in your jurisdiction, get your hands on a sample brief from a colleague or go to the court and ask to see some briefs that are on file. Briefs can be found on the Internet in a form that reveals the true appearance of the caption, such as the portable document format (.pdf) produced by Adobe Acrobat®. A typical format is shown in the following example:

**IN THE
UNITED STATES COURT OF APPEALS
FOR THE FOURTEENTH CIRCUIT**

No. 99-234

BRANCH LOUISIAN OF THE UNITED CHURCH OF
CHRIST THE SAVIOR,

Plaintiff-Appellant,

— *against* —

METROPOLITAN SCHOOL DISTRICT OF GOTHAM,
STATE OF NEW KENT,

Defendant-Appellee.

Appeal from the United States District Court for the Central District of New Kent
Hon. Learned Foot, Judge

BRIEF FOR APPELLANT

Mary Patricia Silverberg
D. Heimlich Maneuver
Large Law Firm LLP25
Commerce Street
Industry, TX 87878
Counsel for Appellant

---

2. Questions Presented for Review (or Issues Presented, Points of Error, Points Relied On, Points for Review)

As you can see from our heading here, the terms that are used to identify this section vary greatly from jurisdiction to jurisdiction. The basic idea is to lay out in one section all of the issues or points of error that are asserted by the appellant or petitioner so that the appellate court easily can see all of the issues that will need to be resolved in the appeal. It is important to list every issue or error that will be discussed in the brief because failure to do so may be interpreted as a waiver of the unlisted arguments, and the court may disregard any issue or argument regarding an issue that is not presented in this section.

a. Questions presented in an intermediate level appellate court

There are two basic methods for drafting the questions presented section in an intermediate level appellate court, and the local rules or case law of the court where the appeal lies will instruct you in which method to employ. The first is the "Notice" method, and the second is the "Complete Disclosure" method. The Notice method is most commonly used. It requires a description of the issue or error **in the form of a question** that mentions the specific error of the court below and the legal standards that show why it was an error. The Complete Disclosure method largely is the same, but you must add a summary of every argument regarding this issue or error that you intend to present in the brief. If you fail to summarize each legal theory and argument in a Complete Disclosure jurisdiction, you run the risk of the appellate court's ignoring the arguments you failed to list. Compare the two methods in the following examples:

> *Notice method:*   Whether the trial court erred in denying Garcia's motion for summary judgment on liability because the evidence cannot support a finding of recklessness under the <u>Dolan</u> standards?

> *Complete Disclosure:*   Whether the trial court erred in denying Garcia's motion for summary judgment on liability because the <u>Dolan</u> standards require proof that Garcia acted with careless disregard for the safety of others and the evidence shows that Garcia undertook the unloading of Fernandez's equipment in a prudent manner, Garcia used the standard methods of unloading approved by the Teamsters' Union and the National Transportation Authority, Garcia postponed the unloading for four hours because Garcia determined that the weather conditions were not safe for unloading, and Garcia undertook to unload the equipment only at the insistence of Fernandez's agent and foreman?

If the Complete Disclosure method looks awkward and over-killed, it is. **Do not use the Complete Disclosure method for your issues presented or questions presented section unless you are compelled to do so by the local rules of the court.**

The phrasing of the questions presented should be neutral, not biased in favor of your client. Do not interject argument and accusations into the issues. An appellate court does not want to read a statement laced with rhetoric that drives the parties apart from a consensus on the issues on appeal. The court would rather see a statement of the issues that both sides can agree upon so that the appellee does not have to draft a competing set of issues for review. <u>See, e.g.</u>, Fed. R. Civ. P. 28(b). When appellant and appellee do not agree, this makes the court's job harder because it will have to determine what separate issues are raised that will need to be resolved in the appeal.

As discussed in the previous chapter, if the standard of review is a standard other than *de novo* review, you should weave this into the statement of the issue. For example, using the Complete Disclosure method, if the standard of review for the point of error you are drafting is "abuse of discretion," you might phrase the issue as:

> ➤ Whether the trial court abused its discretion when it denied Nunez the right to amend its petition, because under Fed. R. Civ. P. 15, leave to amend shall be freely granted when justice so requires, the amendment was required because of new facts and evidence produced to plaintiff just five days before it moved to amend the petition, and there would have been no prejudice to defendant if the amendment were to be allowed?

If the point of error is a pure issue of law, you might use the Notice method to state that the court erred as follows:

> ➤ Whether the trial court erred in its determination that New Hampshire law applied to the contract because the parties chose Rhode Island law in a valid, enforceable forum selection clause?

b. Questions presented in a court of last resort

If you are phrasing a question presented for a court of last resort, you should draft the question so that the individual parties' names are obscured and their roles or the class of persons or entities that they represent are presented instead of the individual parties' names. This method brings to the fore the public policy implications of the dispute for the court to resolve, and reminds the court that it is not just the petitioner and the respondent who will be feeling the effects of their ruling, but all persons in similar situations. Courts of last resort are particularly sensitive to public policy concerns because they will be determining the law and establishing policy for the entire jurisdiction to follow. Consider the following examples:

➤ *Example:* I. Whether a public school district violates a religious organization's First Amendment free speech rights by refusing to post information regarding creationism on the school district's web site created to further the educational mission of the school district?

II. Whether a public school district violates the First Amendment's Establishment Clause by sponsoring a religious organization's web page on the school district's web site created to increase the educational opportunities for students on topics within the curriculum?

Not this: I. Whether Metropolitan Kent School District violated Branch Louisian Church's First Amendment free speech rights by refusing to post information regarding creationism on the Metropolitan Kent School District's web site created to further the educational mission of the school district?

II. Whether Metropolitan Kent School District would violate the First Amendment's Establishment Clause by sponsoring Branch Louisian Church's web page on the Metropolitan Kent School District's web site created to increase the educational opportunities for students on topics within the curriculum?

Note that the first two examples are phrased in the present tense. This reinforces the relevance of the issue for the court—it is a current, troublesome issue for people in similar situations as the petitioner and the respondent. The last two examples were forced to be phrased in the past tense and future tense respectively, in the one case because the party already undertook the action from which the suit arises, and in the other case because the party had not taken the action and now seeks to be heard on what would have happened if it had.

3. Parties to the Proceeding

The rules of the U.S. Supreme Court and other courts require a section that lists all parties to the proceedings in the court whose judgment is sought to be reviewed. If all the parties happen to be listed in the caption, <u>i.e.</u>, there were few enough parties to list all their names in the caption, then the rules of the Supreme Court state that this section is unnecessary. S. Ct. Rule 24.1(b). Parent companies and non-wholly owned subsidiaries may have to be listed, too, as per S. Ct. Rule 29.1.

4. Table of Contents

You have seen tables of contents before, and there is little that is unusual about a table drafted for an appellate brief. Although each individual entry in the table is single-spaced, the entries are separated from each other by two spaces, as shown in the example below. When you provide page references for the argument section, be sure to list in their entirety each of your major and minor headings and subheadings in the argument section. In this way, your table of contents can be a useful outline of your entire argument for the busy judge to look at before or during oral argument. For example:

TABLE OF CONTENTS

QUESTIONS PRESENTED FOR REVIEW i

PARTIES TO THE PROCEEDINGS ii

TABLE OF CONTENTS iii

TABLE OF AUTHORITIES v

OPINIONS AND JUDGMENTS ENTERED IN THE CASE viii

STATEMENT OF JURISDICTION ix

CONSTITUTIONAL AND STATUTORY PROVISIONS ix

STATEMENT OF THE CASE xi

SUMMARY OF THE ARGUMENT xiii

ARGUMENT 1

    I. FORD GAVE PROPER NOTICE TO FIRESTONE BECAUSE
        IT GAVE THE NOTICE REQUIRED BY STATUTE AND
        FIRESTONE ACKNOWLEDGED THE NOTICE 1

        A. Ford Gave Proper Notice because Ford Met Each of the Three
            Requirements for Notice under 15 U.S.C. § 235 1

            1. Ford Gave Notice Through CPSC Notice of Recall 3

            2. Ford Gave Notice Through Telephone, Facsimile Transmission,
               and U.S. Mail 6

            3. Ford Issued a Press Release 8

        B. Firestone Acknowledged the Notice on Three Occasions 9

   II. FIRESTONE FAILED TO PRESERVE ITS ESTOPPEL CLAIM
        BECAUSE IT FAILED TO ASSERT THE CLAIM IN POST TRIAL
        MOTIONS 11

        A. Firestone Failed to Assert an Estoppel Argument in its Motion for
            Judgment as a Matter of Law brought at the End of its Case 11

        B. Firestone Failed to Assert an Estoppel Argument in its Post-Trial
            Motion for New Trial or for Judgment as a Matter of Law 14

CONCLUSION 19

5. Table of Authorities

This is a list in **alphabetical order** of each of the authorities you cite in the brief. A typical way to organize the table is to list cases first, then constitutional and statutory provisions, then rules and administrative law, then treatises and other secondary authorities.

You should italicize or underline the case names (whichever form you are using in the rest of your brief) because you are making a citation to a case in a court document. Jump cites (pinpoint cites, pin cites) to the internal pages of the authorities that you will refer to are ***not*** included. As a rule of thumb, if you cite a case on more than four pages of your brief, you may write *passim* instead of writing all of the page numbers where the case is cited (unless the rules of the court require something else). The page numbers are right justified and preceded by a string of periods. In some word processing programs such as Word Perfect this is referred to as "flush right with dot leaders."

The local rules of the appellate court may ask you to separate the authorities you are using into categories; for example: United States Supreme Court Cases; United States Court of Appeals Cases; United States District Court Cases; State Cases; Constitutions, Statutes and Administrative Regulations; Legislative History Documents; Treatises, Books, and Law Review Articles; Other Authorities. **Alphabetize** the entries in each category. A table of authorities that complies with this rule might look like the following:

TABLE OF AUTHORITIES

United States Supreme Court Cases:

Adams v. Baker, 434 U.S. 456 (1976)	13, 15
Attila v. Romans, 671 U.S. 789 (2005)	*passim*
Rotten v. Vicious, 668 U.S. 123 (2004)	10

United States Court of Appeals Cases:

Able v. Incapable, 786 F.2d 234 (7th Cir. 1989)	23, 24, 27
Farnsworth v. Williston, 678 F.2d 45 (2d Cir. 1972)	6
Goldfarb v. Silverfarb, 333 F.3d 12 (11th Cir. 2005)	6, 8, 22

United States District Court Cases:

Ford v. Chrysler, 155 F. Supp. 2d 246 (E.D.N.Y. 2004)	34
Helena v. Billings, 55 F.R.D. 23 (D. Mont. 1971)	34

State Cases:

Murphy v. O'Brien, No. 96-CIV-2345, 2001 WL 12345 (Mo. Apr. 22, 2001)	35
Uranus v. Mars, 934 N.E.2d 642 (Ill. 1999)	32

Constitutions, Statutes and Administrative Regulations:

U.S. Const. art. I, § 9, cl. 2	20
U.S. Const. amend. XIV, § 2	20
17 U.S.C. § 107 (1999)	*passim*
18 U.S.C. § 1401 (1999)	22
15 C.F.R. § 17.234 (1989)	23, 24

Legislative History Materials:

H.R. 3055, 94th Cong. § 2 (1976) 11, 12, 14, 33

S. Rep. No. 89-910 (1965) 14

Treatises, Books, and Law Review Articles:

E. Allen Farnsworth, *Contracts* (1988) 22, 25

Martin Scorsese, *Film Making* (1992) 13

Terri L. Crocker, *Under the Blood Red Sky: Women's Health and the 1997
Amendments to FIFRA*, 88 Colum. L. Rev. 22 (1988) 21, 31

Other Authorities:

William Rosenthal, *White House Staff Strips Aid to President*, N.Y. Times,
June 15, 2001, at A1 23

Even in the absence of a local rule, it makes sense to separate your authorities into cases; constitutions, statutes, legislative history, and administrative regulations; treatises, books, and law review articles; and miscellaneous authorities, as depicted in the following:

TABLE OF AUTHORITIES

Cases:

Able v. Incapable, 786 F.2d 234 (7th Cir. 1989) 23, 24, 27

Adams v. Baker, 434 U.S. 456 (1976) 13, 15

Attila v. Romans, 671 U.S. 789 (2005) .... *passim*

Farnsworth v. Williston, 678 F.2d 45 (2d Cir. 1972) 6

Ford v. Chrysler, 155 F. Supp. 2d 246 (E.D.N.Y. 2004) 34

Goldfarb v. Silverfarb, 333 F.3d 12 (11th Cir. 2005) 6, 8, 22

Helena v. Billings, 55 F.R.D. 23 (D. Mont. 1971) 34

Murphy v. O'Brien, No. 96-CIV-2345, 2001 WL 12345 (Mo. Apr. 22, 2001) ... 35

Rotten v. Vicious, 668 U.S. 123 (2004) 10

Uranus v. Mars, 934 N.E.2d 642 (Ill. 1999) 32

Constitutions, Statutes, Legislative History, and Administrative Regulations:

U.S. Const. art. I, § 9, cl. 2 20

U.S. Const. amend. XIV, § 2 20

17 U.S.C. § 107 (1999) .... *passim*

18 U.S.C. § 1401 (1999) 22

15 C.F.R. § 17.234 (1989) 23, 24

H.R. 3055, 94th Cong. § 2 (1976) 11, 12, 14, 33

S. Rep. No. 89-910 (1965) 14

Treatises, Books, and Law Review Articles:

E. Allen Farnsworth, *Contracts* (1988) 22, 25

Martin Scorsese, *Film Making* (1992) 13

Terri L. Crocker, *Under the Blood Red Sky: Women's Health and the 1997 Amendments to FIFRA*, 88 Colum. L. Rev. 22 (1988) 21, 31

Miscellaneous:

William Rosenthal, *White House Staff Strips Aid to President*, N.Y. Times, June 15, 2001, at A1 23

6. Opinions and Orders Entered in the Case (or Opinions Below)

In the rules of some courts, such as the Rules of the United States Supreme Court, a section is required that lists the citations of the opinions and orders from courts or administrative agencies from which the appeal arises. Not a very complicated section, but it is necessary nonetheless. If you do not have a full citation for the opinion or judgment, cite as much information as the record gives you and follow citation rules for the citation of slip opinions. At a minimum, you should be able to describe the opinion or judgment and cite the names of the parties, the docket number, the court, and the date of the decision. For example:

OPINIONS AND ORDERS ENTERED IN THE CASE

Order granting summary judgment in favor of defendant Jones and against plaintiff Smith. *Smith v. Jones*, No. 04-CIV-245-DNL (E.D. Cal. Jan. 14, 2005).

Opinion reversing the above order, and remanding the case to the district court for trial. *Jones v. Smith*, No. 05-258-EM (9th Cir. Aug. 24, 2005).

---

7. Statement of Jurisdiction

The Statement of Jurisdiction is a brief section explaining the jurisdictional basis for the case being in the court where it is set. For example:

STATEMENT OF JURISDICTION

This Court has jurisdiction over the subject matter of this case because it is an appeal from the final judgment of the trial court entered on January 12, 2005. 28 U.S.C. § 1291; Fed. R. App. P. 4.

---

8. Constitutional, Treaty, Statutory, and Administrative Law Provisions

Some court rules, including the rules of the U.S. Supreme Court, require a section that quotes the applicable constitutional, treaty, statutory, and administrative law provisions that are implicated by the problem. If the text is short—less than two pages—quote each provision verbatim in this section. If they are lengthy, cite the provision, quote the pertinent language, and then set out the full text in an appendix to the brief, as provided in S. Ct. Rule 24.1(f).

9. Statement of the Case (Including Statement of Facts and Proceedings Below)

In many courts, this section is a summary of the proceedings of the case since the time it was filed to the present. You give only the highlights, such as the date of pleadings and amendments to pleadings, major dispositive motions that were granted or denied, and an explanation of how the case got to the appeals court. This section is not intended to be very argumentative, and it should be kept short. Avoid the temptation to take pot shots at the trial court judge when recounting the history of the case—you will have plenty of opportunity to point out errors in other sections of the brief.

You can draft this section so that it supports your argument by highlighting language used in the courts below, and by trying to summarize and hone down the opinions of the lower courts in such a way that you easily can trounce these opinions in the argument section if you are an appellant or petitioner, or buttress these opinions if you are a respondent. Several of the briefs we have included as sample briefs in this book have excerpted the opinion of the lower court. The skill in choosing what language and what items to highlight in this section parallels the skill you must employ in choosing what facts to highlight in the statement of facts.

In the United States Supreme Court, the rules contemplate that the statement of the case section will encompass **both** a **statement of the pertinent facts** of the case and a **statement of the proceedings below** with citations to the record or joint appendix to support the information in both sections. The facts part of this section should be drafted as a statement of facts as described in the next section, and you would draft both parts (**statement of facts and proceedings below**) under the single heading of statement of the case.

10. Statement of Facts

The statement of facts presents a summary of the historical facts of the case that led up to the date that the case was filed. Since the facts are very important in any appeal, you should take the time to draft them in such a way that your client's position looks strong, by using crisp, active language and strong nouns, adjectives, and adverbs, and by giving appropriate detail to facts that support and sustain your arguments, and limiting the discussion of relevant facts that are detrimental to your arguments. Certainly, there is no need to raise and discuss facts that you believe are irrelevant to the issues on appeal from both your client's and your opponent's perspective, unless you are going to take the time in the argument to demonstrate why certain negative facts are irrelevant. The authors of the **sample briefs** at the end of this chapter have attempted to accomplish these goals with varying degrees of success. Read these samples critically, and note our annotations.

a. Persuasive facts vs. argument

Two principles are at war in drafting the statement of facts. First, the court of appeals would like you to state just the relevant facts, with no argument or innuendo. See Fed. R. App. P. 28(a)(4); Local Rules of the U.S. Ct. App. 7th Cir., Rule 28(d)(1); Il. S. Ct. R. 341(e)(6). Indeed, the local rules of the court of appeals may strictly limit the amount of argument or "bias" that you can interject into the facts. E.g., Local Rules of the U.S. Ct. App. 7th Cir., Rule 28(d)(1); Il. S. Ct. R. 341(e)(6). Even if the local rules do not prohibit argument or comment on the facts, it is advisable to avoid argumentative language and to eliminate any legal conclusions in the facts.

Factual Conclusions:	The truck ***was going fast*** when it approached the curve.
	The driver had trouble steering ***because*** the truck began to rock and sway.
	The trailer became detached from the tractor ***because*** the connector pin was sheared off.
Legal Conclusions:	The truck driver was ***reckless*** for driving at that speed.
	The truck driver ***caused*** the trailer to become detached by his ***driving too fast*** in the curve.
	He ***caused*** the truck to become ***too unstable to control.***
	The driver was ***negligent*** in attempting to take the turn at that speed.

However, the second principle is that a good advocate wants a statement of facts that will persuade the judges to rule in the lawyer's favor as soon as they finish reading the facts. Satisfying both ends requires careful attention to accuracy and advocacy.

b. Accuracy

Accuracy is paramount. You cannot win by misstating facts. If your statement sounds persuasive but your opponent identifies errors or pokes holes in what you told the court, your chances of success will be severely damaged. If evidence is contested, do not recite it as if it were a fact. Give a fair account of the testimony and supporting exhibits, and if you can show why other testimony should be believed or not believed, do so, but do not present one side's witnesses as the only story that was told.

One important part of the requirement of accuracy is to draw only the most logical and most reasonable inferences from the facts in the record.

> *Example:*   If a commission called for a sculpture to be created in two weeks time, and the facts indicate that the artist completed the work in one week, it would be completely safe to point out that the artist did the work "in half the time anticipated by the parties in their contract." It would

not necessarily be fair to say that the artist did the work "quickly," and it certainly would not be fair to infer that the artist "rushed" the job. "Rushing" implies a state of mind, and nothing in the facts we have revealed shows the artist's state of mind. Performing a commission in half the allotted time is not automatically rushing; you do not have enough facts to make that inference. Perhaps the artist routinely does these works in a single day, and one week is a luxurious amount of time.

If the work turned out to be unacceptable to the client—the client found it to be "ugly" and "unappealing"—you could state that "the artist only used half of the allotted time to produce the sculpture, and wound up producing a work that was ugly and unappealing to the client." You could not draw the inference that the artist was "sloppy" or "careless" in producing the work, and certainly could not infer that the artist was "negligent" or "reckless" by producing the work in half the allotted time. Aside from the problem that these are legal conclusions, you do not have enough facts about the artist, her state of mind, her expertise, her prior work production methods, and a host of other factual information that would affect that inference. All you can say is that she produced the work in half the allotted time, and the work was unacceptable to the client because the client found it to be ugly and unappealing.

Missing information from the record necessarily will limit the kind of inferences you logically can draw. Do not get caught up in a spirit of advocacy and fill in details that affect the logical limits of the facts in the record.

➤ *Example:*   If the record states that the commission required the sculpture to be 50% titanium, and tests show that it is less than 50% titanium, you could draw the inference that the sculpture produced "does not meet the terms of the contract," or "does not contain the percentage of titanium that the parties specified in the contract." You cannot automatically draw the inference that the artist "breached the contract." Breach, a legal conclusion, depends on a host of factors relating to performance. The artist may have a lawful excuse or justification for his performance. You cannot state that the artist "purposefully" or "intentionally" left titanium out of the sculpture. You simply do not know what the artist's state of mind was. You only can state exactly what the facts state: "The artist produced a sculpture that did not contain the percentage of titanium that was specified in the parties' agreement."

If you find out additional facts, you might be able to draw other inferences. If you discover that the price of titanium doubled the day after
the commission was signed, you now can state that "the price of titanium doubled the day after the commission was signed, and one week
later, the artist delivered a work that did not contain the percentage of
titanium specified by the parties in their contract." You still cannot
infer that the artist "breached" or "purposefully" or "intentionally"
left titanium out of the sculpture.

c. Highlighting good facts and downplaying bad facts

You can balance the separate duties of accuracy and advocacy with more subtle but still
effective methods. The same set of facts can be drafted differently in ways that better
support the client's position and hinder the opponent's. Fed. R. App. P. 28 requires that
you present the facts relevant to the issues on appeal. That standard offers considerable
latitude in choosing *what* to recite. You can report both favorable and unfavorable facts
on a given point, while still presenting the facts in the best possible light for your client.

You can highlight facts with the amount of detail you present, the sequence in which
you present them, and your own careful choice of words. Instead of using neutral words,
slant the facts with language that carries overtones. Avoid the passive tense and use strong
engaging verbs and descriptive nouns and adjectives in sections that discuss facts favorable
to your client, and do the opposite in sections containing facts unfavorable to your client.

➤ *Example 1 - Common Facts:* Client Jones was going 60 m.p.h. in a 45 m.p.h. zone
on his way to his therapist, a doctor of psychology. He was late. The road was wet.
A poodle came out from behind a parked car and moved into the road in front of
him. Jones swerved, his car slid out of control, and he hit a parked car owned by
plaintiff.

Appellant's Version: Defendant was late for an appointment with his psycho-therapist and was speeding at 60 m.p.h. on rain slick pavement in a 45 m.p.h. zone. A
poodle walked into the path of Defendant's speeding car, and Defendant swerved
and sent his car spinning out of control. Defendant then smashed his car into the
back of plaintiff Smith's parked car.

Appellee's Version: Mr. Jones was proceeding to an important appointment. A dog
jumped out in front of him taking him completely by surprise. In an effort to avoid
hitting the dog, he turned the wheel quickly but the car slid on the damp pavement
and came into contact with the plaintiff's car.

➤ *Example 2 - Common Facts:* ABC Corp. laid off thirteen workers in a reduction in
force (RIF). ABC used a business productivity formula. Six of the workers who were
laid off were over the age of 40, four of these were women. Four more who were

laid off were minorities, two of whom were women. Mr. Smith, a white male age 37, made the final decision of whom to lay off.

Appellant's Version: ABC's most recent RIF was spearheaded by Cliff Smith, a white male. Smith targeted women, minorities, and workers whose age was over 40 for ten of his thirteen cuts. When he fired six elderly workers, he made sure four of them were women, and when he singled out four minorities for firing, he made sure half of them were women. Smith used a formula that ensured that these people could be disposed of with the excuse of increasing productivity.

Appellee's Version: ABC was forced by competitive economic factors to lay off thirteen workers. A formula was used based on a worker's years of service, evaluation grades, and amount of contract revenue generated in the last five years. The thirteen lowest performing workers were laid off.

d. Level of detail

Although the level of detail is one way to highlight important and helpful facts, you can go overboard with too much detail. In a fact intensive appeal, it sometimes is hard to mention all the facts in the statement of facts because it would produce a facts section that is the same length as the argument. In general, ask yourself whether every detail in your recital of the facts is needed. Trial lawyers writing or editing briefs on appeal are especially prone to include facts that seemed important at trial but have little or nothing to do with the issues on appeal. Try to get these weeded out before you send it to the court.

> *Good:*   Defendant Jones was late for an appointment with his psycho-therapist and was speeding at 60 m.p.h. on rain slick pavement in a 45 m.p.h. zone. A poodle walked into the path of Defendant's speeding car, and Defendant swerved and sent his car spinning out of control. Defendant then smashed his car into the back of plaintiff Smith's parked car.

> *Not this:*   Defendant Jones was running approximately eight minutes late for his appointment with his psycho-therapist, Dr. Will Shrinker. He went speeding along on his way to Dr. Shrinker's office on Mulberry Lane, a mixed business and residential street with a 45 m.p.h. speed limit. He was traveling at an average speed of 60 m.p.h. as confirmed by a passive police monitoring unit on Mulberry Lane that Jones passed by; his speed also was generally confirmed by two eye witnesses at the scene, Mrs. Vera Stigmatism and Mr. Esau Nothing. At some point soon after passing by the monitoring unit, a poodle walked out into the path of Defendant's speeding car. Defendant took action immediately. He swerved the car to the left, and sent his car spinning out of control. There is no indication that he was able to regain control

of the car. Jones' car spun out of control for more than two seconds, again, as confirmed by Mrs. Stigmatism and Mr. Nothing. Defendant then smashed his car into the back of plaintiff Smith's parked car. No one witnessed the actions of the poodle after Jones swerved away from it, but the poodle was unharmed in the incident.

The details in the second example above may be interesting, but it is unlikely that they will have any effect on the appeal unless this interchange of the car sliding on the wet road and the collision with the parked car is the only incident from which the appeal arises. If this incident is a tiny part of a much bigger case, and if these details are not relevant for the particular purpose of proving a point of error charged to the lower court, then leave them out. They will wear out your reader and squander her attention span.

e. Divide facts with subheadings

When you have a lot of facts that need to be presented, internal subheadings and topical groupings can help to divide up the facts into more manageable and digestible chunks. Subheadings allow you to focus on separate issues in the facts, presenting only the facts that go with that issue. This paragraph should remind you that you need not present the facts in strict chronological order if that order does little to highlight the important facts of your client's case.

f. Citations to the record

Every fact must be referenced by citation to the record. The appeals court is likely to ignore any facts that are not supported by a citation to the record. Rule 24 of the Supreme Court Rules provides for a cite to the joint appendix, e.g., App. 12, or to the record, e.g., Record 12. Some practitioners place the citations inside parentheses but the rules do not require this method.

➤ *Examples:*   The contract was signed on August 13, 2005 (Record 132, ¶ 12).

Jones testified that he called the police at 10:00 a.m., App. 12, but the police dispatcher records indicate that the call from Jones was received at 10:42 a.m. Plaintiff's Ex. 44, App. 14, ¶ 4.

Other appellate court rules may allow you to shorten the citation to the record to (R. pg. #) or (R-pg. #) as in (R.23) or (R-23), and citations to the joint appendix as (J.A. pg. #) or (JA-pg. #) as in (J.A. 133) or (JA-133).

g. Party names

Describe parties consistently throughout the facts. Do not switch from calling your client "the tenant," to "plaintiff," to "Sam Smith Slaughterhouse Company." Fed. R.

App. P. 28(d) and most appellate judges we have talked to discourage the use of such generic labels as "appellant" and "appellee." Some brief writers believe that it is it acceptable to use the designations used in the trial court (plaintiff, defendant), but we do not agree that this practice promotes the necessary clarity and individuality that you are seeking to achieve in your brief. The authors believe that using the actual names of the parties is the best practice: "McMannis," "Allied Widgets," "Governor Black." Next best is to use descriptive terms, such as "the employer," "the driver," "the taxpayer," "the ship," and so forth.

h. Abbreviations and acronyms

Use abbreviations and acronyms cautiously. You and your client may understand an acronym identifying a party, an agency, a group, a set of laws or regulations, or other items described in the facts, but using abbreviations or acronyms that are not self-explanatory to the court is like using a secret code that taxes the ability and patience of the judges. Most judges know that ACLU refers to the American Civil Liberties Union and RICO refers to the Racketeer Influenced and Corrupt Organizations Act, but how many judges know that FIFRA refers to the Federal Insecticide, Fungicide, and Rodenticide Act or COBRA refers to the Comprehensive Omnibus Budget Reconciliation Act? Be kind to your readers and define all abbreviations and acronyms up front and use them consistently throughout your brief.

i. Tell your client's story

The best possible statement of facts tells a story in which your client is a character, the plot is a straight-forward recounting in lay person's terms of what happened to your client and the opponent and other characters, and the conflict and resolution (if any) is one that shows why your client must win. The moral of the story is the theme of your case, and it should be able to be stated in a single sentence no matter how long it takes you to boil the case down to a single sentence theme. As with most good stories, the reader (the court) should be pulled into it so that they care what happens to the main character (your client) and are eager to know what happens next until they get to the end of the story. Critically evaluate the stories told by the authors of the **sample briefs** at the end of this chapter and decide for yourselves what stories seem the most effective.

11. Standard of Review

In some jurisdictions, the court of appeals' local rules require you to draft a short section laying out what you have determined to be the appropriate standard of review for each issue that is raised on appeal, and stating your legal support for that determination. E.g., Alaska R. App. P. 212(c)(1)(h); Haw. R. App. P. 28(b)(5). In other courts, you will state the standard of review for each point after you list the point in the issues presented section or incorporate the discussion into the argument section, see Fed. R. App. P. 28(a)(6);

Ariz. R. Civ. App. P. 13(a)(6); Ga. Ct. App. R. 27(a)(3), 27(b)(2), so there will be no separate standard of review section.

If the standard of review is obvious, limit the discussion to one sentence for each point of error, and cite one or two powerful authorities that conclusively state the standard. If there is some doubt as to the standard (which might be the case with mixed issues of law and fact), present a short argument with citations to relevant and analogous authority to argue in favor of the standard that benefits your client. Even in this latter situation, you should limit the argument to one or two pages except in the most unusual and complicated of circumstances.

12. Summary of Argument

Federal appellate courts, including the United States Supreme Court, require a separate section entitled "Summary of the Argument" that precedes the argument section. Fed. R. App. P. 28(a)(5); S. Ct. Rule 24.1(h). The drafters of the rule have precluded litigants from simply stringing their argument headings together into roughly connected paragraphs, so avoid the temptation. Instead, make a clear and succinct presentation of the points on review and your arguments on these points, with citation only to the most critical authorities that support your arguments.

Even if the local rules do not limit your pages in this section, we would avoid going over three pages because the judges still have to read your argument section, and you do not want to wear them out with unnecessary repetition, redundancy, duplication, saying the same thing over and over again (see what we mean?).

The reader gets to the Summary first, so even if you draft it second, make it powerful and memorable. That which comes first counts more in legal writing. Judges in a hurry may read only the summary of the argument, not the whole argument section. It definitely is not a section to ignore until the day before the brief is due.

13. Argument

We have now worked our way to the argument section. You must craft the argument with careful attention to organization, citation to authority, as well as the substance of the legal arguments you make. This topic is covered at length in section IV below.

14. Conclusion

Fed. R. App. P. 28(a)(7) requires a short conclusion describing the precise relief sought. The usual question is whether the conclusion should include anything else. The answer typically is "no."

Be as specific as possible about the relief you want. Your request may be in the alternative. The court may deny specific relief that you fail to request. Your request for relief may need some explanation in the argument. If, for instance, you are asking for reversal and remand for the limited purpose of entering judgment in a specified amount, you will need to explain why further evidence is not needed on the question of damages. As a general rule, whenever you seek a remand only for limited purposes, you will need to explain the reasons behind your proposed limits. That explanation belongs in the argument section.

Aside from relief requested, brief writers frequently are tempted to conclude with some rhetoric that does not fit into the disciplined analysis of your argument section. Appellate courts will accept this kind of "traditional" conclusion with appropriate summary and reemphasizing of the arguments you raised. The rule does not forbid this, other than to require that the conclusion be short. If you can keep it brief, a zinger at the end does not hurt. Whether it helps is a matter of some doubt. If your brief has not been persuasive, a rhetorical closing obviously will not save it. Most last-minute points worth making are better included in the argument. You need not worry about coming up with a clever closing—if they did not get it before, they probably will not get it now in the conclusion.

15. Appendices

Sometimes the court requires or allows you include an appendix containing a few choice items—key documents, exhibits, testimony, the full text of statutory and constitutional provisions, unpublished opinions (if the local rules allow you to cite them at all), items such as the contract or instrument sued upon, the final judgment, the notice of appeal, and other important or frequently cited materials. You should be careful about putting things other than the required items into an appendix. You do not want to make the brief twice as fat by virtue of an appendix. But a careful selection can be a great aid to the court by placing the most important documents and authorities at the judges' fingertips.

IV. DRAFTING THE ARGUMENT

The TREAT format (discussed earlier) applies in the argument section, and you should use your questions presented or Points of Error Thesis statements as your major headings, even if the local rules and practices require them to be excessively wordy. Use minor Thesis headings to guide the reader through the sub-issues that require separate TREAT.

A. Use argumentative thesis headings.

Thesis headings should be meaningful so that they can provide a useful summary of your argument to a judge that is skimming your argument section. A good thesis heading not only reveals a conclusion but provides the "because" part—the legal principles and facts that lead up to the conclusion. For example, the following are good argumentative thesis headings:

> ➢ Examples of proper thesis headings in the argument
>   A. The trial court erred in its determination that Bolling provoked the dog prior to the attack because Bolling did not directly attack or threaten the dog as required under Illinois law.

B. The trial court erred in holding that Bolling was trespassing because Bolling was acting peacefully in a place where he had a lawful right to be when he walked on a public sidewalk at Alden Hall without causing any noisy disturbance.

C. The trial court erred in holding that provocation bars Bolling's recovery because the dog's attack on Bolling was vicious and disproportionate to the dusting of snow the Dog received from Bolling.

➢ The following are **not** good headings:

A. Lack of Provocation

B. Bolling was acting peacefully in a place where he had a lawful right to be.

C. The dog's attack was disproportionate.

These last three examples do not suggest enough of the facts and principles of the law to make the headings useful, and the first of these three does not even tell the author's conclusion about the topic. Do not waste a heading by writing something like these. Let your headings be a quick summary of your argument if read one right after the other.

B. Policy counts more on appeal, and precedent becomes a two-way street

In the argument, as in many of the other sections discussed above, you must bear in mind that policy plays a greater role in appellate courts' reasoning, especially in the courts of last resort. Appellate courts do not worry just about following precedent, they have to worry about making it. Appellate courts have to consider the here and now of your case plus the effect that their ruling will have on future cases. You should write briefs with that in mind. If you spend too much effort developing the arguments and equities of your client's position, you may neglect to consider the effect what you are arguing will have on future cases. You should take the time in the discussion of each major issue raised on appeal to address public policy and precedential implications of the arguments you are raising. Usually, the page limits afforded on appeals are ample enough to allow for this, and it may help you persuade more judges of the propriety of your positions even prior to oral argument when the court can drill you in the policies affected by your arguments.

In similar fashion, you might discuss how the case fits into the broader stream of relevant decisions. Fit your appeal into a broader framework of the law and the policies behind the law. Appellate judges are more comfortable applying settled principles than deciding issues of first impression. Many appeals raise something new, but it does not benefit appellant to emphasize that. The law is built on precedent. It seeks the simple and established and avoids the unfamiliar. This means that demonstrating at length the novelty or complexity of your position rarely will help. Make the novel proposition seem familiar or, at most, a natural extension of something that is clearly accepted. The more you can fit your case into established principles, the greater your chance of success.

Start at a logical beginning for the arguments you raise. The page limits generally allow you to present a discussion of the stepping stone principles, both historical steps and steps of a logical progression that lead up to the present principles of the law you are asserting. Too many briefs start in the middle of a legal analysis, rather than building from broad general principles to the specific. Do not go back to the first day or even first semester of contracts, but lay a settled backdrop down before you start throwing the colorful paint around. Put your case into a broader, established legal context first so that judges understand where you are starting. From that they will quickly grasp where you are heading.

C. The continuing benefits of explanatory synthesis

Unless you have controlling precedent that exactly matches your client's case, you should emphasize **principles**, not **cases**. This is another way of looking at the benefits of explanatory synthesis. Individual cases may not say everything you need them to say on exactly what you need them to cover. If you find the magic, controlling, "on all fours" case, use it, but if you do not, you still can convince the court that your appeal fits the broader principles of the law that are illustrated by existing authorities. Synthesize the existing decisions to show how they fit this broader principle. Your argument should show that the cases are not the law itself, but simply illustrations of the law.

If your appeal raises a question of statutory construction, your search for broader principles focuses on what you claim is the statute's objective. Use legislative history to illustrate it. Buttress your construction with interpretations or applications by the implementing agency, and look to the commentators in treatises and law review articles. Whatever the issue, this effort is devoted to assuring the judges that you are not trying to sell them some wild new scheme, but simply that your case fits comfortably into the existing law as you have restated it in plain, straight-forward terms.

D. Be assertive rather than critical about the court below and your opponent's arguments, and remember the standard of review

Too many briefs just try to take pot-shots at the trial judge and the opponents. Even if the judge or opposing counsel have made blatant errors, you first should focus your efforts on what legal principles should apply to the case and only second on what the trial judge or your opponent did wrong. The judges on appeal are far more interested in how to reach and justify the right result. In fact, ad hominem attacks easily can turn the court against you.

You must deal fairly but convincingly with unfavorable authority. We previously have discussed the need to distinguish potentially controlling, negative authority and the decision whether (and **where**) to anticipate and handle negative persuasive authority. Add to that discussion the perception that at the appellate court level, very few dead flies in the bowl of appellate soup are going to go unnoticed. If your opponent does not find the bad case, the judges' clerks probably will. Thus, having the first word on a troublesome authority can make you look upright and truthful and gives you the chance to dull the effect of the authority before your opponent runs amok with it. That said, what is truly "adverse" can be a matter of interpretation. You really need to consider whether the authority is controlling (or just persuasive) and whether your facts are in some way distinguishable.

Finally, remember the standard of review when you are drafting your headings and the rest of the argument section. The standard of review is the keystone to court of appeals decision-making, so you must tailor your argument to it. When the standard is abuse of discretion, for example, it does no good to make arguments that apply only if the court were reviewing a question *de novo*. Define how much discretion is allowed under the law, and argue that the judge exceeded that level using authorities that actually found a violation of the applicable standard.

E. Minimize alternative arguments

Although there is no limit to the number of good arguments you raise (within reason), alternative arguments that simply crowd the brief with imaginative possibilities choke off the best arguments and drown your better arguments in a sea of words. Such scattergun tactics rarely are effective and can dilute your major points. Your time, energy, and space is better spent bolstering your main arguments.

F. As in other litigation documents, limit the use of footnotes, overuse of emphasis, and lengthy quotes

Limit footnotes if you can, and make sure you follow the rules of your jurisdiction. For example, sometimes the court will say that nothing **argumentative** can be in a footnote (i.e., nothing that presents part of the legal support for one of your arguments, as opposed to additional facts, statistics, or a side note of interest about something). Even if the local rules allow you to put argument in footnotes, you run the risk of the argument going unnoticed. Many judges skip footnotes completely, and others will not consider legal arguments mentioned only in footnotes.

Do not stress (underline, bold, italicize) too much in your text—you will stress out the judges! Stated otherwise: no one likes a lawyer who is constantly shouting. Overdoing your underlining or other emphasis has that same effect. Putting key words in all capitals and using exclamation points are artificial devices. Sparing use of underlining or italicizing is useful to highlight key words, but effective emphasis depends on the content and arrangement of your text.

Shorten your quotes. No one likes long quotes for at least three reasons: (1) long quotes are too boring and many readers skip over them; (2) the reader knows you are going to (and should) explain the significance of the quote anyway; and (3) readers want to hear what *you* have to say. So, distill long quotes down to their essential point and avoid long descriptions of cases.

V. DRAFTING AN ANSWERING BRIEF

The most important point for appellee is to make your affirmative case first before you start attacking appellant's. The same points made in discussing appellant's strategy fits here, too: fit your case into a broader framework. You want to set the playing field rather than accept the one set by your opponent. If you do a better job of that than your opponent, then when you start responding to specific arguments you can do so from a position of strength.

Storytelling in the statement of facts is as important for appellee as it is for appellant, and more so if the appellant has done a good job getting out its side of the story. If your opponent told a good story in her opening brief, acknowledge it, but immediately turn the tables around to your side: "Appellant told a good story about XYZ. Now here is the rest of the story." At best you will pull the court's attention and concern away from your opponent and on to your client. At least you should make sure the court is returned to the middle ground, neutral territory, not swayed by the sympathies of either side. This task will be difficult enough if your opponent was an excellent storyteller.

In developing your analytical framework, it will help if you can synthesize the broad principles in a way that highlights the novelty of appellant's position. As mentioned before, appellate judges generally take more comfort in fitting cases into established principles than in breaking new ground. When you can show that appellant is trying to turn the law on its head, you have an excellent chance of winning.

When you start responding to specific arguments, you have the option to follow the sequence of issues used by appellant but you are not bound to follow this structure. Courts appreciate the simplicity of this structure, but you should consider the possibility that this structure might not be the most effective way to structure your arguments. Appellant's third best point might be your best point, and appellant's best point is likely to be your worst point. It is more important to present your best point first and next best point second than it is to limit your brief to the order picked out by your opponent.

What is most important is to make sure you answer all of appellant's arguments. Even if your opponent has raised an argument that obviously lacks merit, you should explain why. Do not leave the court guessing whether you intended to concede something, or force the court to undertake independent research on why appellant's last two arguments should fail, simply because you failed to address them. In addition:

> ➤ Never assume that appellant has laid the necessary foundation for its arguments. Go through a mental checklist on each argument: Did appellant preserve this point below? Are the grounds appellant is advancing now for overturning an evidentiary ruling the same ones it offered below? Is the legal theory appellant advances now the same one presented below? If not, stress that before you even consider a response on the merits.

> ➤ If the appellant seems to have scored points by showing defects in the trial court's approach, remind the court of appeals that it is reviewing the lower court's result, not its reasoning. It can affirm on any basis supported by the law. If you have focused your brief on what should be the controlling principles, you need not worry about defending the lower court's faulty reasoning.

Appellees have the opportunity to call the court's attention to shortcomings in appellant's brief—an inference stated as a fact, an adverse case ignored, and so forth. The tendency is to overdo these comments as if an appeal were a debate where you are scoring points. Keep these comments to a minimum, and stress only those that are substantial. Your goal is to affirm the district court, not eviscerate your opponent.

In rare instances, appellee may want to skip the jurisdictional statement, statement of the issues presented for review, statement of facts, statement of the case (or proceedings below), and the statement of the standard(s) of review (unless, of course, appellee is dissatisfied with appellant's statements of them). This can pose something of a dilemma, especially with the statements of issues or facts. You may find nothing specifically wrong with appellant's statements except their emphasis and implications. Should you accept them for fear the court of appeals will think you a nit-picker? Should you restate them in their entirety, or simply those parts you especially dislike?

You are not required to prove that appellant's statements are wrong before you can write your own. The rule allows you to rewrite whenever you are dissatisfied with one or more of appellant's statements. In other words, it is entirely up to you. You need not apologize. Whether you submit an entire restatement or portions of one will depend on how much needs restating. If your opponent did a decent job of telling its story in the statement of facts, you really must do your best to tell a better story or at least tell "the rest of the story" to restore equilibrium in the case. If your opponent's facts section was mundane, however, you need not go to great lengths to correct the record, but you should take advantage of the situation and tell your own story. Do not miss out on the chance to get the court to care about your client so that it will be happy to listen to your legal arguments that provide the means to the end of victory for your client.

VI. DRAFTING THE REPLY BRIEF

Appellant's right to reply is a valuable right. Do not squander it by rehashing or repeating arguments already covered in your opening brief. Having the last word, as such, does not necessarily have a tremendous effect on the appeal because the judges are likely to wait until the parties have filed all their briefs and then read them all together. Appellant should use its right of reply to focus the appeal down to its core. You know what you said in your opening brief; you now see what appellee has said in response. Refine the issues in light of both. A reply brief is the best vehicle for narrowing the true issues, so sharpen the focus. Now is your chance to tell the court what this appeal is really all about. If appellee did not answer all the issues raised in your opening brief, make the most of that. The reply is your chance to put the issues in their starkest terms that are favorable to your client.

Sometimes you also must use your reply for damage control. If appellee has hurt your position, you must do what you can to repair it. Whatever you do, do not try to interject new issues in your reply. Not only will the court likely ignore them, the judges also will be irritated that you tried to sneak something in without giving your opponent a chance to respond. If something new (a case, statute, rule, regulation, etc.) has come up that the court should know about, use the procedure for submitting supplemental authorities rather than putting it in your reply brief. That way you do not co-mingle the separate functions of replying and submitting supplemental authorities.

A reply brief is optional. However, it is hard to imagine a situation where appellant would not exercise its right to reply where the local rules permit it.

VII. SAMPLE BRIEF GRADING SHEETS

The following are sample brief grading sheets we have used in advocacy and moot court courses and competitions. The first is a general grading sheet for a moot court brief, while the second is a grading sheet created for a particular assignment. In both samples, you can see the breakdown of items and the relative importance of each. By using these forms as a checklist, you can perform a self-guided edit of your own brief.

MOOT COURT BRIEF GRADING SHEET

Student: _____   Argument Section(s) Drafted: _____

INITIAL SECTIONS (40 points possible):
Cover (3):
    Correct color (1 pt); Proper caption, bound at the left (1 pt)   _____
    Identifies team #, students' names, sections drafted (1 pt)   _____
Questions Presented (3):
    Presented in correct order per U.S. S.Ct. Rules (1st) (1 pt)   _____
    Describes issues in proper Supreme Court style (Chap. 3 and
    lecture) (0-2 pts)   _____
    Notes: _____
Table of Contents (3):
    Presented in correct order per U.S. S.Ct. Rules (2nd) (1 pt)   _____
    Listing for Argument section w/ full headings for subsections (0-2 pts)   _____
    Notes: _____
Table of Authorities (3):
    Presented in correct order per U.S. S.Ct. Rules (3rd) (1 pt)   _____
    Separates Cases, Statutes, Legislative History, Secondary Sources
    (0-2 pts)   _____
    Notes: _____
Opinions Below (3):
    Presented in correct order per U.S. S.Ct. Rules (4th) (1 pt)   _____
    Gives citation (1 pt); References record pages where opinion is found
    (1 pt)   _____
Constitutional and Statutory Sections (3):
    Presented in correct order per U.S. S.Ct. Rules (5th) (1 pt)   _____
    Quotes const. & stat. sections <u>or</u> cites them w/ ref. to full text
    in Appdx. (2 pts)   _____
Statement of the Case (10):
    Presented in correct order per U.S. S.Ct. Rules (6th) (1 pt)   _____
    Properly describes facts, proceedings below w/o legal argument (0-5 pts) _____

Section is slanted in favor of client, but not outrageously biased (0-4 pts) _____

Notes: _____

Summary of the Argument (10):

Presented in correct order per U.S. S.Ct. Rules (7th) (1 pt)   _____

Properly summarizes arguments in concise manner (0-5 pts)   _____

Section is strong and punchy, and makes best points clearly and
directly (0-4 pts)   _____

Notes: _____

Conclusion (2): Appears last (1 pt); requests relief properly (1 pt)   _____

SUBTOTAL for INITIAL SECTIONS: _____

ARGUMENT SECTION (60 points possible):

Use of Facts to further arguments (0-10 pts)   _____

Use of Cases and Statutory Authorities - each point is well
researched and supported with proper authority; demonstrates
knowledge of controlling vs. persuasive authority (0-10 pts)   _____

Use of Legislative History and secondary interpretive authorities (0-5 pts) _____

Organization - logical, coherent; uses IRAC or TREAT format;
proper division of argument into main issues and sub-issues (0-10 pts)   _____

Persuasiveness and Advocacy - presents arguments in compelling and
convincing manner; best points are emphasized; weak points are
explained, defused (0-15 pts)   _____

Anticipates Opponent's positions and provides counter-analysis
(0-5 pts)   _____

Public Policy - identifies and explains how arguments further public
policies (0-5 pts)   _____

SUBTOTAL for ARGUMENT SECTION: _____
TOTAL for INITIAL SECTIONS +ARGUMENT SECTION: _____

PENALTY DEDUCTIONS:

Citation Errors (-0.5 pts for each error; max -5 pts)   _____

Format Errors: 2.0 spacing, 12 pt. font, 1" margins, 25/40 pg limit
(-0.5 pts/pg; max -5 pts)   _____

Grammar, Spelling Errors, Typos (-0.5 pts for each error; max -3 pts)   _____

Late Penalty (-5 pts per 24 hour period late)   _____

TOTAL POINTS (out of 100):   _____
FINAL GRADE: _____

APPELLATE BRIEF (FINAL) GRADING SHEET

Student _____   Total Points (out of 100): _____

INITIAL SECTIONS (25 points possible):
Cover (2): Correct color (1); Proper caption, bound at the left (1)   _____
Questions Presented (2): Describes two issues (1) Uses broader, public
policy style - e.g., artist, celebrity (1)   _____
Table of Contents (2): Proper style (1) Listing for Argument section
w/ full headings for subsections (1)   _____
Table of Authorities (2): Proper style (1) Separates Cases, Statutes,
Legislative History, Secondary Sources (1)   _____
Statement of Jurisdiction (1)   _____
Standard of Review (1)   _____
Statement of the Case (6): Properly describes facts, proceedings below
w/o legal argument (3)   _____
Section is slanted in favor of client, but not outrageously biased (3)   _____
Summary of the Argument (7): Properly summarizes arguments in
concise manner (3)   _____
Section is strong and punchy, and makes best points clearly and directly (4)   _____
Conclusion (1): requests relief properly   _____
Sections appear in correct order (1)   _____

SUBTOTAL for INITIAL SECTIONS: _____

ORGANIZATION (5 points possible)   _____
Overall organization-two issues: News, Parody (2)   _____
Sections have an obvious difference in focus even if some authorities
are used in both sections (2)   _____
Brief is coherent and makes intelligent use of transitions, roadmaps
or sub-sections (3)   _____

NEWS (30 points possible)   _____
Statutes and Const.(4):   _____
       Quotes § 3344(a)   _____
       Quotes § 3344(d)   _____
       Quotes U.S. Const. amend. I   _____
       Quotes Cal. Const. art. I, § 2   _____
Discusses commercial speech effectively - distinct from selling speech (3)   _____
Use of controlling authorities (5)   _____
Use of other primary persuasive authorities (5)   _____
Use of secondary persuasive authorities (2)   _____

Explanatory Synthesis (5) _____

Counteranalysis (3) _____

Weaving of public policy into arguments (3) _____

PARODY (30 points possible) _____

Notes and cites authority as to whether parody is defense to right of
publicity (2) _____

Use of controlling authorities (5) _____

Use of primary persuasive authorities (5) _____

Use of secondary persuasive authorities (2) _____

Explanatory Synthesis (5) _____

Counteranalysis (3) _____

Weaving of public policy re: right to criticize public figures and politicians (4) _____

Weaving of public policy re: artistic expression and transformation (4) _____

ADVOCACY AND RESEARCH (10 points possible) _____

Theme: attempted to develop theme for the entire brief that furthered
public policies concerning the issues of the case and tied together the
brief as a whole (3) _____

Advocacy Skills and Persuasiveness: overall demonstration of adversarial
writing skills learned in the course (4) _____

Evidence of Research (3) _____

SUBTOTAL 1 (out of 25) _____

SUBTOTAL 2 (out of 75) _____

POINTS BEFORE DEDUCTIONS _____

Proofreading and Other Errors (Deductions):

Citation errors (-0.5 each/max. -5) _____

Missing citation (-1 each/max. -5) _____

Typo/spelling (-0.5 each/max. -3) _____

Formatting: 2.0-sp, 1" marg, page limit, 25 lines/pg; 12 pt courier
font (-2 each/max. -4) _____

Rules: no name in upper right corner p.1; no page #s (-2 each/max. -4) _____

Lateness: (-20 each 24hr per/-5 late email) _____

Total Deductions _____

TOTAL POINTS _____

VIII. SAMPLE BRIEFS

The samples that follow are two student briefs from an intramural competition that was patterned after the Association of the Bar of the City of New York's National Moot Court Competition, and two actual practitioners' United States Supreme Court briefs from one of the cases that was central to the problem used in the intramural competition briefs. The last sample brief is a practitioner's petition for a writ of mandamus filed in the United States Court of Appeals for the Eleventh Circuit.

We have annotated the briefs with our comments and criticisms. When we have a comment to make, we have inserted it into the middle of the brief, as seen below:

> Naturally, the briefs did not have these comment boxes in them when they were submitted. Do not be confused by the placement of the comment boxes.

Although these briefs appear in the same font as the rest of this book, most of them would have been submitted in Courier or Courier New font. Remember to check the rules of your court or competition when you chose the font of your briefs. We have spaced the briefs with the same line spacing as the rest of this book, when the actual briefs would have been produced with double spacing. Please note that we have left the briefs in original form with regard to citation forms, wording, and other stylistic choices that may not be completely consistent with the rules and recommendations we have given earlier in this text.

Sample Brief No. 1:

Student Brief of Petitioner
in the moot court case:

Metropolitan School Dist. of Gotham
v.
Branch Louisian of the United Church of
Christ the Savior

> This caption follows the form we discussed earlier in this chapter.

DOCKET NO. 00-100

SUPREME COURT OF THE UNITED STATES

March Term 2000

METROPOLITAN SCHOOL DISTRICT OF GOTHAM,
STATE OF NEW KENT,

Petitioner,

——*against*——

BRANCH LOUISIAN OF THE UNITED CHURCH OF
CHRIST THE SAVIOR,

Respondent.

On Writ of Certiorari to the United States Court of Appeals for the Fourteenth Circuit

---

BRIEF OF PETITIONER

Student 1 and Student 2
1234 Streetname Apt. A
St. Louis, MO 63108
Counsel of Record for Petitioner

These Questions Presented work well. They reflect the fact that the case is pending in a court of last resort (the U.S. Supreme Court) that will set a precedent for all courts applying federal law. The questions do not refer to a single party but to the *categories of party* into which the actual parties fit—a school district and a church. The questions have an appropriate level of detail and they are non-argumentative. They are good examples of the proper way to present the issues.

Questions Presented for Review

I. Whether a public school district violates a religious organization's First Amendment free speech rights by refusing to post information regarding creationism on the school district's web site created to further the educational mission of the school district?

II. Whether a public school district violates the First Amendment's Establishment Clause by sponsoring a religious web page on the district's web site created to increase the educational opportunities for students on topics within the curriculum?

This Table of Contents is ineffective primarily because it is too short. The Argument section should display each thesis heading and sub-heading of the Argument, with a page reference for each. Then the table of contents becomes a useful outline for the judges. Note that there is no "Opinions and Judgments Entered in the Case" section. This could have been an oversight because some courts require such a section in addition to the summary of the case. Lesson? Check the local rules.

Table of Contents

Table of Authorities i
Constitutional Provisions iv
Statement of the Case v
Summary of the Argument vii
Argument 1
Conclusion 32

This Table of Authorities is nicely formatted, but it should have been broken down into categories of authorities as shown above in this chapter, and the authors should have left out the jump cites (pinpoint cites). They also should have cited the two lower court opinions from the moot court problem.

Table of Authorities

Adler v. Duval County Sch. Bd.,
174 F.3d 1236 (11th Cir.1999) 23

Agostini v. Felton,
521 U.S. 203 (1997) 31

Arkansas Educ. Television Comm'n v. Forbes,
118 S.Ct. 1633, 1644 (1998) 5, 9

Board of Educ. Of Westside Community Sch. v. Mergens,
496 U.S. 226 (1990) 22, 28

Capital Square Review and Advisory Bd. v. Pinette,
515 U.S. 753 (1995) 27

* * *

U.S. Postal Serv. v. Greenburgh Civic Ass'n,
453 U.S. 114, 129 (1981) 4

Wallace v. Jaffree,
472 U.S. 38 (1985) 22

Erwin Chemerinsky, *Court Takes a Narrow View of Viewpoint Discrimination,* Trial, Mar. 1999, at 90 10

Merriam Webster's Collegiate Dictionary 1244
(10th ed. 1995)... 10

Constitutional Provisions and Statutes

U.S. Const. amend. I:

Congress shall make no law respecting an establishment of religion, or prohibiting the free exercise thereof; or abridging the freedom of speech, or of the press; or the right of the people peaceably to assemble, and to petition the Government for a redress of grievances.

> The students improperly quote Fed. R. Civ. P. 56(c) here. The purpose of the section is to provide the text of substantively controlling constitutional, statutory or regulatory provisions, not procedural rules.

Fed. R. Civ. P. 56(c):

The motion shall be served at least 10 days before the time fixed for the hearing. The adverse party prior to the day of hearing may serve opposing affidavits. The judgment sought shall be rendered forthwith if the pleadings, depositions, answers to interrogatories, and admissions on file, together with the affidavits, if any, show that there is no genuine issue as to any material fact and that the moving party is entitled to a judgment as a matter of law. A summary judgment, interlocutory in character, may be rendered on the same issue of liability alone although there is a genuine issue as to the amount of damages.

Statement of the Case: The first paragraph of this section is done properly, although it does little to advance petitioner's case. To improve the section, zero in on some specifics that the lower courts held, and quote those portions that help your appeal, or at least that box in the lower courts to a position that you can handle. The remaining paragraphs tell a little of the facts. Again, petitioner is holding back a lot. This is a very cautious facts section. You can be more creative in terms of facts to detail and emphasize, and in the way you word the facts so as to paint a picture for the court, and get the court in a frame of mind to agree with your side. Regarding the cites to the record, the U.S. Supreme Court Rules tell you to cite them as Record 3 instead of using the form (R. at 3). Always check Local Rules!

Statement of the Case

Respondent, Branch Louisian of the United Church of Christ the Savior ("Church"), filed a complaint under 42 U.S.C. § 1983 against Petitioner, the Metropolitan School District of Gotham, State of New Kent ("School District"), claiming the School District violated Church's rights under the Free Speech and Establishment clauses of the United States Constitution, Amendment 1, by refusing to allow the Church's religious web pages on the topic of creationism to be displayed on the School District's Internet web site. (R. at 3.) The District Court of New Kent ruled in favor of the School District and denied Church's Motion for Summary Judgment. (R. at 9.) The Church appealed. The United States Court of Appeals for the Fourteenth Circuit reversed the District Court's decision. (R. at 21.) This Court granted certiorari. (R. at 22.)

Petitioner began operating an Internet service provider and managing a web server for the purpose of promoting information about the areas of study currently being taught in the School District. (R. at 11.) The School District invites faculty of the School District and other educational institutions in Gotham to propose web pages for inclusion in the site. (R. at 11.) Any entity seeking access to the web site must submit a proposal to the School District. (R. at 11.) The School District then reviews the proposals and determines whether access should be granted based upon whether the web pages are directly related to a topic currently included in the School District's curriculum guide. (R.. at 11.)

The School District's home page contains an alphabetical listing of all sponsored web sites and pages that have been accepted and linked to the School District's web page. (R. at 12.) Each listing includes a small icon designed by the creator of the sponsored pages, the title of the web site, a short description of the contents of the pages, and a link to the actual "http" address of the pages. (R. at 12.)

Church applied to the School District for permission to post its web site on March 5, 1999. (R. at 13.) The Church described the proposal as a "thorough examination of the doctrine of Creationism from the Book of Genesis in the Bible . . . and a comparison and contrasting . . . with the purportedly scientific doctrines of Evolution and Natural Selection." (R. at 13.) The proposal also included commentary from religious leaders about creationism in text, audio, and video formats and religious depictions of the story of creation in Genesis. (R. at 13.) The School District rejected the proposal because the topic did not directly relate to a subject included in School District's curriculum guide. (R. at 14.)

Summary of the Argument: This section is nicely done. It is punchy, it does not beat around the bush, and it gets a lot of information out in a short space. About the only thing we can point out is that the petitioner did not cite any authority in this section. You may want to consider citing one or two of the major cases or statutes on which your argument is truly based, although not all attorneys follow that practice (in fact, some are strongly against it).

The authors actually disagree with each other on this, and perhaps that underscores a separate point. You will find that no two attorneys you work with will have identical styles, and written work product can never be entirely divorced from personal style. Some attorneys maintain that no cases should be cited in the SOA, while others find it odd if at least the one or two leading authorities are omitted. You will have to use your own best judgment—coupled with the knowledge you can compile about your colleagues (read briefs they have filed in the past) and, of course, a thorough reading of the court's rules.

Summary of the Argument

The Supreme Court should reverse the appellate court's judgment and grant summary judgment to School District because the School District has not infringed on Church's constitutionally protected free speech rights. The web site at issue is a nonpublic forum due to the control the School District maintained over the forum and because the forum was never opened to the general public. Additionally, the School District properly made a content-based, non-viewpoint centered discrimination of the Church's offered statement on creationism because creationism neither relates to any topic in the school district nor does creationism comport to the policy of the School District in teaching evolution. Finally, regardless of the forum or the type of discrimination, the School District's censorship survives strict scrutiny. Both the School District's interest in providing the best education for children and its duty to abide by the Establishment Clause of the Constitution are compelling state interests. The censorship at issue was narrowly tailored to fulfill both of these interests as evidenced by the fact that this has been the only restriction of its kind since the inception of the web site.

The Supreme Court should reverse the appellate court's judgment and grant summary judgment to School District because sponsoring of the Church's religious web pages by the School District amounts to a violation of the Establishment Clause of the First Amendment of the Constitution. The Church's web pages are on creationism, a religious doctrine. The Establishment Clause is violated by the School District's sponsorship of the Church's web pages under any test this Court chooses to apply. Sponsoring of the web pages creates a coercive mechanism in which students are coerced to acknowledge the religious doctrine of the Church. The inclusion of the Church's religious web pages on the School District's home page lead a reasonable person to believe

> The student authors of this brief were not careful about how they referred to the parties. We like the fact that they are not using the confusing terms "petitioner and respondent" or "plaintiff and defendant," but you will see the authors switch from "the School District" to "the District" to "School District," and from "the Church" to "Church" in this brief. Stick to one form of the parties names throughout the brief to preserve your readers' comprehension.

that the District is endorsing the religious doctrine of creationism. The purpose of the web server was to provide educational opportunities for the students. This secular purpose is subverted by inclusion of the Church's religious web pages and creating the effect of endorsement of creationism by the School District. The School District monitoring, reviewing, and surveillance of the sponsored web pages leads to an excessive governmental entanglement with the Church and thus a violation of the Establishment Clause if the School District sponsors the Church's web pages.

Argument

Argument: The first heading is a mouthful. It is almost a Complete Disclosure type drafting job of the issue, but you may remember that the Questions Presented for Review on the second page of the brief were not drafted in Complete Disclosure form, but in proper Notice form. There is nothing inherently wrong with this heading as a grammatical matter, but it is probably too dense. We can see why the petitioners did not want to list their substantive headings and subheadings in the table of contents.

We do like the thesis stated in the heading—it is forceful and bold. "The school district is allowed to discriminate on the basis of content . . ." This is good, affirmative drafting. Take a stand in your theses; make your point and stick to it. So much the better if the heading were put in the table of contents, where the court might read it up front and get very interested in looking into the argument right away.

The "introduction" subsection here is a reasonable start to the argument, but do not waste the reader's time with a one word heading; write an argumentative thesis heading that summarizes the section, or drop the heading. You do not need a heading that says "Introduction" when everyone expects this section to serve that role.

The first paragraph is useful to set up the rest of the section. In the second paragraph, the reference to *de novo* review is a very good thing (check local rules on where Standard of Review should appear), but the reference to Fed. R. Civ. P. 56 is completely unnecessary. You could strike the whole second sentence in the second paragraph and never miss it.

I. THE UNITED STATES SUPREME COURT SHOULD REVERSE THE APPELLATE COURT'S DECISION GRANTING SUMMARY JUDGMENT TO CHURCH AND GRANT SUMMARY JUDGMENT TO SCHOOL DISTRICT BECAUSE THE SCHOOL DISTRICT'S WEB SITE IS A NONPUBLIC FORUM AND THE SCHOOL DISTRICT IS ALLOWED TO DISCRIMINATE ON THE BASIS OF CONTENT SO LONG AS THE DISCRIMINATION IS REASONABLE AND VIEWPOINT NEUTRAL.

A. Introduction

The First Amendment, applicable to the States via the Fourteenth Amendment, provides protection from unnecessary governmental interference in free speech. Cohen v.

<u>California</u>, 403 U.S. 15, 19 (1971). The First Amendment provides, "Congress shall make no law respecting an establishment of religion, or prohibiting the free exercise thereof; or abridging the freedom of speech, or of the press; or the right of the people peaceably to assemble, and to petition the Government for a redress of grievances." U.S. Const. amend. I. In order to invoke First Amendment jurisprudence, the entity claiming a violation of its Constitutional rights ("speaker") must seek access to a "forum." <u>Cornelius v. NAACP Legal Defense & Educ. Fund, Inc.</u>, 473 U.S. 788, 801 (1985). A forum is either public property or private property dedicated to public use. <u>Id.</u>

When a speaker claims a violation of its First Amendment rights after being denied access to a forum, this Court reviews the facts *de novo*. <u>Edwards v. South Carolina</u>, 372 U.S. 229, 235 (1963). Additionally, summary judgment should only be granted when the pleadings, discovery, and all affidavits, if any, "show that there is no genuine issue as to any material fact and that the moving party is entitled to a judgment as a matter of law." Fed.R.Civ.P. 56(c).

> Here, the authors are trying to get the section moving, but the engine is balking a little. The authors jump into the "forum" argument in the first paragraph, but then the second paragraph steps away from the topic and moves on to the "teach and nurture the children" argument. It doesn't sound that bad, but it could be more focused. We take it that authors probably were trying to write an umbrella or roadmap section for the rest of the subsections under section I.
>
> The discussion of education and the courts' "hands off" policy is a very good point for petitioner, especially to get into right up front. Petitioner may be shaky in some areas of the First Amendment law implicated by this case, but not this area. You should try to lead off with your strong points, as these authors did.

Protection of speech rights varies depending upon the nature of the forum. <u>Perry Educ. Ass'n v. Perry Local Educators' Ass'n</u>, 460 U.S. 37, 44-46 (1983). The Court has consistently recognized that a forum is either public, limited public, or nonpublic depending on the historical or present treatment the government has afforded the property. <u>See id.</u> at 44-46. Whether the government can deny a speaker access to a particular forum depends upon whether the forum is public, limited public, or nonpublic.

> We would break up the following paragraph into at least two paragraphs. There are too many connectors—"additionally," "moreover," "finally"—used here trying to keep it all together. It would be better to lose one or more of the connectors and make it two or three paragraphs.

Furthermore, this Court must give deference to school official's decisions regarding educational matters. <u>Hazelwood Sch. Dist. v. Kuhlmeier</u>, 484 U.S. 260, 273 (1988). This Court has long applied the standard that the education of children is primarily the responsibility of parents, teachers, and state and local school officials, not of federal judges. <u>Id.</u> Additionally, the Court has noted that it is only when the government censors with no valid educational purpose that the First Amendment is "directly and sharply implicated." <u>Id.</u> Moreover, when a party asks the courts to review a genuinely academic decision, the courts should show "great respect for the faculty's professional judgment." <u>Regents of the Univ. of Mich. v. Ewing</u>, 474 U.S. 214, 225 (1985). Educators have the primary freedom to determine who may teach, what may be taught, and how it shall be taught. <u>Sweezy v. New Hampshire</u>, 354 U.S. 234, 263 (1957) (Frankfurter, J., concurring). Finally, the Court has most recently held, "When the government appropriates public funds to promote a particular policy of its own it is entitled to say what it wishes, and it may take legitimate and appropriate steps to ensure that its message is neither garbled nor distorted . . ." <u>Rosenberger v. Rector and Visitors of the Univ. of Va.</u>, 515 U.S. 819, 833 (1995). As a final introductory point, web sites, web pages, and web servers are subject to First Amendment forum analysis even though they are somewhat new areas for discourse. <u>See generally</u> <u>Reno v. ACLU</u>, 521 U.S. 844 (1997); <u>Loving v. Boren</u>, 956 F.Supp. 953 (W.D. Okla. 1997); <u>CompuServe, Inc. v. Cyber Promotions, Inc.</u>, 962 F.Supp. 1015 (S.D. Ohio 1997).

The District's decision to exclude the Church's web page discussing creationism was a proper educational decision to which this Court owes great deference. Further, by creating a nonpublic forum, the School District was allowed to engage in content-based discrimination. There is no question that the School District properly made a content-based, non-viewpoint centered censorship in denying access to the Church. Moreover, even if this Court finds that the School District's web page was a limited public forum, the content-based censorship exercised by the School District passes strict scrutiny analysis as it is narrowly tailored to promote a compelling state interest.

> Section B is omitted.

* * *

> Section C is well-structured as it obviously presents an IRAC (or TREAT) discussion. It shows how one issue in the chain of issues suggested by the problem can be dealt with in a clear and succinct manner using the classic IRAC or TREAT format. On the negative side, the heading is incomplete—it does not have the "because" part containing the facts and principles that support the conclusion stated here.

C. <u>The District's web site is a nonpublic forum.</u>

The first issue involves identifying the nature of the forum. The web site at issue is a nonpublic forum. A non-public forum is created when the government does not open the property to the general public. <u>Perry Educ. Ass'n</u>, 460 U.S. at 46. "The First Amendment does not guarantee access to property simply because it is owned or controlled by the government." <u>Id.</u> (quoting <u>U.S. Postal Serv. v. Greenburgh Civic Ass'n</u>, 453 U.S. 114, 129 (1981)). Moreover, "the State, no less than a private owner of property, has power to preserve the property under its control for the use to which it is lawfully dedicated." <u>Id.</u> (quoting <u>Greenburgh Civic Ass'n</u>, 453 U.S. at 129).

> It is regretful that the authors chose to present an unsynthesized explanation section rather than a synthesized explanation. Why not synthesize <u>Perry</u> and <u>Cornelius</u> with other cases to make a better illustration of what is a nonpublic forum? The unsynthesized explanation forces the authors to apply cases instead of principles to the facts in the application section.

In <u>Perry</u>, the Court held that the internal mail system created by the school district to disseminate information to teachers and staff was a non-public forum because neither the district's intent nor its practice opened the mail system to the general public. <u>See generally id.</u> The Court found as dispositive the fact that the district had to grant permission to any person seeking access to the mail system and the fact that permission had not been granted to all who requested it. <u>Id.</u> at 47. The evidence revealed that some groups other than district employees and administrators had been granted access to the mail system. <u>Id.</u> However, the Court concluded that selective access does not create a public forum. <u>Id.</u> <u>See also</u> <u>Cornelius</u>, 473 U.S. at 788 (holding that government run charity drive for nonprofit organizations was nonpublic forum where government retained the power to exclude non-healthcare or non-welfare nonprofit organizations); <u>Arkansas Educ. Television Comm'n v. Forbes</u>, 118 S.Ct. 1633, 1644 (1998) (holding that political debate operated by public television station was nonpublic forum where participation in debate was contingent on the station's permission).

The Court's analysis in <u>Perry</u> strongly supports a finding that the web site at issue here is a nonpublic forum. First, the School District's implementation of standards relating to the type of information the speaker must contribute to the site in order to gain access shows the forum has never been opened to the general public. (R. at 11.) Requiring any speaker's message to relate to a topic of education in the District shows that the forum was not created for the general public because the average person in the community could not be admitted as most people do not possess information pertaining to primary or secondary education. Further, the standards are actively enforced. (R. at 14.) As in <u>Perry</u>, in order to gain access, the speaker must obtain permission from the School District after tendering a written proposal. (R. at 11.) The School District also performs periodic checks of the site for information that is in violation of the policy. (R. at 11.) Finally, the School District maintains the right to remove any non-conforming information. (R. at 11.) Therefore, the District maintained control over the web site by requiring permission, reserving the right to remove information, and setting standards on whom may enter the forum. This control, like in <u>Perry</u>, exhibits the District's purpose that the forum not be opened to the general public. As such, the web site is a nonpublic forum; and the appellate court's decision should be overturned.

> Section D is another clear IRAC or TREAT discussion although it fails to use explanatory synthesis. Once again, bringing in the education of school children is a great idea for petitioner. Always return to your strengths.

D. The District's refusal to allow Church's information regarding Creationism is reasonable, content-based, non-viewpoint discrimination.

Once it has been determined that the web site is a nonpublic forum, the next question is whether the School District properly refused the Church's proposal. It is clear that in this case, the School District properly refused the Church's proposal because its decision was content-based, reasonable, and made irrespective of the Church's viewpoint.

When the forum is characterized as nonpublic, the speaker forbidden access has no First Amendment or other right to the forum. <u>Perry Educ. Ass'n</u>, 460 U.S. at 54. As such, the censorship does not have to be narrowly tailored, the objective does not have to be compelling, and the most efficient means of fulfilling the state's interest do not have to be used. <u>Id.</u> The School District has acted properly as long as its restriction is reasonable and not based on the speaker's viewpoint on the subject. <u>Id.</u> at 46. Distinctions may be drawn between applicants to the site based on subject matter and speaker identity. <u>Id.</u> Furthermore, the reasonableness required need not be the most reasonable or the only reasonable limitation; the state need only show that it was legitimately justified in its actions. <u>Cornelius</u>, 473 U.S. at 808.

> Subsection 1 is strange in that it promises to discuss "Supreme Court precedent<u>s</u>" and then only discusses <u>Cornelius</u>. Do not make a promise and then not keep it. Just say, "under <u>Cornelius</u>" not "under precedent<u>s</u>."
>
> The thesis heading here is a throw-away; it lacks the "because" information to support the thesis.

1. The District's restriction is reasonable.

Any government restriction on speech in a nonpublic forum must be reasonable. Reasonableness of the restriction on access to a nonpublic forum must be determined in relation to the government's purpose and surrounding circumstances of the forum. Id. at 809. The School District's censorship of the Church's proposal is reasonable in light of Supreme Court precedents.

After determining that the forum in Cornelius was nonpublic, the Court analyzed the government's reasonableness in refusing to allow legal defense and other nonprofit litigation organizations from receiving proceeds from the charity drive designed to support health and welfare nonprofit entities. Id. The Court found the restriction reasonable. Id.

In relation to speech restrictions in nonpublic fora, the reasonableness test requires only a threshold showing that the government has appropriate purposes in limiting access. See generally id. The Court has stated that the government acts reasonably when it discriminates in order to maintain administrative manageability; access to the public can be obtained by the speaker through some other means; where it has denied access in order to avoid the appearance of favoritism to one political group over another; and where it restricts in order to avoid controversy. Id. at 809-810. Furthermore, the government does not have to resort to other agencies' restrictions or findings in different circumstances to determine reasonableness. Id.

Applying Cornelius to the case at bar clearly shows the School District's actions were reasonable. The School District's policy was implemented to supplement the topics listed in the curriculum; and creationism neither is nor ever has been a part of the curriculum for the past 150 years. (R. at 15.) Secondly, the School District reasonably restricted access to the Church to avoid controversy because deeply rooted disagreements may arise over any association between the School District and any particular religious beliefs. The School District also feared jeopardizing the success of the program. Allowing the Church to post information about creationism would inevitably lead to other groups seeking access to post information completely unrelated to any part of the curriculum. This slippery slope would result in the weakening of the evaluative process and would inevitably result in a *de facto* public forum as proper research and analysis of each applicant would become overly consuming of both time and money. For these reasons, the School District reasonably denied access to the Church.

> The next three paragraphs extend the application section to discuss three additional points The authors are fond of prefatory phrases such as "further," "finally," similarly." These words are throat-clearing expressions that add nothing to the meaning. Each should be deleted.

Further, it is clear that the School District had an appropriate purpose in restricting access to the Church in order to maintain neutrality. Like Cornelius, where the Court held limiting the appearance of political favoritism provided reasonable justification, restricting access here to avoid the appearance of religious favoritism shows the reasonableness of the School District's actions. Allowing the Church to post the information would lead non-religious parents in the community to believe that because of their beliefs, their children will be treated differently than those who favor creationism.

Finally, the School District acted properly here because the Church can spread its message to both students and non-students through other means. Traditionally, churches and other religious organizations have spread their message throughout the world by active missionary work. Similarly, the Church can spread its message of creationism throughout the community by distributing pamphlets, door-to-door confrontation, rallies, and persuading non-Christians to visit its services.

The factors set out in <u>Cornelius</u>, as applied to the case at bar, show the reasonableness of the School District's actions. Not only has the School District met the threshold requirement, it has persuasively demonstrated that proper measures were taken in order to maintain the vitality of its program.

2. <u>The District's restriction is content-based and not viewpoint centered.</u>

The next issue is whether the School District's restriction is impermissibly viewpoint centered or whether it is appropriate content-based discrimination. The appellate court erred in finding that the School District's restriction was based on the Church's viewpoint.

> In this section, petitioner is referencing a large number of facts. Petitioner should have cited the record where these facts appear. Even if you already did this in the statement of the case, by now your reader may actually decide that she wants to look into the facts. You do not want to make her have to backtrack and dig through the entire statement of the case to find where these facts appear. In this brief, however, petitioner never gave cites to these facts earlier in the brief, which would make it doubly important to give cites now.
>
> The structure of the argument in section 2 breaks down from a clear IRAC or TREAT to something less, but we still can follow the argument.

It is clear that the School District's restriction is appropriate content-based discrimination because creationism does not relate to a topic of education as detailed in the curriculum guide and creationism does not fulfill the School District's purpose in teaching evolution because it is not based on the scientific method. Further, the restriction is content based in the case at bar because creationism does not relate to the areas covered in "Social Studies" or "Sociology" as these courses are taught in the School District. Finally, the deference the Court must give to school districts in educational matters, the recent holding of this Court regarding what constitutes viewpoint discrimination, and the fact that the School District has allowed the communities religious leaders to post information that relates to topics of education in the past lead to the conclusion that the appellate court clearly erred and the School District's actions were appropriately content-based.

"Although a speaker may be excluded from a nonpublic forum if he wishes to address a topic not encompassed within the purpose of the forum, or if he is not a member of the class of speakers for whose especial benefit the forum was created, the government violates the First Amendment when it denies access to a speaker solely to suppress the point of view he espouses on an otherwise includible subject." Cornelius, 473 U.S. at 806. "Viewpoint restrictions pose the inherent risk that the government seeks to suppress unpopular ideals or information." Id. On the other hand, content-based discrimination is acceptable in a nonpublic forum. Perry Educ. Ass'n, 460 U.S. at 54. Although the Court has never explicitly defined viewpoint discrimination, this analysis necessarily involves discussion of public policy, viewpoint discrimination jurisprudence, and the content of the Church's offered material.

Recently, the Court has taken a narrow view on what constitutes viewpoint discrimination. See Arkansas Educ. Television Comm'n, 118 S.Ct. at 1633 (1998); National Endowment for the Arts v. Finley, 524 U.S. 569 (1988). The Court's decisions in these cases allow the government to restrict more liberally without judicial intervention. See Erwin Chemerinsky, *Court Takes a Narrow View of Viewpoint Discrimination*, Trial, Mar. 1999, at 90.

For example, the Finley Court upheld a federal statute requiring artists receiving grants from the NEA to produce art that meets "general standards of decency and respect for the diverse beliefs and values of the American public," as viewpoint neutral. Finley, 524 U.S. at 576. This decision allows an evaluator to use subjective standards when determining whether access should be granted to a nonpublic forum. See Chemerinsky, supra. Therefore, Finley supports the great deference the Court has afforded school faculty and administrators in making access decisions.

In order for the School District's restriction to be viewpoint centered, this Court must find that creationism is related to a topic in the curriculum. If no such relationship exists, creationism information is properly excludable as a content-based restriction. As mentioned previously, the School District's mission in creating the forum was to provide information that has a direct relationship to a specific topic of education included in the curriculum. (R. at 11.) The court of appeals held that evolution was not a topic covered in the curriculum. (R. at 19.) However, it did find that the "origin of humankind" was a topic in the curriculum. (R. at 19.) This is clearly erroneous.

"Topic" is defined as, "a heading in an outlined argument or exposition; the subject of discourse or of a section of discourse." Merriam Webster's Collegiate Dictionary 1244 (10th ed. 1995). Based on this definition, the proper topic for our purposes is what the School District used as a heading in its curriculum. The words "origin of humankind" have never been printed in the curriculum; nor has evolution ever been included in the curriculum. (R. at 15.) On the other hand, biology has been a part of the School District's curriculum of secondary education. (R. at 15.) Instead of interposing its own definition of "topic," the court of appeals should have given deference to the literal meaning of the word. The Court should give deference to the School District and find that for our purposes, biology is the topic covered in the curriculum. As such, creationism is not one view of a topic as listed in the educational curriculum; and the restriction on the Church's proposal to post information regarding the topic was properly declined as a content-based restriction.

> This is a strong part of petitioner's argument. The difference between creationism and a biology class has to be driven home, and petitioner does a good job of it. Petitioner also makes good use of the <u>Edwards</u> case.
>
> Note that the School District has chosen not to capitalize creationism. This is subtle, but it works in Petitioner's favor. They downgrade creationism from the lofty position of a learned academic theory to a mundane subject. Of course, Petitioner matches this by not capitalizing evolution (and not capitalizing other academic subjects of the School District's curriculum). This is the proper approach; you do not want to antagonize any creationism buffs on the court by failing to capitalize only that word, as an intentional slight to the doctrine and its believers. Petitioner goes on to prove its point by showing that evolution is a scientific theory that calls for critical and analytical thinking and the use of the scientific method, while creationism calls for memorization and faith.

Moreover, the School District made a proper content-based restriction in light of its purposes for teaching evolution. Evolution is only part of the biology class offered through the School District. (R. at 15.) The entire course is offered to strengthen and expand students' analytical skills. Biology teaches students to think analytically by introducing them to the scientific method and showing them how scientists in the past used the method to reach a conclusion. <u>See generally</u> Edwards v. Aguillard, 482 U.S. 578 (1987). In other words, through biology, students learn the process of developing a hypothesis based on inferences and observations, testing the hypothesis, making revisions to the hypothesis and re-testing, and eventually drawing a conclusion based on fact. While evolution is discussed, it is not a primary focus of the class and is used overall to teach students how to think for themselves.

In light of the purpose of teaching evolution, it is obvious that creationism is excluded because it was not developed through the scientific method and teaches the students nothing about critical analysis. <u>Id.</u> at 592. Learning creationism requires memorization and regurgitation of material, while biology and evolution forces one to think for one's self both in the laboratory and the outside world. Therefore, the School District denied access to the Church not only because creationism was not listed in the curriculum, but also because, unlike evolution, creationism does not provide an example of the long-standing scientific method. Accordingly, the Court should give deference to the School District as this is an exclusively educational decision and reverse the appellate court's finding that the restriction was based on the Church's views.

> Oops—the authors have started to capitalize all of the curriculum subjects. Inconsistent! They should have stuck to the first plan.

The record further states that the Church sought access to the forum by asking that the creationism information be included under the curriculum topics of "Social Studies" and "Sociology." (R. at 14.) However, they were denied access to the site once against because none of the subtopics of Social Studies and Sociology relate to creationism. The list of subtopics include history, geography, government national and international relations, institutions and movements of social change, the human condition of peoples in America and the world, human interactions, social psychology, mass behavior, gangs and cults, deviant behavior, and analysis of social statistical data. (R. at 14.) However, as the District pointed out to the Church, none of these areas encompass the topics of Theology, Anthropology, religion, or anything related to creationism. (R. at 14.) While the exact areas studied under these subtopics are not contained in the record, this Court should give deference to the District as this decision involves the educational mission in creating the web site and find that creationism does not relate to any of those topics. Accordingly, the appellate court's decision should be reversed as the restriction was based on the Church's content.

Like <u>Finley</u>, the Court should allow the District to use some subjectivity in making a decision that not only affects a program that it has created, but ultimately affects the impressionable students. Further, giving the District deference in this situation allows the Court to place more weight on the reasonableness factor that encompasses many of the policies behind allowing restrictions in nonpublic fora. Clearly, had the District tried to indirectly place creationism in one of the sub-fields of Sociology and Social Studies, more and more people would seek access, the reviewing body would become overloaded, and the success of the program would be jeopardized. The web site would also be jeopardized because of the animosity the School District may have caused in parents and students in the community by allowing such a blatantly non-secular topic to be discussed in an educational forum.

Additionally, the Court should take notice that all of the other non-faculty parties who were allowed to post information on the web site had information that directly involved a topic listed in the curriculum. American History, Art, and Health are all covered in the School District's curriculum. (R. at 12-13.) While the web sites relating to Art and American History clearly relate to those purported topics, the extent to which the "health" sites relate to health is not so clear. However, as discussed below, the District properly allowed inclusion of all of the health pages on the web site. Although the reasons stated below are not grounded in the record, the Court should give deference here as it does in other areas when it applies rational basis analysis. In those cases, if the Court can find a reasonable basis for government action, they uphold the statute even if the reasonable basis was not the actual purpose that the government had in mind when enacting a statute. Here, the Court should apply that same standard and adopt the following reasons why the School District allowed the "health" sites even though the reasons are not founded in the record.

The American Red Cross posted a site relating to health and discussing blood properties, collection, and distribution. (R. at 12.) This not only concerns student personal health by providing them with information as to the contents of blood and the dangers and diseases associated with blood, it also advises students of the importance of blood drives for the promotion of the public health. Additionally, the information regarding student mediation and dispute resolution covers topics relating to mental health and brings the issue to a personal level for the students by informing them of their alternatives to fighting. This information ultimately not only relates to their mental health but also their physical health. (R. at 13.) Finally, the site written by a pastor in the community relates to health by covering the issues of teen pregnancy, drug addiction, gangs, and suicide. This clearly follows the health curriculum as all of these topics relate to physical health of the students, as well as, their mental health and safety.

Based upon the reasonableness of the School District's decision, the content-based nature of the censorship, the lack of viewpoint discrimination, and the fact that this Court has consistently given deference to the government when its purpose is educational and it takes steps to maintain its policy, the censorship of the Church's message regarding creationism is constitutional and this Court should reverse the appellate court's judgment.

> The second sentence under section E must be a typo. Otherwise, it makes little sense. The public is not welcomed to speak in a nonpublic forum. That is why it is called a nonpublic forum. The first two paragraphs of section E are sketchy on the law and make sweeping legal conclusions. That may be one reason why the statements in these paragraphs are completely unsupported by citation to legal authority. Always cite authority for every legal proposition that you state in the argument section.

E. The appellate court erred in finding that the District's web site was not a nonpublic forum.

The appellate court erred in finding that the District's web site is not a nonpublic forum. The general public is welcomed to speak in any nonpublic and public fora. In its holding, the appellate court found that the web site was opened to those of the general public who have information pertaining to a topic of education in the District. However, members of the general public who have information regarding a topic of education in the curriculum are not the general public for purposes of forum analysis. Setting standards on who is to be admitted is a key factor in concluding that a forum is not limited public or public. As such, the District appropriately set limitations on those who could be heard on the web site by requiring a nexus between the speaker's information and the curriculum. This precludes the finding that the web site was opened to the general public.

Furthermore, no speaker ever has to obtain permission from the government in order to gain access to a limited public or public forum. As such, the District's requirement that each applicant obtain the District's permission further supports the fact that the web site is a nonpublic forum. Clearly, the School District's web site cannot be characterized as a public forum or limited public forum. Accordingly, the appellate court erred and this Court should reverse the erroneous conclusion.

> Subsection 1 under section E recovers well from the poor start to this section. It shows clear organization and good use of authority. Subsection 2 is well organized, too. If only the authors had synthesized their authorities.

1. The District's web site is not a public forum.

Public fora are those that "have immemorially been held in trust for the use of the public, and, time out of mind, have been used for purposes of assembly, communicating thoughts between citizens, and discussing public questions." Perry Educ. Ass'n, 460 U.S. at 45 (citing Hague v. Com. for Indus. Org., 307 U.S. 496, 515 (1939)). Public parks and streets are the quintessential public fora. Id. Any content-based restrictions on communication in public fora must survive strict scrutiny. Therefore, the restriction must be narrowly tailored to necessarily achieve a compelling state interest.

In Hazelwood Sch. Dist., 484 U.S. at 260, the Court held that even though students do not shed all of their First Amendment rights at the schoolhouse gate, public schools do not possess all of the characteristics of parks, streets and other traditional public fora. Id. at 267. Furthermore, public schools are only public fora if the administrators "by policy or by practice" welcome the general public for indiscriminate reasons. Id. (citing Perry Educ. Ass'n, 460 U.S. at 37). The Court declared in that the school newspaper at issue in Hazelwood was not a public forum. Id. The Court focused on the school's long-standing policy of keeping the content of the newspaper tied to the school's educational curriculum and retaining ultimate control of the newspaper's content by appointing a teacher to make final decisions. Id. Further, the school had not transformed the paper into a public forum by nonchalance or inaction because the district had not deviated from its long-standing policy. Id.

Like the newspaper in Hazelwood, the web site developed and maintained by the School District in the case at bar is by its very nature not a public forum. Not only has the web site never been likened to public streets and parks, the new and developing nature of the World Wide Web excludes it from this category because of the lack of historical precedence. Furthermore, the school specifically declared that its purpose in creating the site was to further the educational goals of the School District in relation to topics covered in the curriculum, not to freely allow the Internet community to post whatever information it desired. (R. at 11.) Additionally, there is no evidence that the School District has turned the site into a public forum by passively allowing the general public to be heard. Therefore, the web site was not a public forum at its inception; nor has it become a public forum through the School District's passivity.

2. The District's website is not a limited public forum.

The limited public forum is a somewhat less-protected category than the public forum. Perry Educ. Ass'n, 460 U.S. at 45. Although these are not the traditional areas like parks and streets that have been classified as public fora, they are protected from overly prohibitive restrictions because the government has opened them to the general public as a "place for expressive activity." Id. at 45-46. Time, place, and content restrictions are allowed once the state opens the limited forum. Id. at 46. In Perry, the Court held that restrictions in limited public fora must also survive strict scrutiny. Id. Since then, however, the Court has first applied the nonpublic forum test before subjecting the restrictions to strict scrutiny. Rosenberger, 515 U.S. at 829.

In Lamb's Chapel v. Center Moriches Union Free Sch. Dist., 508 U.S. 384 (1993), the Court found a limited public forum where a school district had opened its doors for after-school activities that had "social, civic, and recreational purposes." Id. at 391. Allowing these after-school activities opened the property to the general public because by the terms of the policy almost any activity was allowed after school hours. Id. Therefore, the Court found unconstitutional the school's refusal to allow a group to display a video discussing teenage pregnancy from a religious perspective because a similar video from a non-religious viewpoint would have been admissible. Id.

Comparing the School District's policy in the case at bar with that of the school district's in Lamb's Chapel, it becomes readily apparent that the web site here is not a limited public forum. In Lamb's Chapel, the school's liberal policy of allowing "social, civic or recreational" activity invited the general public onto the school's property. Conversely, the School District here not only restricted the site's participants to those with an educational message, it specifically required that the information be directly related to a topic of education taught in the School District. (R. at 11.) As a result of its policy, the School District maintained control over the web site and forbade the general public from taking part. Therefore, the web site is not a limited public forum.

The District's web site in the case at bar is not a limited public or public forum because the web site is by nature not a long-standing, traditional public forum like parks and streets. Additionally, the School District has created and maintained a strict policy that does not welcome the general public to enlist in the web site. Furthermore, as mentioned previously, the District requires permission to post information on the web site, which is one of the main characteristics of nonpublic fora. For all of these reasons, this Court should reverse the appellate court's erroneous finding and hold that the District's web site is a nonpublic forum.

> We expected this section F below to be part of the argument on the second major issue—avoidance of an Establishment Clause violation as a compelling state interest sufficient to allow prior restraint of speech. We do not think that it belongs here, legally or logically.
>
> The Rosenberger case is twisted by the petitioner in this section; you almost can tell this just from reading the text. Other cases do a better job of spelling out the principle that avoidance of an Establishment Clause violation is a compelling state interest that will justify a prior restraint of religious speech, and they are better than Rosenberger. This section needs work.

F. **If the Court finds that the District's web site is a public or limited public forum, restricting access to the Church in order to maintain separation of church and state as mandated by the Establishment Clause satisfies strict scrutiny analysis.**

Should the Court find that the School District's restriction is viewpoint centered and/or that the web site is a limited public forum, the Court should still uphold the restriction because it meets strict scrutiny.

As mentioned earlier, the Rosenberger Court used viewpoint, content-based, and reasonableness requirements in striking down a restriction in a limited public forum. Rosenberger, 515 U.S. at 829. However, the Court did not overrule Perry and its progeny that require the Court to use strict scrutiny analysis to any restrictions in a limited public forum. Id. at 842. In fact, the Rosenberger Court, after finding that the restrictions were viewpoint-based, performed a strict scrutiny analysis. Id. Thus, the School District's restrictions may still withstand constitutional challenge, even if found to be viewpoint centered, if the School District can show that the restriction was narrowly tailored to a compelling state interest. Id.

The Court in Rosenberger found that the government would not violate the Establishment Clause if it was forced to give funding to a student-run, religious publication where the university had opened the subsidy program to virtually any group but religious ones. Id. In so finding, the Court held that preventing a violation of the Establishment Clause was not a compelling state interest. Id. The Court's decision in Rosenberger, however, does not preclude the Court from finding here that Establishment Clause issues are a compelling state interest as the finding is largely based on facts unique to each situation. The compelling nature of the Establishment Clause issues can be seen in the section below. Essentially, if the Court finds that posting the Church's information on the web site would be a violation of the Establishment Clause, any restriction under free speech analysis should be upheld as a narrowly tailored means of fulfilling a compelling state interest.

Moreover, the School District also has a compelling state interest in educating its students. As mentioned previously, this Court has stated that educating children is the primary concern of the state. Hazelwood Sch. Dist., 484 U.S. at 273. Also mentioned previously, the Court owes great deference to any decision that the School District may make when the decision is purely educational. Id. Educating children so that they become knowledgeable, self-serving, productive citizens is one of the most important tasks the federal government has left for the states. The Framers of the Constitution recognized the importance of such a responsibility and thought best to leave the decisions to the local administrators who could see the results of their decisions first-hand. States, granted with the power given them by the Framers of the Constitution, have a compelling state interest in seeing that their children are properly educated. Therefore, the School District can survive strict scrutiny by narrowly tailoring its policy to achieve the state interest.

Accordingly, the Court must also consider whether the School District's restriction was narrowly tailored to achieve the compelling state interest. Here, the School District's restriction was narrowly tailored to fulfill a compelling state interest because it only restricted information that was violative of its policy and of the Establishment Clause. The School District did not mandate the exclusion of every religious entity or person from the web site. Moreover, the policy was narrowly drawn to only exclude those speakers who had nothing to contribute to the education in the District. The School District evaluated every piece of information that was proposed for inclusion on the web site. Only after determining that the information was violative of its policy and of the Establishment Clause did the School District restrict the Church's information.

> The use of transitional words such as "moreover," "accordingly," or "additionally" can be useful in providing your reader with clear directions and cues for where you are headed and how sentences logically relate. However, you want to be careful not to overuse such words or to use them where, as here, no transitional word or phrase is necessary. These paragraphs would flow nicely without such words or phrases. Do not fall into a pattern of using them as a substitute for a proper transitional sentence at the start of paragraphs if you need to flow the discussion in a new direction.

Additionally, one can find further support for the closely tailored nature of the School District's restriction in the fact that this is the only restriction of its kind and that the School District has allowed other religious leaders in the community to contribute to the web site after finding that the information was not religious in nature and that it pertained to primary or secondary education.

The School District's limited actions at issue, taken only when necessary to fulfill its compelling interest of remaining separated from religion and fulfilling its educational policy, is narrowly tailored and survives strict scrutiny analysis. Therefore, even if the

Court should find a limited public forum and/or viewpoint discrimination, the Court should still uphold the restriction as a constitutionally necessary censorship.

> As discussed above, we saw the second issue (Roman II) as whether Petitioner would have violated the Establishment Clause by hosting Respondent's web pages, because if so, Petitioner would have a compelling interest sufficient to allow a prior restraint of Respondent's speech. This Petitioner split up these two concepts, putting the latter issue first, in the previous section (section F) on the forums and the nature of the discrimination. Altogether, the brief probably covers all of these issues, but we think it would have been easier to understand the argument here if both the potential Establishment Clause violation and its status as a compelling interest were to appear together.
>
> Petitioner treats the Establishment Clause jurisprudence as creating three, disjointed, incoherent, and competing tests—a virtual "Cafeteria plan" of constitutional law. Petitioner's plan is to show that they win under any and all of the three tests. This is a novel idea, and perhaps it is born out by the oftentimes contradictory statements of law in First Amendment cases, but in most cases we would counsel Petitioner to try harder to synthesize the authorities and come up with a more coherent rule on the issue and apply that rule.
>
> Petitioner does provide the reader with a new backdrop on which to discuss all three of the tests: the primary educational requirements and goals in public schools. This was an absolutely wonderful idea because it allows a common theme to be used in the analysis of all three tests and common scenarios to analogize and apply under all three. The backdrop used is incredibly favorable to Petitioner.

II. THE UNITED STATES SUPREME COURT SHOULD REVERSE THE APPELLATE COURT'S DECISION BECAUSE ALLOWING THE CHURCH TO MAINTAIN A WEB SITE HOSTED BY THE SCHOOL DISTRICT VIOLATES THE ESTABLISHMENT CLAUSE UNDER ANY CRITERIA EVER ADOPTED BY THIS COURT.

Violation of the Establishment Clause is determined by application of three complimentary and overlapping tests. Recent Supreme Court decisions have made it unclear which Establishment Clause test is applicable. Therefore, this brief will apply each of the three tests. The first test is the coercion test. If the activity has a coercive effect on the students then it violates the Constitution under the coercion test. Lee v. Weisman, 505 U.S. 577 (1992). The oldest, most developed test is the three-part Lemon test, under which a school district's practice is unconstitutional if it lacks a secular purpose, if its primary effect either advances or inhibits religion, or if it excessively entangles government with religion. Lemon v. Kurtzman, 403 U.S. 602 (1971). A government action violates the Establishment Clause if it fails to satisfy any of the three prongs of the Lemon test. Edwards v. Aguillard, 482 U.S. 578 (1987). Under the third and final test, the endorsement test, a school district's practice is unconstitutional when it conveys a message that religion is favored, preferred, or promoted over other beliefs. County of Allegheny v. ACLU, 492 U.S. 573 (1989).

The Court has an historic awareness of "the sensitive relationship between government and religion and the education of our children." Grand Rapids v. Ball, 473 U.S. 373, 383 (1985). The importance of maintaining strict neutrality toward religion within the public education system is a thread that weaves together all modern Establishment Clause decisions of this Court addressing the issue of religion and public schools. Any analysis of the constitutionality of the Church's posting a web site hosted by the School District must begin with recognition of the special nature of the public school setting.

The web site is an integral part of the School District's educational mission. Official sponsorship of the Church's religious web pages would entangle the religious belief and the School District's governmental authority, provide the Church with an official platform to proselytize to students, and subvert the secular purpose of the web server. The School District's sponsorship of the Church's web pages creates an impermissible endorsement of a particular religious belief.

A. Sponsorship of the Church's religious web pages by the School District amounts to government coercion to participate and believe in a religious doctrine.

The First Amendment, at a minimum, guarantees that government may not directly or indirectly coerce anyone to support or participate in religious exercises or its beliefs. Lee v. Weisman, 505 U.S. 577 (1992). Even subtle coercive pressure by a governmental body violates the Establishment Clause. Id. at 591.

The Court has recognized that there are heightened concerns with protecting students from subtle coercive pressure in the public school setting. See School Dist. of Abington v. Schempp, 374 U.S. 203 (1963); Edwards v. Aguillard, 482 U.S. 578 (1987); Board of Educ. of Westside Community Sch. v. Mergens, 496 U.S. 226 (1990). In a school context, what might otherwise be a reasonable request that the nonbeliever respect religious practice, may appear to the nonbeliever or dissenter to be an attempt to employ the machinery of the State to enforce a religious orthodoxy. Weisman, 505 U.S. at 592. Public schools should be allowed to prevent activities that might appear to advance religion out of their concern for impressionable youth. Wallace v. Jaffree, 472 U.S. 38, 46 (1985).

The specific question addressed in <u>Weisman</u> was whether the school district's practice of inviting local clergy to offer invocation and benedictions as part of high school graduation ceremonies was a violation of the Establishment Clause. 505 U.S. at 592. Although no student was required to attend the graduation ceremonies, the Court noted that students feel psychological pressure to attend such important events in their lives. <u>Id.</u> The school district's supervision and control of graduation ceremonies places public pressure and peer pressure on attending students to observe the religious portion of the ceremony. <u>Id.</u> at 593. This subtle and indirect pressure amounts to a violation of the Establishment Clause. <u>Id.</u>

Recently a school district attempted to subvert the holding in <u>Weisman</u> by delegating decision-making authority to graduating senior students who would determine if religious messages would be delivered at graduation. <u>Adler v. Duval County Sch. Bd.</u>, 174 F.3d 1236 (11th Cir. 1999). The school board did not succeed in dissociating itself from proselytizing prayer at a school-controlled graduation ceremony. <u>Id.</u> at 1248. Similar to <u>Weisman</u>, the policy coerced objecting students to participate in the religious observation and thus amounted to coerced participation. <u>Id.</u>

In the case at bar, the design and purpose of the School District's web server is coercive. The School District encourages teachers to create their own web pages pertaining to the subject they teach. (R. at 11.) The pages sponsored by the School District are to provide resources and links that provide additional educational material not otherwise available to students pertaining to subjects taught. (R. at 11.) In <u>Weisman</u>, the Court found that subtle psychological pressure by the school district to attend graduation ceremonies was sufficient to fail the coercion test. Here, not only does subtle psychological pressure exist to use the web server, but the School District directly coerces teachers to utilize the web server for educational purposes. Requiring the School District to maintain the Church's religious web pages will force the teachers to refrain from encouraging students to use the web server in order to prevent direct coercion of participation in a particular religious belief.

The School District periodically reviews all web sites accepted for sponsorship to ensure compatibility with the curriculum. (R. at 5.) To be accepted, the applicant must submit a written proposal describing the contents of the proposed web pages for review. (R. at 11.) In <u>Weisman</u> and <u>Adler</u>, it was precisely the schools supervision and control over the ceremonies that created the coercive behavior violative of the Establishment Clause. Here, the School District is also supervising and controlling the web site. Allowing the Church to post its message on the web site would create enough supervision and control over the Church's information to create a violation of the Establishment Clause.

Like the graduation ceremonies in <u>Weisman</u> and <u>Adler</u>, a student may choose not to participate in a particular web site. However, an icon present on the School District's home page creates a subtle coercive pressure that a particular religious belief is being promoted. If a student chooses not to visit the School District's web site altogether because of the church's message, then the student must forsake access to other academic opportunities and information.

The School District's web site was created to promote information about areas of study taught in the schools, and all participating web pages are controlled and supervised by the School District. (R. at 11.) Just as the religious benediction at graduation in <u>Weisman</u> created a subtle coercive pressure, in the case at bar the prominent display of the Church's icon on the home page acts as a coercive mechanism. The various links to other web pages are meant to entice students to partake of the particular learning experience available at each site. This is not only subtle coercive activity, but the very nature of the web site creates direct coercion due to the School District's control over the information therein contained.

The fact that the Church's site is listed on the School District's home page constitutes a coercive pressure that this religious belief is a part of the District's curricula and must be believed or learned. Allowing the Church's religious web pages to be sponsored by the School District creates an impermissible inference that the State is endorsing a particular religious orthodoxy. Therefore, the School District would inevitably violate the Establishment Clause by coercing students to participate in the Church's religious message.

> In section B, we would have liked to have seen a definite IRAC or TREAT here concerning the <u>Lemon</u> test and its three elements. We think it would have improved this section. Instead, we are dropped into the middle of a good discussion of "secular purpose" as if we would know that this is the first element under <u>Lemon</u>. The reader probably can stay afloat in this section, but only through her own efforts, not through careful drafting by the authors.

B. <u>The School District's sponsorship of the Church's religious web pages violates the Establishment Clause because it subverts the secular purpose, creates the primary effect of endorsement, and results in excessive entanglement of the government and religion.</u>

   1. <u>Creationism is a religious belief and as such would subvert the secular purpose of the School District's web server.</u>

The theory of creation is a religious belief and is not a scientifically based theory. <u>Edwards</u>, 482 U.S at 593. Local policies and state laws promoting the teaching of creationism in public schools are unconstitutional because they violate the secular purpose requirement of the <u>Lemon</u> test. <u>See</u> <u>Edwards</u>, 482 U.S. at 586; <u>Epperson v. Arkansas</u>, 393 U.S. 97, 106 (1968). The First Amendment does not permit the state to require that teaching and learning be tailored to the dogma of a religious sect. <u>Epperson</u>, 393 U.S. at 106.

In <u>Edwards</u>, a state law requiring that "creation science" be taught in conjunction with evolution was struck down as unconstitutional. 482 U.S. at 594. The Court refused to entertain the argument that creationism is a legitimate scientific theory. <u>Id.</u> at 593. Thus, any attempts by the Church to portray 'creation science' as anything more than a religious belief must be rejected based on <u>Epperson</u> and <u>Edwards</u>.

In a recent California case, a local school board initiated an advertising sponsorship program to benefit the high school baseball team. <u>DiLoreto v. Board of Educ.</u>, 87 Cal. Rptr. 2d 791 (Cal. Ct. App. 1999). One of the advertisers sued when the school district refused to allow the advertiser to display the Ten Commandments in his ad. <u>Id.</u> Applying the <u>Lemon</u> test, the court determined the original purpose of the fund-raiser to be secular and concluded that the secular purpose would be subverted if the board of education were to begin accepting signs of a religious nature. <u>Id.</u> at 276.

Like the board of education in <u>DiLoreto</u>, the School District's web server and home page have a secular purpose as required under the <u>Lemon</u> test. The purpose of the web server was to promote information about the areas of study currently being taught throughout the District. (R. at 11.) If sponsored by the School District, the Church's religious web pages would subvert the secular purpose of the web server and Internet provider service, resulting in a violation of the Establishment Clause.

The School District's purpose in establishing the web server is secular. Creationism, the topic of the Church's web pages, is a religious belief. Sponsoring of the Church's web pages by the School District would violate the Establishment Clause because the secular purpose would be subverted.

> Sub-sections 2 and 3 below are drafted as sub-TREATs or sub-IRACs of the elements of the <u>Lemon</u> test, and as such, they are much easier to read and understand. We are not dropped headfirst into the discussion as we were in the previous sub-section. The analogies used in the Application sections of sections 2 and 3 are very strong.

2. <u>Sponsorship of the Church's religious web pages will have the primary effect of improper endorsement of a religious orthodoxy.</u>

The second prong of the <u>Lemon</u> test is whether compelling the School District to sponsor the Church's religious web pages will have the primary effect of either advancing or inhibiting religion. <u>Lemon</u>, 403 U.S. at 612. This is similar to analysis under the endorsement test in which a government practice may not aid a religion or favor one religion over another. <u>County of Allegheny</u>, 492 U.S. at 576. The appellate court erred because a reasonable person would believe the School District is endorsing the Church's religious belief.

Under the endorsement test, the Establishment Clause is violated where government operation of a forum has the effect of endorsing religion. <u>County of Allegheny</u>, 492 U.S. at 577. The test is whether a reasonable observer would be likely to perceive the activity as an endorsement by the government of a particular religious belief. <u>County of Allegheny</u>, 492 U.S. at 631. Even where the government does not intend nor actively encourage the appearance of endorsement, the Establishment Clause is violated if a reasonable person might perceive such.

> Use of a dissenting opinion always is a risky venture. Since Justice O'Connor is such an Establishment Clause maven, it makes more sense to cite one of her dissents than some of the other judges, but it still is weak authority.

Capital Square Review and Advisory Bd. v. Pinette, 515 U.S. 753, 777 (1995) (O'Conner, J., dissenting).

> This section really could use some explanatory synthesis. Not only does it walk the reader through several cases, one after the other, it also applies each case to the facts as if each case were a law unto itself. Lesson: SYNTHESIZE!

In Capital Square, this Court determined that a display of the Ku Klux Klan's cross on public property historically designated an open forum would not lead a reasonable person to believe that the state was endorsing a religious doctrine. Id. at 765. The reasonable person would be aware that the property has been designated as an open forum and thus not conclude that the state was sponsoring the Ku Klux Klan's cross. Id.

In the case at bar, the School District's web site is a new innovation. Established case law regarding the Internet has not been well developed. The Internet has not been historically designated as a public forum. Thus, unlike the historically designated public forum property in Capital Square, the School District's web site is not a public or a limited public forum.

In Lamb's Chapel v. Center Moriches Union Free Sch. Dist., this Court found that permitting a religious group to use school facilities to show religious films did not constitute a violation of the Establishment Clause. 508 U.S. 384, 395 (1993). The Court found dispositive the fact that the films would not be shown during school hours and were in no way sponsored by the school. Id. at 394. Similarly, in Mergens, allowing a religious student group to form and meet on school property during non-instructional time was found not to be a violation of the Establishment Clause. 496 U.S. at 250. The Court found the following facts dispositive: (1) the school policy strictly forbade school officials' participation in the student groups; (2) meetings had to take place during non-instructional time; and (3) no classroom activities were involved. Thus, the Court concluded that there was no danger that a student might believe the school was endorsing the religious group's belief. Id. at 228.

Applying Lamb's Chapel to the case at bar clearly shows that the reasonable person would conclude that the School District is endorsing a religious belief. Unlike the school facilities in Lamb's Chapel, the Internet and the School District's home page is accessible during instructional time and available for teachers to use in the classrooms as an instructional tool. Also, unlike the religious films in Lamb's Chapel, the School District is sponsoring organizations whose links are displayed on the home page. A reasonable person or student would be led to believe that the School District is endorsing the religious doctrine of creationism. In Mergens, allowing religious organizations access to school property was not endorsement only because no school officials participated, meetings were during non-instructional times, and no classroom activity was involved. Unlike Mergens, in the case at bar, the School District is encouraging participation by faculty and the web server is not only accessible during instructional times but involves classroom activities and topics. (R. at 11.) A student could easily believe that the School District is endorsing the Church's religious doctrine.

In Church of Latter Day Saints v. Amos, 483 U.S. 327 (1987), employees filed a religious discrimination suit against the Church of Latter Day Saints for terminating their employment because they were not members of the church. This Court upheld a state law exempting religious organizations from Title VII employment discrimination charges. Id. at 335. The Court held that to be unconstitutional the government entity itself must be advancing religion through its own activities. Id. at 337. The State was merely exempting religious organizations, thus allowing churches to base hiring decisions on the religion of its employees. Id.

In Amos, the government was merely acting passively to prevent its interference or entanglement with religious organizations. Whereas, in the case at bar, the School District's own affirmative activity established the web server and home page. Unlike Amos, the School District would be advancing religion through its own affirmative activity if it sponsors the Church's web pages.

The Internet's accessibility during instructional time, its lack of historical precedent or analogy as a public forum, and the School District's sponsoring of the web pages lead a reasonable person to conclude that the School District is endorsing the Church's religious belief. The School District's affirmative activity of establishing the web server and encouraging faculty involvement and classroom activities through the home page would amount to an improper endorsement of a religious doctrine if the Church's web pages are sponsored by the School District.

3. **Sponsoring of the Church's religious web pages by the School District is an entanglement of government and religion and is a violation of the Establishment Clause.**

* * *

The Supreme Court is not in the business of awarding summary judgment to litigants, so petitioner's prayer for relief is inappropriate. We simply would ask the Court to reverse the 14th Circuit and order that the order and judgment of the District Court be reinstated.

CONCLUSION

For the reasons stated above, the decision of the United States Court of Appeals for the Fourteenth Circuit should be reversed, and this Court should grant summary judgment to School District as there are no genuine issues as to any material fact and School District is entitled to judgment as a matter of law.

Sample Brief No. 2:

Student Brief of Petitioner
in the moot court case:

Metropolitan School Dist. of Gotham
v.
Branch Louisian of the United Church of
Christ the Savior

IN THE SUPREME COURT OF THE UNITED STATES

March Term 2000

———————

NO. 00-100

———————

METROPOLITAN SCHOOL DISTRICT OF GOTHAM,
STATE OF NEW KENT

Petitioner,

v.

BRANCH LOUISIAN OF THE UNITED CHURCH OF
CHRIST THE SAVIOR,

Respondent.

———————

On Writ of Certiorari to the United States Court of Appeals for the Fourteenth Circuit

———————

BRIEF OF RESPONDENT

Student 1 – Issue 1

Student 2 – Issue 2

These Questions Presented would be acceptable if this brief were drafted for an intermediate level appellate court such as the United States Court of Appeals. The questions are phrased in a very neutral manner and give sufficient information about the case to inform the court of the issues. However, this brief was to be filed in a court of last resort, the United States Supreme Court, so the questions presented should have been drafted as a general issue of federal or constitutional law with broad application to persons in the same class as the petitioner and respondent. Petitioner had the right idea about this in sample brief #1 above. In addition, we do not like the use of the term "Fourteenth Circuit Appellate Court." The appropriate term is "United States Court of Appeals for the Fourteenth Circuit."

QUESTIONS PRESENTED

1. Whether the Fourteenth Circuit Appellate Court erred in holding that Petitioner violated the First Amendment by denying Respondent access to its web site solely on the basis of the religious content of its proposal?

2. Whether the Fourteenth Circuit Appellate Court erred in holding that Petitioner's conduct in initiating a web site, open for general use to all members of the community, created a limited public forum for the purpose of the right to free speech under the First Amendment?

3. Whether the Fourteenth Circuit Appellate Court erred in holding that Petitioner's denial of Respondent's proposal, based upon its religious content, is in violation of the First Amendment regardless of the type of forum because the denial constitutes viewpoint discrimination?

4. Whether the Fourteenth Circuit Appellate Court erred in holding that the hosting of Respondent's creationism web pages on Petitioner's web site did not violate the Establishment Clause?

Underlining all of the entries in the Argument section of the Table of Contents clutters up this section and makes it hard to read. We see no advantage to doing it this way, and a lot of disadvantages. Eliminate the underlining (unless the local rule specifically requires it).

TABLE OF CONTENTS

QUESTIONS PRESENTED i

TABLE OF AUTHORITIES iv

DECISIONS BELOW 1

CONSTITUTIONAL PROVISIONS, STATUTES, AND REGULATIONS............ 2

STATEMENT OF THE CASE 3

SUMMARY OF ARGUMENT 6

ARGUMENT 8

I. THE JUDGMENT OF THE APPELLATE COURT SHOULD BE AFFIRMED BECAUSE PETITIONER'S DISCRIMINATORY EXCLUSION OF RESPONDENT'S PROPOSED WEB PAGES, SOLELY ON THE BASIS OF RELIGIOUS CONTENT AND IDEOLOGY IS IN VIOLATION OF THE FIRST AMENDMENT'S FREE SPEECH CLAUSE AND AGAINST PUBLIC POLICY. 8

    A. Petitioner has created a public forum by initiating a web site open to all members of the community and other organizations for the purpose of promoting information regarding current curriculum and providing alternative sources of information that may not be available in the curriculum. 10

        1. Petitioner's conduct in devising the web site for the sole purpose of expressive activities has created a designated public forum. 12

        2. Even if Petitioner's web site is not found to be a pure designated public forum it must qualify as the subset, a limited public forum. 15

    B. Petitioner's denial of Respondent's web pages solely based upon the religious content therein, constitutes content-based discrimination in violation of the First Amendment's Free Speech Clause. 16

        1. Petitioner's content-based exclusion of Respondent's web pages from its public forum triggers a strict scrutiny analysis, which Petitioner cannot meet. 17

2. Petitioner offers no compelling state interest to justify content-discrimination; hence, Petitioner fails to satisfy strict scrutiny. 19

C. Regardless of the nature of the forum, Petitioner's conduct of excluding Respondent's web pages based upon Respondent's religious ideology constitutes viewpoint discrimination which is a per se violation of the First Amendment's Free Speech Clause. 21

II. THE ESTABLISHMENT CLAUSE DOES NOT BAR THE METROPOLITAN SCHOOL DISTRICT FROM HOSTING RESPONDENT'S WEB PAGES AS PART OF A CURRICULUM FOCUSED WEB SITE. 23

A. The hosting of Respondent's web pages by the Metropolitan School District respects rather than offends the School District's neutrality towards religion as required by the Establishment Clause. 25

B. The hosting of Respondent's web pages by the Metropolitan School District comports with the three-pronged Lemon test and, therefore, does not violate the Establishment Clause. 28

1. The purpose of the Metropolitan School District's web site is secular. 28

2. The primary effect of including Respondent's web pages is not the advancement of religion. 29

3. The inclusion of Respondent's web pages does not create an excessive government entanglement with religion. 30

C. By including Respondent's web pages on the Metropolitan School District's web site, petitioners are not intending to endorse nor are they perceived to endorse a particular religious belief. 31

D. The School District's inclusion in its web site of Respondent's web pages does not create a policy of religious coercion. 35

CONCLUSION 37

This is the strangest Table of Authorities we have seen in quite some time. The authors have abandoned the "flush right with dot leaders" way of formatting in favor of this strange design. The authors also failed to separate the table into different categories of authorities, and they failed to cite the opinions of the lower courts in the instant case.

TABLE OF AUTHORITIES

Abrams v. U.S.,
250 U.S. 616 (1919). --- 18

Arkansas Educ. Television Communication v.
Forbes,
523 U.S. 666 (1998). --- 19, 21

Bernal v. Fainter,
467 U.S. 216 (1984). --- 9, 18

Board of Educ. of Westside Community Sch.
(Dist.566) v. Mergens,
496 U.S. 226 (1990). --- 26

Capitol Square Review and Advisory Bd. v. Pinette,
515 U.S. 753 (1995). --- 9, 10, 31-35

Cornelius v. NAACP,
473 U.S. 788 (1985). --- 10, 22-23

County of Allegheny v. ACLU,
492 U.S. 573 (1989). --- 31, 35

East High Gay/Straight Alliance v. Board of Educ.
of Salt Lake City Sch. Dist.,
No.CIV.A.2:98-CV-193J, 1999 WL 1103365,
(D. Utah Oct. 6, 1999). -- 8

Edwards v. Aguillard,
482 U.S. 578 (1987). --- 28

Epperson v. Arkansas,
393 U.S. 97 (1968). -- 28, 29

* * *

> This Decisions Below section is adequate. The problem did not give citations for either case, and yet, we are not sure where Respondent came up with these versions of the case names. Compare this section with the example we gave in this chapter, above.

DECISIONS BELOW

The decision of the court of appeals finding for the Church is reported as <u>Branch of the United Church of Christ the Savior v. Metropolitan School District of Gotham</u> (14th Cir. 1999).

The decision of the district court finding for the School District is reported as <u>Branch of the United Church of Christ the Savior v. Metropolitan School District of Gotham</u> (C.D.N.K. 1999).

> Aside from the title, this Constitutional Provisions section is nicely done. The Respondent is quite correct to cite the Fourteenth Amendment—it is what makes the First Amendment apply directly to the states. We quibble with the title because readers would think this means "public policy," and they would be confused because they will expect this section to be about constitutional, statutory, and administrative law, not public policy. The Respondent meant to refer to the School District's web site policy, but few readers would pick up on this.

CONSTITUTIONAL PROVISIONS AND POLICY

The First Amendment to the United States Constitution provides as follows:

> Congress shall make no law respecting an establishment of religion, or prohibiting the free exercise thereof; or abridging the freedom of speech, or of the press; or the right of the people peaceably to assemble, and to petition the Government for a redress of grievances.

U.S. Const. amend. I.

The first section of the Fourteenth Amendment to the United States Constitution provides as follows:

> All persons born or naturalized in the United States, and subject to the jurisdiction thereof, are citizens of the United States and of the State wherein they reside. No State shall make or enforce any law which shall abridge the privileges or immunities of citizens of the United States; nor shall any State deprive any person of life, liberty, or property, without due process of law; nor deny to any person within its jurisdiction the equal protection of the laws.

U.S. Const. amend. XIV, § 1.

The policy of the Metropolitan School District pertaining to the hosting of web pages on its web site is set forth in the Record of Transcript, R-11.

> The Statement of the Case is very well done. The most important facts are highlighted and Respondent's case is furthered, but it still does not read as argumentative and divisive. This is good drafting. Note that citations to the record should be in the form of Record 3 not (R. at 3).

STATEMENT OF THE CASE

Petitioner School District ("Petitioner") is a political subdivision of the State of New Kent. (Record of Transcript [R.] at 10). For the last 150 years, Petitioner has operated all of the public schools in Gotham, New Kent. (R. at 10-11). Petitioner brings this case to the United States Supreme Court on appeal from a decision of the United States Court of Appeals for the Fourteenth Circuit. This Appellant Court found for Respondent, Branch Louisian of the United Church of Christ the Savior ("Respondent"), a religious organization, registered and operating in the State of New Kent. Respondent, a proponent of Judeo-Christian doctrine of Creationism, conducts religious education and worship services each week in a church located in Gotham, New Kent. (R. at 4, 10).

Petitioner is an Internet service provider and hosts web sites from sources outside of the School District system. (R. at 4). Petitioner began operating as an Internet service provider in June 1998. (R. at 11). Petitioner manages the Internet server and operates a web site for the purpose of hosting other web pages on its site. (R. at 11). The home page site reads:

> This site was created by the [School District] for the purpose of promoting information about the areas of study that are currently being taught in the schools of the [School District]. The pages we hope to sponsor will not only highlight topics of interest in the curriculum of the [School District], but also provide resources and information and links to other sources of information that may not be available in the textbooks and other materials provided to our students in the courses taught in the [School District]. In this spirit of expanding the educational potential of this site, we invite faculty of the [School District] and other educational institutions in Gotham, members of the community, and other organizations to propose web pages for inclusion in the site, as long as the subject matter of each page is tied to topic of education in this [School District]." (R. at 11).

All persons seeking inclusion in the site must submit a written proposal to Petitioner for review describing in detail the title and contents of the proposal. (R. at 11). Petitioner will also review the web site periodically to insure the pages posted on the site meet the requirement being "tied to a topic of education" in the School District's curriculum and are created in such a way "as to uphold the high academic standards of the School District." (R. at 11).

On March 5, 1999, Respondent made a proposal for Petitioner to host its web site on the subject of "Theological Anthropology" the title of which was "Creationism: Past and Present." (R. at 13). The proposal was further described as an examination of the doctrine

> Respondent needs to proofread the word "form" and change it to "from" in several places here. This is one of many examples we could offer of why running a "spell check" in your word processing program is not the same as proofreading. Spell check would not catch the "form" error because that is the correct spelling—albeit of a word other than the one that the author intended.

of Creationism form the Book of Genesis and a comparison and contrasting of the "purportedly scientific" doctrines of Evolution and Natural Selection. (R. at 13). The contents of the proposal were described as a multimedia presentation of commentary form scholars and educators regarding the doctrine of Creationism and five centuries of religious artwork regarding the doctrine of Creationism. (R. at 13). On March 7, 1999, Petitioner denied Respondent's proposal stating that, "its subject matter is not directly related to a topic of education in the district." (R. at 14). On March 11, 1999, Respondent resubmitted its proposal but changed the description of the subject matter to "Social Studies" and "Sociology". (R. at 14) On March 12, 1999, Petitioner once again denied Respondent's proposal on the same grounds as stated before. (R. at 14).

The topics of "Social Studies" and "Sociology" are topics listed under the School District's curriculum guide, however, they do not encompass the topics of Theology, Anthropology, or anything relating to Creationism. (R. at 14). On the other hand, the curriculum guide does include the Darwinian theories of Evolution and Natural Selection, which are currently taught in Biology courses in the School District and have been taught in the District since 1922. (R. at 14-15). Prior to Respondent's proposal, Petitioner had never rejected a proposed web page form a member of the community. (R. at 15). A variety of web pages created by entities having no affiliation with the School District are currently being sponsored on Petitioner's web site. (R. at 12). These entities include, but are not limited to, The Council for Alternative Dispute Resolution with a site on health that features an interview with its founder and director, Reverend Carla Boulevardier, Pastor of St. Peter's AME Church of Gotham, and The Greater Gotham Youth League with a site on health that features an article on suicide written by Fr. John Berrigan, a Roman Catholic Priest of the Gotham Cathedral Church. (R. at 13).

Respondent has made several additional oral requests to have its web pages posted on the Petitioner's web site. Each request was denied. In the hope of exercising it's constitutional right to free speech, Respondent filed this lawsuit against the School District on May 15, 1999.

> The Summary of Argument is very good, but once again, we would like to see a few citations to Respondent's best legal authorities. What if the justices only read your summary of the argument before your oral argument? Would you not want them to get in their minds the names of the four or five cases that really hold up your argument? Otherwise, this section is very effective. One note: in the first sentence, we would not say "not so new." This sounds a little too informal. We would say "not new."

SUMMARY OF ARGUMENT

Although the constitutional issues raised pertaining to the right of Free Speech under the First Amendment and the requirement that there be a separation of church and state under the Establishment Clause are not so new, the issue of how these two vital constitutional components are addressed as they pertain to the internet is novel. The judgment of the Fourteenth Circuit Appellate Court should be affirmed because the Metropolitan School District's discriminatory exclusion of the Branch Louisian Church's proposed web pages, solely on the basis of religious content and ideology is in violation of the First Amendment's free speech clause and against public policy. The School District has created a public forum by initiating a web site open to all members of the community and other organizations for the purpose of promoting information regarding current curriculum and providing alternative sources of information that may not be available in the curriculum. Therefore, the School District's conduct in devising the web site for the sole purpose of expressive activities has created a designated public forum. Even if the District's web site is not found to be a pure designated public forum it must qualify as the subset, a limited public forum. Based upon finding the web site a limited public forum, the District's denial of the Respondent's web page solely based upon the religious content therein, constitutes content-based discrimination in violation of the First Amendment's Free Speech Clause. The School District's content-based exclusion of Respondent's web page from its public forum triggers a strict scrutiny analysis. The District offers no compelling state interest to justify content-based discrimination, therefore, the strict scrutiny standard cannot be met. Regardless of the nature of the forum, however, the District's conduct of excluding Respondent's web page based upon Respondent's religious ideology constitutes viewpoint discrimination which is a per se violation of the First Amendment's Free Speech Clause.

The Establishment Clause does not bar the Metropolitan School District from hosting a creationism web page as part of a curriculum focused web site. The inclusion of Respondent's web pages by the Metropolitan School District will be found constitutional because it meets every test articulated by this Court to determine violations of the Establishment Clause. The hosting of Respondent's web pages by the Metropolitan School District respects rather than offends the School District's neutrality towards religion as required by the Establishment Clause. The hosting of Respondent's web pages by the Metropolitan School District comports with the three-pronged <u>Lemon</u> test and, therefore, does not violate the Establishment Clause. The purpose of the District's web site is secular, its primary effect is not the advancement of religion, and the inclusion of the creationism web pages does not create an excessive government entanglement with religion. By including Respondent's web pages on the Metropolitan School District's web site, Petitioners are not intending to endorse nor are they perceived to endorse a particular religious belief. Finally, the District's inclusion in its web site of Respondent's web pages create a policy of religious coercion. Based upon Respondent's arguments, the Appellate Court's ruling should be upheld.

> Respondent is in the enviable position of having a United States Court of Appeals agree with it, and it makes the most of that here by wrapping itself in the flag in the third and fourth paragraphs in this section. It is fine to try this once in a while in a brief, but it is even better to leave out the flag waving and let the court salute the flag when they write up the opinion agreeing with your legal position, after you have bowled them over with your argument.
>
> This entire section from Roman I to the first section heading (A) is devoted to setting the mood (the background) for the brief. It is not an IRAC or TREAT of any of the main issues, nor is it a roadmap or "umbrella" section. But we like the mood it creates. The stage is set up nicely for the rest of the argument in this section. The initial issues are dealt with smoothly and concisely in this section. It flows nicely right to the first major contested issue in section A. We also like the thesis heading here. Very good work, Respondent.

ARGUMENT

I. THE JUDGMENT OF THE APPELLATE COURT SHOULD BE AFFIRMED BECAUSE PETITIONER'S DISCRIMINATORY EXCLUSION OF RESPONDENT'S PROPOSED WEB PAGES SOLELY ON THE BASIS OF RELIGIOUS CONTENT AND IDEOLOGY IS IN VIOLATION OF THE FIRST AMENDMENT'S FREE SPEECH CLAUSE AND AGAINST PUBLIC POLICY.

The Appellate Court made a proper decision, in support of public policy, holding that Petitioner's denial of Respondent's web pages violates the Free Speech Clause of the First Amendment. (R. at 19). The Appellate Court accurately found that Petitioner created a public forum by opening its web site to any member of the community wishing to be heard on educational topics that are tied to the School District's curriculum. Moreover, Petitioner's denial was solely based upon Respondent's religious viewpoint; an act that is presumed unconstitutional. (R. at 19).

The First Amendment provides, in part, that "Congress shall make no law...abridging the freedom of speech." U.S. Const. amend. I. The First Amendment's guarantee of free speech is applicable to restrictions enacted by state and local governments, including public school boards, by way of the Due Process Clause of the 14th Amendment. East High Gay/Straight Alliance v. Board of Edu. of Salt Lake City Sch. Dist., No.CIV.A.2:98-CV-193J, 1999 WL 1103365, at *1 (D. Utah Oct. 6, 1999).

The guarantee of free speech is a vital fundamental right to citizens of the United States upon which our democratic society is built. In <u>Ferlauto v. Hamsher</u>, 88 Cal.Rptr.2d 843 (Cal. Ct. App. 1999). California court held that the "First Amendment's free speech guarantee safeguards a freedom, which is the matrix, and the indispensable condition of nearly every other form of freedom." <u>Id.</u> at 848.

This enumerated freedom, which is the matrix of our great democracy, has begun a recent evolution with the inception of the Internet and cyberspace. This evolution has crept into the realm of authority of the United States Supreme Court, which has set precedent for how this issue must be resolved. In <u>Reno v. ACLU</u>, 521 U.S. 844 (1997), this Court recently addressed the nature of the Internet and held that it most closely resembles books and newspapers and is therefore deserving of the utmost freedom from content-based restrictions. <u>Id.</u> at 885.

> We like the interjection of the Internet into the discussion. It makes this argument punchier. And look at what case Respondent uses to set out the standard of review: <u>New York Times v. Sullivan</u>. Classy! Even though <u>New York Times v. Sullivan</u> is not a religion case, it is effective to use a monumental First Amendment case like this for the standard of review because it reminds the court of the importance of the issues and policies in First Amendment litigation.

In reviewing a constitutional claim, this Court will apply a de novo review of the issue. <u>New York Times Co. v. Sullivan</u>, 376 U.S. 254, 285 (1964). However, when a fundamental right, such as free speech is at issue and the State restriction is content-based, the restriction is subject to strict scrutiny. <u>Widmar v. Vincent</u>, 454 U.S. 263, 263 (1981). Under a strict scrutiny analysis, the restriction is found unconstitutional unless the State can prove that the restriction advances a compelling state interest by the least restrictive means available. <u>Bernal v. Fainter</u>, 467 U.S. 216, 219 (1984). Petitioner is unable to meet this heavy burden.

A private religious expression is entitled to the same protection under the Free Speech Clause as secular private expression. <u>Capitol Square Review and Advisory Board v. Pinette</u>, 515 U.S. 753, 760 (1995). The State may not discriminate against speakers, by denying them the ability to speak based upon their religious viewpoint. Although the State may not endorse or assist religious activities in a way that violates the Establishment Clause, the State is limited by the First Amendment's Freedom of Speech Clause when it denies benefits to, or imposes burdens on religious speakers. <u>Id.</u> at 760. Petitioner's decision to deny Respondent's proposal based upon its religious content and ideology constitutes an egregious form of discrimination in violation of the First Amendment. The Appellate Court carefully reviewed this vital issue and made a fair and proper ruling in support of Respondent's fundamental right of free speech. Therefore, the decision by the Appellate Court should be affirmed.

Here we see the first use of the IRAC or TREAT format. The first five sentences are definite legal statements, but no citation to authority is given. This is a loose style of which we do not approve. *Always cite authority for legal propositions.* Do not reserve your citation(s) until the end of the paragraph, as Respondent did here. The reader cannot tell if the single cite (here to <u>Cornelius</u>) is supposed to support all six sentences or just the sixth sentence.

A. <u>Petitioner has created a public forum by initiating a web site open to all members of the community and other organizations for the purpose of promoting information regarding current curriculum and providing alternative sources of information that may not be available in the curriculum.</u>

In analyzing a regulation of speech under the First Amendment, the nature of the forum involved must be determined because the extent to which the State may restrict access depends upon the type of forum. There are two general categories, public and nonpublic forums. Within the public forum category, however, there are subsets, traditional and designated public forums. The designated public forum category also has a subset, limited public forums. Access to a public forum may only be restricted when necessary to serve a compelling state interest and the exclusion is narrowly drawn to achieve that interest. Access to a nonpublic forum may be limited as to subject matter and speaker identity as long as the distinctions drawn are reasonable in light of the purpose served by the forum. <u>Cornelius v. NAACP</u>, 473 U.S. 788, 807 (1985). This Court first recognized and classified three types of forums in <u>Perry Educ. Ass'n v. Perry Local Educators Ass'n</u>, 460 U.S. 37, 45-46 (1983).

The Court in <u>Perry</u> described a traditional public forum as a place that has a history of being devoted to assembly, debate, and communication between citizens. <u>Id.</u> at 45. Parks, sidewalks, plazas, and streets define a traditional public forum. The rights of the State to limit expressive activity in this type of forum are sharply circumscribed and subject to strict scrutiny. Further, content-based discrimination is only allowed when the State can prove that the regulation is necessary to serve a compelling state interest and the regulation is narrowly drawn to achieve that interest. <u>Id</u>.

We said this was the first attempt at IRAC or TREAT, and the attempt was short-lived. Perhaps this is a long, extended Rule section.

The second type of public forum described in <u>Perry</u> is a designated public forum which is public property not traditionally open to assembly and debate, but which the State has intentionally designated for the purpose of expressive activity. <u>Id</u>. The State is bound by the same standards as a traditional public forum, and strict scrutiny will be applied in reviewing a State regulation. <u>Id.</u> at 46. Therefore, content-based discrimination is prohibited except when it is necessary to serve a compelling state interest and the regulation is narrowly drawn to achieve that end. 460 U.S. at 46. Unlike a traditional forum, however, the State is not required to keep this forum open indefinitely.

A designated public forum may be created for a limited purpose, such as use by certain groups, e.g., <u>Widmar v. Vincent</u>, 454 U.S. 263 (1981) or for the discussion of certain subjects, e.g., <u>Madison Joint Sch. Dist. v. Wisconsin Pub. Employment Relations Comm'n</u> 429 U.S. 167 (1976). This subset of a designated public forum is categorized as a "limited public forum". Within a limited public forum, the State must still show that the restriction is "narrowly drawn to effectuate a compelling state interest". <u>Perry</u>, 460 U.S. at 46. However, the State may also confine the forum's use to the limited purposes for which it is created as long as the regulation is reasonable and not an effort to suppress a speaker's viewpoint. <u>Rosenberger v. Rector of Univ. of Virginia</u> 515 U.S. 819, 829 (1995).

The third type of forum described in <u>Perry</u> is a non-public forum, which is public property that is not by tradition or designation a forum for public communication. 460 U.S. at 46. The State may preserve this forum for its intended purpose, expressive activities, or otherwise, as long as the regulation on speech is reasonable and not an effort to suppress a speaker's viewpoint. 460 U.S. at 46. However, the State has the right to make restrictions to access based upon subject matter and speaker's identity. <u>Id.</u>

> Sub-section 1 appears to be an Explanation and Application section if you view section A as one long Rule section. This appears to be what Respondent intended. After considering this structure, we can see that these sections show a decent amount of organization, and Respondent just had a complicated Rule to get through.
>
> Sub-section 1 is nicely drafted. We especially like the last paragraph of this sub-section that analogizes the Internet to a traditional public forum—the quintessential public forum—in the words carefully chosen by Respondent. Strong stuff.

1. <u>Petitioner's conduct in devising the web site for the sole purpose of expressive activities created a designated public forum.</u>

As stated earlier, the court in <u>Perry</u> addressed the distinctions between the three forums. While the Court did not offer a precise test to determine between a designated public forum and a nonpublic forum, the Court did define the designated public forum as being created by the State for the allocated purpose of expressive activity. 460 U.S. at 45. The nonpublic forum has no such allocation. In <u>Perry</u>, the school district's internal mail system was placed in the third category, nonpublic forum. 460 U.S. at 46. This Court found that the intended function of the mail system was only to facilitate internal communication of school matters and therefore not open to the general public. <u>Id.</u> at 46. This

Court further surmised that if the school district's policy was to open the mail system for indiscriminate use by the general public, then it could be considered a designated public forum of the second category. Id.

Petitioner's open access policy clearly meets this "indiscriminate use by the general public" set out in Perry, 460 U.S. at 47. Petitioner created the web site for the sole purpose of sharing ideas related to the curriculum among members in the community. The web site is open to faculty, other educational institutions, members of the community, and other organizations who wish to be heard. This policy is far from the restricted policy of the internal mail system in Perry, which provides a paradigm of a nonpublic forum. Unlike Perry, Petitioner opened its web site to "members of the community, and other organizations" who wished to be heard. (R. at 11). This policy of open access more closely resembles the forum created in Widmar, where a state university made its facilities generally available to all registered student groups. This court held that the university, having opened the forum for use by all registered student groups, created a public forum. 454 U.S. at 263. The forum in the instant case is even more expansive, as it is not open only for use by students or school employees but also for all members of the community, other educational institutions in the community, and other organizations.

Further, this Court held that public school facilities become designated public forums when "school authorities have, by policy or practice, opened those facilities for indiscriminate use by the general public, or by some segment of the public, such as student organizations." Hazelwood Sch. Dist. v. Kuhlmeier, 484 U.S. 260, 267 (1988). In the instant case, both "policy and practice" compel the conclusion that the web site is a designated public forum. Petitioner states that its policy invites "faculty of the School district, any other educational institution in Gotham, members of the community, and other organizations" to propose web pages for inclusion in the site. (R. at 11). Through its policy, Petitioner has created a forum "generally open to the public" as stated in Hazelwood Sch.Dist. Id. at 267. It is difficult to imagine a more expansive use policy than one explicitly open to "members of the community and other organizations" as expounded in the instant case.

It has been the consistent practice of Petitioner to allow a wide diversity of groups access to the web site. Numerous organizations from the League of Women Voters' to the American Red Cross, to articles written from heads' of churches for the Council for Alternative Dispute Resolution and The Greater Gotham Youth League, have been allowed to post web pages on Petitioner's web site. (R. at 12-13). In fact, no other web pages have been previously denied. (R. at 15). This is a classic example of "indiscriminate use by the general public" as this court called for in Perry and Hazelwood School Dist. 460 U.S. at 47; 484 U.S. at 267.

The very nature of the forum as a web site argues in favor of defining it as a public forum. While the Internet's modernistic nature precludes it from being a traditional public forum it does share many of the same characteristics. Similar to traditional forums, the Internet is devoted to assembly, debate, and expressive communication. Arguably, the Internet is even more dedicated to expressive activities than traditional forums. Traditional forums, such as parks and plazas were not created solely for the purpose of public discourse. One may visit a park for the purpose of relaxing, recreation, or simply to observe and enjoy the serene setting. The Internet, on the other hand, was created for the sole purpose of communication. The "information super-highway" is slowly replacing traditional public forums as an outlet for citizens to express and exchange ideas. As this medium of expression evolves so must our legal definitions.

> Subsection 2 is a good alternative argument. It clearly is secondary to the first position, but it is strongly supported by authority and convincing in its own right. We think this section would be vastly superior and much more readable if the Respondent had drafted it in an IRAC or TREAT format. This free flow of legal principles and application of same is a little confusing and hard to puzzle through. It needs some paragraph breaks, at the very least.

2. Even if Petitioner's web site is not found to be a pure designated public forum it must qualify as the subset, a limited public forum.

The Appellate Court found Petitioner's web site to be a limited public forum as defined in Rosenberger and Perry. (R. at 18). The Court stated that the web site is far from a limited forum where only certain groups or certain subjects may be accommodated to preserve the essential purpose of the forum. Rather, this Court found it to be a limited public forum in that it is open to anyone wishing to be heard as long as the material has some relation to the subjects found in the School Districts curriculum. (R. at 18). It may be argued that the web site is not a "pure" public forum, but rather a "limited" public forum. It is limited in that the material presented on the proposed web pages must be "tied to a topic of education in the School District". (R. at 11). Under a limited public forum, reasonable exclusions made in order to preserve the forum's purpose may be allowed. Perry, 460 U.S. at 46. Petitioner claims that Respondent's web pages were rejected because they were not related to a subject found in the School District's curriculum. (R at 14). Therefore, Respondent is not being discriminated against but being rightfully barred based on the purpose of the forum. However, Petitioner's claim is erroneous. The School District's curriculum includes the creation of humankind as viewed through Darwin's theory of evolution and natural selection. (R. at 15). Respondent's web pages are clearly "tied to a topic of education in the school district" as required by Petitioner's policy. Creationism is merely another theory of the origin of humankind.

Furthermore, Petitioner states the exclusion was necessary to preserve the purpose of the forum it created. Petitioner's purpose explicitly set out on its home web page, states:

[T]his site was created for the purpose of promoting information about the areas of study currently being taught in the schools. The pages we hope to sponsor will not only highlight topics of interest in the curriculum, but also provide resources and information and links to other sources of information that may not be available in the textbooks and other materials provided to our students in the courses taught. (R. at 11).

Respondent's web pages clearly further the web site's purpose by providing readers with an alternative theory of the creation of humankind, which is not found within the materials taught. Consequently, Petitioner's claim that Respondent's web pages are rightfully barred based on the restrictions of the forum is meritless because the web pages are directly "tied to" theories of the origin of humankind which is included in the District's curriculum and the web pages clearly further the purpose for which the web site was created.

> Section B repeats the abuse of IRAC and TREAT. We suppose section B might be interpreted as one long Rule section, but there is an Application section right in the middle, so Respondent is not building an IRAC or TREAT structure. We understand the points that are being made here, but we attribute that to our familiarity with the law. An IRAC or TREAT structure would help even the uninformed reader to keep up with the issues.

B. Petitioner's denial of Respondent's web pages solely based upon the religious content therein, constitutes content-based discrimination in violation of the First Amendment's Free Speech Clause.

By creating a public forum open to all members of the community, Petitioner is barred by the First Amendment from refusing to accommodate Respondent based upon the content of speech. Rosenberger, 515 U.S. at 819. Content-based discrimination is based upon the ideas or information contained in speech. If a restriction occurs because the State objects to the communicative impact of the expression, the State is not being content-neutral. This type of content-based regulation directly suppresses the communicative impact of the speech and therefore must be analyzed under the rigid review of strict scrutiny. Id.

In the instant case, Petitioner's refusal to allow Respondent access to its web site was obvious content discrimination based upon Respondent's religious ideology of creationism. Petitioner has created a public forum by opening up its web site to all members of the community, or organizations who wish to be heard on educational topics that have a connection to the subjects taught in the School District. Concerned with endorsing the separation of church and state, Petitioner objected to the communicative impact of Respondent's web pages because they were based on the religious theory of creationism.

If Respondent wished to address the same topic, the origin of humankind, with the focus on the scientific theory of evolution rather than the religious theory of creationism, then Petitioner would probably have no objection to Respondent's web pages. However, because the web pages include a religious content, Petitioner has denied Respondent's proposal. This is blatant and unconstitutional State content-discrimination of private religious speech.

> Now, in sub-section 1, we see a return to a true IRAC or TREAT structure, and this section absolutely shines with clarity.

1. Petitioner's content-based exclusion of Respondent's web pages from its public forum triggers a strict scrutiny test, which Petitioner cannot meet.

When a fundamental right, such as free speech is at issue and the State restriction is content-based, this Court has subjected the regulation to strict scrutiny. Widmar, 454 U.S. at 276. Under a strict scrutiny analysis, the restriction is found unconstitutional unless the State can prove (1) its regulation is necessary to serve a compelling state interest, and (2) that it is narrowly drawn to achieve that interest. Bernal, 467 U.S. at 219. With a fundamental right at issue, such as free speech, few regulations can meet this stringent test.

The strict scrutiny analysis applied to content-based discrimination is based upon policy which was expounded by Justice Holmes in Abrams v. United States, 250 U.S. 616 (1919). Justice Holmes stated that there must be "free trade in ideas" and truth will become accepted through the "competition of the market." Id. at 630.

The instant case is analogous to Widmar, where members of a registered religious student organization brought a First Amendment action challenging their exclusion from using university facilities. This Court held that the state university created a public forum by making its facilities available to all registered student organizations, and having done so the university could not discriminate among student groups on the basis of religious content. 454 U.S. at 263. This Court applied the strict scrutiny test and found that the university's discrimination violated the First Amendment. Id. at 268.

Respondent can be analogized to the religious student organization in Widmar. Both Respondent and the student organization are within a class for which the public forum was generally available. Here, the forum is open to all members of the community, and other organizations. In Widmar the forum was open to all registered student organizations. Both Respondent and Widmar were denied access to a public forum based upon religious content of their speech. In accordance with Widmar, this Court should apply strict scrutiny, a constitutional standard that Petitioner cannot satisfy, and find that Petitioner's denial of access to Respondent based on religious content of the proposed web pages constitutes content discrimination which is unconstitutional under the First Amendment's Free Speech Clause.

> Sub-section 2 is another true IRAC or TREAT, and it is powerful and persuasive as a result.

2. <u>Petitioner offers no compelling state interest to justify content-discrimination; hence, Petitioner fails to satisfy strict scrutiny.</u>

A State may exclude a speaker from a public forum without violating the First Amendment when the exclusion is necessary to serve a compelling state interest and is narrowly drawn to achieve that interest. <u>Arkansas Educ. Television Communication v. Forbes</u>, 523 U.S. 666 (1998). Petitioner has offered no legitimate compelling state interest for excluding Respondent. Petitioner merely argues that the exclusion was necessary to preserve the separation of church and state. While separation of church and state is a compelling state interest on its face, it is ensured under the Establishment Clause and is not violated in the instant case.

The university in <u>Widmar</u> also claimed separation of church and state as a compelling interest allowing content-based discrimination. This Court addressed the claim and held that the State's interest in achieving greater separation of church than is already ensured under the Establishment Clause and is limited by the Free Speech Clause is not sufficiently "compelling" to justify content-based discrimination against religious speech. <u>Widmar,</u> 454 U.S. at 277. Furthermore, this Court found that the forum created by the State was open to a broad spectrum of groups and would provide only an incidental benefit to religion. <u>Id.</u> at 274. In accordance with its prior finding, this Court held that "an open forum in a public university does not confer any imprimatur of state approval on religious sects or practices." <u>Id.</u> Therefore, separation of church cannot be a compelling state interest justifying content-based discrimination.

> We have not been dwelling on Respondent's failure to use explanatory synthesis in these explanation sections. We hope you are starting to notice this for yourself. If Respondent synthesized <u>Lamb's Chapel</u> and <u>Widmar</u>, Respondent could derive principles from these two cases concerning how the rule is to be interpreted and applied, and apply these principles to the facts in the application section. Instead, it must apply the cases to the facts as if the cases themselves were rules.

In <u>Lamb's Chapel v. Center Moriches Union Free School District</u>, 508 U.S. 384 (1993), this Court also rejected the Establishment Clause defense as a compelling state interest. This Court reasoned that the school property, although found to be a nonpublic forum, was open to a wide variety of uses. Moreover, this Court stated that the school district was not directly sponsoring the religious group's activities, and "any benefit to the church would have been no more than incidental." <u>Id.</u> at 395.

Quite obviously, the factors considered by this Court in <u>Lamb's Chapel</u> and <u>Widmar</u> exist here. Petitioner created a public forum open to all members in the community for the purpose of expressing alternative ideas and avenues of materials related to current school curriculum. Petitioner would not be endorsing Respondent's religious ideology on the creation of humankind, it merely would be providing an open public forum allowing alternative viewpoints, whether the viewpoints be religious or secular. Under these circumstances, as in <u>Widmar</u> and <u>Lamb's Chapel</u>, there would be no realistic danger that viewers of the web site would think that Petitioner is endorsing Respondent's religious ideology. Permitting Respondent's web page onto the public web site is not an establishment of religion under any of the Establishment Clause tests articulated by this Court and further illustrated in section two of this argument.

Petitioner offers no compelling state interest to trump the content-based discrimination it imposed on Respondent, therefore, there is no need to look into whether the regulation was narrowly draw to achieve that interest. Unable to prove a compelling state interest, Petitioner has violated Respondent's First Amendment constitutional right to Free Speech.

> Section C flip-flops the explanation and application sections, but it otherwise is nicely drafted.

C. Regardless of the nature of the forum, Petitioner's conduct of excluding Respondent's web pages based upon Respondent's religious ideology constitutes viewpoint discrimination which is a per se violation of the First Amendment's Free Speech Clause.

Regardless of the type of forum, restrictions that seek to suppress a speaker's viewpoint are per se unconstitutional in violation of the First Amendment's Free Speech Clause. <u>Arkansas Educ. Television Comm'n</u>, 523 U.S. at 676, <u>Rosenberger</u>, 523 U.S. at 827. Viewpoint discrimination is an egregious subset of content-based discrimination. <u>Id.</u> at 827. While content-based discrimination may be justified by a compelling state interest narrowly drawn to achieve its ends, viewpoint discrimination can never be justified.

As previously stated, Petitioner claims that its web site is a nonpublic forum and the restriction is based not on the content of the web pages or on Respondent's viewpoint, but rather on the religious subject matter of the web pages and this type of subject-matter discrimination is reasonable in light of a nonpublic forum. (R. at 6). Even if the web site is found to be a nonpublic forum, Petitioner's defense of subject-matter discrimination is not supported by the facts because Petitioner has authorized other web pages that contain religious subject matter. For instance, The Council for Alternative Dispute Resolution has posted a site on "health" which includes an article with founder, Reverend Carla Boulevardier, Pastor of St. Peter's AME Church of Gotham. The Greater Gotham Youth League and North Gotham General Hospital also has a site on "health" including an article written by Fr. John Berrigan, Roman Catholic priest of Gotham Cathedral Church.

(R. at 13). Petitioner cannot successfully claim that Respondent is being denied access based on the religious subject matter of the web pages when Petitioner has granted access to web sites that focus on articles written by heads of church.

Moreover, Respondent's perspective on creationism provides a specific premise, a perspective, and a standpoint from which the subject of the origin of humankind may be discussed and considered. The prohibited perspective, creationism, not the general subject matter, origin of humankind, resulted in the refusal to allow Respondent access to Petitioner's public web site, because the subject of the proposed web pages was within the approved category of subjects taught in the School District's curriculum. In arguing subject matter discrimination, Petitioner is merely providing a façade for viewpoint discrimination. Petitioner is not placing the entire topic of the origin of humankind off-limits as it is covered in the School District's curriculum. Instead Petitioner is rejecting Respondent's web pages based upon Respondent's religious ideology of the origin of humankind.

In <u>Lamb's Chapel</u>, this Court found the school district's denial of a church's request to exhibit a film dealing with family and child-rearing issues, to constitute viewpoint discrimination. 508 U.S. at 393. Moreover, this Court found that while opening the school facilities for after school use created a non-public forum, the restriction placed on the church's film was not viewpoint neutral and therefore a violation of the First Amendment. <u>Id.</u> at 393. Furthermore, this Court rationalized its holding by finding that the subject matter of child rearing would ordinarily be permitted; however, it was not permitted in this instance because it was presented from a religious perspective. <u>Id.</u> This rationale was in accordance with this Court's previous finding in <u>Cornelius</u> which held that:

> [A]lthough a speaker may be excluded form a nonpublic forum if he wishes to address topics not encompassed within the purpose of the forum or if he is a member of a class of speakers for whose benefit the forum was created, the government violates the First Amendment when it denies access to speaker solely to suppress point of view he espouses on otherwise includible subject.

473 U.S. at 805.

As established herein, Respondent's proposal encompasses a topic within the purpose of the forum, Respondent is a member of the class of speakers for which the forum was created, and Petitioner has not designated religion as an impermissible subject matter. Therefore, Petitioner's conduct in excluding Respondent's proposal constitutes viewpoint-discrimination, which blatantly violates the First Amendment's Free Speech Clause.

Respondent starts off issue II with another big background and introduction section. This one sounds a little more like an umbrella or roadmap section. It is a good section, and worth doing if you have the space. Because Respondent knows that it is drafting an introduction and background section, it left out a lot of the citations to legal authority. Once again, we do not approve of this tactic. You certainly do not have to explain each case you cite, but *always* give a cite to support your sweeping legal statements.

II. THE JUDGMENT OF THE APPELLATE COURT OF THE FOURTEENTH CIRCUIT SHOULD BE AFFIRMED BECAUSE THE INCLUSION OF RESPONDENT'S WEB PAGES IN THE METROPOLITAN SCHOOL DISTRICT'S WEB SITE DOES NOT VIOLATE THE ESTABLISHMENT CLAUSE.

The Metropolitan School District claims that hosting the Branch Louisian's creationism web pages violates the Establishment Clause. Creationism is defined as "a doctrine or theory holding that matter, the various forms of life, and the world were created by God out of nothing and usually in the way described in Genesis."[4] There is no constitutional provision that prohibits a public school from exposing its students to religion. The Establishment Clause was intended to protect against "sponsorship, financial support, and active involvement of the sovereign in religious activity." Lemon v. Kurtzman, 403 U.S. 602, 612 (1971). Chief Justice Burger stated in writing the opinion for this Court in Lynch v. Donnelly, that the Constitution does not "require complete separation of church and state; it affirmatively mandates accommodation, not merely tolerance, of all religions, and forbids hostility toward any." Lynch v. Donnelly, 465 U.S. 668, 673 (1984). It is upon this foundation that the argument for the inclusion of Respondent's web pages is made. The School District cannot claim to violate the Establishment Clause solely on the basis that creationism is tied to religion. The web site, sponsored by the School District, is comparable to a school's library. Both contain educational materials to enhance the students' appreciation and interest in the areas taught at the schools. The inclusion of religious materials in a school library, in and of itself, has never been found by this Court to violate the Establishment Clause. Neither can a web page with religious content hosted by a public school on its web site, one among many other web pages pertaining to the school's curriculum, be found in violation of the Establishment Clause.

---

[4] Merriam-Webster Dictionary, Inc. (2000).

> Perhaps Respondent still thinks it is in an introduction mode, but it is killing the reader with these endless paragraphs. Break them up—please! It also needs to adopt an IRAC or TREAT structure. It is easier for the uninformed reader to follow that kind of rule-based logical syllogism than this "stream of legal principles" format, followed by intermittent application of the principles.
>
> Compared to the sample brief above, it is much more apparent in this brief that Respondent has switched authors from the first major issue to the second; one student did Section I and a different student did Section II. Just the length of the paragraphs tells us this much. It should not be so obvious. Moot Court teams should take the time to edit and meld separately authored work together so that the final product is seamless. There is no question that Respondent #2 is a good legal writer, but he or she can improve things if he or she constantly tries to employ IRAC or TREAT, and breaks up these monster paragraphs into proper chunks.

The hosting of Respondent's web pages by the Metropolitan School District will be found constitutional because it meets every test used by this Court to determine violations of the Establishment Clause. First, the hosting of the creationism web page by the School District does not offend the requirement that the school remain neutral with regards to religion. Neutrality towards religion is not synonymous with exclusion or absence of religion. Second, the hosting of the creationism web page meets the three-prong test articulated by this Court in Lemon, 403 U.S. at 612-613. The purpose, primary effect, and entanglement issues all support the finding that including Respondent's web pages in the School District's web site would not violate the Establishment Clause. Lemon has its critics, however, and other tests have been recommended by this Court to determine whether the Establishment Clause has been violated.[5] Finally, it will be argued, therefore, that the endorsement and the coercion tests both support a finding that a violation of the Establishment Clause would not occur with the inclusion of a creationism web page on the School District's web site. The hosting of a creationism web page on a School District's web site presents unique issues regarding the Establishment Clause and because of that this case cannot solely be determined by the decisions in other Establishment Clause cases. Chief Justice Burger stated that the line of separation between church and state "is a blurred, indistinct, and variable barrier depending on all the circumstances of a particular

---

[5]   See Justice Scalia's concurring opinion in Lamb's Chapel when criticizing the Court's usage of the Lemon test in deciding the case, he states that Lemon is "like some ghoul in a late-night horror movie that repeatedly sits up in its grave and shuffles abroad, after being repeatedly killed and buried." Lamb's Chapel v. Center Moriches Union Free School District, 508 U.S. 384, 398 (1993).

relationship." Lemon, 403 U.S. at 614. The circumstances of the this particular relationship support a finding that the School District would not violate the Establishment Clause by including Respondent's web pages on its web site.

A. The hosting of Respondent's web pages by the Metropolitan School District respects rather than offends the School District's neutrality towards religion.

"Neutrality, in both form and effect, is one hallmark of the Establishment Clause." Rosenberger, 515 U.S. at 846 (O'Connor concurring). The inclusion of Respondent's web pages ensures a policy of neutrality toward religion. The School District, however, has chosen to exclude the creationism web page under the guise that it would create an impermissible relationship between church and state in violation of the Establishment Clause. The web page pertaining to creationism is directly related to the topic of the origin of humankind. The fact that the School District has opened its web site to others and has shut its door to Respondent's web pages "demonstrates not neutrality but hostility toward religion." Board of Educ. of Westside Community Sch. (Dist.566) v. Mergens, 496 U.S. 226, 248 (1990). The School District's contention that the inclusion of the creationism web page would violate their web site policy is warrantless. Like Lamb's Chapel, the basis for the exclusion is due to this particular religious belief. They have opened up a forum under a policy that states that for a web site to be hosted it must "directly relate to a topic" taught in the schools. Evolution is a scientific theory regarding the origin of humankind. Creationism is a theory with a religious foundation regarding the origin of humankind. The fact that Darwin's theory of evolution is taught and has been taught for over 70 years in the School District supports the inclusion of a creationism web page. The School District's policy is focused on curriculum based and enhancing web pages. This policy as stated, therefore, is neutral towards religious web pages which are related to an area in the District's curriculum. The Bible, when integrated into a public school's curriculum, may be constitutionally used as an appropriate study of history, civilization, ethics, or comparative religion. Stone v. Graham, 449 U.S. 39, 42 (1980). Creationism is related to an area covered in the curriculum, the origin of humankind, whether that topic is taught under biology or anthropology. "A significant factor in upholding government programs in the face of attack under the establishment of religion clause is such programs' neutrality towards religion." Rosenberger, 515 U.S. at 839. Because the School District's policy maintains its neutrality even when hosting a creationism web page, refusing the web pages in order to prevent a violation of the Establishment Clause is an invalid argument.

The School District's web site is neutral in design. As in Rosenberger, there is no suggestion that the School District created its web site with the intention of advancing religion or that they "adopted some ingenious device with the purpose of aiding a religious cause." Id. at 840. A government program that is neutral in design cannot use the Establishment Clause to justify "a refusal to extend free speech rights to religious speakers." Id. at 839. The Establishment Clause was intended to protect against "sponsorship, financial support, and active involvement of the sovereign in religious activity." Lemon, 403 US at 612. In the present case, the School District's inclusion of the creationism web pages does not offend any of those objectives. The Branch Louisian Church sponsors the web pages. Any cost to the School District of hosting the web pages is incidental to the Church because the Church is already paying for the web pages and the School District is solely supplying a link to those pages. The School District has little involvement with the web pages it hosts with the exception of creating the link and following their own written policy. The School District would not be actively involved in any manner in the Branch Louisian web pages any more than the District is involved with the other web pages it hosts. The District policy is a neutral curriculum based policy. The sponsorship by the Branch Louisian Church, the lack of financial support, and the limited involvement in the creationism web pages all support the argument that the inclusion of the creationism web pages would maintain the District's neutrality towards religion and would, therefore, not violate the Establishment Clause.

> Sections B(1) and (2) are trying to get into IRAC or TREAT form but ultimately cannot because there is no break in the paragraphs. The semblance of a Rule and Explanation is present, and a little Application here and there. It is just plain difficult to get through these sections because you do not know when to come up for air. IRAC or TREAT structures are much easier to read and comprehend.

B. The hosting of Respondent's web pages by the Metropolitan School District comports with the three-pronged Lemon test and, therefore, does not violate the Establishment Clause.

1. The purpose of the Metropolitan School District's web site is secular.

Under the Lemon test if one prong fails, the statute or policy will be found to be in violation of the Establishment Clause. The first prong of the Lemon test looks at the government's purpose in implementing the policy under question. In order for a policy to be found constitutional, the government's purpose for implementing the policy must be found to have been secular rather than religious. The purpose of the School District's web site, as stated on the home page, was to both promote and supplement those areas of study currently being taught in the District's primary and secondary schools. (R-11). The purpose, therefore, is secular in nature. The purpose prong, however, has been the most effective in finding statutes requiring the exclusion of the teaching of evolution or the inclusion of creationism in violation of the Establishment Clause. Two cases pertaining to the teaching of creationism in public schools have gone before this Court, and both were found to violate the Establishment Clause. Epperson v. Arkansas, 393 U.S. 97 (1968); Edwards v. Aguillar, 482 U.S. 578 (1987). In both Epperson and Edwards this Court found a lack of secular purpose in the enacted statutes. This Court found in Epperson that the purpose of the Arkansas statute was to prevent evolution from being taught in the schools because it was contrary to creationism. "It is clear that fundamentalist sectarian conviction was and is the law's reason for existence." Id. at 108. In Edwards, Justice Brennan stated that the Court would not defer to a State's articulated secular purpose when it obviously does not have such a purpose and in fact is really a "sham". Both cases, however, are easily distinguishable from the present creationism case due to the fact that the statutes enacted did not have a secular purpose. The School District in the present case had only a secular purpose when it implemented its web site. Justice Fortas wrote in Epperson that "while [the] study of religions and of the Bible from a literary and historic viewpoint, presented objectively as part of a secular program of education, need not collide with the First Amendment's prohibition, the State may not adopt programs or practices in its public schools or colleges which 'aid or oppose' any religion." Epperson, 393 U.S. at 104. Epperson and Edwards do not purport to prohibit the teaching of creationism in public schools. It is only when creationism has been required to be taught or evolution prohibited from being taught for religious reasons that the First Amendment is violated. It is the actions and intentions of the government, not the church, that the Establishment Clause restricts. In the case at hand, the School District's policy is secular, and the inclusion of a creationism web pages does not change that purpose from a secular one to a religious one.

2. The primary effect of including the creationism web pages is not the advancement of religion.

The second prong of the Lemon test looks at whether the questioned policy has a primary effect of advancing religion. The primary effect of the School District hosting a creationism web page on its web site is to achieve its secular purpose of enhancing and supplementing the District's curriculum, not the advancement of religion. The study of creationism can certainly be part of a secular curriculum without having the primary effect of advancing a religious ideology. Requiring the teaching of creationism would almost certainly be found to violate the Establishment Clause, however, allowing a greater understanding of the origin of humankind through an exposure to evolution, creationism, and other theories is a valid secular purpose without the effect of advancing any particular belief. It is certainly possible to present information that contains religious content in a public school as an objective part of a secular education program and not violate the Establishment Clause. School Dist. of Abington Township v. Schempp, 374 US 203, 225 (1963). In fact, this Court stated that, "it might well be said that one's education is not complete without a study of comparative religion or the history of religion and its relationship to the advancement of civilization. . ." Id. The inclusion of a creationism web page as part of the School District's web site does not have the effect of advancing religion but rather has the effect of enhancing an objective secular educational program.

> Did we mention that these paragraphs are too long? To save you from the abuse of these paragraphs, we are going to skip to the Conclusion.

* * *

CONCLUSION

> A long winded Conclusion almost never is seen in trial court and appellate briefs. By the time a judge lurches to the conclusion at the end of a 30+ page brief, she is ready to be done, and does not want to read two more pages of a clever rehash of the same arguments she has been pouring over for the last hour or two. Especially if the two pages of conclusion are one long paragraph. Instead, state your prayer for relief and sign off.

As Chief Justice Burger stated in <u>Lynch v. Donnelly</u>, "in our modern, complex society, whose traditions and constitutional underpinnings rest on and encourage diversity and pluralism in all areas, an absolutist approach in applying the Establishment Clause is simplistic and has been uniformly rejected by the Court." <u>Lynch</u>, 465 U.S. at 678. This case and questions involved cannot be dealt with simplistically. In the case before us, the School District elected to sponsor a web site for the purpose of hosting web pages that would "highlight topics of interest in the curriculum" and provide "information that may not be available in the textbooks" (R-11). Petitioner chose to initiate this web site for the purpose of expressive activities and to promote alternative information tied to the School District's curriculum. By opening this web site to all members of the community, Petitioner created a designated public forum. In doing so, Petitioner must abide by the rules of free speech in accordance with this type of forum. While Petitioner chooses to keep this forum open for general use to all members of the community, it must not discriminate against Respondent's religious viewpoint or the religious content of the proposed web pages. This type of content-based discrimination clearly violates Respondent's First Amendment right to free speech. Ergo, the Appellate Court correctly found that Petitioner's discriminatory behavior in denying Respondent's proposed web pages, violated Respondent's constitutional right to Free Speech.

The School District attempts to justify this First Amendment discriminatory behavior by arguing that it was compelled to do so in order to avoid violating the Establishment Clause. However, the Establishment Clause is not implicated in this case. Every Establishment Clause test articulated by this Court finds the separation of church and state well in place. Allowing the School District to prohibit the Branch Louisian's web pages only does an injustice to the children attending the District's schools. "The classroom is peculiarly the marketplace of ideas. The Nation's future depends upon leaders trained through wide exposure to that robust exchange of ideas which discovers truth out of a multitude of tongues, [rather] than through any kind of authoritative selection." <u>Keyishian v. Board of Regents</u>, 385 U.S. 589, 603 (1967). The School District is failing the children, education, and the Constitution by refusing to host Respondent's web pages and casting a "pall of orthodoxy over the classrooms." <u>Id.</u> The School District's argument loses on both issues. Respondent, therefore, requests that this Court affirm the Appellate Court's decision.

Sample Brief No. 3:

Brief of Petitioners in the
U.S. Supreme Court case:

Capitol Square Review and Advisory Board
v.
Pinette

515 U.S. 753 (1995)

Docket No. 94-780

SUPREME COURT OF THE UNITED STATES

October Term, 1994

CAPITOL SQUARE REVIEW AND ADVISORY BOARD,
RONALD T. KELLER, DANIEL SHELLENBARGER, AND
OHIO SENATOR RICHARD T. FINAN,

Petitioners,

— *against*—

VINCENT J. PINETTE, DONNIE A. CARR, AND KNIGHTS
OF THE KU KLUX KLAN,

Respondents.

ON WRIT OF CERTIORARI TO THE UNITED STATES COURT OF
APPEALS FOR THE SIXTH CIRCUIT

BRIEF OF PETITIONERS

> Question Presented: The question here is adequate, but somewhat densely-worded. It does not flow very well. We would drop the references to the Latin cross and the Ohio statehouse—they are too case-specific for a Supreme Court QP. We also do not like the "such as a . . ." phrasing. Our version would read:
>
> > Whether the unattended display on government property of a purely religious symbol, directly in front of a seat of government, violates the establishment clause, even if such display is sponsored by a private group in a public forum?
>
> We understand the desire to get your facts up front as soon as possible, but the bare rendition of the legal issue seems engaging enough to get the reader to look further.

QUESTION PRESENTED FOR REVIEW

Whether the unattended display on government property of a purely religious symbol, such as a large, Latin cross, directly in front of a seat of government, such as the Ohio statehouse, violates the establishment clause, even if such display is sponsored by a private group in a public forum?

> We cut out the **TABLE OF CONTENTS** and **TABLE OF AUTHORITIES** to save space. You have seen enough examples of these by now. What follows is the "Opinions Below" section. It is a necessary section in some briefs (check local rules), and this one is adequate.

OPINIONS BELOW

The opinion of the Court of Appeals for the Sixth Circuit is reported at 30 F.3d 676 (6th Cir. 1994) and is reprinted in the Appendix to the Petition for Writ of Certiorari ("App.") at A1-A12. The Sixth Circuit's opinion affirmed the December 21, 1993 Order and Opinion of the United States District Court for the Southern District of Ohio. The District court's opinion is reported at 844 F. Supp. 1182 (S.D. Ohio 1993) and is reprinted at App. A13-A26. The Report and Recommendation of the Administrative Hearing Examiner, adopted in full by the Capitol Square Review and Advisory Board, is reprinted at App. A27-A37.

The unreported opinion of the Sixth Circuit denying Petitioners' request for an emergency stay of the district court's injunction pending appeal is reprinted at App. A40-A42. The in-chambers opinion of Justice Stevens, sitting as Circuit Justice, denying Petitioners' request for an emergency stay of the district court's injunction pending appeal is reported at 114 S. Ct. 626 (Stevens, Circuit Justice 1993) and is reprinted at App. A38-A39.

> The Statement of Jurisdiction is another required section. This one is adequate.

STATEMENT OF JURISDICTION OF THE COURT

The decision of the Court of Appeals for the Sixth Circuit was entered on July 25, 1994. See App. A1. The petition for writ of certiorari was filed on October 24, 1994, and was granted on January 13, 1995. This Court has jurisdiction pursuant to 28 U.S.C. § 1254(1).

> This Constitutional Provisions section is fine. Note that none of these required sections should be argumentative. The Question Presented in this brief was a little too argumentative, but these other required sections are properly neutral.

CONSTITUTIONAL PROVISIONS INVOLVED

Constitution of the United States, Amendment I.

Congress shall make no law respecting an establishment of religion, or prohibiting the free exercise thereof; or abridging the freedom of speech, or of the press, or the right of the people peaceably to assemble, and to petition the Government for a redress of grievances.

Constitution of the United States, Amendment XIV, Section 1.

All persons born or naturalized in the United States and subject to the jurisdiction thereof, are citizens of the United States and of the State wherein they reside. No State shall make or enforce any law which shall abridge the privileges or immunities of citizens of the United States; nor shall any State deprive any person of life, liberty, or property, without due process of law; nor deny to any person within its jurisdiction the equal protection of the laws.

> In the Statement of the Case, the brief writers take the opportunity to bolster their case in an otherwise non-argumentative section by using compelling language and by the selection of the facts they choose to emphasize. They quickly bring out in section 1 the respondents' overtly religious message that is intended to go along with the cross. The petitioners continually refer to the cross as "large," even though we have not yet heard the actual dimensions of the cross. This is a neat trick, because it allows the readers to envision whatever they might come up with when they hear "large cross"—the readers might get a mental picture of a fifty foot high, shining white cross with spotlights on it. Allowing the readers' minds to run amok helps the petitioners in this instance.
>
> This section shows the proper Supreme Court combination of a statement of facts and proceedings below section, all under the single heading of "Statement of the Case." This statement of the case is a great deal longer than that of any of the preceding briefs. We would venture to say that it is far too long to keep the readers' attention, but it is well drafted.

STATEMENT OF THE CASE

1. Respondents in this action, the Knights of the Ku Klux Klan (Ohio Realm) and two of their officers, brought this suit originally against the Capitol Square Review and Advisory Board, its executive director, spokesperson, and chairperson. Joint Appendix (J.A. 22-23). The lawsuit sought in effect to compel the State of Ohio to allow Respondents to erect a large, unattended Latin cross directly in front of the Ohio Statehouse during the Christmas season, between December 8, 1993 and December 24, 1993. (J.A. 26). Respondents openly acknowledged that their purpose in seeking to erect the display at this location was to erect "a symbol for our Lord, Jesus Christ" (J.A. 173) in furtherance of their more general purpose to "establish a Christian government in America." (J.A. 144-147).

> Section 2 of the statement of the case does a nice job of setting out how visible the state house is – details here paint a clear and compelling picture of the scene. Petitioners downplay the other religious items they have allowed to be displayed in the square; there is no point in dwelling on these bad facts.

2. The Capitol Square is owned by the State of Ohio and located in downtown Columbus. It is the site of Ohio's state capitol building, also known as the Ohio Statehouse, which is a large rectangular building that centers the Capitol Square. The Ohio Statehouse, which is a distinctive example of Greek Doric architecture, is topped by a large rotunda. For well over a century, it has housed both chambers of the Ohio General Assembly as well as the offices of the Ohio Governor and other statewide officeholders. (J.A. 96-97). The Ohio Statehouse is the dominant feature of the Capitol Square, and it is plainly and unavoidably visible from every vantage point on the Capitol Square. See App. A43 (photograph). The District Court held in this case that the Capitol Square is a public forum. See App. A18.

For the past several years, the State of Ohio has allowed certain holiday seasonal displays to be placed on the Capitol Square for limited periods during the month of December. (J.A. 98). The State's traditional policy is to allow a broad range of speakers and other gatherings of people to conduct events on the Capitol Square. (J.A. 98). These displays are generally an exception to that policy because they are unattended structures. The holiday seasonal displays permitted by the State in the past have included a Christmas tree and a menorah. (J.A. 98).

On November 18, 1993, the Capitol Square Review and Advisory Board, which is authorized by law to regulate the uses of the Capitol Square, voted not to permit unattended displays on the Capitol Square during December of 1993. (J.A. 98). That vote was later declared invalid, and on November 23, 1993, the Board voted to approve displays of a Christmas tree and menorah. (J.A. 98-99). The State displayed its own Christmas tree, and a permit application to erect a menorah on the Capitol Square from December 8-16, 1993, which was explicitly stated to be a "seasonal display," was granted. (J.A. 99).

> Section 3 – okay, ***now*** we find out the cross is only ten feet high and six feet across.
>
> Footnote 1 is fine here, but in general, you should limit footnotes to nonessential matters. Footnotes should not contain information that is important to the analysis of the case. Footnotes are for additional facts or minor legal issues that pop up in the discussion, but have no bearing on the main argument you are making. If the material in the footnote does have a bearing on the main argument, put the material in the text where it will not be missed.

3. On November 29, 1993, Respondents applied for a permit to display a cross on the Capitol Square from December 8-24, 1993. (J.A. 99). The application described the type of event as being to "erect a cross for Christmas." (J.A. 99). Executive Director Keller denied the application on December 3, 1993, "upon the advice of counsel, in a good faith attempt to comply with the Ohio and United States Constitutions, as they have been interpreted in relevant decisions by the Federal and State Courts." (J.A. 99). Respondents

later clarified that they sought to erect a cross in the style of a Latin cross,[6] about ten feet high and six feet across and accompanied by a suggested disclaimer open to negotiation. (J.A. 100).

On December 9, 1993, Respondents filed an administrative appeal of this action to the full Board; the appeal was perfected on December 13, 1993. (J.A. 100-101). On December 17, 1993, a state administrative appeal was conducted by a hearing examiner who took evidence and heard argument from both sides. On December 21, 1993, the administrative hearing examiner issued a report and recommendation which found that the initial denial of a permit to Respondents was proper. App. A27. The hearing examiner held, among other things, that whereas holiday seasonal symbols have by virtue of that association taken on "cultural significance extending well beyond the religious sphere," the Latin cross "is generally regarded as having a purely sectarian purpose (i.e., to advance or endorse the Christian religion)." App. A34-A35. For that reason, the display of a Latin cross directly in front of the Ohio Statehouse, unlike the display of a Christmas tree or a menorah, was held to violate the Establishment Clause. App. A36. The Board unanimously adopted this report and recommendation as its own final ruling later that day. App. A16.

> Sections 4, 5, 6, and 7 of the Statement of the Case really drive home some important points by focusing on the language used by the lower courts when they rejected petitioners' arguments. This sets the scene nicely for petitioners' attempt to get a reversal by reasserting the same arguments that failed below. Hopefully, they will reassert them with new emphasis and stronger support. But petitioners need to confine the opinions below to a more manageable—and refutable—size. They do this by quoting the court's language and passing off these excerpts as the holding of the cases below.
>
> Note the language used here. Strong action verbs, adverbs, and adjectives are used—such as "immediately"—to connote a sense of rush to the proceedings below. A sense of urgency is also communicated by the fact that these hearings took place right in the middle of the holiday season. "Rushing around" is not an admirable description when you are considering weighty legal questions. If petitioners can

---

[6] "Latin cross" is the proper term for any "cross whose base stem is longer than the other three arms." American Civil Liberties Union v. City of St. Charles, 794 F.2d 265, 271, cert. denied, 479 U.S. 961 (1986) (affirming preliminary injunction against display of lighted Latin cross on top of city fire department building during Christmas season because it would violate the Establishment Clause).

suggest to the Supreme Court that the courts below rushed their decisions, it may be easier to convince the Court that these decisions are wrong. Never mind that the petitioners probably wanted the proceedings to go as quickly as possible below; you take the cards dealt to you and play them to your advantage.

We like that the sense of urgency here is more implicit than explicit. If petitioners had come out and said, "The proceedings below were rushed because of the holiday season," then respondents undoubtedly would respond with something like, "Respondents will not sit by and let petitioners impugn the decisions of a United States District Judge, three judges of the United States Court of Appeals for the Sixth Circuit, and Justice Stevens of this Court. The proceedings were not rushed. Careful deliberation and explanation of the decisions were undertaken. In any event, whatever need to proceed forthwith was procured by petitioners' own timing of their decision to refuse to display respondents' cross."

Mentioning in section 6 the vandalism of the first cross erected by the Ku Klux Klan is a tactical move, most likely thrown in to remind the high court of the widespread popular sentiment against the Klan. There really is no other reason to mention it here. But we think it was a great idea.

Having photos to refer to is a great advantage here because, visually, the scene described must have been quite a compelling one. Petitioners' reference to it serves two purposes: first, to remind the Supreme Court of the sentiment against the Klan, and second, to remind the Court that separation of church and state symbols is a good idea; otherwise, you get chaotic scenes like this one. Nice work, petitioners.

4. In the meantime, on December 15, 1993, Respondents filed this lawsuit in District court, asserting that the denial of their application for permit to erect a cross violated their constitutional right of free speech. (J.A. 27). The court set the matter for hearing on December 20, 1993, and consolidated the hearing on Respondents' motion for a preliminary injunction with a trial on the merits. At the close of this hearing, the court deferred its ruling pending the outcome of the state administrative appeal process. Once that process was completed on December 21, 1993, the court granted a permanent injunction requiring Petitioners to approve a permit for Respondents to display a cross on the Capitol Square through December 24, 1993. App. A26.

> Note: we will not comment on the citation forms, spac-
> ing, or other formatting of the brief. The text we were able
> to obtain was not formatted and did not have standard
> Bluebook citations, so do not rely on the forms and format-
> ting depicted here.

In its ruling, the District Court considered whether Respondents' display of a large, unattended Latin cross directly in front of the Ohio Statehouse would constitute an impermissible "endorsement" of religion under Lemon v. Kurtzman, 403 U.S. 602 (1971), as subsequently interpreted and applied in such "holiday seasonal display" cases as Lynch v. Donnelly, 465 U.S. 668 (1984), and County of Allegheny v. American Civil Liberties Union, 492 U.S. 573 (1989). On the basis of a recent en banc decision by the Sixth Circuit Court of Appeals that addressed essentially the same issue, Americans United for Separation of Church & State v. Grand Rapids, 980 F.2d 1538 (6th Cir. 1993) (en banc), the District Court held that the unattended religious display in this case would not constitute an impermissible endorsement of religion so as to violate the Establishment Clause. App. A7-A8.

5. Immediately after the District Court issued its ruling, Petitioners moved for a stay pending appeal, which the court denied. Petitioners filed a Notice of Appeal to the Sixth Circuit on the same day — December 21, 1993 — and filed a motion for an emergency stay of the injunction pending appeal, which the Sixth Circuit denied on December 22, 1993. App. A40. Petitioners then filed an emergency application for a stay of injunction with Circuit Justice Stevens, which was denied on December 23, 1993. App. A38.

6. Respondents erected a cross on the Capitol Square sometime during the night of December 21, 1993, and it was displayed there the following day until it was apparently vandalized. The cross was displayed by itself in the middle of the lawn directly in front of the Ohio Statehouse, see App. A43 (photograph), located at some distance from the Christmas tree.[7] On December 22, 1993, Petitioners received yet another application from a group of Christian ministers, who sought to erect twenty more Latin crosses in front of the Ohio Statehouse. Petitioners believed themselves obligated, by the force of the District Court's ruling, to grant this further application, and thereafter numerous other crosses were erected and displayed in the same vicinity on December 23-24, 1993. (J.A. 60) (Appendix to Brief In Opposition To Writ Of Certiorari p. RA 31 ("Opp. App.")).

7. On appeal, the Sixth Circuit affirmed the District Court's ruling. App. A1. The Sixth Circuit adhered to its recent en banc decision in Americans United, which "held that a private organization's unattended display of a religious symbol in a public forum does not violate the Establishment Clause." App. A8. The court focused in particular on the nature of the display and the nature of the forum. It essentially held that because this display was privately sponsored, it did not matter what was contained in the display — for

---

[7] The menorah had been removed almost a week earlier, when that permit expired on December 16, 1993.

example, a Latin cross in this case as opposed to a menorah in cases like *Americans United* and *County of Allegheny*. Because this display was to be located in a public forum, moreover, it did not matter what kind of location was to exhibit the display — for example, the Ohio Statehouse in this case as opposed to a public park

> The Sixth Circuit is made to look foolish by the wording of the court's holding (that a big Latin cross sitting right in front of the Ohio statehouse would not suggest any approval of or endorsement of Christianity). The point is a good one, but this section is phrased too strongly—it is an insult to the Sixth Circuit, not a neutral report of its findings. It should have been toned down for equal legal effect, but less insult.

in cases like *Americans United* and *Lynch*. The Sixth Circuit thus determined that a reasonable observer could not conclude that the State of Ohio endorsed Christianity after viewing a large, unattended Latin cross standing directly in front of the Ohio Statehouse because "truly private religious expression in a truly public forum cannot be seen as endorsement by a reasonable observer." App. A9 (quoting *Americans United*, 980 F.2d at 1553) (emphasis in original). On this ground, the Sixth Circuit held that Respondents' display of a Latin cross directly in front of the Ohio Statehouse did not constitute an impermissible endorsement of religion under the Establishment Clause.

> The Summary of Argument is a critical section. Never shortchange this section by writing it at the last minute, when you are exhausted and could care less what goes in there. This section is *definitely* going to be read by even the busiest judge or justice. They may tire of your actual argument section, but they most likely will read your entire summary of argument. So give it your best shot. Write it *after* you have completed the argument, and take the same care in drafting—and especially in editing and revising—the section as you do with the full argument.
>
> Petitioners have done a good job with this section. They make their points clearly and concisely. You should never beat around the bush in this section. Notice how short the paragraphs are—two or three sentences each, in most cases. This makes it easy to read and drives home the points quickly and smoothly. The most important authorities are cited in this section, *not all* of the authorities, which improves readability.
>
> On the other hand, we do not think this section is perfect. We seriously question the suggestion that the free speech clause should not trump the establishment clause because the establishment clause is listed first in the First Amendment. This sounds flaky, and it is phrased almost as a rhetorical question. You should avoid such flippant remarks in something as grave as a Supreme Court brief.

SUMMARY OF ARGUMENT

Displays of purely religious symbols at the seat of government, such as the large solitary and unattended Latin cross placed directly in front of the Ohio Statehouse in this case, violate the Establishment Clause of the First Amendment.

A purely religious symbol, such as a Latin cross, the ultimate sectarian symbol of Christianity, conveys a clear message of religion. See American Civil Liberties Union v. City of St. Charles, 794 F. 2d 265 (7th Cir.), cert. denied, 479 U.S. 961 (1986). At the same time, the symbol of the seat of government, in this case the Ohio Statehouse, conveys a clear message of government authority. Kaplan v. City of Burlington, 891 F. 2d 1024 (2nd Cir. 1989), cert. denied, 496 U.S. 926 (1990). The conjunction of the two communicates powerfully to an observer that the message conveyed by each symbol comes from the same source — the government. Id.

In most circumstances, an observer can easily identify those responsible for speech: the speaker at the microphone, the group chanting a slogan, the person holding a sign or passing out brochures. But when speech is conveyed by an unattended display, the author of the speech is not readily ascertainable and usually is perceived by most reasonable observers to be the owner of the property on which the display stands.

The Establishment Clause protects against religious messages bearing the government's imprimatur. Widmar v. Vincent, 454 U.S. 263 (1981). The juncture of the cross and the government building in an unattended setting creates the danger against which the Establishment Clause guards.

The Court has not addressed whether a union of church and state is legally permissible if it occurs in a public forum. The Sixth Circuit adopted a per se rule that, because a display is privately sponsored in a public forum, there can never be a misperception of the message. But nothing in the Court's precedents removes, for Establishment Clause purposes, the obligation of a court to determine the nature of the message being sent and received. The fact that the message is delivered in a public forum does not give the government the right to advocate religion. Nor may it permit a private party to proffer speech which is likely to be perceived as government speech endorsing religion. Public forum or no public forum, government may not throw its weight behind sectarian evangelism, nor may it permit a private party to create the impression that government supports religion. But just such an impression is created when an unattended, purely religious symbol, such as the Latin cross, is positioned with the state capitol as its backdrop.

The court below incorrectly held that one part of the First Amendment — the free speech clause — always trumps another part of the First Amendment — the Establishment Clause — when speech is uttered in a public forum. Under such rationale, no inquiry ever need be made whether, under the circumstances of the case, the speaker in the public forum appears to be the government and the speech appears to be endorsement of religion. If the Framers had intended such power of the Free Speech Clause, one would think that they would at least have placed it before the Establishment Clause.

The Court's cases dealing with holiday seasonal displays offer two tests for evaluating the issues in the instant case. See County of Allegheny v. American Civil Liberties Union, 492 U.S. 573 (1989). Each test attempts to strike a proper balance so that government neither advances nor inhibits religion. See Lemon v. Kurtzman, 403 U.S. 602 (1971). This includes not preferring the religious practices of one group at the expense of other groups, or even religious non-adherents. County of Allegheny.

The union of an isolated and unattended religious icon and the seat of government upsets this constitutional balance. Kaplan; Smith v. County of Albemarle, Va., 895 F. 2d 953 (4th Cir.), cert. denied, ___U.S.___, 111 S. Ct. 74 (1990). There is a significant risk that observers of the message conveyed by this union will perceive it as emanating from the government. For that reason, the unattended display in this case violates either test previously established by the Court.

Neither the Court's opinions nor reasoning in its "equal access" line of cases alters this conclusion. The equal access cases dealt with whether the message conveyed by government when allowing or denying access to government property communicates government preference for or intolerance to religion. Widmar; Board of Education of Westside Community Schools v. Mergens, 492 U.S. 226 (1990); Lamb's Chapel v. Center Moriches

Union Free School Dist.,___ U.S.___, 113 S. Ct. 2141 (1993). The Court concluded in the context of those cases that equal access was necessary to convey government neutrality toward religion. Although in those cases the Court found no significant risk of misperception of the message conveyed by government, the inquiry was directed toward the perception of the listener or observer under each set of circumstances. See generally id.

In stark contrast, the Sixth Circuit's analysis in this case ceased once the court established that speech was uttered in a public forum by a private non-governmental party. The court below incorrectly limited its analysis to a factual determination of who spoke, rather than, in the circumstances presented, who a "reasonable observer" might rationally conclude spoke.

Government may make distinctions in speech if compelling interests exist for doing so. Lamb's Chapel. Here government has a compelling interest to avoid violating the Establishment Clause. A complete prohibition on purely religious symbols at the seat of government is the only, and, therefore, the most narrowly tailored way to accomplish that goal. Disclaimers are entirely ineffectual and themselves create the risk of government entanglement with religion.

> The petitioners take quite a risk by opening their Argument section with *criticisms* of the Supreme Court (<u>e.g.</u>, that it engages in the "jurisprudence of minutiae" in establishment clause cases). There does not seem to be any purpose for this kind of commentary, and it is best to avoid openly criticizing the Court from which you are seeking relief. Petitioners do go on to say in effect, that "you won't have to do that in our case," but the sting nevertheless remains.
>
> Beyond that, we think the "symbols" discussion petitioners lead off with is a good topic, but we question the argument petitioners have drafted. The talk of "symbolism" is a little esoteric. We wouldn't lead off with this kind of argument if we had lost twice in the courts below. We would have led with a simpler, more direct, and absolutely well supported argument.

ARGUMENT

I. A PURELY RELIGIOUS SYMBOL, SUCH AS A LARGE UNATTENDED LATIN CROSS, CLOSELY ASSOCIATED WITH THE SEAT OF GOVERNMENT, CONVEYS AN UNMISTAKABLE MESSAGE OF GOVERNMENT IMPRIMATUR OF RELIGION.

In the Court's line of seasonal holiday display cases, the Court has confronted the fact-specific nature of each case. That inquiry has been criticized as dealing with "jurisprudence of minutae". County of Allegheny v. American Civil Liberties Union, 492 U.S. 573, 674 (1989) (Kennedy, J., concurring in the judgment in part and dissenting in part). The Court need not engage in the same analysis in this case. Any isolated, unattended display of a purely religious symbol at the seat of government violates the Establishment Clause. The combination of symbols representing church and state conveys too powerful a message that can easily be misunderstood, especially in a context where an observer has no readily identifiable source to which to attribute the message, other than government itself.

Symbols elicit direct and immediate emotions due to their strong and enduring meaning. A religious, especially sectarian, symbol, no matter what the particular physical setting may be, conveys the unmistakable message of that symbol's religious doctrine. The Latin Cross is a powerful example of just such a symbol: ". . . the cross is a symbol par excellence of Christianity itself as well as of Christ its head. . . . [T]he cross is endowed with transcendent significance." Anderson Affidavit PP 8 and 11 (J.A. 131-132). No ambiguity about the symbolic meaning of the Latin cross exists.

Similarly, a seat of government such as the Ohio Statehouse stands inexorably as a symbolic "metaphor for government." American Jewish Congress v. City of Chicago, 827

F.2d 120, 128 (7th Cir. 1987). When the universal symbol of Christianity is placed directly in front of the Ohio Statehouse, it is inseverably linked to the symbolic center of government. In West Virginia State Board of Education v. Barnette, 319 U.S. 624, 632 (1943), the Court recognized the inescapable association between various symbols:

> Symbolism is a primitive but effective way of communicating ideas. The use of an emblem or flag to symbolize some system, idea, institution, or personality is a short cut from mind to mind. Causes and nations, political parties, lodges and ecclesiastical groups seek to knit the loyalty of their followings to a flag or banner, a color or design. The State announces rank, function, and authority through crowns and maces, uniforms and black robes, the church speaks through the Cross, the Crucifix, the altar and shrine, and clerical raiment. Symbols of State often convey political ideas just as religious symbols come to convey theological ones. (emphasis added).

The meaning of a symbol must be viewed in the overall context of its setting. "The context in which a symbol is used for purposes of expression is important, for the context may give meaning to the symbol." Spence v. Washington, 418 U.S. 405, 410 (1974). Scholars have observed that "people's responses to a symbol will be contingent upon their assessments of the circumstances of its usage." C. Elder & R. Cobb, The Political Uses of Symbols 57 (1983). This is especially true if the symbol is visually linked to other symbols. "When a particular symbol is used in conjunction with several other symbols, they may all become linked in the eyes of the general public." Id. at 77.

Respondents in the instant case were permitted, based upon the lower courts' decisions, to erect a Latin cross at the seat of secular government. Just as the Latin cross conveys a powerful message of religion, the Ohio Statehouse conveys a powerful message of governmental authority. See American Jewish Congress, 827 F.2d at 128 (discussing the symbol of city hall); Kaplan v. City of Burlington, 891 F.2d 1024, 1029-30 (2nd Cir. 1989), cert. denied, 496 U.S. 926 (1990) ("the park involved is not any city park, but rather City Hall park. This Park is bounded on the east by City Hall, the seat and the official symbol of Burlington city government. . . ."). And, just as the Latin cross is the most recognizable symbol of Christianity, the Ohio Statehouse is the single most visible and recognizable symbol of government in the State of Ohio. Any association of the two threatens to blur the distinction between church and state because the observer will view it as government's sponsorship of religion.[8]

---

[8]   The Latin cross was not erected as part of a holiday seasonal display but stood majestically by itself in the middle of the front lawn of the Capitol Square. App. A43. Respondents' application specifically requested this location which was apart from and a distance away from where the Christmas tree and menorah were located. (J.A. 43).

We like the footnote on this page because it really paints a picture. But petitioners snuck in the word "majestically," which doubtfully was in the appellate court record cited here. As much as we like the word, we think is a little over-the-top. Perhaps in a footnote it is okay, but in general, *do not get carried away with cute language.* The discussion of the symbolic meaning and effect of the Latin cross that follows is effective.

The Establishment Clause protects against "any imprimatur of state approval of religious sects or practices." Widmar v. Vincent, 454 U.S. 263, 274 (1981). The combination of the cross and government, in a context where the latter is perceived to support the former, creates this danger.

It has long been recognized that speech may take many forms, including such nonverbal forms as symbolic displays. Not all forms of speech, however, have equivalent impact. Sometimes, such as in this case, speech must be evaluated not only on the basis of its content, but also as to the identity of the speaker. A determination of authorship often is directly determinable from the columnist, the television commentator, the rally speaker, the sign holder. All can be noted directly by the reader or the listener. But in the case of an unattended display, the source of the communication must be inferred. In the absence of clear and direct information to the contrary, an observer reasonably perceives the message conveyed by an unattended display as the message of the landowner.

The grounds of the Ohio Statehouse, in addition to being a public forum, as observed by the Sixth Circuit, are home to statutes of historical figures important to Ohio and Columbus. As the record reflects, these grounds have previously housed only two other temporary, unattended displays — a secular and pluralistic seasonal display and a chart showing the progress of the community's United Way campaign. Observers of these unattended displays correctly will perceive the message conveyed by these symbols as messages supported and approved by the State of Ohio.

The Sixth Circuit declared that since the unattended display of the Latin cross was presented in a public forum, only a "hypothetical dolt" would not realize this message came from private citizens, not the government. Because government can and does convey symbolic unattended messages from the very grounds upon which private speech rallies frequently occur, however, the mere fact that private speech is permitted does not remove the inference that an unattended display on government property is government endorsed.

Starting here, we find the first, clear, powerful, and concise argument that petitioners have made so far: No federal case has ever found the display of a Latin cross on public land by a state or state subdivision to be constitutional. We

> would have led with this argument, first thing out of the gate. Arguing that the Supreme Court has to make new law to force a state to put a KKK cross up on the state's front lawn will give the justices pause.

A battery of cases has held that the display of a cross on government property "dramatically conveys a message of governmental support for Christianity, whatever the intentions of those responsible for the display may be." American Civil Liberties Union v. City of St. Charles, 794 F.2d 265, 271 (7th Cir. 1986), cert. denied, 479 U.S. 961 (1986). See Gonzales v. North Township of Lake County, 4 F.3d 1412, 1423 (7th Cir. 1993) (court held that the cross "does not bear secular trappings sufficient to neutralize its religious message," and indeed "does not convey any secular message, whether remote, indirect, or incidental").

For this reason, courts regularly and persistently have granted injunctions and other proper relief when an Establishment Clause challenge is raised against an attempt by anyone to display a Latin cross on government property. See, e.g., Mendelson v. City of St. Cloud, 719 F. Supp. 1065, 1069 (M.D. Fla. 1989) ("no federal case has ever found the display of a Latin cross on public land by a state or state subdivision to be constitutional"); American Civil Liberties Union v. Mississippi General Services Admin., 652 F. Supp. 380, 384-85 & n.2 (S.D. Miss. 1987) ("in no other federal case either before or since Lynch v. Donnelly has the public display of a cross by a state or subdivision thereof been found to be constitutional").

This judicial result has been the same whether the Latin cross on government property is large, see, e.g., Jewish War Veterans v. United States, 695 F. Supp. 3, 5 (D.D.C. 1988) (65' illuminated cross serving as war memorial on Marine Corps base; permanent injunction granted); Mendelson, 719 F. Supp. at 1066 (12' cross on city water tower; injunction granted), medium-sized, see, e.g., Libin v. Town of Greenwich, 625 F. Supp. 393, 394 (D. Conn. 1985) (3' X 5' illuminated cross on firehouse; preliminary injunction granted), or quite small, see, e.g., Harris v. City of Zion, 927 F.2d 1401, 1402-04 (7th Cir. 1991), cert. denied, ___U.S.___, 112 S.Ct. 3054 (1992) (Latin cross appeared in one quadrant of municipal corporate seals; permanent injunction granted); Friedman v. Board of County Commissioners, 781 F.2d 777, 779 (10th Cir. 1985) (en banc), cert. denied, 476 U.S. 1169 (1986) (Latin cross appeared on county seal; injunction granted).

In addition, this has been true even when the display of the Latin cross on government property has existed for many years, see, e.g., American Civil Liberties Union v. Rabun County Chamber of Commerce, 698 F.2d 1098, 1101 (11th Cir. 1983) (cross in state park originally dated back almost 30 years; permanent injunction granted); Jewish War Veterans, 695 F. Supp. at 5 (cross on Marine Corps base more than 22 years; permanent injunction granted), and even where it was privately sponsored. See Gonzales, 4 F.3d at 1422-23 (crucifix in public park for more than 40 years; permanent injunction granted). It is this judicial recognition of the inability of an observer to separate the state from the message of the Latin cross that undermines the decision below.

> Petitioners are too loose in their citation usage. They occasionally make a sweeping statement about the law without citation to legal authority. You can attribute some of these unsupported statements to their placement in "umbrella" or "road map" paragraphs, but we recommend a more "religious" use of citations. ***Whenever*** you make a statement about the law, a legal conclusion, or a statement about a legal rule (or element thereof), you should include a citation to authority. Unsupported rhetoric in appellate briefs is not going to win you very many appeals. Find a source that comes close to what you are saying and cite it.

II. THE ESTABLISHMENT CLAUSE MAY REQUIRE A FINDING OF THE UNCONSTITUTIONALITY OF AN UNATTENDED RELIGIOUS DISPLAY, EVEN IF SUCH DISPLAY STANDS IN A PUBLIC FORUM

The decision of the court below is sweeping in scope, creating a per se rule obviating the need to examine how the message is perceived by a reasonable observer. The lower court focused not on the risk that the government's message will be misperceived, but only on the public nature of the forum in which the message is relayed.

The nature of a public forum guarantees broad communication. The Court first recognized the concept of the public forum in Hague v. CIO, 307 U.S. 496 (1939). The Court observed that streets and parks in this country universally have been considered public forums:

> Wherever the title of streets and parks may rest, they have immemorially been held in trust for the use of the public and, time out of mind, have been used for purposes of assembly, communicating thought between citizens, and discussing public questions. Such use of the streets and public places has, from ancient times, been a part of the privileges, immunities, rights, and liberties of citizens.

Id. at 515. See also Lamb's Chapel v. Center Moriches Union Free School District, ___U.S. ___, 113 S. Ct 2131, 2146 (1993) ("parks and sidewalks are traditional public fora"); International Soc'y for Krishna Consciousness v. Lee, ___ U.S. ___, 112 S. Ct. 2711, 2717 (1992) (Kennedy, J., concurring) ("types of property that we have recognized as the quintessential public forums are streets, parks, and sidewalks").

In these traditional public forums, as well as in so-called "designated" or "limited" public forums, the government may not prohibit all communication. Cornelius v. NAACP Legal Defense and Education Fund, Inc., 473 U.S. 788 (1985); Perry Educ. Assn. v. Perry Local Educators' Assn., 470 U.S. 37, 45 (1983) ("[I]n places which by long tradition or by government fiat have been devoted to assembly and debate, the rights of the State to limit expressive activity are sharply circumscribed.") (emphasis added).

The public forum doctrine by itself, however, does not require the State of Ohio to permit the erection of any symbol upon government property characterized as a public forum. Just as "[t]he principle that government accommodation of the free exercise of religion does not supersede the fundamental limitations imposed by the Establishment Clause", Lee v. Weisman, ___U.S.___, 112 S.Ct. 2649, 2655 (1992), the public forum doctrine should not be permitted to "swallow up" the Establishment Clause. Kaplan, 891 F.2d at 1029. That a message is delivered in a public forum does not give government the right to advocate religion. Nor may it permit a private party to proffer speech that is likely to be perceived as government speech endorsing religion. Public forum or not, government may not lend its support to a particular religious message or allow private parties to manipulate government for that purpose.

In Burson v. Freeman, ___U.S.___, 112 S.Ct. 1846 (1992), Justice Kennedy squarely recognized the inherent clash between competing constitutional doctrines:

> The same use of the compelling interest test is adopted today, not to justify or condemn a category of suppression but to determine the accuracy of the justification the State gives for its law. There is a narrow area in which the First Amendment permits freedom of expression to yield to the extent necessary for an accommodation of another constitutional right.

Id., 112 S.Ct. at 1859 (Kennedy, J., concurring). And just as competing doctrines were balanced in that case, they must be balanced here. The Sixth Circuit's holding does not balance competing doctrines. It allows one to trump the other.

We are skipping to the Conclusion.

---

* * *

> This is the typical kind of Conclusion you will see at the end of a long brief. Pray for relief and end it.

CONCLUSION

For the reasons set forth, this Court should reverse the decision of the court below.

Respectfully submitted,

BETTY D. MONTGOMERY, Ohio Attorney General
MICHAEL J. RENNER, Chief Counsel, Counsel of Record
CHRISTOPHER S. COOK
ANDREW S. BERGMAN
SIMON B. KARAS
ANDREW I. SUTTER
Assistant Attorneys General,
State Office Tower
30 East Broad St.,17th Fl.
Columbus, Ohio 43215-3428
(614) 466-5026
Attorneys for Petitioners

Sample Brief No. 4:

Brief of Respondents in the
U.S. Supreme Court case:

Capitol Square Review and Advisory Board
v.
Pinette

515 U.S. 753 (1995)

Docket No. 94-780

SUPREME COURT OF THE UNITED STATES

October Term, 1994

CAPITOL SQUARE REVIEW AND ADVISORY BOARD, RONALD T. KELLER, DANIEL SHELLENBARGER, AND OHIO SENATOR RICHARD T. FINAN,

Petitioners,

— *against*—

VINCENT J. PINETTE, DONNIE A. CARR, AND KNIGHTS OF THE KU KLUX KLAN,

Respondents.

ON WRIT OF CERTIORARI TO THE UNITED STATES COURT OF APPEALS FOR THE SIXTH CIRCUIT

BRIEF OF RESPONDENTS

Question Presented: It is interesting to note that respondents chose to call the item in question a "Ku Klux Klan cross." This may be accurate, but it is a loaded term that easily could distract the court away from the pure legal issue on which the respondents twice have prevailed in the courts below. It would have been more neutral to call the item a "Latin cross" or simply a "cross." Otherwise, this question is appropriate because it is drafted broadly to encompass more of the public policy at stake in a brief directed to a court of last resort.

QUESTION PRESENTED FOR REVIEW

Whether the temporary, unattended display of a Ku Klux Klan cross on a public forum open to all other political and religious expression violates the Establishment Clause solely because the public forum is in proximity to the seat of government.

The Respondents respectfully urge this Court to affirm the judgment of the United States Court of Appeals for the Sixth Circuit in this proceeding.

Once again, we cut out the **TABLE OF CONTENTS** and **TABLE OF AUTHORITIES** to save space. What follows is an "Introduction" section. It is not required by the rules. In general, we like introductions, and this one turns the tables on the petitioners.

INTRODUCTION

The State asserts that the primary issue in this case is whether the Establishment Clause creates a flat ban on the private, unattended display of a Klan cross on a public forum open to all other political and religious communication where the forum is near the seat of government. The State's assertion is wrong. The record in this case makes clear that the State's reliance on the Establishment Clause is pretextual. The State's objection to the Ku Klux Klan cross had much less to do with the cross than with the Ku Klux Klan itself. The discriminatory denial of access to a public forum under these circumstances is clearly prohibited by the First Amendment.

> Proceedings Below: Pure housekeeping. This section is adequate.

PROCEEDINGS BELOW

Following the filing of the complaint in this case, the District Court sua sponte divided its proceedings into two segments. An Opinion and Order was entered for each segment. Both shared a common nucleus of operative facts. The District Court opinion directly resulting in the Petition for Certiorari is reported at 844 F. Supp. 1182 (S.D. Ohio 1993). It is also appended to the Petition at A13-A26;[9] n1 the other opinion and order is reported on Westlaw at 1994 WL 749489 and is included in the Respondents' Appendix at RA1-RA10.[10] The December 20 and 21 hearings focused on injunctive relief regarding the cross which the District Court granted on December 21, 1993. A26. The January 3 hearing focused mainly on discriminatory treatment, injunctive relief related to the rally, and a claim for damages; the Court issued the injunction permitting the rally and denied damages. RA10, Pinette v. Capitol Square Review and Advisory Board, Case No. C2-93-1162, U.S.D.C. S.D. Ohio, Opinion and Order of January 4, 1994, (1994 WL 749489). The subject of the Petition before this Court is the injunction ordering the Petitioners to grant the permit to erect the Klan's cross; the State did not appeal the injunction ordering the State to grant a permit for the rally. The record of both hearings constitutes the record on appeal, together with a supplemental record from the District Court.

The opinion of the United States Court of Appeals for the Sixth Circuit is reported at 30 F.3d 675 (6th Cir. 1994) and is appended to the Petition for Certiorari at A1-A12.

---

[9] References to the Appendices contained in the Petition are identified herein as A1, A2, etc. References to the Respondents' Appendices contained in the Brief in Opposition to a Writ of Certiorari are identified herein as RA1, RA2, etc. References to the Appendices included in this Brief of Respondents are identified as 1a, 2a, and 3a.

[10] The Respondents' Complaint and Amended Complaint raised two issues: one was related to erection of the Klan's cross on the same forum as the menorah; the other related to the denial of a permit to the Klan to hold a rally on Capitol Square in January 1994. Two hearings were set: one was primarily devoted to the cross issue, and the other was primarily devoted to the rally. References herein to the record include R. 9: TR I (record of hearing of December 20 and 21, 1993), and R. 23: TR II (record of the morning portion of the hearing of January 3, 1994) and R. 23: TR III (record of the hearing of the afternoon of January 3, 1994).

> Statement of the Case: Look at the rest of the story here, the parts petitioners left out (and with good reason). Bringing these facts to light will help in small part to mollify respondents' negative public persona.
>
> But this section is too long (seven pages when double spaced). Starting in section (b) of the Statement of the Case, Respondents include too much detail and minutiae. We are not certain that the court needs to hear all of these facts. Some of the "This is unfair" innuendo also is a little forced and not at all compelling when uttered by Respondents. The discussion of the "Klan cross" as "a symbol of freedom to rally men against political oppression and tyranny" also sounds like a stretch. Nevertheless, this is respondents' position.

STATEMENT OF THE CASE

The Knights of the Ku Klux Klan filed this case on December 15, 1993, to challenge, inter alia, the discriminatory refusal of the Capitol Square Review and Advisory Board[11] to grant a permit allowing display of a Ku Klux Klan cross on the public forum on the west side of the Capitol Building in Columbus, Ohio. Hearings to consider the Plaintiffs' requests for injunctive relief were held on December 20-21, 1993 and on January 3, 1994. The order that is the subject of the Petition was entered on December 21, 1993.

a. Background

On October 29, 1993, prior to initiating this case, the Knights of the Ku Klux Klan had applied for a permit to hold a public assembly in the Capitol Square forum. The purpose of the public assembly, which the Klan planned to hold the following January 15, 1994, was to express the organization's political views.

On November 18, 1993, while the application for the January 15th rally was still under consideration, the members of the Capitol Square Review Board met in executive session and discussed the issue of Ku Klux Klan access to the same forum during the holiday season. They feared that the Knights of the Ku Klux Klan might follow the example of another Klan group in Cincinnati by seeking to put up a Ku Klux Klan cross during the Christmas season. RA14, RA18; RA19-RA21. As a result of its discussion in executive session, the Board reconvened in public and voted sua sponte to bar display of both the State Christmas tree and the private display of the Lubavitch sect's menorah from Capitol Square during December 1993. A14. At the time, the Lubavitch Sect had

---

[11] The Capitol Square Review and Advisory Board is alternatively referred to as the "Board" or the "State" in this brief.

not yet applied for its 1993 permit nor had the Klan yet sought a permit to erect a cross in Capitol Square. Nevertheless, the Petitioners decided to bar the Christmas tree and the anticipated Lubavitch display of its menorah solely to foreclose any claim to equal access that the Klan might present. RA12 (Plaintiffs' Exhibit 33, Broadcast No. 5).

The decision of the State to bar the tree and menorah resulted in a great public uproar. A statement was released by the Office of the Governor objecting to imposition of a ban on all symbols as a means to prevent display of a Klan cross. According to the statement, the "[p]eople of this great State think that we ought to have a Christmas tree and think that we ought to have a menorah at the Statehouse and so do we. We've had a Christmas tree at the Statehouse for tens of years, and you can't let a single group or groups of people dictate to the people of Ohio what they are and aren't going to do." RA14 (Plaintiffs' Exhibit 33, Broadcast No. 6, Statement of Mike Dawson, Press Secretary to the Governor.) Newspaper accounts described the Governor as "disappointed and upset." RA20 (Defendants' Exhibit D, The Columbus Dispatch, November 20, 1993, front page). The Governor was also quoted as saying: "The Board's initial decision was a mistake. I trust this matter will be resolved quickly." Id.

Consistent with these public statements, the Governor and the other State officials who appoint the members of the Board[12] signed and delivered to the Board a letter calling upon the Board to permit the tree and menorah. Id.; RA14; RA19-RA20; JA 167-168, TR I 94. The Board met in special session on November 23, 1993, and resolved into executive session. Immediately following the executive session, the Board reconvened in public to formally declare its earlier vote invalid. In addition, it approved the State display of its Christmas tree and the private display of a menorah by a nine-to-zero vote. A15; JA 167-168, TR I 94. The vote to approve both the Christmas tree and the menorah was made even though no permit applications for displays on the Capitol Square had been filed. The reason for the change in vote was explained by Board Chairperson Richard Finan (a Petitioner herein): "I've been in politics for twenty-one years. When you get a letter from the Governor, the Speaker, and the President of the Senate, you do respond," he said. RA16 (Plaintiffs' Exhibit 33, Broadcast No. 8).

b. Capitol Square Public Forum

The public forum in question is a large park-like area, a block wide, on one side of the State Capitol building in Columbus.[13] Temporary, unattended[14] displays have been per-

---

[12] Ohio Revised Code Section 123.022.

[13] The forum area at issue in this case is one city block wide and approximately 240 feet deep, JA 96-97 (Stipulations, P12), about 3 1/2 acres. The entire Capitol Square block consists of ten acres, some 435,600 square feet. REDI REALTY ATLAS, City Map Volume I (22nd ed. 1991) p. 397. Views of the public forum are included at Brief of Petitioners, Appendix, at 1a (Plaintiffs' Supplemental Exhibit 104), 3a, (Plaintiffs' Supplemental Exhibit 106), JA 64 (Defendants' Supplemental Exhibit 109), and JA 65 (Defendants' Supplemental Exhibit 110).

[14] As used in this brief, "unattended" means that the given display has been permitted to remain at least overnight without accompanying personnel or ongoing ceremonies.

mitted in the public forum for many years. For example, the State of Ohio has erected a Christmas tree annually and has hung a "Seasons Greetings" banner from two of the Statehouse's pillars. 2a. The Lubavitch sect has been granted annual permits to display a large Chanukah menorah in Capitol Square. A14. And, permission has been granted for secular displays, such as United Fund campaign "thermometers" and arts festivals exhibits and booths. JA 159-160. There is no rule or regulation that confines unattended displays to any particular time of year, and they have in fact been present at various times over the years. A16.

In addition to these unattended displays, Capitol Square has been the site of numerous speech activities including gay rights demonstrations, anti-war demonstrations, and religious rallies and marches. A18. It is undisputed that Capitol Square has "been used from time immemorial for all manner of public gatherings and demonstrations by groups of all kinds, including political parties, charitable and religious groups, labor unions, civil rights groups, and the proponents and opponents of all manner of social and political issues." RA6. As the District Court summarized the record, the Capitol Square "grounds have been made available for speeches and public gatherings by various groups advocating various causes both secular and religious." A14.

c. Administration of the Capitol Square Forum

The Capitol Square Review and Advisory Board is authorized by law to regulate the uses of Capitol Square. Ohio Revised Code Section 123.022. According to Section 128-4-02 of the Ohio Administrative Code, "Capitol buildings and grounds are available for use by the public . . . for free discussion of public questions" if the applicant adheres to a stated procedure for requesting such use, and if the proposed use:

(1) Does not interfere with the primary use of the capitol buildings or grounds;
(2) Is appropriate to the physical context of the capitol buildings or grounds;
(3) Does not unduly burden the managing authority;
(4) Is not a hazard to the safety of the public or state employees; and
(5) Does not expose the state to the likelihood of expenses and/or damages which cannot be recovered.A32 (Report and Recommendation of Hearing Examiner, Conclusions of Law, P2).

Ronald Keller, Executive Director of the Board, is responsible for management of the Capitol Square complex. In this capacity, he grants and denies permits for the use of Capitol Square. TR I 84-85; JA 97, Stipulations, P19. Persons desiring to use Capitol Square submit their requests on the Board's form, "Application For Permit to Use Statehouse Grounds." JA 99, (Stipulations, P27-28); JA 103-111 (Exh. 3,4).

d. Display of the Menorah and the Tree

On November 29, 1993, Rabbi Chaim Capland submitted an official application for the display — previously approved by the Board — of a menorah on Capitol Square from

December 8 through December 16, 1993, to coincide with the days of Chanukah. Keller issued Capland's permit on November 29, 1993, the same day the application was submitted. A15, JA 168-169, TR I 97-98. The menorah was erected at the Capitol Square on December 8, 1993.

The State Christmas tree was erected on December 7, 1993. A16.

e. Denial of a Permit to Display the Ku Klux Klan Cross

The Klan's application for a permit to display its cross on the Capitol Square forum from December 8 through December 24 was also submitted on November 29, 1993. A15. The period covered by the application overlapped the period during which the menorah would be displayed. Executive Director Keller denied the Klan's application by letter of December 3, 1993. Id. Mr. Keller wrote that:

> [The denial] . . . was made upon the advice of counsel, in a good faith attempt to comply with the Ohio and United States Constitutions, as they have been interpreted in relevant decisions by the Federal and State Courts. We would direct your attention in particular to controlling decisions recently rendered by the United States Supreme Court under the First Amendment to the United States Constitution.JA 91-93 (Plaintiffs' Exhibit 5); A15 (District Court Findings of Fact, P9).

The Klan filed an administrative appeal of the permit denial. Although the administrative appeal was denied on December 21, 1993, the hearing examiner concluded that:

> The evidence adduced at the [administrative] hearing in this matter does not offer a complete explanation of the process or basis for the Board's denial of the Appellant's request. Board Executive Director Keller did, however, advise the Appellant that the Board denied its request on advice of counsel, who had raised constitutional objections to the request. . . .A33 (Report and Recommendation of Hearing Examiner, Conclusions of Law, P4).

Respondents had filed the instant action prior to the issuance of the hearing examiner's report. On December 21, 1993, following the report, the District Court issued a permanent injunction ordering the State to grant a permit which would allow the Klan to display its cross through December 24. Pursuant to that injunction, the cross was set in place in the early morning hours of December 22, 1993. RA24-RA30 (Plaintiffs' Supplemental Exhibits 102, The Columbus Dispatch, December 23, 1993, front page, and 103, The [Akron] Beacon Journal, December 23, 1993, page B5). It was vandalized a short time later. RA28-RA29, RA31. Meanwhile, on December 22 the Board granted permits to several religious groups that applied to display crosses around the Klan Cross; the purpose of those crosses was to protest the presence of the Klan cross.

f. The Menorah as a Religious Symbol

At the hearing before the District Court, Cantor Jack Chomsky of Tifereth Israel Congregation in Columbus, Ohio, testified that the menorah permitted by the State of Ohio, like other Chanukah menorahs, "is a religious symbol. It is used in conjunction with fulfilling the obligations incumbent upon a Jew for the celebration of the festival of Chanukah." JA 152, TR I 70. Cantor Chomsky explained that Jews have an obligation to "put candles in it as appropriate, as prescribed by our tradition, and they recite blessings which state as part of the blessings that we were commanded to perform this act. Blessings such as this make this into very much a ritual act." JA 155, 75-76. Rabbi Harold Berman also stated that the menorah "is a religious symbol. . . ." JA 53.

g. The Klan Cross

Plaintiff Carr testified that he applied for a permit to display the Klan cross because he had heard that the State was going to permit a tree and a menorah but not a Klan cross. JA 134-137, TR I 42-44. Mr. Carr said that his motivation for filing the request was that "since we were being excluded by the city or the state, the Capitol Square Review and Advisory Board, that we would attempt to obtain a permit to erect a cross for the Christmas season." Id. Mr. Carr also testified that while the cross communicates a religious message, it also conveys a political message: "To us, it is a sacred symbol, but it is also a symbol of going against tyranny, a symbol of freedom." JA 142, TR I 51. He noted that the "Klan's use of the cross originated from the early Scottish clans in Scotland in the 1300's which used the cross as a symbol to rally the clans together to fight against their English oppressors." JA 143. And Mr. Carr observed "the cross was also incorporated in the Confederate battle flag. . . ." JA 150.

In addition, counsel for the Klan informed the State that accompanying the cross would be a disclaimer stating that "this cross was erected by private individuals without government support for the purpose of expressing respect for the holiday season and to assert the right of all religious views to be expressed on an equal basis on public property." A15-16.[15]

h. The Opinion of the District Court

In granting the injunction, the District Court found that the area in question was a traditional public forum, A18, that there was no policy against free-standing displays in Capitol Square, and that for many years a variety of unattended displays have been permitted on Capitol Square for limited periods, including, during December, a free-standing Christmas tree and a free-standing menorah. A16.

---

[15] Counsel for the Klan also invited State suggestions concerning the content of the disclaimer. Id.

The Court observed that one of the Board's reasons for denying the Klan's application — the purported failure of the Klan to post a bond — was "not a proper ground for the denial of the permit . . ." and that the State "does not contend that the erection of a cross poses a security risk of any kind." A16. The Court concluded, based on all of the facts, that "the State of Ohio is in no way associating itself with the Klan's display," that there was no appearance of endorsement of religion, and that "the reasonable observer should conclude that the government is expressing its toleration of religious and secular pluralism" in the public forum. The Court then held that "freedom of speech would be meaningless if it did not apply to all groups, popular and unpopular alike." A26.

i. The Opinion of the Sixth Circuit

The Sixth Circuit affirmed the District Court on Free Speech, Free Exercise, and Equal Protection grounds. A6-A7, A11-A12. It rejected the Petitioners' claim that there was any endorsement of religion by the State in this case. Instead, it held that a reasonable observer could not conclude that the display of the Ku Klux Klan cross on Capitol Square was a state endorsement of religion. It also concluded that religious groups and groups communicating controversial or offensive messages could not be selectively denied access to a public forum in the name of the Establishment Clause. A11-A12.

> Summary of Argument: This section is well-drafted. However, respondents share the belief of the student authors that no legal citation should be used in the Summary of Argument.
>
> As stated in the comment on the Summary of Argument in sample brief #1, the authors actually disagree with each other on this. Some attorneys maintain that no cases should be cited in the SOA, while others find it odd if you fail to cite one or two of the most important authorities that support your argument.

SUMMARY OF ARGUMENT

The Free Speech and Free Exercise Clauses of the First Amendment and the Equal Protection Clause of the Fourteenth Amendment require a state to permit the temporary unattended display of a Ku Klux Klan cross in a traditional public forum that is open to other political and religious symbols — even if that forum is near the seat of government — absent any special indicia of endorsement.

1. The State's discriminatory refusal to permit the display of the Ku Klux Klan cross in a traditional public forum where the State has permitted other secular and religious symbols violates the Free Speech and Free Exercise Clauses of the First Amendment.

In this case, the State has singled out the Ku Klux Klan and has refused to permit the Klan to display its cross in the Capitol Square forum. The cross is symbolic of the Klan's view about politics and religion.

The record establishes that the denial was based upon the controversial communication of a controversial speaker. On that record, the State clearly discriminated among political and religious symbols. Moreover, the discrimination was unlawfully accomplished by means of standardless procedures permitting the exercise of unbridled discretion.

The State's only response to the claim of discrimination is that the Board relied upon the Establishment Clause; however, this explanation rings hollow given the State's tolerance of other religious symbols at the same site.

2. Given the facts of this case, both courts below correctly held that no reasonable observer could conclude that the Ku Klux Klan display of its cross on the Capitol Square public forum constituted an endorsement or appearance of endorsement of religion.

The State erroneously insists that, because of the inherent power of an unattended cross as a symbol, the Establishment Clause automatically bans from the Capitol Square forum the unattended display of the Klan cross at any location at any time under any circumstances. This flat ban is wrong as a matter of law precisely because it forecloses consideration of all relevant facts and circumstances.

The State's contention that the Establishment Clause flatly bans all symbols alleged to be "purely religious" precludes the application of the "reasonable observer" standard set forth by this Court in County of Allegheny v. Greater Pittsburgh ACLU, 492 U.S. 573

(1989) and followed by the courts below. While the State claims that banning the Klan cross is necessary to serve its interest in obeying the Establishment Clause, it ignores its parallel obligation to fulfill the requirements of the Free Speech and Free Exercise Clauses. These interests must be reconciled on a case-by-case basis by use of the "reasonable observer" standard.

The State fails to acknowledge that providing a public forum is not an endorsement of the speech thereon. It also ignores the distinction, recognized in Allegheny, between private religious expression in a public forum and government religious expression.

3. Privately sponsored displays of religious symbols cannot be excluded from a quintessential public forum even at the seat of government, absent some indicia of state endorsement. Indeed, the defining characteristic of a public forum is that the state may not discriminate against speech on the basis of content.

Respondents do not quarrel with the endorsement test under the Establishment Clause as it has been developed by this Court. But, endorsement cannot be presumed from the mere fact of private speech in a public forum. Yet, without this inference, there is no plausible claim of endorsement on the facts of this case, as both lower courts found. The judgment below should therefore be affirmed.

> Argument: Respondents begin their argument by recit-
> ing the facts again. We do not like this decision. Get your
> rule and explanation out there, and then do the application
> to the facts. Moreover—where is the IRAC or TREAT struc-
> ture? It is not clear to us that it is present anywhere in the
> first section of their argument. We hear a lot of facts, and
> then get some rule (or is it explanation?) material at the end
> of the section. This is not our recommended drafting style.

ARGUMENT

I. THE STATE'S DISCRIMINATORY REFUSAL TO PERMIT DISPLAY OF THE KU KLUX KLAN CROSS IN A TRADITIONAL PUBLIC FORUM VIOLATES THE FREE SPEECH AND FREE EXERCISE CLAUSES OF THE FIRST AMENDMENT AND THE EQUAL PROTECTION CLAUSE OF THE FOURTEENTH AMENDMENT

The record in this case clearly establishes that officials of the Capitol Square Review and Advisory Board persistently engaged in a series of discriminatory actions to prevent the Ku Klux Klan from displaying the Klan cross in the public forum at Capitol Square. The maneuvering began after the Ku Klux Klan filed an application to hold a rally at Capitol Square on the birthday of Martin Luther King, Jr. On October 29, 1993, the Board received, but did not act upon, the Klan's permit request. Then, on November 18, 1993, Board Chairman Richard Finan conceded that there was no legal basis to prevent the Klan from holding its rally. RA11.[16] The Board's attention shifted to efforts to fore-stall the possibility that the Klan might obtain a permit to erect a Klan cross in Capitol Square, because similar applications had been filed in Cincinnati by another Klan group. RA12.

The Capitol Square Review and Advisory Board announced its strategy to forestall possible display of the Klan cross on November 18, 1993. On that date, Board officials stated that the traditional state Christmas tree would not be erected in the Capitol Square during the 1993 Christmas season. They also stated that the Board would not allow the Lubavitch sect to display a menorah that had been permitted in previous years.

The Board's initial strategy crumbled on November 23, 1993, after vigorous public protests and after strong political pressure from the Governor and legislative leaders who appointed the members of the Board. In response to this pressure, the Board suddenly changed course and agreed to permit the menorah and to display the tree. A15; JA 167-

---

[16] The Board did not issue a permit for the Klan rally until ordered to do so by the District Court on January 4, 1994. RA1.

168. A few days later, Rabbi Capland applied for a permit to erect the Lubavitch menorah. His permit was granted the same day. A15.

The Board's change of position, which was reported in detail by the press, caused Donnie Carr to file a permit application to display the Klan cross. According to Carr, the permit application was filed to protest the Board's gratuitous policy of denying Klan access to Capitol Square while granting access to the Lubavitch sect. During his testimony at the hearing below he explained that "since we were being excluded by the City or the State, the Capitol Square Review and Advisory Board, that we would attempt to obtain a permit to erect a cross for the Christmas season." JA 136-137.

A. The Constitution prohibits discrimination based on political or religious viewpoint.

It was against this record detailing the State's plan to bar the Klan cross that the Court of Appeals for the Sixth Circuit concluded, in a gross understatement, that "there was no indication that Ohio treated the Klan or its display favorably." A10. Indeed, as the Circuit made clear, this case has much less to do with endorsement of the Klan's speech than with discrimination against it. Thus, it commented: "Zealots have First Amendment rights too. Some speech may be distasteful, unpopular and outright offensive, but as Thurgood Marshall so persuasively wrote, the protection found in the First Amendment does not depend on popular opinion[.]" A11. The Sixth Circuit underscored its point by quoting Justice Marshall's statement in Police Department of Chicago v. Mosley, 408 U.S. 92 (1972):

Necessarily then, under the Equal Protection Clause, not to mention the First Amendment itself, government may not grant the use of a forum to people whose views it finds acceptable, but deny use to those wishing to express less favored or more controversial views. And it may not select which issues are worth discussing or debating in public facilities. There is an "equality of status in the field of ideas," and government must afford all points of view an equal opportunity to be heard. Once a forum is opened up to assembly or speaking by some groups, government may not prohibit others from assembling or speaking on the basis of what they intend to say. Selective exclusions from a public forum may not be based on content alone, and may not be justified by reference to content alone. A11-A12 (30 F.3d at 680), 408 U.S. at 96 (footnote omitted by the Circuit).

This Court has consistently restated this principle in cases decided since Mosley. For example, in Carey v. Brown, 447 U.S. 455, (1980), this Court stated that "[a]ny restriction on expressive activity because of its content would completely undercut the 'profound national commitment to the principle that debate on public issues should be uninhibited, robust, and wide open.'" Id. at 462-63, quoting New York Times v. Sullivan, 376 U.S. 254, 270 (1964). Similarly in R.A.V. v. St. Paul, U.S., 112 S. Ct. 2538 (1992), this Court stated, "The First Amendment generally prevents government from proscribing speech, see, e.g., Cantwell v. Connecticut, 310 U.S. 296, 309-311 (1940), or even expressive conduct, see e.g. Texas v. Johnson, 491 U.S. 397, 406 (1989), because of disapproval of the ideas expressed. Content based regulations are presumptively invalid." R.A.V.,

112 S. Ct. at 2542. According to FCC v. Pacifica Foundation, 438 U.S. 726 (1978)," . . . the fact that society may find speech offensive is not a sufficient reason for suppressing it. Indeed, if it is the speaker's opinion that gives offense, that consequence is a reason for according it constitutional protection." Id. at 745-46.

We are all the way to section I(B), and we see no sign of the IRAC or TREAT paradigm. Legal points are argued, but they appear in a form that we would call "legal narrative reasoning." We do not believe that a presumption of victory—even if you are 99.9% certain the court will go your way—trumps the need to organize your arguments in a clear, concise, and convincing manner. Some form and structure would make this a much stronger section—and, remember, most cases are won or lost on the briefs.

If you were to read on to the end, you would see that there is no attempt to use a traditional legal writing structure for this Argument. Ultimately, this is more like a legal essay than anything else.

Finally—this brief clearly is written in response to petitioners' brief. Many of the headings used directly address points raised in petitioners' brief. This limits its usefulness as a model for moot court briefing, but as a model for appellees' and respondents' briefs, it is a decent example.

B. The State's Establishment Clause claim is a pretext for discrimination.

Faced with this overwhelming authority, the State fails to address whether its efforts to prevent display of the Klan cross were motivated by the unpopularity of the Ku Klux Klan and its symbol. Instead, the State prefers to argue that its efforts to prevent display of the Klan cross were motivated solely by a desire to avoid an Establishment Clause violation. According to the State's brief, display of the Klan cross at Capitol Square conveys the "message of government imprimatur of religion" because it is a Latin Cross which, in turn is the symbol of Christianity. Pet. Br. 12-17.

The disingenuousness of the State's Establishment Clause claim is patently apparent. First, contrary to the State's assertion, the Klan itself clearly regards the cross as both a political symbol and a religious symbol. Second, even if it is assumed that the Klan cross is a purely religious symbol, the State may still not discriminate against it nor engage in "maneuvers to bring about a legal ascendancy of one sect over another." Thomas Jefferson, Letter to Elbridge Gerry, January 26, 1799, reprinted in SAUL K. PADOVER, A JEFFERSON PROFILE (1956) 112. Yet, the evidence of discrimination on this record is undeniable. When the menorah was erected in December of 1993, the governor participated in the lighting ceremony. RA23 (The Columbus Dispatch, December 9, 1993). In addition, the menorah has been displayed without state objection for several years. Unlike the permit application for the Klan cross, the application for the menorah was approved in advance of the day it was filed.

Under this Court's well-established precedents, the State may not permit the menorah and bar the cross by selectively invoking the Establishment Clause. For example, in Niemotko v. Maryland, 340 U.S. 268 (1951), the Court unanimously struck down the discriminatory refusal of government officials to allow a Jehovah's Witness group from holding a bible meeting in a public park. Similarly, in Fowler v. Rhode Island, 345 U.S. 67 (1953), this Court found that the First Amendment was violated when a Jehovah's Witness religious service was treated differently than those of Catholics or Protestants. Id. at 69-70.

In Larson v. Valente, 456 U.S. 228 (1982), this Court underscored the constitutional prohibition against discrimination among religions. "The clearest command of the Establishment Clause is that one religious denomination cannot be officially preferred over another." Id. at 244. And, as this Court stated in Allegheny, "[w]hatever else the Establishment Clause may mean . . ., it certainly means that at the very least that government may not demonstrate a preference for one particular sect or creed. . . ." 492 U.S. at 605.

The State's discriminatory motives were highlighted by the Capitol Square Review and Advisory Board's use of ad hoc procedures designed to obstruct Klan access to the Capitol Square. The Board's vacillation over whether to impose a flat ban on all unattended displays at Capitol Square during the Christmas holidays was justified by no published rule or regulation. Nor was any rule or regulation cited as a basis for the anticipatory denial of a permit for the display of the Klan cross.

The ad hoc quality of the Board's permit denial in this case was noted in the findings of the Board's administrative hearing officer. According to these findings:

The evidence adduced at the [administrative] hearing in this matter does not offer a complete explanation of the process or basis for the Board's denial of the Appellant's request. Board Executive Director Keller did, however, advise the Appellant that the Board denied its request on advice of counsel, who had raised constitutional objections to the request. The record does not establish whether other objections were raised by the Board's counsel. A33, P4. The standards applied to the Klan are thus unpublished and unknown. The use of such ad hoc procedures to facilitate discrimination against disfavored speakers is forbidden by the First Amendment. Forsyth County, Ga. v. Nationalist Movement, U.S. , 112 S. Ct. 2395 (1992); Lakewood v. Plain Dealer Publishing Co., 486 U.S. 750 (1988).

The rule against discrimination is thoroughly consistent with the command of this Court, more than fifty years ago, that no public official "can prescribe what shall be orthodox in politics [or] religion . . .," West Virginia Board of Education v. Barnette, 319 U.S. 624, 642 (1943). The decisions of the District Court and the Court of Appeals were based on this command and therefore should be affirmed.

> Sections II and III of the argument are omitted.

* * *

> An appropriately short Conclusion that simply asks for the relief sought.

CONCLUSION

For the foregoing reasons, the Respondents respectfully urge this Court to affirm the decision of the United States Court of Appeals for the Sixth Circuit.

Respectfully submitted,

BENSON A. WOLMAN, Counsel of Record, MOOTS, COPE & STANTON, 3600 Olentangy River Road, Building 501, Columbus, Ohio 43214-3913, (614) 459-4140

DAVID GOLDBERGER, c/o The Ohio State Univ. College of Law, 55 West Twelfth Avenue, Columbus, Ohio 43210, (614) 292-6821

BARBARA P. O'TOOLE, Roger Baldwin Foundation of ACLU, 203 N. LaSalle Street, Chicago, IL 60601, (312) 201-9740

STEVEN R. SHAPIRO, American Civil Liberties Union Foundation, 132 West 43rd Street, New York, NY 10036, (212) 944-9800, Attorneys for Respondents

Of Counsel

PETER JOY, Case Western Reserve Univ. College of Law, 11075 East Boulevard, Cleveland, Ohio 44106, (216) 368-2766

KEVIN FRANCIS O'NEILL, American Civil Liberties Union of Ohio Foundation, 1223 West Sixth Street, Cleveland, Ohio 44113, (216) 781-1078

Sample Brief No. 5:

Petition for a Writ of Mandamus

IN THE
UNITED STATES COURT OF APPEALS
FOR THE ELEVENTH CIRCUIT

No. 12345

In re ABC CAROLINAS, INC.,
ABC SOUTHEAST, INC., and
ABC SOUTHWEST, INC.,

Petitioners.

PETITION FOR WRIT OF MANDAMUS

I.M. Madashell
Big Law Firm LLP
One Address Square, Suite 123
St. Charles, Missouri 64102
Phone: (555) 555-2000
Fax: (555) 555-2001

[We have eliminated the required sections on Interested Persons and Corporate Relationships, the Table of Contents and the Table of Authorities]

> The first section here is the most important. You must grab the court of appeals' attention right away and convince them that a grave injustice has occurred and action needs to be taken. Fortunately for the author here, he had the authorities to back up this claim.

SUMMARY OF THE ARGUMENT AND REASONS WHY MANDAMUS SHOULD ISSUE

This petition for writ of mandamus presents two issues that have been conclusively determined by binding precedent of this circuit: *first*, that the district court clearly abused its discretion by failing to enforce a valid contractual forum selection clause requiring the dismissal or transfer of the underlying lawsuit. In re Fireman's Fund Insurance Companies, 588 F.2d 93, 95 (5th Cir. 1979) (forum selection clause preempts statutory venue provision); In re Ricoh Corp., 870 F.2d 570, 572-74 (11th Cir. 1989) (district court clearly abused its discretion in failing to enforce forum selection clause), petition for writ after remand from Stewart Org., Inc. v. Ricoh Corp., 487 U.S. 22 (1988); and *second*, that mandamus should issue to correct this manifest error. Ricoh, 870 F.2d at 571-72 (writ of mandamus is to be issued to correct district court's failure to enforce forum selection clause).

This lawsuit arises from a dispute among partners concerning the proper disposition of approximately $23 million in proceeds from the sale of partnership properties in three related partnerships. The partnership agreements contain a forum selection clause calling for any partnership disputes to be brought either in Delaware, the state in which the partnerships are organized, or one of the venues where the partnership properties are located. No properties are located in Florida. Nevertheless, the general partner filed an interpleader action in the U.S. District Court for the Southern District of Florida. The general partner claimed that it was an innocent stakeholder of the disputed proceeds as between the two limited partners, Petitioners and a sister company of the general partner. Plaintiff invoked 28 U.S.C. § 1397, which provides that venue for statutory interpleader actions is appropriate wherever any claimant resides. Both the general partner and its affiliate/limited partner are based in southern Florida.

Petitioners moved pursuant to Fed. R. Civ. P. 12(b)(3) and 28 U.S.C. § 1406 for the case to be dismissed for improper venue because Florida was not one of the contractually agreed-to venues. Alternatively, Petitioners sought transfer to the District of Delaware where a separate action, filed by Petitioners, is pending. The Honorable William J. Zloch, United States District Judge, Southern District of Florida (Respondent), issued two opinions on Petitioners motion. In his initial opinion, he found that:

- The forum selection clause was valid and applicable to this controversy.
- The forum selection clause did <u>not</u> permit venue in Florida.
- The forum selection clause was not preempted by 28 U.S.C. § 1397 because even exclusive statutory venue provisions can be waived by contractual agreement of the parties.

After requesting further briefing on the issue of whether 28 U.S.C. § 1404(a) or § 1406 was the proper vehicle to effectuate transfer or dismissal of the case, Judge Zloch issued a second opinion. Without altering any of his initial conclusions, Judge Zloch held that <u>neither</u> § 1404(a) <u>nor</u> § 1406 authorized dismissal or transfer of the case. Judge Zloch held that venue in Florida was not improper as that term is used in 28 U.S.C. § 1406 because venue in Florida was available under the interpleader venue statute, 28 U.S.C. § 1397; therefore, he could neither dismiss nor transfer the action pursuant to § 1406. Judge Zloch also refused to transfer the case pursuant to 28 U.S.C. § 1404(a), holding that § 1404(a) was inapplicable because the case could not originally have been brought in the District of Delaware under 28 U.S.C. § 1397. Judge Zloch refused to reconsider his ruling and refused to certify it for interlocutory appeal.

Although mandamus is an extraordinary remedy, it is appropriate where there has been a clear abuse of discretion. Here, Judge Zloch clearly abused his discretion by refusing to enforce the contractual forum selection clause between the parties. The applicable precedent leaves no doubt that the parties contractual selection of venue should be honored even if other venues are specified by statute. <u>Fireman's Fund</u>, 588 F.2d at 95. Indeed, Judge Zloch so found in his initial opinion. His subsequent decision not to give effect to the forum selection clause because of the venue provisions of § 1397 simply cannot be reconciled with his original holding. Nor can it be reconciled with the law.

Petitioners have no other adequate alternative remedy. The option of seeking reversal on venue grounds only after being forced to endure full discovery, litigation, and trial in southern Florida is not only inadequate but is terribly wasteful. This Court has determined that mandamus is appropriate to correct a district court's refusal to enforce a forum selection clause. <u>Ricoh</u>, 870 F.2d at 571-72. This remedy should be granted here.

STATEMENT OF THE ISSUE PRESENTED AND RELIEF SOUGHT

Whether the venue provisions of 28 U.S.C. § 1397 are subject to contractual waiver through a forum selection clause and, if so, whether an action filed in violation of the forum selection clause should be dismissed or transferred to a contractually agreed forum pursuant to either 28 U.S.C. § 1406 or 28 U.S.C. § 1404(a). The district court's opinion denying dismissal or transfer of this case is directly contrary to the following controlling authorities:

<u>In re Fireman's Fund Insurance Companies</u>, 588 F.2d 93 (5th Cir. 1979).

<u>In re Ricoh</u>, 870 F.2d 570 (11th Cir. 1989), <u>petition for writ after remand from Stewart Org. v. Ricoh</u>, 487 U.S. 22 (1988).

The Bremen v. Zapata Off-Shore Co., 407 U.S. 1 (1972).

Carnival Cruise Lines, Inc. v. Shute, 499 U.S. 585 (1991).

Petitioners request this Court to issue a writ of mandamus ordering the district court to dismiss this action for lack of proper venue or, alternatively, to transfer the action to the United States District Court for the District of Delaware pursuant to the forum selection clause applicable to this matter, and to order such further and other relief as the Court deems appropriate in the circumstances.

[We have eliminated the statement of facts and proceedings below sections]

> The argument uses the words "clear" and "clearly" a lot, which normally would make a reader cringe, but in this case, the trial judge really did make an obvious mistake. Arguably, "clear" errors are the *only* kind that ever warrant the issuance of a writ of mandamus. Nevertheless, we would limit or omit the use of these words.

ARGUMENT

I. MANDAMUS IS AN APPROPRIATE REMEDY TO CORRECT RESPONDENT'S CLEAR ABUSE OF DISCRETION

Mandamus is a proper remedy where the trial court fails to enforce a forum selection clause that requires the dismissal or transfer of an action. In re Ricoh, 870 F.2d 570, 571-72 (11th Cir. 1989), petition for writ after remand from Stewart Org. v. Ricoh, 487 U.S. 22 (1988). It is particularly appropriate for the Court of Appeals to issue the writ when the district court has failed to certify the issue for interlocutory appeal. Id. at 572 n. 4.

> The author makes heavy use of Ricoh because it was an 11th Circuit case that granted a writ in the exact same circumstances as the instant case. It does not get much better than that.

The district court clearly abused its discretion when it failed to enforce a valid forum selection clause. In Ricoh, this Court was explicit about the necessity to enforce forum selection clauses by transfer under 28 U.S.C. § 1404(a):

> In considering Ricoh's motion under section 1404(a) to transfer this action to the Southern District of New York, the district court . . . clearly abused its discretion . . .

. . . [The district court's] deference to the filing forum would only encourage parties to violate their contractual obligations, the integrity of which are vital to our judicial system. See Stewart, [487 U.S. at 33], 108 S.Ct. at 2246 ([E]nforcement of valid forum selection clauses, bargained for by the parties, protects their legitimate expectations and furthers vital interests of the justice system.) (Kennedy, J., concurring); see also Stewart, 810 F.2d 1066, 1075 (11th Cir. 1987) (en banc) (Where, as here, the non-movant has not shown that it would be unjust to honor a forum selection clause that it has freely given, the interest of justice requires that the non-movant be held to its promise.) (Tjoflat, J., concurring). We conclude that when a motion under section 1404(a) seeks to enforce a valid, reasonable choice of forum clause, the opponent bears the burden of persuading the court that the contractual forum is sufficiently inconvenient to justify retention of the dispute.

In so concluding, we adhere to the reasoning advanced by the Supreme Court in its opinion in this case. See Stewart, [487 U.S. 22] , 108 S.Ct. 2239, 101 L.Ed.2d 22 (1988). . . . [T]he clear import of the Court's opinion is that the venue mandated by a choice of forum clause rarely will be outweighed by other 1404(a) factors.

Ricoh, 870 F.2d at 572-73. The facts of Ricoh parallel the instant case:

Looking to the specific facts of this case, we note that the instant contract was freely and fairly negotiated by experienced business professionals. . . . Stewart has neither alleged nor shown the presence of fraud, duress, misrepresentation, or other misconduct that would bar the clause's enforcement. Nor has Stewart demonstrated that because of intervening and unexpected occurrences between the contract's formation and the filing of the suit, the contract's purpose would be frustrated if we were to mandate the transfer of this case to a Manhattan forum. This suit, therefore, does not present the type of exceptional situation in which judicial enforcement of a contractual choice of forum clause would be improper. See Stewart, [487 U.S. at 33], 108 S.Ct. at 2246 (Kennedy, J., concurring). The district court clearly abused its discretion in concluding otherwise.

Ricoh, 870 F.2d at 573-74.

In these circumstances, Petitioners have no other adequate alternative remedy. The only conceivable alternative remedy, "inevitable reversal by this court after the defendants have been forced to endure full discovery, full litigation, and a full trial is scarcely . . . adequate." In re Cooper, 971 F.2d 640, 641 (11th Cir. 1992) (citing In re Watkins, 271 F.2d 771, 775 (5th Cir. 1959)). Therefore, this Court should issue a writ of mandamus to order the Respondent to dismiss or transfer the underlying action.

II. RESPONDENT CLEARLY ABUSED ITS DISCRETION BY DENYING THE MOTION TO DISMISS OR TRANSFER

There is an unbroken line of controlling authorities that require the enforcement of contractual forum selection clauses. The Bremen v. Zapata Off-Shore Co., 407 U.S. 1 (1972); Carnival Cruise Lines, Inc. v. Shute, 499 U.S. 585 (1991); Stewart Organization v. Ricoh, 487 U.S. 22 (1988); Ricoh, 870 F.2d 570; In re Fireman's Fund Insurance Companies, 588 F.2d 93 (5th Cir. 1979). This point is not disputed by the parties. Judge Zloch concluded, however, that neither § 1406 nor § 1404(a) empowered him to dismiss or transfer the action. This conclusion was clearly in error.

Judge Zloch determined that 28 U.S.C. § 1404(a), rather than § 1406, applied to the motion to dismiss or transfer. Judge Zloch followed what Petitioners believe is a minority opinion among the courts that was triggered by a footnote in the Stewart case, 487 U.S. at 28 n. 8. See, e.g., Jumara v. State Farm Ins. Co., 55 F.3d 873, 878-79 (3d Cir. 1995). This position holds that cases are not subject to dismissal under Rule 12(b)(3) or 28 U.S.C. § 1406 on the basis of a forum selection clause because the venue where the case is filed is not made improper by operation of the forum selection clause. Id. Instead, these courts apply 28 U.S.C. § 1404(a) to determine whether the case is to be transferred. Id.

Judge Zloch concluded, however, that § 1404(a) was inapplicable because this case could not have been brought in Delaware under the interpleader venue provision, 28 U.S.C. § 1397. This conclusion is directly contrary to the established law of this circuit, In re Fireman's Fund Ins. Co., 588 F.2d 93, 95 (5th Cir. 1979).

In Fireman's Fund, this Court held that the specific, exclusive venue provision of the Miller Act, 40 U.S.C. § 270b(b), mandating that [e]very suit instituted under this section shall be brought . . . in the United States District Court for any district in which the contract was to be performed and executed and not elsewhere, was nonetheless subject to a forum selection clause between the parties which called for a transfer to a forum where the contract was not to be performed or executed. 588 F.2d at 95. The Court noted that a motion to transfer under 28 U.S.C. § 1404(a) applies to any civil action. Id. Furthermore, the Court noted that even an exclusive venue provision containing the phrase, and not elsewhere, was still subject to alteration by the parties forum selection clause, because venue may be varied by contract. Id.

The Miller Act's exclusive venue provision is worded much stronger than 28 U.S.C. § 1397, yet this circuit recognized that a party's power to contract into another forum is even stronger. This opinion is buttressed by numerous other cases cited by Judge Zloch in the 10/22/96 Order (at pp. 6-7) holding that forum selection clauses preempt the operation of venue statutes, including exclusive venue provisions. B & D Mechanical, 70 F.3d at 1117; FGS Constructors, Inc. v. Carlow, 64 F.3d 1230, 1233 (8th Cir. 1995); Pittsburgh Tank, 62 F.3d at 36; Bense v. Interstate Battery System of America, 683 F.2d 718 (2d Cir. 1982).

Judge Zloch initially followed these authorities in the 10/22/96 Order, specifically holding that section 1397 . . . is a venue provision and thus subject to contractual waiver. 10/22/96 Order at 7. But he then ignored these authorities in the 12/5/96 Order, concluding that a contractually designated forum that would not be an appropriate venue for the action under the interpleader venue statue, section 1397, is not a court where the action might have been brought under section 1404(a). 12/5/96 Order at 8.

Judge Zloch cited <u>Hoffman v. Blaski</u>, 363 U.S. 335 (1960), as his sole authority for this proposition. 12/5/96 Order at 8. However, this case is inapposite to the issue because it has nothing whatsoever to do with a forum selection clause or the parties right to make a prior selection of venue by consent or agreement. In <u>Hoffman</u>, the defendants moved under section 1404(a) for transfer to a forum where the defendants had not been amenable to service of process and had no contacts, and where venue was obviously improper at the initiation of the action by plaintiffs. 363 U.S. at 336-37 and n. 2, 338-39 and n. 5. Defendants' motion stated that defendants were willing to submit themselves to the jurisdiction and venue of the alternative forum, if the court would consider the transfer on the basis of convenience to the parties and witnesses. <u>Id.</u> The forum to which defendants sought to be transferred was clearly one in which the case could <u>not</u> have been brought by the plaintiffs when the suit was filed. <u>Id.</u> In these circumstances, the court determined that a transfer to the forum under section 1404(a) was not proper. 363 U.S. at 342-43.

<u>Hoffman</u> is inapposite because in the instant case, plaintiff had every right to bring this action in the forum selected by the Agreements forum selection clause. The controlling authorities hold that forum selection clauses must be enforced unless the opponents of the motion prove that there are exceptional circumstances that render the enforcement of the clause unreasonable and improper. <u>Ricoh</u>, 870 F.2d at 572-74; <u>Stewart</u>, 487 U.S. at 33 (Kennedy, J., concurring). Respondent ignored these authorities, and made a clearly erroneous determination of Petitioner's motion to dismiss or transfer that flies in the face of these authorities and even contradicts Respondent's prior order in the instant case. Therefore, the Court should issue a writ of mandamus to remedy Respondent's clear abuse of discretion and usurpation of judicial power.

CONCLUSION

WHEREFORE, Petitioners respectfully request this Court to issue a writ of mandamus ordering the district court to dismiss this case for lack of proper venue, or to transfer this action to the United States District Court for the District of Delaware pursuant to the forum selection clause applicable to this matter, and to order such further and other relief as the Court deems appropriate in the circumstances.

Chapter 26

Oral Advocacy at Pretrial, Trial and Appellate Stages

We have concentrated on the use of writing for communication in the practice of law. It is true, however, that any lawyer will have at least as many and sometimes more occasions to use oral communication in the practice of law:

> ➤ to provide advice to a client or other attorneys in the lawyer's office
> ➤ to discuss matters or negotiate with other attorneys
> ➤ to orally communicate and argue motions, requests, objections, and other legal arguments to a decision maker such as a judge

If we were to compare the amount of time we have spent on the telephone and talking on our feet as an attorney to the amount of time hunched before a keyboard drafting documents, we are sure we would find that the former balances out and sometimes even outweighs the latter.

Clear and effective communication skills in person and over the phone are a great asset for any attorney. Many times your clients or your superiors who vote on your future in the law office will only have these types of encounters with you—they never will have read a single thing you have written, and the only impression they will have of you as an attorney is from your oral communication skills. This should be a great incentive to try to refine your skills. Talk in complete sentences. Avoid excessive slang, and fillers such as "ya know," "uhhhhh," "like," and others. Be concise in speaking—an economy of words and a depth of meaning should be your goal.

This chapter focuses on the more particular skills required in litigation settings. Unlike most legal method and legal writing texts, we will discuss argument in the trenches of the trial level courts before going to the mountaintop of appellate level oral argument. The skills needed in the former type of forum are slightly different and somewhat more crude than the skills needed in the latter.

I. BACKGROUND PRINCIPLES OF THE PRACTICE OF ORAL ARGUMENT

Lawyers often puzzle over the true meaning of oral argument. As with writing, we think it is prudent to look at oral argument from the perspective of the audience, the trial or appellate court judge. Judges have several ends that are achieved by oral argument:

A. It is an efficient use of the court's time and resources.

At the trial court level, complicated motions can be summarized and reported orally in capsule form to the court, who, after hearing the argument, might have an immediate answer for the parties on the merits of the motion. If the court is one in which the judge has an abundance of cases and no law clerks, oral argument enables the court to process a great number of cases in the shortest possible time. Even if the judge is forced to take a motion "under advisement" after the oral argument, the argument still may have served its purpose to educate the court enough to allow it to proceed rapidly through the briefs and memoranda filed on the motion, and ultimately lead to a quicker decision.

On appeal, the judges generally have law clerks who can summarize the legal briefs for the judges in the form of a bench memo, but appellate court judges often will take the time to personally consult the parties' briefs before the oral argument. In these instances, oral argument still can assist the court to make sense of complicated issues and provides the judges with a forum to question the litigants, as discussed in the section below, which can assist the court in reaching its decision in a shorter period of time.

B. It allows a judge to question the two sides about the motion or appeal.

If a judge did read and digest the motion or appellate briefs ahead of time, or her clerks did, and they summarized the case for the judge, the judge still may have questions that need to be answered before she can rule. Oral argument is just the place for this. Many advocates think of oral argument as "their time" to present their arguments, but judges quite properly think of argument as the court's time to clarify and explore the issues.

An advocate may spend days preparing a wonderful fifteen minute oral argument just to show up and have the court use up thirteen of the fifteen minutes with questions. This is not a failure, it is exactly what the advocate should expect and even welcome. The days spent working on and thinking hard about the case will enable the advocate properly to address those thirteen minutes of questions, and the judges will leave this argument with a much better understanding of those aspects of the case that troubled them the most.

C. It can assist a judge in making up her mind.

Trial court judges often have no idea that a motion was filed in your case until you step up to the podium and address the court on the motion. The only time you will have the judge's undivided attention on your motion is during these brief periods of argument. If the judge cannot devote long periods of time to the briefs filed by the parties and has no law clerks to help her, the oral argument is the most important time for the judge to make up her mind about the merits of the motion.

Of the appellate court judges we have heard on this issue, most have reported that they make up their minds based on the briefs of the parties. The arguments serve as a chance to reconfirm this initial opinion or perhaps to have one or two questions answered that might push the judge a little farther in one direction or the other. These judges do allow for the possibility that from time to time the parties might explain their case orally in such a way that the judges actually will change their minds solely because of the oral arguments. This should be enough incentive for you to take the argument process seriously.

II. ORAL ARGUMENT IN TRIAL LEVEL COURTS PRIOR TO TRIAL

An oral argument in the pretrial stage can happen several ways. The ways will depend on the local rules and local practices of the jurisdiction and occasionally on the individual judge to which your case is assigned.

A. "No oral argument" jurisdictions

You may find yourself practicing in a jurisdiction that does not allow oral argument on motions except when it is specifically ordered by the court. This is what we characterize as a "no oral argument" jurisdiction, because the rule commonly is interpreted to mean that oral argument will be extremely rare on motions, and reserved only for the most complicated motions where the parties and the court think it will be of benefit.

The parties might request oral argument because they think it will lead to an earlier ruling on the motion. They also might think that the court will benefit from having the parties run through the motion in person, so that they can address any problems that the court might have with the facts, or the law, or the positions of the parties.

The court might go along with the request or, even more rarely, *sua sponte* order oral argument on a motion for the same reasons as stated above. Different judges have different opinions about the benefits and costs of oral argument. Some judges love to see and hear the attorneys in the case, others started their judicial career in a court where oral arguments were routinely heard, and they think of the process as a great way to clear their docket of a number of motions in a short period of time. Other judges would rather reserve their court time for trials and hearings and will not be bothered to hear motions argued.

B. "Motion Day" or "Law Day" jurisdictions

In some courts, one or two days a month or sometimes one or two days a week are set aside for motions to be heard on oral argument pursuant to local rules. <u>E.g.</u>, Ala. R. Civ. P. 78; Ariz. R. Civ. P. 78; Ark. R. Civ. P. 78; Colo. R. Civ. P. 78; Haw. R. Civ. P. 78. These days are called "motion days" or sometimes "law days." The movant generally will have to schedule a place on the motion docket with the court, and then give notice of the date and time to all parties and the court. Occasionally, a court will allow any and all parties with pending motions simply to show up and sign up on the motion day, without prior scheduling or notice to the court. It will be necessary to notify your opponents that you are going, because if you show up by yourself, the court is unlikely to entertain an *ex parte* argument on the motion.

C. "Open Court" Jurisdictions

Occasionally, a court will hear oral arguments on motions any day that the court is in session. A simple call to the court to confirm that they are in session on the chosen day, perhaps to sign up on the docket, too, and notice given in writing to all parties and to the court will secure your oral argument whenever it is convenient for you and the other parties.

D. Informal matters and "show up" jurisdictions

Courts sometimes will set aside a short period of time, usually in the morning when the court first opens for business, for the hearing of informal matters and motions, and any party with such a request or motion simply can show up and present their request to the court. Prior notice to the court is not required, although it will be necessary to contact the other parties to let them know what you are up to. These sessions usually are reserved for smaller, often uncontested motions, such as requests for extensions of time to answer or to respond to discovery or to file an amended complaint, requests to file a brief with additional pages over the local page limit, for attorney admission to the court, for a minor amendment to pleadings, or other fairly simple requests. Discovery motions, such as motions to quash or motions to compel might be brought here, especially if the timing of the discovery (a deposition, for example) demands expedited attention from the court. Substantial requests, such as dispositive motions to dismiss or for summary judgment, motions for preliminary injunctions, and complicated discovery motions or motions in limine generally will not be entertained in informal matters, and the court may get angry at you for trying to bring up a complicated, contested motion in these sessions.

E. The necessity to "notice up" motions

In many courts, other than those in category A above, the parties must call for oral argument by "noticing up a hearing" on a motion because that is the only way their motions are going to get ruled on. Notice of a hearing on a motion alerts the other parties that if they have not filed an opposition to the motion yet, do it now or before the hearing. Notice also puts the court file in the judge's hands on the day of the hearing, and gives him a strong incentive to deal with the motion then and there, rather than hear the oral argument, let the motion go under advisement, and forget about it.

F. Style of oral argument in trial courts in the pretrial period

Oral argument at the pretrial stage differs from the appellate level oral argument in several ways: usually, you do not get a fixed period of time to talk. You talk until the judge shuts you up, or your opponent interrupts you and cuts you off, or until you run out of things to say, or until the judge walks out and they turn the lights off in the court. You do not get just one chance to argue your position; you can go back and forth several times arguing your side then listening to your opponent argue hers, then interrupting her and trying to command the judge's attention, until she cuts you off or the judge calls it quits.

In the best instances, the judge will control the argument and demand an orderly presentation so that each side gets a chance to say what it wants to say. The best judges will not tolerate counsel interrupting each other and will quash such rudeness quickly. The judge may question each side so as to explore the strengths and weaknesses of their positions. The judge, not the parties, decides when she has heard enough on the motion.

At its worst, the court will not regulate the argument, and will sit by while counsel interrupt and cut each other off, and bluster and rage so as to command the most attention. In these situations, it matters much less whether or not you have a structured and logical outline, and a start and finish to the argument worked out on a pretrial motion; rather, what is important is the ability to divert the judge's attention away from your opponent and capture it long enough to say your two or three points any way that you can. Being quick of tongue, loud, blustery, and ready and willing to interrupt and cut off your opponent will help in these dismal situations.

III. ORAL ARGUMENT DURING A TRIAL

Aside from the opening statement and the closing argument, which are directed to the jury of laypersons, not to the court, and which have nothing to do with our topic here, oral arguments to the court are not regularly scheduled during trials. However, in our experience, we have more often than not been called on to make miniature oral arguments during a trial to argue evidentiary points, to argue motions made during the trial, and to argue or defend motions for directed verdict or for judgment as a matter of law.

These arguments usually are conducted like the pretrial motions described above—you do not get a set amount of time and you get to go back and forth several times, but far fewer of the same "style" advantages carry over to this setting because a sense of decorum prevails during a trial that is absent in the average pretrial hearing. As a result, the arguments generally are cleaner with fewer interruptions. Nevertheless, the content of the arguments typically are no more organized, detailed, or thought-provoking than the average pretrial argument.

IV. APPELLATE ORAL ARGUMENT

The rest of this chapter focuses on the more particular skills required in appellate court and moot court settings. The paradigm of oral argument for law students is appellate level oral argument. This is the model followed by most law schools in first year oral arguments and in the moot court programs and competitions in the second and third year.

Compared to oral arguments in the trial courts, appellate level argument is a "mountaintop" experience, because you get a certain amount of time to speak, no one interrupts you (except the panel), and getting out your full argument does not depend on your ability and willingness to interrupt and cut off the other side.

The standard procedures for oral argument are remarkably similar from place to place and competition to competition: usually there is more than one judge on the panel. Each side (appellant - appellee, or petitioner - respondent) gets a specific period of time in which to speak. It can be as little as ten minutes or as long as the court wants to give you, although most courts will not give each side more than forty-five minutes or an hour for any argument. No one except the panel can interrupt the oralist. No counsel can yell, "Objection," or "She's misstating the facts!" during their opponent's argument. A bailiff or clerk keeps time, and periodically will hold up a card, light up a small light in front of you, or rap a gavel to let you know how many minutes you have left. Each oralist makes her arguments and answers the panel's questions and sits down.

Generally, the appellant or petitioner oralists speak first and the appellee or respondent oralists speak second. The appellant usually can reserve a few minutes for one oralist to do rebuttal, and once in a great while the rules of the court or the moot court competition will allow the appellee to reserve time for an oralist to do surrebuttal. If you have a partner or associate with you, your side will have to pre-determine how to split the time between the two oralists. Most of the time, an even split is the best idea. You do not want to deny the panel the opportunity to have a good look at both oralists.

Where there is more than one issue at stake in the appeal, some courts allow an appellant or petitioner to argue issue one followed by the appellee or respondent's argument on issue one, followed by the appellant or petitioner's argument on issue two, followed by the appellee or respondent's argument on issue two, and so on. Some moot court competitions follow this procedure, too.

The classic and expected practice is for the judges to interrupt your argument with questions. Panels will vary from how **active** they are (lots of questions), how **hostile** they are (how much they show their dislike for one or both sides' arguments), or how "**hot**" they are ("hot" means they read the parties' briefs or the bench briefs carefully, and are prepared to question you on the issues and authorities; "cold" means they did not read anything before hand, and will just give you a cold indifferent stare when you start). A good panel for almost any oral argumentative is an active, hot, but not hostile panel.

V. HOW TO PREPARE FOR ORAL ARGUMENT

Appellate oral argument follows the briefing of the case in which the appellant or petitioner files its opening brief, the appellee or respondent files its answering brief or opposition brief, and the appellant or petitioner files its reply brief. An argument date is set by the court. A panel of judges from the court is selected unless the matter is to be heard by the court *en banc*. As the day of the argument approaches, counsel should be doing the following things to prepare themselves for the argument:

A. Know every case and legal authority inside and out.

You probably will be nervous before your first two or three oral arguments, but use this energy to drive you through the preparation. Channel your nervous energy into reviewing the points you will make and the points raised by your opponent in her brief. Read all of your cases and authorities again for facts, holding, rationale, and policies. Key Cite or shepardize them one more time. Now do the same for your opponent's cases: find her bad cases.

If you have one or more partners, you should spend some time discussing all of the good and bad cases as a team when you are preparing for oral argument. Everyone on the team should have a working knowledge of the issues and the authorities in the case, both good authorities and bad. It is common in oral arguments to hear an oralist beg off a question by disclaiming "That is a question that my co-counsel will address," or worse yet, "That issue has been discussed in my co-counsel's part of the argument, and I am not able to discuss it." The only time you should be uttering these words in oral argument is if you are completely stumped by a question thrown at you by the panel, **and** it happens to be an issue that your co-counsel, who is going next, will address. If you are well up to speed on the case, you should not have to beg off. Some judges are looking to see how up to speed on the whole case you really are, and if you handle an "off your position" question well, they will be very impressed.

B. Write an outline, not a script.

Draft an **outline** of what you want to say. You do not want to write out things word for word because if you then read from a prepared text, this will not sound conversational, sincere, and from the heart. Good oral arguments sound more conversational than speeches delivered from a podium. You also are supposed to make eye contact with everyone on the panel, and you cannot do that if you are looking down at your notes. Oral arguments have the illusion of being an impromptu discussion from someone who knows and cares, and thus are more persuasive than the average lecture. If you write out your entire argument, you will have too much paper up there with you at the podium, and in trying to follow it, you may get distracted by a question and lose your place.

Your outline does not have to follow the exact order of arguments that you put in your brief. Think about ways to get to the best argument quickly and work on a transition from that to the next best argument and so on. The judges have your brief, and they can read the whole story of your case if they want to. Oral argument is the place for you to drive home your best points and make them stick in the judges' minds, so that when the judges retire to the conference that follows the arguments, they will remember these points and be more inclined to vote in your favor.

C. Prepare an introduction.

The only exception to the rule against scripting that we encourage you to follow is for you to script the first forty-five seconds or so of your oral argument and to commit this portion to memory. The start of the argument has certain formal requirements expected of counsel in most jurisdictions:

➢ Most oralists will start their argument with the phrase, "May it please the court." This is a convention, not a rule in most jurisdictions, but it is a convention followed by the vast majority of oralists. If you decide to buck the convention, you should be aware that from time to time you will encounter a judge who will view your free-spirited thinking as rebellion. You will not necessarily win points for originality; instead, judges will think you started the argument incorrectly. Many oralists soften the formality by adding, "Good morning, your honors" or other greeting appropriate for the time of day. Oralists at the United States Supreme Court begin by stating, "Mr. Chief Justice, may it please the court."

➢ Personal introductions come next. Introduce yourself and your co-counsel, and the party you represent. Remind the court of the reason for your argument and your prayer for relief. Explain the breakdown of the points you and your co-counsel will be addressing.

Example: May it please the court. Good afternoon, your honors. My name is Walter Scott and I, together with my co-counsel, Edith Wharton, represent petitioner George Elliot. Mr. Elliot asks the court to reverse the order granting summary judgment in favor of respondent Twain issued by the United States District Court for the Western District of Tennessee. I will be addressing the issues of news reporting and political speech. My co-counsel will address the issues of parody and the right to comment on and criticize political figures under the First Amendment.

➢ The next portion should be an introduction to your argument and your theme. Most counsel draft a short statement of the two or three major bullet points of their argument, followed by a statement of the theme of the case from your client's perspective.

Example: {**introduction**} Mr. Elliot requests that you reverse the lower court for three reasons: first, that the First Amendment protects and encourages political commentary to such a degree that respondent Twain's publicity rights must give way to Mr. Elliot's commentary. Second, that the Tennessee Personal Rights Protection Act specifically provides an exception for "news reporting" and commentary on "public affairs," and Mr. Elliot meets the requirements of this exception. Third, that Mr. Elliot's commentary is not commercial speech. {**theme**} Your honors, the protection of the right of political commentary is the core value protected by the First Amendment. The preservation of all other topics of expression is secondary to the goal of preserving an open and robust dialogue on politics in a democracy.

Some counsel will flip the theme and the introduction:

Example: {**theme**} Your honors, the protection of the right of political commentary is the core value protected by the First Amendment. The preservation of all other topics of expression is secondary to the goal of preserving an open and robust dialogue on politics in a democracy. {**introduction**} Mr. Elliot requests that you reverse the lower court for three reasons: first, that the First Amendment protects and encourages political commentary to such a degree that respondent Twain's publicity rights must give way to Mr. Elliot's commentary. Second, that the Tennessee Personal Rights Protection Act specifically provides an exception for "news reporting" and commentary on "public affairs," and Mr. Elliot meets the requirements of this exception. Third, that Mr. Elliot's commentary is not commercial speech.

Still others will combine the theme and the introduction in one statement of the case:

{**thematic introduction**} Mr. Elliot requests that you reverse the lower court for three reasons: first, that the First Amendment protects and encourages political commentary to such a degree that respondent Twain's publicity rights must give way to Mr. Elliot's commentary. Indeed, this is the core value protected by the First Amendment, which outweighs the protection of all other topics of speech. Second, that the Tennessee Personal Rights Protection Act specifically provides an exception for "news reporting" and commentary on "public affairs" so as to ensure an open and robust dialogue on matters of public interest in a democracy. Mr. Elliot meets the requirements of this exception. Third, that Mr. Elliot's commentary is not commercial speech and thus deserves the full protection that the First Amendment affords to political commentary.

A bullet point introduction of the two or three main points of your argument notifies the court of what you think are your most important points. The judges will appreciate the outline if it is short and manageable. An outline of five or six major points is excessive. Rarely would even the most skilled oralist be able to cover six points adequately in fifteen minutes even if the judges withheld all of their questions. The judges will be discouraged if you ask them to try to keep that many major points straight in their heads as you make the effort to cover them. It is much better to distill your argument down to two or three points. Telling the judges your two or three best points up front also allows them to direct you to address whichever of the points the judges are the most interested in, which most likely will be the points that the judges are having the most trouble with. You might be disappointed that the judges do not want to hear point one, your best point, but if they already have resolved that point in their minds, argument over this point would be a waste of your time and theirs.

Do not be misled into thinking that our recommendation of scripting your opening means that you might plan on reading from the script. Nothing could be further from the truth. The script is there for you to memorize well before you step up to the podium. After memorizing your opening, practice it several times each day leading up to the argument. Memorization and practice allows two things to happen simultaneously in your argument: first, you will be assured that you have command of the first forty-five seconds of your argument. If you are tense or nervous about the argument process, at least you will know that you can speak confidently without stumbling or getting tongue tied for the first forty-five seconds. This allows you precious time to get comfortable with the process and get into the flow of a conversation. Second, memorization allows you to make eye contact with the entire panel and to establish rapport during the opening seconds. A smooth opening relaxes the panel and draws them in. They will be happy to be listening to a competent oralist who can begin smoothly and who invites them to join the conversation by making eye contact with each member of the panel. That is why reading from your script is a cardinal sin.

If you have not had much experience memorizing passages of this length, here are two tips:

➢ Copy over your script by hand at least three times. The exercise of copying engages the mind in several activities at once—considering the words individually, considering how they flow one to the other, and directing your hand to write them down correctly. Actors use this technique to memorize their scripts, and on average they have a lot more lines to commit to memory than you will have.

➢ Practice your opening several times a day. If you stumble, go back and copy over your script three more times. Repeat this process until you have the opening committed to memory.

If you still are uncomfortable with the thought of forgetting your opening, do not bring your script to the podium. Instead, outline your opening on an index card:

(1) May it please the court
(2) Introduce yourself and your co-counsel–what are each of you arguing
(3) Ask the court to reverse
(4) Give your outline:
    point one: political speech
    point two: statutory exception
    point three: not commercial speech
(5) Give theme: political speech and First Amendment

At least then you will have a crutch, but you will not be encouraged to read off of the card.

D. Themes are not just for briefs.

As mentioned in the section above, you should work on a theme for your argument that fits with your facts and the majority of your written arguments. Hopefully, you already had a good theme in your brief, but if not, there still is time to come up with one. A good sound bite that sums up your arguments, that you can return to frequently in your argument and in answers to questions, can drive home your arguments faster than a long winded explanation. Try to find the best (and safest) analogy for your situation, and use it whenever you want to remind the court of the equities or legal realities that drive your arguments to their conclusions. Short and vivid themes are the best. Paint a small picture—or come up with a one panel editorial cartoon with a one line zinger that sums up you case, and build the argument around that. Do not get too wordy or complicated—think advertising copy, not a treatise discussion.

E. Try to anticipate likely questions, and work out good answers to them.

Try to think up questions your panel of judges might ask, and work out answers that are good, complete responses to the questions and which can segue you back to the points you want to raise.[1] Judges will ask about the strengths of your case and your opponent's case, and explore the weaknesses of both sides. Judges will ask about the public policy and precedential implications of the arguments you are making. They will ask questions about specific cases and authorities—What were the facts of that case? Who was the plaintiff? Did that case have anything to do with [XYZ topic]? When was that statute enacted? When did that regulation go into effect? Do not neglect your opponent's authorities and the major points of your opponent's argument; you must be prepared to discuss these, too. You can put these questions and the outline of your sample answers on a flip stack of 3X5 cards to include with the materials you will bring to the podium.

F. Organize your materials for easy access.

Ideally, your outline should fit on one or two pages. Try pasting it or stapling it to the inside of a legal size manila folder. With a manila folder, you can add a flip stack of 3X5 cards with all your important cases and authorities, your rebuttal points, and perhaps some details of the areas of law you will be discussing summarized on the cards, and a flip stack of question and answer cards described in the section above. If you think of additional points or questions, you still can stick Post-it™ notes on to the pages all the way up

---

[1]   See also section IX infra, "Questions from the panel."

to the argument. We also have used three ring binders with well marked tabs leading you to your outline, your questions and answers, your rebuttal points, and your authorities information pages.

Put tabs on your brief and the opponent's brief, in case you need to look up something in these documents. If you think you might use the record, go through and tab the parts that you think might come up.

What you bring up to the podium matters less than your ability to use what you have brought quickly, quietly, and neatly. In most cases we will bring one binder or a legal size manila folder for our outline and our question-answer cards and authority cards, the briefs of the two sides, and whatever parts of the record we think we might absolutely have to use. We will expect to look at only ten percent of what we bring to the podium— usually only the outline. Your preparation for the argument should have instilled in your brain the information needed to answer the panel's questions and to make your argument without reference to the note cards and briefs.

At the very least, do not be the person who drags up several bulging file folders, full of papers sticking out this way and that, who takes five minutes to get set up before he can begin, and another six minutes to clean up after he is finished, while the judges stare at him with mixed feelings of ire and pity. You are trying to make an impression on the court that will cause them to vote in your favor. You do not want to lose points for sloppiness, of all things.

G. Go and do some field research – see how this is done.

Go watch real life oral arguments and moot court arguments. Get a feeling for what goes on, and pay attention to the kinds of questions that are asked and how they are answered. Note the tone of the oralists. Very few of them will be shouting. Theatrics probably will not be evident. It will probably sound like a conversation, one in which the oralist dominates but the judges can join at any time.

If you cannot leave home or cannot pry yourself away from the law library, you still can take advantage of the work of Prof. Jerry Goldman at Northwestern University Law School, who has prepared Real Audio® files of hundreds of oral arguments of U.S. Supreme Court cases that you can access and listen to at the Oyez Project web site, www.oyez.org (last visited April 11, 2005). The U.S. Supreme Court typically is a very active and hot panel, so you can listen to how the oralists handle intense questioning in their arguments. Court TV's site, www.courttv.com/video/ (last visited April 11, 2005), allows you to browse for video clips of trial level arguments (particularly opening statements and closing arguments).

H. How do you get to the Supreme Court? – practice, practice, practice.

Practice arguing in front of a camcorder or mirror; then practice in front of your friends and teammates. You do not necessarily have to give a legal argument in order to get the feeling of standing at a podium; present any kind of argument for some position, and answer questions from your "judges." Whatever topic you choose, take the process seriously, because you will not learn much from a session that breaks down into kidding and laughing. Just getting the feeling of talking and answering questions on your feet can make you more comfortable with the process.

After this, hold regular moot court practice sessions with your classmates or teammates—at least two or three a week in the weeks that precede the arguments. You and your teammates should grill each other as best as you can on the weaknesses and trouble spots of the case. It may seem foolish and tiresome the fourth or fifth time you do it, but practice rounds of oral argument are like batting practice or shooting free throws: the more you drill yourself to respond cooly and competently to hard questions, the more likely it will be that you will respond cooly and competently to these same questions when you are at your oral argument and the pressure is on. Have someone videotape these practice sessions. Watching yourself on tape will reveal all kinds of amazing things you never imagined yourself doing.

VI. MOOT COURT JUDGES

Whether you are facing an oral argument as part of your first year curriculum or you are facing it in the context of an upper division moot court competition, you are likely to face the same kinds of judges. The common pool for intramural and interscholastic competitions are alumnae of the school where the competition is being held, whether they be private practitioners, government lawyers, public defenders and prosecutors, in-house counsel, or actual judges. Even a regional moot court competition is going to be housed by local lawyers and judges.

The sponsors of a national competition may draw in a number of judges from out of town (the Jessup International Law Moot Court competition coordinates their international final rounds with the yearly convention of the American Society of International Law, so they have a bunch of conventioneers to choose from). You are more likely to get high powered judges who are actually judges at a regional or national competition finals.

Almost all judges you will face had a strong interest in moot court in law school, and most will have had several years of experience in litigation and oral advocacy. Most will know that they should ask questions, and many of them even will know how to ask short, cogent questions without droning on for a minute or more. (Just kidding, judges!). Judges will try to test your arguments with worst case scenarios, parades of horrors, and the edge of the slippery slope.[2] They may try to test your composure by interrupting you frequently and trying to quarrel with you about the law or the facts. Do not take the bait; they are testing you to see if you will get angry and fire back at them, but they are expecting you not to.

Actual judges are not necessarily the best oral argument judges. Actual members of the judiciary have a habit of listening to arguments rather than spicing them up with a lot of

---

[2] See also section IX *infra*, "Questions from the panel."

questions. This carries over from actual courtroom practices. Something about wearing a black choir robe every day makes a person more dignified and ready to listen, rather than fostering a desire to stir things up and test the knowledge and abilities of the advocates before them. Do not expect real judges to behave like television's "Judge Judy" and give you a good tongue lashing. A panel of actual judges can get all riled up in moot court as well as in real court, but in our experience, practitioners ask more and harder questions on average than actual judges.

VII. DECORUM, APPEARANCE, AND DELIVERY

Strict rules of decorum apply in appellate level oral argument. You must show respect for the panel at every turn. You always should address a judge as "Your honor," or two judges as "Your honors," and the whole panel as "the Court."

Disagree with a judge or judges gracefully and respectfully. When you want to say "no" to a judge, say "I respectfully disagree" or "Your honor, the answer is not [XYZ]" or "With all due respect, your Honor, the cases in [PDQ jurisdiction] do not support the argument that . . ." Avoid saying "No" or "No, your honor" directly to a judge unless the judge asked you a "yes-no" question that demands a "yes-no" answer. This is a matter of decorum and politeness, not substance. The judges expect you to disagree with them when they try to undo part of your case, but you should explain your disagreement with grace and respect.

Polite attention and eye contact is expected and is effective in oral argument. Staring or glaring at a judge for minutes at a time is not. Grinning, laughing, or otherwise goofing or joking at oral argument is not acceptable. If a judge makes a joke, you should politely laugh (not bust a gut and slap your knee), and smile and move on with your answer or with your argument. Resist the temptation to make a follow-up joke. Oral argument is serious business, not open-mike night at the local comedy club.

There is no "backstage" in the courtroom, so behave yourself at the counsel table. Sit patiently and listen attentively and respectfully or quietly take notes during your opponent's oral argument. Do not roll your eyes or snort or slam your pen down; these theatrics cost you much more than they will ever gain you. If you have a partner, pay close attention to the back of her head and give her focus in this way when she is arguing. Resist the urge to nod vigorously or pump your fist in the air when she makes a good point. You do not want to draw focus away from her and to yourself by nodding, fidgeting, picking your fingernails, slouching on the table, leaning way back in your chair, spinning your chair back and forth, or other such distracting conduct. Do not try these things on your opponents, either; it is very unprofessional and detrimental to the judges' opinion of you. Beaming happily at the back of your partner's head is permitted.

In every oral argument, whether it be in a real appellate court or in moot court, your appearance must be professional and appropriate. Wear your best job interview suit for an interview at a stodgy law firm. Wear your hair in a conservative lawyerly way. Jewelry and accessories (men's ties, women's scarves, chains, and earrings) should be somewhat subdued and preferably conservative. Do not wear a watch or jewelry that is loose and clunky that you might bang the podium with in the middle of your argument.

You should stand fairly still at the podium with your hands gently placed on the edge near you or gently intertwined at your stomach; the latter is especially good if you have no podium and have to argue in front of a table or desk. The reason for this is to keep your hands where you need them and not where you do not want them—it gives your hands something to hold on to in a tidy way. Often the panel will not be able to see your hands in these positions because of the podium. In these positions, your hands can rise up to make a gesture of emphasis, or flip pages, or lift a note card smoothly, quickly, and quietly.

If you can stand and comfortably deliver your argument with your hands at your sides, that can look very impressive. The trouble is that few people can do this for a long enough period of time, and wind up letting their hands go somewhere they do not want them to go; they snake into a pocket, or one or both hands wind up on your hips, or your hands start swinging back and forth, which are inappropriate places for them to be during the argument.

Do not sway back and forth or from side to side at the podium. You will make the panel seasick. Do not wander from your spot—this is not a closing argument before a jury where you may want to walk the rail and make eye contact with all of the jurors. Do not grip the podium like a dying man or lean your full weight on it or slouch with your elbows on it as if you are exhausted or lazy.

Arms crossed are hostile. Arms forced behind the back or nailed to your sides will look peculiar and should be avoided unless you were in the military or other occupation where you were asked to stand in a rigid, formal posture and you are the most comfortable standing that way. Putting one or both hands in your pockets looks cavalier or disrespectful; it is too casual for this situation. Hands on the hips look impatient or disapproving .

Small gestures used sparingly for emphasis can be effective, but do not point or shake a finger directly at a judge or take any other subliminally hostile action. Arm waving or fist shaking is beyond the pale. Any arm gesture that puts your hands above the level of your shoulders is suspect. Think friendly counselor, not fire-and-brimstone preacher. Never pound the pulpit no matter how worked up you get. It is too comical and theatrical for a serious situation like oral argument.

A conversational tone may come naturally to you, or you may have to work at it. Tape yourself and listen to what you sound like. Ask your friends and associates to listen to you and evaluate your tone. Does it sound like a normal tone of voice for speaking? Does it sound like the start of a conversation that a person would feel comfortable joining? Or does it sound like preaching, shouting, addressing a large crowd from a stage, or other public speaking style that no one would characterize as conversational.

High speed is your enemy. It is hard enough to be understood when explaining something orally, speeding up just a little can lose your audience a lot. If your normal conversational tone is rushed, consciously slow yourself down a little bit. But — do — not — talk — abnormally — slowly — because — this — does — not — allow — your — argument — to — sound — conversational. Ask your co-counsel to evaluate how well you are doing.

Above all, try to consciously eliminate verbal fillers such as "uhhh," "ahhh," "ummm," and lackluster vernacular phrases such as "uh-huh," "ya-know," "like" (as in "It's like so illegal," or "The Constitution like bans this conduct."). These phrases are distracting and can make a judge tune you out. Worse yet, the judge might start a score card with how many "uhhh's" and "ummm's" you say in the argument; take it from us—that judge is not paying proper attention to the substance of your argument any more.

VIII. CONSTRUCTING THE ARGUMENT

As mentioned above, you do not have to rigidly follow your brief. Truly consider what is your best argument, and find a way to get to that argument quickly and logically. Then plan the transition to the next best argument and so on.

Certainly do not plan to argue using just the table of contents from your brief as your outline. Presume that the judges have read that much. Instead, focus on planning a route to your best issue so that you have a shot of getting that out before the questions start firing.

It is customary in some courts for the first person who argues to ask if the court requires a recitation of the facts (note that this is not expected of the second, third, or fourth person to argue in the session). If you are lucky, they will turn you down and not waste five to ten minutes of your allotted time on background facts. Of course, if you want to talk about the facts, just launch into them; this applies whether you are arguing first or last in the session. If the judges really do not want to hear about the facts, they will tell you to move on. If you absolutely do not want to present a summary of the facts, ask the court for permission to **dispense with a recitation of the facts**. State: "With the court's permission, may I dispense with a recitation of the facts?" This should help to remind the panel that you do not have enough time to dwell on facts.

As mentioned above, you should write a theme for your argument and interject it whenever the point you are arguing or the question you are answering touches on the theme. It helps you drive home points and tie things together in a memorable way. Your theme must fit the case and your facts, of course.

Be prepared to be interrupted and distracted with questions from the panel, so make sure you have in mind the few points you absolutely want to make in the argument, so that you can fight to return to them each time you are sidetracked.

IX. QUESTIONS FROM THE PANEL

Aside from showing up and being respectful in your argument, the most important part of oral argument is effectively dealing with and responding to the questions from the panel. These questions are your friends—in real life and in moot court. In real life, they represent the issues that the court is sticking on and needs to be resolved by you before they are willing to vote for your side. This is information you want them to have, so you should be happy to get questions. In moot court, the ability to answer questions well and still transition back to your argument and make points along the way is what you are being graded on. At the very least, questions indicate that the judges are listening to your argument. Welcome the questions; pray that your argument does not end without a single question being asked.

You must never show annoyance or frustration over being interrupted by a question. Do not ever snort or roll your eyes or fume when you are repeatedly interrupted. It is much more important to answer all the panel's questions than it is to get through your outline.

Decorum and respect require you to stop talking the instant a judge on the panel starts talking. Literally stop in mid-sentence—in mid-syllable if necessary.

If your time runs out during a question or during your answer to a question, the proper thing to do is to politely point out to the panel that your time is up and ask permission to complete your answer to the question. 99% of the time permission will be granted, but do not take this as an opportunity to drone on for five more minutes. Answer the question completely and correctly, but as succinctly as you can. Never bring up a new argument or issue in this "grace" period.

There is great value in answering questions quickly and succinctly, but do not leave out important information in the process. Complete answers are better than quick answers. Impress the judges with your candor.

If you can, during your answer (thinking on your feet, remember), try to plan a **transition** from the answer you are giving back to a point of your own that you want to make. For example:

> ➤ Question: What about the appellee's Internet cases? Do they answer this issue and go against you?
>
> Answer: Your Honor, the Internet cases relied on by my opponent do not cover the situation of transaction of business via the Internet. This is an issue of first impression in this jurisdiction and, I might add, in this country, and there is no controlling authority on this point. However, the analogous area of law covered in the controlling law of this jurisdiction is business conducted over telephone wires and electronically by facsimile and telephone and email. The cases on this point, including <u>Scullin</u>, definitively support my argument, because they hold . . .

Try once, and perhaps twice not to concede an important point even if it is clear that the judges are not buying your argument. It is especially important not to concede the ultimate issue of the case (are we liable or not, for instance)—never give in on the ultimate issue. But if one section of your argument definitely annoys the panel and you cannot convince them that you are right the first two times, **and** you have alternative arguments to rely on if you give in on that sticking point, then concede the point and move on. Do not keep beating the dead horse three and four times. If you do not concede, the panel may tell you to move on, and at that point you had better do what they tell you.

Oral argument judges tend to gravitate to certain types of questions, so we have prepared a chart of the most common questions and what you should try to do when answering them:

Form of Question	Why are they Asking it?	What you should do to Answer it
The Information Seeking Question - What is the holding of that case? When did that statute go into effect? Did your client telephone the authorities that night or not?	These are fairly mundane questions designed to illicit information about the record or the authorities. Usually, the court is seeking the information for a simple reason: they want to know the answer. Occasionally, a judge will ask this type of question to test your knowledge of the record or the authorities.	Be prepared to discuss the facts from the record and the authorities on the law. Re-read your own authorities and your opponent's authorities. Study the most important documents and testimony from the record. Make sure when you do your practice rounds that your "judges" quiz you on details such as these so that you will not be thrown when you get your first question of this kind.
The Slippery Slope Question - Aren't you opening the floodgates to ...? Aren't you asking the Court to set a dangerous precedent for ...? Aren't you asking the Court to plunge into uncharted and dangerous territory?	Appellate courts in general, and courts of last resort in particular, must be cognizant of the fact that they are not just deciding the single case before them but also are setting a rule and precedent for all future cases in that jurisdiction. They do not want to issue an overly broad opinion. They do not want to create a rule that might work fine in the case before them, but it might be applied to other situations to produce unintended negative results.	Be aware of the impact of your arguments on future cases. Take a long view and a broad view when you are drafting your brief and preparing for oral argument. Think of the ways your arguments might affect future cases, related and analogous areas of the law, and other kinds of parties (plaintiffs and defendants) than are in the case at hand. Be prepared to discuss how your arguments can and should be limited to the parties in the case at hand and other future parties just like them. Show how the impact of your arguments is limited to the case at hand, and only will control future situations just like the one at hand. Alternatively, if you think a broader precedent should be set, be prepared to discuss the parameters of the new rule you would have the court set and the public policies that are furthered by the new rule.

Form of Question	Why are they Asking it?	What you should do to Answer it
The Drawing the Line Question - How do we draw the line? Where do we need to draw the line?	Related to the above type, drawing the line here does not refer to an aggressive act to defy someone (<u>i.e.</u>, drawing a line in the sand), but rather to finding the place where the strength and logic of the arguments you are making ends. The court wants to know where your arguments should be cut off so that they can articulate reasons in their opinion why the precedent they will create will be limited to certain types of situations, such as the situation involving the parties in the case before them, and not to other situations. The court is searching for a way to write a more limited rule and precedent.	Once again, you should be prepared to discuss the reasonable, logical, and lawful boundaries of your arguments. How and why should your arguments be limited to the parties in the case at hand and other future parties just like them? Show how the impact of your public policy arguments is limited to the case at hand, and why the precedent to be set by the court need only control future situations just like the one at hand. Show how the logic of your arguments easily answers the issues in the case at hand but does not need to be extended further. Try to articulate standards for drawing the line that you have derived from the authorities, rather than simply describing individual factual situations from cases that are "good" and cutting off the situations of cases that are "bad." Alternatively, if you think a broader precedent should be set, be prepared to discuss the parameters of the new rule you would have the court set and the public policies that are furthered by the new rule.
The Roving Hypothetical - What if the plaintiff were a ...? What if a defendant came along and tried to ...? What if the next case involves a ...?	Law students probably are familiar with this kind of question because it is part and parcel of the Socratic method. Yet, sometimes they are surprised to find Socrates wearing a black robe and bearing down on them in an oral argument. The purpose of these questions is twofold:	Because the purpose of these questions is to try to test your ability to think on your feet, you might think it is hard to prepare for them. But, as with the categories of questions discussed above, you should prepare ahead of time by thinking through the impact of your arguments on future cases. Think of the ways

Form of Question	Why are they Asking it?	What you should do to Answer it
	first, the judges are testing you to see how well you are able to think on your feet; second, they may indeed be trying to find the limits of your argument—the future situations you think will be controlled by their decision and which will not be— which relates to the category of questions discussed above.	your arguments might affect future cases, related and analogous areas of the law, and other kinds of parties (plaintiffs and defendants) than are in the case at hand. The first answer to these questions should not be, "Well, your honor, that is not our case." After wrestling with a hypothetical or two, you may wind up having to bring the court back to the case at hand somewhat more skillfully—"Your honor, that might be true if the plaintiff were to . . . but in our case, plaintiff did not do X-Y-Z and so . . ." Do not get lost in a sea of hypotheticals. If the court is marching into stranger and stranger territory, calmly bring them back to reality and drive home that your arguments easily answer the issues raised by the case at hand. As with all of these question types, when you hold your practice sessions, have your "judges" drill you on hypotheticals. Have them force you to think on your feet so that you can become comfortable addressing strange and troubling hypotheticals while standing at the podium.
The "If we do X-Y-Z, do you lose?" Question - If we do not buy your argument that . . . do you lose? If we do not	This question is testing you on your knowledge of the law and your knowledge of the issues of the case and the arguments needed to answer them. The judges are looking	In order to address this type of question, you must be well versed in the law and the necessary steps in the pathway to victory. Very often there are multiple pathways to victory, but some paths are

Form of Question	Why are they Asking it?	What you should do to Answer it
accept your position on . . ., can you still win? If we rule against you on this claim, is your case finished?	to see if you have the ability to recognize alternative arguments that are alternative pathways to victory; or they want to see if you understand that in order to prevail, you must convince the court of at least some parts of your argument. This type of question also is used as a test to see how strongly you feel about some of the alternative arguments you are raising, and whether you are willing or able to abandon some claim or alternative argument you are raising.	harder to get through than others. Most of this book is devoted to getting you to think through your strongest arguments and present them first and foremost in your brief and oral argument. In preparing for oral argument, you must be certain of the necessary steps that the court must pass on in order for you to win. As for the alternative steps, you should be aware of those that can be abandoned with little or no impact on the rest of your arguments, and those whose abandonment might have a negative impact on your legal or public policy arguments elsewhere in the case. Do not concede an argument just because you have others—if you have raised it in your brief or oral argument, the judges will expect you to be able to defend it as far as it goes—but you must know the distance you are willing to go on alternative arguments, and do not dig in your heels past the necessary and logical end of your arguments when the panel is trying hard to knock you off your position. Defending your positions is expected, but being flexible about the pathway to victory when you can be flexible also is a virtue. Of course, you never should concede a necessary step on the pathway to victory.

Form of Question	Why are they Asking it?	What you should do to Answer it
The "What would you have this Court do?" Question - What would you like our opinion to say? What precedent would you have this court set? What is the rule of law that you think we should write on this issue? What cases are you arguing that we should overrule? What relief are you seeking here?	This type of question is asking you to clarify what you want the court to do. As an aid to drafting their opinion, the court may want to know what you think their opinion should hold, what prior cases should the court reconsider or overturn, and what new law should the court write as a precedent for future cases. At a minimum, the court is testing you to see if you understand the relief you are seeking, but more often, the court is testing you to see if you really understand what the court needs to do in order to rule in your favor.	Strangely enough, this type of question can be a real stumper in moot court. Having been alerted to it, you should prepare for oral argument by writing a page or an index card that lays out exactly what you would like the court to do. Do not just focus on the obvious—<u>e.g.</u>, please reverse the decision of the court of appeals—but also lay out the essentials of the opinion you think the court should write, and the precedent to be set, which discusses the factual situations that should be covered by the rule that you are stating should be applied, and the cases and other authorities that should be clarified or overruled by the court's decision. This type of inquiry really is not intended to be a trick question, and it will not be one if you have prepared for it ahead of time. Your response to the question may prompt the court to inquire further—why do you think the <u>Smith</u> case should be overruled?—but that is true of any solid response to a question.

X. OTHER CONSIDERATIONS

A. Winning points

You win points by proper argument and proper answers to questions. It is proper and customary to address points raised by your opponent in her brief, and to respond to things she said in her oral argument if you are going second. Do so in a professional way, countering the legal or factual points of your opponent's position. You do not win points by beating up and ridiculing your opponent or your opponent's brief or her argument, or by beating up the lower court.

B. Candor toward the court

Do not pretend to know things you do not really know. If you are asked about a case or a law review article that you never have heard of, confess that you are not familiar with it and ask for more details. If it is a major case that you should have found, you may be marked down for failing to uncover it in you research, but you cannot take the chance of being shown to be a liar and a cheat as well as a poor researcher by pretending that you are familiar with the case and that you are ready to discuss it.

If the panel asks about facts and details that are not in the record, it is appropriate to state that they are not in the record. If you are wrong, so much the worse for your score, but in most cases, the judge is trying to see if you know the limits of the facts that are in the record. Often a judge will not be as up to speed on the facts as she needs to be, and your job is not to assume that the judge knows something about the facts that you have forgotten.

If the question really is addressed to an inference from the facts, and you think it is a proper and logical inference, go ahead and address it as an inference—you actually might say, "That is logical to infer from the facts"—but be prepared to stop and remind the panel that the record does not expressly indicate that a fact exists. Inserting facts into the record is fraught with peril. The panel might call you on it, and your opponent might beat you up about it when they get up to argue second or on rebuttal. In most instances, the court will know when the record is silent on a certain topic, and they will expect you to respect this situation.

C. Finishing your argument

If you finish your outline and still have a minute or two left in your allotted time, the safest practice in moot court and even in real court is to simply conclude by reciting the relief you request (<u>e.g.</u>, "For these reasons, appellant respectfully requests the court to reverse the decision of the district court and remand this case for a new trial"). Then say, "Thank you, your honors," and move to sit down. If the panel is not through with you, they will jump in with more questions. They might do this even if your time has expired. Asking the panel if they have any additional questions before you sit down is a risky business. This invitation usually prompts a mean old question or two, usually the ones the judges were holding onto for a while, just waiting for a chance to dump them on you.

D. Pay attention to the stop sign.

As discussed above, if you still are talking when time runs out, ask for permission to finish your sentence or the point you were making (<u>e.g.</u>, "I see that my time is up. May I finish what I was saying?"), or simply ask for permission to conclude, which generally means stating your request for relief, as shown in the example in the paragraph above. If you were in the middle of answering a question, ask permission to finish your answer. Do not ignore the stop sign, and never use the permission granted by the court as an opportunity to continue your argument for a minute or more. It is especially bad to try to use the grace period to make a new point. The panel may decide to cut you off altogether, and that can be embarrassing.

E.   Wait and listen to the whole question.

Wait and listen to the whole question that is being asked. Do not start answering before the judge gets the whole question out just because you are sure you know where the question is going. Judges can give amazingly long and rambling questions, and sometimes they change their minds midstream and the question takes a turn at the end that you were not expecting. If at the end of the question you realize you have no idea what the judge wants you to answer, do not just launch into something; explain that you do not understand and politely ask the judge if he might clarify or restate the question.

F.   Give a direct "yes-no" answer to a "yes-no" question; then explain.

Give a direct answer to a "yes-no" question first (<u>i.e.</u>, answer "Yes" or "No"), then immediately proceed to explain your answer. Above all, do not attempt to dodge the substance of the question because you are uncomfortable with it or because you are not quite sure what answer the judge wants you to give. If you try to avoid answering, the judge simply will point out that you did not answer her question, and she will ask it again.

G.   Unexpected events

Do not be worried if you sneeze or cough or if you lose your train of thought in mid-sentence. The judges know you are human. Pick up where you can and move on. If you completely lose your entire train of thought, take a moment to try to get back on track, but if the thought is gone forever, simply confess to the court: "I'm sorry, I have completely forgotten what I was about to say." If you think a question was asked, but you do not remember what it was, ask: "Is there a question pending?" or "May I hear the question again?" or if you simply do not know what end is up, say "May I proceed with my next point?", and jump back into the argument wherever you can. A charley-horse of the brain sometimes happens, and these are appropriate ways to massage it out.

If a cellular phone or pager goes off in the room, it is best to ignore it. Let the judges comment on it if they choose. Your own cellular phone or pager never will go off because you **never** should have an activated telephone or pager with you in any courtroom or moot court room.

H.   Poker face

A good poker face is an asset for an oralist. If your opponent makes a great point, do not blanch and furiously start looking up things in your materials in a panic. Stare forward as if nothing has happened. If you realize that your argument is coming apart at the seams during questioning, keep a stiff upper lip and remain calm. Judges may not immediately know that your opponent has made a great point or that the panel has hit on the lynch pin of your case which, if removed, will pull the whole thing apart. But if your face reveals it, they will know it immediately.

Chapter 27

Strategies for Moot Court and Beyond

I. MOOT COURT COMPETITIONS

A. A taste of practice

Moot Court competitions simulate appellate practice in particular and all types of adversarial practice in general. By briefing your side and arguing it in person, you learn important skills in advocacy that will carry on into your practice if you do any kind of litigation or contested matter practice.

Moot court may be your first foray into a simulated litigation experience. Some law schools allow you the chance to experience this in your first year. Most law schools run intramural competitions and sponsor interscholastic moot court teams for second and third year students.

Moot court is a lot like the situation in real life of taking on an appeal, particularly if you are an appellate specialist in your firm or law office. Appellate specialists take on a case after it has been tried and someone has won and someone has lost. Most general practice litigators have the privilege of living with the case for a couple of years, then trying it, then losing it, before they get to take the appeal.

Certainly, the simulation does not exactly duplicate actual practice. For one thing, the record in moot court typically is extremely limited. An actual practitioner probably will get a large record to plow through. This record likely will consist of the entire court file with all of the pre-trial motions and orders in it, all the documents and things produced in discovery, deposition transcripts, trial preparation materials, a complete trial transcript along with all the exhibits entered into evidence and any that were refused, and any post-trial motions. Although some moot court directors tell us that they have at times gone so far as to buddy up with a prosecutorial appellate department, and from them they have obtained actual appellate files with complete "records" in criminal cases for their students to use in moot court classes—including, for example, little glassine pouches containing the actual bullets that killed the actual person whose homicide prompted the prosecution— most moot court records consist of only a few documents. You might get a stipulation of facts, an exhibit or two, and the orders and opinions of the lower courts.

Moot court forces you to engage in a process of in depth review of a client's case, to research and analyze that case as thoroughly as possible with no holds barred. You must write a significant document laying out your arguments, and stand on your feet and defend your client's position against an onslaught of questions. Rarely in law school do you get to work up a single case as thoroughly as you will in moot court. You will know your client's facts and the law that governs the case intimately. In the several months that you will work on your moot court problem, you will become an expert on the particular issues implicated by this client's case. This is what litigation practice is like.

If you wind up working on an appeal when you get out of law school, it will feel very much like your moot court experience. But moot court is not just a good experience for future appellate litigators. Much of your time in practice will involve researching and writing your analysis of legal issues, explaining your analysis orally, and defending it before your colleagues, clients, and the courts. Your first "oral arguments" in practice will not be in front of an appellate panel, but rather in an armchair in front of your boss's desk, as you explain your research to her, and she probes the strengths, weaknesses, and troubling spots of your analysis with questions. Corporate attorneys, banking and real estate attorneys, even trusts and estates attorneys all have to face this kind of probing and explain themselves to senior colleagues in their office when these colleagues want to explore their research and legal conclusions. Being able to calmly and competently think on your feet—even if you actually are sitting in an armchair—and address your colleagues' concerns will further your professional career at the firm.

Some of your toughest audiences will be your clients. One of the authors recalls that his toughest, most unpleasant oral arguments were before an in-house counsel at one of his firm's clients. She would drag him back and forth on his findings and recommendations, working him over like an old punching bag. He would welcome a chance to be vetted by the state supreme court before going back to her "court" again. Then, there were the oral arguments with clients over legal bills. Try explaining why it cost $10,000 to produce a 10 page research memorandum to an irate client some time. You will long for the patient attention of a moot court panel after going through that exercise once or twice. An experience in moot court will help you prepare for these and other real practice encounters.

B. Devil's advocacy skills

There are some twists in moot court that do not appear in real practice. You may be called upon to switch sides and argue "off brief"—argue the position you did not brief—during one or more of the oral argument rounds. This requirement will force you to look at the case as a whole, to evaluate the strengths and weaknesses of your brief position and the opposite side's position, and to make a convincing argument for either side.

Once again, this is not just a trick invented by law professors to amuse themselves and befuddle their students. We are not perpetuating a joke about lawyers who can talk out of both sides of their mouth, or trying to teach you that there is no such thing as truth or right and wrong in representing a client. The skill we are promoting is objectivity about your client's case. Objectivity is an asset to any litigator. Too often lawyers get caught up in their client's cases and fail to see the weaknesses and shortcomings until their opponents shove them in their faces at some critical juncture in the case. Being a good devil's advocate is an excellent skill to develop, and moot court often forces you to work on that skill.

If you are confident and skilled enough to present a coherent and credible argument for either side of the case, then you will have excellent skills for law practice. It takes a lot of thought, an in depth examination of all of the issues and all of the authorities, and sufficient attention to the policies and themes of the area of law to pull off this task in a coherent and credible manner. If you can be this objective in each of your cases, then you will be much sought after as a lawyer, even if the devil never pays you a retainer.

II. IDEAL TRAITS FOR A MOOT COURT PARTNER

The model for moot court success presented in this chapter relies on a team effort. The power of a good team effort can make a huge difference in moot court. Try to imagine the Lone Ranger without a Tonto; Batman without a Robin; George W. Bush without a Dick Cheney.

A moot court partner should not be a silent partner in this business. Both partners, or as many partners as are on the team, should plan to take on the same amount of work and the same amount of responsibility. It will do no good if one person on the team winds up doing 90% of the work. This will require careful selection of your teammates. It will not help you to figure out that you made a bad choice when you are several weeks into the drafting of the brief.

An ideal teammate should have the following traits:

A. Dedicated and hardworking

Find teammates who are as driven and devoted to excellence as you are. Your drinking buddies and best friends are not necessarily good candidates. Your boyfriend, girlfriend or significant other may or may not be a great candidate; you will have to decide.

Ask the following questions about any prospective partner: Have you and your prospective partner ever worked or studied well together on legal matters? Does she study as much as you do, or is she always several rounds ahead of you when you run into her at the local hangout after the library has closed?

Even a hard worker may not be a good match. Ask whether your work styles are compatible—do you like late nights and weekends and she likes early days and ruthless scheduling between classes? Is he an exercise fanatic?—"I can't work on the brief this weekend because I am in an Iron Man competition." Is she single and you are married with significant childcare responsibilities. All of this can affect your ability to work together.

B. Available

The hardest working student in the law school still is not an ideal partner if she never is available to sit down with you and discuss the brief or do a practice oral argument. Many of the best students are over-committed. If you are equally over-committed, and will have to carve out the time to edit and revise the brief through ruthless time management, then a workaholic partner may be ideal for you. But consider the downside if you have put moot court as your number one priority for the semester, and your partner is on a journal and has a part-time job and has several other high priority time commitments.

Note well that being on a journal and doing moot court and carrying a full load of classes is not an impossible task for an upper division law student. Do not shy away from an otherwise perfect match just because she wants to squeeze the most out of her second or third year of law school. The point is to pick a partner who you can work with. So, if you plan to spend twenty hours each week working on moot court, and there is no way your prospective partner can do that in her schedule, face up to that fact, discuss it, and figure out whether you can work with it. It is the unspoken resentment building up over time that destroys most moot court partnerships.

C. Balanced

Moot court competitions grade heavily on both brief writing and oral argument. Neither skill can be counted out of the equation when forming your team. If you have the luxury of having three or more team members, and only two need to argue at the competition, then you can cherry pick a team with a brief writing specialist and two oral argument specialists. Add to that an editing and proofreading specialist, and you will have a juggernaut that cannot be stopped. But in most intramural competitions and some interscholastic competitions, you only will have two members on the team, so each one must be adept at brief writing, editing, proofreading, and oral argument. A team with one good brief writer may do fine in the brief judging portion of the competition, but oral argument scores always are based on the scores of both oralists, so you will trip up in that portion of the competition if your team lacks two strong oralists.

You may be attracted to a partner because you have seen his dazzling oral argument skills. Some people's gifts in that area are obvious. It is harder to evaluate someone's writing and editing skills. Experience on a journal or law review may indicate something, as will disclosure of someone's first year legal writing grade. But the most important thing to do is ask: "Are you comfortable at brief writing, editing, and proof-reading?" "Have you had success doing these things in law school?" You may be a great brief writer, editor and proofreader, but unless you plan to carry the bulk of the writing load, and the responsibility for that part of the grade, be wary of persons who disclaim that they really are only in it for the oral argument experience.

Not everyone is able effectively to criticize legal writing, but it is hard to test this skill except under actual practice. Certainly, a partner who is or was a law journal editor or a legal writing teaching assistant has the resume credentials to do a better job at this task. It would be of great interest to us to see how a potential partner would edit our own work—and not just a trashy throw-away piece of work, but something with real effort put into it. Exchanging writing for mutual editing is a lot to ask a potential partner, but you would learn valuable things about your partner in the process. And having a process to learn these things is better than never knowing them at all.

D. Good match for your strengths and weaknesses

A good partner should complement your team, not throw it out of kilter. If you are a better oralist than a brief writer, you should try to find someone who is a great brief writer, and at least a decent oralist. Two great oralists with no brief writing and editing skills will look good at the arguments, but rarely can progress to the advanced rounds. The same goes for two excellent brief writers and editors who cannot stand up and do a decent oral argument. You may win the best brief award, but you will be going home from the competition on Friday afternoon instead of late Saturday night or Sunday morning.

There is room for different styles of oral argument. You can match two oralists who have very different argument styles, as long as each style is effective and will score well based on the criteria laid out in this book in the chapter on oral argument. But two brief writers with very different writing styles may be a problem. If you are a flamboyant writer and your partner is low key, you may have to decide whose style will give way when you get around to the editing process and are striving to make a single coherent document out of the two parts of the brief each of you has drafted. Are you willing to go toe to toe over whether that paragraph will remain in section II(B) on page 18 of the brief and still walk away friends?

Having someone on the team who is a meticulous editor, proofreader, Bluebook checker, and grammarian will be a great asset to a moot court team—as long as everyone knows their work will be ruthlessly edited and corrected. Being able to take criticism is a must in this process. As a potential partner on a moot court team, you must ask yourself whether you can you give and receive constructive criticism on writing and oral argument in a way that will not drive you and your partners apart forever. Our advice is to drop your ego at the door. This is a team effort to produce a team brief and to maximize the team's oral argument performance. It is not about you, it is about the team, and there is no "I" and no "U" in the word "Team."

III. INTERPRETING MOOT COURT RULES

More than a few tears of frustration are shed trying to figure out some of the rules that arise in intramural and interscholastic moot court competitions. The following is our take on some of the more common and troublesome rules we have seen. Be aware that this is *only* our personal interpretation—the final arbiter of any competition's rules is the organization or committee that sponsors and runs the competition and writes the rules. Our interpretation is based on our own experience in reading rules, trying to comply with rules, and seeing the kinds of penalties that are handed down for non-compliance. It certainly is possible that we may be wrong on some of these rules, but we believe our reading would be better than average.

A. Read the rules

The first advice we can give you is to read the rules. In fact, do not just read them, parse them. Pour over them. Outline and summarize them, and discuss them as a team.

There is a hidden educational aspect of moot court competitions: they can teach you the importance of reading and interpreting rules. Litigation in the real world is full of rules—local rules, administrative orders of the court, rules of procedure, standing orders, and more. Failing to follow these rules will quicky cause your case to be jammed up, and this will embarrass you in front of your opponent, the court, and your client. Failing to follow moot court rules will cause you to incur penalties, and when you lose points that way, you really are taking yourself out of contention in the competition. As recently as November 2000, the last time one of the author's law school hosted the regional of the Association of the Bar of the City of New York's National Moot Court competition, he observed that a Best Brief contender was edged out of the title by a competitor who scored lower on the substance of the brief, but had less penalty points than the contender. We are sure that this happens frequently in competitions across the country each year.

B. United States Supreme Court rules

It is very popular for competitions to adopt the Rules of the Supreme Court of the United States regarding briefs. If your competition has adopted these rules, pay attention to the following:

1. Rules on typesetting and printing

The Supreme Court rules require briefs to follow strict typesetting and printing rules, to be permanently and professionally bound, and to use a reduced paper size of 6 X 9¼ inches (more like a "Monarch" sized stationery page than a standard 8½ X 11 inch page). See U.S. Supreme Court Rule 33.1(a, d). Most competitions have recognized the impracticality of these rules, and have opted out of them. But if your competition has adopted the Supreme Court rules and has not seen fit to opt out of the printing rules, you should immediately write to the sponsors to request clarification of the rule. Otherwise, you may find yourself looking for a commercial printer to produce your multiple copies of the brief at great expense to you or your law school.

2. Brief covers

The brief cover rules for the U.S. Supreme Court are complicated only because there are a lot of colors to choose from. To make things simple, you are looking for the brief color for a brief on the merits, and you want the color for the petitioner or the respondent. Petitioner's brief on the merits is light blue, and respondent's brief on the merits is red. See U.S. Supreme Court Rule 33.3(e, f). The rules say "light red," but we do not know what a light red is, and neither will the guy at Kinkos®. We know the Supreme Court does not mean pink, and we assume you will not interpret "red" to mean maroon or deep crimson.

3. Brief length

Look at the page limits in U.S. Supreme Court Rule 33.3(e, f): if your brief is commercially printed, it can be 50 pages long! If it is typed and double-spaced, it can be 110 pages long!! That is why competitions invariably will write their own page limitation rules.

C. Page limits and typeface rules

There are a number of ways to express page limitations. The idea is to make sure everyone has a level playing field and turns in a brief with no more than a certain number of words. You can imagine the chaos if everyone could decide their line spacing, text size, characters per inch, and so on.

If page limits are used, they usually are straightforward. There most often will be a limit on the number of pages you can devote to the argument section, and sometimes a limit on the number of pages for the other parts of the brief, or a limit on the total length of the brief.

The trickier parts are the rules that prevent you from cramming fifty pages of material into the allotted thirty pages of argument. You may see a "characters per inch" rule, such as "type at no more than 12 characters per inch," or "type size not capable of producing more than 12 characters per inch." Competitors that trip up on this rule usually do so because they use a non-uniformly spaced font. Here is a word to the wise: Courier is a uniformly spaced font; Times Roman and CG Times are not. What this means is that in Courier font, every character and space between characters is the same width. If you set the type size of 10 or 12, you can measure how many characters you will get per inch on your printout. In Times Roman and CG Times, certain characters are narrower than others; t's and f's and i's and l's are especially narrow. (Get out a ruler and compare the length of this word in both fonts if you do not believe us: Illustration (Courier) and Illustration (Times Roman)). If you use Times Roman or CG Times, you will not know how many characters per inch you will get when you use 12 point font. More particularly, under the language of the rule, 12 point font size in Times Roman or CG Times is capable of producing more than 12 characters per inch. Brief graders are attuned to this fact, and they probably will assess a penalty if they see Times Roman or CG Times anywhere in your document, even if you increase the font size to try to compensate for the uneven spacing. If the rules of your competition have a limit on the characters per inch your font can generate, use Courier to be on the safe side, not Times Roman or CG Times.

Some competitions avoid all of this font measuring by setting a limit on the number of words that can be in the Argument section. You will have to use a spell checker or some other word processor function to do the counting unless you want to go word by word and count them yourself. We suspect that the brief graders will not sit and count each word either, so you probably will have to turn in a copy of your brief on a floppy disk or by email attachment so that the graders can run it through a program that counts the words.

Line spacing also is regulated. Many competitions use double spacing as the rule; others use a limit of so many lines of text per vertical inch, or so many lines of text per page, which usually comes out to mean double-spacing. We can tell you from experience in grading papers that when you cheat and try to use 1.9 or 1.8 spacing or anything less than 2.0 spacing, it is painfully obvious to the grader, and you will get penalized for it.

The "shrink to fit" function on many word processing programs—used to "shrink to fit" your argument into the 30 pages allocated for such—merely compresses the line spacing, font size, and kerning (spacing between characters) so that the text will fit the number of pages you tell it to fit. All of this tweaking stands out like a sore thumb when the brief grader reads several correctly formatted briefs in a row, and then gets to the "shrunken to fit" brief. You will be penalized for this.

D. Binding

Binding of briefs usually is covered in the rules of the competition because no one wants to go through the requirements of the U.S. Supreme Court rules. Sometimes a specific binding is identified, such as "three staples on the left margin." Other times, it will be more cryptic, such as "bound in a volume." We read "bound in a volume" to mean some kind of nonremovable binding that creates a booklet, such as tape binding. Velo-binding might satisfy this requirement. We do not think it necessarily includes spiral binding or comb binding, but a lot of people disagree with us on this. In any event, if there is a certain kind of binding that is identified as acceptable in the rules, go with that kind of binding rather than taking a chance of being wrong, even if that means using three staples.

E. Outside assistance

The rules of moot court competitions typically limit the kind of help you can get when writing the brief, and sometimes even when preparing for oral argument. There are at least three ways of going about this: first is the absolute prohibition on assistance; second is the prohibition of "direct" or "specific" assistance; and third is the allowance of assistance on specific topics, such as allowing assistance on issues, organization, and strategy, but prohibiting assistance on research, brief writing, editing and proofreading.

In the absence of a rule limiting outside assistance, presumably, you can talk to anyone about anything, and use any material you find, as long as you do not plagiarize. We never have seen an interscholastic competition that did not put some limit on outside assistance. Some intramural competitions may allow open, unabated assistance, but we doubt it.

An absolute prohibition is easy to understand—do not look for assistance from anyone, and do not take any.

We take "no direct assistance" or "no specific assistance" to mean direct or specific assistance in researching, writing, editing, and proofreading the brief, and direct assistance in answering or organizing a response to the very issues presented by the problem. You cannot have a faculty member review your draft of the brief and offer advice on how to revise it, nor can you ask them how to complete your research to pump up your brief with better authorities. But this rule should not prohibit general questions about the subject matter of the problem, or questions about the area of law in which the problem arises, or general advice and assistance about brief writing in the area of law in which the problem arises. This does allow a significant gray area to tread in, and it might be easy to stray from the gray into the black (or red, as it were).

> ➤ *Example:* If the problem involved the effect of the 1999 OPRAH amendments to ERISA (we made up these amendments—do not get excited) regarding Medicare disclosure requirements for home health care workers who follow the teachings of television's Dr. Phil, we would find it a violation of the "no specific assistance" rule to approach an ERISA expert (faculty member or practitioner) and ask, "In general, in what ways are home health care workers affected by the new Medicare disclosure requirements in the 1999 OPRAH amendments to ERISA." We would find it acceptable to ask about the OPRAH amendments in general, or the process of Medicare disclosure in general, but not the process as currently applied to home health care workers.

Other competitions liberally allow outside assistance. For example, the Jessup International Law Moot Court Competition states in its rules:

All research, writing and editing must be solely the product of Team members. However, faculty members, coaches, librarians and other research professionals, and other Team advisors may provide advice to a Team. Such advice shall be limited to: general discussions of the issues; suggestions as to research sources; consultations regarding oral advocacy technique; the location of legal sources; general legal research methods; general commentary on argument organization and structure, the flow of arguments, and format; and advice during Competition elimination rounds as to pleading option or similar strategy.

Philip C. Jessup International Law Moot Court Competition, 2005 Official Rules, Rule 2.4.

No one can draft and edit your brief (the "memorial," as it is called in Jessup) for you, or tell you how they would answer the problem, but they can help you with almost anything else.

Some competitions, such as the National Health Law Moot Court Competition, have a rule that states, "No participants shall procure a copy of any pleadings or papers actually filed in any trial or appeal of any case upon which the record is founded. Contact with the actual litigants or their attorneys is prohibited." 2004-2005 National Health Law Moot

Court Competition, Official Rules, Rule 8(a). This would seem to us to be a dead give-away that the sponsors of the competition use an actual lawsuit as the basis of their problem. The rule creates an interesting "Catch 22" situation—the rule does not prohibit the procurement of materials from a case that the problem is not based on, but how do you know if the materials you procured from an actual case are from the actual case the problem is based on unless you procure the materials and read them? We do not know how to answer that one. We suppose the sponsors could come right out and tell you, this case is based on *Jones v. Smith*, 234 F.3d 123 (9th Cir. 2001), but we do not think they do this. In any event, the rule reminds you to look beyond case reporters and treatises in the preparation of your case.

IV. ANALYZING A MOOT COURT PROBLEM

A. Careful reading

The best advice we can give you about your moot court problem is to read it carefully. Yes, this should go without saying, but we have read enough briefs and seen enough oral arguments to know that students do not always get the facts right, whether they be the historical facts that led up to the lawsuit, or procedural facts about how the case wound its way through the court system to get to the court where the problem is set.

Some people like to read through a problem and highlight parts that interest them, much like they are reading a case for class. We like to take notes as we read and re-read the problem, and then write up a summary of the entire case—historical facts and procedural facts—before moving on to the next step. Summarizing and synthesizing the facts should force you to come to grips with them, and the process of writing often reveals gaps or areas that you glossed over on your earlier readings. All of this is time well spent in the process of getting ready to research and analyze the problem.

B. Handling the facts

Once you have read through the problem a few times, it is time to get serious with the facts. The facts determine what you can argue, how you can argue it, and the strength of the various arguments you can make. Facts dictate the law that determines the case—is it a contracts problem, a torts problem, a tax problem, or a combination of several areas?— the way the law is going to be applied to the case, and the play of the public policies around the area of law you are briefing. In order to succeed at moot court, you must be adept at organizing and marshaling the facts that support your client, and at explaining, defusing, and otherwise handling the facts that hurt your client.

1. Put the facts in chronological order.

In order to start the process of mastering the facts of the problem, you first should put all of the facts in chronological order. The problem may not present the facts in this kind of sequence. As lawyers, we often look at facts in chronological order, and getting the facts down in date sequence probably will help you make sense of the case.

The significance of certain facts may jump out at you more readily when you put them next to other facts that happened at the same time. Gaps in the factual information provided to you may become obvious when you lay out the facts in date sequence. At the very least, putting the facts in chronological order will produce an orderly version of the facts to refer to in later stages of the process.

2. Separate good facts from bad facts.

The next step is to separate the good facts from the bad. You may not be able to complete this task your first time through because your research and analysis into the law will often reveal that certain facts are indeed bad, and others are good. You can start with your gut feeling about the facts, and then return to the facts again and again as you are researching the law to make sure you have the good and the bad facts straight.

The point of this exercise is to compile those facts that you will want to emphasize in the statement of the facts and throughout the brief, and those that you will want to downplay or put your best spin on. Moot court writing is adversarial writing, and you should never be satisfied with a complete chronological approach to the facts in your writing and argument unless you are in that rarest of situations where all the facts seem to go your client's way.

3. Make reasonable and logical inferences from the facts.

It is appropriate to draw reasonable and logical inferences from known facts. What you must avoid is drawing inferences that are too extreme and are unsupported by the facts. This is the equivalent of inventing facts that are not in the record. The judges certainly will mark you down for inventing facts, and your standing similarly will be discounted if you try to stretch the facts to the breaking point.

Be conservative and draw only the most reasonable and logical inferences from the facts:

➤ *Example:*   If the facts indicate that the Maryland Board of Healing Arts describes two hours as the average time for a surgical procedure, and a certain doctor did the procedure in one hour, it would be a logical inference to state that the doctor operated "quickly." It is completely safe (and obvious) to point out that the doctor did the procedure "in half the time provided by the Maryland Board of Healing Arts."

What would not be reasonable is to infer that the doctor "rushed" the procedure. "Rushing" implies a state of mind, and nothing in the facts we have revealed shows the doctor's state of mind. Performing the procedure in half the time is not automatically rushing; you do not have enough facts to make that inference. Perhaps the doctor is the most skilled surgeon in the state, and twenty experts would testify that she ought to take half as much time to do the procedure because of her expertise.

You also cannot draw the inference that the doctor was "negligent" or "reckless." Aside from the problem that these are legal conclusions, you do not have enough facts about the doctor, her state of mind, her expertise, and a host of other factual information that would affect that inference. All you can say is that she performed the operation "quickly" and "in half the time provided by the Maryland Board of Healing Arts."

Missing information from the record necessarily will limit the kind of inferences you logically can draw. As stated above, in moot court, your record will be more limited than in a typical real life litigation. Do not get caught up in a spirit of advocacy and fill in details that affect the logical limits of the facts in the record.

➤ *Example:*   If the record states that the defendant had five alcoholic drinks in a two hour period, you should not automatically draw the inference that the defendant became intoxicated. Intoxication depends on a host of factors (such as the defendant's weight, percentage of fatty tissue to lean tissue in the body, whether the alcohol was consumed with other food or beverages that might limit its rate of absorption into the body). The concept of intoxication also depends on the context; do you mean too intoxicated to drive, or too intoxicated to sit in a chair and watch television? You can state exactly what the facts state: "the defendant drank five alcoholic drinks in two hours."

If you know the blood alcohol content of the defendant, you then can combine this with other facts to make further inferences. For example, if the record indicates that the defendant had a blood alcohol content of 0.12, you can perform research that might indicate that "defendant's blood alcohol level was above the legal limit for operating a motor vehicle in all fifty states of the United States."

4. Group the facts by topic and subject matter and look for themes.

The next step is to group the facts by topic and subject matter so that you can evaluate what the potential themes of the case will be. The theme of the case is different from the legal issues raised by a case and the subject matter of the applicable law that governs these legal issues. Themes are a rhetorical device, designed to reinforce your arguments and persuade the reader to accept your position and vote for your client. A theme is used in the brief and in oral argument as a focal point to tie together the facts of the case, the legal arguments you will make, and the policy issues you will argue. Thus, you cannot have a theme that lacks one of the essential elements of facts, law, and public policy. The facts you are studying will reveal potential, viable themes. You cannot superimpose a popular theme onto your case if the facts will not support the theme.

> ➤ *Example:* One potential theme in a business dispute over the performance of a contract is that the larger company took advantage of the smaller company, and exerted improper pressure and used abusive tactics rather than performing the contract in good faith. When you begin to group the facts by topic, you notice that the two companies had a long working relationship, and the relationship was punctuated by fairness and equity at every point discussed in the record. Your theme is doomed—there is no point to asserting a factually unsupportable theme to the case, because sooner or later your theme is going to be shot down by your opponent, and the brief grader and oral argument judges will mark you down for this.
>
> On the other hand, if the problem throws you some bones that make it look like your company was trying to do business with a Microsoft-type giant or other functional monopolizer, it would behoove you to pursue a theme that the reason the court should accept your legal interpretation of the contract and your argument that the contract was breached is because your opponent is an arrogant giant that uses its superior size and market position to wrest improper demands from its contractual partners. This argument uses the facts to bring the public policy against monopolizers and unfair competitors into view, and thus to cast a favorable light on your legal arguments regarding the contract and its performance.

Themes are the sunshine and pleasant breeze of legal rhetoric that make the brief graders and oral argument judges want to hang out in the backyard of your argument. Cheap window dressing that is not held up by solid facts in the record will crash down on your head, and cause these same brief graders and judges to walk out on your party early, leaving low scores behind. Thus, a careful review of the facts that are available for various topics and themes is essential.

5. Return to the facts again and again.

You will need to return to the facts at every stage of the moot court process: spotting the issues, researching the issues, analyzing the case, drafting and revising the brief, and preparing for oral argument. The facts determine the issues, and if you think that an issue might be present, you must confirm that the facts exist to create an appropriate question for appellate review, as discussed further in the section that follows. At the research and analysis stage, certain facts that you reviewed at the initial run through will take on new meaning and new importance to your case. At the drafting stage, you must return to the facts again and again for the drafting of the statement of facts or statement of the case, and to confirm and provide citations to details that your are using in your argument section. At the oral argument stage, you must determine which facts and themes you will present first and will return to in answers to questions and transitions from answering questions back to your argument.

All of this means that your initial review of the facts is only an initial review. The facts are too important to the moot court process to allow you to visit them once and learn them wrong. You should be reciting the facts in your sleep before the moot court competition is over.

C. Issue spotting

Issue spotting is the next important task in the moot court process. In some competitions, it can be a relatively straightforward process. The problem might set out the issues as "questions presented" as part of the packet. In other competitions, the notice of appeal or petition for certiorari in the packet might set out the issues in clear and straightforward language. In these instances, there is no guesswork involved.

The authors of moot court problems for intramural or interscholastic competitions often do not want you to guess at the issues either, so they too will take great pains to write a problem that makes the issues obvious. When we say obvious, we mean they will write one or two lower court opinions for the record that state two issues as Roman numerals one and two in the lower court opinions, and they will attempt to create documents and other factual sources for the record that only can lead to those two issues. If you miss those two issues, you are done for, and there will be little hope for you.

On occasion—and perhaps too often for comfort's sake—the author intentionally or unintentionally obscures the issues, or intentionally or unintentionally allows issues into the record that can be spotted and briefed. The record may leave the door open for a jurisdictional argument, or a preservation of issues argument, or reveal a constitutional defect in the proceedings. The material that follows will help you to spot these issues and to determine whether and to what extent they present questions that should be briefed and argued on review.

1. Harmless error, appealable error, preservation, and clear error

Not every error or mistake that occurred in the trial court presents a proper issue for review. No one is guaranteed a perfect trial or perfect handling of their case in the trial court. The doctrine of **harmless error** provides that if an error caused no harm to your client, you cannot raise it on appeal. If a jury instruction was requested and not given, the instruction that was given in its place must be more favorable to the party that prevailed on that issue; if the instruction given was less favorable, or your client actually prevailed on this particular claim or defense, you cannot appeal from this error. If a witness was barred from testifying, but the substance of the witness's testimony presented in an offer of proof obviously duplicates testimony from other witnesses that were allowed to testify, then the barring of this one witness may be harmless error.

In general, an issue must have been raised and preserved in order for it to be an **appealable error**. If you never asked the trial court to do something, and the court winds up not doing it, you cannot later raise the court's failure to do that thing as an error. Thus, if you did not request a continuance to allow a witness to appear, or did not ask for leave to amend a petition to insert a new claim, you cannot later complain on appeal that a continuance was not granted to you and the witness did not appear, or that your additional claim was not heard. In general, an issue must have been raised and the trial court must have had the opportunity to address the issue and correct the mistake in order for the error to be raised on appeal.

Preservation is a trickier concept. Some errors require a formal procedure to preserve the issue, such as a defect in venue or personal jurisdiction, which must be raised through the timely assertion of a motion to dismiss, and not later abandoned by a general appearance in the case without preserving the error in the pleadings. Evidentiary issues raised in motions in limine or during trial generally must be preserved by the aggrieved party through a formal statement on the record and sometimes with an offer of proof that is received into the record but not presented to the jury. In many jurisdictions, the rules of procedure require a litigant to raise all points of error in a post-trial motion for new trial in order for them to be preserved for appeal.

If the record presented in your moot court problem is complete enough to make a determination whether the issues have been preserved or not, you should use the record to prove that each issue you will argue was properly raised and preserved. However, your moot court problem may prevent you from resolving these questions because it may not give you any indication whether or not an issue was properly preserved at or before trial. Some moot court problems consist of a trial level opinion and an appellate level opinion, with nothing before or in between. One or both of the opinions may make a catch all saving phrase to the effect that "This issue was properly raised at trial and preserved for appeal," in which case the author of the problem wants you to forget about objection and preservation as issues in the case. But the problem might be silent. Unless the issue is one of venue or personal jurisdiction (discussed in the next section), if the issue is discussed by both courts, you most likely are to presume that the issue is preserved for review even if there are no facts in the problem that expressly spell this out.

An exception to the objection and preservation requirements is the doctrine of **clear error** or **plain error**. If an error is so egregious that it should have been taken up by the court *sua sponte* and a mistrial ordered, the fact that no party raised the issue in the trial court does not bar it from being raised on appeal for the first time. A potential clear error is not subtle. It should leap out at you from the record, and cry out for justice. Even if you think you have found one, research the applicable law of your jurisdiction to make sure that this type of error has been identified as clear error or plain error before. Appellate court judges and moot court judges will not readily accept an issue as clear error or plain error if you do not have the goods to prove to them that it is one.

2. Jurisdictional errors in the trial court

You should always review the jurisdiction and venue of the trial court over the subject matter of the action and the parties to the action, because improper jurisdiction can present an appealable issue. You will recall from legal research and writing and civil procedure that a court must have three kinds of power in a case:

- subject matter jurisdiction over the claims raised in the action;
- personal jurisdiction over the parties to the action effectuated by proper service of process; and
- venue over the place where the action occurred or arose, or over the parties or the subject matter of (the *res* or property involved in) the suit.

A clever author of a moot court problem may sneak a jurisdictional issue into the problem. A not so clever author might let one in without knowing it. It will most likely be a problem with the subject matter jurisdiction of the trial court, because questions regarding personal jurisdiction and venue must be raised and properly preserved or they are waived, and if the author has gone to the trouble of putting enough information into the record to indicate that a personal jurisdiction or venue issue is preserved, then it should be obvious to you that the issue is present and appealable.

3. Appellate court jurisdictional issues

You also should verify that the appellate courts that heard the case had proper jurisdiction over the case. Appellate courts can only take jurisdiction over an action by three means:

- extraordinary writ,
- interlocutory appeal, or
- appeal after final judgment.

A petition for an extraordinary writ may be filed at any time, and if the record indicates that an extraordinary writ was issued and the lower court was required to answer, then there is little else to stick up the works in the form of appellate procedural error. Your moot court problem may or may not include the petition for a writ, the response of the opponent, and any orders requiring an answer or issuing a preliminary writ. The problem may simply state that the petition for a writ is granted, in which case there is little to question in the way of appellate jurisdiction.

Interlocutory appeals also may be filed at any time. In federal court, 28 U.S.C. § 1292(b) provides that the trial court may certify one or more issues for immediate review, and the appellate court may accept review of the certified issues under Fed. R. App. P. 5. This is a popular way for the author of a moot court problem to get two discreet issues of law sent up for review.

If your problem involves an interlocutory appeal, you should look to see that the requirements of 28 U.S.C. § 1292(b) and Fed. R. App. P. 5 have been met. At a minimum, the district court opinion should have stated that the court's "order involves a controlling question of law as to which there is substantial ground for difference of opinion and that an immediate appeal from the order may materially advance the ultimate termination of the litigation." 28 U.S.C. § 1292(b). However, the author of the moot court problem may not have given you enough information to resolve the question. If the problem indicates that an intermediate level appellate court took up and resolved an issue arising from an interlocutory order of the trial court, it probably is safe to presume that the requirements of the rule and statute were met.

An appeal after final judgment must be initiated by a timely filed notice of appeal, as per the requirements of Fed. R. App. P. 3 and 4, or their state rule equivalents. The author of your moot court problem may inadvertently have allowed an untimely appeal to have been filed by not being careful with the dates in the record. This almost assuredly was unintentional, because the issue of timeliness is jurisdictional, and if the appeal is untimely, there is nothing the appellate court can do to help the parties out. Your moot court argument would end right then and there. If you figure out that the dates in the problem indicate that an appeal was not timely, contact the sponsor of the moot court program and request a clarification of the dates. You most likely will get a clarification.

A shrewd author might allow an issue as to whether a judgment was final or not when the notice of appeal was filed. If this was inadvertent, then the record probably will be corrected rather than allowing this defect to destroy the entire appeal. If you suspect that a claim or defense of a party was not resolved by the order and judgment of the trial court, you should request clarification, and if none is given, you should research the definition of finality in your jurisdiction to see if your author has created a dispositive issue for briefing and argument.

In addition, check the record to see that the steps required for the filing and docketing of the appeal appear to have been followed in the case, but do not be surprised if the record is silent on these facts. Authors of moot court problems rarely attempt to confound law students by inserting an issue regarding the filing or docketing of the appeal, so if the record says nothing, assume that this means the problem intends no issue regarding filing or docketing. Only worry about these factors if the author inserts facts into the record that affirmatively indicate that a filing or docketing was botched.

There may be a subject matter jurisdiction issue in the appellate court. An appellate court's subject matter jurisdiction is governed by the applicable constitution, statutes, or court rules of the jurisdiction. An example of this is the rule set out in 28 U.S.C. § 1295 that provides that all appeals from patent cases litigated in the U.S. District Courts are to be heard by the U.S. Court of Appeals for the Federal Circuit, rather than the court of appeals that would normally entertain appeals from the district court in question. If you stumble on an appeal from a patent case that is filed in the U.S. Court of Appeals for the

Eighth Circuit, you have a bona fide appellate court subject matter issue to research and brief.

The courts of last resort most often have limited jurisdiction whereby parties seeking to have a case heard in these courts must **request a transfer** to the court or **petition** the court for the issuance of a **writ of certiorari**, or **writ of mandamus**, or other writ, to allow the case to be heard by the court. If the record does not indicate that one of these procedures was used to get to the court, but the problem indicates that the current appeal is pending in the court of last resort, it is probably attributable to poor attention to detail on the part of the writer of the problem. You can point it out in your brief and oral argument, but the record probably will not contain enough information to actually argue the effect of the omission.

4. Constitutional defects of justiciability

There are several constitutional law doctrines regarding the justiciability of actions:

Case or Controversy: In federal court, Article III of the U.S. Constitution provides that the courts shall only hear cases or controversies, which means that if a party has yet to be injured by the conduct of the opponent, the case should not be heard. Federal courts are not to issue advisory opinions. There are some kinds of cases that present a clear enough picture of the type and amount of injury that will occur that they can be heard prior to the actual injury's occurrence, such as an imminent breach of a contract or licensing agreement, and there are some procedures, such as temporary restraining orders and preliminary injunctions, that might stop the impending injury in its tracks. But if someone has jumped the gun and gone to court before an injury has taken place, it is worth researching the issue to see if a case or controversy is present. The same defense might apply in a state court, but you should research the constitutional and procedural law of the jurisdiction to be certain (if the problem identified an actual state, as opposed to the "State of Apex" or other fictional jurisdiction).

Ripeness: Ripeness is related to the concept of case or controversy. If the injury complained of in the action is speculative, and has not occurred and may not occur, a ripeness issue may exist.

Mootness: Although moot court is the name of the game, if the cause of action and the injury, and the position of the parties in the underlying action cannot be affected or resolved by the order of the court, then the problem is moot and should not be litigated. There are some exceptions, such as an injury that is capable of repetition yet evading review. See Roe v. Wade, 410 U.S. 113 (1973). If it looks like the court's handling of the case might be futile no matter who prevails in the case, then you should research the mootness issue for possible inclusion in your brief and argument.

Standing: The standing of the plaintiff to bring the action has got to be the sleeper issue of the century for moot court oral argument judges. No competitor ever thinks it is an issue, because those old Supreme Court cases on standing—Baker v. Carr, 369 U.S. 186, 204 (1962); Flast v. Cohen, 392 U.S. 83, 101 (1968); Sierra Club v. Morton, 405

U.S. 727, 732 (1972); and others—do not make any impact on you when you cover them in two or three class periods in your first year civil procedure or constitutional law courses. Nevertheless, in real life, judges get very agitated when they suspect that someone is trying to stand as a private attorney general, or assert the rights of others by assignment or by some other actual or implied legal relationship, or is trying to sue as a third party beneficiary of an agreement. You should spend some time thinking about standing, and if there is any indication in the problem that the plaintiff was not the person directly and personally harmed by the action of the defendant, you should research and resolve the issue in your brief and oral argument.

D. Appellant's determination of which issues to raise

After the issue spotting and research is done, students briefing the appellant's or petitioner's or applicant's position still might want to weed out their issues before they start to draft the brief. This is particularly necessary if you think you have found five or more main issues to argue. Moot court is supposed to simulate actual appellate practice, and in actual appellate practice, when you are evaluating the possible errors committed by the lower court, quality is far more important than quantity.

The authors of moot court problems typically intend to present two significant issues to brief—often identified by upper-case Roman numerals I and II in the court opinions found in the record—and most authors probably hope that there are no other issues suggested by the facts. Although two main issues is the norm, occasionally, a moot court problem will present three or more main issues. We discussed above how an author may intentionally or inadvertently insert a jurisdictional or constitutional issue into the problem. When additional issues are suggested by the facts of the problem that are not part of or related to the issues that were discussed in the problem in the sections under the big Roman numerals, then you will have to decide if these side issues are worth briefing. If you have undertaken the analysis described in this chapter, and you have determined that the issue is an appealable error (e.g., it was raised and preserved), and is not harmless error, then the issue should be briefed.

If, however, you are in a situation where it appears obvious that the author only intended for there to be two issues, and you are stuck on a third, an appellant safely can jettison a side issue as long as it has absolutely no bearing on the main issues that are presented in the problem. We can say this, because every appellate court judge and every worthy appellate practitioner will tell an appellant that less is more. It is better not to go fishing for issues or sub-issues to write about. In moot court, as in actual appellate practice, you will do much better if you find and argue the two horrible, unforgivable errors that are set out in the record, rather than "finding" and briefing a dozen somewhat troublesome errors that arguably might be raised. In real life, certain litigators will throw up as many assertions of error as they can think of, hoping that one will stick and cause the case to be overturned. This is a tactic of desperation, not of effective advocacy. Moot court judges are sensitive to this tactic, and they will not want you to develop such bad habits, so they will punish you on your score if you let a quantity of "also ran" errors drown out the effectiveness of your arguments on the main issues of the case.

However, appellants should make sure that the "side issue" you are thinking about discarding does not have an impact on the analysis of the other, main issues in the case. The validity of a signature on a contract in a licensing case, or inconsistent testimony about the road conditions in a car accident case may not stand alone as separately appealable issues, but they might have an impact on the main issues of liability and defenses to liability in the case. If the side issue has a direct bearing on the "main" issues, it should not be discarded, but instead you should brief it. You may wind up briefing it as a sub-issue or threshold issue that leads up to one or more of the ultimate issues in the case. Err on the side of briefing an issue that has a direct bearing on the main issues if you are in doubt.

If you find three or more issues, and the problem does not clue you in on how to split them up, you may have to figure out how to divide them up with your partner. There is no magic to this, and the decision is not so critical under our plan for drafting and revising the argument section because all teammates will wind up looking at the brief as a whole when the first complete draft of the brief is written.

E. Appellee's determination of which issues to rebut

An appellee or respondent must analyze the problem in a similar way as the appellant in order to anticipate what issues the appellant is likely to raise. One of the serious limitations in moot court as it is practiced today is that the appellee does not have the opportunity to see and respond directly to the appellant's brief and the issues the appellant chooses to raise. Appellees most likely will be required to turn in their brief at the same time as appellants. Most moot court problems fail even to provide the notice of appeal filed by the appellant, which also would give a strong indication what the questions presented will be. (This is intentional, and it has more to do with testing the appellants to see if they can spot appealable issues than with punishing appellees by not giving them enough information.) Unfortunately, you may have to make an educated guess as to what issues are going to be raised by your opponent.

As discussed above, authors of moot court problems usually do not want you or the appellant to have to guess about the issues. These authors often will go to great lengths to point out that there are two main issues that they want both sides to address. But sometimes your review of the record will uncover a potential appealable issue that is not one of the two main "Roman numeral" issues presented by the problem. You may have identified an issue regarding the subject matter jurisdiction of the trial court or the appellate court, or one regarding ripeness or mootness, or the standing of the plaintiff—who might be you—to have brought the action in the first place. Appellees do not have as much discretion to jettison issues as appellants have. Even if you think an issue is tenuous, not likely to produce a reversal, and easily refuted, it will be in your best interest to raise it and rebut it as quickly and competently as you can. Spend a page or less on a straightforward issue that is resolved by controlling authority; spend more time on a more complicated error that requires analysis of the facts, controlling and persuasive authority, and public policy.

You will not be penalized for discussing actual appealable issues found outside the main "Roman numeral" issues. In fact, it may separate your brief from the pack and boost your score if your keen analysis reveals a thorn that almost everyone else overlooked. On the other hand, chasing after hobgoblins that are not reversible errors, or raising straw men issues just so you can tear them down in your brief, will not be a credit to your analytical skills. You also must be cognizant of not spending too much time and too many pages on tertiary issues that crowd out more important analysis and discussion of the main issues. Being able to budget your space is one of the skills on which you will be graded in moot court.

V. THE COLLABORATIVE WRITING PROCESS

Moot court may be your first foray into the collaborative process of legal writing, the style of writing which is used most often in actual legal practice. Through this process, each team member edits, comments on, and redrafts the work of the other member or members of the team to produce the best possible final product. You should take advantage of this opportunity, not only to get a very accurate taste of what real law practice is all about, but also to employ the premise that two or three heads are better than one. If done properly, following the advice given below, your moot court brief will be a much better product than if you follow the lazy and undemanding method of splitting your writing between team members who do not comment on each other's work, and merely agree to meet the evening before the brief is due to try to cram the individual work of each team member into one somewhat coherent brief.

The advice below is hard, demanding, and time-consuming, and it will sound extraordinary in comparison to what you have done for other writing assignments in law school and elsewhere. That is the great thing about advice—you can take it or leave it. If you cannot devote the time to do it all, do as much as you can.

A. Write a complete first draft of the brief as early as you can

The first advice we have is to write a complete first draft of the brief as early as you can, preferably three to four weeks before the final brief is due. Note that we said a *complete* first draft—we mean everything but the table of contents and table of authorities. Draft the questions presented, statement of jurisdiction, statement of the case or statement of facts, and summary of the argument, as well as a complete draft of the argument section.

The purpose of this is to allow yourself the time properly to review the problem and evaluate the brief. You should leave yourself the time to make mistakes, to change your mind, to add new issues and to drop others. You must leave the time for your teammates to edit and critique the brief. This amount of time is generous, but not overly generous when you think about how busy you will be in the middle of a semester with your other classes and responsibilities.

If you have a teaching assistant or advisor who, under the rules of the competition, can comment on the drafting of the brief itself, producing a complete product for them to look at and evaluate is much better than an outline and a few notes about things you promise to fill in. No one knows what to say about notes you write in the draft such as: "Add section on preemption," "Find cases," or "Here I'm going to argue that the award is unconstitutional under Perry."

B. Write multiple drafts

Do not just do one complete draft and then the final. Take advantage of the time you saved and write a draft every two or three days. You should know from experience that the first two or three drafts take a lot of time to write and revise, but the next two or three will take a lot less time, and each draft after that will take even less time to turn around. When you get to the level of fine tuning each sentence and paragraph, you may be able to turn around drafts in a matter of one or two hours.

C. Meet frequently with your teammates and let them comment on each draft

We mentioned choosing people who can give constructive criticism on legal writing, and that you should leave your ego at the door on a team project such as this. The sessions you spend hashing over the brief and discussing its contents will be some of the most valuable time you will spend in your legal education if you have top notch teammates who all can contribute to the effort. Rarely in private practice did we ever get to sit down for an hour or two and hash through a brief that we were working on with several other lawyers; you simply do not get the time to do it, or the client will not pay for these consultation sessions. When this did occur on major projects, we savored the experience. We invite you to have a taste of it while you still are in law school.

Do not cut yourself short in these sessions. Anything less than two hours is a rush. Schedule four two-hour sessions a week—three meetings on weekdays and one on the weekend. If you are on a vacation or break, meet every day. If you have a teaching assistant, try to get them involved two or three times a week.

D. Talk about each section the first week, each paragraph the second and third weeks, and each sentence and word the last week

Start big in your evaluations of the brief by looking hard at each major section of the brief and the Argument section. Ask yourself: Is this section coherent? Is there enough authority here? Does this argument ring true? Are these facts sufficient, or are they too detailed? Is this Summary of the Argument strong and punchy enough? Does the whole section flow easily and read quickly without having to go back and reread it one or more times? Am I transitioning to the next section adequately?

Next, look at each paragraph: Does it have a good topic sentence? Is the idea stated in the paragraph clear enough? Is it coherent? Is it short enough, or is it too wordy? Does it flow easily? Can you easily understand it without having to read it two or three times?

Remember that three sentences can be an excellent paragraph, and even two sentences will work when you want to be extremely direct and punchy. We have not met any brief judge who will bust you for having a paragraph that is too short, but many will comment on a paragraph that is too long. Readers will get lost in a long paragraph, and will start to ask themselves questions—"Why did I get into this discussion? How did this start? Are we still talking about the same topic?" Our rule of thumb is that no paragraph should be more then five sentences or more than one third of a page in length. Use the editing process to cut every paragraph down to size.

The last effort is word-smithing; going sentence by sentence and word by word, and making the language as tight and convincing as possible. Do we need this word? Why do we say "immediately" instead of "quickly"? Let's rephrase this sentence and make it shorter.

This part of the process usually is where we get into the most trouble with our cohorts—we like a certain word or phrase, and they do not. Try to get along, but remember, your ego should not matter and the end result should be a team effort. If you have three or more people, vote on final changes if you need to.

E. Thoroughly discuss each authority

When you are working through each draft, discuss each authority that you citing: Why are we citing this case? What does it mean? What are the facts? Does this authority stand for this exact proposition? Can we rephrase the sentence so that we do not have to say *See* or *See also* or *Cf.* when we cite the authority? Isn't there a stronger case for this point? Are there any negatives associated with using this case? Are we opening ourselves up to a counterattack because we are using this case?

The value of this exercise to your brief should be apparent, but you also will be doing yourself a favor when it comes time for oral argument. All this discussion and review will help you learn everything you need to know about the authorities for oral argument. You will be a walking, talking expert on this little area of the law before you are through, and that will make you a deadly force in oral argument.

F. Use another team or persons briefing the opposite position if the rules allow it

If you are in a situation where the rules of the competition allow you to consult with another team or persons that are briefing the opposite position on the problem (usually a team from the same school), take the opportunity to consult with them. If you can, use this opportunity. You will learn a lot from the fresh and contrary perspective of an opponent. They can try to poke holes in your argument, question your sources, present their take on the issues, and discuss how the authorities support or do not support certain positions. Of course, you can help them with their brief, too.

G.   Use all the outside help the rules allow

Outside assistance typically is limited by the moot court competition's rules. Where it is permitted, you should plan to take advantage of it, and scheduling a date and time with one or more faculty members and practitioners will help you to stay on track and get your act together before these meeting dates arrive. Unless you really are struggling with the issues or the research, you should wait until your research is fairly complete and your brief is well on the way to completion before inviting a law professor or practitioner to comment on it. Every legal professional values her time, and law professors are no exception. Law professors also tend to be a very critical audience, so you should strive to have a strong product in place before you fly it past them. We never felt comfortable in law school dogging our professors to ask them advice on moot court briefs until we were good and prepared on the law, and had specific questions to ask.

Remember, too, that even if you ask for help, you may not get very good outside assistance regarding a moot court problem because the issues chosen for moot court treatment usually are cutting edge issues for which people do not have a good answer. You can get direction, and a sense of what track is right and which tracks are wrong, but the answer will be up to you and your team. At the end of the process, your team will be better experts on this narrowly focused area of the law than anyone else who has not handled an actual case with the same issues. That is what actual litigation practice in the real world is like, too.

Appendix A

Preparing a Case Brief or Case Analysis for Class

The decades-old tradition of teaching first year classes of torts, contracts, property, civil procedure, and criminal law by examining reported judicial opinions ("cases"), one after the other, will continue for the foreseeable future. Therefore, in order to attempt to prepare yourself for class and especially for the bombardment of questions that is part and parcel of the Socratic Method (so named because it can drive you to a point where drinking poison is a more acceptable alternative than continuing with the class), you should try to brief the cases you are assigned to read. Hopefully, then you will have something to refer to when the professor turns her sights on you and starts firing.

Why do we care so much about cases?

The Common Law tradition in the United States and other British-influenced countries allows the courts to make binding law through a process of interpreting, and sometimes modifying or reversing legal rules from earlier sources (cases, statutes, rules, and commentary), and applying the newly crafted rule to the case at hand (the parties and their situation) so as to create a **precedent** that future lawyers and judges can use to evaluate and determine the cases before them. Throughout much of the history of England, this process of developing and advancing the law was more important than the passage of laws by Parliament or by royal decree. Thus, in the ancient bedrock areas of the law (torts, contracts, property, etc.), we still discuss the law and its development by reference to cases.

What kinds of things are we looking for in the cases we read?

A precedent can be **binding** (also referred to as **controlling**) on future courts, or it can merely be **persuasive**. A binding or controlling case is supposed to dictate the action of the court bound by the case—the court must handle the legal matter at hand in the same way as was done in the precedential case. A persuasive opinion only is used to try to persuade the court that it should do things the same way. If an opinion is binding, it still is only binding on cases that involve the same type of situation and similar facts as those of the precedential case. Therefore, the **facts** (what happened in the case that led up to a lawsuit being filed—the who, what, when, where, and how of the case) and the **issues** involved (the individual legal questions that the court addresses and usually answers) in the cases you read are very important.

Everyone wants to know who won, so the **judgment** rendered in the case is very important. In addition, only the **holding** of the court in the case is deemed to be controlling on future cases. The holding is a sentence or a short discussion (no more than a paragraph), which explains in legal terms the rule of law that ultimately applied to resolve the legal issue in the case, and how it was applied, so as to explain why the prevailing party won. If the discussion in part of the case has no bearing on the outcome of the case, or is a discussion of what would be or should be the law, or discusses what the result would be in different situations or on different facts, then all of this discussion is called **dicta** and it is not binding on future courts in future cases. Although it is not binding, it is important to lawyers and judges in predicting how a court would handle a future case where the facts and issues were as discussed in the dicta, and thus dicta should be considered valuable persuasive authority. Accordingly, you should lay out the holding of the case in your brief, but also make note of the dicta.

The **procedural history** of the case discusses the things that happened in the case after it was filed, and in particular, it identifies the stage of the case in the litigation process when the opinion was issued. For instance, was the opinion issued from a trial court or an appellate court? At what stage of the case did the court issue the opinion—before a trial or after? Was it an intermediate level appellate court or the court of last resort in the jurisdiction? (See Chapter 3 above). This often can be important, because a ruling in a case from the trial court issued before trial will have a much different effect on future cases than a ruling from the state supreme court (court of last resort) on appeal from the intermediate level appellate court in the state which handled the first appeal after a full jury trial in the case.

The **level** of the court matters—is it a **trial court** or an **intermediate level appellate court** or a **court of last resort**? The **jurisdiction** of the court matters—is it a **state court** or **federal court** or court from a foreign country? (**Tip:** a **federal court** is a court that has "United States" in its title). Is it a special court, such as a chancery court, that only handles cases of a specific kind? The name of the **judge** matters—he or she may have a great reputation, so the opinion will command a lot of respect. All of these factors are worthy of attention in a case brief. (Note: you may not think these are important right now, but trust us—your professors will.)

What does it look like?

The case brief should include the **name of the case**, called the **style** of the case, the **court**, the **judge**, the **facts** (also known as **historical facts**), the **procedural history**, the **issues** in the case, the **judgment** (who won and what they won), the **holding**, and any **dicta** that sounds important. You may also write up a brief discussion of the **rationale** employed by the court beyond what you wrote in the holding part. As for organization, that is up to you, but it seems logical to organize these topics into an outline.

For example:

CASE BRIEF

Style of the Case:

Court:

Judge:

Facts and Procedural History:

Issues:

Judgment:

Holding:

Discussion (and Dicta):

How long should a case analysis be?

At first, your analysis of each case probably will be a full page and often longer. You soon will tire of preparing that much, and after a few weeks of Socratic examination from your professors, you hopefully will learn what you should focus on with each professor, and you probably will winnow down the briefs to two thirds of a page or less. For example, a civil procedure professor will be very interested in the procedures employed in the case—how it got into the court, why were the defendants able to be sued there, how did the plaintiff's claim get dismissed. In contrast, a contracts professor will be very interested in any agreements discussed in the case—the discussions that led up to the agreements, the form and meaning of the agreements, and how the parties performed or did not perform their agreements.

You still don't understand holding vs dicta?!

Holding and dicta not easy concepts, and they will cause you a lot of trouble in your first year classes.

Holding:

A sentence or a short discussion (no more than a paragraph), which explains in legal terms the rule of law that ultimately applied to resolve the legal issue in the case, and how it was applied, so as to explain why the prevailing party won.

This definition suggests that a thorough discussion of holding will mention facts used by the court in rendering its decision, as well as the rule of law applied and the actual results of the application.

The trickier question is what is dicta. Consider the following definition:

Dicta:

Anything in a case (any statement, any analysis, any discussion of an element or factor or consideration) that is irrelevant to and unnecessary for the outcome of the case. If the item you are looking at has no impact on the outcome of the case (the decision of the court as to who won and who lost and why), then it is dicta.

When you are confused as to whether something is holding or dicta, think about the following:

◆ Did the court make its decision halfway through the case, and announced it, but went on to discuss several elements, items, or factors anyway? If so, the items that are discussed after the court made up its mind most likely are dicta.
◆ Did the court predict an outcome for a future case if the facts or circumstances were different? That kind of prediction is dicta.
◆ Did the court say that it was not reaching certain issues? That is a dead giveaway that any discussion of these issues is dicta.
◆ If you simply dropped the issue or the discussion of the issue from the case—removed every mention of it—would it still be possible to:
  a. Figure out why the prevailing party prevailed?
  b. State the factors, policies, and considerations that brought about the decision?
  c. Explain the rule(s) or element(s) that were analyzed and applied to determine the outcome?
  d. State the facts that the court found to be important to the decision?

If you answer YES to a, b, c, and d, you have dicta.

You can't go wrong?!

Don't expect to get the holding and dicta, the court's rationale, and even the judgment in the case right all the time. No one expects you to, least of all your professors. The first semester of law school is like baseball—if you get a hit one third of the time, you are doing great. If your batting average is .500 or higher, you will disappoint your professors who want to be able to stump you with their questions. Therefore, do the best you can, but expect to be wrong a good percentage of the time. All your fellow first year students are in the same boat—don't go overboard with frustration and worry, and when you are not "on call" in class, sit back and enjoy the cruise.

Appendix B

Common Errors in Grammar and Punctuation

I. GRAMMAR

Lawyers have a terrible reputation for writing long-winded sentences replete with "legalese," which includes everything from antiquated expressions (such as "heretofore," and "aforementioned") to "throat-clearing" expressions that announce a thought rather than stating it outright (common offenders are "it is obvious that" and "it is interesting to note that") to redundant words and phrases ("full and complete," "each and every," "the reason is because," "in my past experience"). In short, lawyers tend to be overly verbose, using 10 words to state what could be said in 5 or 6. We could write an entire book about the need to be precise and concise in your writing but, fortunately, others beat us to it. Richard C. Wydick's <u>Plain English for Lawyers</u> is a particularly good manual to purchase early on in law school and keep close at hand for the entirety of your legal career.

Here, we have chosen not to provide tips for better usage, but to point out the grammatical errors we have found most prevalent in law students' writing. For most people, learning grammar is as a much fun as learning legal citation (though the authors oddly are fond of both), but the importance of good grammar cannot be overstated (unless we wrote: "Using proper grammar is the only way to ensure that your legal writing professor does not stab you with a sharp pencil"—that might be an overstatement). Without it, you risk damaging your credibility before your audience has time to processes the substance of your writing. And that perhaps is the best case scenario. The worst is that poor grammar actually risks *confusing* your reader to the point of her thinking that you meant the opposite of what you actually intended.

A. Parallelism

Parallel structure requires that you use the same grammatical structure for things that are logically parallel.

    Rule   Use parallel adjectives to describe parallel qualities

    Example:
    The plaintiff was disoriented, confused, and agitated.

Not:
The plaintiff was disoriented, confused, and walking down the street.

Rule   Use parallel structure in lists

Example:
The defendant shov<u>ed</u> the gun into the cabinet, jump<u>ed</u> out the window, and hurr<u>ied</u> down the street.

Not:
The defendant shoved the gun into the cabinet, jumped out the window, and was running down the street.

Rule   Use parallel structure to compare or contrast cases

Example:
In *Smith*, the court found that the defendant's agitated state should not be considered where he passed a drug test. In contrast, in *Jones*, the court found that the defendant's agitated state should be considered where he passed a drug test.

Not:
In *Smith*, the court found that the defendant's agitated state was evidence of his drug use. In contrast, in *Jones*, the court found that the defendant's disposition was irrelevant.

Rule   Use parallel structure to add emphasis

Example:
The defendant failed to show up at his probation meeting, failed to appear at his hearing, and failed to obtain employment as condition of his probation.

Not:
The defendant failed to show up at his probation meeting, did not appear for his hearing, and is refusing to obtain employment as condition of his probation.

B. Word choice

Word choice is of paramount importance because every word counts in legal writing. Misusing words, moreover, can detract from the credibility and validity of your legal analysis.

Rule   Be careful with use of legal terms, or terms of art, because incorrect usage can damage your reputation as a legal writer

Example:
The <u>Marbury</u> Court *held* that judicial review is appropriate.

Not:
The <u>Marbury</u> Court *found* that judicial review is appropriate.

Note: Juries make findings of facts, courts do not unless the courts are holding a bench trial (non-jury trial). Courts make holdings; holdings are also known as rules of law. Other words to describe what courts do: conclude, determine, decide.

Rule   Avoid unnecessary modifiers (adverbs, adjectives, etc.)

Example:
An alcoholic father

Not:
A habitually alcoholic father

Rule   Use pronouns at your own risk; be absolutely, unequivocally, categorically sure that it is clear to what or whom the pronoun refers

Example:
Christopher and Paulie disagreed about whether Paulie should kill the restaurant owner.

Not:
Christopher and Paulie disagreed about whether he should kill the restaurant owner.

Rule   Make sure each "this" is unambiguous

Example:
This ruling is a miscarriage of justice.

Not:
This is a miscarriage of justice.

Rule   That vs. which

Use "which" when the modifier is a completely separate clause

Example:
Your car, which was still in the lot at midnight, was towed.

Otherwise, use "that" (i.e., when there is no comma in the sentence)

Example:
All cars that remain in the lot after 10 p.m. will be towed.

Rule   Since vs. Because

Since refers to a relationship in time

Example:
It has been a while since I've seen you.

Because denotes an explanation (one event or thing is the cause of something else)

Example:
It has been a while since I've seen you because I don't like you.

Not:
It has been a while since I've seen you since I don't like you.

C. Dangling modifiers

A dangling modifier is a modifying phrase that does not modify any word in the sentence. To avoid this problem, always make sure the subject of the verb in the modifying phrase is included in the remaining portion of the sentence.

Example:
Upon reviewing the exams, the results exceeded expectations.

Better Example:
Upon reviewing the exams, the professor realized that the results exceeded her expectations.

D. Misplaced modifiers

A misplaced modifier modifies any potential subject other than the subject of the word or phrase that most closely follows it. To avoid this problem, place the modifying word or phrase right next to the modified word.

Example:
The robber was described as a tall man with a black moustache weighing 150 pounds.

Revised:
The robber was described as a six-foot-tall man weighing 150 pounds with a black moustache. ("150 pounds" describes the man, not the moustache.)

"Only" is a frequently misplaced modifier.

Example:
I only run in the Spring.

Note: This is confusing because it is not clear if the subject runs only during the three months of the Spring season or if the subject only runs instead of walking, driving, etc. during this time.

Revised:
I run only in the Spring.

E. Active vs. passive voice

The passive voice consists of a "be"-verb (<u>e.g.</u>, are, is, am), or a form of "get," combined with the past participle of a verb.

Examples:

<u>Active</u>: "The 1L pulled his rolly-bag up the stairs and clogged traffic."

<u>Passive</u>: "The rolly-bag was pulled up the stairs by the 1L."

Note: This is confusing because we do not know who pulled the bag—the 1L or someone else who pulled the bag past the 1L?

<u>Even worse</u>: "The rolly-bag was pulled up the stairs and traffic was clogged."

Note: This is confusing because we do not know who pulled the bag or who or what clogged the traffic, nor do we know if there was a connection between the two events.

Active: "Betty ignored Bob after 'hanging out' with him at the bar last Thursday, but only because she forgot what he looked like."

Passive: "Bob was ignored after 'hanging out' at the bar with Betty last Thursday, but only because his looks were forgotten."

Note: Did everyone ignore Bob or just Betty? Were his looks forgotten by everyone or just Betty?

If after reading the sentence, the specific actor in the sentence is not clear, you probably used the passive voice. We suggest reviewing your paper specifically to change passive voice into active voice.

There are a few instances where passive voice, in moderation, is acceptable. These instances are limited to where the actor is unknown, unimportant, or intentionally concealed; and where the emphasis is on the recipient of the action instead of the actor. However, generally avoid using passive voice.

II. PUNCTUATION

Punctuation errors can be common even among the most polished writers, in part because we don't mark differences among punctuation marks in speaking. In other words, we "pause" in speaking where we might use a comma, period, or a semicolon, and nothing about our mastery of spoken English indicates which of these marks is appropriate in writing. Moreover, some punctuation marks—including ellipses and, often, colons—are not revealed at all in speech. As writers transcribe thoughts into written words, they may have to think twice about proper punctuation, or they may not use much punctuation at all at first-draft stage. Proper punctuation may thus be a necessary focus at the editing and polishing stage.

A. Comma Usage

1. Commas and independent clauses

Rule   Use a comma before a coordinating conjunction joining two main, or independent clauses. (An independent clause is one that can stand on its own as a sentence.)

Example
"The study group ordered pizza, and the slackers went out for a beer."

Rule   Do not use a comma when there is just one subject for the two clauses.

Example:
"The study group ordered pizza and went out for a beer."

2. Commas in a series

Rule Place a comma at the end of each item listed, including the item listed immediately before the *and*. Adding the comma before *and* avoids any possible confusion about how many items are listed.

Example:
Bring your pencils, pens, and paper to the exam.

Example:
Your writing assignments are due in October, November, and March.

3. Commas in dates

Rule When referencing a specific date including the month, day, and year, place a comma between the day and year and another between the year and the rest of the sentence.

Example:
We enjoyed the August 18, 2004, legal writing presentation immensely.

Rule However, when referencing only the month and year, no comma after the year is necessary.

Example:
The November 2000 election inspired tremendous controversy.

B. Quotation marks

1. Quotation marks with other punctuation marks

Rule Place periods and commas *inside* closing quotation marks

Examples:
"Janice said to put the gun in the cabinet."
"Put the gun in the cabinet," she testified.

Rule Place semicolons and colons *outside* the quotation marks

Example:
Her three favorite expressions were: (1) "hakuna matata"; (2) "don't worry be happy"; and (3) "carpe diem."

Rule   Question marks or exclamation marks can go inside or outside the quotation marks, depending on whether it is part of the quotation

Examples:
"Put the gun in the cabinet!"
I can't believe that she said, "You are a terrible shooter"!
She asked me, "Where is the gun?"
Did she say, "The gun is in the cabinet"?

Note: In the third example that the quotation itself is a question, whereas in the fourth example, the quotation is part of the question.

2. Single quotation marks

Rule   Use single quotation marks only for quotes within other quotes.

Example:
The plaintiff testified, "Mark told me to 'hide the gun in the cabinet.'"

C. <u>Ellipsis Dots</u> . . .

Ellipsis dots are used in legal writing in two major ways: to indicate that words in a sentence or paragraph have been omitted or, when quoting legal passages, to eliminate unnecessary or repetitive language.

Rule   <u>Three dots</u>: Use three ellipsis dots to indicate the omission of one or more words inside a quotation. Be sure to press the space bar between each dot.

Example—Without Ellipsis
"Law school students have been known to fall asleep during class because of lack of sleep and malnutrition."

With Ellipsis
"Law school students have been known to fall asleep . . . because of lack of sleep and malnutrition."

Rule   <u>Four dots</u>: Use four dots to indicate the omission of (a) content at the end of a sentence, (b) content after a completed sentence when the quotation continues, (c) content at the end of the sentence when the quotation continues, and (d) a complete paragraph.

Example—Without Ellipsis
"Law school students have been known to fall asleep during class because of lack of sleep and malnutrition. In addition, they occasionally snore."

With Ellipsis

• Content at the end of a sentence.

Example:
"Law school students have been known to fall asleep during class . . . ."

• Content after a completed sentence when the quotation continues.

Example:
"Law school students have been known to fall asleep during class . . . . In addition, they occasionally snore."

• Content at the end of the sentence when the quotation continues.

Example:
"Law school students have been known to fall asleep during class because of lack of sleep and malnutrition. . . . they occasionally snore."

Rule   <u>Four Dots</u> are needed to show the deletion of a complete paragraph

Example:
Section 8. The Congress shall have the Power to lay and collected Taxes, Duties, Imposts and Excises, to pay the Debts and provide for the common Defence and general Welfare of the United States; but all Duties, Imposts and Excises shall be uniform throughout the United States;

. . . .

To make all Laws which shall be necessary and proper for carrying into Execution the foregoing Powers, and all other Powers vested by this Constitution in the Government of the United States, or in any Department or Officer thereof.

Rule   It is never appropriate in legal writing to begin a quotation with an ellipsis. A bracketed capital letter indicates that something has been omitted.

Example:
"[S]tudents have been known to fall asleep during class because of lack of sleep and malnutrition."

D. Colons

Proper use of the colon is extremely important in legal writing. It helps lead the reader down a chain of reasoning and serves as an arrow or pointing finger to the second clause.

> *Note: Make sure you know the difference between use of a colon and use of a semi-colon (see below).*

There are a few specific rules you should remember when using colons.

Rule   Use a colon to introduce a quotation, list, or statement (*e.g.*, a block quote or categorical list)

> *Note: It may be helpful to use a colon when listing the elements of a rule; however, remember to use a semicolon to separate each particular element of the rule.*

> *Example:*
> There are 3 elements of a valid contract: (1) offer; (2) acceptance; and (3) consideration.

Rule   Do not use a colon directly after a verb when introducing a list

> *Example:*
> Your knapsack should include the following: a knife, a piece of wood, and a slingshot.

> *Not:*
> Your knapsack should include: a knife, a piece of wood, and slingshot.

- Use a colon to join two independent clauses with a colon if the second interprets or amplifies the first

> *Example:*
> Things got worse in a hurry: our co-defendant turned state's evidence.

> *Note: a semicolon can also be used in the above example; but remember, a colon emphasizes the second phrase, which can be extremely helpful in legal writing.*

E. Semi-colons

Legal writing usually requires using semi-colons on two occasions.

Rule   Semi-colons separate two independent clauses. Independent clauses are statements that could stand alone or can be combined using a conjunction, an adverb, or nothing at all. When two or more independent clauses are joined by an adverb or by nothing, use of a semi-colon is appropriate (whereas a conjunction serves the same purpose as a semicolon and is preceded only by a comma).

Examples:
Adverb: "Law school barely relates to legal practice; nonetheless, most students tend to work too hard and too long."

Note: Other common adverbs include: accordingly, also, besides, consequently, further, furthermore, hence, however, indeed, instead, later, likewise, meanwhile, moreover, nevertheless, now, still, then, therefore, thus

Nothing: "One L's think the first year of school is the hardest; the second year will disabuse them of that notion."

Conjunction: "One L's may appear tired and overwhelmed, but they are still learning time management."

Rule   Semi-colons are used to separate elements in a series when the individual elements are complex or contain internal commas. This most commonly occurs in a statute or a contract.

Example:
"As commonly defined for the charge of murder, 'malice' means the specific intent to kill; the specific intent to inflict serious bodily harm; the specific intent to commit a felony; or reckless indifference to human life."

Appendix C

Preparing For and Taking Exams

I. OUTLINING and OUTLINES (Your's, Other Students', Commercial Outlines)

A. What is outlining?

Taking the material assigned and the material covered in the class and putting it into an organized structure in outline form.

You lay out the big picture issues, the policies, and perform a synthesis of the cases and other sources of the law assigned and discussed in class in order to have an organized capsule summary of the law on the topic.

An outline is a "digested" compilation of the material that came thick and fast in the semester.

B. Why outline?

The discipline of outlining forces you to tackle the material (again, that came thick and fast in the semester) and think hard about it, break it down, organize it, and synthesize it into a cohesive summary of the law on the topic.

Merely reading the material, even reading it twice, is not enough. You have to try to make something out of the material—make connections, think about the big picture issues and the policies at work; think about how the holding of one case adds to the holding of previous cases, or modifies, expands, limits the rules and legal standards learned in other cases.

The material was not chosen at random, and it was most likely presented in a way that exemplifies both the current law and the development of the law in the area. Therefore, outlining the material also will help you to understand the current law and the way the law developed and hopefully why it developed in that way

Reading is too passive. Outlining engages the mind. Being forced to write down what you know about the area exposes your thoughts and your understanding to the light of day. If your outline looks like a mess, your thinking on the law of this area probably is messy.

Outlining aids in learning and memorizing the law in the area in a way that simply reading and rereading the material does not. This will really help on closed book exams!

There is an analogy to preparing to act in a theatrical production—when you are learning lines for a play, active practice (writing out you lines, running lines) beats passive reading and rereading.

C. What about other people's outlines or the commercial outlines?

For all the reasons above, there is no substitute for doing your own outlines. Reading and rereading someone else's outline is not going to force you to think critically and synthesize and digest the material.

If you never read the material in the first place, obviously, you cannot outline what you have not read, or at least not very effectively. Therefore, read what you can. Try to read and understand a commercial outline and one or more student outlines and your notes from class (if you did go to class and took notes and did not just soak up the atmosphere). If you never read the material assigned for the class, don't expect to do very well.

If some person from a previous year got an "A" in the class and made it on to law review, you still should not simply follow her outline for the course. Once again, for the reasons stated above, doing your own outline has important benefits in digesting and learning the material. This is of particular importance with closed book exams.

Nevertheless, comparing your outline to the outline of a very successful student can expose areas that you glossed over or misconstrued and areas that you may need to reexamine. These outlines can improve you outline and your overall understanding of the course. But make sure the student had your professor and make sure she was an "A" student—you are not shooting for a "B" are you, so why use the "B" student's outline even if it is nicely typed, formatted, and easy to read?

You may be wondering, what is wrong with commercial outlines? Commercial outlines were written by someone who did not attend your classes, most likely did not have your professor, did not necessarily look at the material you were supposed to read, and is going to try to explain the law in terms that your professor may not have used. Thus, be wary.

Commercial outlines may have been written for the textbook you were assigned—that is one point in their favor, but the other problems above still apply. Of course, you can try to use a commercial outline to make sure your outline of the law looks correct and makes sense. In this way they can be a partial substitute for the "A" student outline mentioned above.

II. TAKING EXAMS

A. Closed book vs. open book

The closed book exam requires you to take the test without the benefit of your notes, the casebook, your outline, other outlines, flash cards, prayer cards, what have you—so you have to have learned the material ahead of time. As mentioned above, having read, digested, and outlined the material is a big step toward that goal.

Do not rejoice in the open book exam—often the professor feels entitled to make them harder and more detailed because they are open book, with all your materials in front of you. In any event, it is going to be hard to find the material you need quickly unless you have read, digested, and—you guessed it—outlined the material. Flipping to the correct section of your own outline is much faster that trying to find the material in your notes, the casebook, a 200 page commercial outline or even someone else's outline that you did not create.

> **NOTICE TO STUDENTS: THE RULES DIFFER FROM CLASS TO CLASS AND FROM PROFESSOR TO PROFESSOR ON WHAT YOU CAN BRING TO AN OPEN BOOK EXAM. LEARN THEM AHEAD OF TIME, NOT ON THE MORNING OF THE EXAM WHEN THE PROCTER WRENCHES THAT COMMERCIAL OUTLINE OUT OF YOUR CLUTCHING HANDS.**

B. Types of questions

1. ISSUE SPOTTING

The typical law school exam question. A fact pattern is presented and you must figure out the most relevant facts and the legal issues implicated by the facts, then discuss the legal rules and legal standards that address the issues, and do the application of the law to the facts to answer the question, typically in 50 minutes or less per question.

> Example: Mr. Jones, a resident of Blackacre, the largest city in the State of Slu, was standing on the platform of the Blackacre Transportation Company's downtown subway station at rush hour. The trains were packed, and employees of the transportation company were helping to shove passengers into the over-packed subway cars. One such employee, Mrs. Smith, noticed a passenger standing on the platform near the front of the train who looked very ill and appeared to be having a mild seizure. This passenger swayed back and forth, and Smith thought she was in danger of toppling into the path of the train that was preparing to depart. Smith jumped and ran to aid of the swooning passenger. In her zeal, she knocked over a trash can that rolled into a small freestanding billboard for Winston cigarettes, which caused the billboard to topple over on to the head of Mr. Jones. Mr. Jones suffered severe lacerations requiring 100 stitches and much pain and discomfort.
>
> Discuss Mr. Jones' ability to recover for his injuries from Mrs. Smith and Blackacre Transportation Companies.

In this example, you would have to discuss issues of negligence, including the duty of care of a common carrier, whether that duty applies to someone on the platform, whether the duty was violated by the Transportation Co. or its agent Mrs. Smith, whether there was causation of Mr. Jones' injuries; issues regarding responsibility for the actions of an employee which involves issues of agency and *respondeat superior* liability (if those were covered in class); "Good Samaritan" liability to the extent it might change the outcome of the above analysis.

Points generally are awarded for correctly identifying all the issues implicated in the facts, for identifying and spelling out the rules and legal standards that apply to the issues, and for doing a logical, plausible application of the law to the facts. Additional points may be awarded for exploring alternative outcomes based on different theories of the law, or based on facts that are not discussed in the fact pattern but would impact the outcome if they were present.

If you have read and digested the law ahead of time, you will tend to spot more issues, and you generally will come up with the correct rules and legal principles to apply. If you have not, you will probably miss issues, apply the wrong law, or on an open book exam, you will be scrambling to find a case or a Restatement provision that covers the issues you think are there.

2. BIG PICTURE, POLICY QUESTIONS

Essay questions ask you to explain why the law is the way it is today, or why it developed in a certain way, or the reasons for doing it one way or the other. This question requires you to show off a broader understanding of the meaning of the law by revealing your understanding of the big issues and policies of this area.

> Examples: Discuss the pros and cons of the "Good Samaritan" rule that modifies the rules on liability for negligence.
>
> Discuss the reasons for and against the comparative negligence rule and the contributory negligence rule.

Points will be awarded for discussing the policies, the pros and cons and whys and wherefores of these big picture issues, and doing so in a thoughtful, well organized way.

3. INFORMATION SEEKING—SHORT ANSWER

This is the "you know it or you don't" question. On an open book exam, you will know when your classmates have reached this section because they will start madly flipping through the casebook or an outline or their notes or whatever is allowed to be brought in to the exam.

> Examples: A legislative enactment that allows a state to exert its jurisdiction over nonresidents is called: _____

The U.S. Supreme Court case that said you can only exert jurisdictional power over someone if they are physically present in the jurisdiction is: _____

The doctrine of tort law (expressed in a Latin phrase) covering an employer's liability for the actions of its employees, servants and agents is: _____

The elements of a claim for promissory estoppel are: _____

Fill in the blank. Sometimes the blank will suggest the average length of the answer; sometimes not (i.e., all the blanks will be the same length).

4. MULTIPLE CHOICE (MULTIPLE GUESS)

The prepared student or the optimist will call this section multiple choice. The unprepared or pessimistic student calls it multiple guess. These will look familiar. Again, you always have a one in four or one in five chance of getting the right answer. Or, if they are true/false, it's 50/50.

Examples: The person bringing an appeal can properly be referred to as the: (a) plaintiff; (b) defendant; (c) appellant; (d) appellee.

The party who prevailed in Siewerth v. Charleston was: (a) Roy Siewerth; (b) Robert Siewerth; (c) June Charleston; (d) Ruben Charleston.

In promissory estoppel, the claimant's reasonable and foreseeable reliance on a definite promise, to her detriment, can replace the element of consideration in the typical breach of contract case—True or False?

C. Time Management

Exam taking not only tests your knowledge of the subject matter and skills as a lawyer, but also tests your ability to manage time. Look for clues (direct or indirect) as to how much of your time to spend on a given question or section of questions—occasionally the professor is nice enough to spell out the time or the percentage that each question or section is worth (e.g., they may state, "spend no more than 45 minutes on each question"—meaning each question is weighted equally; or they may state, "question 1 (35%), question 2 (20%), . . ." etc., so that you can allocate your time accordingly). Spending two hours on one of six equally weighted questions and fifteen minutes on each of the other five will cost you on the overall grade in most instances.

Follow these directives: **Plan ahead**—actually put your watch in front of you and when the allotted time is gone, wrap up quickly or simply leave it and move on to the next question. **Leave a space** at the end of the "not so finished answer" to come back to if you finish the other questions early and can come back to the unfinished. **Try to leave ten minutes at the end** to read all of your answers and correct the obvious typos, complete your incomplete sentences and thoughts, and clarify the messiest areas.

One technique to consider is to outline your answers to each of the major essay questions in the exam booklet (where the professor can read it quickly). Then go back and write the essays answering the question and filling in the particulars. If you run out of time to write a nice essay, an outline can reveal a lot of what you know and understand about the law—the issues you spotted, the rules and standards that apply, and so on. Obviously, a detailed outline is more informative than a sparse outline. If you show in outline form that you recognized the five issues that were there to be "spotted," that you knew the five rules and the three exceptions to the general rule that were implicated, and gave the correct elements of the rule in the outline, and briefly outlined how you would apply the law to the facts and what the outcome will be, you can get a lot of credit on the question; maybe not full credit, but a lot more credit than you will get from a blank space.